Lecture Notes in Computer Science   15377

Founding Editors

Gerhard Goos
Juris Hartmanis

Editorial Board Members

The series Lecture Notes in Computer Science (LNCS), including its subseries Lecture Notes in Artificial Intelligence (LNAI) and Lecture Notes in Bioinformatics (LNBI), has established itself as a medium for the publication of new developments in computer science and information technology research, teaching, and education.

LNCS enjoys close cooperation with the computer science R & D community, the series counts many renowned academics among its volume editors and paper authors, and collaborates with prestigious societies. Its mission is to serve this international community by providing an invaluable service, mainly focused on the publication of conference and workshop proceedings and postproceedings. LNCS commenced publication in 1973.

Jessie Y. C. Chen · Gino Fragomeni ·
Norbert A. Streitz · Shin'ichi Konomi ·
Xiaowen Fang

Editors

HCI International 2024 – Late Breaking Papers

26th International Conference on
Human-Computer Interaction, HCII 2024
Washington, DC, USA, June 29 – July 4, 2024
Proceedings, Part IV

 Springer

Editors
Jessie Y. C. Chen
U.S. Army Research Laboratory
Adelphi, MD, USA

Norbert A. Streitz (ID)
Smart Future Initiative
Frankfurt, Germany

Xiaowen Fang
DePaul University
Chicago, IL, USA

Gino Fragomeni
U.S. Army Combat Capabilities Development
Command Soldier Center (DEVCOM SC)
Orlando, FL, USA

Shin'ichi Konomi
Kyushu University
Fukuoka, Japan

ISSN 0302-9743   ISSN 1611-3349 (electronic)
Lecture Notes in Computer Science
ISBN 978-3-031-76811-8   ISBN 978-3-031-76812-5 (eBook)
https://doi.org/10.1007/978-3-031-76812-5

Foreword

This year we celebrate 40 years since the establishment of the HCI International (HCII) Conference, which has been a hub for presenting groundbreaking research and novel ideas and collaboration for people from all over the world.

The HCII conference was founded in 1984 by Prof. Gavriel Salvendy (Purdue University, USA, Tsinghua University, P.R. China, and University of Central Florida, USA) and the first event of the series, "1st USA-Japan Conference on Human-Computer Interaction", was held in Honolulu, Hawaii, USA, 18–20 August. Since then, HCI International is held jointly with several Thematic Areas and Affiliated Conferences, with each one under the auspices of a distinguished international Program Board and under one management and one registration. Twenty-six HCI International Conferences have been organized so far (every two years until 2013, and annually thereafter).

Over the years, this conference has served as a platform for scholars, researchers, industry experts and students to exchange ideas, connect, and address challenges in the ever-evolving HCI field. Throughout these 40 years, the conference has evolved itself, adapting to new technologies and emerging trends, while staying committed to its core mission of advancing knowledge and driving change.

As we celebrate this milestone anniversary, we reflect on the contributions of its founding members and appreciate the commitment of its current and past Affiliated Conference Program Board Chairs and members. We are also thankful to all past conference attendees who have shaped this community into what it is today.

The 26th International Conference on Human-Computer Interaction, HCI International 2024 (HCII 2024), was held as a 'hybrid' event at the Washington Hilton Hotel, Washington, DC, USA, during 29 June – 4 July 2024. It incorporated the 21 thematic areas and affiliated conferences listed below.

A total of 5108 individuals from academia, research institutes, industry, and government agencies from 85 countries submitted contributions, and 1271 papers and 309 posters were included in the volumes of the proceedings that were published just before the start of the conference. Additionally, 222 papers and 104 posters were included in the volumes of the proceedings published after the conference, as "Late Breaking Work". The contributions thoroughly cover the entire field of human-computer interaction, addressing major advances in knowledge and effective use of computers in a variety of application areas. These papers provide academics, researchers, engineers, scientists, practitioners and students with state-of-the-art information on the most recent advances in HCI. The volumes constituting the full set of the HCII 2024 conference proceedings are listed on the following pages.

I would like to thank the Program Board Chairs and the members of the Program Boards of all thematic areas and affiliated conferences for their contribution towards the high scientific quality and overall success of the HCI International 2024 conference. Their manifold support in terms of paper reviewing (single-blind review process, with a minimum of two reviews per submission), session organization and their willingness to act as goodwill ambassadors for the conference is most highly appreciated.

This conference would not have been possible without the continuous and unwavering support and advice of Gavriel Salvendy, founder, General Chair Emeritus, and Scientific Advisor. For his outstanding efforts, I would like to express my sincere appreciation to Abbas Moallem, Communications Chair and Editor of HCI International News.

September 2024   Constantine Stephanidis

HCI International 2024 Thematic Areas
and Affiliated Conferences

- HCI: Human-Computer Interaction Thematic Area
- HIMI: Human Interface and the Management of Information Thematic Area
- EPCE: 21st International Conference on Engineering Psychology and Cognitive Ergonomics
- AC: 18th International Conference on Augmented Cognition
- UAHCI: 18th International Conference on Universal Access in Human-Computer Interaction
- CCD: 16th International Conference on Cross-Cultural Design
- SCSM: 16th International Conference on Social Computing and Social Media
- VAMR: 16th International Conference on Virtual, Augmented and Mixed Reality
- DHM: 15th International Conference on Digital Human Modeling & Applications in Health, Safety, Ergonomics & Risk Management
- DUXU: 13th International Conference on Design, User Experience and Usability
- C&C: 12th International Conference on Culture and Computing
- DAPI: 12th International Conference on Distributed, Ambient and Pervasive Interactions
- HCIBGO: 11th International Conference on HCI in Business, Government and Organizations
- LCT: 11th International Conference on Learning and Collaboration Technologies
- ITAP: 10th International Conference on Human Aspects of IT for the Aged Population
- AIS: 6th International Conference on Adaptive Instructional Systems
- HCI-CPT: 6th International Conference on HCI for Cybersecurity, Privacy and Trust
- HCI-Games: 6th International Conference on HCI in Games
- MobiTAS: 6th International Conference on HCI in Mobility, Transport and Automotive Systems
- AI-HCI: 5th International Conference on Artificial Intelligence in HCI
- MOBILE: 5th International Conference on Human-Centered Design, Operation and Evaluation of Mobile Communications

Conference Proceedings – Full List of Volumes

https://2024.hci.international/proceedings

26th International Conference on Human-Computer Interaction (HCII 2024)

The full list with the Program Board Chairs and the members of the Program Boards of all thematic areas and affiliated conferences of HCII2024 is available online at:

http://www.hci.international/board-members-2024.php

HCI International 2025 Conference

The 27th International Conference on Human-Computer Interaction, HCI International 2025, will be held jointly with the affiliated conferences at the Swedish Exhibition & Congress Centre and Gothia Towers Hotel, Gothenburg, Sweden, June 22–27, 2025. It will cover a broad spectrum of themes related to Human-Computer Interaction, including theoretical issues, methods, tools, processes, and case studies in HCI design, as well as novel interaction techniques, interfaces, and applications. The proceedings will be published by Springer. More information is available on the conference website: https://2025.hci.international/.

General Chair
Prof. Constantine Stephanidis
University of Crete and ICS-FORTH
Heraklion, Crete, Greece
Email: general_chair@2025.hci.international

https://2025.hci.international/

Contents – Part IV

Playing Experiences

Virtual Experiences in XR
and the Metaverse

Study and Development of Machine Learning Models Designed for Extended Reality Interactivity in Real-Time

Geovana Amorim Abensur[ID], Agustín Alejandro Ortiz Díaz[✉][ID], Sergio Cleger Tamayo[ID], and Delrick Nunes De Oliveira[ID]

Sidia Institute of Science and Technology. Av. Darcy Vargas, 654, 69055-035 Manaus, Brasil
{geovana.abensur,agustin.diaz,sergio.tamayo,
delrick.oliveira}@sidia.com

Abstract. The continuous development of hardware has allowed immersive technologies to be accessible for application in various daily tasks. It is currently possible to access immersive experiences through mobile devices, head-mounted displays, and other technologies. Extended reality (XR) is the term that encompasses a spectrum of various immersive and interactive technologies. Interactions are part of the hard core of immersive experiences and provide the possibility of interacting with the world around us. However, there are currently some SDKs intended for machine learning, such as ML-Kit. This SDK includes functionalities such as face and object detection and tracking, pose detection, and so on. However, there is a diverse set of functionalities, which are not yet grouped within some reusable structure (API or SDK). Many of these functionalities have proposed solutions using deep learning techniques. A characteristic of these techniques is that they tend to be complex in their space-time dimension. For this and other reasons, they are usually more difficult techniques to adapt for real-time use and other limiting characteristics of devices that reproduce immersive experiences. This work aims to study a viable architecture in which a set of ML methods that can be adapted to work in XR environments can be organized and grouped. These methods will have special characteristics since they must be adapted to provide real-time responses to users' interactions with the environment. That is, they must adjust to the characteristics and limitations of immersive environments. Within the study, some of the main SDKs for immersive environments are analyzed and several ML methods are analyzed, related to the areas of computer vision and speech recognition, which should be included within the proposed architecture.

Keywords: Immersive Technologies · ML methods · Extended Reality · Head-Mounted Displays

1 Introduction

The continuous development of hardware has allowed immersive technologies to be accessible for application in various daily tasks. Extended reality (XR) is the term that encompasses a spectrum of immersive and interactive technologies. XR covers augmented reality (AR), mixed reality (MR), and virtual reality (VR). Interactions are part

J. Y. C. Chen et al. (Eds.): HCII 2024, LNCS 15377, pp. 3–19, 2025.
https://doi.org/10.1007/978-3-031-76812-5_1

of the hard core of immersive experiences, some authors consider that these experiences are exceptional due to the possibility of interacting with the world around us. It is currently possible to access immersive experiences through mobile devices, head-mounted displays (HMD), virtual reality glasses, and other technologies. [1].

Both VR and AR are interactive, computer-based experiences that are increasingly integrated into commonly used applications. VR allows users to immerse themselves in a digital world and experience the true depth and visual richness of digital objects as if they were real. For its part, AR makes it possible to enrich scenarios taken directly from the physical world with virtual objects. In this way, when a user interacts with a virtual object, she feels as if she is interacting with a real-world object. MR describes the continuity between the virtual and physical worlds. Any intermediate point between these two realities (AR and VR) can be considered within MR [1].

Many companies are integrating XR experiences into their workflows to drive design reviews, virtual production, and location-based entertainment. There are many software developments kits (SDKs) that are particularly aimed at the AR and XR area in a general sense. Arcore, Arkit, Ar-Foundation, Vuforia, and Artoolkit are some of the SDKs that are widely used due to features like environmental awareness, scanning, and object creation [2].

On the other hand, machine learning (ML) is a subset of artificial intelligence techniques that allows the creation of computer models that learn from previous experiences to make predictions about the behavior of future experiences. There are currently some SDKs aimed at ML; for example, ML-Kit is an SDK developed by Google that offers mobile app developers a suite of powerful methods, including machine learning techniques. This SDK includes functionalities such as face detection, facial mesh detection, object detection and tracking, pose detection, selfie segmentation, and so on [3].

However, there is a diverse set of functionalities, including ML techniques, that are not yet grouped and organized within some type of reusable structure, such as application programming interfaces (API) or SDKs. Many of these functionalities involve situations that already have proposed solutions using deep learning (DL) techniques. DL is a branch of ML that uses artificial neural network models built, typically including multiple hidden layers, to train and learn from large data sets. A particular characteristic of DL techniques is that they tend to be complex in their spatio-temporal dimension [4]. For this and other reasons, these techniques are often more difficult to adapt for real-time use and other limiting features that appear within devices that reproduce immersive experiences. Among these features we can mention:

- Recognition of people through face,
- Detection of facial expressions,
- Pose classification,
- Gesture recognition,
- Speech recognition,
- Semantic segmentation,
- Depth Estimation,
- Plane and scene detection, and so on.

New lines of work have recently emerged, such as Real-time Multi-Task Multi-Model, which are laying the foundation for efficient use of ML techniques in areas such as

XR. The core idea is to combine user interactivity in XR environments with computationally complex machine-learning activities. This combination generates a strong synergy that solves different problems by offering more pleasant and sophisticated applications within immersive environments [5].

Following this line of research, this work aims to study a viable architecture in which a set of ML (or DL) models and methods that can be adapted to work in XR environments can be organized and grouped. These methods will have special characteristics since they must be adapted to provide real-time responses to users' interactions with the environment; In a general sense, they must adjust to the characteristics and limitations of immersive environments. These methods are essential and useful to improve the performance of current and future systems.

This work analyzes some of the main SDKs for immersive environments today, some existing SDK options for ML are discussed; The use of different ML techniques and models is proposed, mainly in the areas related to computer vision and speech recognition; and we suggest some limitations, strengths, and methods to achieve this goal. The proposal of a new architecture to organize and group ML techniques aimed at XR is studied. Bundling and making available this set of functionalities will bring great benefits to both the industry and the scientific community.

For better organization and description of the work results, the article has been divided into 7 sections: Related Works (Sect. 2), AR specialized SDKs. (Sect. 3), SDK ML_Kit. (Sect. 4), Architectural proposal. (Sect. 5), and some ethical considerations (Sect. 6). Finally, in Sect. 7, we present our Conclusions, Acknowledgments, and References.

2   Related Work

To date, many research projects have been published that aim to combine artificial intelligence techniques, others more restricted to machine learning, with augmented reality techniques in various areas of application. In 2021, a very exhaustive compilation of works was published that explores the current scope of AI in AR-assisted manufacturing applications, that is, it attempts to mark the place of AI and AR in industrial processes [6]. This work, despite highlighting some important limitations in the area, supports the idea and highlights the inclusion of AI techniques as a tool within AR as a current need.

Another survey, also published in 2021, directs its objective to the study of systems created within mobile augmented reality (MAR) [7]. MAR systems integrate computer-generated virtual objects with physical environments for mobile devices. This paper carries out a study of existing MAR systems (37 frameworks or SDKs) through an approach from the perspective of user-centered design, potentially empowered by ML methods. Additionally, the authors provide a compilation of research organized by application areas: entertainment, education, health, and so on [7].

In the same year, another compilation performed a performance analysis of several works aimed at immersive systems [8]. This is because these types of systems are experiencing greater application in different work areas. This review includes applications in which experiments have been done to evaluate the proposed systems. The results outline current and future research areas where the use of new techniques may be necessary.

Current machine learning and deep learning techniques, adapted to the characteristics of these systems, could greatly favor this type of system [8].

More recently, in 2023, another compilation of scientific articles that have been applied to AR systems using machine learning techniques was published [9]. This survey group works, between 2010 and 2021, that are within the health domain. This work addresses several topics in the field of health, but there are two interesting points to highlight due to their relationship with this work: (1) Artificial intelligence and machine learning algorithms used in AR systems and how they are used, and (2) Comparison between different display modalities (web, mobile and HMD) [9].

Recently, in 2023, new lines of work have emerged, such as Real-time Multi-Task Multi-Model, which are laying the foundations for the efficient use of ML techniques in areas such as XR. The central idea is to combine user interactivity in XR environments with computationally complex machine-learning activities. This combination generates a strong synergy that solves different problems by offering more pleasant and sophisticated applications within immersive environments [5].

3 AR Specialized SDKs

A software development kit (SDK) is a set of tools and libraries used to create software. ARCore, ARKit, AR-Foundation, Vuforia, and ARToolKit are some of the most used SDKs to develop AR applications due to features such as environment recognition, scanning, and object creation. In addition, they are compatible with the most popular program for creating AR applications, "Unity 3D" [10]. This session describes some of the characteristics of these well-known SDKs (Table 1) and the possible inclusion of machine-learning techniques.

3.1 ARCore

ARCore is Google's augmented reality application development platform. It offers a variety of APIs to work with several key functionalities [11, 12].

- **Motion tracking:** This makes it possible to obtain the device's location coordinates relative to the world.
- **Anchors:** This makes it possible to track the position of an object over time.
- **Environmental understanding:** Makes it possible to detect the size and location of all types of surfaces.
- **Deep understanding:** This makes it possible to measure the distance between different surfaces from a certain point. Depth calculation.
- **Light estimation:** This makes it possible to always calculate the lighting conditions of the environment. Provides information about the color correction of the environment and the average light intensity.

ARCore uses computer vision technology to understand the scene in real-time, allowing AR experiences to be accurate and immersive. Additionally, it is compatible with a wide range of Android devices, making it accessible to developers and users around the world [11].

On the other hand, ARCore incorporates machine learning techniques to create intelligent augmented reality experiences. For example, it uses the ML kit and the Google Cloud Vision API to build an ML model that virtually classifies and labels real-world objects in the camera view [11].

3.2 ARKit

ARKit is Apple's solution to incorporate Mobile Augmented Reality (MAR). ARKit is compatible with a wide range of devices using VisionOS or iOS operating systems; Among these devices are the iPhone, iPad, and iPod. ARKit is an SDK that integrates hardware detection functions to produce augmented reality applications and games. Like ARCore, it offers APIs for device motion tracking, world tracking, scene understanding, and display amenities to simplify creating an AR experience [13].

According to [14], two of the most important technical features of ARKit are its tracking system and its function to control a gyroscope. Furthermore, according to [12], another important feature is visual-inertial odometry, which is used to analyze notable features of a scene taken by a device's camera to provide a physical tracking of the world.

To incorporate Machine learning techniques, Apple has several tools [13]:

- The Core_ML framework contributes to much more efficient and faster loading and inference of ML models. This framework includes several APIs, such as Async Prediction and Module, such as Core ML Tools. These tools help simplify, compress, and optimize models for implementation in device hardware.
- Create_ML framework makes the creation of custom ML models on top of visual feature extractors.
- Other ML APIs, within the Vision framework, offer options such as image segmentation, and the detection of animal and human body postures.

3.3 AR Foundation

AR-Foundation is a framework specially designed for augmented reality development that allows you to create new experiences that can then be implemented on multiple mobile and wearable AR devices. It is a cross-platform framework, developed by Google, that allows you to create AR experiences with Unity in a simple way and without the need for specific adjustments when generating compilations for the Android or iOS operating systems [15]. Some of the SDKs that it integrates and makes available are Google's ARCore (for Android) and Apple's ARKit (for IOS). According to [15], Unity supports the following plugins:

- Google ARCore XR plugin on Android
- Apple ARKit XR plugin on iOS
- Magic Leap XR Plugin in Magic Leap
- OpenXR plugin on HoloLens-2

When AR-Foundation builds and runs your app on an AR device, it enables these features using the Platform's native AR-SDK. This SDK is highly integrated with other technologies in the AR ecosystem, such as ARCore. AR Foundation SDK allows us to work with different augmented reality platforms, to carry out this work it provides the following functionalities [16]:

- Tracking: Device position and orientation tracking, face tracking, 2D and 3D image tracking, and body tracking.
- Plane detection: Detects horizontal planes and vertical surfaces.
- Anchor: Positions and tracks the device.
- Light estimation: Estimates on average the color temperature and brightness.
- Environmental Probe: Represents on a cube map a particular area of the physical environment.
- Meshing: generates triangular meshes to represent physical space.
- Collaborative participants: Position and track other devices allowing shared experiences.
- Human segmentation and occlusion: Apply distance and depth to virtual and physical world objects.

AR foundation SDK can incorporate machine learning techniques because it imports the features of two SDKs described earlier in this session ARCore and ARKit.

3.4 Vuforia

Vuforia is an SDK developed by Qualcomm that allows the creation of AR applications. This SDK is one of the most used in the AR market, despite being a proprietary platform (PCT: "Power_To_Create") [17]. Vuforia works on a wide range of devices, including smartphones, tablets, and augmented reality glasses, allowing developers to create immersive experiences in a variety of contexts.

Among the most appreciated features of this SDK, we can mention:

- Position tracking: It is possible to overlay virtual and physical objects on a single video in real-time [18].
- Marker technology: Use AR markers to determine relative positions of objects. There is no dependency on the type of marker, that is, it can identify any marker. Furthermore, it allows the use of numerous markers in the same video scene [18].
- Object and Function Library: Provides a library of target objects, object identification, and additional tracking functions [19].
- Mapping technology: Depth mapping and timing [20].

Vuforia incorporates several ML techniques into its Model Target Generator (MTG). MTG uses deep learning techniques to convert an existing 3D model into a Vuforia database that is used, among other purposes, for Model Target tracking [17]. Another research report has compared some object detection techniques based on ML and augmented reality techniques using Vuforia. According to their results, the Machine Learning-based approach detected objects with an accuracy of around 96% and the Vuforia-based approach detected objects with 100% [21].

Other recent work highlights that Vuforia can use several different types of images and objects as targets by scanning objects to produce 3D models. Additionally, you can use video data from cameras external to the devices to improve your recognition and tracking capabilities [12].

3.5   ARToolKit

ARToolKit is an SDK developed by the Human Interface Technology Laboratory at the University of Washington. This kit is a collection of software libraries, created to integrate into application programs. For this reason, it is distributed as source code and must be compiled for use. The project remained active until November 2017. From this date, the developers focused on a new open-source project, ARToolKitX. The latest version of ARToolKit is completely cross-platform. This SDK supports Android, iOS, and JavaScript [12, 22].

ARToolKit integrates some functionality using the ARKit SDK; among features, we can mention light estimation, True-Depth camera, visual-inertial odometry, scene identification, and rendering optimizations [14]. On the other hand, other features are specific to the ARToolKit SDK [22]:

- Individual or stereo cameras for position/orientation tracking.
- Tracking simple black squares.
- Flat image tracking.
- Camera calibration, optical stereo calibration.
- Support for optical head-mounted displays.

Some AR frameworks developed based on ARToolKit are: AndAR, which enables the use of AR on the Android platform; FLARManager, which is a framework built for flash-based AR applications; FLARToolKit, which is the Flash Actionscript version of ARToolKit; NyARToolkit, provides natural and marker-based feature tracking; and SLARToolkit, which is a flexible AR library created for developing AR applications with Silverlight [23].

Table 1. Some relevant characteristics of the SDKs: ARCore, ARKit, ARToolKit, ARFundation, and Vuforia.

SDK	ARCore [11]	ARKit [13]	ARToolKit [22]	ARFundation [15]	Vuforia [17]
Platform support	Android, iOS, United, and Web.	iOS	iOS, Android, Linus, Windows	Android, iOS, United, and Web.	iOS, Android, Windows
Tracking	Markers, NFT, Device, plane.	Markers, NFT, Device, plane, hand, body, facial.	Markers, plane.	Markers, NFT, Device, plane, hand, body, facial.	Markers, NFT, Device, plane.
Meshing	No	Yes	No	Yes	No
Occlusion	Yes	Yes	No	Yes	No
Open source	Yes	No	Yes	Yes	No
Sensors	Camera, IMU, GPS.	Camera, LiDAR IMU, GPS.	Camera.	Camera, LiDAR IMU, GPS.	Camera, GPS.

4 SDK ML_Kit

Machine Learning Kit (ML_Kit) is an SDK that includes a method package where several machine learning techniques are grouped. These methods enable the development of higher quality products, as they offer more attractive, personalized, and optimized solutions. ML_Kit was developed by Google and is primarily aimed at mobile app developers, whether Android or iOS. All these methods can be executed in real-time. This is because it has the particularity of being processed within the device itself, thus reducing the execution time. Each method can work offline, that is, using only elements stored within the device [3].

ML-Kit is an SDK that groups, within APIs, several sets of functionalities aimed at solving different work problems. In this section, the main APIs that are specifically directed to the area of computer vision will be highlighted [3].

4.1 Face Detection API

Using the ML Kit face detection APIs, it is possible to solve the following tasks:

- **Recognize and locate facial features.** Within each detected face, the coordinates of some of its main parts can be obtained. For example, eyes, cheeks, ears, nose, and mouth.
- **Obtain the contours of facial features.** Returns the contours of the detected human faces.
- **Recognition of facial expressions.** For example, it might be possible to determine whether a person is smiling or whether their eyes are closed.
- **Face tracking**. Each detected face is tagged with a unique identifier. In this way, it is possible to follow each face through the frames of a video.

4.2 Face Mesh Detection API

Using the ML Kit face mesh detection APIs, it is possible to solve the following tasks:

- **Recognize and locate faces.** It is possible to obtain a bounding box for each face detected in an image.
- **Face mesh.** It is possible to obtain all 468 3D points and triangle information for each detected face.

4.3 Object Detection and Tracking API

Using the ML Kit object detection and tracking APIs, it is possible to solve the following tasks:

- **Fast object detection and tracking**. Detect objects in real-time within images and return their relative location. Track each detected object through the stream of frames.
- **Detection of the prominent object**. Automatically determine the object that stands out the most in an image.
- **Approximate classification.** It is possible to classify objects into various general categories. Some of the supported categories are: Home Items, Fashion Items, Food, Plants, and Places.
- **Use a custom model to classify.** The classification model of objects detected within the images can be customized.

4.4 Pose Detection API

Using the ML Kit pose detection APIs, it is possible to solve the following tasks:

- **Body tracking.** To track the body, the model returns 33 reference points of the human skeleton. These points reference different parts of the entire body, for example ears, eyes, mouth, nose, hands, and feet.
- **InFrameLikelihood Score.** Returns, for each reference point, the probability that it is within the image frame.
- **Z coordinate for depth analysis.** Returns a depth value for each reference point. This coordinate allows us to know which part of the body is in front and which is behind, taking the hip as a reference.

4.5 Selfie Segmentation

Using the ML Kit selfie segmentation APIs, it is possible to solve the following tasks:

- **Face segmentation.** It allows one or more faces to be separated from the background of the analyzed image.
- **Half-body and full-body compatibility.** It allows you to separate, in portraits, the complete bodies from the background of the image. In addition, it allows each body to be separated into its upper and lower parts.

4.6 Image Labeling

Using the ML Kit selfie segmentation APIs, it is possible to solve the following tasks:

- **Image classifier into categories.** It allows you to recognize around 400 categories of objects whose frequency of appearance in photos is high.
- **Customize pre-trained models.** It allows adapting pre-trained models to your custom models and allows post-processing of images. The methods are supported by the TensorFlow library.

5 Architectural Proposal

We introduce a new architecture for organizing, grouping, and executing ML methods suitable for XR environments. This proposal builds upon the modular and layered architecture and incorporates the concepts of Real-Time Multi-Task Multi-Model (RT-MTMM) workloads [5] and the limitations of current SDKs. This architecture aims to provide real-time responses to user interactions while considering the limitations and characteristics of immersive environments. The key considerations of this Architecture are:

- **Real-time Performance:** The architecture needs to support low latency processing to ensure immediate responses to user interactions.
- **Resource Constraints:** XR devices often have limited processing power and battery life, requiring efficient resource utilization [3].
- **Adaptability:** The architecture should adapt to various XR environments and user interactions.

- **Scalability:** The design should allow for adding new functionalities and models as needed.
- **Heterogeneity:** The architecture needs to handle various ML task types (e.g., object recognition, speech recognition, gesture recognition) and model complexities [3].
- **Concurrency:** The architecture must support concurrent execution of multiple tasks and models to achieve real-time responsiveness [5].
- **Cascading and Cascaded-Concurrency:** The architecture should be able to handle scenarios where the output from one task is used as input for another, both concurrently and sequentially [5].
- **Privacy:** The architecture emphasizes privacy-preserving techniques throughout the pipeline, including data anonymization, secure storage and transmission, and user consent for data collection [24].

5.1 Proposed Architecture

Our proposed architecture consists of six principal components, Fig 1:

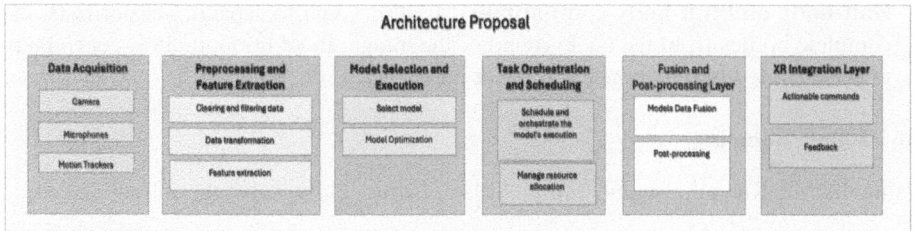

Fig. 1. Architecture Proposal for XR with Real-Time Multi-Model Capabilities.

Data Acquisition. This layer would be responsible for collecting various user input data from sensors like cameras, microphones, and motion trackers, using encryption techniques to protect data during transmission and storage. **It would also handle pre-processing and cleaning initial sensitive data for further processing** [24, 25].

Preprocessing and Feature Extraction. This layer takes the raw sensor data from the previous layer and performs essential processing steps before feeding it into the ML models. These steps can involve:

a) *Cleaning and filtering:* Removing noise reduction, and unwanted artifacts from the data, removing after this step sensitive data [24].
b) *Data transformation:* Resizing images, normalizing audio levels, or converting data to suitable formats for specific ML models.
c) *Feature extraction:* Extracting relevant features from the data that are most informative for the intended tasks (e.g., identifying key points in an image, extracting features for gesture recognition from motion tracker data).

Model Selection and Verification. This layer houses a library of pre-trained and optimized ML models, categorized based on their functionalities (e.g., object recognition, speech recognition, gesture recognition). These models are chosen specifically to be suitable for XR environments, considering factors like [3]:

a) *Real-time performance:* Models need to be able to process information and provide results quickly to maintain user engagement.
b) *Resource efficiency:* The limited processing power and battery life of XR devices necessitate computationally efficient models.
c) *Accuracy:* While efficiency is important, the models must still maintain acceptable accuracy in their respective tasks.
d) *The layer acts as a "model zoo":* dynamically selecting the most appropriate model for a given task based on the extracted features, user interactions, and real-time requirements. It may also employ techniques like model pruning (reduces the size of the model) or quantization (reduces the precision, improving speed) to further optimize efficiency without sacrificing significant accuracy.
e) The model would be downloaded from a signed service or local storage, loaded, and verified according to its signed key. Once the model has been verified to the expected functionality, the service provider will return the signed version of the model [24, 25].

Task Orchestration and Scheduling. This layer manages the concurrent execution of multiple models based on the extracted features and user interactions.

a) *Schedule and orchestrate the execution of multiple models concurrently:* this step utilizes RT-MTMM workloads or similar techniques that help in efficiently scheduling tasks simultaneously, such as recognizing people, detecting facial expressions, and recognizing gestures, all in real-time based on real-time deadlines, resource availability, and potential task dependencies. For example, the output of a face recognition model might be used as input for a facial expression detection model, creating a cascading workflow [5].
b) *Manage resource allocation:* Ensures that available resources (processing power, memory) are distributed efficiently among the concurrently running models.

Fusion and Post-processing. This layer receives the outputs from various models that were executed concurrently in the previous layer. It also guarantees that the results provided to the XR integration layer are meaningful, accurate, and ready for interaction within the immersive experience. Its primary functions include:

a) *Data fusion:* Combining the results from different models to create a single, improved output. This can involve techniques like averaging, weighted averaging, or more sophisticated methods depending on the specific tasks and models involved [26].
b) *Post-processing:* Refining the fused outputs to ensure they are interpretable and actionable within the XR environment. This could involve tasks like removing outliers, smoothing results, or adjusting the outputs based on context.

XR Integration. This final layer bridges the gap between the ML processing layers and the XR development environment. By seamlessly integrating with the XR environment, this layer ensures that the user receives real-time feedback and interacts with the environment based on the processed information from the previous layers. It translates the processed and refined outputs from the previous layer into:

a) *Actionable commands:* These commands might control virtual objects, trigger animations, modify soundscapes, or adjust user interfaces within the XR experience.
b) *Feedback:* This could involve generating visual, auditive or haptic feedback based on the received information, creating a seamless and responsive experience for the user.

5.2 Contributions of this Architecture

- **Improved User Experience:** Real-time responses and efficient resource utilization enhance the overall user experience in XR environments.
- **Adaptability:** The architecture adapts to various XR scenarios and user interactions through dynamic model selection and task scheduling.
- **Scalability:** The modular design allows for incorporating new functionalities and models as needed.
- **Privacy:** Ensures that sensitive data from users are not processed and stored, also that trusted models with signed permission perform declared tasks provided by their developers.

5.3 Methods, Models, or Tools that Could be Incorporated

This section proposes some methods and models that should be included within the proposed architecture. Some of the ideas proposed below arose from the needs highlighted in the previous works studied. [3, 5]. These ideas are fundamentally related to computer vision and speech processing.

5.4 Face Detection [3]

- **Recognition of people through the face.** With this functionality, you could customize the work within the devices.
- **Detect, from facial expressions, various types of human emotions.** For example, players' expressions could be used in certain applications such as video chat or games.
- **Modify portraits of people.** For example, the image of a person could be transformed during a video transmission. This would be possible if the video frames could be processed in real-time.
- **Generate avatars.** Create new avatars from user photos.

5.5 Face Mesh Detection [3]

- **Automatic adjustments in the meshes.** Automatic adjustments could be made to the meshes obtained for each face. These adjustments would consider the types of emotions detected with previous functionalities. Add more precise operations on faces, such as AR filters and selfie capture.

5.6 Object Detection and Tracking [3]

- **Create more specialized classification models:** Design new classification models that include more general categories. Additionally, they could include more specific subcategories within each added category.

5.7 Pose Detection [3]

- **Pose classification:** Create a model that can classify different known poses of the human body.
- **Repetition counting.** Given a pose of the human body, representative of a given training exercise, calculate the repetitions of the exercise.
- **Recognition of simple gestures.** Using the body's reference points and the relationship of their positions in space, recognize some simple gestures such as: touching the face, hands on the waist, and so on.

5.8 Selfie Segmentation [3]

- In addition to separating the background of faces or bodies within a scene, it allows adding effects within selfies or automatically inserting new backgrounds of interest.
- Automatic recognition of people in selfies.

5.9 Image Labeling [3].

- Adapt this API to classify different types of objects in images, for example: books, chairs, and so on. The Object Detection and Tracking API could be a starting option.

5.10 Other Methods [5]

- Gesture recognition.
- Speech recognition.
- Semantic segmentation.
- Depth Estimation.
- Plane and scene detection, and so on.

6   Some Ethical Considerations

Artificial intelligence is a technology that has revolutionized the world in the last decade. This technology has brought notable benefits in various research areas such as health, education, transportation, etc. However, it can also carry a high potential for damage and misuse. Below are some of the possible current concerns [27]:

Bias and Fairness. When we train a prediction or classification system based on historical data, this system could create biased learning. This is because the system will reproduce historical biases. That is, the application that does not consider these existing biases in the training data will create AI models of algorithmic decisions with the potential to reinforce or aggravate existing biases [28].

Explainability. Deep learning systems, typically based on neural network models, can have billions of parameters to tune. These types of schemes work like black boxes and generally, there is no way to understand or explain the decision-making process. This situation has led to the emergence of the subfield of explainable AI. This subfield studies how to make the decision-making process in complex models transparent [29].

Weaponizing AI. Like all major technologies that have been developed over time, AI is undoubtedly being and will be used in the military context directly or indirectly. AI will enhance war technology in a very short time [30].

Concentration of power: Many of the most powerful companies in the world know that AI-related technologies will allow them to obtain enormous benefits. For this reason, these companies are making large investments in the area. As with any advanced technology, AI is likely to concentrate power in the hands of the major organizations that control it [31].

Existential Risk. Many of the existential risks that humans suffer have arisen from the negative results of advanced technologies. As humans, we should be very cautious when building systems that are more powerful and capable than ourselves. These technologies, at best, will put great power in the hands of those who control it; or worse yet, we could become unable to control it in the future [32].

Data Collection. Regarding collecting and processing final user data that will be used with this ML architecture, we intend to follow the main ethical and privacy recommendations that comply with the General Data Protection Regulation (GDPR) [36]. Among these recommendations are: Make users aware of the data collection, storage, and processing processes; Give the user the possibility of revoking consent to data capture and informing them of the moment they were collected; Give the user control over which applications will use their data; Collect only needed data and store only until necessary.

In general, modern deep learning methods are based on processing large crowd-sourced data sets. These datasets may contain sensitive or private information. Among the proposals to be included within the ML architecture presented are some facial recognition methods. Facial recognition systems have a particularly high risk in terms of misuse of information, given that they need to process sensitive and private data such as images of faces. Controlling entities such as authoritarian states or large private technology companies could misuse this information to limit citizen rights, violate the privacy of potential users, and commercialize personal data [33]. For these and other reasons, some researchers or political activists have questioned whether this technology should exist [34].

Therefore, it is important to create designs that guarantee the privacy and security of people's information, especially when applying these techniques in high-risk areas such as healthcare and finance [35].

7   Conclusion

In recent decades, continuous hardware development has allowed immersive technologies to be accessible within different types of mobile devices for application in various daily tasks. Extended reality technologies and the development of virtual environments have been gaining ground and have been integrated to improve the quality of solutions to many everyday problems. On the other hand, machine learning techniques are another area that has had a new awakening in the last decade, particularly the deep learning subarea.

This work presented a viable architecture proposal in which different machine-learning methods and models can be grouped and organized. The objective is to create an efficient tool from which these models can be integrated into immersive environments. This architecture is made up of six main components:

- Data Acquisition.
- Preprocessing and Feature Extraction.
- Model Selection and Verification.
- Task Orchestration and Scheduling.
- Fusion and post-processing.
- XR Integration.

This architectural design guarantees that the methods and models to be inserted can adjust to the limitations of the different devices that support extended reality technologies. These methods must provide real-time responses to user interactions with high levels of accuracy.

Within the study, the characteristics of some of the main SDKs designed to support immersive technologies were analyzed. ML_Kit, one of the main SDKs designed for machine learning on mobile devices, was also analyzed and characterized. Finally, an analysis of some ethical considerations to be considered at work is carried out. This section is important because most of these proposed techniques will use sensitive and personal data. As a guideline for future work, each of the machine learning methods described will be developed. These methods will be adapted to the characteristics of the proposed architecture.

Acknowledgments. This paper was presented as part of the results of the Project "SIDIA-M_AR_Internet_For_Bondi", carried out by the Institute of Science and Technology - SIDIA, in partnership with Samsung Eletrônica da Amazônia LTDA, in accordance with the Information Technology Law n.8387/91 and article at the. 39 of Decree 10,521/2020.

References

1. Gupta, Y.P., Mukul, Gupta, N.: Deep learning model-based multimedia retrieval and its optimization in augmented reality applications. Multimed Tools Appl. **82**, 8447–8466 (2023). https://doi.org/10.1007/s11042-022-13555-y
2. Amin, D., Govilkar, S.: Comparative study of augmented reality Sdk's. Int. J. Comput. Sci. Appl. **5**, 11–26 (2015). https://doi.org/10.5121/ijcsa.2015.5102
3. ML Kit|Google for Developers (2024). https://developers.google.com/ml-kit
4. Alaskar, H., Saba, T.: Machine learning and deep learning: a comparative review. In: Singh Mer, K.K., Semwal, V.B., Bijalwan, V., Crespo, R.G. (eds.) Proceedings of Integrated Intelligence Enable Networks and Computing. Algorithms for Intelligent Systems. Springer, Singapore (2021). https://doi.org/10.1007/978-981-33-6307-6_15
5. Kwon, H., et al.: XRBench: an extended reality (XR) machine learning benchmark suite for the metaverse. In: Proceedings of the 6th MLSys Conference, Miami Beach, FL, USA, 2023.2211.08675, arXiv, http://arxiv.org/abs/2211.08675/ (2023)
6. Sahu, C., Young, C., Rai, R.: Artificial intelligence (AI) in augmented reality (AR)-assisted manufacturing applications: a review. Int. J. Prod. Res. **59**(16), 4903–4959 (2021). https://doi.org/10.1080/00207543.2020.1859636

7. Cao, J., Lam, K., Lee, L., Liu, X., Hui, P., Su, X.: Mobile Augmented Reality: User Interfaces, Frameworks, and Intelligence (2021). https://doi.org/10.1145/3557999
8. Liberatore, M., Wagner, W.: Virtual, mixed, and augmented reality: a systematic review for immersive systems research. Virtual Reality **25**, 773–799 (2021). https://doi.org/10.1007/s10 055-020-00492-0
9. Orji, J., Chan, G., Orji, R.: Augmented reality and machine learning in health: a systematic review, 59–67 (2023). https://doi.org/10.1145/3603421.3603430,
10. Karacif, E., Gurer, E.A.: Decision support system proposal on the usage of extended reality SDKs. In: Architecture Symposium 16th DDAS (MSTAS) - Special Issue 2022 **23**, 17–30 (2022). https://doi.org/10.18038/estubtda.1165368
11. Google. ARCore. https://developers.google.com/ar. Accessed 30 Mar 2023
12. Syahputra, M., Hardywantara, F., Andayani, U.: Augmented reality virtual house model using ARCore technology based on android. J. Phys. Conf. Ser. (2018)
13. ARKit|Apple Developer Documentation (2023). https://developer.apple.com/documentation
14. Ashour, Z., Yan, W.: BIM-powered augmented reality for advancing human-building interaction. eCAADe **1**, 169–178 (2020)
15. AR   Foundation|5.1.3   (2024).   ttps://docs.unity3d.com/Packages /com.unity.xr.arfoundation@5.1/manual/index.html
16. Chaudhry, T., Juneja, A., Rastogi, S.: AR foundation for augmented reality in unity. Int. J. Adv. Eng. Manag. (IJAEM) **3**(1), 662–667 (2021). www.ijaem.net ISSN: 2395-5252 https:// doi.org/10.35629/5252-0301662667
17. PTC. Vuforia Documentation. https://www.ptc.com/en/products/vuforia. Accessed 30 Mar 2023
18. Yao, J., Lin, Y., Zhao, Y., Chang-lin, L., Yuan, P.: Augmented reality technology-based wind environment visualization. In: CAADRIA, pp. 369–377 (2018)
19. Gül, L.F.: Studying architectural massing strategies in co-design mobile augmented reality tool versus 3d virtual world. eCAADe **35** (2017)
20. Goepel, G.: Augmented construction: Impact and opportunity of mixed reality integration in architectural design implementation. In: ACADIA, pp. 430–437 (2019)
21. Upadhyay, G., Aggarwal, D., Bansal, A., Bhola, G.: Augmented reality and machine learning based product identification in retail using Vuforia and MobileNets. In: 2020 International Conference on Inventive Computation Technologies (ICICT), Coimbatore, India, pp. 479–485 (2020). https://doi.org/10.1109/ICICT48043.2020.9112490
22. Lamb, P.: ARToolKit (2004). http://www.hitl.washington.edu/artoolkit/
23. Amin, D., Govilkar, S.: Comparative study of augmented reality SDK'S. Int. J. Comput. Sci. Appl. (IJCSA) **5**(1) (2015). https://doi.org/10.5121/ijcsa.2015.5102
24. Lehman, S.M., Alrumayh, A.S., Kolhe, K., Ling, H., Tan, C.: Hidden in plain sight: exploring privacy risks of mobile augmented reality applications. ACM Trans. Priv. Secur. **25**(4), 1–35 (2022). https://doi.org/10.1145/352402
25. Chen, C., et al.: Privacy computing meets metaverse: necessity, taxonomy and challenges. Ad Hoc Netw. 103457 (2024). ISSN 1570–8705. https://doi.org/10.1016/j.adhoc.2024.103457 (https://www.sciencedirect.com/science/article/pii/S1570870524000684)
26. Sharma, M., Kushwaha, P., Kumari, P., Kumari, P., Yadav, R.: Machine learning techniques in data fusion: a review. In: Sharma, H., Shrivastava, V., Bharti, K.K., Wang, L. (eds.) Communication and Intelligent Systems. ICCIS 2022. Lecture Notes in Networks and Systems, vol. 686. Springer, Singapore (2023). https://doi.org/10.1007/978-981-99-2100-3_31
27. Prince, S.: Understanding Deep Learning. MIT Press (2024). https://mitpress.mit.edu
28. Binns, R.: Algorithmic accountability, and public reason. Philosophy Technol. **31**(4), 543–556 (2018)
29. Grennan, L., et al.: Why businesses need explainable AI—and how to deliver it. McKinsey (2022)

30. Heikkilä, M.: Why business is booming for military AI startups. MIT Technol. Rev. **7** (2022)
31. David, H.: Why are there still so many jobs? the history and future of workplace automation. J. Econ. Perspect. **29**(3), 3–30 (2015)
32. Tegmark, M.: Life 3.0: Being human in the age of artificial intelligence. Vintage (2018)
33. Smith, M., Miller, S.: The ethical application of biometric facial recognition technology. AI Soc. **37**(167–175), 2022 (2022)
34. Barrett, L.: Ban facial recognition technologies for children — and everyone else. Boston Univ. J. Sci. Technol. Law **26**(2), 223–285 (2020)
35. Boulemtafes, A., Derhab, A., Challal, Y.: A review of privacy-preserving techniques for deep learning. Neurocomputing **384**, 21–45 (2020)
36. Wolford, B.: Editor in Chief, GDPR EU. General Data Protection Regulation (GDPR) (2024). https://gdpr.eu/what-is-gdpr/

Optimizing AR Application Testing: Integrating Metamorphic Testing to Address Developer and End-User Challenges

Dibyendu Brinto Bose, Brendan David-John, and Chris Brown[✉]

Virginia Tech, Blacksburg, VA, USA
{brintodibyendu,bmdj,dcbrown}@vt.edu

Abstract. The rapid proliferation of Augmented Reality (AR) applications in gaming, education, and healthcare underscores the urgent need for effective testing methodologies. As AR applications become more complex and widely used, ensuring their robustness and reliability is increasingly challenging. Traditional methods, like Junit and Unity tests, often fall short due to AR's inherent complexities, including 3D interactions and immersive environments. Our research addresses these challenges by integrating Metamorphic Testing (MT) to enhance AR application testing processes. MT overcomes traditional testing limitations by focusing on Metamorphic Relations (MRs) - expected relationships between inputs and outputs without a reliable test oracle. We define specific MRs tailored for mobile AR to facilitate fault identification and rectification. Our study presents a comprehensive framework for applying MT in mobile AR, detailing the MR identification and implementation process. We identified a set of MRs for mobile AR. These MRs, including Object Scaling with Distance, Raycast within Boundary, Visibility and Occlusion, Overlapping with Game Objects, and Orientation Consistency Relative to Gravity, address crucial aspects of AR functionality. They ensure realistic object scaling, consistent placement, correct occlusion handling, prevention of object overlap, and maintained orientation consistency. Adopting Metamorphic Testing significantly advances AR application testing. We are developing a tool to automatically incorporate these MRs into mobile AR applications, streamlining testing processes and enhancing system reliability. Future work will refine these relations and expand their scope to cover a broader range of AR functionalities.

Keywords: Metamorphic testing · Mobile AR · End users · Metamorphic relations

1 Motivation and Problem Statement

Augmented Reality (AR) and Virtual Reality (VR) technologies have significantly transformed various sectors, including gaming [2], entertainment [3],

© The Author(s), under exclusive license to Springer Nature Switzerland AG 2025
J. Y. C. Chen et al. (Eds.): HCII 2024, LNCS 15377, pp. 20–33, 2025.
https://doi.org/10.1007/978-3-031-76812-5_2

education [18,29], the military [32], and medicine [23,34]. These technologies offer immersive experiences that blend the physical and digital worlds, providing users with interactive and engaging environments. Moreover, the applications of AR/VR technologies are critical in various sectors. For example, in the medical field, AR is used for preoperative planning and intraoperative guidance, where accuracy and reliability are paramount to patient safety [31]. AR enhances learning by providing interactive and immersive content in education, which requires thorough testing to deliver consistent educational benefits [4]. Similarly, in the military, AR is used for training simulations that demand high reliability to ensure effective and realistic training outcomes [13,24]. The significance of AR/VR technologies across diverse fields clearly underscores the necessity for reliable and effective testing methodologies.

However, the development and deployment of AR/VR applications pose unique challenges, particularly in testing these systems to ensure their reliability and performance. The complexity of AR/VR environments, characterized by 3D interactions and real-time responses, demands innovative testing approaches beyond traditional software testing methods. Previous studies have emphasized the importance of robust testing to ensure software quality and system behavior [16,25,36]. Despite this, testing AR/VR applications remains challenging due to the lack of development knowledge among end-users [5] and the inadequacy of existing testing tools to address the specific needs of VR applications [33].

To better understand these challenges, in our preliminary work we conducted a comprehensive survey distributed to AR/VR developers. The survey identified specific hurdles in mixed-reality application testing, including difficulties in visualizing test results, managing complex feature requirements, and dealing with the obsolescence of traditional Q&A forums. Both developers and end-users highlighted the unpredictable outcomes and complex input-output relationships inherent in AR/VR environments.

Our research proposes the use of *Metamorphic Testing* (MT), a software testing approach that does not rely on a traditional test oracle [10], to address these challenges. MT uses Metamorphic Relations (MRs), which define the expected relationships between inputs and outputs, to identify and rectify faults that conventional testing methods might miss. This approach is particularly suitable for AR/VR applications, where the complexity and variability of user interactions make traditional testing less effective.

In our initial exploration of this approach, our research focuses on mobile AR environments. We started with mobile AR because, in our previous survey, we found that mobile devices are one of the main platforms that developers use mostly to build AR applications, and it was also available to us. We aim to enhance the testing process by integrating MT principles and improving user experiences. By identifying and implementing MRs tailored to mobile AR, we seek to create a robust testing framework that addresses the practical challenges developers and end-users face.

By proposing Metamorphic Testing as a robust methodology for AR application testing, we aim to address the unique challenges of AR application testing and contribute to the advancement and reliability of these transformative technologies. The rapid adoption and diverse applications of AR/VR technologies necessitate advanced testing methodologies to ensure their reliability and effectiveness. Through our proposed approach, we seek to provide a practical and scalable solution to the complex challenges of AR/VR application testing, fostering the development of reliable and high-quality AR/VR experiences.

2   Related Work

The related work section is divided into two main subsections: one focusing on the testing challenges and methodologies in AR/VR development and the other on the application and benefits of metamorphic testing in software engineering. This structure allows for a comprehensive understanding of the current state of research in these areas. It highlights the relevance of our study in addressing existing gaps for applying MT to AR development.

2.1   Testing in AR/VR Development

Various studies have identified AR/VR developers' challenges at multiple levels. Krauß et al. [22] analyzed the interactions between different roles of AR/VR creators in the development of extended reality (XR) applications, which encompass AR, VR, mixed reality (MR), and related technologies [12]. They provided insights into collaboration practices for cross-disciplinary AR/VR application development. Nebelling et al. [14] discussed the limitations of AR/VR authoring tools, emphasizing the need for tools accessible to users without extensive coding skills. Ashtari et al. [5] highlighted the obstacles end-user developers face, who are often professionals from various fields learning to code to support their tasks [26].

End-user development is a significant focus within the HCI community [6,21]. Interviews with AR/VR creators with minimal formal training revealed numerous barriers to XR application creation. Gandy et al. [15] explored how non-technologists can effectively develop XR applications using the Designer's Augmented Reality Toolkit (DART), underscoring the necessity for supportive tools. Speicher et al. [37] identified technical challenges in cross-device AR applications, highlighting six major issues: limited field of view and gesture recognition.

While Ashtari et al. [5] focused on barriers for end-users, Krauß et al. [22] discussed interdisciplinary development challenges, and Speicher et al. [37] examined cross-platform application issues. Addressing these barriers requires robust testing frameworks that can ensure the reliability and functionality of AR/VR applications across different use cases. Our paper aims to contribute to this need by providing a set of Metamorphic Relations (MRs) tailored for mobile AR applications and showcasing their proof of concept. By focusing on Metamorphic Testing (MT), we aim to enhance the robustness and reliability of mobile AR applications through a structured and innovative testing framework, thus addressing the practical challenges developers and end-users face.

2.2   Metamorphic Testing in Software Engineering

Metamorphic Testing (MT) has emerged as a robust solution to the oracle problem, which complicates the verification of program correctness [35]. MT addresses this issue by using metamorphic relations (MRs), which are necessary properties that relate multiple inputs to their expected outputs.

Chen et al. [9] compared the effectiveness of different test case generation methods, finding that random testing combined with MT generates more comprehensive test data sets than manual methods alone. Wu et al. [38] concluded that random source test cases are particularly effective for MT. Additionally, Segura et al. [35] demonstrated that combining random and manual testing enhances fault detection efficiency.

Batra and Sengupta [20] presented a genetic algorithm for selecting source test cases that maximize path coverage in the program under test. Similarly, Chen et al. [8] proposed generating source test cases by partitioning the input domain into equivalence classes.

MT has been applied across various domains, including numerical programs, computer graphics, and machine learning [19,30]. For example, Mayer and Guderlei [28] utilized MT for testing image processing programs, while Chan et al. [7] applied it to mesh simplification programs. Additionally, Jameel et al. [17] demonstrated MT's effectiveness in detecting faults in morphological image operations. No work so far has used MT in augmented reality application testing. In our work, we introduce a set of MRs specifically for improving testing and ensuring the behavior of mobile AR applications.

3   Approach

Metamorphic Testing (MT) presents an innovative approach to software testing, concentrating on identifying and leveraging relations between inputs and outputs in software systems [10]. This method addresses two primary challenges in software testing: the creation of additional test cases from existing ones, and the Oracle problem, which pertains to verifying outcomes when a definitive correct result is not available [11]. Central to MT are Metamorphic Relations (MRs), which define the expected relationships between inputs and outputs for a particular function or algorithm. These relations are crucial for predicting how changes in the input should affect the output, thereby providing a structured testing methodology that does not rely on known expected results.

To illustrate the utility of MT, consider the scenario of evaluating a search engine. If a user searches for "car", the engine returns a set of results. A meaningful MR in this context would be that a search for "electric car" should yield a subset of the results from the "car" search, as all electric cars are a subset of cars. MT excels in scenarios where the correct results are difficult to determine directly, as it generates new test cases (follow-up test cases) from original inputs (source test cases) using these MRs [39]. In the context of AR applications, defining effective MRs involves understanding the complex interactions within these immersive environments. Our approach employs an ad hoc method informed by existing research [11]. Although there are promising systematic approaches like swarm optimization for MR identification [40], current MT practices often rely on less structured methods. Nonetheless, ad hoc approaches have effectively detected faults [27], and we have tailored these methods to suit AR applications.

The proposed MRs for AR testing are designed to address the unique challenges these environments pose. Each MR specifies the inputs, expected outputs, and transformations tailored to mobile AR contexts. For example, one MR ensures that objects maintain their relative positions as the user navigates the AR space. Another MR checks that virtual objects scale appropriately with changes in the user's perspective or distance. Identifying these MRs involved a detailed analysis of typical AR interactions and the needs of both developers and end-users. We focused on core AR functionalities such as object placement, scaling, and occlusion to develop a comprehensive testing framework. This framework facilitates fault detection and enhances the overall user experience by ensuring consistent and expected behavior under various conditions.

Our MR identification process is iterative and collaborative. We refine our MRs based on AR developers' feedback and empirical testing results. This ongoing refinement ensures that our MRs remain effective and relevant as AR technology evolves. Incorporating insights from both developers and end-users helps us address practical challenges and real-world scenarios, making our approach robust and adaptable.

By adopting Metamorphic Testing, we aim to advance the testing methodologies for AR applications. The structured approach provided by MRs enables systematic fault detection and improves the reliability of complex AR environments. Our contributions lie in developing enhanced testing frameworks that support the growing demands of AR technologies, ultimately leading to more reliable and user-friendly AR applications.

4   Identified Mobile AR Metamorphic Relations

Our MR identification approach is informed by insights from end-users [5] and developers. The empirical studies focusing on end-users [5] and developers both highlighted several critical challenges inherent to the immersive nature of augmented reality (AR) applications. Key issues include verifying if an object resides within the detected plane, ensuring correct object spawning in the presence of other objects, confirming the accurate instantiation of objects, validating the proper functioning of the environment tracker, and maintaining consistent performance across varying environments. Addressing these complexities often entails a process of trial and error.

Our research specifically targets these areas by introducing meticulously designed metamorphic relations (MRs), aiming to address the concerns raised by practitioners in the field comprehensively. Utilizing their feedback, we identified fundamental features within AR applications that serve as a basis for MRs. The design of these MRs was guided by two usability heuristics as proposed by Nielsen [1]: *Recognition rather than recall* and *Error prevention*. The former informs our MR design by ensuring that testing processes and criteria are intuitively structured, reducing the cognitive load on developers by making test conditions and expected outcomes clear and easily identifiable. For example, MRs such as "Object Scaling with Distance" and "Raycast within Boundary" provide clear and predictable behaviors that developers can recognize without needing to recall specific details about the implementation. Similarly, the latter plays a pivotal role in shaping our MRs by prioritizing anticipating and eliminating potential errors in AR application testing. For instance, MRs like "Overlapping with Game Objects" and "Visibility and Occlusion" are designed to preemptively address common issues such as object overlap and occlusion errors, enhancing AR applications' overall reliability and user experience.

For example, the identified MRs *Object Scaling with Distance* embody these heuristics. This MR stipulates that as an object's distance from the AR camera changes, its scale should adjust accordingly to maintain a realistic appearance. This relation promotes recognition over recall by facilitating the ability to predict and recognize the correct behavior of virtual objects in physical space without the burden of memorizing specific distances or scaling factors. Moreover, it helps to prevent errors by explicitly defining expected outcomes for object scaling behavior, thereby preemptively outlining potential discrepancies in object appearance. For example, if an object significantly diminishes in size when moved a short distance, this would be immediately recognized as an error to be corrected. Table 1 delineates MRs specific to AR applications. Moreover, the we provide a detailed description of each of our metamorphic relations below. The implementations of our relations are available online.[1]

- **Raycast within Boundary**: This metamorphic relation ensures that when an object is spawned within the initial AR plane, it remains within the boundaries of any newly detected planes as the camera moves. The AR camera may detect multiple planes as it scans the environment. The object's position must be recalculated to ensure it stays within the boundaries of the newly detected plane. This is achieved by calculating the dot product for each plane's transform and checking if the value is within tolerance, iterating for each plane. This MR supports *Recognition rather than recall* by providing clear guidelines for verifying object placement within plane boundaries, making it easier for developers to predict object behavior. It also enhances *Error prevention* by ensuring that objects do not erroneously appear outside intended boundaries, thereby maintaining spatial accuracy. In Fig. 1, we displayed our implementation of this MR. Here, on the left, display information regarding the game object, showing if it is within the plane. Otherwise, it will display that it is outside the boundary.
- **Overlapping with Game Object**: This relation focuses on preventing the overlap of spawned game objects. When a touch event occurs on the screen to spawn a new game object, it must check for existing objects. If an existing game object is detected, the new one should not be spawned. Unity's layer

---

[1] https://github.com/brintodibyendu/metamorphic_test_ar.

Table 1. List of identified metamorphic relations (MR)

Name	Input	Expected output	Transformation	Transformed output	Implementation
Raycast within Boundary	Spawn an object in initial plane	Spawn object should be inside the plane boundary	While changing the camera AR camera adds multiple planes	Position of the placed objects should remain consistent within the boundary of the newly detected plane	Calculate the dot product for each plane's transform to check if the value is within tolerance. Iterate for each plane
Overlapping with Game Object	Simulate touch event over the screen.	Game object should be spawned	After spawning game object, any new game object should look for existing objects	If there is an existing game object, it should not be spawned	Use Unity's layer masking technique and apply raycasting to prevent overlapping by detecting other spawn objects instead of the plane layer
Visibility and Occlusion	Place an object partially behind another gameobject.	Part of the virtual object is occluded by the other gameobject object	Move the camera to view the object from different angles	The occlusion should adjust correctly as the perspective changes	Use depth sensing and spatial mapping to understand the environment and manage occlusion
Object Scaling with Distance	Place a spawn object at a known distance	Object appears at a size proportional to its distance	Change the position of the camera, moving closer to or further from the object	The object should scale up or down depending on the camera's distance	Calculate the distance between the camera and the object and adjust the scale of the object accordingly
Orientation Consistency Relative to Gravity	Place an object with a specific orientation relative to gravity	Object maintains its orientation	Rotate or tilt the AR device	The object should adjust its orientation to maintain consistency relative to gravity	Monitor device orientation and adjust the object's orientation accordingly
Varying Rotation	Simulate rotation	The rotation angle should be the same	Change the initial angle and speed	The rotation angle should be within a specific threshold	Assess the object's rotation parameters
Check Correct Object Instantiation	Spawn an object by touching	Touch and instantiate object should be the same	N/A	N/A	Comparing touch and instantiated object

masking technique and raycasting detect other spawned objects instead of the plane layer, ensuring no overlap occurs. This MR promotes *Recognition rather than recall* by using straightforward checks to ensure no object overlap, making it intuitive for developers to understand object interaction rules. It also supports *Error prevention* by automatically preventing new objects from spawning in occupied spaces, reducing the likelihood of visual and functional conflicts. In Fig. 2, we displayed the implementation of this MR. Here, if a

Fig. 1. Display of our implementation of proposed MR(Raycast within Boundary)

touch happens in any spawned objects (blue one), it will provide text to the audience that they click on the spawn object(in the display).

- **Visibility and Occlusion**: This MR deals with the occlusion of virtual objects by other game objects. When a virtual object is placed partially behind a real-world object, part of the virtual object should be occluded. The occlusion must adjust correctly as the camera moves to view the object from different angles. Depth sensing and spatial mapping are used to understand the environment and manage the occlusion effectively. This MR enhances

Fig. 2. Display of our implementation of proposed MR(Overlapping with Game Object). (Color figure online)

Recognition rather than recall by ensuring occlusion behaviors are predictable and consistent, making it easier for developers to recognize correct object visibility. It aids *Error prevention* by dynamically adjusting occlusion based on real-world interactions, thereby preventing unrealistic visual artifacts.

- **Object Scaling with Distance**: This relation ensures that virtual objects appear at a size proportional to their distance from the camera. When the camera's position changes, moving closer to or further from the object, the object's size should scale up or down accordingly. This is achieved by calculating the distance between the camera and the object and adjusting the object's scale based on this distance. This MR supports *Recognition rather than recall* by providing a clear and intuitive relationship between object size and distance, making it easy for developers to predict and recognize correct scaling behavior. It also ensures *Error prevention* by defining explicit scaling rules, thereby preventing anomalies in object appearance due to incorrect size adjustments.

- **Orientation Consistency Relative to Gravity**: This MR ensures that a virtual object maintains its orientation relative to gravity. When the AR device is rotated or tilted, the object should adjust its orientation to remain consistent with the gravitational pull. This is monitored by continuously tracking the device's orientation and adjusting the object's orientation accordingly. This MR enhances *Recognition rather than recall* by making orientation adjustments predictable and aligned with real-world gravity, simplifying the developer's task of ensuring correct object orientation. It supports *Error prevention* by continuously monitoring and adjusting the orientation, preventing objects from appearing misaligned or floating unnaturally.
- **Varying Rotation**: This relation focuses on ensuring the consistency of rotation angles. When a rotation is simulated, the rotation angle should remain consistent regardless of changes in the initial angle and speed. The rotation angle should be within a specific threshold, and the object's rotation parameters are assessed to ensure this consistency. This MR supports *Recognition rather than recall* by providing clear criteria for consistent rotation, making it easier for developers to predict and verify correct rotation behaviors. It aids *Error prevention* by defining rotation thresholds and monitoring parameters, thereby preventing rotational inconsistencies that could lead to visual and functional errors.
- **Check Correct Object Instantiation**: This MR verifies that the object instantiated by a touch event on the screen matches the touch input. The comparison is straightforward, ensuring that the touch and the instantiated object correspond correctly. This MR supports *Recognition rather than recall* by ensuring that the instantiation process is direct and predictable, making it easy for developers to confirm correct object creation. It enhances *Error prevention* by verifying the correspondence between touch input and instantiated object, preventing incorrect or unintended object creation.

5   Threats to Validity

In conducting this research, we acknowledge several threats to the validity of our findings and propose measures to mitigate them.

5.1   Generalization to Other AR Devices

One primary threat to validity is the limited scope of our study, which focused exclusively on mobile AR applications. Other AR devices like Magic Leap 2 and

HoloLens possess different hardware and software capabilities. Consequently, the Metamorphic Relations (MRs) identified in this study might not directly apply to these other AR platforms. We concentrated on the MR relations rather than specific implementations to mitigate this threat. This focus ensures that, while the implementations may vary across different AR devices, the underlying principles of the identified MRs can be adapted by practitioners to suit various platforms. By providing a flexible framework, we aim to support the broader application of our findings across diverse AR technologies.

5.2 Identification of Metamorphic Relations

Another threat to validity arises from our approach to identifying MRs. As highlighted by previous research, there is no standardized method for MR identification, leading us to adopt an ad-hoc approach. This lack of a systematic methodology could affect the comprehensiveness and reliability of our identified MRs. To address this threat and enhance the external validity of our results, we incorporated feedback from core AR developers and end-users. By involving practitioners in the MR identification process, we aimed to ensure that the identified MRs are practical, relevant, and address real-world needs. This collaborative approach helps validate and align our findings with the requirements of AR application developers and users.

6   Future Work

Building on the promising results of our study, future work will focus on several key areas to further enhance the effectiveness of Metamorphic Testing in AR applications.

Firstly, we plan to develop and implement an automated tool that integrates the identified MRs into the testing processes of AR applications, particularly on mobile platforms. This tool will aim to seamlessly incorporate MT principles into existing AR development environments, offering developers an intuitive and efficient testing interface without requiring significant changes to their workflow.

Secondly, we will comprehensively evaluate our automated tool, comparing its performance and usability against traditional AR testing methodologies. These evaluations will involve extensive user studies and feedback sessions with AR developers and end-users to gather insights and refine the tool's features. This process will help validate our approach's practicality and effectiveness in real-world scenarios.

Our future research will also explore identifying and integrating new MRs to cover a broader range of AR functionalities. This includes emerging technologies such as spatial audio integration, multi-user interactions, and advanced gesture recognition. We will continuously update our MR framework to stay ahead of the evolving AR landscape and provide comprehensive testing solutions that address various AR application scenarios. Collaboration with industry partners and AR application developers will be critical to our future work. We intend to engage in pilot projects and case studies to demonstrate the practical benefits of MT in diverse AR application contexts. These collaborations will validate our testing framework and foster innovation and adoption of MT in the industry.

Ultimately, our goal is to contribute to the advancement of AR technology by providing robust, automated testing solutions that enhance the development and quality of AR applications. Through ongoing research and development, we aim to support the growth of the AR industry and ensure that users can enjoy seamless, immersive experiences across various applications and platforms.

7   Conclusion

The increasing prevalence of Augmented Reality (AR) applications in various fields, such as gaming, education, and healthcare, necessitates the development of robust and reliable testing methodologies. Traditional testing approaches often struggle with the unique challenges presented by AR environments, including complex 3D interactions and immersive user interfaces. Our research aims to bridge this gap by integrating Metamorphic Testing (MT) into the AR application testing process.

Our study introduces a novel framework for applying MT to mobile AR applications. By identifying specific Metamorphic Relations (MRs) tailored for AR, we provide a method to detect faults that traditional testing methods might overlook. These MRs help in defining the expected relationships between inputs and outputs, even in the absence of a reliable test oracle. This approach not only enhances the accuracy of testing but also ensures that the AR applications deliver consistent and reliable user experiences.

The research involved a detailed process of MR identification and implementation, ensuring that the testing criteria are intuitive and effective. By focusing on usability heuristics such as "Recognition rather than recall" and "Error prevention", we designed MRs that anticipate potential errors and facilitate easier testing processes. Our findings underscore the potential of MT to significantly advance AR application testing by providing a structured methodology that addresses the unique complexities of AR environments.

References

1. 10 usability heuristics for user interface design. https://www.nngroup.com/articles/ten-usability-heuristics/
2. Microsoft hololens. https://www.microsoft.com/en-us/hololens/
3. Oculus quest. https://www.oculus.com/experiences/quest/
4. Ardiny, H., Khanmirza, E.: The role of ar and vr technologies in education developments: opportunities and challenges. In: 2018 6th RSI International Conference on Robotics and Mechatronics (IcRoM), pp. 482–487 (2018)
5. Ashtari, N., Bunt, A., McGrenere, J., Nebeling, M., Chilana, P.K.: Creating augmented and virtual reality applications: current practices, challenges, and opportunities. In: Proceedings of the 2020 CHI Conference on Human Factors in Computing Systems, CHI 2020, pp. 1–13. Association for Computing Machinery, New York (2020)

6. Burnett, M., Cook, C., Rothermel, G.: End-user software engineering. Commun. ACM **47**(9), 53–58 (2004)
7. Chan, W., Ho, J., Tse, T.: Piping classification to metamorphic testing: an empirical study towards better effectiveness for the identification of failures in mesh simplification programs, vol. 1, pp. 397–404 (2007)
8. Chen, T., Cheung, S.-C., Yiu, S.: Metamorphic testing: a new approach for generating next test cases (2020)
9. Chen, T., Huang, D., Tse, T., Zhou, Z.Q.: Case studies on the selection of useful relations in metamorphic testing (2004)
10. Chen, T.Y., Cheung, S.C., Yiu, S.M.: Metamorphic testing: a new approach for generating next test cases. Technical Report HKUST-CS98-01, Department of Computer Science The Hong Kong University of Science and Technology (1998)
11. Chen, T.Y., et al.: Metamorphic testing: a review of challenges and opportunities. ACM Comput. Surv. (CSUR) **51**(1), 1–27 (2018)
12. Chuah, S.: Why and who will adopt extended reality technology? literature review, synthesis, and future research agenda (2018)
13. Doer, K.-U., Schiefel, J., Kubbat, W.: Virtual cockpit simulation for pilot training, p. 8 (2001)
14. Eswaran, M., Bahubalendruni, M.R.: Challenges and opportunities on AR/VR technologies for manufacturing systems in the context of industry 4.0: a state of the art review. J. Manuf. Syst. **65**, 260–278 (2022)
15. Gandy, M., MacIntyre, B.: Designer's augmented reality toolkit, ten years later: implications for new media authoring tools. In: Proceedings of the 27th Annual ACM Symposium on User Interface Software and Technology, UIST 2014, pp. 627–636. Association for Computing Machinery, New York (2014)
16. Ikeda, B., Szafir, D.: An ar debugging tool for robotics programmers. In: 4th International Workshop on Virtual, Augmented, and Mixed Reality for HRI (2021)
17. Jameel, T., Lin, M., Chao, L.: Test oracles based on metamorphic relations for image processing applications. In: 2015 IEEE/ACIS 16th International Conference on Software Engineering, Artificial Intelligence, Networking and Parallel/Distributed Computing (SNPD), pp. 1–6 (2015)
18. Kamińska, D., et al.: Virtual reality and its applications in education: survey. Inf. **10**, 318 (2019)
19. Kanewala, U., Bieman, J.M.: Using machine learning techniques to detect metamorphic relations for programs without test oracles. In: 2013 IEEE 24th International Symposium on Software Reliability Engineering (ISSRE), pp. 1–10 (2013)
20. Kaur, G., Jyotsna, S.: An efficient metamorphic testing technique using genetic algorithm, vol. 141, pp. 180–188 (2011)
21. Ko, A.J., et al.: The state of the art in end-user software engineering. ACM Comput. Surv. **43**(3) (2011)
22. Krauß, V., Boden, A., Oppermann, L., Reiners, R.: Current practices, challenges, and design implications for collaborative ar/vr application development. In: Proceedings of the 2021 CHI Conference on Human Factors in Computing Systems, CHI 2021. Association for Computing Machinery, New York (2021)
23. Kuechenmeister, C.A., Linton, P.H., Mueller, T.V., White, H.B.: Eye tracking in relation to age, sex, and illness. Arch. General Psychiat. **34**(5), 578–579 (1977)
24. Lee, W.-S., Kim, J.-H., Cho, J.-H.: A driving simulator as a virtual reality tool. In: Proceedings. 1998 IEEE International Conference on Robotics and Automation (Cat. No. 98CH36146), vol. 1, pp. 71–76 (1998)

25. Lehman, S.M., Ling, H., Tan, C.C.: Archie: a user-focused framework for testing augmented reality applications in the wild. In: 2020 IEEE Conference on Virtual Reality and 3D User Interfaces (VR), pp. 903–912 (2020)
26. Lieberman, H., Paternò, F., Klann, M., Wulf, V.: End-user development: an emerging paradigm, vol. 9, pp. 1–8 (2006)
27. Liu, H., Kuo, F.-C., Towey, D., Chen, T.Y.: How effectively does metamorphic testing alleviate the oracle problem? IEEE Trans. Softw. Eng. **40**(1), 4–22 (2013)
28. Mayer, J., Guderlei, R.: An empirical study on the selection of good metamorphic relations. In: 30th Annual International Computer Software and Applications Conference (COMPSAC'06), vol. 1, pp. 475–484 (2006)
29. Mileva, G.: How is augmented reality transforming special education? AR Post (2021). https://arpost.co/2021/06/25/augmented-reality-special-education/
30. Murphy, C., Kaiser, G., Hu, L., Wu, L.: Properties of machine learning applications for use in metamorphic testing, pp. 867–872 (2008)
31. Nicholson, D., Chalk, C., Funnell, W., Daniel, S.: Can virtual reality improve anatomy education? a randomised controlled study of a computer-generated three-dimensional anatomical ear model. Med. Educ. **40**, 1081–1087 (2006)
32. Parkin, S.: How vr is training the perfect soldier (2015). https://www.wareable.com/vr/how-vr-is-training-the-perfect-soldier-1757/
33. Rzig, D.E., Iqbal, N., Attisano, I., Qin, X., Hassan, F.: Virtual reality (vr) automated testing in the wild: a case study on unity-based vr applications. In: Proceedings of the 32nd ACM SIGSOFT International Symposium on Software Testing and Analysis, pp. 1269–1281 (2023)
34. Samadbeik, M., Yaaghobi, D., Bastani, P., Abhari, S., Rezaee, R., Garavand, A.: The applications of virtual reality technology in medical groups teaching. J. Adv. Med. Educ. Professional. **6**(3), 123 (2018)
35. Segura, S., Fraser, G., Sanchez, A.B., Ruiz-Cortés, A.: A survey on metamorphic testing. IEEE Trans. Softw. Eng. **42**(9), 805–824 (2016)
36. Correa Souza, A.C., Nunes, F.L., Delamaro, M.E.: An automated functional testing approach for virtual reality applications. Softw. Test. Verificat. Reliabil. **28**(8), e1690 (2018)
37. Speicher, M., Hall, B.D., Yu, A., Zhang, B., Zhang, H., Nebeling, J., Nebeling, M.: XD-AR: challenges and opportunities in cross-device augmented reality application development. Proc. ACM Hum.-Comput. Interact. **2**(EICS), 1–24 (2018)
38. Wu, P., Xiao-Chun, S., Jiang-Jun, T., Hui-Min, L.: Metamorphic testing and special case testing: a case study. J. Softw. **16**, 07 (2005)
39. Yoo, S.: Metamorphic testing of stochastic optimisation. In: 2010 Third International Conference on Software Testing, Verification, and Validation Workshops, pp. 192–201. IEEE (2010)
40. Zhang, J., et al.: Search-based inference of polynomial metamorphic relations. In: Proceedings of the 29th ACM/IEEE International Conference on Automated Software Engineering, ASE 2014, pp. 701–712. Association for Computing Machinery, New York (2014)

Comparing Vibrotactile and Visual Feedback in Virtual Reality Motion Guidance: An Investigation on Workload and Performance

Yunlu Ding, Hualin Zhang, and Jiaxin Zhang[✉]

School of System Design and Intelligent Manufacturing, South University of Science and Technology, Shenzhen 518071, Guangdong, China
zhangjx@sustech.edu.cn

Abstract. Virtual reality (VR) technology has become increasingly prevalent in telerehabilitation, due to its potential for providing immersive environments to enhance situation perception. Practical motion guidance optimizes motor training outcomes and facilitates skill learning and rehabilitation progress. Vibrotactile feedback has garnered attention due to the popularity of multimodal applications and has been shown to optimize motion guidance performance. However, the effectiveness and mental workload associated with visual and vibrotactile feedback instruction are currently unclear, and the research on the motion guidance mode is insufficient. Furthermore, the guidance performance (including direction accuracy, speed control accuracy, and completion time) and subjective mental workload of each guiding mode under static and dynamic movement states remain uncertain. To estimate the effectiveness of different feedback modalities, a 2×2 factorial within-subject design experiment involving 16 participants was conducted to assess the impact of feedback modalities and movement states on subjective mental workload. The results indicated a strong preference among participants for visual feedback, which was attributed to its higher motion accuracy and lower mental workload. Additionally, the dynamic movement state was associated with decreased motion guidance performance and increased mental workload. Future studies should explore performance under various motion-guiding scenarios to inform precise feedback mode design.

Keywords: Virtual Reality · Motion Guidance · Vibrotactile and visual Feedback · State of Motion · Workload and performance

1 Introduction

Many chronic diseases or mechanical injuries that can be cured require adequate rehabilitation training [1]. Additionally, the population affected by chronic diseases and mechanical injuries increases every year. Many rehabilitation programs are traditionally conducted offline under unified guidance, which allows patients to receive direct supervision from rehabilitation physicians and achieve better therapeutic effects. However, this approach faces several challenges. For instance, there is a severe shortage

J. Y. C. Chen et al. (Eds.): HCII 2024, LNCS 15377, pp. 34–45, 2025.
https://doi.org/10.1007/978-3-031-76812-5_3

of rehabilitation physicians when dealing with many patients. This scarcity of medical resources results in a significant portion of individuals not receiving sufficient rehabilitation training. Furthermore, many patients themselves have physical impairments and compromised mobility, making it impossible for them to participate in on-site treatment. Therefore, a method that enables remote guidance for rehabilitation training is crucial.

Due to these issues, remote rehabilitation is becoming increasingly popular because remote rehabilitation systems can overcome geographical and time barriers, allowing patients to receive treatment guidance anytime, anywhere. In recent years, the continuous development of virtual reality (VR) technology has provided new means for remote medical rehabilitation guidance [2]. Many rehabilitation therapies have been published with the assistance of VR technology. For instance, rehabilitation from stroke [3, 4], brain injury [5], and neurorehabilitation [6, 7]. VR technology can provide users with better immersion and experience, enhancing their sense of presence and improving rehabilitation learning outcomes [8]. The guidance methods for action learning in VR involve visual and tactile feedback. However, it still needs to be made clear which guidance method is more accurate for static and dynamic movements, and further research is needed on the cognitive load imposed on users.

Motion learning in virtual reality is becoming gradually popular and there are three primary modalities: visual, audio, and haptic. Vision is commonly used as our first and prior information receiver, so visual feedback is widely studied and almost inevitable. In many studies, audio or vibrotactile feedback is considered as an augment for visual feedback, creating a multi-modality mode to enhance the feedback effect [9–11]. Vibrotactile feedback has been widely used for motion guidance in virtual reality, for instant navigation [12], dancing [13], snowboarding [14, 15], and instrument learning [16].

Several studies have explored the use of vibrotactile in different motor tasks, such as guiding a 1DOF arm movement [17], posture control [18], and balance maintenance [19]. Vibrotactile feedback allows users to discern the tactile cues on specific body parts in the motor tasks, potentially enhancing motion guidance performance and reducing motor error by engaging closely with the proprioceptive and kinaesthetic systems [20]. The research suggests that vibrotactile feedback can be as effective as visual feedback in a virtual environment [21]. Moreover, vibrotactile feedback was estimated to increase direction clarity and reduce system utility for collision feedback in a virtual reality environment [22].

In addition to behavioral performance, a series of subjective perceptions serves as evaluation indicators for the sustainability of a feedback modality for given tasks. Previous studies have investigated the impact of haptic feedback on mental workload during a room boundary experiment in virtual reality, finding that while haptic feedback may increase mental workload, performances remain comparable to visual guidance [23]. Some studies have reported that tactile feedback, such as a 3D virtual reality car race, led to shorter completion times, outperforming visual cues due to reduced information load [24]. However, limited research has delved deeply into the effect of mental workload on motion guidance. Motor skill retention performance has improved with visual-haptic cues despite increased cognitive workload [25]. Additionally, although vibrotactile feedback may result in higher response speed, visual feedback tends to be rated as having a higher preference than other modalities [26].

Several studies have explored the impact on behavioral performance and mental workload in different movement states. Previous research has indicated that the higher walking speed is associated with increased motion errors [27], leading to longer reaction time and reduced feedback detection [28]. For movement states, prior studies found that mental workload tends to be higher during tasks involving high moving speeds with visual feedback [29].

Our long-term objective is to develop precise feedback patterns to guide motor learning in virtual reality, thereby contributing to remote rehabilitation efforts. The initial step towards achieving this objective is to assess the effectiveness of various feedback modalities for motion guidance. To determine which guidance method, visual or tactile, is more effective in enhancing arm movement direction and speed accuracy in both static and dynamic states, as well as evaluate users' subjective experiences with each method (perceived difficulty, mental workload, and behavioral intention), we designed a 2×2 virtual reality motor learning experiment. Participants were recruited in the testing phase, and the results were subsequently analyzed using appropriate data analysis methods.

We hypotheses the result would be as follows:

- H1: In static tasks, in either visual or vibrotactile feedback conditions:
- H1a. Participants perform better at the static level than at the dynamic level of the task.
- H1b. Participants have a lower mental workload at the static level than at the dynamic level.
- H2. Compared with visual feedback:
- H2a. Participants report no performance and mental workload difference at a static level between the two feedback modes.
- H2b. Participants perform better and have lower mental workload with vibrotactile feedback at the dynamic level.

In Sect. 1, we introduce this research and related work. The Sect. 2 exhibits our methods, including participants, apparatus, experiment design, procedure, and data collection. In Sects. 3 and 4, we present our results and discuss the findings and limitations. The Sect. 5 contains the conclusion and future work.

2 Method

An experiment was designed to estimate the impact of motion guidance performance under dynamic and static motion states and visual and vibrotactile feedback. Initially, we developed a haptic armband and a pair of leg bands capable of providing vibrotactile feedback. The learning tasks were conducted within a virtual reality created using the Unity3D platform (version 2021.3.9) with VR functionality supported by SteamVR (version 2.2.3) and VIVE VR wearable devices. Data collection comprised two components: behavioral data captured by the devices and subjective mental workload assessed by a scale adapted from NASA-TLX [30]. Following the preparation of the experiment, a total of 16 participants were recruited to complete tasks.

2.1 Participants

Sixteen right-handed participants (5 males, 11 females, aged 21–28, mean = 22.86, median = 22.5, SD = 1.67) voluntarily participated in this experiment, all of whom had no cognitive impairment. All the participants were undergraduate and postgraduate students from the Southern University of Science and Technology.

2.2 Experiment Design

In our experiment, we utilized the following devices:

- A VIVE VR head-mounted display (HMD) will provide the virtual environment, and a VR hand controller will be used for task completion.
- A vibrotactile armband designed to offer direction feedback and two vibrotactile leg bands aimed at maintaining a steady pace during dynamic tasks.

The vibrotactile armband was designed with an Arduino ESP32 chip and four GPIO digital pins. Each vibrotactile leg band was created using an Arduino ESP8266, controlled by a single GPIO digital pin.

Figure 1 depicts our devices, including armbands (A) and vibrotactile position (A, B), vibrotactile leg bands and position (C, D), and all the equipment (E).

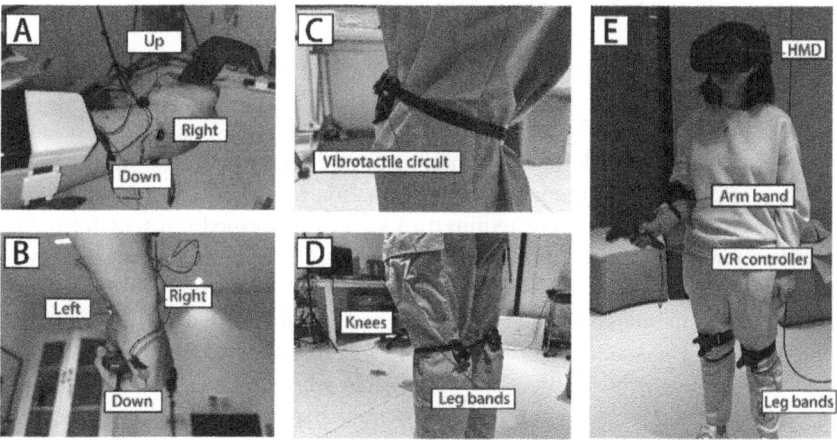

Fig. 1. Apputuses utilized. A and B show the vibrotactile location. C and D show the leg bands' location. E shows all the wearables that were equipped during the tasks.

The VR environment for tasks was developed using Unity3D, and the scripting was programmed in the C# language. The VR functionality was executed with the SteamVR application. In the VR environment, participants were required to navigate a random path with a VR controller. The path contained a total of a total 20 steps, randomly generated by the C# program (see Fig. 2). Visual or vibrotactile feedback was provided to guide the direction and movement speed in each task.

In the visual static task, arrows were designed to guide the ball's direction at each step. These arrows were color-coded to indicate the t participant's arm movement speed: red for fast-moving speed (over 0.4 m/s), yellow for slow speed (less than 0.1 m/s), and green for the expected speed (between 0.1 m/s−0.4 m/s). In the visual dynamic task, two bulbs would be positioned behind the maze, one on the left and one on the right within the participant's field of vision. These bulbs alternated between red and green, with each color lasting 1.5 s. Only one bulb was green at any given time, guiding the frequency of leg movements to maintain a dynamic state.

In the vibrotactile static task, the vibrotactile armband on the right arm received signals from the Unity3D application and activated one of four directions vibrotactile circuits accordingly. These circuits were designed to guide the movement direction to participants with vibrations signaling upward, downward, leftward, or rightward. Participants received only vibrotactile cues with no visual guidance apart from the presence of balls and the maze.

Additionally, the intensity of the vibrotactile cues guided speed: an intensity of 255 Hz (in the C program of the Arduino chip) indicated the highest intensity for slow speed, 100 Hz indicated fast speed, and 176 Hz indicated the correct speed. Each vibrotactile feedback lasted 200 ms long, with a 500 ms interval between every two feedbacks. In the vibrotactile dynamic task, the two vibrotactile leg bands delivered one-second-long vibrotactile cues repeatedly, with only one leg band giving cues at a time. The switching frequency of these matched that of the visual bulbs, ensuring participants maintained a consistent dynamic state throughout the task.

2.3 Procedure

Participants began to experiment individually, with each session booked in advance. An announcement was made to the participants at the experiment's outset, providing an objective explanation of the tasks and information regarding privacy. Following the announcement, participants were required to sign an informed consent form. Subsequently, they put on all the devices mentioned earlier, familiarizing themselves with the task requirements and rules in preparation for the learning section. Before the formal experiment, participants conducted a learning section using two feedback modes for motion guidance. The sequence of the learning section is as follows: visual static (VS), visual dynamic (VD), vibrotactile static (VTS), and vibrotactile (VTD) was fixed. Tasks within each learning section were conducted until participants indicated their understanding of the task requirements and rules. After the learning phase, participants were asked to provide basic information and then commence the experimental tasks. To mitigate any potential learning or prediction effects on the results, each participant was randomly assigned a sequence of four tasks. Participants completed a survey between each task containing the criteria outlined in the appendix.

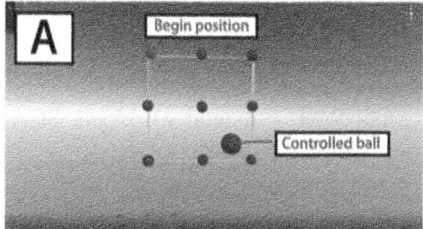 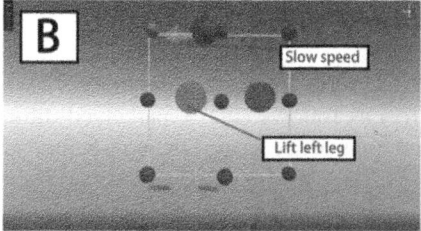

Fig. 2. Interface design. A shows that vibrotactile tasks have no visual cues and B shows the task under visual dynamic conditions, and the red and green squares are the legs pace cues (Color figure online).

2.4 Data Collection

Data from Devices. The VR sensors recorded the 3D distance every 0.5 s, capturing the virtual ball's "X", "Y" and "Z" coordinates. These coordinates were utilized to calculate the movement distance between two consecutive records. The distance was then divided by the time scale according to the following formula:

$$CS = \frac{\sqrt{x_{i+1}^2 + y_{i+1}^2 + z_{i+1}^2} - \sqrt{x_i^2 + y_i^2 + z_i^2}}{TI}$$

where CS refers to current speed, and TI refers to time interval. A 'right' tag was recorded when the CS was within the range of 0.1 m/s to 0.4 m/s. Fast and slow tags were recorded if the CS exceeds 0.4 m/s or below 0.1 m/s, respectively.

The definition of calculation of the speed control accuracy ratio was defined as follows:

$$SCA = \frac{N_{rt}}{N_{tt}}$$

where SCA refers to speed control accuracy, N_{tt} refers to the number of total tags and N_{rt} refers to the number of proper tags.

Direction accuracy. Participants were tasked with navigating a randomized maze path without making a partial step. Failure to adhere to this rule, such as touching a non-destination ball, resulted in the termination of the task. At the onset of each task, participants were allocated three points, one point deducted for each misstep. Consequently, participants had three chances to complete each task, and failure occurred when their points reached zero.

The definition of direction accuracy ratio was defined using the following formula:

$$DA = \frac{N_{rp}}{N_{tp}}$$

where DA refers to direction accuracy. N_{tp} refers to the number of all points for one task, and N_{rp} refers to the number of points remaining for one task.

Data from the Survey. The survey assessed several constructs, including per-ceived difficulty (PD) and subjective mental workload (MW) scale adapted with NASA-TXL (Hart & Staveland, 1988).

3 Results

The data were analyzed using the Spyder platform (version 5.4.3) with Python (version 3.11.2) as follows (PD = perceived difficulty, and WM = mental workload, SCA = speed control accuracy, DA = direction accuracy) (Tables 1 and 2):

Table 1. Mean value and standard deviations of data

		VS	VD	VTS	VTD
Component	Variable	Mean (SD)	Mean (SD)	Mean (SD)	Mean (SD)
Subjective	PD	1.312 (0.479)	3.625 (1.544)	2.625 (1.310)	4.566 (1.632)
	MW	2.838 (0.794)	4.360 (1.564)	3.700 (1.321)	5.675 (1.771)
Behavioral	SCA	62.83% (3.61%)	32.96% (3.84%)	42.07% (1.67%)	26.37% (1.35%)
	DA	100% (0)	100% (0)	87.5% (26.87%)	81.25% (32.13%)

We conducted a Kruskal-Wallis test among four groups to determine the statistical significance. The results are as follows:

Table 2. P-value of four groups among all criteria

	PD	MW	SCA	DA
h	30.489	19.926	24.726	10.584
p	0.000	0.000	0.000	0.014

These results indicate significant differences in all criteria between at least two groups among four tasks. Then, we conducted Dunn's test to examine the statistical significance between each pair of groups. All results are as Fig. 3 shows (***: $p <= 0.001$; **: $0.001 < p <= 0.01$; *: $0.01 < p <= 0.05$):

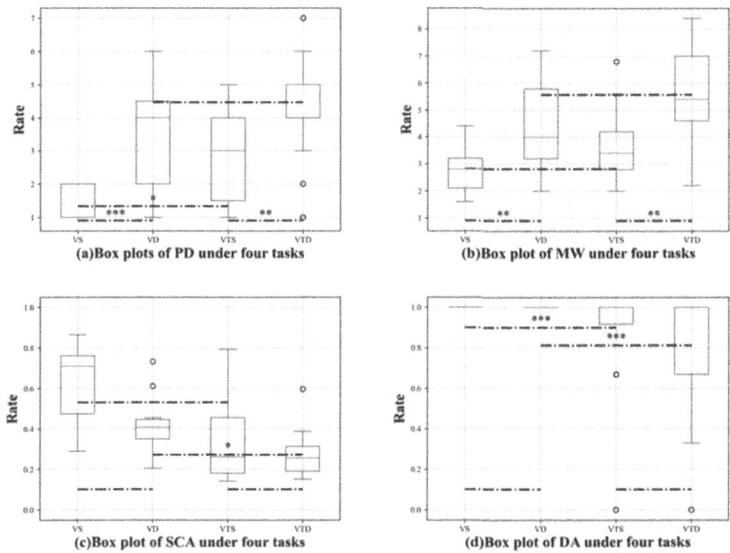

Fig. 3. Box plots of criteria. All results support H1, and no result supports H2.

4 Discussion

4.1 Motion Performance of Different Tasks

Based on the results above, it was observed that the SCA in tasks utilizing vibrotactile feedback was consistently lower compared to those with visual cues. Regardless of whether the movement state was static or dynamic, the DA never reached one hundred percent when the vibrotactile feedback task was used (p $<=$ 0.001 in both movement states), indicating its inferiority to visual cues. This discrepancy may be attributed to visual cues being more commonly relied upon for direction guidance in daily activities, while fewer individuals depend on vibrotactile cues.

Interestingly, the results for SCA revealed subtle differences, showing that only under dynamic state visual feedback reported increased SCA compared to vibrotactile feedback. It was noted that the SCA assessment not only encompassed speed accuracy during movement but also included the time taken for feedback direction distinguishing. The continuous detection process resulted in lower speed determinations if participants paused to interpret direction and speed cues, indicating a compromise between feedback accuracy and processing time. This outcome may also be attributed to prior studies suggesting a decrease in the perception of vibrotactile cues during dynamic states, leading to similar conclusions that vibrotactile guidance does not offer significant advantages in position control experiments [30, 31].

Furthermore, the results indicated that tasks involving arm motion guidance performed better in static conditions compared to dynamic situations, aligning with the result of previous research findings [28], probably due to decreased movement speed reducing the perceived intensity of vibrotactile feedback [32].

4.2 Mental Workload Between Visual Feedback and Vibrotactile in Two Movement States

Our subjective perception analysis indicates that participants consistently prefer visual feedback over vibrotactile feedback due to its precision and ease of use in both static and dynamic tasks. Participants reported lower mental and physical demands when using visual feedback compared to vibrotactile feedback, aligning with previous research findings [23]. Additionally, participants' preference for visual feedback corroborates previous studies [26]. Furthermore, tasks conducted under dynamic states were associated with worse perception, including higher mental workload, increased perceived task difficulty, lower perceived ease of use, worse attitude towards use, and decreased behavioral intention.

The result indicated that, under a static state, visual feedback outperforms vibrotactile feedback in terms of mental performance and perception. This suggests that for static tasks, visual feedback provides straightforward motion guidance due to precise visual cues ($0.01 <= p <= 0.05$). However, during dynamic states, PD and WM of tasks with vibrotactile feedback show significant differences compared to those with visual feedback ($p > 0.05$). This indicates that while visual feedback is easy to learn, understand, and utilize for motion guidance in static states, the gap between visual feedback and vibrotactile feedback decreases during dynamic tasks, possibly due to the distraction of visual focus, whereas vibrotactile feedback imposes no concentrating pressure. This suggests that vibrotactile feedback has potential application for dynamic movement motion guidance if the clarity of vibrotactile mode and intensity are increased. These findings provide valuable insights for future studies, suggesting the possibility of designing specific modes for vibrotactile feedback to enhance the accuracy of motion guidance and subjective user perception.

5   Conclusion

To determine if there is any difference between visual feedback or vibrotactile for motion guidance in VR, we conducted a 2×2 experiment with parameters containing movement state (dynamic or static) and feedback modalities (visual or vibrotactile). We recruited 16 participants to finish the experiment and the survey. With the data analysis, we found that both at static and dynamic states, visual feedback presented higher accuracy in direction and speed, resulting in lower mental workload. The data collection of this study can be comprehensive, and the time calculation method could be more reliable. This limitation causes the feedback related to better performance to remain uncertain. Further studies are going to fix these shortages and find more effective feedback modes.

Acknowledgments. This study was funded by National Natural Science Foundation of China (grant number 72301122); Shenzhen Higher Education Stability Support Program (grant number 20231121100550002); the Startup Fund of Southern University of Science and Technology (grant number Y01966117 & Y01966223).

Disclosure of Interests.   No conflict of interest was declared by the authors.

References

1. Seim, C.E., Wolf, S.L., Starner, T.E.: Wearable vibrotactile stimulation for upper extremity rehabilitation in chronic stroke: clinical feasibility trial using the VTS Glove. J. Neuro Eng. Rehabil. **18**, 14 (2021)
2. Levin, M.F., Weiss, P.L., Keshner, E.A.: 2015. Emergence of virtual reality as a tool for upper limb rehabilitation: incorporation of motor control and motor learning principles. Phys. Ther. **95**(3), 415–425 (2015)
3. Kim, W.S., et al.: Clinical application of virtual reality for upper limb motor rehabilitation in stroke: review of technologies and clinical evidence. J. Clin. Med. **9**(10), 3369 (2020). https://doi.org/10.3390/jcm9103369
4. Huygelier, H., Mattheus, E., Abeele, V.V., Van Ee, R., Gillebert, C.R.: The use of the term virtual reality in post-stroke rehabilitation: a scoping review and commentary. Psychol Belg. **61**(1), 145–162 (2021). https://doi.org/10.5334/pb.1033
5. Choi, J.Y., et al.: Virtual reality rehabilitation in children with brain injury: a randomized controlled trial. Dev. Med. Child Neurol. **63**(4), 480–487 (2021). https://doi.org/10.1111/dmcn.14762
6. Kumar, N., Vibhuti, Kataria, C.: Efficacy assessment of virtual reality therapy for neuromotor rehabilitation in home environment: a systematic review. Disabil. Rehabil. Assistive Technol. **18**(7), 1200–1220 (2023). https://doi.org/10.1080/17483107.2021.1998674
7. Nath, D., Singh, N., Saini, M., Srivastava, V.P., Mehndiratta, A.: Design and validation of virtual reality task for neuro-rehabilitation of distal upper extremities. Int. J. Environ. Res. Public Health **19**(3), 1442 (2022). https://doi.org/10.3390/ijerph19031442
8. Thumm, C., Giladi, N., Hausdorff, J., et al.: Rehabilitation with virtual reality: a case report on the simultaneous, remote training of two patients with parkinson disease. Am. J. Phys. Med. Rehabil. **100**(5), 435–438 (2021)
9. Gibbs, J.K., Gillies, M., Pan, X.: A comparison of the effects of haptic and visual feedback on presence in virtual reality. Int. J. Hum. Comput. Stud. **157**(2022), 102717 (2022). https://doi.org/10.1016/j.ijhcs.2021.102717
10. Adilkhanov, A., Yelenov, A., Reddy, R.S., Terekhov, A., Kappassov, Z.: VibeRo: vibrotactile stiffness perception interface for virtual reality. IEEE Robot. Autom. Lett. **5**(2), 2785–2792 (2020). https://doi.org/10.1109/LRA.2020.2972793
11. Fang, C., Zhang, Y., Dworman, M., Harrison, C.: Wireality: enabling complex tangible geometries in virtual reality with worn multi-string haptics. In: Proceedings of the 2020 CHI Conference on Human Factors in Computing Systems (CHI 2020), pp. 1–10. Association for Computing Machinery, New York, NY, USA (2020). https://doi.org/10.1145/3313831.3376470
12. Xiong, Z., Huang, X.: Comparison of the static and dynamic vibrotactile interactive perception of walking navigation assistants for limited vision people. *IEEE Access* **10**, 42261–42267 (2022). https://doi.org/10.1109/ACCESS.2022.3167407
13. Senecal, S., Nijdam, N.A., Aristidou, A., Magnenat-Thalmann, N.: Salsa dance learning evaluation and motion analysis in gamified virtual reality environment. Multimedia Tools Appl. **79**(33), 24621–24643 (2020). https://doi.org/10.1007/s11042-020-09192-y
14. Hoffard, J., Zhang, X., Wu, E., Nakamura, T., Koike, H.: SkiSim: a comprehensive study on full body motion capture and real-time feedback in VR Ski training. In: Proceedings of the Augmented Humans International Conference 2022 (AHs 2022), pp. 131–141. Association for Computing Machinery, New York, NY, USA (2022). https://doi.org/10.1145/3519391.3519400]

15. Okada, Y., et al.: Virtual ski training system that allows beginners to acquire ski skills based on physical and visual feedbacks. In: 2023 IEEE/RSJ International Conference on Intelligent Robots and Systems (IROS), pp. 1268–1275 (2023). https://doi.org/10.1109/IROS55 552.2023.10342020
16. Fang, L., Müller, T., Pescara, E., Fischer, N., Huang, Y., Beigl, M.: Investigating passive haptic learning of piano songs using three tactile sensations of vibration, stroking and tapping. In: Proceedings of the ACM on Interactive, Mobile, Wearable and Ubiquitous Technologies, vol. 7, no. 3, Article 95, p. 19 (2023). https://doi.org/10.1145/3610899
17. Bark, K.: Effects of vibrotactile feedback on human learning of arm motions. IEEE Trans. Neural Syst. Rehabil. Eng. **23**(1), 51–63 (2015). https://doi.org/10.1109/TNSRE.2014.232 7229
18. Meinke, A., Peters, R., Knols, R., Karlen, W., Swanenburg, J.: Exergaming using postural feedback from wearable sensors and exercise therapy to improve postural balance in people with nonspecific low back pain: protocol for a factorial pilot randomized controlled trial. JMIR Res. Protocols **10**(8), e26982 (2021). https://doi.org/10.2196/26982
19. Ballardini, G., Florio, V., Canessa, A., Carlini, G., Morasso, P., Casadio, M.: Vibrotactile feedback for improving standing balance. Front. Bioeng. Biotechnol. **8**(94), 1–13 (2020). https://doi.org/10.3389/fbioe.2020.00094
20. Van Breda, E., Verwulgen, S., Saeys, W., Wuyts, K., Peeters, T., Truijen, S.: Vibrotactile feedback as a tool to improve motor learning and sports performance: a systematic review. BMJ Open Sport Exerc. Med. **3**(1), e000216 (2017). https://doi.org/10.1136/bmjsem-2016-000216.PMID:28761708;PMCID:PMC5530110
21. Islam, M.S., Lim, S.: Vibrotactile feedback in virtual motor learning: a systematic review. Appl. Ergon. **101** (2022)
22. Weber, B., Sagardia, M., Hulin, T., et al.: Visual, vibrotactile, and force feedback of collisions in virtual environments: effects on performance, mental workload and spatial orientation. Virtual Augmented Mixed Reality **8021**(2013), 313–320 (2013)
23. George, C., Tamunjoh, P., Hussmann, H.: Invisible boundaries for VR: auditory and haptic signals as indicators for real world boundaries. IEEE Trans. Vis. Comput. Graph. **26**(12), 3414–3422 (2020)
24. Cooper, N., Milella, F., Pinto, C., et al.: The effects of substitute multisensory feedback on task performance and the sense of presence in a virtual reality environment. Plos One **13**(2), e0191846 (2018)
25. Simpson, T.G., Rafferty, K.: Evaluating the effect of reinforcement haptics on motor learning and cognitive workload in driver training. Augmented Reality Virtual Reality Comput. Graph. **2022**, 203–211 (2022)
26. Yoshida, K.T., Kiernan, J.X., Okamura, A.M., Nunez, C.M.: Exploring human response times to combinations of audio, haptic, and visual stimuli from a mobile device. In: Proceedings of the 2023 IEEE World Haptics Conference (WHC), pp. 121–127 (2023). https://doi.org/10. 1109/WHC56415.2023.10224375
27. Dim, N.K., Ren, X.: Investigation of suitable body parts for wearable vibration feedback in walking navigation. Int. J. Hum. Comput. Stud. **97**(5), 34–44 (2017). https://doi.org/10.1016/ j.ijhcs.2016.08.002
28. Karuei, I., MacLean, K.E., Foley-Fisher, Z., MacKenzie, R., Koch, S., El-Zohairy, M.: Detecting vibrations across the body in mobile contexts. In: Proceedings of the SIGCHI Conference on Human Factors in Computing Systems (CHI 2011), pp. 3267–3276. Association for Computing Machinery, New York, NY, USA (2011). https://doi.org/10.1145/1978942.197 9426
29. Syrett, E.D., Holman, M.E., Bhargava, T., et al.: The effect of movement speed on mental workload during a simple visually guided task: 1946 board #207 May 31 3. Med. Sci. Sports Exerc. **50**(5S), 470 (2018)

30. Hart, S.G., Staveland, L.E.: Development of NASA-TLX (Task Load Index): results of empirical and theoretical research. Adv. Psychol. **52**, 139–183. North-Holland (1988)
31. Mödinger, M., Woll, A., Wagner, I.: Video-based visual feedback to enhance motor learning in physical education—a systematic review. Ger. J. Exerc. Sport Res. **52**(2022), 447–460 (2022)
32. Sigrist, R., Rauter, G., Riener, R., et al.: Augmented visual, auditory, haptic, and multimodal feedback in motor learning: a review. Psychon. Bull. Rev. **20**(2013), 21–53 (2013)
33. Machida, T., Dim, N.K., Ren, X.: Suitable body parts for vibration feedback in walking navigation systems. In: Proceedings of the Third International Symposium of Chinese CHI (Chinese CHI 2015), pp. 32–36. ACM, New York, NY, USA (2015)

Improving Virtual Workspaces Based on Sense of Embodiment

Ryusei Fukuda[1], Naomi Kuwata[1(✉)], and Daiji Kobayashi[2(✉)]

[1] Graduate School of Chitose Institute of Science and Technology, Hokkaido, Japan
{m2230290,m2240200}@photon.chitose.ac.jp
[2] Chitose Institute of Science and Technology, Hokkaido, Japan
d-kobaya@photon.chitose.ac.jp

Abstract. Factories and plants increasingly employ virtual reality (VR) for training, focusing on the optimization of workers' movements based on ergonomics. This study investigates the impact of sense of embodiment (SoE) in a virtual workspace on workers' task performance to elucidate SoE's role as a performance measure in such environments. Participants, tasked with assembling an office chair consisting of eight parts using VR controllers, were observed. The results revealed that participants had difficulty perceiving the distance between parts, leading to difficulty in picking up parts. Therefore, it was concluded that the sense of self-location (SoSL) component of SoE influences assembly tasks in virtual workspaces. Additionally, we reveal how differences in SoE affect skill acquisition and subsequent real-word tasks, using brick stacking as an example. SoE was assessed through responses to fourteen questions rated on a 7-point scale. Higher SoE corresponded to faster skill acquisition, with participants displaying increased confidence and focus in the real workspace following high SoE conditions. This study revealed that SoE influences assembly tasks in virtual workspaces. Furthermore, it became evident that training in virtual workspaces with higher SoE leads to smoother operations in real workspaces. Thus, SoE serves as an important metric for task performance.

Keywords: Virtual Reality · Assembly Operation · Sense of Embodiment

1 Introduction

Many companies are increasingly introducing virtual reality (VR) into their operations. For example, an automobile manufacturing company uses VR for practicing movements necessary for assembling automobiles, such as "tightening screws" and "installing parts in vehicles" [1]. Another automobile manufacturer is developing 3D models of cars for VR gaming and corresponding systems, which is also being expanded to include a driving simulation system within VR [2]. A venture company is developing a VR system for firefighting training simulations, allowing firefighters to undergo training in environments that closely mimic real situations [3]. Additionally, a space agency has introduced a VR system for astronaut training. Using this system along with devices providing physical feedback, astronauts can safely undergo mission training [4].

J. Y. C. Chen et al. (Eds.): HCII 2024, LNCS 15377, pp. 46–57, 2025.
https://doi.org/10.1007/978-3-031-76812-5_4

Various factories and plants are optimizing workers' movements based on ergonomics and using these results for training the workers. By incorporating principles of human factors engineering into VR simulations, it is possible to design workspaces that reduce physical strain and fatigue for workers.

Furthermore, VR technology can be adopted to optimize workspaces by considering accessibility, visibility, and safety, thereby enhancing efficiency. In the virtual workspace displayed on head-mounted displays (HMDs), temporal and spatial inconsistencies between human vision and other sensory inputs can diminish the sense of self-location (SoSL), which is a component of the sense of embodiment (SoE). This is linked to diminished task performance and an increased rate of errors [5].

However, there are few studies that focus on SoE in assembly tasks in virtual workspaces. Additionally, there are hardly any studies that examine the effect of SoE differences on task mastery or their effect on tasks in real workspaces. Considering that there are factors that remain unnoticed by the workers in task performance in the virtual workspace, in this study, we focused on the sense of embodiment (SoE). A recent study focusing on SoE includes geospatial education in VR. In the study, researchers compared the score of SoE between immersive VR and desktop VR regarding the geo-visualization of global earthquake locations [6]. Another study compared the influence of active and passive transformation on SoE while embodying a virtual avatar, focusing on the score of SoE [7]. In this study, we investigated the influence of SoE on tasks in virtual workspaces, using the assembly of an office chair as an example. Furthermore, we examined the effect of SoE differences on task proficiency and their effect on task performance in real workspaces, using brick stacking as an example.

2 Method

In this study, we aimed to clarify the relationship between SoE and assembly work in a virtual workspace. We conducted an experiment in which the participants were instructed to assemble an office chair in a virtual workspace and their movements were examined. In addition, we aimed to clarify the influence of SoE on skill acquisition in the virtual workspace. Thus, we conducted an experiment in which the participants were instructed to perform a brick-stacking task and their movements were examined.

2.1 Experiment: Investigating the Relationship Between SoE and Assembly Work

Participants. Seven healthy male and seven female student volunteers, with ages ranging from 20 to 24 years (mean = 21.9, SD = 1.0), participated in the study. The Research Ethics Committee of the Chitose Institute of Science and Technology (Reception No. 2023–7) approved and reviewed this study. Informed consent was obtained from the participants prior to the experiment.

Experimental Virtual Environment and Apparatus. We created a simulated environment as a simple virtual workspace for testing office chair assembly and evaluated the workers' task performance. The virtual workspace featured white floors and walls, with the components of an office chair randomly placed within it. This environment was developed using the Unity game engine, a powerful tool for creating interactive 3D experiences. The 3D models of the office chair parts were created using Blender, a software for 3D computer graphics production (refer to Fig. 1).

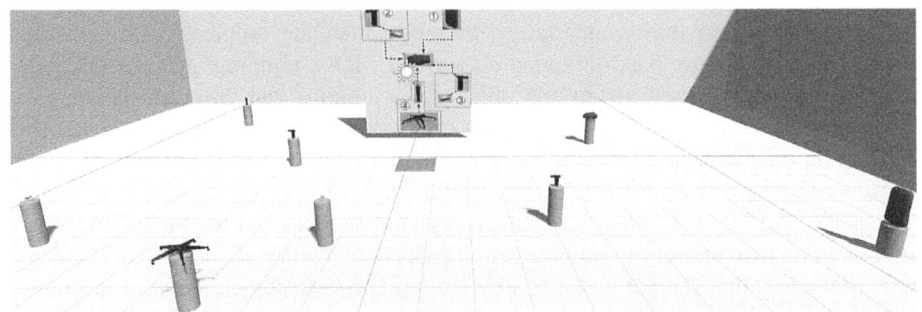

Fig. 1. Environment for assembling the office chair.

During this experiment, we connected the HTC VIVE Pro Eye, an HMD, to the PC (Lenovo Legion T730) to display the virtual environment. The participants wore the HMD and utilized controllers for their tasks. The directional keys on the controllers were used for moving closer to the parts and adjusting the field of view, while the triggers on both controllers were assigned the action of grabbing the part. All these controls were programmed using Unity.

Procedure and Metrics. Participants operated controllers held in both hands to collect parts while navigating the virtual workspace and assembling an office chair. First, we provided participants with an overview of this experiment. Participants then practiced grabbing and connecting cubes of various sizes within a simulated workspace to familiarize themselves with controller usage. After this practice session, participants proceeded to assemble the office chair. During the assembly task, participants referred to an assembly diagram placed in front of them to guide them through the assembly process.

To measure work efficiency, two metrics were used: assembly time and assembly errors. Assembly time was defined as the duration from when the participant began the task to when the final component was connected. The number of assembly errors were recorded, including instances in which components were connected in different aspect or incorrect components were connected. Furthermore, the assembly process within the virtual workspace was recorded for analysis. After completing the experiment, participants provided us with subjective opinions regarding the experimental task.

2.2   Experiment: Investigating the Influence of SoE on Skill Acquisition

Participants. Ten healthy male and female student volunteers, with ages ranging from 21 to 27 years (mean = 22.6, SD = 1.73), participated in the study. The Research Ethics Committee of the Chitose Institute of Science and Technology (Reception No. 2023–7) approved and reviewed this study. Informed consent was obtained from the participants prior to the experiment.

Experimental Virtual Environment and Apparatus. We developed a simulated environment as a simple virtual workspace for testing brick stacking and evaluated the workers' task performance. Bricks for the task and a sample stack were prepared on the desk. Additionally, a stopwatch was provided to track the elapsed time for participants. This virtual workspace was developed using the Unity game engine (refer to Fig. 2).

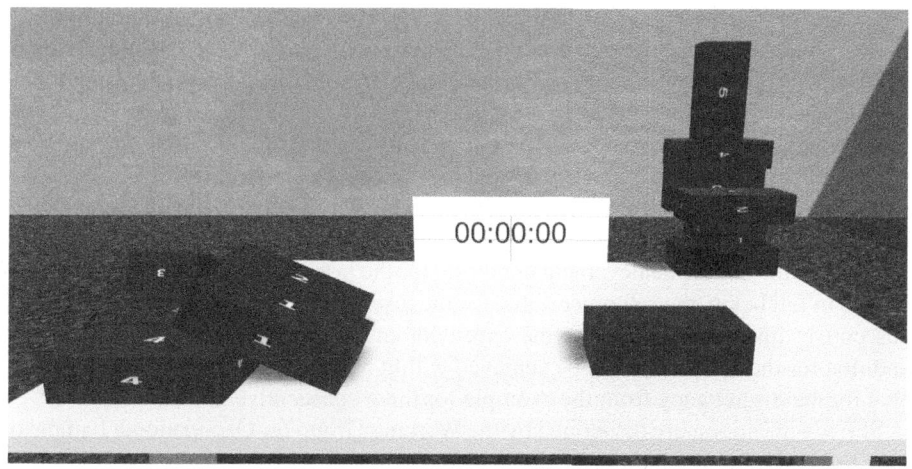

Fig. 2. Virtual workspace for stacking bricks.

During this experiment, we connected the HTC VIVE Pro Eye, an HMD, to the PC (Lenovo Legion T730) to present the virtual environment. Participants wore the HMD and used controllers to interact with the virtual environment. The triggers on both controllers were assigned the action of grabbing the part.

Two different virtual workspaces with distinct conditions were prepared as working environments. One environment featured tactile stimuli, where upon touching a brick, a vibration device attached to the hand would vibrate, and the bricks that could be grasped were highlighted with light (with Tactile Stimuli (with TS)). The other environment had no feedback from the vibration device or highlighting of the bricks with light, and the movements of the hands in the virtual workspace appeared delayed (without TS). The order of two conditions was varied for every five participants. The vibration device was constructed using an eccentric motor (CL-0614–13103-3 by S.T.L.JAPAN) covered with a rubber cover (RC-VM612 by S.T.L.JAPAN), and the motor was energized with a voltage of 1.2 V. All these controls were programmed using Unity.

Procedure and Metrics. Initially, we provided participants with an overview of the experiment. Following this, participants were instructed to wear HMDs and underwent a single practice session of stacking bricks to familiarize themselves with the use of the controllers. The task involved stacking five bricks to match the example shape provided. Subsequently, participants stacked bricks in the virtual workspace while we conducted various measurements. This task was repeated until a certain condition was met. Subsequently, participants stacked bricks in the real workspace three times. Following this, the conditions in the virtual workspace were altered, and the task was repeated once more.

Subjective fatigue was assessed using the Subjective Feelings of Fatigue (SFF) before the single practice session and after conducting the brick stacking task [9, 10]. Psychological stress was evaluated using the Brief Job Stress Questionnaire (BJSQ) [11]. Subjective mental workload was evaluated after conducting the actual assembly using the National Aeronautics Space Administration Task Load Index (NASA-TLX) [12]. Participant's attitudes towards the real workspace task after the virtual workspace task was assessed using the concept of FLOW [13, 14]. All subjective checklists were presented on a PC screen, and participants responded clicking with a mouse. At the conclusion of the experiment, participants engaged in introspection sessions where they shared their impressions of the experiment.

We recorded the time it took for participants to begin moving for the task after the experiment started until they finished stacking the last brick. Additionally, we quantified and measured the discrepancy between the stacked result and the example. These measurements were conducted until participants achieved the condition in both cases. In the case with TS, the achievement condition for the task was set to be achieved within 30 s and to fall below the reference value for the discrepancy from the example for three consecutive times. In addition, in the case without TS environment, the achievement condition for the task was set to be achieved within 50 s and to fall below the reference value for the discrepancy from the example for three consecutive times.

SFF is a questionnaire developed by the Working Group for Occupational Fatigue of Japan Society for Occupational Health to assess changes over time in the state of fatigue induced by work [8] Participants were asked to rate twenty-five questions on a 5-point scale for each of five groups: drowsiness, instability, uneasiness, local pain or dullness, and eyestrain [9, 10].

BJSQ is a questionnaire provided by the Ministry of Health, Labour and Welfare that assesses work stressors and psychological and physical stress reactions [11]. In this study, only eighteen items related to psychological stress reactions were used. Participants were asked to rate eighteen items on a 4-point scale. The results of the responses were evaluated in five groups: liveness, irritability, fatigue, anxiety, and depression. Depression was calculated on a 24-point scale because it included six items. Each of the other four groups included three items, so the score was calculated on a 12-point scale.

NASA-TLX is a subjective evaluation tool used to assess mental workload. In this evaluation, participants were asked to rate six items; mental demand (MD), physical demand (PD), temporal demand (TD), own performance (OP), effort (EF), and frustration level (FR) on a visual analog scale ranging from 0 to 100 points, and the average value was calculated. Additionally, in this study, Raw TLX (RTLX), which represents the simple average of the six items, was also calculated [12].

FLOW experiences were investigated using a flow experience checklist [13]. The checklist comprises three factors: immersion (conscious experience through positive emotions and immersion), ability (confidence in ability), and challenge (goal challenge) [14]. We calculated the average scores for each factor. As the checklist does not include a criterion for determining when a "flow state has occurred," we considered scores of 5 or higher to indicate the occurrence of the flow state. This is because the checklist employs a 7-point rating scale, with 3 being considered a neutral score. Subsequently, the SFF and BJSQ scores were compared before and after the experiment using the paired t-test, with a significance level set at $\leq 5\%$.

SoE Questionnaire. SoE refers to a comprehensive concept of human sensory integration, consisting of the following three components [15]:

- Sense of body ownership (SoBO) – Indicates the sense that one's body belongs to oneself.
- Sense of agency (SoA) – Indicates "the overall muscle movement control, including subjective experiences such as action, control, impulses, which muscles to use, and conscious experiences" (Blanke and Metzinger, 2009).
- Sense of self-location (SoSL) – Indicates the sense of self-presence within a virtual workspace and awareness of one's own position.

In this experiment, following a previous study, the sense of vibration was also incorporated into the items of SoE as sense of tactile (SoT) [16]. After the virtual workspace task, participants were asked to evaluate SoBO, SoA, SoSL, and SoT using a questionnaire. The questionnaire items were created to align with this study based on the previous study (refer to Table 1) [16]. In this experiment, scores for SoBO, SoA, SoSL, and SoT were calculated as follows:

- SoBO score = (Q1 – Q2 – Q3)/3
- SoA score = (Q4 + Q5 + Q6 – Q7)/4
- SoSL score = Q8 – Q9 + Q10)/3
- SoT score = (Q11 + Q12 + Q13)/3
- SoE score = SoBO score + SoA score + SoSL score + SoT score.

3 Results

3.1 Office Chair Assembly Task

The experimental results revealed that the average assembly time for the fourteen participants was 388.3 ± 136.5 s. The standard deviation of the participants' assembly time was approximately one-third of the mean, indicating that the virtual workspace constructed may not have been conducive to efficient assembly. Consequently, we examined the participants' assembly process captured in video recordings. Our observations revealed that the participants encountered difficulties in reaching and grasping parts as they moved to the positions where the parts were located.

3.2 Brick-Stacking Task

SFF Scores. We present the calculation results of SFF in Fig. 3. In the case with TS, there was a tendency for local pain or dullness to be higher after the task compared to before the task ($p < .1$). Furthermore, in the case without TS, there was a tendency for local pain or dullness to be higher after the task compared to before the task ($p < .1$).

Table 1. Thirteen questionnaire items for investigating SoE in the virtual workspace.

Category	Question
SoBO	1. I felt as if the virtual hands were my hands
	2. It felt as if the virtual hands I saw was someone else's
	3. It seemed as if I might have more than one hand
SoA	4. It felt like I could control the virtual hands as if they were my own hands
	5. The movements of the virtual hands were caused by my movements
	6. I felt as if the movements of the virtual hands were influencing my own movements
	7. I felt as if the virtual hands were moving by themselves
SoSL	8. I felt as if my hands were located where I saw the virtual hands
	9. I felt out of my body
	10. I felt as if my (real) hands were drifting toward the virtual hands or as if the virtual hands were drifting toward my (real) hands
SoT	11. It seemed as if I felt the touch of the bricks in the location where I saw the virtual hands touching them
	12. It seemed as if the touch I felt was caused by the hands touching the virtual bricks
	13. It seemed as if my hands were touching the virtual bricks

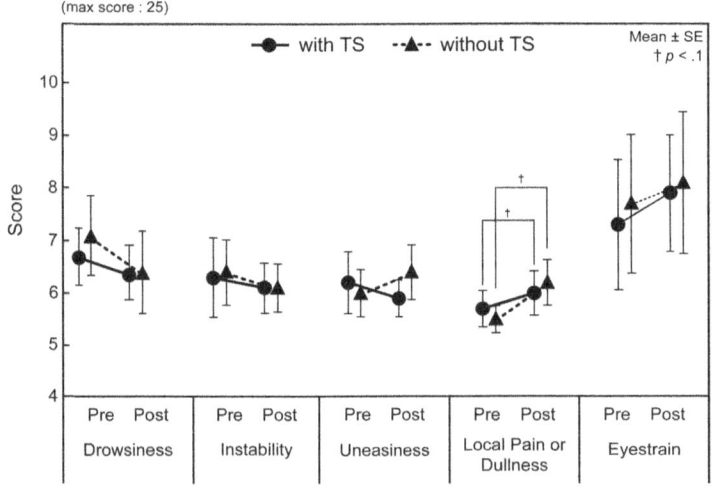

Fig. 3. SFF scores (n = 10).

BJSQ Scores. We present the calculation results of BJSQ in Fig. 4. No significant differences were observed in any of the items with TS. In the case without TS, there was a tendency for fatigue to be higher after the task compared to before the task ($p < .1$).

(max score of Depression : 24)

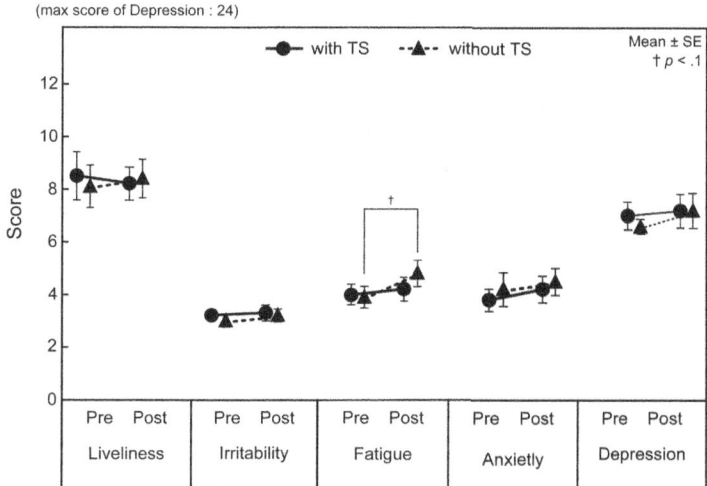

Fig. 4. BJSQ scores (n = 10).

NASA-TLX Scores. We present the calculation results of NASA-TLX in Fig. 5. Compared to the case without TS, TD was significantly higher with TS ($p < .05$). Furthermore, FR was significantly higher in the case without TS compared to with TS ($p < .01$).

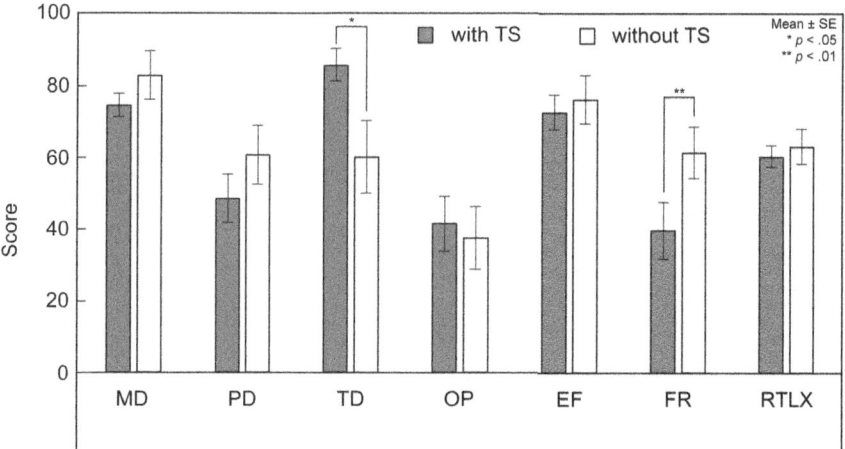

Fig. 5. NASA-TLX scores (n = 10).

SoE Scores. We present the calculation results of each term related to SoE in Fig. 6. In terms of SoA, the score with TS was significantly higher than the case without TS ($p < .01$). Similarly, in terms of SoBO, the score with TS was significantly higher than the case without TS ($p < .05$). Additionally, in terms of SoT, the score with TS was significantly higher than the case without TS ($p < .05$).

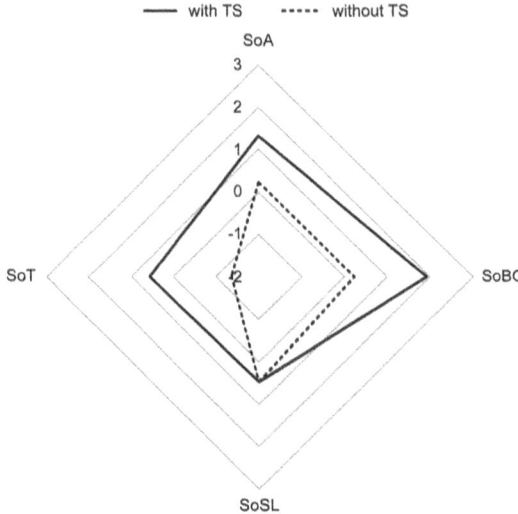

Fig. 6. SoE scores (n = 10).

FLOW Scores. We present the calculation results of each term related to FLOW in Fig. 7. No significant differences were observed between cases for any of the terms. Focusing on the scores in the case with TS, it was found that they had reached the criterion of 5 points for all terms. This suggests that the work in the real workspace after training in the case with TS was in a state of FLOW.

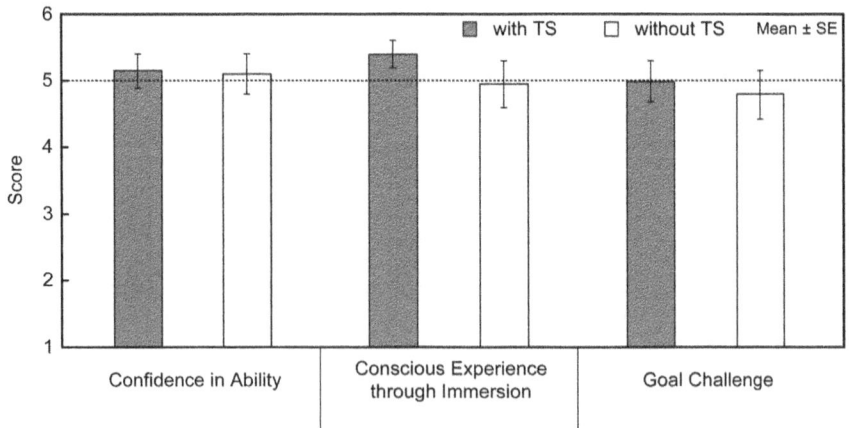

Fig. 7. FLOW scores (n = 10). The dotted line indicates the boundary of state of FLOW.

Task-Performance Comparison. We focused on the number of task repetitions required to meet the task completion criteria for each case. As a result, it was found that the number of task repetitions for participants who worked in the case without TS later was fewer than those who worked in it earlier. Furthermore, it was found that the number of task repetitions for participants who worked in the case with TS later was fewer than those who worked in the case with TS earlier.

Next, we focused on the discrepancy in the position of each brick in the real workplace compared to the reference. The comparison of discrepancies between the reference and the position of each brick after working in the virtual workplace under each case revealed no significant differences in the position of any brick.

In addition, we focused on the relationship between the evaluation of various indices of SoE and task performance. We found that participants who rated SoA highly completed the task more quickly. On the other hand, participants who evaluated SoA lowly repeated the task multiple times before completion.

4 Discussion

Focusing on the results of the office chair assembly task, it was observed that the failures to pick up parts were due to visual measurement errors, which were caused by a deficiency in accurately perceiving the distance between the parts and the participants' own position within the virtual environment. Therefore, in the virtual workspace prepared for the experiment, there was an increased probability that the lack of a clear perception of one's own position and the distance to the parts, grounded in SoSL, could lead to failures in the "grab the part" aspect of the assembly task. This may have significantly affected the overall assembly time.

Now we focus on the result of the brick-stacking task. From the calculation results of NASA-TLX, it was found that TD was significantly higher in the case with TS compared to the case without TS. This may be attributed to the participants' feedback indicating that "Time limit was too short, and there was not enough time to complete the work." Furthermore, compared to the case with TS, FR was higher in the case without TS. This factor may be related to the participants' feedback indicating that "The movement of hands in the field of view was slow, making it difficult to control as planned."

From the calculation results of SoA, SoBO, and SoT, the scores were significantly higher in the case with TS compared to the case without TS. These factors may explain the mismatches in hand movements in the case without TS, which led to participants not being able to recognize their own hands and control them effectively, as well as the lack of sensation when touching the bricks.

From the calculation results of FLOW, focusing on the scores of each factor in the case with TS, it was found that they had reached 5 points for all factors, indicating a state of FLOW. The participants could identify the hands within the virtual workspace as their own, enabling them to train effectively. It is assumed that this recognition also led to increased confidence and concentration in the real workspace.

The number of tasks completed by participants who worked without TS in the latter half was fewer than those who worked in the first half. This may be attributed to the feedback from participants who worked in the case without TS in the latter half, indicating that "We could work with more ease in the latter half of without TS tasks because of the tempo from the case with TS tasks in the first half." Furthermore, the number of tasks completed by participants who worked in the case with TS in the latter half was fewer than those who worked in the case with TS in the first half. This may be attributed to the feedback from participants who worked in the case with TS in the latter half, indicating that "Repeating the task multiple times in the case without TS in the first half familiarized them with the task and in the latter half in the case with TS, feeling the sensation of the bricks through vibrations made the task easier."

5 Conclusion

Through this study, we have established that SoE influences assembly tasks in the virtual workspace. Moreover, it has become apparent that the ease of tasks in the virtual workspace is closely related to differences in SoE, and that when conducting training, a workspace with higher SoE facilitates smoother task acquisition. Additionally, differences in SoE in the virtual workspace do not affect the difficulty of task in the real workspace. However, changes were noted in confidence, concentration, and goal clarity during tasks, underlining that training in a virtual workspace with higher SoE enables smoother task performance. Therefore, it is evident that SoE is a crucial metric for task performance.

In future studies, our aim will be to determine the threshold of SoE in the virtual workspace for achieving smooth task performance in the real workspace, and to establish guidelines for essential considerations when using the virtual workspace for training purposes.

References

1. Audi uses modular solution for virtual-reality training, Audi MediaCenter. (https://www.audi-mediacenter.com/en/press-releases/audi-uses-modular-solution-for-virtual-reality-training-10767)
2. BMW Group uses virtual reality engineering in its vehicle development, BMW. (https://www.bmw.com/en/events/nextgen/global-collaboration.html)
3. FLAIM Trainer^{TM}, the world's first immersive technology enables firefighter training solution, Flaim. (https://flaimsystems.com/products/trainer)
4. Using Hybrid Reality to Explore Scientific Exploration Scenarios, NASA. (https://nvite.jsc.nasa.gov/presentations/b3/D2_2_Virtual_Reality_Panel_Young.pdf)
5. Kobayashi, D., et al.: Effect of artificial haptic characteristics on virtual reality performance. In: Yamamoto, S., Mori, H., (eds.) HCII 2019, LNCS, vol. 11570, pp. 24–35. Springer Nature, Switzerland (2019)
6. Bagher, M.M., Sajjadi, P., Wallgrün, J.O., LaFemina, P., Klippel, A.: Virtual reality for geospatial education: immersive technologies enhance sense of embodiment. Cartography Geogr. Inf. Sci. **50**(3), 233–248 (2023)
7. Otono, R.,et al.: I'm transforming! effects of visual transitions to change of avatar on the sense of embodiment in AR. In: 2023 IEEE Conference Virtual Reality and 3D User Interfaces (VR) (2023)
8. Subjective Fatigue Feelings, Working Group for Occupational Fatigue of Japan Society for Occupational Health. (https://square.umin.ac.jp/of/service.html)
9. Sasaki, T., Matsumoto, S.: Actual conditions of work, fatigue and sleep in non-employed, home-base female information technology workers with preschool children. Ind. Health **43**, 142–150 (2005)

10. Matsumura, T., et al.: Fundamental study on fatigue measurement in VDT work from speech analysis. Electron. Commun. Jpn. **102**(1), 10–17 (2018)
11. Brief Job Stress Questionnaire, Ministry of Health, Labor and Welfare. (https://www.mhlw.go.jp/bunya/roudoukijun/anzeneisei12/dl/stress-check_j.pdf)
12. Hart, S.G., Staveland, L.E.: Development of NASA-TLX (Task Load Index): results of empirical and theoretical research. Adv. Psychol. **52**, 139–183 (1988)
13. Ishimura, I.: Psychological study on enhancing factors and positive functions of flow experiences. doctoral thesis from the School of Comprehensive Human Sciences, University of Tsukuba (2008). (in Japanese)
14. Jackson, S.A., Marsh, H.W.: Development and validation of a scale to measure optimal experience: the flow state scale. J. Sport Exerc. Psychol. **18**, 17–35 (1996)
15. Kilteni, K., Groten, R., Slater, M.: The sense of embodiment in virtual reality. Presence Teleoperators Virtual Environ. **21**(4), 373–387 (2012)
16. Gonzalez-Franco, M., Peck, T.C.: Avatar embodiment. towards a standardized questionnaire. Front. Robot. AI **5**(74) (2018)

Working in Extended Reality: A Study on the Relationship Between Concentration and Work in Immersive Environments

Yuri Inhamuns[(⊠)] [iD], Fernanda Pimentel[iD], and Marcos Silbermann[iD]

Sidia Instituto de Ciência e Tecnologia, Manaus - AM 69075-830, Brazil
yuri.vidal@sidia.com

Abstract. This article presents an exploratory study, which, using qualitative tools, sought to understand, from the users' perspective, aspects of their work experience in immersive environments and their relationship with focus and concentration. The study involved ten participants with an intermediate level of familiarity with Head Mounted Devices, who were recruited for the study and were structured in two phases. In the first phase, participants were[1] (This article is the result of the RD&I Platform project, carried out by Sidia Institute of Scienceand Technology in partnership with Samsung Eletrônica da Amazônia Ltda.) interviewed about their perceptions of productivity and corporate work. In the second phase, we carried out an experiment simulating a work environment, with which all participants were familiar. A controlled experiment methodology was applied (Gil 2017), dividing the volunteers into two groups made up of five participants: a Control Group and an Experimental Group. The results revealed important user perspectives on focus, concentration and productivity, demonstrating that this aspect is not related to the quality of the environment, but rather to daily rituals that help users build an environment of focus, such as screen layout at the workstation, customizing and adding objects to the desktop.

Keywords: Working · Extended reality · Productivity

1 Introduction

Between mid-2021–2022 it was possible to observe the rise of Extended Reality HMD (Head Mounted Device) in the technology market. Extended Reality (XR) is a common term linked to technologies that can modify or generate realities through the addition of virtual elements projected into the environment or through a wearable device, usually glasses (Rauschnabel et al. 2022). The term XR covers these technologies, in this context we can find 3 types of technologies that encompass extended reality: Augmented Reality (AR), Mixed Reality (MR) and Virtual Reality (VR).

According to Alnagrat (2022), the concept of Augmented Reality (AR) technologies refers to the projection of digital elements in a real environment, to provide a more

---

This article is the result of the RD&I Platform project, carried out by Sidia Institute of Science-and Technology in partnership with Samsung Eletrônica da Amazônia Ltda.

J. Y. C. Chen et al. (Eds.): HCII 2024, LNCS 15377, pp. 58–68, 2025.
https://doi.org/10.1007/978-3-031-76812-5_5

realistic experience for users, these elements are positioned in such a way that they stand out or make up the environment. In this sense, for the author, these technologies expand the reality of users, making them perceive and interact with the real environment more effectively (Alnagrat 2022). On the other hand, Virtual Reality (VR) technologies enable immersion in three-dimensional environments in 360-degrees, completely filling the user's field of vision, thus modifying their perception of physical dimensions such as time and space and, especially, when they are playing games in VR (Alnagrat 2022).

As the concept suggests, Mixed Reality (MR) technologies offer the user environments in which it is possible to move between VR and AR environments. While in the AR environment the user is limited to only observing certain digital elements, in MR the user is able to interact with these elements in a more direct way. A good example for this technology is Micorsoft's Hololens hardware that enables this transition between realities (Speicher 2019).

Today we can find several Head Mounted Devices on the market, currently, the most prominent devices on the market are Quest 2/Quest Pro (Meta) and Vision Pro (Apple). In 2022, Mark Zuckerberg's company Meta managed to reach approximately 20 million sales with the Meta Quest 2 and Quest Pro, reaching the highest number of extended reality devices sold to date.

On the other hand, the company Apple promises the launch of its first reality device, the Vision Pro for the first half of 2024. This device presented to the public in 2023 brings with it the promise of becoming the new reference in the technology market XR, with its hardware composition of sensors and cameras, eliminating the need to use physical controls or keyboards through the combination of inputs such as eye gaze and hand-tracking, eliminating limitations of other XR devices. (Waisberg 2023).

Despite this context of expansion of the consumer market for XR technologies, as well as the number of devices present on the market with the entry of large technology companies in the fight for space in this expanding market, research indicates that HMDs are still a technology of niche. XR devices are purchased with the main objective of playing immersive games, in the USA around 70% of consumers claim to have purchased their devices to enhance their gaming experiences. In this sense, the use of this type of technology is still strongly associated with this usage scenario, producers of this report point out that XR devices were unable to penetrate this niche due to the limited content offering for this platform and the difficulty of demonstrating to users the possibility to insert this technology into your daily life, as a relevant tool in resolving daily demands and activities. The question to be asked for XR technologies is how to break into this niche and expand their consumer market, large technology companies have been trying to break through by producing productivity applications and defending to consumers that XR devices have the potential to revolutionize way the user works.

Through an experimental approach, this article questions some assumptions about the value of extended reality technologies on work activities, their ability to improve users' level of concentration. In the next section we will discuss a little more broadly the attempt to build this vision about XR technologies and their supposed capacity to revolutionize the corporate work context and then we will present an experiment carried out at our institute with the aim of deepening our knowledge about the hypothesis that working in immersive environments would increase users' concentration and focus, therefore being a tool for increasing productivity, mainly for corporate work.

2   A New Niche for XR: Work and Productivity Apps

Along with the popularization of HMDs, it is possible to observe the launch of a variety of XR applications with different themes. The spectrum of content for XR technologies is broad and ranges from healthcare applications like FitXR – Box. HIIT (2019) to productivity applications like Meta Horizon Workrooms – Beta (2021). This occurs because HMDs create experiences comparable to reality, thus providing a way to change people's behavior with traditional technologies available on the market today. From this, a much-discussed example is the use of HMDs for students. Due to the lockdown, many students were forced to abandon traditional learning methods, thus having to migrate to remote collaboration platforms such as ZOOM, Google Meet and others (Kellner 2020). In this way, using VR it would be possible to recreate a completely immersive, attractive and collaborative environment, which would meet students' main needs for effective education (Alnagrat 2022).

2.1   Adherence to XR in a Productivity Scenario

If you noticed a big investment by companies in wanting to break everyday limitations, one of these limitations would be non-face-to-face collaborative work. Since 2019, tools for remote collaboration such as ZOOM, Microsoft Teams, Google Meet have been gaining more and more prominence in the global market. (Krodel 2023) In 2020 during the COVID-19 lockdown, due to social distancing safety measures, rapid and major changes in the market had to happen, one of these changes being the adoption of remote work in public and private organizations (Kellner 2020). Accompanied by increasing digitalization in certain areas of the market. Due to this digitalization, the traditional market needed to adapt, thus influencing the previously established model in the production of services and products. (Dragan 2021).

One type of application that has gained a lot of prominence in the current XR market is Dimensions of Collaborative Environments (CE). With the advancement of remote collaboration tools, CEs are three-dimensional environments, where people from different parts of the world can collaborate remotely and share the same virtual environment, using XR. (Mayer 2023) Unlike conventional remote collaboration tools, which limit the user to a 2D interface, CEs seek to immerse the user in a collaborative space, simulating the artifices and interactions of a real work environment, in order to try to engage productivity and teamwork within of the environment.

With the rise of HMD devices, it is now possible to find a range of XR applications for remote collaboration purposes, such as Meta Horizon Workrooms, immersed, vSpatial and others. However, despite the constant evolution of XR technology, there is still much debate within large communities about what the real benefits of using an HMD for productivity purposes are and how immersive experiences will restructure tools already consolidated on the market. Because, although these emerging XR technologies are constantly maximizing their potential with each new release, the sensation of motion sickness is still present in some users, which in turn ends up limiting the time these people use with an HMD (Chandra 2022).

3 Research Questions

At the beginning of this research, our institute's UX Design team was discussing some hypotheses about how the immersive environment can influence a person when carrying out their work activities. VR provides more focus on work: VR can influence users' concentration, directly affecting the development and performance of their activities. The VR environment can influence the way the user works: The VR environment can impact functionally/emotionally, making users more inspired and productive in their work routine. VR can cause visual discomfort: When the user spends a lot of time using VR applications, they end up experiencing some visual discomfort (red eyes, headaches). These hypotheses were raised based on the monitoring of new productivity applications launched on the market and which presuppose the association between improving users' concentration on common work activities, when carried out with the aid of an HMD. This article presents an exploratory study, which, through qualitative tools, sought to understand from the users' perspective aspects of their work experience in immersive environments and their relationship with focus and concentration.

4 Methodology

According to Suh and Prophet's (2018) systematic literature review, XR experiments involving human participants can be broadly categorized into two groups: (1) studies on XR and (2) studies on the use of XR. The first group focuses on the effects of XR system features on the user experience (e.g., monitoring presence results based on the amount of physical interaction), while the second category examines how the use of a technology XR modifies a measurable attribute of the user (for example, if leveraging physical interaction in XR affects learning outcomes).

Experimental research (GIL 2007) constitutes an important procedure for testing hypotheses that establish cause and effect relationships between variables. Due to their control possibilities, experiments offer a much greater guarantee than any other design that the independent variable causes effects on the dependent variable.

In our case, the design of an experiment aimed to simulate a workflow in a conventional environment to observe user reactions and the influence of using an HMD on performing work tasks. We structured the experiment around an agnostic corporate workflow, that is, this flow of work activities did not focus on a specific area. It was broad enough so that we could observe differences in the execution of tasks without the bias of a specific work area. Based on this, the Office ecosystem tools were chosen, as they are conventional tools that are not exclusive to specific areas, making it possible to observe how participants would behave carrying out more detailed activities in the immersive environment.

The application chosen for the experiment was Horizon Workrooms – Beta (2021), from Meta. As it is a productivity application that seeks to recreate a traditional collaborative environment in an immersive space, it provides the migration of some tools from the conventional work environment into the experience, in addition to allowing the user some minimal customizations. Certain elements in the environment. Being a reference application in the productivity category of Meta devices, Horizon Workrooms – Beta presents highly outstanding technical features, such as meeting rooms with the ability to immerse up to 16 people using VR devices, physical keyboard pairing and screen mirroring. Computer, into the immersive application.

Within Horizon Workrooms – Beta, participants had to perform 6 activities. Initially, the participant immersed himself within the application and briefly narrated what were the most noticeable elements for him within that immersive environment, then the participant was asked to open the Microsoft Teams application on the mirror screen of the computer within Horizon Workrooms – Beta, in order to receive instructions for the next activities to be developed, shortly after the participant was asked to do a search on Google Chrome and put together a presentation in Microsoft Power-Point, after finishing this activity the participant needed to create a table in Microsoft Excel, with the price of 5 XR devices, after completing the previous activities, the participant was asked to enter a meeting on Microsoft Teams and present their activities to the experiment moderator and finally, upon completing their presentation, the participant needed to transcribe what they developed in a board inside Miro.

It was necessary to divide this experiment into two stages. In the first stage, an in-depth interview was carried out with each sample, with the aim of understanding the participants' perceptions of what they understand by productivity, what influences their productivity and understanding what they expect from an application focused on productivity. For the second stage of the experiment, participants followed a script of certain activities using Horizon Workrooms – Beta, on Meta Quest Pro devices. The experiment aimed to create an everyday corporate work situation to observe user behavior in terms of concentration and focus in an XR environment and assess whether there is a relationship between working in an immersive environment and increased user concentration. The flow of tasks proposed to participants consisted of activities such as reading and writing documents, web research and structuring tables. We must emphasize that this experiment did not aim to create a sample with population representation, but rather to build a context to describe the qualitative aspect of the experience of working in an immersive environment.

Following the defined methodological requirements of our experiment, the 10 participants were divided into two different groups. This division aimed to observe differences in the level of concentration:

- **Control Group:** Participants within this group had a time limit of just 5 min to carry out each activity; if the participant did not finish the activity, they would have to move on to the next one.
- **Experimental Group:** In this group, participants did not have any type of set time limit, leaving them free to complete the activities in the most conventional time for each one.

5 Results

This experiment made us understand people's perspectives on what it means to be productive, what parameters they consider influencing their productivity and what rituals they develop to maintain focus on developing their activities. Peculiarities about the characteristics of an ideal environment more likely to increase productivity were also discussed, as well as aspects of form factor, accessibility, cybersickness and multidevice experiences. Opening the possibility for the discussion of how the HMD device can influence a conventional work routine and what benefits and limitations this current XR technology can provide to its users.

The results of our experiment are organized into two main axes. Firstly, we present some insights into the perspectives and values presented by the research participants, which point to how they conceive notions of productivity and how these notions imply behaviors and rituals that structure their daily work. In the second part we present the results related to the answers provided by the participants in each of the groups in the experiment. The data collected was organized and categorized, being divided into two types: results from a group with stress and results from a group without stress, thus enabling a broader and more detailed view of the results.

5.1 What is Productivity from the Participants' Perspective?

Among the research participants, we found different perceptions about what productivity is. These perceptions vary depending on the participant's activity and behavior. From his perspective, productivity is not a notion associated with a context of activities, but an index of quantity and volume of work. This dissociation of understandings about the notion of productivity is an important finding, which helps us define the scope and values that should be offered by these applications.

On the other hand, it is necessary to point out that the notion of productivity is directly associated with the optimization of activities and the ability to carry them out more easily and in less time. In other words, for participants, productivity is a quality of people and tools that produce in large quantities. As we see in the statements collected in the interviews.

In this sense, something that facilitates and expands skills in developing an activity, being able to optimize time and quality in delivery. All participants are part of the same corporate environment, so the perception of productivity is closely related to this work environment and specific considerations about what makes up this scenario. "Productivity for me is being able to concentrate and perform a task with ease, being able to focus on a task and finish it in a reasonable time, without taking too long" – Participant 7. Or as pointed out by one participant, productivity is related to focusing on work and the consequent increase in the number of tasks carried out in a shorter period of time: "Productivity is being able to concentrate and carry out a task with ease, being able to focus on a task and finish it in a reasonable time, without taking too long." – Participant 6

5.2 Focus and Concentration

The focus is not necessarily related to the quality of the environment but is linked to practices and rituals carried out by users to increase focus on work. Participants develop these rituals to avoid distractions. So, this is a way for them to increase concentration and focus on the activities they are performing. Some of these rituals described by the participants were: Listening to music, Layout of screens on the workstation, Organization of desktop files, personalization and addition of objects. "Music is my ritual, so I can concentrate and stay focused." – Participant 3.

5.3   Adaptation to the VR Environment

The introduction within the Horizon Workroom – Beta application meant that participants needed to interrupt and adapt habits that they already used in their work routines, into the immersive environment, one of these habits observed was the ability to type without having to look at the keyboard, however, when performing this action within the VR application, participants demonstrated difficulties when writing a sentence, claiming that the simulated keyboard within Horizon Workroom – Beta, did not have the same dimensions as the real paired keyboard, as yes, forcing participants to constantly look at the keyboard while typing "I usually type without looking at the keyboard, but here I had to keep moving my head to type" – Participant 2. Participants' adaptation to the immersive environment in the The general experience was frustration, the flow designed to simulate a VR work environment meant that they had to interrupt the development of the experiment activity to adapt to the HMD. This fact was highlighted by them as a problematic point (Fig. 1).

Fig. 1. Experiment participant using the paired keyboard within the application Horizon Workrooms – Beta.

5.4   The HMD Can Impact the User in Different Ways, Depending on the Specificity of Which It is Used

Experiment participants reported feeling a clear difference in using an HMD between leisure activities and work activities. According to a report obtained during the experiment "I played for 3 h, and my eyes didn't get tired, but now doing more delicate activities, my eyes got tired." – Participant 5. Noted that using an HMD for activities that require more concentration and focus causes fatigue faster. This may occur due to the need for focus and mental effort to carry out work activities in the virtual environment. Furthermore, in VR, the incidence of light and visual elements very close to the user's eyes can amplify the feeling of tiredness and even cause physical discomfort (Fig. 2).

Fig. 2. Participant using Horizon Workrooms – Beta on Quest 2 to perform experiment activities.

5.5   Immersive Environments Help with Focus and Concentration

Aspects present in the external environment can have a major influence on productivity. Users who used workrooms in search mention the fact that the virtual scenario brings an aspect of tranquility due to its calm and individual characteristics. However, in normal work routines, noise can cause distraction and divert focus, such as traffic noise, loud conversations between people nearby, and so on. "I prefer to work from home because there aren't many noises that end up distracting me, which easily happens when I'm face to face." – Participant 1.

The neutral environment provided by the Horizon Workroom application contributed to increasing the concentration of participants during the experiment, due to the fact that the virtual experience scenario does not have very prominent visual or sound elements, thus inducing the user to remain focused on the main issues. -main elements of task execution (screen, keyboard and table), thus causing only a feeling of immersion in a pleasant environment without distractions, allowing the user to carry out tasks with attention.

Another positive factor of the VR environment is the isolation from the real world. In the interviews, it was observed in the participants' reports that one of the negative points of the real work environment is the noise that affects the concentration of users, such as noise and movement of objects. People in the environment, however the use of the HMD helps to eliminate these inconveniences, making the user concentrate on specific activities – favoring their concentration on work.

However, as it is a virtual reality application, the participants' perception of the real world was affected, leaving them alienated from the real environment around them, thus allowing them to collide with or forget other objects that were around him "I lost my water bottle." – Participant 3 (The participant's water bottle was in front of her, but the immersive environment did not allow her to see it). We identified this specific context as an opportunity to use the complete Video See-Through feature, as it is a tool that has been gaining great notoriety in the area of security and complementing the user experience. (Pimentel, 2023).

5.6 Concertation on Task Execution

Group with Stress. Because the time limit required participants to deliver an activity more quickly, it was observed that the level of focus required was higher than the participant in the non-stress group. The participants in this group observed the detailed results of each activity in the experiment with greater attention. Participants indicated that the real hand overlay and mesh/hand tracking confused them when using the keyboard, it was also pointed out that the inability to move and resize the screen was also highlighted as an issue.

Stress-Free Group. Although this group also had an adequate level of concentration for the tasks, the freedom of time allowed participants to observe other points within the application. Redirecting their attention to peripheral tools, such as environmental details, support actions and extra functions, not observed by the limited group.

5.7 Microsoft Office Usability in an XR Environment

Group with Stress. The participants in this group complained most emphatically about the time, pointing out the difficulty in performing some legibility activities within the mirrored software, mainly the difficulty in identifying the separation lines of each cell in Excel, as well as small details in the table. Tools in the PowerPoint interface, such as adding new slides, finding and applying slide templates, have been described as too small for users.

Stress-Free Group. As in the previous group, participants pointed out the lack of legibility of Office System tools and functions on the shared screen. However, due to the fact that they were able to carry out the activities with less haste, they were able to overcome and carry out the most difficult actions, in addition to observing problems with the peripherals and within the software they used.

5.8 When the Immersive Experience Gets in the Way or Takes Away the User's Focus

- **Form Factor:** During the experiment, participants constantly reported the constant heating of the HMD after a certain period of use, thus making the experience uncomfortable and consequently distracting them from carrying out their activities. In addition to constantly reporting the discomfort of the HMD pressing on their faces.

- **Excessive exposure to light:** The white color of the VR environment causes visual fatigue and on computer screens there are many windows with a predominantly white color. The user's high exposure to a tonality causes discomfort in the experience, making it difficult to view and read texts, functions and tools in mirrored screen software.
- **Lack of familiarity with the device:** The learning curve in using new equipment to work meant that participants spent more time and effort to focus on discovering how to use the HMD and software in the best possible way, in addition to trying to adapt the experience's features to their tastes, rather than really focusing on performing the task.
- **Unable to adjust mirrored computer main screen:** The mirrored computer screen within the XR application is locked in a single position, preventing the participant from resizing it or positioning it so that they would be more comfortable, thus forcing the user to rotate and move their head to view parts specific tasks, often making screen accessibility difficult, making users take longer to perform certain activities that needed more attention, such as filling out an Excel table.
- **The user bumps into interface elements:** Users often bumped into and activated tools on the interface accidentally, this factor happened more recurrently in the main menu interface, due to the distance between the interface and the hands of the participants who were using the keyboard. In this scenario, a certain difficulty faced by participants in the usability of the Horizon Workroom main menu was also analyzed in this scenario, as they did not know how to close the configuration interface.
- **Using multiple inputs to perform the same activity:** The user uses handtracking to type and the device controllers to interact with the main interface of Horizon Workroom, as it was observed that participants had difficulty in carrying out certain interactions in the interface with manual tracking, so participants often felt obligated using more than one input to perform the same activity. Users complained of feeling confused about the appropriate inputs to carry out required activities.

References

Kellner, B., Korunka, C., Kubicek, B., Wolfsberger, J.: flexible working studie 2020: wie COVID-19 das Arbeiten in ¨Osterreich ver¨andert. Deloitte Consulting GmbH, 1–24 (2020). https://www2.deloitte.com/at/de/seiten/humancapital/artikel/flexible-working-studie.html

Krodel, T., Schott, V., Mayer, A., Ovtcharova, J.: Impact of XR-enabled collaboration in businesses—an economic. Ecolog. Soc. Perspect. (2023). https://doi.org/10.1007/978-3-031-42085-6_66

Dragan, I.: Digital transformation during lockdown. Inform. Econ. **25**(1/2021), 86–93 (2021). https://doi.org/10.24818/issn14531305/25.1.2021.07

Mayer, A., Chardonnet, J.R., Häfner, P., Ovtcharova, J.: Collaborative work enabled by immersive. Environments (2023). https://doi.org/10.1007/978-3-031-26490-0_6

Gil, A.C.: Como elaborar projetos de pesquisa (4.ed.) São Paulo: Atlas, 2002 Hip$\sqrt{}\geq$teses que foram levantadas durante a pesquisa

Rauschnabel, et al.: What is XR? Comput. Hum. Behav. **133**, 107289 (2022). https://doi.org/10.1016/j.chb.2022.107289

Chandra, A.N.R., Jamiy, F.E., Reza, H.: A systematic survey on cybersickness in virtual environments. Computers **11**(4), 51 (2022). https://doi.org/10.3390/computers11040051

Alnagrat, A., Ismail, R.C., Idrus, S., Zulkarnain, S.: A review of extended reality (XR) technologies in the future of human education: current trend and future opportunity. J. Hum. Reproduct. Sci. **1**, 81–96 (2022). https://doi.org/10.11113/humentech. v1n2.27

Speicher, M., Hall, B., Nebeling, M.: What is Mixed Reality? (2019). https://doi.org/10.1145/329 0605.3300767

Waisberg, E., et al.: Apple vision pro and why extended reality will revolutionize the future of medicine. Irish J. Med. Sci. (1971 -). 193 (2023). https://doi.org/10.1007/s11845-023-03437-z

Alnagrat, A., Ismail, R.C., Idrus, S., Syed, Z.: A review of extended reality (XR) technologies in the future of human education: current trend and future opportunity. J. Hum. Reproduct. Sci. **1**, 81–96 (2022). https://doi.org/10.11113/humentech. v1n2.27

Qayyum, A., et al.: Secure and Trustworthy Artificial Intelligence-Extended Reality (AI-XR) for Metaverses (2022). https://doi.org/10.48550/arXiv.2210.13289

Pimentel, F., Inhamuns, Y., Silbermann, M.: Exploring new futures in video see-through: experience-es and scenarios using XR technologies. In: Stephanidis, C., Antona, M., Ntoa, S., Salvendy, G. (eds.) HCI International 2023 Posters. HCII 2023. Communications in Computer and Information Science, vol. 1836. Springer, Cham (2023). https://doi.org/10.1007/978-3-031-36004-6_38

Influence of Color on Asthenopia of VR Based on Real-Time Teleoperating Lunar Rover

Ao Jiang[1,2,3(✉)], Jinglin Zhang[1,3], Yan Zhao[4], Hao Fan[5], Kun Yu[6], and Haihai Zhou[1]

[1] Nanjing University of Aeronautics and Astronautics, Nanjing, China
aojiang@nuaa.edu.cn
[2] Imperial College London, London, UK
[3] EuroMoonMars, ILEWG ESA, Beatenberg, The Netherlands
[4] Key Laboratory of Biomimetic Robots and Systems of Chinese Ministry of Education, Beijing Institute of Technology, Beijing, China
[5] Southeast University, Nanjing, China
[6] China Ship Development and Design Center, Shanghai, China

Abstract. Many countries and companies are increasingly delving into applying Virtual reality (VR) to lunar rovers. Research institutions including NASA, EAS and the China Space Center have published reports related with online control platforms based on VR technology to control an unmanned lunar rover exploring the moon surface. One of the main research directions of VR human-machine interface is Visual interaction interface. The visual interaction interface will cause visual fatigue more easily. The purpose of this paper is to explore the relationship between asthenopia, teleoperation efficiency and the color of VR interface in a simulated lunar surface environment, to make suggestions for improvement of color selection, to improve VR interface and relieve long hours operation fatigue. 30 participants were recruited and asked to use Likert scale to express. We design a teleoperation interface of unmanned lunar rover to simulate the color contrast of interface including background color and element color (Text and patterns). The hue samples of VR interface were extract from foreground color. Our task is to test user's ability to recognize objects and environments, make real-time decisions, and control rover movements. The results show that blue and green had the weakest visual fatigue under gray background, while red had the highest visual fatigue. This study explores the visual fatigue level of different hues in the VR display of the moon environment based on the principle of visual perception levels, and finds the color and visual fatigue rules of the VR interface of teleoperating the unmanned lunar rover. The results provide a reference basis for the color level design of the VR interface of the unmanned lunar rover.

Keywords: Teleoperate lunar rover · VR interface · Color · Asthenopia · Online control

1 Introduction

Over the past decades, the employment of teleoperation systems has spread to numerous domains. Teleoperation represents any technical implementation that via a communication medium extends the human operator's capacity to manipulate objects to a

J. Y. C. Chen et al. (Eds.): HCII 2024, LNCS 15377, pp. 69–78, 2025.
https://doi.org/10.1007/978-3-031-76812-5_6

manipulator positioned within a remote environment. Remotely operated vehicles and vessels are used in warfare and underwater exploration. Robotic teleoperation systems are increasingly being used in the medical field, especially in surgery, and teleoperation systems are being used in a variety of applications such as search and rescue operations, education, and care of the disabled and elderly [1].

However, in the aerospace field, teleoperation is still in the early stage of development and is a hot research topic from now to the future. Remote operation of the lunar rover, controlling the rover to walk in the complex terrain environment on the moon surface under the condition of large delay, is a high-risk, high-investment and highly complex system engineering with the outstanding features of huge cost, long development cycle, complex environmental constraints, numerous variable parameters, high reliability of system design and control, etc., which makes it difficult to realise real-time control in the traditional control mode. Currently, many countries and companies are increasingly delving into applying VR to lunar rovers. Research institutions including NASA, EAS and the China Space Center have published reports related with online control platforms based on VR technology to control an unmanned lunar rover exploring the moon surface. Combined with pictures taken by the lunar rover and the telemetry data, a virtual full scene of the mission can be generated. And commands can be transmitted to the rover at any time. This online control platform can greatly improve the effectiveness and safety of teleoperation [2].

In remote control tasks, the operator's perception of understanding the environment and objects and the accuracy of the operation is very important for the whole task. Increased telepresence through properly implemented Virtual Reality (VR) technology is believed to improve the interpretability of and control over remote environments [3].

Virtual reality (VR) VR is a medium capable of providing a high degree of verisimilitude with the real world, accessed via head-mounted display (HMD) and accompanying peripheral devices (e.g., hand controllers) [4, 5]. In the realisation of a remotely controlled lunar rover, the key to the accuracy and continuity of the operation is the use of VR. One of the main research directions of VR human-machine interface at present is Visual interaction interface. The visual interaction interface mainly uses the user's visual perception, that will cause visual fatigue more easily. The research of Pei [6]. Shows that the reading efficiency in virtual reality environment is lower than in flat display interface [7]. Also, prolonged exposure to virtual reality head-mounted displays (VR-HMDs, is more likely to cause digital Eye Strain (DES), produces dry eyes, headaches and other adverse physiological reactions seriously reducing work efficiency and accuracy [8]. Therefore, it is important to alleviate real-time teleoperation fatigue in VR interface. SEEV model [9] explains the allocation of visual attention during activities based on top-down and bottom-up processes Among them, colour is the main factor affecting saliency. Among the information in the human-machine interface, colours are the most visually expressive and guide the user's attention. Research says that different coloured displays give users a different visual experience [10]. In area of head Up Display (HUD) and helmet Mounted Display (HMD), DereFeldt et al. [11] and Blundell et al. [12] found that colour coding improved pilots' visual search efficiency compared to monochrome coding. Ling Bai [13] conducted a pilot study on the problem of matching two-colour coding with environmental colours by extracting pictures of mountain ranges and snow-capped mountains and concluded that the cognitive performance of HUD two-colour coding is higher than that of monochrome coding. Xiao et [14] demonstrated experimentally that the use of red is superior to yellow for anomalous information in the colour coding of HUDs, while green is not suitable for anomalous information. Colour coding in the interface can effectively reduce visual information confusion and improve cognitive performance [15]. It is important to rationally allocate visual attention to alleviate visual fatigue and optimise the visual experience. However, relieving visual fatigue of VR interface color under teleoperating lunar rover and exploring the effect of color on information delivery under VR is still insufficient [16]. The moon is a colourless environment, the lunar environment is dominated by grey and black, and a theoretical basis is needed to design VR interactive interface colours in a grey background.

An experiment to simulate remote manipulation of a lunar rover by designing an interactive interface, with special attention to the effect of different colour schemes on visual fatigue. The purpose of this paper is to explore when using a VR headset for teleoperation: 1. Whether colour affects visual fatigue and productivity 2. Choosing the right colour scheme to minimise visual fatigue and maximise productivity, by exploring the relationship between asthenopia, teleoperation efficiency and the color of VR interface in a simulated lunar surface environment, to make suggestions for improvement of color selection, to improve VR interface and relieve long hours operation fatigue.

2   Method

2.1   Participants

In this study, we recruited 30 participants from a local research institute (male = 15, female = 15, aged 23–36 years, M = 26.58, SD = 3.74). Most participants reported normal vision, normal/corrected vision (with glasses),5 Participants wear glasses. We asked participants to rate their familiarity with the VR (M = 3, SD = 1.36) using a 5-point Likert scale (1 = not at all, 5 = very well).

2.2   Experimental Set-Up

We designed an unmanned lunar rover telecontrol interface to simulate the contrast between the background colour and the elemental colours (including fonts and patterns) in the interface during an interaction scenario. The VR interface is designed to have two main views:1) Mini overview with bird's eye view for real-time traversal monitoring. 2) Immersive view that provides annotatable on surface ground view. The mission used for this test is a teleoperated lunar rover mobile operations mission that is equipped with an immersive first view, with both sides of the view including front and rear movement routes, movement commands, and movement speeds (see Fig. 1). The mission procedures are designed to test the user's ability to recognise objects and environments, make real-time decisions, coverage path planning, and complete lunar rover movement tasks in a VR environment.

Fig. 1. Simulation of remote manoeuvring of the lunar rover VR interactive interface

2.3 VR Display Interface Colour Extraction

The hue samples of the VR interface are extracted from the foreground colour of the collected pictures, and the extraction process is as follows: use PS to extract and summarize the colours of characters, logos and graphics in the aerospace display interface, and then extract the colours of the summarized foreground colours in accordance with the hue ranges of red, orange, yellow, green, cyan, blue, violet, and magenta through the Image Color Summarizer program, and set the saturation and luminance to 100, and use grey as the background colour. Following the above process, finally we obtain 5 hue samples, as shown in Table 1.

Table 1. Sample display interface hues

N	Hue	R	G	B	L	a	b
A1	red	255	8	0	53.2	80.1	67.2
A2	orange	255	179	0	78.2	16.6	81.1
A3	yellow	255	255	0	97.1	−21.6	94.5
A4	green	0	255	89	97.4	−19.2	75.9
A5	cyan	0	255	166	89.1	−70.0	28.7

2.4   Experimental Procedure

The lunar rover movement operations task was first explained to participants, including the objectives (e.g., object recognition, real-time decision making, coverage path planning) and the controls they would use. Participants were randomly assigned to different colour schemes of the VR interface to ensure that each participant experienced all colour schemes throughout the experiment. A different colour scheme should be used for each session to avoid adaptation effects. Engage participants in lunar rover locomotion tasks in each colour scheme, including forward and backward navigation. Monitor their ability to recognise objects, make decisions and complete tasks in a simulated VR environment. Participants' visual fatigue was assessed after each task using an established visual fatigue scale and subjective feedback. Record any reported difficulties or discomfort related to the colour scheme of the VR interface. Collect data on task completion times, error rates and any other relevant performance metrics. This data will be used to assess the efficiency of remote operation under different colour schemes.

2.5   Data Statistics

In this study, statistical analyses will begin with data cleaning and then descriptive statistics will be calculated to summarise participant characteristics and key indicators. The core analysis will involve repeated measures of variance (RM-ANOVA) to assess the effect of VR interface colour on visual fatigue, supplemented by mixed design ANOVA to investigate the interaction between VR familiarity and interface colour on task performance. Post hoc tests (e.g. Tukey's HSD) will be used to identify specific colour schemes that have a significant impact on the results. All analyses followed hypothesis checking and model fit assessment to ensure reliability and validity. Results will be interpreted in the context of the design implications of the VR interface and results will be reported comprehensively, including measures of centralised trends, variability, significance levels and effect sizes.

3   Result

Statistical analysis of data collected from 30 participants revealed important insights into the effect of VR interface colour on visual fatigue and task performance during real-time teleoperating lunar rover∘ Descriptive statistics showed that participants had a mean age of 26.58 years (SD = 3.74) and a moderate familiarity with VR technology (M = 3, SD = 1.36).

A repeated-measures (ANOVA) showed a statistically significant effect of VR interface colour on visual fatigue, $F (6, 174) = 5.23$, $p < .001$, $\eta2 = .15$, suggesting that VR interface colour significantly affected participants' visual fatigue levels. Post-hoc analyses using Tukey's HSD test showed that interfaces in shades of blue resulted in significantly lower visual fatigue scores compared to interfaces in shades of red ($p < .05$) and yellow ($p < .01$), suggesting that cooler colours may be more conducive to reducing visual fatigue.

A mixed-design ANOVA exploring the interaction between VR familiarity and interface colour on task performance did not produce a significant interaction effect, $F (6,$

174) $= 1.89$, $p = .09$, suggesting that the effect of interface colour on task performance was consistent across VR familiarity. However, there was a significant main effect of interface colour on task performance, $F(6, 174) = 4.56$, $p < .01$, $\eta2 = .12$, with green and cyan shades associated with faster task completion times and lower error rates.

Correlation analyses revealed no significant relationships between age or VR familiarity and visual fatigue levels or task performance metrics (all ps $> .05$), suggesting that these factors did not substantially influence the outcomes of interest. Multiple regression analyses further confirmed that interface colour was a significant predictor of visual fatigue ($\beta = -.32$, $p < .01$) and task performance ($\beta = .27$, $p < .05$) even when controlling for age and VR familiarity.

Effect size calculations highlight the practical implications of the findings, with cooler colours (blue, green, cyan) showing moderate to large effects on reducing visual fatigue and improving task performance. These results suggest that the choice of interface colours in lunar rover teleoperation VR applications can significantly affect user experience and operational efficiency.

4 Discussion

Currently, there is little research on colour and human factors ergonomics in VR interaction interfaces, especially in the aerospace field, and little is known about the relationship between colour and visual perception, visual fatigue, and work efficiency. This study evaluated the effects of different colour backgrounds and elemental colours (including fonts and patterns) of the interaction interface on the degree of visual fatigue and the participants' ability to identify objects and environments, make real-time decisions, plan traversals, and complete rover mobility tasks in a VR environment during simulated interactions with an unmanned rover's telecontrol interface. The results showed that within the range of commonly used colours in aerospace, the visual fatigue values of blue, yellow, and green in the grey background of the VR interactive interface were significantly lower than those of red and orange ($p < 0.05$), and the average reaction times of red and orange were higher than those of other colours, but not significantly so. Different colour combinations have different effects on the visual fatigue values. When used as elemental colours, both blue and green hues have the weakest visual fatigue values on a grey background, and red has the highest visual fatigue value when used as an elemental colour.

This study obtained that different colour shades produce different fatigue values for participants in the same background, and participants' reaction time to different colour shades varies. This shows the value of research on colour, especially the colour matching of the interaction interface, and this study can provide a reference for the design of the VR interaction interface for remote implementation of the control of the lunar rover, and is also conducive to the improvement of the reasonableness of the VR interaction interface in more fields, to better serve the users and to reduce the visual burden.

4.1 The Effect of Different Colours and the Efficiency of Identification Decisions

The results of this study show that different colours require different reaction times for participants, with red and orange having higher average reaction times than other colours. In the VR interactive interface, participants reacted more quickly to cooler colours such as blue and blue, and were able to identify and make decisions faster. This is consistent with the findings of Hyun K. Kim [17] in the context of AR interactive interfaces, where orange consistently had the lowest average task completion and blue the highest in either context. Mean response times for red, orange, yellow and green were also found to be greater than those for magenta and greater than those for cyan, blue and violet in a study of HUD flat panel displays [18]. This suggests that the speed with which users respond to colours in a display interface is likely to be related to the warmth of the colour, with warmer colours having a greater reaction time than cooler colours, and people recognising and responding more quickly to cooler colours. This is consistent with other research findings that "cool" colours such as blue and green can promote relaxation, sleep, reduce head pressure and make people calmer [19] Therefore, in the colour design of the VR interaction interface, more use can be made of blue, cyan and purple hues, and less use of red and orange hues.

4.2 The Effect of Colour on Visual Fatigue When Interacting with VR for Long Periods of Time

It was found that both blue and green hues had the weakest visual fatigue on a grey background when used as elemental colours, and red had the highest visual fatigue when used as an elemental colour. This illustrates that different colours produce different levels of visual fatigue in participants. This corresponds to the reaction time of colours, and colours with large reaction time are more likely to cause human eye fatigue, resulting in dizziness, slow reaction and blurred vision, which is not conducive to lunar rover control and real-time decision-making. Meanwhile, some studies have shown that different colour backgrounds also cause different degrees of visual fatigue [17, 18, 20]. For the lunar environment, grey and black backgrounds predominate, and grey backgrounds are easier to identify and have fewer handling errors than black backgrounds. In addition to colour, visual fatigue increases significantly with time, and the lighting environment also affects visual fatigue to varying degrees.

4.3 The Role of Different Colour Schemes on VR Interface Design

Colour matching is not only reflected between different patterns and text colours, but also between elemental and background colours. The results of the study showed that the interaction between elemental and background colours was significant. Different combinations of background and target colours affect how quickly and to what extent subjects identify the target, and the effects of combinations of background and foreground colours vary depending on the brain load and the type of task [21, 23]. Both blue and green hues had the weakest visual fatigue against a grey background, and red had the highest visual fatigue when used as an elemental colour. The effect of colour matching on maneuvering efficiency was not studied in depth in this study, but it was found that on the flight plane display, the two-color display was superior to the monochrome and three-colour displays; green + magenta was superior to other colour configurations [22]. Therefore, when designing the remote telemanipulation lunar rover VR interaction interface, the roles of colour, colour scheme, background, time, and lighting should be considered comprehensively.

4.4 Limitations and Future Prospects

Regarding the limitations of this study, the sample was broadly representative of the general research population in China (M = 15, F = 15, ages 23–36). However, the sample originated from local research institutes, mostly from Eastern cultural backgrounds, and the participants' perception and preference of colours can be influenced by culture and geography, thus limiting the applicability of the results to other cultural regional groups. In the next study, the sample should be expanded to other cultural groups to include practical application populations such as astronauts and space centre controllers for experiments.

In this study, the selection of colour samples and background colours was small, and the analysis was mainly carried out on the interface design of five colour samples on a grey background. Therefore, it is difficult to provide sufficient support for VR interface design for non-lunar surfaces and non-spaceflight domains. In addition, some literature suggests that colours in black and grey backgrounds produce different effects on visual fatigue [17]. Therefore, the next study should extend the analysis to black background and other colour samples to further improve the experimental data.

At present, XR technology is developing rapidly, and the comprehensive use of VR, AR and MR has become a hot trend of current research. In the future, for the interactive interface design colour research, it is necessary to extend to AR and MR, etc., to come up with more universal matching schemes and suggestions, and to explore more comprehensively the visual fatigue hierarchy of different hues under the visual environment of the Moon and the law of the display interface's colour and visual fatigue. Remote VR operation of unmanned lunar rovers is a trend in the development of lunar exploration technology, and the design of the colour hierarchy of the VR interface is crucial for improving the visual perception of the operator. In the future, we will further study the effect of interface colour on visual fatigue and visual perception in VR, AR and XR, further expand the colour sample size, and explore the overall laws of colour coding and visual perception. We will focus on: 1. Different interactive interface presentation forms 2. More available colour samples 3. The effect of colour on visual perception in different environments, in order to get a more universal colour design reference. Aiming at the mission scenario of lunar exploration, this design explores the visual fatigue hierarchy of different hues under the visual environment of the moon based on the visual perception hierarchy principle, and discovers the colour and visual fatigue law of the remote VR display interface of an unmanned lunar rover, which provides a reference basis for the design of the colour hierarchy of the remote VR interface of an unmanned lunar rover, which is of certain reference significance. Meanwhile, this study explores the colour coding for the VR interactive interface, which also provides an important reference for virtual interface colour design in other fields.

5 Conclusion

This paper investigates the effects of the colour of the VR interaction interface on manipulation efficiency and visual fatigue of manipulators in a simulated remote manipulation of a lunar rover scenario. The interaction between five colour samples as elemental colours and background colours was tested on a simulated VR interaction interface by experimentally assessing and studying participants' physiological data and subjective feelings, using methods such as the CIE Lab* colour space model and Likert scales. We found a significant interaction between elemental and background colours ($F = 2.011$, $p = 0.050$). The results showed that the visual fatigue time of blue, yellow and green was significantly lower than that of red and orange in grey background ($p < 0.05$), and the mean reaction time of red and orange was higher than that of other colours but not significant. In summary, when used as elemental colours, both blue and green hues have the weakest visual fatigue on a grey background, and red has the highest visual fatigue when used as an elemental colour. This provides a valuable reference for the design of VR interaction interface for remote real-time remote control of lunar rover.

References

1. Nitsch, V., Frber, B.: A meta-analysis of the effects of haptic interfaces on task performance with teleoperation systems. IEEE Trans. Haptics **6**(4), 387–398 (2013). https://doi.org/10.1109/TOH.2012.62
2. Yang, C., Song, J., Sun, J., et al.: On real-time teleoperation of lunar rover. Sci. Sin. Informationis **44**(4), 461 (2014). https://doi.org/10.1360/N112013-00228
3. Freund, E., Rossmann, J.: Projective virtual reality: bridging the gap between virtual reality and robotics. IEEE Trans. Robot. Autom. **15**(3), 411–422 (1999). https://doi.org/10.1109/70.768175
4. Jiang, A., Yao, X., Schlacht, I.L., Musso, G., Tang, T. Westland, S.: Habitability study on space station colour design. in advances in human aspects of transportation. In: Proceedings of the AHFE 2020 Virtual Conference on Human Aspects of Transportation, July 16–20, 2020, USA, pp. 507–514. Springer International Publishing (2020)
5. Jiang, A., Foing, B.H., Schlacht, I.L., Yao, X., Cheung, V., Rhodes, P.A.: Colour schemes to reduce stress response in the hygiene area of a space station: a Delphi study. Appl. Ergon. **98**, 103573 (2022)
6. Rau, P.L.P., Zheng, J., Guo, Z., et al.: Speed reading on virtual reality and augmented reality. Comput. Educ. **125**, 240–245 (2018)
7. Bo, Z.: Research on virtual reality interactive interface design based on cognitive psychology – taking VR simulation product structure teaching system as an example. Shandong Univ. (2022). https://doi.org/10.27272/d.cnki.gshdu.2022.001214
8. Jiang, A., Yao, X., Hemingray, C., Westland, S.: Young people's colour preference and the arousal level of small apartments. Color. Res. Appl. **47**(3), 783–795 (2022)
9. Wickens, C.D., Helleberg, J., Goh, J., Xu, X., Horrey, W.J.: Pilot Task Management: Testing an Attentional Expected Value Model of Visual Scanning, p. 23: Aviation Research Lab, Institute of Aviation (2001)
10. Law, D., Yip, J., Wong, C.W.Y.: How does visual merchandising affect consumer affective response? an intimate apparel experience. Eur. J. Mark. **46**(1), 112–133 (2012). https://doi.org/10.1108/03090561211189266

11. Derefeldt, G., Skinnars, Ö., AL fredson, J., et al.: Improvement of tactical situation awareness with colour-coded horizontal situation displays in combat aircraft. Displays, **20**(4), 171–184 (1999)
12. Jiang, A., et al.: Space habitat astronautics: multicolour lighting psychology in a 7-day simulated habitat. Space Sci. Technol. (2022)
13. Jiang, A., et al.: Short-term virtual reality simulation of the effects of space station colour and microgravity and lunar gravity on cognitive task performance and emotion. Build. Environ. **227**, 109789 (2023)
14. Xiao, X., Wanyan, X.R., Zhuang, D.M., et al.: Ergonomic design and evaluation of visual coding for aircraft head-up display. In: 2012 5th International Conference on BioMedical Engineering and Informatics, Chongqing, pp. 748–752 (2012)
15. Jing, L., Chengqi, X.: Color encoding research of digital display interface based on the visual perceptual layering. J. Mech. Eng. **52**(24), 201–208 (2016)
16. Zhou, X., Yin, G.: Research on symbol color of automotive augmented reality head-up display. J. Phys. Conf. Ser. **1875**(1), 012013. IOP Publishing (2021)
17. Jiang, A., Zhu, Y., Yao, X., Foing, B.H., Westland, S., Hemingray, C.: The effect of three body positions on colour preference: an exploration of microgravity and lunar gravity simulations. Acta Astronaut. **204**, 1–10 (2023)
18. Jiakang, Z., Xiang, Y., Wenhao, Y.: Color design for helmet mounted display interface of lunar spacesuit. J. Mach. Des. **40**(09), 156–162 (2023). https://doi.org/10.13841/j.cnki.jxsj. 2023.09.012
19. Dalke, H., et al.: Colour and lighting in hospital design. Opt. Laser Technol. **38**(4–6), 343–365 (2006). ISSN 0030–3992, https://doi.org/10.1016/j.optlastec.2005.06.040
20. Jiang, A., et al.: The effect of colour environments on visual tracking and visual strain during short-term simulation of three gravity states. Appl. Ergon. **110**, 103994 (2023)
21. Lei, Z., Damin, Z.: Color matching of aircraft interface design. J. Beijing Univ. Aeronaut. Astronaut. **35**(08), 1001–1004 (2009). https://doi.org/10.13700/j.bh.1001-5965.2009.08.013
22. Ruiqin, X., Jing, H., Qingjun, Z.: Effects of multicolor display on HUD information in dynamic simulated flight. Space Med. Med. Eng. **29**(02), 127–132 (2016). https://doi.org/10.16289/j.cnki.1002-0837.2016.02.009
23. Jiang, A.O.: Effects of colour environment on spaceflight cognitive abilities during short-term simulations of three gravity states (Doctoral dissertation, University of Leeds) (2022)

Effects of Avatar Design on Alarm Resolution in a Virtual Reality Physical Security Scenario

Aaron P. Jones[1]([✉]), Michael C. S. Trumbo[1], Andrew Mcfarland[1], Allen Bagwell[1], Bradley M. Robert[1], Aundre J. Marzulli[1], Stephanie M. Roldan[2], and David A. Band[2]

[1] Sandia National Laboratories, Albuquerque, NM 87123, USA
ajones3@sandia.gov
[2] Transportation Security Administration, Springfield, VA 22150, USA

Abstract. Transportation Security Officers (TSOs) must resolve alarms from On-Person Screening (OPS; i.e., body scanner) systems quickly and accurately. Previous work discovered that TSOs' accuracy in identifying alarm locations is influenced by how the body of the passenger is represented by the avatar. To reflect the operational environment more accurately, a virtual reality (VR) methodology was developed to measure the effect of avatar and alarm design on pat-down performance in a simulated screening scenario. Results comparing performance between two displays suggest that the display type influences pat-down behavior. Specifically, the officers in the prototype display group had greater location accuracy and patted down less extraneous area on the passenger compared to a legacy display. In addition, officers reported moderate to high levels of engagement and immersion and indicated that the VR task was highly representative of their job environment. Realistic scenarios like this can help improve training and operational performance and are not limited to pat-down applications.

Keywords: Virtual Reality · On-Person Screening · Physical Security · Immersion · Human Performance · Visual Search

1 Introduction

Domestic airports in the United States require the search of persons and property prior to authorizing their presence on an aircraft. As part of this screening procedure, passengers may walk through systems that use millimeter wave technology to detect prohibited items, which is part of the On-Person Screening (OPS) procedure. In the event of an alarm, the screener will initiate a pat-down procedure to adjudicate that alarm. An alarm location is presented to security screeners on a generic avatar colloquially referred to as the "gingerbread man" [1], which consists of a largely featureless outline of the human body. This generic avatar was selected to protect passenger privacy via exclusion of individual features as mandated by the FAA Modernization and Reform Act of 2012 [2]. One consequence of this generic avatar is that it contains few cues for spatial scaling – relating locations and distances on an avatar that exist on the small 2D space of a monitor to a larger passenger that exists in 3D space [3]. This design may contribute

© The Author(s), under exclusive license to Springer Nature Switzerland AG 2025
J. Y. C. Chen et al. (Eds.): HCII 2024, LNCS 15377, pp. 79–98, 2025.
https://doi.org/10.1007/978-3-031-76812-5_7

to security screeners examining larger areas of the passenger than necessary, leading to perception of pat-down procedures as overly invasive, drawing frequent complaints from passengers, and creating an uncomfortable situation for both passengers and screeners, as well as slowing down the screening process and passenger throughput [1, 4]. To facilitate spatial scaling, alternative avatar designs have been evaluated. These include varying the level of body detail and placement of gridlines to demarcate body segments [5]. The provision of landmarks – indications of features that apply to both the avatar and the referent passenger – has previously been shown to be a useful tool in facilitating judgement of distances [6]. Indeed, both body detail (e.g., joints, figure outlines) and grid lines improved Transportation Security Officers' (TSOs) target location estimates [5]. However, detailed silhouettes are unlikely to be deployed in aviation security screening due to technical and privacy challenges. Instead, avatars with a generic outline of joints and gridlines can be compared against the typical "gingerbread man" avatars for performance benefits. In previous work, TSOs indicated target locations using a mouse interface on a standard computer monitor [5]. The current study builds upon this previous work by employing a virtual reality (VR) methodology to measure TSOs' target location accuracy and pat-down coverage area with higher precision and real-world fidelity than that of a standard computer task. VR refers to a three-dimensional computer-generated environment that enables stereoscopic depth which can result in immersion in a virtual space. As a technology solution, VR can provide a safe environment that can mimic real-world challenges while avoiding time-consuming and costly setup/travel as well as materials and human coaching expenses. VR provides additional advantages that are difficult to achieve in real-world scenarios, including unlimited variability within simulated environments, increased opportunities for experience via easily repeatable scenarios, and improved enjoyment and motivation [7]. Due to the ability to allow stereoscopic depth, VR has become a popular research tool for tasks requiring visual search, defined as a goal-oriented activity that involves the active scanning of the environment to locate a particular target among irrelevant non-targets [8]. Use of VR in visual search experiments has suggested that search speed, accuracy, memory, and workload may benefit from representation of scenes in VR as opposed to naturalistic viewing or viewing on a standard 2D monitor, with improved performance thought to result from immersivity, depth of field, and clarity of the visual experience [9–13]. Additionally, VR enables task performance in ecologically valid virtual environments while also enabling the capture of objective metrics during task execution that can be used to quantify performance or provide user feedback, as seen in standard cognitive science experiments or training. For the current experiment, we developed a VR methodology to collect data on TSO search performance in a simulated pat-down scenario. Conducting the experiment in VR provides detailed control over the location of alarms, the physical attributes of passengers that may influence TSO search (e.g., body size, clothing fit), and search area metrics (e.g., search area size, location, duration) in a quantifiable, replicable manner that better reflects the circumstances of an airport security checkpoint. A VR approach is expected to provide a more accurate evaluation of TSO search behavior than previously employed methods of collecting responses using 2D passenger images and mouse input to indicate search areas. This increased precision should allow for a more accurate assessment of on-body search behavior in relation to Standard Operating Procedure (SOP).

1.1 Hypotheses

Based on previous work [5], the hypotheses for this experiment were that, compared to the less-detailed System 1 avatar currently deployed in the field, the Prototype Avatar (also called OPS Mockup) that includes joint depictions and gridlines as landmark references would lead to (1) more accurate identification of the alarm location, (2) more accurate pat-down metrics, and (3) reduced pat-down time (see Fig. 1). Additionally, the opportunity presented itself to collect data from officers who had yet to begin on-the-job (OJT) training but had finished the classroom portion of training (this group is referred to as NOJTs). This allowed for the direct comparison of officers with and without OJT (i.e., officers who have used the System 1 avatar to adjudicate alarms in the field versus officers who have not yet performed the pat-down procedure in the field). It was further hypothesized that (4) TSOs would outperform NOJT officers on the task with either avatar type.

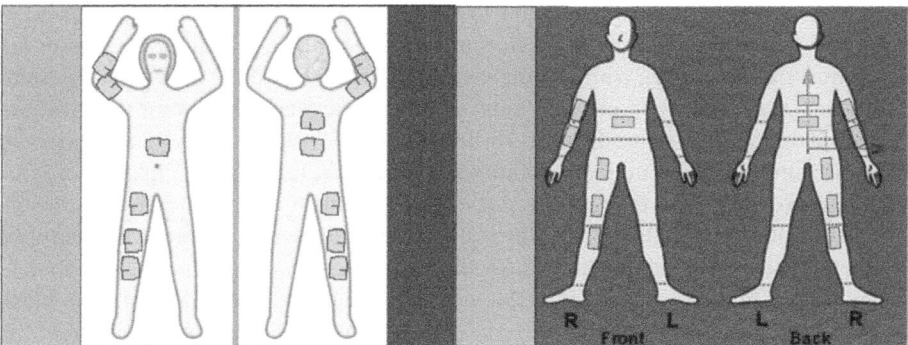

Fig. 1. Avatar/Alarm Indicator type for System 1 (left) and Prototype (right) trials. The red and green arrows were not included in the experimental display.

2 Methods

2.1 Hardware and Software

Stimuli were presented on the HTC Vive Focus 3 Standalone VR headset (https://www.vive.com/us/product/vive-focus3/overview/). This system has 5K resolution, a 120-degree field of view (FOV), and a 90 Hz refresh rate (the higher refresh rate is designed to minimize motion sickness). The Focus 3 can operate tethered to a VR capable machine and has the option to operate as a completely untethered (wireless) system that allows for deployment in a much broader range of environments, since it does not have to be physically connected to a computer. The tethered configuration was used in the current study. The headset has dual 2.88-in. Liquid Crystal Display (LCD) panels, dual speakers (not earbuds), which allows the user to be aware of ambient sound while still being immersed in the VR experience. The Focus 3 has two ergonomic controllers that allow the user to interact with the virtual environment in a more natural way compared to a mouse or joystick. The system has 128 GB of onboard storage with microSD support up to 2TB. The system uses four tracking cameras, a g-sensor (accelerometer), gyroscope, and proximity sensor, as well as a "Pass-Through" mode that allows the user to see the physical environment on the system's LCD panels if they step out of a predefined "play area." The battery life is also ample for field data collection activities, boasting up to 15 h on a charge. The batteries are also hot-swappable if necessary.

2.2 Participants

The criteria for entry to this assessment were completion of training for an OPS scanner system. The study was approved and overseen by our local Human Studies Board (HSB) and was conducted in accordance with the Declaration of Helsinki. Participants were asked to read and sign an informed consent document explaining the nature of the experiment, procedures, and their responsibilities prior to their participation. The Visually Induced Motion Sickness Susceptibility Questionnaire (VIMSSQ) [14] was administered to prospective participants to screen out participants predisposed to experiencing symptoms of visually induced motion sickness. The VIMSSQ-Short uses six questions about experience with moving visual media scored from 0 (Never) to 3 (Often) to measure susceptibility to visually induced motion sickness. Scores for this measure are summed, and thus range from 0–18. Indication of "often" to any question would result in exclusion (no participants in this sample were excluded). Participants were free either to choose not to participate or to leave the experiment at any time, for any reason, without penalty. A total of 91 screening staff from two domestic airports were recruited for the experiment. Three did not finish the experiment (two had headaches prior to putting the VR headset on and decided not to participate, and one was not able to finish the post-experiment questionnaires due to a scheduling conflict), leaving a total of 88. The experiment lasted less than 1.0 h for each participant. Please see Table 1 for number of participants per group.

Table 1. Participant Groups.

Group	Avatar/Alarm Type	Participant/Passenger Sex	No. of Participants
1	System 1	Male	25
2	System 1	Female	19
3	Prototype	Male	25
4	Prototype	Female	19
Total			**88**

2.3 General Overview of Experimental Procedures

Participants were first invited to read and sign an informed consent document, outlining the purpose of the study, the study procedures, and participant responsibilities. They were given the opportunity and encouraged to ask questions regarding the experiment prior to signing the informed consent document. Upon providing consent, a demographic questionnaire was administered. They were then oriented to the VR equipment and were provided instructions to complete the task. During task execution to measure pat-down performance, simulated passengers appear in a scanner. The participant presses a scan button, and an alarm overlaid on an avatar is displayed on the scanner's control panel. The passenger then moves to the pat-down area for alarm adjudication. The TSO uses the controller to reach out and indicate where they believe the center of the alarm to be, and then performs the pat-down according to their understanding of the SOP. The area "touched" by the TSO is highlighted with green paint to let them know where they conducted the pat-down. That painted area becomes the metric for accuracy and coverage area. Note that performance is measured against the alarms' defined center and size as well as a "buffer zone" search area stipulated by SOP. Please find more details in the sections below.

2.4 Instructions and Training

Participants were guided to put the VR headset on with the help of an experimenter. They were allowed to get comfortable in the environment (i.e., look around) before beginning the experiment. They were assigned to one of two conditions (System 1 Avatar/Prototype Avatar) and were assigned a matched-gender passenger set (male/female) based on their response to the gender question in the demographic questionnaire. Participants were provided written and verbal instruction to indicate with the virtual hand (Vive controller) with pointer finger extended (grip button pressed) where they believed the center of the alarm was located on the simulated passenger by colliding with, or "poking," the passenger model in the desired location. Next, after releasing the grip button, the officer "painted" the area on the passenger that they would pat-down given the alarm output from the virtual scan as if they were at the checkpoint. TSOs were presented with four sample/practice trials to familiarize themselves with the VR device, experimental procedures, and to allow them to ask questions of the experimenter prior to the initiation of the experiment.

2.5 Experimental Procedures

The virtual environment included one simulated body scanner system. The virtual scanner system was complete with a basic interactive interface (control panel) that allowed TSOs to initiate and then view the results of the scan. Simulated passengers appeared within the scanner during the scan and outside of the scanner, in the pat-down area, once the scan was complete. Passengers were modeled in three dimensions, with predefined options for clothing (2 levels – baggy or form-fitting) and body size (2 levels – thin, wide). A total of eight simulated passenger models were used (4 male, 4 female). Officer and passenger gender were matched, such that female officers interacted with female passenger models, and likewise for male officers, to reflect the current SOP that requires same-gender pat-downs for screening. TSOs initiated a scan by selecting the appropriate button on the simulated scanner interface. The interface on the simulated control panel then displayed one alarm indicator on a 2D avatar in one of 13 predetermined locations.

Two avatar designs and two alarm indicator designs were used, with paired avatars and alarm indicators manipulated across participants. TSOs completed 56 total trials, seeing each of the 13-alarm location/passenger type/clothing type combinations once. Please see Fig. 1 for avatar/alarm type examples and Fig. 2 for simulated passengers.

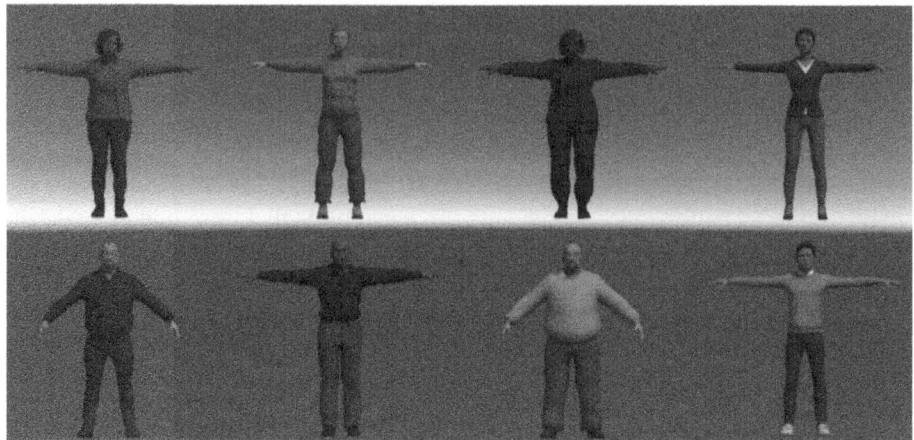

Fig. 2. Simulated passengers. Factors included gender (male/female), clothing type (loose/fitted), and body type (thin/wide).

TSOs initiated the pat-down by selecting the appropriate button on the scanner interface. Passengers exited the scanner facing the TSO and could be rotated 180° by selecting the appropriate button on the control interface (Fig. 3A). TSOs were then able to indicate the perceived center of the detected alarm by reaching out a virtual finger and touching the passenger model (Fig. 3B). They then indicated the area where they would search for the alarm by guiding the virtual hand over the intended search area on the passenger. During the virtual pat-down, a painting function was used, such that a new color texture was painted over the passenger to indicate where the TSO determined the pat-down should occur (Fig. 3C). Once the TSO indicated their search area and confirmed that the search area is accurate to their intended pat-down region, the TSO cleared the passenger using the scanner interface and initiated a new scan with a new passenger. See Fig. 4 for a graphical depiction of the timeline.

2.6 Data Collection Within the Unity Application

The VR scenario records data during participant sessions via the Data Capture Controller (DCC). This is a software element built into the Unity application and written in the C# programming language. The VR scene can also use this system for simple event handling (e.g., informing the DCC when a new passenger pat-down begins or when a given participant's session has concluded). Most data are captured as raw values; however, some are calculated by the DCC for convenience. These data are: (1) the distance from the center of the alarm to the participant touch point, (2) percent of total area inside SOP

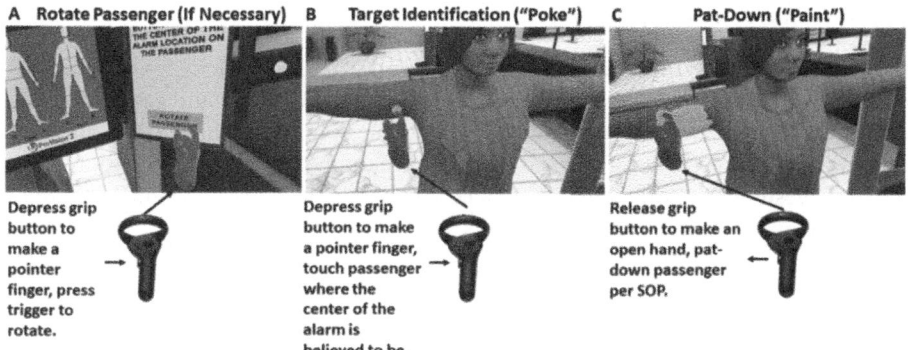

Fig. 3. Rotation of passenger (A), Target Identification (B), and Pat-Down (C) procedures. If the alarm was determined to be on the back of the passenger, the participant would depress the grip button to make a pointer finger, then squeeze the trigger while touching the "Rotate Passenger" button to rotate the passenger. To identify the center of the alarm, the participant would depress the grip button to make a pointer finger, then touch the passenger, which painted the touched location green (indicating that the participant contacted the passenger). Finally, the participant would release the grip button and pat down the passenger per SOP. Any area touched by the participant was painted, serving as a visual indicator for the participant.

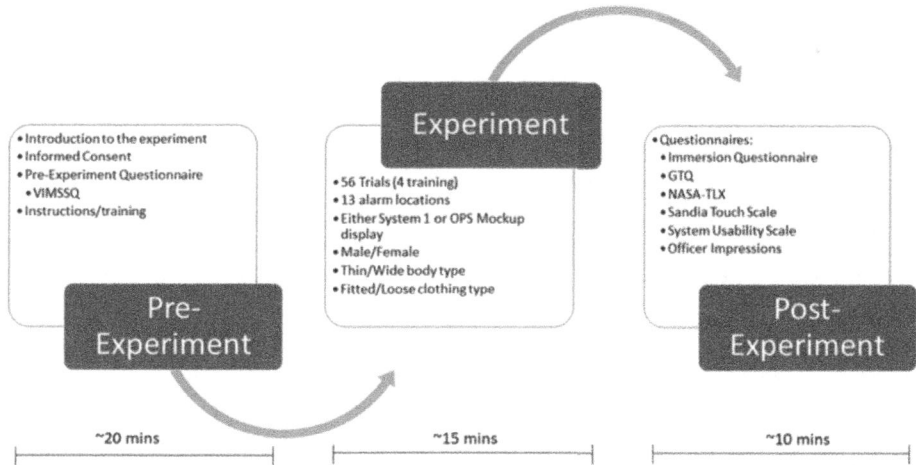

Fig. 4. Experimental Timeline.

covered by the pat down relative to the total size of the SOP area, (3) percent of area patted down outside of the SOP relative to the total pat down area, and (4) percent of pat down inside of the SOP area relative to total pat down area. All data are captured in-memory on the VR headset until the end of the experiment is reached. Once that occurs, the DCC writes out the data to a file in JSON format. JSON is a text-based interchange format and was chosen for its human-readability and its universal compatibility with other programming languages.

2.7 Outcome/Performance Metrics

Data regarding the TSO's response time, size of pat-down area, and location accuracy relative to SOP for pat downs, and the true location of the target for location accuracy, were recorded. Other metrics included a demographic questionnaire, which asked questions regarding time in role, education, and age, as well as a post-experiment debrief, which included questions regarding the officer's experience in the experiment and preference for specific avatars and alarm indicator types.

2.8 Post-experiment Questionnaires

Following the experiment, TSOs were asked to complete a short questionnaire asking them about their experience in the experiment and preferences for specific avatars and alarm indicator types. This questionnaire included the Gas Tank Questionnaire (GTQ) [15]. The GTQ was developed to assess remaining mental resources using a simple, single-item question. Participants are instructed to "Think about your brain as an engine. Please indicate inside the fuel tank below how much gas you had left after interacting with the VR Activity." The questionnaire graphically presents participants with a simple rectangle that has five equally spaced tick marks inside of it and responses are recorded according to where the participant marks. The questionnaire also included a visual Likert scale representing a person's emotion using seven faces and was used to measure TSOs' overall impression of the VR Activity. Finally, the questionnaire included two questions from the National Aeronautics and Space Administration – Task Load Index NASA-TLX [16, 17] regarding mental and physical effort required to complete the task. The System Usability Scale (SUS) [18] was then administered to gauge how easy the VR system is to use in terms of factors such as physical comfort, interface, and complexity. Lastly, an Immersion Scale adapted from [19] was used to gauge how immersed the participants felt while performing the task. Participants rated questions from 0 (not at all/definitely not) to 6 (a lot/definitely yes). All scales and questionnaires were hosted on TSA's Survey Monkey site and were administered via iPad.

2.9 Survey and Questionnaire Scoring Approach

Data from all surveys were combined into a master database for scoring, and each instrument was scored using the recommended approach. For the post-experiment questionnaire, GTQ scores ranged from 0 (no gas left in the tank) to 100 (complete gas left in the tank). Scores from the other questions were aggregated depending on the scale of the question. For the Immersion Scale, subscale scores were calculated for the 6 subscales (basic attention, temporal dissociation, transportation (from reality), challenge, emotional involvement, and enjoyment), according to [19]. Only subscale scores are reported here, as the approach for the current experiment differed significantly from previous tasks in which this instrument was used. Specifically, since we were trying to simulate a realistic environment, we did not predict that participants would feel "transported" to another reality. Likewise, since we were attempting to recreate the officers' work environment, we didn't anticipate it being overly challenging. For the SUS, individual item scores were transformed to produce a summary score on a scale of 1–100.

In web usability, a score at or above 80 is a solid 'A;' scores below 68 indicate problems [18].

2.10 Inferential Statistics Approach

Two databases were first compiled, where the first database included only TSOs from both airports to assess the performance of the alarm visualization types in the primary population of interest, to test the hypotheses that participants in the prototype avatar condition would be faster and more accurate (for target identification and area patted down) than participants in the System 1 condition. A second database was compiled with TSOs (from both airports) and NOJT officers (from Airport B only) to address the hypothesis that TSOs would perform faster and more accurately than NOJT participants, as well as any effects of alarm visualization types between officers that have on-the-job experience versus those who have completed basic training at the TSA Academy but have yet to perform their job in the field. Five performance metrics were calculated and included in the analyses. These metrics included accuracy, called the "poke," percentage of alarm area painted relative to the total area of the alarm, percentage of area patted-down ("painted") outside of the SOP relative to total area painted, poke time (time elapsed from pressing the pat-down button to making initial contact with the passenger model), and paint time (time elapsed from poke to completing pat-down). These metrics were chosen because they relate to pat-down efficiency and effectiveness via searching in the right place (accuracy) and searching an appropriate coverage area (pat-down). Data were inspected for normality and outliers. For each dependent measure, outlier trials were removed based on a 3-standard deviation cutoff. Each of these dependent variables was entered into separate mixed model Analysis of Variance (ANOVAs) with gender, age, airport, experience, body type, clothing type, alarm location, and alarm type as fixed effects predictors. Subject was entered as a random effect. Akaike Information Criteria (AIC) was used to assess model fit. The most parsimonious model with relevant factors included (based on the minimum AIC) was chosen. Interactions were investigated up to the 3-factor level. Simple effects testing of any significant interactions were investigated using contrast testing. Pearson's r was used for correlation analysis. The significance level was set to $p < 0.05$. All inferential analyses were conducted in JASP 0.16.3 [20]. Demographics data were processed and visualized using Minitab 19.2020.1 [21].

3 Results

3.1 Demographics

A total of 91 participants provided informed consent. Two officers decided after providing consent, but prior to starting the VR experiment, not to continue (both reported headaches unrelated to the VR scenario). An additional participant completed the VR portion of the task without incident but decided to cease participation without completing the post-experiment questionnaires, and thus was dropped from subsequent analyses. A total of 88 screening staff completed all phases of the experiment (ages 19 – 67, mean age = 37.89, SD = 12.13, 33 female). This included 55 TSOs (ages 19 – 67, mean age

= 38.51, SD = 13.21, 23 female), 3 instructors (ages 27 – 39, mean age = 32.33, SD = 6.11, 1 female), 9 lead TSOs (LTSOs) (ages 27 – 54, mean age = 36.00, SD = 9.75, 4 female), 11 NOJTs (ages 24 – 53, mean age = 33.55, SD = 9.89, 5 female), and 10 supervisory TSOs (STSOs) (ages 30 – 61, mean age = 42.60, SD = 10.46, 5 female). See Fig. 5 for a plot of age by rank and airport (left) and a plot of gender by rank and airport (right).

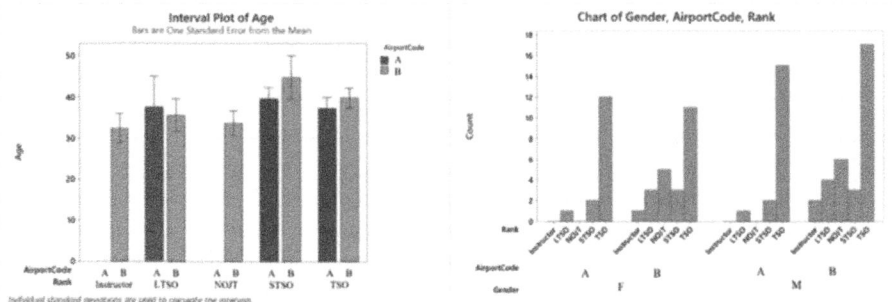

Fig. 5. Average age by rank and airport location (left) and count of gender by rank and airport location (right). Error bars = ± 1 Standard Error of the Mean (SEM).

3.2 Participant Impressions/Questionnaires

Please see Table 2 for descriptive statistics for all the questionnaires. For the immersion scale, participants felt like the scenario was very engaging and held their attention well, but did not feel like they were temporally dissociated or transported from reality. Participants found the scenario challenging, but not extremely so, were involved in the task and wanted to do well (as evidenced by the emotional involvement subscale scores), and neither disliked nor necessarily enjoyed the scenario. Since they were being asked to perform a task which mimicked their normal job duties, we did not expect to see extremely high scores for the enjoyment subscale. Considering this was a repetitive task, the fact that participants' average scores indicated ambivalence is reassuring in that they did not dislike or feel negatively about the task. For the SUS, participants found the scenario and hardware very usable. For the GTQ and the two questions (mental and physical effort) from the NASA-TLX, results suggest that participants did not find the scenario or task too mentally or physically demanding. For the post-experiment questionnaire, results suggest that participants felt like the hardware was comfortable and that the scenario and the way they interacted with it highly simulated their experience in an actual checkpoint environment. Participants felt like the length of time spent in the scenario was ideal, had a very high overall impression of the task, and almost every participant was willing to participate in similar experiments in the future.

3.3 TSO Only Performance Results

Note that there were main effects for Alarm Location for every model run. Those results will not be reported for brevity, but any interactions with alarm type and location (and

Table 2. Participant Questionnaire Responses.

Scale/Subscale (Maximum Possible Score)	Mean	SD
Immersion Scale		
Basic Attention (24)	17.943	3.337
Temporal Dissociation (36)	19.727	4.367
Transportation (36)	16	5.045
Challenge (36)	24.034	3.508
Emotional Involvement (30)	19.92	5.213
Enjoyment (24)	12.307	3.123
System Usability		
System Usability Scale (100)	79.18	14.52
Mental and Physical Demand		
Gas Tank Questionnaire (100)	80.23	21.96
NASA-TLX Mental Demand (100)	29.94	26.66
NASA-TLX Physical Demand (100)	39.23	29.98
TSO Questionnaire		
Physical Comfort (5)	3.78	1.12
Simulate Checkpoint Environment/Job Duties (5)	4.05	0.84
Length of Time on Task (5)	3.06	0.76
Overall Impression (7)	6.09	0.89
Willingness to Participate (1)	0.98	0.15

other factors) will be reported. For accuracy, which measures the distance from the center of the alarm location to the initial touch/poke by the participant, results revealed a main effect of clothing type, where participants were on average closer to the center of the alarm for fitted clothing type compared to the loose clothing type ($F_{(1, 2704.06)} = 4.814, p = 0.028$). There was also a trend level effect for alarm type overall; on average, participants in the Prototype condition were closer to the center of the alarm compared to System 1 ($F_{(1, 51.01)} = 3.217, p = 0.079$). Two interactions for accuracy were observed: a two-way alarm-type*alarm location interaction ($F_{(12, 2704.09)} = 13.083, p = 1.469e\text{-}26$; Fig. 6), and a three-way airport*alarm type*alarm location interaction ($F_{(12, 2704.09)} = 1.884, p = 0.032$; Fig. 8). Simple effects for the two-way interaction suggest that participants in the Prototype condition were more accurate than the System 1 condition for alarm locations 1, 3, 7, 8, and 9, while participants in the System 1 condition were more accurate than the Prototype condition for location 11.

For the three-way interaction, simple effects testing suggests significant differences between alarm locations across airport, where the Prototype resulted in greater accuracy than System 1 for both airports at body locations 1, 7, and 9, and at body location 8 for

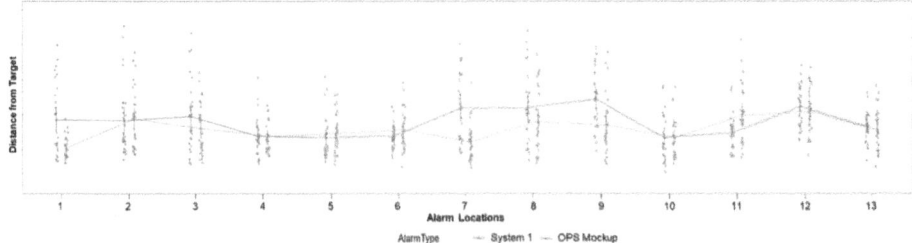

Fig. 6. Alarm Type*Alarm Location Interaction. The Prototype (referred to as OPS Mockup in the results figures) was superior to System 1 in accuracy at several locations, while System 1 was superior only for one location. No other significant differences were observed between conditions. Error bars = 95% CI of the mean.

Airport A only. System 1 performed better than the Prototype only at location 11 for Airport A (see Fig. 7).

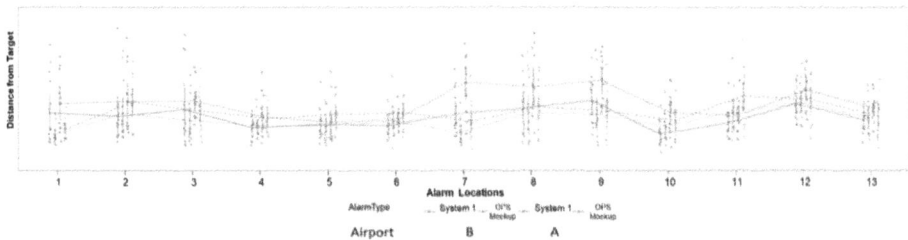

Fig. 7. Airport*Alarm Type*Alarm Location Interaction. The prototype avatar was superior to System 1 at several locations for both airports, and for one location at Airport A only. System 1 was superior to the Prototype only for one location at Airport A. No other significant differences were observed between conditions. Error bars = 95% CI of the mean.

For percentage of alarm area painted relative to total alarm area, two significant interactions were observed. One two-way interaction of alarm type*alarm location (F(12, 2757) = 5.780, p = 5.794e-10), and a three-way interaction of gender*alarm type*alarm location (F(12, 2757) = 1.904, p = 0.029; Fig. 9) Simple effects testing of the two-way interaction revealed effects at location 1 where, on average, the Prototype performed better than System 1, and at location 6 where System 1 performed better than the Prototype. No other effects were found. For the three-way interaction of percentage of alarm area painted relative to total alarm area, simple effects testing revealed effects only for the male participants. At location 1, the Prototype was better than System 1 for the percentage of alarm area painted relative to total alarm area, while for locations 6 and 13, System 1 was better than the Prototype (see Fig. 8).

For percentage of area painted outside of the alarm area, main effects were observed for passenger body type ($F_{(1, 2699)} = 16.267$, $p = 5.655e-5$), where performance for the wider body type was better than for the thinner body type, and for clothing type ($F_{(1, 2699)} = 19.311$, $p = 1.153e-5$), where performance for fitted clothing was better than for loose clothing. Two significant interactions were observed: a two-way interaction

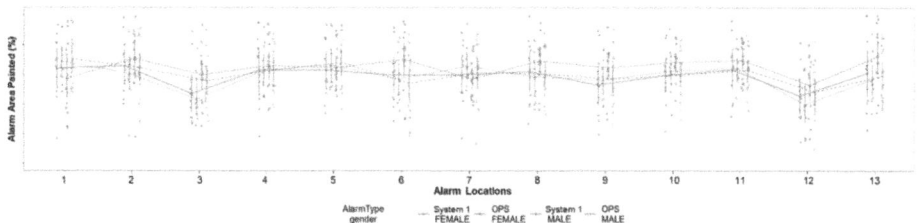

Fig. 8. Alarm Area Painted (%). Effects were found of alarm type within male participants only. The Prototype was superior to System 1 for one location, while System 1 was superior to the Prototype at two locations.

of alarm type*alarm location ($F_{(12, 2699)} = 5.071, p = 2.003e\text{-}8$; Fig. 9, and a three-way interaction of gender*alarm type*alarm location ($F_{(12, 2699)} = 2.648, p = 0.001$; Fig. 10). Simple effects testing of the two-way interaction revealed that the Prototype resulted in significantly better performance than System 1 at locations 1, 4, 5, 7, 9, and 11. No other effects were observed.

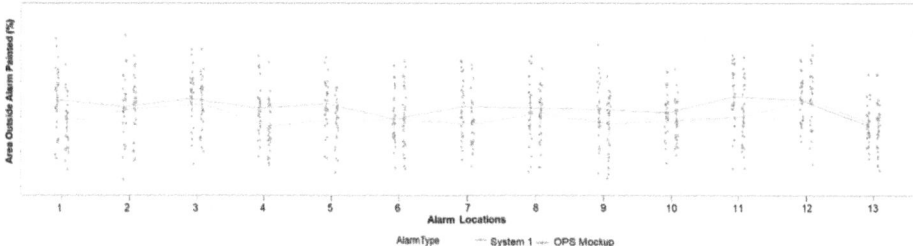

Fig. 9. Percentage painted outside of alarm area, alarm type*alarm location interaction. Effects were found where the Prototype performed better than System 1 for several locations. Error bars = 95% CI of the mean.

Simple effects testing of the three-way interaction for percentage of area painted outside of the alarm area revealed effects of alarm type and location within both male and female participants. All effects were in the same direction as the two-way interaction, in that the Prototype condition performed better than the System 1 condition. Effects were found for female participants at locations 9, and 11. For male participants, effects were found at locations 1, 4, and 11.

For poke time, which measures the time from when the passenger model appears in the Passenger Pat Down Position to when the first contact between the pointer finger of the virtual hand and the passenger model occurs, there were significant main effects observed for body type ($F_{(1, 2686.99)} = 10.421, p = 0.001$), where poke time was faster for wider body types compared to thinner body types. There was also an effect of clothing type ($F_{(1, 2686.96)} = 17.703, p = 2.667e\text{-}5$), where poke time was faster for fitted clothing trials compared to the loose clothing trials. There was also a trend-level effect for alarm type ($F_{(1, 50.95)} = 2.909, p = 0.094$), where the System 1 condition was faster than the Prototype condition. No interactions with alarm type were observed.

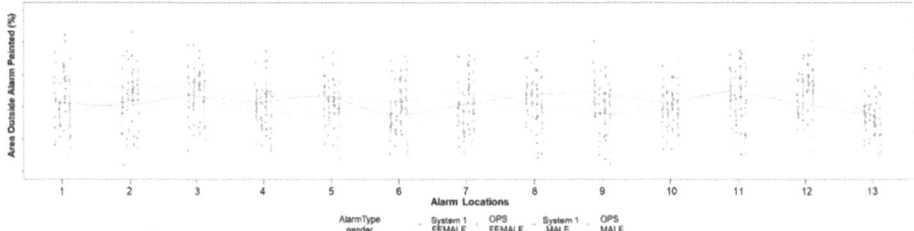

Fig. 10. Percentage painted outside of alarm area, Gender*Alarm type*Alarm location interaction. Effects were found in female participants at two locations, and in male participants at three locations. All effects suggest the Prototype performed better than System 1. No other effects were observed. Error bars = 95% CI of the mean.

For paint time, which measures the time from the initial poke to when the participant indicates they are finished with the trial, there was a significant main effect observed for clothing type ($F_{(1, 2615.99)} = 49.459$, $p = 2.575e$-12), where paint time was faster for fitted clothing compared to loose clothing. There was a significant two-way interaction of alarm type*alarm location ($F_{(12, 2615.99)} = 2.268$, $p = 0.001$). Investigation of this interaction revealed that at location 13, paint time for the System 1 condition was faster on average than for the Prototype condition. No other simple effects were significant.

3.4   TSO Versus NOJT Performance Results

Note: there were main effects for Alarm Location for every model run. Those results will not be reported for brevity, but any interactions with alarm type, location, rank (and other factors) are reported. Performance results were compared between TSOs and NOJTs to explore the effects of training and experience on pat-down behavior. Results revealed main effects of clothing type for pat-down accuracy, where participants were closer to the center of the alarm for fitted clothing type compared to the loose clothing type ($F_{(1, 1757.95)} = 4.783$, $p = 0.029$). There was also a main effect of body type, where participants were closer to the center of the alarm for thinner body type compared to wider body type ($F_{(1, 1757.95)} = 11.861$, $p = 5.866e$-4). There was a trend level effect for rank overall, where on average TSO participants were closer to the center of the alarm compared to NOJT participants ($F_{(1, 34.95)} = 3.217$, $p = 0.069$). A two-way alarm type*alarm location interaction was observed ($F_{(12, 1758.21)} = 6.460$, $p = 2.300e$-11). Simple effects testing for the two-way interaction suggested that participants in the Prototype condition were more accurate than the System 1 condition for alarm locations 1, and 7, while participants in the System 1 condition were more accurate than the Prototype condition for location 11.

For percentage of alarm area painted relative to total alarm area, three significant interactions were observed: one two-way interaction of alarm type*alarm location ($F_{(12, 1941)} = 5.259$, $p = 8.694e$-9), one two-way interaction of rank*alarm location ($F_{(12, 1941)} = 4.765$, $p = 9.723e$-8), and a three-way interaction of rank*alarm type*alarm location ($F_{(12, 2757)} = 1.904$, $p = 0.029$). Simple effects testing of the three-way interaction between rank, alarm type, and alarm location revealed effects at locations 1 and 7 in the NOJT group, where on average the Prototype performed better than System 1.

Investigating the effect of rank within levels of alarm type and location revealed that NOJTs outperformed TSOs at location 1 and 4 in the Prototype condition. In the System 1 condition, NOJTs performed better than TSOs at location 13.

For percentage of area painted outside of the alarm area, main effects were observed for: rank ($F_{(1, 35)} = 16.162, p = 2.944\text{e-}4$), where TSOs outperformed NOJTs; passenger body type ($F_{(1, 1789.01)} = 10.325, p = 0.001$), where performance for the wider body type was better than for the thinner body type, and for clothing type ($F_{(1, 1789.01)} = 10.975, p = 9.421\text{e-}4$), where performance for fitted clothing was better than loose clothing. Three significant interactions in performance between NOJTs and TSOs were observed: a two-way interaction of alarm type*alarm location ($F_{(12, 1789.01)} = 1.853, p = 0.036$); a two-way interaction of rank*alarm location ($F_{(12, 1789.01)} = 3.374, p = 3.374\text{e-}5$), and a three-way interaction of rank*alarm type*alarm location ($F_{(12, 1789.01)} = 2.645, p = 0.002$; Fig. 11). Simple effects testing of the three-way interaction investigating alarm type and location within levels of rank revealed effects in the TSO group only, where the Prototype resulted in better performance than System 1 at locations 1, 5, and 11. No other effects were observed.

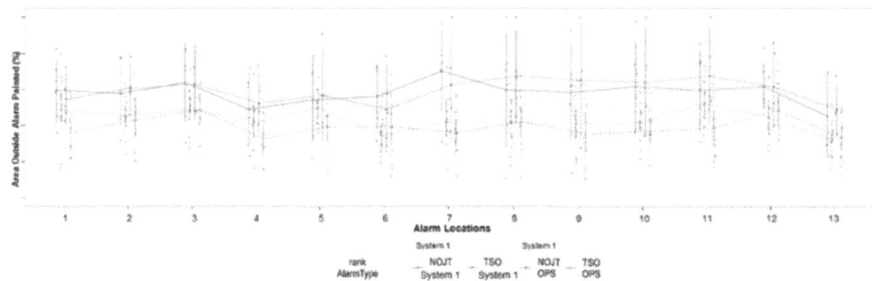

Fig. 11. Outside Alarm Area Painted, Rank*Alarm Type*Alarm Location interaction. Within rank, the Prototype outperformed System 1 at three locations in the TSO group. Error bars = 95% CI of the mean.

For poke time, there were significant main effects observed for rank, where TSOs were faster overall than NOJTs ($F_{(1, 35)} = 12.342, p = 0.001$), and body type ($F_{(1, 1773)} = 8.928, p = 0.003$), where poke time was faster for wider body types compared to thinner body types. A significant two-way rank*alarm location interaction ($F_{(1, 1773.01)} = 2.331, p = 0.006$; see Fig. 12) and a three-way rank*alarm type*alarm location were also observed ($F_{(1, 1773.01)} = 2.856, p = 6.654\text{e-}4$). The nature of the interactions was driven by rank, where TSOs were overall faster than NOJTs.

For paint time, there were significant main effects observed for rank ($F_{(1, 34.98)} = 14.979, p = 4.359\text{e-}4$), where paint time was faster for TSOs compared to NOJTs, and clothing type ($F_{(1, 1756.99)} = 34.547, p = 3.689\text{e-}23$), where paint time was faster for fitted clothing compared to loose clothing. There was a significant two-way interaction of rank*alarm location ($F_{(12, 1756.99)} = 2.787, p = 8.927\text{e-}4$; see Fig. 13). The nature of this interaction was similar to poke time, in that TSOs were faster at every alarm location compared to NOJTs.

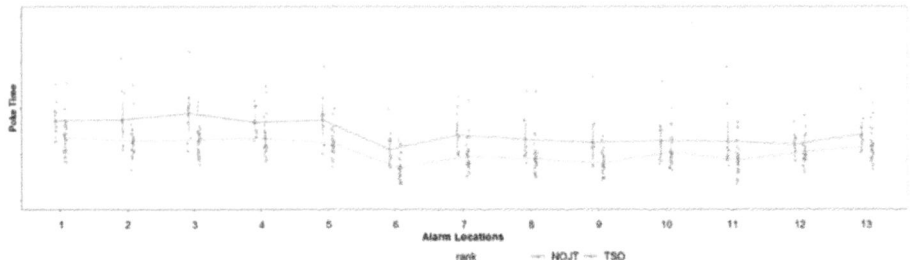

Fig. 12. Poke time, two-way interaction of Rank*Alarm location. TSOs were faster than NOJTs at all alarm locations. Error bars = 95% CI of the mean.

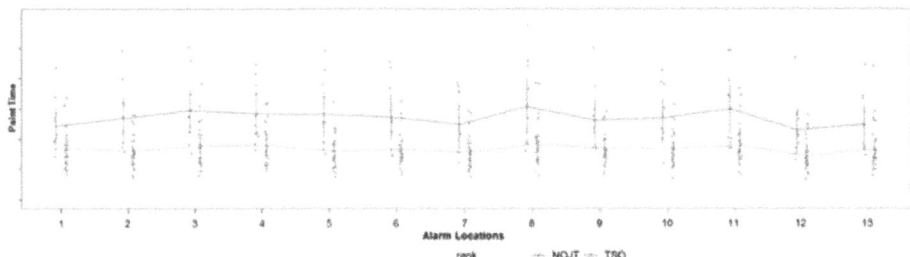

Fig. 13. Paint time, two-way Alarm Type*Alarm Location interaction. TSOs were faster than NOJTs at all locations. Error bars = 95% CI of the mean.

4 Discussion

In this experiment, we report data on TSO search performance in a simulated pat-down scenario. Conducting the experiment in VR allowed detailed control over the location of alarms, the physical attributes of passengers that may influence TSO search (e.g., body size, fitting of clothes), and search area metrics (e.g., search area size, location, duration), in a quantifiable, replicable manner that better reflects the circumstances of an airport security checkpoint than traditional methods. Results indicate that the Prototype condition was superior to System 1 for accuracy and area painted outside of the alarm area for TSOs. This effect appeared to be strongest in certain areas of the body but not others. There was no operational difference in reaction time between conditions.

In general, passenger gender and clothing type did not interact with alarm type to effect pat-down metrics, suggesting that those variables were not influenced by the alarm display type, though there were some nuanced effects on some metrics. Overall, across different passenger types, the Prototype condition resulted in improved target location accuracy and more accurate pat-downs for most alarm locations, compared to the System 1 condition. TSOs were superior to NOJTs for location accuracy and reduced percentage of area painted outside of the SOP target area and were faster than NOJTs across all alarm locations for initial alarm localization (i.e., poke time) and time to complete the search (i.e., paint time). Experience, measured as number of years with TSA, predicted performance for painting outside of the alarm area for TSOs, but did not significantly predict accuracy, paint inside the alarm area, or poke or paint time.

For participant impressions, officers reported being engaged in the task and that it held their attention. While they did not feel strongly negatively or positively about the task, this was an expected finding since we were asking them to simply perform their job duties (i.e., we were not asking them to pilot a spaceship or other tasks that would have been more enjoyable than merely doing their job). The task was not overly mentally or physically demanding, and the system was comfortable and rated as user-friendly. Critically, officers described the scenario as highly representative of their work environment and procedures at the checkpoint and had a very high overall impression of the scenario, and almost all were willing to participate in experiments like this in the future. As this was the first time VR was used for research at TSA, this finding is of particular importance for future endeavors.

Overall, this experiment demonstrated the successful novel application of VR to the study of search behaviors performed by TSOs conducting on-person pat-downs. The findings support previous research suggesting that avatar and alarm features can influence TSO pat-down performance [5]. The VR system builds upon two-dimensional, computer-based tasks by capturing more precise and realistic pat-down performance metrics such as alarm location accuracy and estimated search coverage area in three dimensions. These and other behaviors are of interest for task evaluation and improvement because they influence not only security effectiveness – by ensuring that TSOs perform SOP to maximize chances of locating concealed threats – but also passenger throughput, as focusing searches on the appropriate region around the identified threat can expedite the resolution process. These findings also support design features for OPS interfaces that better support TSO performance and threat detection. VR as a methodology for pat-down performance assessment provides unique access to precise metrics that can inform the effectiveness and accuracy of on-person pat-downs, which can ultimately support aviation security and passenger convenience. VR can be used to overcome certain challenges in pat-down training, namely replicability of item location, ability to control passenger appearance, and recording precise metrics related to pat-down speed and coverage area. VR can be used for other physical security research or training applications. For example, using VR to visualize 3D computed tomography (CT) data could provide a more realistic and intuitive way to interrogate CT-scanned luggage images compared to viewing such data on a 2D screen. Using VR as a research testbed or training tool for physical security allows for officers (and researchers) to explore ways to improve performance in a safe-to-fail, cost effective, ecologically valid way.

5   Limitations and Future Directions

The experiences and opinions expressed by participants in this study reflect those of individual TSOs and may not be generalizable across all TSOs or airports. In fact, we observed differences related to airport location on the accuracy analysis, which could be due to numerous factors, including nature of the demographic makeup of the officers and/or passengers, local training techniques, time-of-day effects, etc. Quantitative data may not be representative of all airports, as data collection occurred in a small number of locations, though every effort was made to collect as representative a sample as possible. Differences in security screening procedures around the world would have to be taken into consideration if this study were to take place outside of the United States. The stimulus set is limited in nature and does not reflect the variability in passengers or alarms seen in the field. However, the data we obtained help us evaluate how well VR captures search performance behaviors in simulated screening scenarios.

VR, along with Augmented Reality (AR), has been mostly used as a training tool in the domains of first responders, medical professionals, military operators, and transportation professionals [22]. Numerous studies, across multiple fields, have indicated that VR is as effective of a training method as current commonly accepted methods [23]. VR environments can address several time and cost constraints that are frequently at issue with real-world training. As a technology solution, VR can provide a safe training environment that can mimic real-world challenges while avoiding time-consuming and costly setup/travel as well as materials and human coaching expenses. VR as a training solution provides additional advantages that are difficult to achieve in real-world simulated training scenarios by allowing for nearly unlimited variability within simulated environments and training scenarios, increased opportunities for experience via easily repeatable scenarios, and improved enjoyment and motivation [7]. Additionally, the controlled nature of the VR environment is easily combined with established protocols of physiological measurements proven to be sensitive enough to distinguish different levels of arousal, valence, anxiety, stress, or cognitive workload during task performance [24].

While VR represents a potentially valuable training technology, there are several limitations and future directions to consider prior to widespread application. The version of the experiment reported here did not include alarms in sensitive areas, and alarms were limited to one side of the body (namely the right side of the passenger). As sensitive area alarms are associated with a different SOP, the inclusion of sensitive alarm areas as well as distribution of alarms across the entire body would need to be evaluated prior to implementing a comprehensive VR training program. The simulated passengers in this study appeared somewhat stylized. Increased realism, along with an expanded cast of passenger models, is easily achievable and could be incorporated into a training environment that is designed to better mimic the variety an officer might encounter in the course of job performance. Additionally, for the purposes of this experiment, all passengers alarmed, which does not mimic the real-world base-rate. The frequency of alarms could be adjusted for either research (e.g., fatigue) or training purposes. As results indicate differences between NOJT officers and TSOs regarding area painted and speed of pat-down completion, it seems evident that experience at a checkpoint leads to improvements in these domains. It is possible that VR training could serve as a surrogate, supplement, or bridge to OJT, thereby improving officer preparation and experience levels before they reach a live checkpoint. For example, a VR training scenario could provide real-time feedback to the training officer, instructor, or both, while performing pat downs to help scaffold their learning.

While participants in the current study received some rudimentary feedback regarding collision of the hand models with the passenger models via controller vibration, feedback regarding pressure was not provided. Application of appropriate level of pressure has previously been voiced as a concern for TSOs [25], and is important for threat detection, with one previously tested solution involving construction of training mannequins equipped with pressure sensors [26], though these were expensive to procure and subject to deterioration and are not currently in use by TSA. The existing technology space for VR deployment allows for expansion beyond the traditional visual experience to the inclusion of auditory, haptic, kinesthetic, and olfactory simulation [22]. Pressure-sensitivity and feedback can be incorporated into a VR training experience via gloves designed to allow for simulation of physical objects in a virtual space (e.g., https://haptx.com/). This could allow tactile feedback and performance metrics regarding the appropriate amount of pressure for TSOs to apply when learning how to perform a pat-down. Though this capability would require some investment in basic research, including the development of easily deployable tactile feedback to identify appropriate levels of pressure, it would allow for a high-fidelity representation of virtually modeled objects that can be manipulated and felt in a fashion analogous to a real-world experience. Such technologies are relevant to agencies beyond TSA; many other security professionals perform similar search tasks, like Customs and Border Protection (CBP). As such, these technologies could be applied to a wide variety of screening operations in numerous domains.

Acknowledgments. Sandia National Laboratories is a multi-mission laboratory managed and operated by National Technology & Engineering Solutions of Sandia, LLC (NTESS), a wholly owned subsidiary of Honeywell International Inc., for the U.S. Department of Energy's National Nuclear Security Administration (DOE/NNSA) under contract DE-NA0003525. This written work is authored by an employee of NTESS. The employee, not NTESS, owns the right, title and interest in and to the written work and is responsible for its contents. Any subjective views or opinions that might be expressed in the written work do not necessarily represent the views of the U.S. Government. The publisher acknowledges that the U.S. Government retains a non-exclusive, paid-up, irrevocable, world-wide license to publish or reproduce the published form of this written work or allow others to do so, for U.S. Government purposes. The DOE will provide public access to results of federally sponsored research in accordance with the DOE Public Access Plan.

Disclosure of Interests. The authors have no competing interests to declare that are relevant to the content of this article.

References

1. Ehsan, Z.: What are your rights at screenings and checkpoints? GPSolo **30**, 34 (2013)
2. U.S. House of Representatives. FAA Modernization and Reform Act of 2012 (2012)
3. Möhring, W., Newcombe, N.S., Frick, A.: Using mental transformation strategies for spatial scaling: evidence from a discrimination task. J. Exp. Psychol. Learn. Mem. Cogn. **42**(9), 1473 (2016)
4. Thomas, D.S., Hobson, H., Hubbard, J.C., Forcht, K.A.: Technology in practice: airport scanning privacy Issues. Issues Inf. Syst. **14**(1), 47–53 (2013)
5. Zish, K., Band, D., Korbelak, K., Endres, D., McKee, C., McKnight, S.: Designing and evaluating an avatar for on-person screening. In: Proceedings of the Human Factors and Ergonomics Society Annual Meeting, vol. 65, pp. 106–110 (2021)
6. Frick, A., Newcombe, N.S.: Getting the big picture: development of spatial scaling abilities. Cogn. Dev. **27**(3), 270–282 (2012)
7. Makransky, G., Borre-Gude, S., Mayer, R.E.: Motivational and cognitive benefits of training in immersive virtual reality based on multiple assessments. J. Comput. Assist. Learn. **35**(6), 691–707 (2019)

8. Eckstein, M.P.: Visual search: a retrospective. J. Vis. **11**(5), 14 (2011)

9. El Beheiry, M., et al.: Breast magnetic resonance image analysis for surgeons using virtual reality: a comparative study. JCO Clin. Canc. Inform. **5**, 1127–1133 (2021)

10. Figueroa, J.C.M., Arellano, R.A.B., Calinisan, J.M.E.: A comparative study of virtual reality and 2D display methods in visual search in real scenes. In: Cassenti, D. (eds.) Advances in Human Factors in Simulation and Modeling. AHFE 2017. Advances in Intelligent Systems and Computing, vol. 591, pp. 366–377. Springer, Cham (2018). https://doi.org/10.1007/978-3-319-60591-3_33

11. Ijaz, K., Ahmadpour, N., Naismith, S.L., Calvo, R.A.: An immersive virtual reality platform for assessing spatial navigation memory in predementia screening: feasibility and usability study. JMIR Mental Health **6**(9), e13887 (2019)

12. Nevalainen, S.: A Comparative Study of Monitoring Data Center Temperature Through Visualizations in Virtual Reality Versus 2D Screen (2018)

13. van den Oever, F., Gorobets, V., Fjeld, M., Kunz, A.: Comparing visual search between physical environments and VR. In: 2022 IEEE International Symposium on Mixed and Augmented Reality Adjunct (ISMAR-Adjunct), pp. 411–416. IEEE (2022)

14. Keshavarz, B., Saryazdi, R., Campos, J.L., Golding, J.F.: Introducing the VIMSSQ: measuring susceptibility to visually induced motion sickness. Proc. Hum. Fact. Ergon. Soc. Ann. Meet. **63**, 2267–2271 (2019). https://doi.org/10.1177/1071181319631216

15. Monfort, S.S., Graybeal, J.J., Harwood, A.E., McKnight, P.E., Shaw, T.H.: A single-item assessment for remaining mental resources: development and validation of the gas tank questionnaire (GTQ). Theor. Issues Ergon. Sci. 1–23 (2017)

16. Hart, S.G., Staveland, L.E.: Development of NASA-TLX (Task Load Index): results of empirical and theoretical research. [W]: PA Hancock, N. Meshkati (eds.): Human Mental Workload (1988)

17. Hart, S.G.: NASA-task load index (NASA-TLX); 20 years later. In Proceedings of the Human Factors and Ergonomics Society Annual Meeting, vol. 50, no. 9, pp. 904–908. Sage CA: Los Angeles, CA: Sage publications (2006)

18. Brooke, J.: SUS: a "quick and dirty" usability scale. In: Jordan, P.W., Thomas, B., McClelland, B.W., (eds.), Usability Evaluation in Industry, p. 189. CRC Press (1996). https://doi.org/10.1201/9781498710411

19. Jennett, C., et al.: Measuring and defining the experience of immersion in activities. Int. J. Hum. Comput. Stud. **66**(9), 641–661 (2008)

20. JASP Team. JASP (Version 0.16.3) [Computer software] (2022)

21. Minitab 19 Statistical Software. [Computer software]. State College, PA: Minitab, Inc. (2020). (www.minitab.com)

22. Xie, B., et al.: A review on virtual reality skill training applications. Front. Virtual Reality **2**, 645153 (2021)

23. Kaplan, A.D., Cruit, J., Endsley, M., Beers, S.M., Sawyer, B.D., Hancock, P.A.: The effects of virtual reality, augmented reality, and mixed reality as training enhancement methods: a meta-analysis. Hum. Factors **63**(4), 706–726 (2021)

24. Halbig, A., Latoschik, M.E.: A systematic review of physiological measurements, factors, methods, and applications in virtual reality. Front. Virtual Reality **2** (2021)

25. Korbelak, K., Dressel, J., Band, D., Blanchard, J.: Teaming with technology at the TSA: practical methods for enhancing human performance with automation in operational environments. In: Proceedings of the Human Factors and Ergonomics Society Annual Meeting, vol. 62, no. 1, pp. 639–640. Sage CA: Los Angeles, CA: SAGE Publications (2018)

26. Matteson, R.: Pat-down accuracy training tool–development and application of a quantitative tool to measure applied pressures during a pat-down. In: 17th International Conference on Human-Computer Interaction. Springer (2015)

Enhancing Augmented Reality (MAR) Interaction Experience: A Design Framework Grounded in User Mental Model Construction

Xiaozhan Liang⬤ and Xiaona Ma$^{(\boxtimes)}$

Beihang University, No. 37 Xueyuan Road, Haidian District, Beijing,
People's Republic of China
`dearzhan1019@163.com`

Abstract. Purpose: This study introduces a novel approach to enhance handheld mobile augmented reality (MAR) experiences through user mental models. By analyzing MAR characteristics, we construct a user mental model based on "execution" and "evaluation" dimensions alongside six attributes, guiding MAR interaction design. **Methods:** We analyze MAR traits like interactivity, information display, and physical comfort, deriving two dimensions (execution and evaluation) and six attributes (usage habits, information attention, interactive behavior, usage experience, cognitive experience, and workload). Through user interviews and affinity diagrams, we construct the mental model. To demonstrate its practical application, we utilize a MAR exhibition with a miniature model theme. **Results:** Through case application and user testing, we validate the effectiveness of the mental model-driven design in enhancing MAR interaction. Users perceive improvements in ease of use, learnability, and satisfaction with systems designed using this approach. **Conclusion:** This study underscores the value of leveraging user mental models rooted in "execution" and "evaluation" dimensions to guide MAR system design. Utilizing the affinity diagram method, our approach not only enhances system adaptability but also boosts user satisfaction, marking a significant advancement in MAR HCI research.

Keywords: User mental models · Mobile augmented reality · User experience

1 Introduction

Augmented reality (AR) seamlessly merges virtual information with the real world environment, exhibiting traits such as real-virtual integration, real-time interaction, and three-dimensional alignment. Scholars, notably Milgram, have conceptualized mixed reality as a continuum bridging the virtual and real realms [1]. Milgram's classification delineates four states-real environment, augmented

© The Author(s), under exclusive license to Springer Nature Switzerland AG 2025
J. Y. C. Chen et al. (Eds.): HCII 2024, LNCS 15377, pp. 99–116, 2025.
https://doi.org/10.1007/978-3-031-76812-5_8

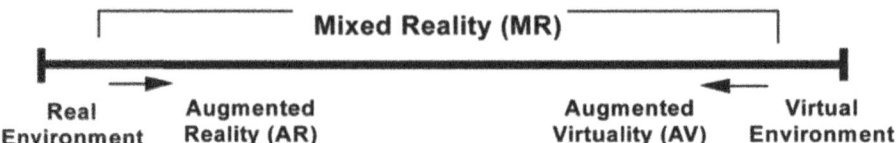

Fig. 1. Reality-Virtual Continuum.

reality, augmented virtual reality, and virtual reality-based on the proportion of real and virtual information within the system (see Fig. 1).

In comparison to virtual reality, augmented reality offers distinct advantages in user experience, notably heightened authenticity and natural interactivity. Through the organic fusion of real-world settings and virtual elements, AR delivers multi-sensory stimuli, transcending material constraints and affording users a heightened sense of real-time immersion and natural interaction. Moreover, the inherent characteristics of mobile devices further enhance AR's interactive versatility, albeit with constraints such as limited information display capabilities and increased physical demands.

In this context, our paper delves into an analysis and synthesis of existing design principles governing mobile augmented reality, shedding light on potential limitations and laying a robust foundation for future research endeavors. By elucidating the nuances of AR user experience and its interaction with mobile platforms, we aim to advance understanding and pave the way for optimized AR experiences in diverse application domains.

2   Characteristics and Research Status of Mobile Augmented Reality

2.1   Characteristics of Mobile Augmented Reality

Augmented reality technology aims to enrich the perception of the real world by adding digital knowledge. AR can be divided into two categories: mobile augmented reality (MAR) and fixed augmented reality (FAR). MAR allows users to move flexibly when using the device, breaking the constraints of space and time [2]. For example, applications such as Pokemon GO are typical examples of MAR. By combining the real environment with the digital world, it provides a new way of spatial exploration and interaction (see Fig. 2). In addition, there are applications such as Historik application, which allows users to explore historical places in the city and display urban landscapes in different historical periods through AR technology (see Fig. 3).

Fig. 2. Pokemon GO application.   **Fig. 3.** Historik application.

Augmented reality has the characteristics of real-time, authenticity and naturalness in terms of user experience. MAR not only has these characteristics, but also has the characteristics of strong interactive versatility, limited information display capabilities and high physical load based on the characteristics of mobile device carriers.

Based on the high popularity of mobile devices such as mobile phones and tablets, MAR has become more and more universal, showing the characteristics of universality and low threshold. Google Trend data shows that the search popularity of the term "Mobile Augmented Reality" has increased significantly since 2010 (see Fig. 2). In addition, according to the *2023 China Augmented Reality (AR) Industry Research Report*, the number of global AR consumer users continued to rise from 3.6 million in 2020 to 5.4 million in 2021; it reached 9.7 million in 2022, with a two-year compound growth rate of 64%, howing that it has a wide range of applications in education, medical care, culture and entertainment. Therefore, with the high popularity of mobile device carriers and MAR applications, MAR's interaction has gradually unified under the WIMP interface paradigm based on windows, icons, menus and pointers, making it highly universal (Fig. 4).

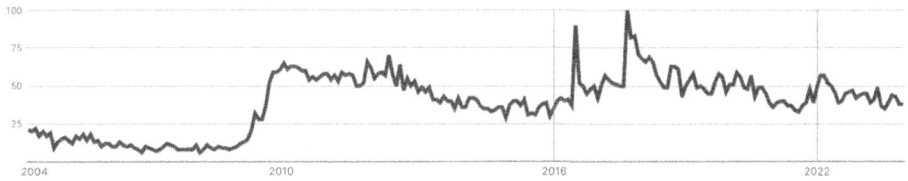

Fig. 4. Trend of the popularity of Mobile Augmented Reality over time.

Limited Information Display Capability: A key limitation of MAR technology is its ability to display information [3,4]. Due to hardware and screen size limitations, MAR systems can only present a limited amount of information, which may affect the user's ability to acquire and process complex data [5]. How to effectively perceive the relative movement of the device relative to the environment or the user within a limited computing range and prompt and guide the user's attention is one of the key points of interaction design in MAR.

High Physical Strain: When using MAR, users may experience high physical strain. This is mainly because users need to hold the mobile device or wear the head-mounted display for a long time, which may cause arm fatigue or neck pressure [6]. This physical strain is particularly significant in application scenarios that require frequent interaction or long-term use.

2.2   Interactive Experience of Mobile Augmented Reality System

Table 1. Interactive experience cases of AR

Project name	Place	years	Features
Archeoguide	Greece	2001	AR technology displays digital reconstructions of archaeological sites
Carnuntum APP	Austria	2011	AR tour guide applications provide real-time information and interactive experience
Tate Britain	U.K.	2021	Dynamically display artworks to enhance understanding and experience
Yunnan Province ICH AR	China	2023	Use AR technology to showcase Yunnan's bronze civilization and culture

Since the mid-20th century, AR technology has been widely used in museums, exhibition spaces and other occasions, and has gradually changed the traditional way of interaction. According to the Trend Watch report, most MAR experiences tend to use the new generation of mobile devices as display carriers. Through the combination of AR's virtual and real, visitors can acquire knowledge more quickly, realize digital reconstruction, display the emotional value of exhibition content, and provide content experience beyond materiality.

Table 1 shows multiple interactive experience cases of AR. For example, the application of the Archeoguide [7] (Greece, 2001) in the digital display of cultural heritage allows visitors to observe the digitally reconstructed original architectural forms next to archaeological sites through smartphones; Carnuntum application (Austria, 2011) provides users with real-time updated scenic spot information and a time-travel tour experience; the Tate Britain Museum in the UK (UK, 2021) displays static artworks in a dynamic and three-dimensional way to help the audience understand the stories behind the art; the Yunnan Province

Intangible Cultural Heritage AR Project (China, 2023) uses augmented reality technology to display Yunnan's ancient bronze civilization, allowing users to experience the integration of history and modernity in a three-dimensional way.

2.3   Limitations of Mobile Augmented Reality Design Principles

Based on the popularization of mobile devices such as smartphones and the widespread application scenarios such as exhibition spaces, MAR has become a common information technology. Users' demand for MAR experience continues to increase, prompting researchers to explore relevant design principles. In 2004, Traskback et al. summarized the usability guidance and user needs of augmented reality applications; in 2007, Dunser et al. combined the particularity and usage context of augmented reality systems with user-centered design principles, and proposed the following guidelines for MAR applications based on the traditional general design principles of human-computer interaction; in 2012, Huang [8] et al. proposed a relatively complete set of design principles for mobile AR applications, including: text information should be clear; virtual information needs to have a high contrast; virtual information should be classified and managed; prompt information must be obvious enough to attract user attention, etc. However, the existing design principles have certain limitations: First, they mainly focus on the interface and visual performance of MAR applications, and lack attention to information architecture, interaction design, etc. At the same time, although these principles are based on the 'user-centered" perspective, they always take "designers" as the subject of principle formulation, and are not really based on user preferences and demands. Therefore, the applicability and guidance of such principles for MAR interactive experience design are questionable. However, since the development of augmented reality has long been driven by technology, it is difficult for users to clearly express their interaction preferences and experience demands for MAR applications, which makes it difficult for user-centered design methods to be used in the design practice of MAR applications.

Aiming at the limitations in MAR interactive experience design, this paper innovatively proposes a new design method based on the relationship between user behavior and mental models. The method covers two main dimensions and their six related attributes to obtain users' mental information more comprehensively and accurately. In addition, this study applies this method to the interactive experience design of MAR exhibitions based on miniature models to explore new design points. Through usability testing, the effectiveness of these dimensions and attributes is verified, providing new guidance for MAR-based interactive experience design.

3   Research Methods of Mobile Augmented Reality Based on Mental Model

Kenneth Craik [9] first proposed that mental model is a reconstruction or mapping of the real world in the human brain after observing the real world. In the field of human-computer interaction, Norman [10] defines mental model as "the knowledge in the user's mind about the concepts and behaviors that a product should have. This knowledge may come from the user's previous experience, or the user's expectation of the product's concepts and behaviors based on the goals to be achieved by using the product." The higher the degree of match between the user model and the design model, the higher the usability of the product. Therefore, understanding the user's MAR-oriented mental model will help improve the usability of the MAR system, thereby improving the user experience.

3.1 Two Dimensions and Six Attributes

Table 2. Evaluation dimensions and dimension properties

Dimensions	Dimension attributes	Corresponding MAR characteristics
	Uusage habit	Strong interactive versatility
Implemention	Information attention	Limited information display capabilities
	Interaction Behavior	Higher physical load used
Evaluation	Experience feelings	Strong interactive versatility

Mental models influence people's thinking, cognition and behavior patterns. They are systematic knowledge that people use to determine behavioral decisions and cognitive understanding. User behavior is the expression of mental models in the external world. Norman pointed out in Design Psychology that behavior consists of two parts: "execution" and "evaluation" [10], where "execution" refers to actions acting on the external world, and "evaluation" refers to comparing the external world situation with the user's expected state.

This article will start from the two dimensions of "execution" and "evaluation". Based on the characteristics of MAR's strong versatility in interaction, limited information display capabilities, and high physical load, the "execution" dimension and the "evaluation" dimension are subdivided into "usage habits", "information attention", "interaction behavior", "usage experience", "cognitive experience", and "load level", as shown in Table 2. This article will construct an interview outline based on these six dimensional attributes, so as to obtain users' mental information about MAR experience in a targeted manner.

To build a user mental model, we first need to obtain user mental information. Mental information, as an internal representation, is difficult to capture and measure. However, the user behavior and ideas expressed by the mental model can be relatively easily obtained through interviews and observations. This article will diverge from the above two dimensions and six dimension attributes to formulate a user interview outline, see Table 3, and adjust the interview outline according to the user's expression and actual situation in the actual interview, so that users can express their opinions smoothly and naturally, thereby comprehensively and specifically obtaining users' mental information for MAR experience, laying the foundation for more usable MAR design.

Table 3. User interview outline

Dimensions	Dimension attributes	Corresponding MAR characteristics
Implementation	Usage habit	When using MAR apps, how do you typically interact with content (e.g., select, manipulate)? Please describe or demonstrate how you typically use this type of application How do you typically get started with MAR apps? Do you use these interactions out of habit or because the app is designed to do so? ......
	Information attention	During use, what types of information do you pay more attention to, such as text, pictures, videos or models? Do you feel that the screen size limits your information viewing experience? If you feel constrained, do you proactively move to see more information? ......
	Interaction behavior	Which device do you use more for MAR interaction, such as tablet, mobile phone or other devices? In your past experience, was it mainly handheld device operation or did you place the device somewhere for control? ......
Evaluation	Experience feelings	What is your overall experience with the MAR-based applications you have used in the past? Do the interactions for these experiences match your device usage habits? What MAR experiences have been particularly memorable to you? ......
	Cognitive experience	Do you think MAR applications have improved your information cognition efficiency? Do you think the information presented in the MAR is clear? Which type of information is more helpful in improving your cognitive efficiency and cognitive experience? Which type of interaction is more helpful in improving your cognitive efficiency and cognitive experience? ......
	Load level	Does the weight of the device's hardware bother you? How long can you tolerate the physical strain of the MAR experience? ......

3.2   Construction of User Mental Model

The ultimate goal of analyzing mental information is to form a mental model. This process mainly involves abstracting individual psychological behavior activities from the user's interview description, and then summarizing them into "tasks". The affinity diagram method (KJ method) is used to cluster tasks with the same attributes into "task towers" according to their mutual affinity (similarity). The "task towers" are then clustered again to form "mental spaces". Finally, the relationship between each mental space is clarified to complete the construction of the user's mental model [11]. This study invited 10 users with certain MAR usage experience as respondents, including 4 males and 6 females. The information of the respondents is shown in Table 4. Semi-open interviews were conducted according to the interview outline.

Table 4. Respondent information

Serial number	Gender	Age	Education level	Occupation/Profession	Usage of MAR applications
1	Male	26	Postgraduate	Market Analyst	More skilled
2	Male	15	Junior high school	student	More skilled
3	Male	48	Undergraduate	Media practitioners	More skilled
4	Male	20	Undergraduate	student	skilled
5	Female	23	Postgraduate	student	skilled
6	Female	22	Undergraduate	student	More skilled
7	Female	39	Undergraduate	Scientific Researcher	More skilled
8	Female	17	High school	student	Not very skilled
9	Female	13	Primary school	student	skilled
10	Female	50	PhD	Office staff	Not very skilled

Table 5. Extraction tasks

User description	Extraction tasks
The main way to interact with the buttons and 3D models that have appeared is to click and drag them. I will also zoom in and out to adjust the viewing angle to see if there are any new discoveries. In addition, I may also want to see if there are any other hints.	Click to interact with the button
	Drag to interact with 3D models
	Adjust the view to see new information
	Note the additional interaction prompts

Extraction Task. This article will extract valid information from 10 user interviews and analyze a single "task" from the valid information. For example, based on the user's description of the question "When using MAR applications, how do you usually interact with the content (such as selection, operation)?", it is mentioned that "(I) interact with the buttons and 3D models that have appeared mainly by clicking and dragging them, and I will also zoom in and out to adjust the perspective to see if there are any new discoveries. In addition, I may also need to see if there are other prompts." From this, four tasks can be extracted: "click to interact with buttons", "drag to interact with 3D models", "adjust the perspective to view new information", and "pay attention to additional interaction prompts", as shown in Table 5. This study extracted a total of 27 tasks from the user's description.

Table 6. Cluster task tower

Extraction tasks	User description
Prefer to try common interactions first	
When encountering complex interactions, users will exit directly	Focus on the naturalness
No difficult-to-understand interactions or prompts	of interaction
Note the additional interaction prompts	

Clustering Task Tower. After extracting user tasks, this paper clusters tasks with similar meanings into task towers. For example, the tasks "tend to try general interaction behaviors first", "users will exit directly when encountering complex interactions", and "do not have difficult-to-understand interactions and prompts" are discussing that users pay more attention to the naturalness of interaction, and can be clustered into the task tower "pay attention to the naturalness of interaction", see Table 6. Thus, 27 tasks are clustered into 10 task towers.

Clustering Mental Space. After clustering the tasks into 10 task towers, this paper further clustered the task towers into mental spaces. For example, the task tower "Pay attention to the naturalness of interaction" and the task tower "Master the mapping of interaction and change" both discuss the user's "interaction behavior and feedback". Based on this, this study clustered and formed 4 mental spaces (see Fig. 5).

This paper deeply analyzes the logical relationship of the four mental spaces, revealing how "experience motivation" and "information acquisition and processing" affect the way users obtain content; at the same time, "interactive behavior and feedback" and "experience load and feelings" respectively show the user's behavioral response based on intuitive cognition or through learning after receiving information and the evaluation of the experience itself and its influencing factors. Based on these analyses, this paper constructs a user mental model with the goal of "users using MAR applications" (see Fig. 6).

3.3 MAR System Requirements Analysis Based on User Mental Model

In this paper, based on the mental model formed by users in the process of using MAR systems, we analyze in detail the content acquisition path and the interactive perception after information reception, in order to deeply explore the specific needs of users for MAR systems.

Analysis of User Demand for Content Acquisition Paths. 1) Analysis of "Experience Motivation": Accurate positioning function is a key prerequisite for user experience of MAR system. The survey found that users have a clear preference for the diversification of information display dimensions in MAR system. When choosing devices for content acquisition, users prefer those with lower physical and cognitive burden, such as smartphones and tablets. In addition, innovative interaction methods are also favored by users.

2) "Information acquisition and processing" analysis : Users mainly acquire information through visual and auditory channels during the experience, and pay close attention to visual changes (such as color and shape changes) dur-

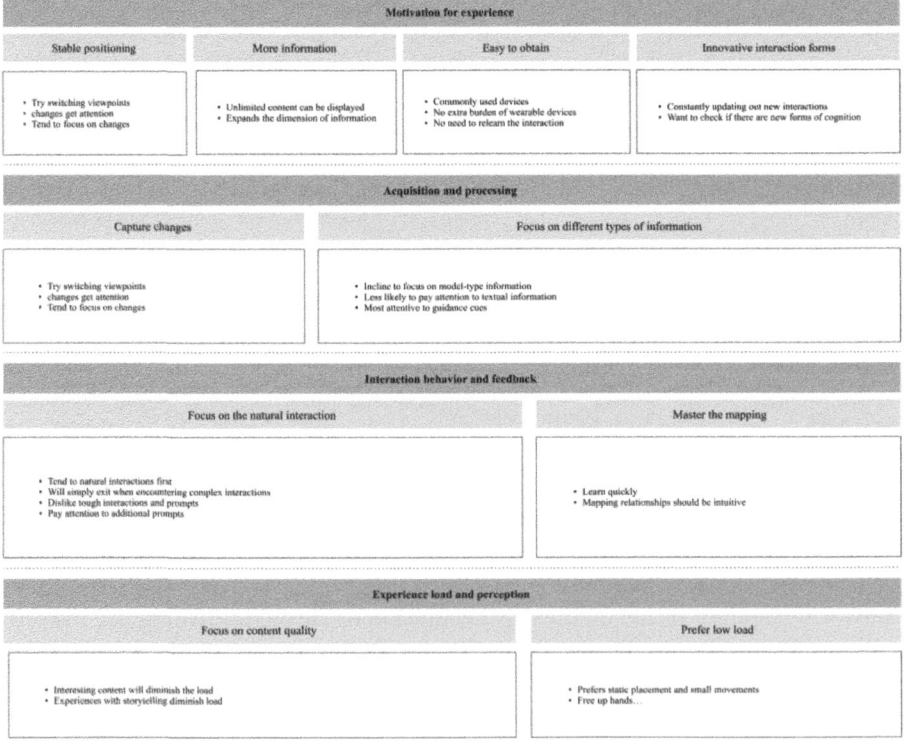

Fig. 5. The mental space of users using handheld MAR systems.

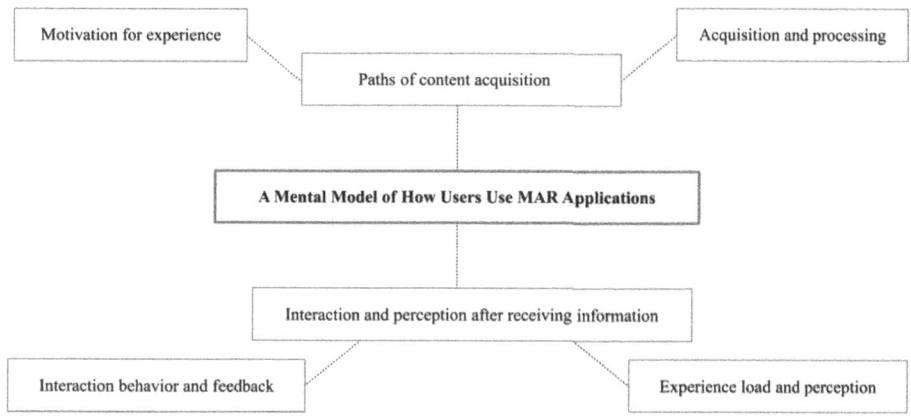

Fig. 6. The mental model of users using handheld MAR systems.

ing the interaction process. As for the type of information, users prefer graphical and dynamic video content rather than pure text information.

Analysis of Users' Needs for Interaction and Perception After Receiving Information. 1) Analysis of "interaction behavior and feedback": Users value the naturalness and intuitiveness of the experience during interaction, and prefer conventional and easy-to-understand interaction methods. For the introduction of new interaction methods, necessary guidance and prompts are key. At the same time, there should be a direct and clear connection between the interaction behavior and the feedback it causes.

2) Analysis of "experience load and feelings": Since devices are often needed during the experience process, users feel a certain experience load. Improving content quality can alleviate this burden to a certain extent. In addition, users are more inclined to use an experience method based on statically placed devices, which helps to enhance immersion.

Based on the analysis of mental space, we summarize the user needs for using the MAR system, and take four types of needs, namely functional needs, interaction needs, content needs, and visual needs, as the objects of system design, see Table 7.

4   Design of Mobile Augmented Reality Interaction System Based on Mental Model

This paper takes the design of MAR interactive system for miniature models as an example, taking the four types of requirements summarized in the previous article, namely functional requirements, interaction requirements, content requirements, and visual requirements, as the objects of system design, and systematically carries out the information architecture design, interaction points and process design, interface and visual expression design of the MAR system.

Table 7. Requirements analysis of MAR system based on user mental model

Mental models	Mind space	User needs	Requirement type
Content acquisition path	Experience motivation	Diversified information dimensions	Content requirements
		Interaction method is easy to learn	Interaction requirements
		Stable positioning	Functional requirements
	Information acquisition and processing	Interactive feedback is obvious	Interaction requirements
		Multi-model class information	Content requirements
		Add guidance tips	Functional requirements, visual requirements
		A chance to choose again	Functional requirements
After receiving the information Interaction and perception	Interaction and feedback	More natural interaction	Interaction requirements
		The mapping of interactions and changes is more intuitive	Interaction needs, visual needs
	Experience load and feeling	Make content more interesting	Content requirements
		More statically placed devices	Functional requirements

4.1 Information Architecture Design for Mobile Augmented Reality Applications

When designing an AR system for iPad-based miniature models, we should design the information architecture based on the display requirements of the functional purpose, hierarchical structure, internal space, etc. of these contents in the AR experience, combined with the user mental model built in the previous article.

In the information architecture design, this paper corresponds the function points with user needs and mental spaces, and regards the function points that appear in multiple mental spaces as the first-level page functions. Taking the "multi-label selection pop-up corresponding model" as an example, this function point can meet the "interaction method is easy to learn" requirement under the "experience motivation" mental space, and at the same time can meet the "multi-model type information" requirement under the "information acquisition and processing" mental space, proving that this function point has a great impact on the user's mental model and can meet multiple user needs, so it should be located on the first-level page. Therefore, this paper designs and constructs the information architecture of the MAR system, see Table 8.

4.2 Key Points and Processes of Interactive Design of Mobile Augmented Reality System

Based on the logical order of "content acquisition path" and "interaction and perception after receiving information" in the user's mental model, this study constructed a framework for user demand sequence and information architecture design, and developed the key points and processes of system interaction design for miniature models based on this. First, users can use the fun guidance of three-dimensional images in the initial welcome page to understand the interaction methods and processes involved in the system. After entering the main

Table 8. Information architecture of MAR system based on user mental model

User requirements description	Feature design	Function number of mental spaces	Information hierarchy
Add guidance tips	First function guided teaching	1	Home page
Stable positioning A chance to choose again	Reload button	2	First level page
Interaction method is easy to learn Multi-model class information	Multi-label selection pop-up corresponding model	2	First level page
The mapping of interactions and changes is more intuitive Interactive feedback is obvious	Click animation and sound feedback	2	First level page
Diversified information dimensions	Multiple buttons correspond to multi-dimensional information	1	Secondary interface
More natural interaction	Scale and rotate the model	1	Secondary interface
More natural interaction	Model structure split	1	Three-level interface
Make content more interesting	Play function animation	1	Three-level interface
Make content more interesting	Play internal demonstration video	1	Three-level interface

scene of the miniature model, users can scan, and based on the system's spatial positioning of the three-dimensional model, the corresponding name label will float above the corresponding area. This is the starting point of the interaction design process and the first step of information architecture design, ensuring that users can intuitively obtain regional information. Users can click to enter the next level of interaction to view the regional model.

Furthermore, the dynamic appearance and jumping behavior of the characters can further strengthen the user's visual cognition of the selected area. The system design displays a guiding label of "click to view details" after three seconds to guide users to interact in depth. After the user responds to the guidance, the virtual model is enlarged and brought closer to the user. The user can now rotate, zoom and observe the model in all directions. This process not only meets the user's needs for content acquisition paths, but also provides a rich interactive experience.

When users explore the structure, space, and function of the regional model, they can click the corresponding bubble button, and the system will present the functional purpose, structural hierarchy, and internal space of the region. These interactive steps reflect the hierarchy and detail in information architecture design, allowing users to explore and perceive different aspects of the content in order according to their own needs. Specifically, the three-dimensional animation activated by clicking the "Functional Purpose" button shows the functional attributes of the region to the user; after the user clicks the "Structural Hierarchy" button, the system provides a vertical split function to display the layered structural information, enhancing the user's understanding of the regional structural hierarchy; in the exploration stage of the internal space, the user clicks the "Internal Space" button, and the character appears again as a dynamic guide to assist the user in a virtual tour of the internal space based on video animation.

The interactive design process of the MAR system proposed in this article, which takes the miniature model as an example, is a practice based on the user's mental model. It aims to improve the user's cognitive efficiency and experience quality through structured information display and interaction methods.

4.3   Interface and Visual Performance of Mobile Augmented Reality System

In order to effectively design the user interface of the MAR system to improve the efficiency of information transmission and the user's interactive experience, this study will explore the best practices of interface layout and the selection and arrangement of visual elements, as well as how these factors affect the user's perception and use of the MAR system. Through this discussion, this section aims to provide specific and practical guidance and suggestions on the visual level for the design of the MAR system interface.

Interface Layout Design. Augmented reality is an interactive experience that couples virtual information with real objects. In order to ensure that users can fully observe the superposition of virtual and real content on mobile devices, this paper proposes an interface layout strategy that renders virtual models and dynamic information on top of real objects to reduce visual occlusion and cognitive interference. This upper-layer display strategy allows users to obtain an enhanced view of information without losing their perception of the real environment.

At the operational level, this paper designs an interactive user interface that allows users to zoom in and out through gestures or controls to adjust the personalized perspective. This design not only improves the flexibility of the interface, but also increases the depth of user exploration of virtual content. By implementing this scalable interactive function, this study promotes users' information exploration from a personalized perspective and meets the observation needs at different levels from micro to macro.

Furthermore, based on the design object examples of miniature models, this study also explores the dynamic layout of auxiliary interface elements such as role models, controls, and explanatory texts. These elements use real-time spatial positioning technology to dynamically position themselves around the regional model according to the user's interactive behavior and perspective. This is intended to provide seamless operation guidance and information feedback, thereby reducing the cognitive difficulty of user operation. For example, when the user's line of sight focuses on a specific building, the relevant interactive controls and explanatory texts appear immediately, directly guiding the user to take the next step, which not only enhances the guidance of the interface, but also optimizes the efficiency of information presentation.

Interface Color and Icon Design. First of all, based on the characteristics of the miniature model object, this paper positions the visual style of the system as simple and technological, and formulates specifications for the design content of page layout, color, icons, text, and controls. Taking the AR interactive system of the future lunar base as an example, this paper uses blue-purple, which matches the sense of technology and space, as the main color of the content, and uses gradient colors to make the overall hierarchy of the control richer. Among them, the colors of the "selected" and "selected" states of the control change based on the "default" state, giving users more obvious visual feedback. Taking the bubble control of the regional optional function as an example, the controls in three states present three different color states.

In order to avoid cognitive impairment and cognitive load of reading a large amount of text information, this article uses relatively common icons as symbols of visual information. In the text part, this article mainly uses Microsoft YaHei font, setting the title to 16 px bold, the body size to 12 px, and the description text to 10 px; the controls are uniformly chamfered with 6 px to make the visual effect more rounded and unified.

5   Testing and Evaluation

5.1   Participants and Tasks

The study further iterates and optimizes a real-world application case of MAR, conducting user experience tests on the case based on the mental model.

Participants. We recruited 20 participants (8 males, 12 females), aged 18–40 (M = 22.9, SD = 4.15), for our study, 9 of whom had extensive experience in handheld AR across various fields (e.g., computer science, HCI, art, economics). A sandbox comprising a 120×150 cm base and several 3D-printed miniature buildings was 3D scanned and reconstructed. Utilizing a high-end Windows 11 desktop as a server, the experiment was set up and deployed in a handheld AR. We using an Android 13 vivo iPA2375 device (12.1 in., 619 g) with a 2800*2000 resolution. The sandbox's images were collected and 3D reconstructed to create a cloud-based positioning map, enabling real-time image capturing and AR interaction. Participants could freely move 360° around the sandbox for AR scanning.

Tasks. Participants were asked to use paradigms separately to perform the same tasks in handheld AR:

(1) **Positioning task:** reload the positioning and adjust to the appropriate viewing angle by clicking a button;

(2) **Select the task:** find the tag with a specific name and complete the selection;

(3) **Operation task:** translate, rotate and scale the 3D model corresponding to the selected label.

The tests employed **(1) the SUS Usability Scale** for assessing Usability, Learnability, and overall user satisfaction and **(2) semi-structured interviews** to provide users with more discussion opportunities. The comparison validates that the mental model-based design approach effectively enhances the interaction experience of MAR systems.

5.2   Experimental Process and Data Collection

After the user enters the system test, there will first be an interactive welcome page to briefly introduce the system content and guide the user. Then, the user will follow the task arrangement and guidance of the staff to gradually complete the task.

During the experiment, we recorded the user's operation time and accuracy. At the same time, after each round of experiments, we issued a targeted questionnaire to the users. Users were required to rate the ease of use and learnability of the three groups on a scale of 1–5 based on SUS. In addition, we also required participants to provide corresponding reasons and participation experience for their answers. Subsequently, we conducted a comparative analysis and summary of the three groups, and verified the rationality and adaptability of this innovative user mental model design method for MAR system design by evaluating the usability of the system.

Table 9. SUS Score of MAR system based on user mental model

Descriptive statistica of SUS (n=20)					
statistic	n	total	mean	sd	min	max
	10	727.5	72.75	7.12	65.0	85.0
Descriptive statistica of Usability (n=20)					
statistic	n	total	mean	sd	min	max
	10	685	68.5	10.62	65	96
Descriptive statistica of Learnability (n=20)					
statistic	n	total	mean	sd	min	max
	10	770	77.0	10.46	62	94

In this study, the SUS was used to evaluate the usability and learnability of this miniature-oriented MAR system, as shown in Table 9. This study thus evaluated the usability of the mental model design method based on the two dimensions of "execution" and "evaluation" and six attributes. In addition, through qualitative user interviews, this study further explored the user's interactive experience and perceived needs after receiving information.

(1) Usability analysis: Considering the importance of user interaction experience, usability evaluation pays special attention to the user's intuitive operation of the MAR system. The analysis revealed that users generally recognize the intuitive and user-friendly nature of the system, with an average score of 68.5. However, the lower score of "complexity" indicates potential room for improvement in interface design and visual representation.

(2) Easy to learn analysis: Easy to learn analysis focuses on the speed at which users learn new systems. Among them, the score for "learning needs" is relatively low, indicating that users may face challenges such as positioning control when using this MAR system for the first time. Based on the results of qualitative interviews, this study found that users can quickly adapt after becoming familiar with basic operations, but clearer guidance is needed for advanced features.

(3) Comprehensive availability analysis: The average score of SUS overall is 72.75, reflecting a relatively high level of user satisfaction with the overall availability of the system. According to the SUS rating table, the system's usability is at a "good" level. Although the data analysis results indicate that the system performs well in terms of usability and learnability, some users have also mentioned that there is room for improvement in the operation process and technical support of advanced functions. The research team will optimize and iterate the system and design methods based on this in future work.

In summary, this study combines quantitative analysis and qualitative user interviews to effectively confirm the application value of user mental models in guiding the design of MAR systems. This method not only evaluates the usability and learnability of the system, but also deeply understands the user's interactive needs and perceived experience, providing important guidance for future system design (Fig. 7).

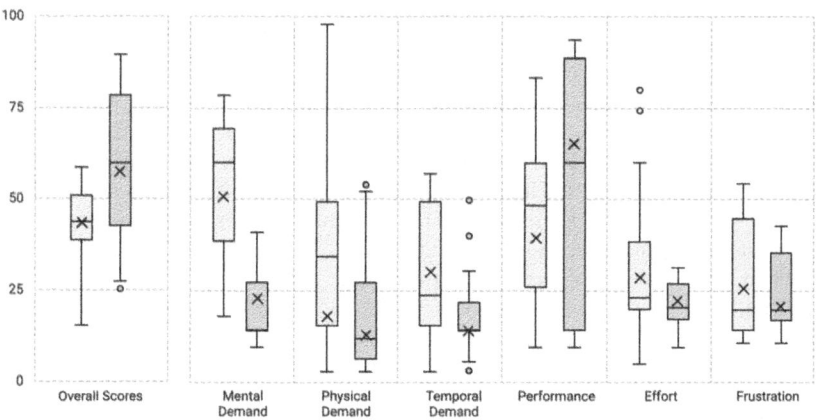

Fig. 7. Boxplots for the overall scores of the NASA TLX, and its scores broken down into subscales.

6   Conclusion and Future Work

This study indicates that acquiring psychological information from the Implementation and evaluation dimensions of user behavior and constructing a mental model using the affinity diagram method (KJ method) can effectively guide the design of MAR system interaction experiences, enhancing the system's applicability and user satisfaction.

This design method provides a new perspective on MAR system design. At the application level, this study provides valuable guidance for the practical application of MAR technology in multiple fields such as education, entertainment, and professional training.

References

1. Milgram, P., Kishino, F.: A taxonomy of mixed reality visual displays. IEICE Trans. Inf. Syst. **77**(12), 1321–1329 (1994)
2. Kipper, G., Rampolla, J.: Augmented Reality: An Emerging Technologies Guide to AR. Syngress Publishing, Rockland (2012)
3. Lamberti, F., Manuri, F., Sanna, A., Paravati, G., Pezzolla, P., Montuschi, P.: Challenges, opportunities, and future trends of emerging techniques for augmented reality-based maintenance. IEEE Trans. Emerg. Top. Comput. **2**(4), 411–421 (2017)
4. Cao, J., Lam, K.-Y., Lee, L.-H., Liu, X., Hui, P., Xiang, S.: Mobile augmented reality: user interfaces, frameworks, and intelligence. ACM Comput. Surv. **55**(9), 1–36 (2023)
5. Ekanayake, I., Gayanika, S.: Data visualization using augmented reality for education: a systematic review. In: 2022 7th International Conference on Business and Industrial Research (ICBIR), pp. 533–537 (2022)
6. Siriwardhana, Y., Porambage, P., Liyanage, M., Ylianttila, M.: A survey on mobile augmented reality with 5g mobile edge computing: architectures, applications, and technical aspects. IEEE Commun. Surv. Tutor. **23**(2), 1160–1192 (2021)
7. Vlahakis, V., Ioannidis, M., Karigiannis, J., Tsotros, M., Gounaris, M., Stricker, D., Gleue, T., Daehne, P., Almeida, L.: Archeoguide: an augmented reality guide for archaeological sites. IEEE Comput. Graphics Appl. **22**(5), 52–60 (2002)
8. Huang, W., Alem, L., Livingston, M.A.: Human Factors in Augmented Reality Environments. Springer, New York (2012)
9. Craik, K.: The nature of explanation (1944)
10. Norman, D.: Emotional Design: Why We Love (or Hate) Everyday Things, vol. 27 (2004)
11. Young, I.: Mental models: aligning design strategy with human behavior. Ubiquity **1–1**(04), 2008 (2008)

Advantages of Virtual Reality Tool for Helping Personal Sketch Modeling

Ming-Huang Lin[1], Yun-Wen Lee[1,2]([✉]), Yu-Cheng Lin[1], and Hao-Xuan Lu[3]

[1] National Taiwan University of Science and Technology, Taipei, Taiwan
wen4877@gmail.com
[2] National Tsing Hua University, Hsinchu, Taiwan
[3] Eindhoven University of Technology, Eindhoven, Netherlands

Abstract. This study examined the strengths and weaknesses of Gravity Sketch, which is a virtual-reality (VR) sketching and modeling tool, in the later stages of personal sketch creation. Seven designers with at least 4 months of experience with this tool were invited to sketch out ideas in VR and on paper, and their sketches were examined through qualitative analysis based on retrospection interviews and grounded theory. The results of this study highlight the strengths and weaknesses of VR sketching in product design; clarify designers' timing of switching between paper and VR sketching; and confirm the inference of our previous study that VR sketching is suitable for designers to verify, modify, and explore shapes intuitively in a three-dimensional (3D) space after they have generated a preliminary design idea. In contrast to paper sketches, VR sketches are created in an environment with highly precise visual information, and VR sketching involves additional creation steps compared with paper sketching, thereby reducing the speed and abstractness of sketching. These characteristics of VR sketching prompt designers to focus more on modeling instead of sketching when using VR tools. In contrast to regular 3D modeling software, VR sketching tools do not limit the ability of designers to create shapes and sketch out ideas, even when they are more proficient in creating paper sketches and lack experience with VR modeling.

Keywords: Virtual Reality (VR) · Sketch · Product Design · Computer-aided Design (CAD)

1 Introduction

An increasing number of young designers are inexperienced in converting their design ideas into paper drawings (Aldoy & Evans 2011) and instead rely on computer-aided design (CAD) software for quickly creating simplistic designs that fully express their ideas and conform to the latest design trend. However, unfamiliarity with the complex operation of such software can limit the ability of designers to create drawings (Lawson 2002). Alcaide-Marzal et al. (2013) noted that CAD software is considerably less flexible than is paper sketching for developing designs and expressing design concepts. However, breakthroughs in the development of immersive hardware technology have

© The Author(s), under exclusive license to Springer Nature Switzerland AG 2025
J. Y. C. Chen et al. (Eds.): HCII 2024, LNCS 15377, pp. 117–132, 2025.
https://doi.org/10.1007/978-3-031-76812-5_9

improved the monitor refresh rate and provided greater intuitive control for designers to experience realistic and smooth interaction in virtual environments. Accordingly, virtual-reality (VR) design software, such as Gravity Sketch, has become an alternative option to paper sketching and CAD modeling and enables designers to create curves and surfaces, simulate materials, and experiment with colors in a three-dimensional (3D) space. Therefore, VR technology provides innovative design tools for industrial designers to develop and express their design ideas.

VR involves the use of computer simulation to generate a realistic 3D space that simulates visual, auditory, and tactile senses. Head-mounted displays enable users to enter a realistic virtual environment, in which they can move around by using a controller and gain a strongly immersive experience similar to that achieved in a real-word environment. According to their precision, digital tools are divided into those used for high-fidelity modeling and low-fidelity modeling. High-fidelity modeling is achieved using CAD software such as Rhino and Creo and is mostly applied in later design stages, in which precision modeling is required. By contrast, Gravity Sketch, which is a sketching and modeling software, focuses on low-fidelity modeling in preliminary design stages. Therefore, this study explored the vertical thinking process in early design stages by comparing the ease of use and complementarity of VR and conventional paper drawing tools, thereby clarifying approaches for the effective creation of design shapes in VR environments.

2   Literature Review

The development of CAD software has led to the integration of digital tools in design processes. In particular, the emergence of multiple artificial intelligence software programs in 2022 has considerably enhanced the work efficiency of humans (Noy & Zhen 2023). However, conventional sketches are still used frequently during initial design thinking and exploration to examine different abstract concepts and viewpoints. Sketches are inexpensive one-time drawings with rich and abstract content that are created quickly. They are based on a well-defined composition with minimum details and on abstract concepts and are used to explore possible design solutions (Buxton 2010). Sketches can also be used to configure critical details flexibly, identify the relationships between such details, deconstruct multiple design problems, determine design solutions, and facilitate vertical thinking through interpretation (Cross 1999). Currently, the comfort and freedom of drawing sketches on paper cannot be replicated by a digital tool. Sketching is an indispensable fundamental skill in industrial design. Sketching involves more than the sole manifestation of ideas; designers must develop their thinking and identify new connections and possibilities when creating sketches (Israel et al. 2019). In general, designers engage in horizontal and vertical conversions when generating a new sketch from an old one. Horizontal conversion focuses on the generation of new solutions from existing sketches, whereas vertical conversion focuses on improving previous sketches by adding details to them (Goel 1995). However, various problems occur when paper sketches are used in early design stages. For example, converting front-view and side-view images into 3D images is often difficult because designers might be unable to create a mental image of the 3D structure or might create an incorrect image, which results in inconsistencies between sketches for different view angles. VR technology can address this problem by creating an immersive environment, in which intuitive 3D structures are provided to help designers to construct the 3D appearance of the designed object. Rieuf et al. (2017) asserted that during the sketching stage, immersive VR tools enable a simple 3D evaluation of the designed object and thus allow designers to comprehend their design more effectively. Seyi Sosanya, the co-developer of Gravity Sketch, stated in the official blog of their company that according to customer feedback statistics, Gravity Sketch reduces design time by 30%–60%, depending on how well designers utilize this tool during their design process, and the number of designs created by a designer within the same period increases 10-fold when Gravity Sketch is used. Moreover, a previous study indicated that VR design tools are more advantageous in vertical conversion than in horizontal conversion (Lin et al. 2022). In practical settings, sketching is the most irreplaceable, efficient, and common medium used by designers in various design stages. Therefore, the present study invited participants to use conventional sketches (which facilitate horizontal thinking) and VR design sketches (which facilitate vertical thinking) in alternation at their will under specific design goals and conditions (reference images, 3D modeling, background images, and reference sketches). The objective was to explore the strengths of VR design tools, examine designers' work procedures, and clarify the timing of designers' switching between conventional and VR sketching.

Ferguson (1994) and Olofsson and Sjolen (2005) have divided the sketching process of the design and engineering fields into three sequential stages with different purposes: the thinking sketch, talking sketch, and prescriptive sketch stages. In the thinking sketch stage, designers engage in brainstorming for rapidly noting various ideas and creating a line sketch without shading. In the talking sketch stage, designers present their design concepts and receive feedback from the client or collaborators to select the most suitable design solution; the content of each candidate solution is usually based on different variations of the same concept and might focus on specific details, features, or functions. In the prescriptive sketch stage, the final design solution is created, and sketches created for the solution include rendered images for different view angles, specific proportions of design details, and the interaction between various details. In the engineering field, such sketches might also include part diagrams, CAD models, and technical drawings for product manufacturing. McGown et al. (1998) divided sketches into five levels according to their complexity (lines, colors, and 3D shading) and the provided information (arrow labels and footnotes); sketches of higher levels contain more details. Sketches in Level 1 are simple line drawings without shading or footnotes; they only contain arrow labels to indicate the movements of parts. Sketches in Level 2 are also simple line drawings without shading, but they contain one or two short footnotes and lines of different thicknesses. Sketches in Level 3 are single-colored line drawings with simple shading and contain footnotes that describe the design thinking. Sketches in Level 4 are single-colored or multicolored line drawings, and shading is used in them to highlight the 3D appearance; colors are used to describe specific design concepts but do not represent the actual colors of the final product. Sketches in Level 5 present the actual colors of the final product; considerable highlighting and shading are used to illustrate the 3D appearance, and footnotes or questions for the client are left on the sketches. Pei et al. (2011) adopted a product development perspective for systemically classifying conventional sketches commonly used by designers into four categories: personal, shared, persuasive, and handover sketches. Personal sketches, which are sketches made in early design stages, are usually created in a large quantity and contain simple shapes and colors to present critical details in designs; shared sketches are used to express clear design information and simulate discussion with the client to reach a consensus; persuasive sketches are used to illustrate the appearance of the final product and must be highly realistic and specific; and handover sketches are used to express fine product details, including the mechanical structure, manufacturing procedures, materials, and product size. The diverse categories of sketches defined by these researchers reflect the prevalent use of sketches in all design stages. On the basis of their categorization, we propose five levels of sketches that can be created in the VR environment of Gravity Sketch to help individuals understand the experimental configuration.

Free Sketches. In a virtual design environment, free sketches are similar to conventional personal sketches (see Fig. 1) or thumbnails and are created without referencing any structural models or other sketches. The main goal of free sketches is to generate multiple conceptual images through horizontal thinking. Such sketches might include coarse lines, basic geometrical shapes, and unadjusted contours to enable users to rapidly obtain the correct perspective and form conceptual outlines as references for subsequent design stages.

Fig. 1. Free sketch produced in a VR design environment.

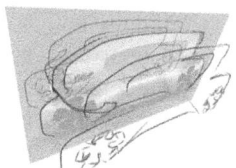

Fig. 2. Inputting a two-dimensional paper sketch into a VR design environment.

Fig. 3. Inputting a 3D structural model into a VR design environment.

3D Sketches Based on References. Paper sketches (see Fig. 2), 3D structural models of moderately accurate proportions (see Fig. 3), or human figure models are input into VR design software. A 3D sketch is then produced or adjusted according to the input sketch. The main goal of such a 3D sketch is to explore the relationship between the internal elements and outer appearance of a design when two-dimensional (2D) sketches are converted into 3D contours. Rough 3D sketches mostly contain coarse lines, basic geometric shapes, and unadjusted contours, and such sketches do not require fine adjustment. References are used to limit the content of the sketch to ensure that the design concepts and perspectives are rational and render the ideal design.

3D Sketches for Exploring Curved Surfaces. In VR design software, structural models and ergonomic factors are used as the basis for the 3D sketch that clearly defining the contours of the designed object. This stage is similar to the aforementioned shared sketches. The designer also attempts to create rough curved surfaces and ensure that the product is proportionally aesthetic and rational (see Fig. 4).

Fig. 4. Rough curved surfaces created in a VR design environment.

Fig. 5. Precise 3D curved surfaces created in a VR design environment.

Fig. 6. Accurate expression of colors, materials, and finish to review the product design.

3D Sketches with Precise Curved Surfaces. Sketches with highly precise curved surfaces are created in VR design software. Such sketches are mainly composed of curved surfaces and only comprise a few curved lines to assist with illustrating the product contours. The overall product appearance in this stage is more detailed, accurate (within thinner lines), and less abstract than that in the previous stage for clearly defining the product contours and the orientations of curved surfaces (see Fig. 5). Only a few basic colors are used in the sketch because its main goal is to confirm the orientation and details of curved surfaces. This is the last stage before the sketch is input into other modeling software (e.g., Alias and Rhinoceros), and the sketch serves as the basis for creating a precise final 3D model.

Precise Modeling of Curved Surfaces. In VR design software, a highly precise model is created for clearly reflecting the form of the designed object and the shading of the curved surfaces. Such a model is nearly 100% identical to the final product and is similar to a persuasive sketch. In this stage, the model completely transcends the initial line sketch and is fully composed of curved surfaces, which reflect the actual thickness and physical form of the product. The precision of the final model is comparable to that of a CAD model, and the final model precisely defines the colors, materials, and finish of the final product, thereby allowing designers to review the product design. (see Fig. 6).

3 Research Method

According to a previous study (Lin et al. 2022), VR tools are more useful in the vertical thinking stage than in the horizontal thinking stage. Therefore, the present study focused on the later stages of personal sketch creation. Participants were asked to use both VR and conventional paper drawing tools so that the ease of use of these tools could be compared and their complementarity in the vertical thinking stage could be examined. Given that the VR environment, which facilitates vertical thinking, can make users overly immersed in its special experience, the VR sketching stages used in the conducted experiment were "3D sketches for exploring curved surfaces" and "3D sketches with precise curved surfaces." Similar to our previous study, the present study was based on grounded theory and involved the recruitment of participants with at least 4 months of experience with

Gravity Sketch to explore the value of VR technology as a sketching tool for creating designs. This study was divided into two phases. In the first phase, the participants used paper drawing and VR tools in alternation to create 3D sketches in an experiment. In the second phase, audio records were collected from retrospective interviews with the participants. The two phases were conducted no more than 1 h apart from each other. After all the participants completed the experiment, the collected data were analyzed using grounded theory and coded using NVivo ver.12, qualitative data analysis software, in which open coding, axial coding, and selective coding were used to simplify relevant concepts and describe observations. The experimental procedures are detailed in the following section.

3.1 Objective

The literature review and the present authors' observations of designers and design students revealed that designers in Taiwan rarely engage in automotive design, either because of their lack of expertise in this field or the nature of local industries. Compared with conventional tools, VR tools are more suitable for designing objects with a large volume. Considering that the experiment had a time limit, the requirement of designing a normal passenger car would have been ill-suited to the experiment because this task would involve more detailed design than would the design process for a truck. Therefore, In the experiment, the participants were asked to design a truck individually by using the same proxy model and referential images. The participants could use the conventional paper sketching tool or VR sketching tool to begin their design process. This study explored how designers used the two tools alternately, thereby identifying the strengths and complementarity of the two tools and the timing of switching between the two tools. Moreover, this study investigated whether VR sketching helped designers to quickly grasp each aspect of an unfamiliar product that was to be designed, thereby enabling them to work more efficiently.

3.2 Materials

Three VR systems [Oculus Quest 2 (Meta Platforms, Inc.) with Oculus Link connection and Gravity Sketch] were used in the experiment. Fifty pieces of A3 paper, ten 2B pencils, five black and blue ballpoint pens, five erasers, two laptops (for storing questionnaire and interview data), and two smartphones (12 million pixels; $\geq$ 60 fps) were also used in the experiment.

3.3 Stimuli

A total of 12 reference images were provided in the experiment for the participants to study the appearances of trucks and other vehicles.

3.4 Participants

Purposive sampling was used to recruit five university students, one graduate student, and one designer aged 21–26 years. The seven participants received at least 4 months of training in Gravity Sketch. In the experiment, one researcher was tasked with observing the participants in the VR space to confirm their familiarity with the software. Another researcher used a form to record the score of each participant. The results revealed that one participant (D6) was unfamiliar with the software, five participants (D1, D3, D4, D5, and D7) were familiar with the software, and one participant (D2) was very familiar with the software. Members of the research team stood in the VR space to help participants who encountered problems while using Gravity Sketch.

3.5 Procedures

The research team members informed the participants of the experiment content and sketch object, provided reference images, recited the definitions of the five 3D sketching stages proposed in this paper, and provided examples for each stage. Subsequently, the participants took a basic categorization test for approximately 20 min to ensure that they understood the definition of each stage. Next, the participants were asked to nearly reach to "3D sketches for exploring curved surfaces " or "3D sketches with precise curved surfaces" by using pen and paper as well as the VR equipment. They were allowed to switch freely between the two tools, and the sketch time was approximately 80 min when excluding breaks and the buffer time for switching tools. The research team members assisted the participants in outputting VR sketches and scanning paper sketches when they had to switch tools. The research team members also used a camera to record the drawing process of the participants when they created paper sketches. Moreover, the movements of the participants while drawing in the VR space were recorded from the first- and third-person views. After all sketches were completed, the records were used during retrospective in-depth interviews for the participants to recall their drawing process and movements in the VR space. The interviews lasted for approximately 120 min, and the interview content was audio-recorded. The entire experiment was completed in approximately 4h (see Fig. 7).

Fig. 7. Photographs of the experiment and interviews captured by the research team.

4   Results

4.1   Basic Observation and Data Analysis

In our previous study (Lin et al. 2022), participants created sketches by using VR equipment or pen and paper. However, the immersive experience provided by VR caused the participants to focus overly on a single sketch idea during horizontal thinking. Accordingly, the present study adopted a different experimental configuration by allowing the participants to switch freely between conventional drawing and VR tools. The observation results revealed that the participants experienced the constraints of the VR space when engaging in vertical thinking. In this scenario, the participants could switch to the conventional paper drawing tool to gain new inspiration or ideas. Therefore, switching between the two tools enabled the participants to understand the 3D structure of the relevant object by observing stimuli in the VR space and to brainstorm their design ideas on a paper to prevent excessive focus on vertical thinking in the VR space. Figure 8 displays a sketch created by Participant D3.

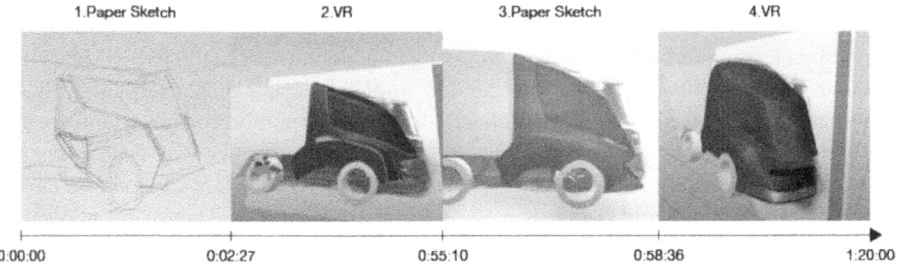

Fig. 8. Timeline of the sketching process completed by Participant D3.

The experimental results revealed that the participants spent more time sketching in the VR space than on paper. Simple statistics indicated that during the 80-min sketching process, the mean time spent in the VR space was considerably higher (by approximately 6.5 times) than that spent on paper (see Fig. 9). Participants D1, D6, and D7 only switched their tool once; specifically, they began their sketching process on paper and then switched to Gravity Sketch to conduct vertical thinking. Participants D2 and D3 began with paper sketches, switched to the VR tool, and then switched back to paper sketches again. Participants D4 and D5 first used VR to create their design and then spent a very short period adjusting their design on paper. This phenomenon might have been caused by the relatively low hand-drawing skills of these two participants.

The observation and interview results revealed that the participants adopted different strategies. One of the strategies involved the use of side-view images drawn on paper (D1, D6 and D7), and another strategy involved the direct creation of 3D outlines in the VR space by identifying the intersecting lines between planes (D2, D3, and D4). An additional strategy involved the creation of side-view images in the VR space; this approach requires participants to use their skillsets for other CAD software programs to create sketches in VR. When sketching on paper, most participants understood that the paper sketches would eventually be input into the VR tool for vertical thinking. When creating sketches in VR, the participants mostly drew curves for quickly illustrating their design ideas; they spent most of the sketching time on editing curves and curved surfaces to form a single design concept.

4.2 VR Modeling or VR Sketching

The participants mostly engaged in vertical thinking when sketching in the VR space. By adjusting curved lines and surfaces, they attempted to create smooth images. The

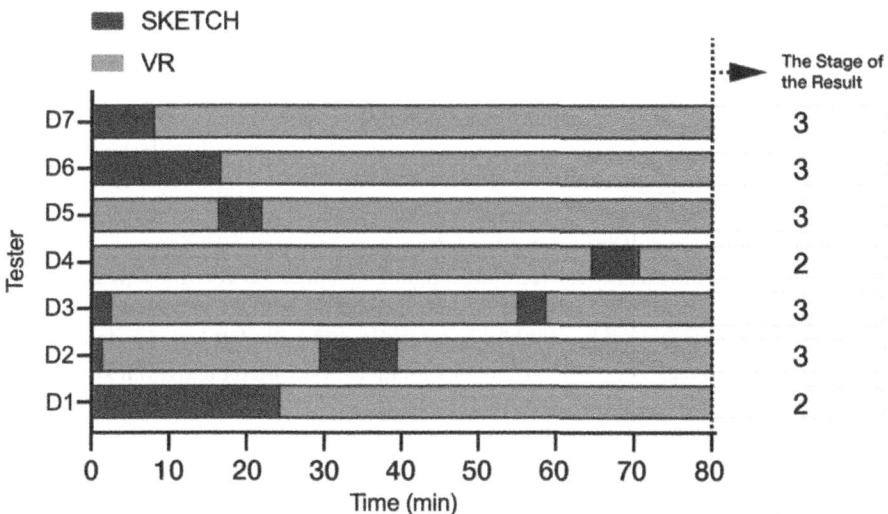

Fig. 9. Distribution of the time spent by each participant in using the conventional paper drawing and VR tools.

participants had to generate ideas continually while sketching; consequently, the sketching process was time-consuming. For example, when rotating an object or changing the view angle, the participants often discovered that their curved lines or surfaces were unsmooth or were drawn irrationally and thus required adjustment. Participant D6 stated, "When entering VR, I discovered that the location of a curved surface did not match that shown in the paper sketch, and this [mismatch] violated my understanding of the original shape." To prevent the design from deviating from its original concept and to prevent themselves from becoming overly focused on vertical thinking, Participant D7 adopted a certain strategy. They stated that "I wanted to complete the overall model first because I did not want to get my hands tied when working on the surfaces. I used to complete all the surfaces at the front first, only to find that they matched very poorly with the rear part. Now, I always complete the overall model before focusing on the details." Participant D4 stated, "I feel that modeling is similar to sanding Polyurethane foam (PU) and scraping oil-based clay. In VR, [modeling] is similar to scraping an oil-based clay model. Each step involves using different tools, and this allows me to express my ideas within a shorter time."

Timing of Switching to VR. The observation results revealed that most of the participants could independently determine when to switch between VR and paper sketching. For example, Participants D2 and D3 switched decisively from paper sketching to VR sketching within 3 min after the experiment began. This phenomenon was observed mainly because these participants were confident in their paper sketching ability and were familiar with the characteristics of VR. Accordingly, they could switch to the VR tool as soon as they sketched 80% of their design ideas on paper. Participant D2 stated, "It's mainly because I'm quite familiar with this program. If I were unfamiliar with a program, I would complete the 2D sketches before working on 3D sketches. Because this experiment involved designing a truck, which is cuboid in shape, I was able to perform VR sketching immediately after a concept formed in my mind." Participant D1 stated, "I allocated my time for paper and VR sketches according to their suitability for each design task." Most of the participants were unfamiliar with vehicle design. Therefore, they found the perspective guiding function of the VR tool to be highly helpful when attempting to design a large vehicle. For example, Participant D7 stated, "Because I am not good with drawing on paper, I could not draw anymore after the sketch was completed to a certain degree. Therefore, after a rough outline of my design was completed, I switched to the VR tool." Moreover, Participant D4 stated, "When drawing on paper, I had to image the 3D structure of the object and painstakingly make sure that the perspective was rational. However, this could be done easily in the 3D VR space, where I could quickly adjust my sketch according to my design ideas. I decided the overall shape of the truck and then started to draw conventional freehand sketches because freehand sketches allow you to quickly expand the details, like 'I want the doors to be adorned with this pattern.'" According to the observation and interview results, the following characteristics of VR sketching were found to determine the timing of participants switching to the VR tool. First, an essential single-view-angle image (usually the side-view image) was created in the paper sketch, and other view angles and perspectives were addressed in the VR space. Second, participants who were familiar with VR operation did not have to sketch out the design model on paper first; they used their paper sketches as base layers to develop details and improve their design ideas. Third, the VR tool enabled the easy adjustment and replication of contours to ensure consistency across all lines, thereby allowing the participants to create clean and sharp lines. Fourth, in the VR space, the participants could easily review the shapes of curved planes and how they differed from those in paper sketches, thereby ensuring design rationality. Fifth, the participants captured images of the VR sketches from different perspectives and used them as references to confirm the details of the final product in paper sketches.

Designer Behavior During VR Modeling. The results revealed that after Participants D1, D6, and D7 created 2D sketches on paper through horizontal thinking (whereas Participant D5 directly created 2D sketches in VR), they switched to Gravity Sketch to enhance their sketches. Specifically, they converted the abstract paper sketches with coarse details into 3D images with clearly defined outlines. This step enabled the participants to create preliminary truck models with rational proportions by revising their contours in the 2D sketches. During this revision, they mostly engaged in vertical thinking and adjusted curved lines and surfaces to create smooth images; this process was highly time-consuming. For example, Participant D1 stated, "When creating curved shapes, I thought about how they would work in a [3D] model." He further noted, "After I learned to use the SubD function in VR, I considered not only [the aesthetics of] my design shape but also whether this shape would be suitable for creating SubD curved surfaces and more realistic models that closely resemble the curved surfaces of an actual vehicle." Moreover, Participant D7 stated, "When I started to create sketches in VR, I thought about how to create curved surfaces, and I felt that I should complete all structural lines in the sketches first." To help designers to create sketches, Gravity Sketch provides functions similar to those provided in other modeling software programs (such as Rhino and Alias), and the most notable function provided by Gravity Sketch is SubD.

Although Gravity Sketch does not provide Boolean algebra or curve trimming functions, it offers greater freedom than that provided by other modeling software programs, and it provides a modeling experience comparable to that achieved when using modeling clay or PU foam. In the present study, all the participants used modeling functions to assist with sketching; this behavior is consistent with that observed in our previous study.

Utilization of Previous Design Habits. The process through which the participants developed and constructed their designs was observed in the experiment, and retrospective interviews revealed that most of the participants used their existing modeling or sketching habits when working with the VR tool. For example, most of the participants habitually drew contours before creating curved surfaces along the contours. An interesting finding regarding VR operation was that Participant D6 used his left hand to create paper sketches but his right hand to control the mouse for VR modeling. Observation of the ambidextrous behavior of this participant revealed that when he used his left hand to create VR sketches, he directly produced curves as if he was drawing on paper. By contrast, when he used his right hand to create a model, he produced a random curve before adjusting the direction points on the curve to finalize its shape. These finding questions whether the primary function of VR tools is more oriented toward modeling or sketching.

4.3 Advantages of VR Sketch

After open coding, tree coding, and selective coding the interviews, we extracted several key points; Table 1 presents the content of axis coding and repression parts of open coding. Base on the findings of last experience where the participants agreed that VR enabled a 3D view of the drawing, and more detail about its advantages have been identified rather than general conclusion last time: (a) higher degree of freedom and efficiency than modeling software (b) simple color and material simulations that enable users to evaluate their designs (3) Model duplicability and editability. (Lin et al. 2022).

Essential content was extracted from the interview responses after open, axial, and selective coding. Table 1 presents representative content obtained after axial and open coding. Similar to our previous study, the participants in the present study agreed that the VR tool has several advantages, namely (a) higher freedom and efficiency than other modeling software programs, (b) simple color and material simulation that enables users to evaluate their design, and (c) ability to create replicable and editable models (Lin et al. 2022). Table 1 lists the advantages of Gravity Sketch determined after coding. The advantages were revealed using grounded theory, and the alternating use of 2D and 3D sketching environments accentuated these advantages because smooth conversion between 2D and 3D outlines was enabled by the assistance provided by designated researchers, which allowed the participants to further notice the advantages of the VR tool. Compared with sketching on paper, Gravity Sketch enables users to improve 3D design ideas more rapidly and reduces the delay caused by perspective adjustment. In the case of truck design, users can easily view a design in its full scale from different angles and inspect large objects in the design. This feature allowed the participants to recall images of real trucks and use them for comparison to create rational design shapes.

Table 1. Overview of axis codes from tree nodes and their categories and subcategories from open codes.

Axis codes	Categories	Subcategories		
1. initial step	1-1 timing of switching to VR	unable to do much lateral thinking with ordinary drawing	poor drawing ability	complete around 70-80% of the drawing first
		features available in VR	allocate task time according to VR characteristics	
	1-2 convert paper sketches to VR sketches	assign tasks between VR and hand drawing	sufficient for next stage of modeling	
	1-3 additional Steps for VR sketching	set baseline	fix baseline	adjust working environment
		re-position	remove unnecessary frames	meet expectations
		name layer	aligning reference images	adding missing views to provide extra information
		complete top view	issues only found in VR	problems caused by initial uncertainty
		redo	start building surfaces and solving issues as they arise	free play
		considering modeling commands	symmetry	reduce control points
		unlock layers	zoom out the model	reduce transparency
		sketch complex surfaces	SubD vs Nurbs	convert Nurbs to SubD
		consider creating quad mesh		
2. unfolding ideas	2-1 design habits	finish the surfaces one by one	add thickness	sketching habit
		having fewer control points	get used to step-by-step model completion	past design experience
		put the whole set together and think about it separately	adjust the transparency of a layer	
	2-2 general starting point	for some reason, it seems appropriate to start here	outline the important lines first	try first even without ideas
		much look like to play puzzles	more impressed with a certain reference	exploration
	2-3 think while drawing	build up details with outlines	roughly capture the proportions and contours	capture styling vocabulary
		specific sketching perspective	characteristic surface	characteristic curve
		pen follows the mood	let the pen wander	check position
		styling coherence		
	2-4 altering after seeing the reference	abandon the ones that don't look good	modeling is smooth	happens to be suitable
		fit into a similar look		
	2-5 adding details	add shading to enhance expression	3D perspective sense	outline local areas
		the sharpness of the surface	sketch iteration	use markers to create a three-dimensional effect
		iso curve		
	2-6 surface verification	zoom out	observe 3D surfaces and blend contour lines together	start building surfaces and adapt to changing ideas
		hiding the sketch layer		
	2-7 restarting a new sketch	evaluate references	evaluating the aesthetics and adjusting proportions	

(continued)

Table 1. (continued)

3.modifications	3-1 comparison	more like a truck	relatively trendy	more masculine semantics
	3-2 Refinement	surfaces must be modified from 2D to 3D / print the file from VR and refine the sketches by hand / get closer to reality / redrawing is better / discover incomplete details / sketching, thinking, and refining	3d drawing in VR has some minor flaws / fill in the contours by going back to VR / check the overall design / unified Design Vocabulary / make up for omissions	change it if it doesn't look good / insert or remove control points / should be some changes / design rationalization / association
	3-3 getting stuck	stuck on the use of tools / forgot to center the object, causing difficulties in subsequent processing / try more other tools	hesitation due to the conflict between rationality and beauty / didn't know enough about SubD / worried about losing proportion	mistakes due to improper operation of tools / breakthrough
	3-4 discovered by VR Sketch	correct proportions	comments generated by the tool	evaluating the design characteristics
4. time constraints	4-1 time factor	time is running short	running out of time	
5. references	5-1 learning from references	refer to their structure and proportions / carefully studying reference images	reference features	learning from references
	5-2 references baffle original ideas	being influenced unconsciously by references	adding details based on references	
6. drawing on paper vs in VR	6-1 advantages of VR sketching	SubD / VR allows for visualizing 3D shapes / more convenient and faster to draw details in VR / able to express ideas quickly / easier to explore in VR / VR sketching helps with thinking about contours, overall structure, local surfaces, and details	easier to control in VR sketching / able to change colors in VR / painting 3D in VR is clearer / clay modeling takes a long time / not good at sketching on paper	able to complete side view and perspective at same time in VR / able to positioning accuracy in VR / VR assists in perspective drawing / faster to express directly in VR / modeling the desired shape in a short time / easier to duplicate
	6-2 disadvantages of VR sketching	terrible mirror function / easy to miss top or front view / easy to miss some places in VR drawing / sketch on paper are more comprehensive	drawing 2D shapes in VR is difficult / easily distracted in VR / forgetting to turn on the snap point / forgot to consider how to build the surface when sketching	easy to miss details because of complex information in VR / failure due to unfamiliar with the tool / SubD without NURBS is not very user-friendly / sweeping 2 rails is difficult to use
	6-3 VR-related issues	continuing the Habit of Rhino modeling / VR operation skills / no time to think of better modeling methods / the burden of switching sketch from VR to paper is small / the first impression of entering VR is modeling / familiarity	convert 3D mode to 2D mode / baselines in VR / follow the habit of paper sketching / sketches on paper looks different as those made in VR / distinguishing the modeling process	personal initial setting / personal modeling method / the flat line indicates the direction of the surface / a surface along exactly the curves / past design experience
	6-4 related issues about drawing on paper	visualize 2D curves as 3D surfaces / sketching helps thinking	sketching 3D objects requires patience / the tactile sensation of sketching on paper	sketching for necessary section line / sketching on paper has better focus
7. ambiguity	7-1 ambiguity of paper sketch	ideas are still ambiguous / adding curves to surfaces to express shape transitions and reduces ambiguity	reduce ambiguity	erase inaccurate lines to reduce ambiguity / sketching and shading to reduce ambiguity
	7-2 ambiguity of VR sketches	zoom in to reduce ambiguity	make lines thinner to reduce blur	
8. others		perspective is the most difficult view to draw accurately by hand / muscle memory	trace the shape of the VR painting on paper to deepen the impression	

4.4   Weakness of VR Sketch

According to the results obtained in our previous study (Lin et al. 2022) and the present study, the following weaknesses (Cell 6-2 in Table 1) and constraints of Gravity Sketch were identified.

User Discomfort.   Wearing the head-mounted display is often uncomfortable because of its heavy weight and unfavorable weight distribution; it also tires the eyes after prolonged use.

Low Precision.   A key constraint of Gravity Sketch is that it lacks precision. As its name suggests, the current version of Gravity Sketch is more suitable for creating rough sketches. The value of Gravity Sketch lies in rapidly visualizing 3D design ideas for subsequent precise modeling or oil clay modeling based on computer numerical control, not in achieving a model precision comparable to that of other modeling tools.

Lack of Tactile Feedback.   Gravity Sketch does not provide tactile feedback similar to that obtained when using pen and paper. It also lacks the ergonomic and tactile feedback provided by physical models.

Unsuitable for Horizontal Thinking.   Although Gravity Sketch is designed for users to create sketches in VR, users can engage in horizontal thinking more easily when performing paper sketching than when performing VR sketching.

Difficulty in Time Control.   Because VR provides an excellent immersive experience, users are likely to focus excessively on specific details, thereby spending excessive time on VR modeling instead of VR sketching.

Low Abstractness.   Because VR provides clear spatial information, the lack of spatial abstractness might reduce users' imagination.

Nonintuitive Functions.   Because some functions of Gravity Sketch are nonintuitive, users might forget to turn on these functions and thus might need to restart the design process.

4.5   Ambiguity

Reduced Ambiguity Due to Extra Design Work and Steps in VR. When the participants used Gravity Sketch to create designs, they had to complete additional steps required by this tool. Cell 1-3 in Table 1 lists the additional steps required for using the VR tool. Typical additional steps included (a) adjusting the VR environment to suit one's working habits or aligning VR objects with reference images, (b) creating a scale bar to determine the contour proportion, (c) deleting or adding direction points on curves to adjust curve smoothness, (d) ensuring that the rendered structural lines clearly define the intersections between curved surfaces, (e) drawing feature lines on rough curved surfaces to identify specific shapes, and (f) using the zoom-in tool to examine the connections between objects. These steps indirectly improve model precision and reduce design ambiguity, which might be inconducive to horizontal thinking in early design stages because the lack of ambiguity limits designers' imagination.

Increasing Ambiguity in the VR Design Environment Through Specific Procedures. Our previous study (Lin et al. 2022) indicated that designs produced using VR tools are less abstract and more precise than are designs produced through paper sketching, and these characteristics of VR tools might impede horizontal thinking in early design stages. In the present study, multiple participants who were familiar with Gravity Sketch attempted to increase the ambiguity of VR sketches through specific procedures, including (a) the use of curves with fading edges to create the initial contour, (b) the use of multiple flat planes to create a curved surface, (c) the use of geometric shapes to create blocks, and (d) the use of SubD clay tools to create shapes. The aforementioned steps adequately preserve in VR sketches a level of ambiguity comparable to that of paper sketches; thus, such steps enable VR tools to retain the freedom of paper sketches.

5 Discussion

The present study indicated that VR sketches are suitable for the middle and later stages of personal sketch creation. In an experiment, the alternating use of VR and paper sketches in the design process enabled a preliminary verification of the applicability of Gravity Sketch to early product design. In the middle and later personal sketch design stages, rendered 3D outlines still comprise a certain degree of ambiguity and allow for the adjustment of curved surfaces. In the design of a large product, the conversion of 2D paper sketches into 3D VR sketches reduces the ambiguity of the product design, enables the designer to improve their ideas rapidly, and facilitates an intuitive transition from horizontal thinking to vertical thinking. In contrast to regular 3D modeling software, VR sketching tools do not limit the ability of designers to develop or create shapes, even when they possess a limited understanding of computer modeling. Such tools help designers to construct and render their design concepts easily.

The selection and coordination of design tools is a part of the design process. Because designers have different knowledge backgrounds and habits, they might exhibit a doubtful attitude toward VR design tools and regard them as a gimmick or entertainment. However, although the participants of this study differed considerably in their ability to use Gravity Sketch, they did not experience difficulty with the complex operation and other limitations of CAD software (Lawson 2002) after undergoing adequate training, learning by trial and error, and acquiring sufficient skills. The results of this study indirectly verified the ease of use of Gravity Sketch in creating sketches of vehicles with a streamlined design. Accordingly, Gravity Sketch can be an innovative tool that enables flexible design procedures in practical settings.

6 Conclusions

This study mainly focused on the design process of switching between VR sketching and traditional paper sketching and verified the advantages of VR in the middle and later stages of personal sketching. In response to the continual advancement of immersive design tools, we will incorporate focus group interviews in future research to explore the advantages of VR sketching, examine the effect of including VR operation in design curricula to help students to complete their designs, and investigate the timing of using VR to assist in design tasks and the applications of VR in practical scenarios. Moreover, because Gravity Sketch provides functions similar to those used for computer modeling, its user interface might exert an increased mental load on designers, and this effect might not be reflected in the comparison of VR and paper drawing tools in the present study. Therefore, in a future study, we will focus on Level-4 sketches with refined curved surfaces to ensure that the study samples solely comprise 3D VR sketches and exclude rendered 3D VR models. The goal will be to compare the advantages of VR sketching and other digital illustration such as Graphic s tablet or iPad in creating clean curves, precise shapes, and nonabstract designs.

Acknowledgments. This work was financially supported by the Ministry of Science and Technology of Taiwan by grant number 109-2410-H-011-007-MY2. We thank the design students who participated in our experiment.

References

Alcaide Marzal, J., Diego-Más, J.A., Asensio-Cuesta, S., Piqueras Fiszman, B.: An exploratory study on the use of digital sculpting in conceptual product design. Des. Stud. **34**(2), 264–284 (2013)

Aldoy, N., Evans, M.: A review of digital industrial and product design methods in UK higher education. Des. J. **14**(3), 343–368 (2011)

Buxton, B.: Sketching user experiences: getting the design right and the right design. Morgan Kaufmann (2010)

Cross, N.: Natural intelligence in design. Des. Stud. **20**(1), 25–39 (1999)

Ferguson, E.S.: Engineering and the mind's eye. MIT press (1994)

Goel, V.: Sketches of thought. MIT press (1995)

Israel, J.H., Wiese, E., Mateescu, M., Zöllner, C., Stark, R.: Investigating three-dimensional sketching for early conceptual design-Results from expert discussions and user studies. Comput. Graph. **33**(4), 462–473 (2009)

Lawson, B.: CAD and creativity: does the computer really help? Leonardo **35**, 327–331 (2002)

Lin, M., Chiang, I., Lee, L., Lu, H.: Examining performance of VR sketch modeling tool in personal sketches. In: Lockton, D., Lloyd, P., Lenzi, S. (eds.) DRS2022: Bilbao, Spain (2022)

McGown, A., Green, G., Rodgers, P.A.: Visible ideas: information patterns of conceptual sketch activity. Des. Stud. **19**(4), 431–453 (1998)

Noy, S., Zhang, W.: Experimental evidence on the productivity effects of generative artificial intelligence. Available at SSRN 4375283 (2023)

Olofsson, E., Sjolen, K.: Design sketching. Design Books AB, Klippan, Sweden (2005)

Pei, E., Campbell, I., Evans, M.: A taxonomic classification of visual design representations used by industrial designers and engineering designers. Des. J. **14**(1), 64–91 (2011)

Rieuf, V., Bouchard, C., Meyrueis, V., Omhover, J.F.: Emotional activity in early immersive design: sketches and mood boards in virtual reality. Des. Stud. **48**, 43–75 (2017)

Effects of Redirected Walking on Cybersickness in an Applied Virtual Environment

Matthew D. Marraffino[1]([✉]), Kristen M. Schmidt[2], Allison E. Garibaldi[2], and Nicholas W. Fraulini[2]

[1] Naval Air Warfare Center Training Systems Division, Orlando, FL 32826, USA
matthew.d.marraffino.civ@us.navy.mil
[2] StraCon Services Group, Fort Worth, TX 76109, USA
{kristen.m.schmidt.ctr,allison.e.garibaldi.ctr,
nicholas.w.fraulini.ctr}@us.navy.mil

Abstract. Virtual reality (VR) is becoming increasingly common and desirable for training applications due to its accessibility and flexibility. However, VR often requires large physical space if training requires one to walk around freely. Two locomotion techniques, redirected walking (RDW) and 2:1 resets, have been recommended as a solution to fit a larger virtual space into a smaller physical space. However, few studies thoroughly examined these techniques and their impact on cybersickness (CS), particularly in applied and confined environments. This study aimed to investigate the effects of RDW and 2:1 resets within a VE based on a confined, real-world environment. Our findings suggest that the presence of RDW causes significantly more CS compared to free walking and resets alone. Additionally, participants who noticed the RDW manipulations tended to experience more CS. Implications of these findings and future directions are discussed.

Keywords: Virtual Reality · Redirected Walking · Cybersickness

1 Introduction

In recent years, the widespread availability of affordable virtual reality (VR) systems has opened the door for game designers, training specialists, and instructional system developers to explore new approaches using highly immersive digital experiences. Advances in VR availability and technology have garnered particular interest for military training, as they offer the opportunity to train in environments that are impractical or unsafe to train in the real world [1, 2]. Concerns for widespread implementation of VR-based training remain, though, as the consequences of certain VR features for both training outcomes and user experience are not understood fully. Training in VR is most effective when it directly leverages the immersive properties of VR [3]. Locomotion, or moving around the virtual environment (VE) is one of the most basic interactions a user will experience within VR. The ability to walk in a VE offers a seamless method of locomotion that is intuitive, beneficial for training outcomes [4–6], and helps mitigate issues arising from cybersickness (CS) [7]. However, allowing users to explore VEs through

J. Y. C. Chen et al. (Eds.): HCII 2024, LNCS 15377, pp. 133–145, 2025.
https://doi.org/10.1007/978-3-031-76812-5_10

walking requires considerable physical space requirements, such that the physical space available must be 1:1 with the VE. Although designers have developed several artificial locomotion interfaces that significantly reduce physical space requirements, such as tele-porting and joystick [8–12], these interfaces have three primary drawbacks. First, they are artificial and require the user to interact with an interface, thus reducing intuitive-ness and immersion [13, 14]. Second, they remove proprioceptive and visual cues that assist in wayfinding and spatial knowledge acquisition [e.g., 4, 15, 16]. Finally, artificial locomotion interfaces can induce CS [17], which may negatively affect the user expe-rience and potentially impact training outcomes. Despite their clear benefits, the large space requirements to support a free walking experience in VR are often not tenable. Recent locomotion techniques, such as redirected walking (RDW; i.e., imperceptibly manipulating the users' walking path to fit a smaller space) and 2:1 resets (i.e., having the user turn 180 degrees when they reach the tracking boundary), may help overcome the practical limitations of free walking [18, 19]. However, their effects on CS have not been studied extensively in the context of constrained real-world virtual environments, which are especially common in the military domain. Thus, the present study examined the effects of RDW and 2:1 resets on participants' levels of CS as they navigated a virtual submarine to determine the feasibility of these approaches to support military training.

1.1   Redirected Walking, 2:1 Resets, and Cybersickness

First demonstrated by Razzaque et al. [20], redirected walking techniques subtly adjust the virtual scene to allow a user to walk around a VE freely in a smaller physical space. To achieve this, RDW employs various techniques, including rotation and curvature gains that imperceptibly manipulate the user's perception of movement to encourage physical walking paths that differ from the virtual space [see 18, 19 for reviews]. Rotation gain biases the user towards the center of the tracking space and away from boundaries by increasing or decreasing the speed of the virtual rotation mapping in the scene from the physical head movements of the user [21, 22]. Similarly, curvature gains adjust the virtual scene such that users walk in curved paths in the physical space to move along a straight-line path in the VE [e.g., 23, 24]. Both compress the physical space required for free walking in VR. However, even when RDW techniques are used, there is still the possibility that users reach the tracking space boundaries. Resets can alleviate this problem by repositioning the user using an overt cue when they approach a physical boundary. The present study implemented 2:1 resets, where the user turns in place 180 degrees while the virtual environment rotates 360 degrees [24]. As a result, the user faces the opposite direction in the physical space but perceives a full turn within the VE. This reorients them towards the inside of the tracking space and away from the boundary. Although resets are frequently used in conjunction with RDW to maximize space reduction, the current paper examines resets as a separate feature from the space compression techniques employed with RDW algorithms.

The extent to which RDW gains can be maximized before being noticeable has been studied extensively [e.g., 25–28]. However, RDW techniques can create conflict between the visual and vestibular senses, which may lead users to experience CS even if the redirection is imperceptible [29, 30]. CS can be characterized as a set of symptoms experienced while in immersive environments that are similar to classic motion sickness, including nausea, oculomotor fatigue, headache, and vertigo [30]. In addition to negatively affecting the user experience, CS is particularly problematic in the use of VR for training, as it can cause research participants to end their participation in VR-based activities early [e.g., 7, 31, 32]. As a result, trainees may end their training before reaching a desirable level of knowledge acquisition. Thus, features of VR that exacerbate CS must be carefully considered if VR-based training is to be implemented in operational settings.

CS has been studied across a broad range of locomotion interfaces, [e.g., 7, 17, 33], but research on how RDW and resets in particular affect CS is insufficient and presents conflicting results. Steinicke et al. [27, 28] and Grechkin et al. [25] reported increased CS after experiencing RDW, but the papers did not conduct tests of statistical significance. Similarly, Hodgson et al. [31] noted CS-related attrition during their experiment, but subjective measures of CS were not reported. In a subsequent study, Schmitz et al. [32] found significantly higher levels of CS when participants experienced rotation gains compared to a free walking control group. In contrast, Langbehn et al. [34] compared CS across multiple locomotion methods and found that RDW did not produce significantly higher Simulator Sickness Questionnaire (SSQ) scores after VR exposure, though they did not include free walking in their comparison. Despite research from Paris et al. [35] reporting no evidence that resets increased CS, resets are understudied in the context of CS. The conflicting findings and gaps in previous research complicate recommendations for implementing RDW into real-world, virtual reality-based training.

1.2   The Present Study

The goal of the current experiment was to investigate whether applying RDW and/or 2:1 resets would result in higher levels of CS than a free walking control condition without any manipulations. To test our research question, we used a VE based on an Auxiliary Machinery Room (AMR) located aboard a submarine. This environment enabled us to examine these techniques in a real-world operational environment to better understand the implications for training. Much of the research on RDW and CS takes place either in open, unconstrained environments, or in environments that may not be applicable to real-world training needs (e.g., open desert; [36]; small office; [34]; open city [27, 28]). Real-world training scenarios may involve spaces that are difficult to navigate either by being space-constrained or by containing large obstacles. Researchers have speculated that this leads to higher CS by causing higher levels of optic flow (i.e., information about relative movement of objects; [37] and claustrophobia [31]). Additionally, the constraints of the VE may affect whether RDW techniques are noticed, and subsequently increase levels of CS [31]. Therefore, despite some research suggesting that RDW does not affect levels of CS, we hypothesized that participants would report higher SSQ scores in the RDW and 2:1 reset conditions than the control condition.

2 Method

2.1 Participants

Twenty-five participants were recruited from the Orlando, Florida area based on a power analysis for repeated measures ANOVA (alpha level of .05, 80% estimated power) using G*Power [38]. Participants received a $50 gift card as compensation for participation. This study was approved by the U.S. Navy Institutional Review Board. All participants were given information about the study, including a warning that the study might induce motion sickness, and signed a consent document prior to participation. Participants were told they could stop the study at any time.

Of the 25 participants, 12 identified as male and 13 as female, with a mean reported age of 23.2 ($SD = 5.19$) and normal or corrected to normal vision. Overall, 71% of participants reported having had experience with VR/AR systems, but only 25% reported having used VR within the last three months. Of those reporting having previous experience with AR/VR systems, none reported using the technology daily, and only 13% reported using it at least monthly. Regarding video game usage, 92% of participants reported playing video games of any kind at least monthly.

2.2 Design

This study utilized a within-subjects design; all participants experienced all four experimental VR conditions. The four conditions were Free Walk, RDW-Only, Reset-Only, and RDW-Reset. The Free Walk condition was used as a control where participants explored the submarine AMR by completing a scavenger hunt task with both RDW and resets turned off. The remaining three conditions were presented in a randomized order and took place in the AMR with the same task. In RDW-Only, participants completed the scavenger hunt while experiencing RDW manipulation (but not 2:1 resets). In the Reset-Only and RDW-Reset conditions, participants were placed in smaller tracking space to induce resets (with or without the RDW manipulation) and simulate conditions where the VE was larger than the physical space available. In these conditions, a 2:1 reset prompted participants to turn in place when they encroached on the buffer of the walking space.

2.3 VR Equipment and Environment

Participants used the HTC Vive Pro 2 as the VR headset for this study alongside two HTC Vive controllers. Four base stations (1 per corner) were used for the tracking space. The Vive was powered by an HP VR Backpack G2 with a NVIDIA GeForce RTX 2080 graphics card. Surveys were administered on a separate laptop.

The virtual environment for this experiment was the AMR, a 30ft x 30ft space located on board a submarine. The VE was created using a modified version of the Virtual Interactive Shipboard Instructional Tour (VISIT), which is a Unity-based training platform used to introduce and orient sailors to the location of critical safety equipment onboard ships and submarines. A tracking space of 32ft × 32ft was utilized for the Free Walk and RDW-Only conditions as this was the minimum space necessary to avoid collisions and/or resets. However, the tracking space was reduced to 20ft x 20ft for the RDW-Reset and Reset-Only conditions to simulate a smaller room that would benefit from RDW and resets.

The Redirected Walking Toolkit [39], developed as an open source RDW library designed within Unity, was used to drive the RDW engine in the VE. In the conditions where RDW was enabled, defaults from the toolkit were used such that a 7-m radius curvature gain was applied to forward movement. Additionally, rotation was biased towards the center with a [−.2, .3] rotation gain. This toolkit was also used to implement the 2:1 resets in this study. A 2ft buffer was made within the 20ft × 20ft tracking space. When a participant approached the buffer, the simulation prompted them to turn in place. The simulation would turn twice as fast as the participant. As such, participants would turn 180 degrees in the physical space while it appeared they did a full 360 degrees turn in the simulation, reorienting them back towards the middle of the tracking space and away from the boundary [24].

During each VR session, participants completed a scavenger hunt task where they located 16 pieces of equipment throughout the AMR by following a blue line. The path through the VR had participants traverse the space roughly twice; first counterclockwise, and then clockwise. The task was identical for all VR sessions (Fig. 1).

Fig. 1. Example scavenger hunt item.

2.4 Measures

This study utilized a variety of questionnaires to assess the simulations and the loco-motion techniques. These included the Simulator Sickness Questionnaire (SSQ), a demographics questionnaire, and a measure to assess whether the participant noticed a mismatch between their physical movements and the movements in the VR.

The SSQ [40] is a 16-item questionnaire used to measure simulator sickness symptoms. The SSQ contains three scales gauging simulator sickness (SS): Nausea, Oculomotor, and Disorientation. Although the symptoms of CS may be distinct from simulator sickness [41], the SSQ remains the most used method of measuring CS, as several studies have demonstrated its suitability for measuring both types of sickness [7; but see 42, 43]. The SSQ has participants rate the severity of 16 symptoms on a four-point scale (0-None, 1-Slight, 2-Moderate, 3-Severe). The measure was administered 5 times during this study, once prior to entering the VR to capture baseline symptoms, which cannot be assumed to be zero [44], and once after each of the four experimental conditions.

The demographics questionnaire was administered to gather information regarding participants' age, gender, VR/AR, and video game experience. At the end of the study, a single-item question developed by the researchers asked participants to self-report whether they noticed discrepancies between their movement in the VR versus the physical space (i.e., "Did you notice a mismatch between your actual movements and the movements in the VR in any of the machinery room simulations?). The response was recorded using a five-point Likert scale (1-Definitely not, 2-Probably not, 3-Might or might not, 4-Probably yes, 5-Definitely yes).

2.5 Procedure

After giving consent, participants completed the SSQ to obtain a baseline measure of CS, as well as the demographics questionnaire. Next, they read through tutorial instructions to learn how the VR system works. This included information on the study purpose and schedule, putting on the headset, how to walk around, how to reset, how to select objects, and how to complete the scavenger hunt task.

Experimenters then set up participants in the VR system. Participants were first asked to complete a practice scavenger hunt in a pier-side environment to learn how the VR system and resets worked. After finishing the practice scavenger hunt, participants exited the VR and returned to the computer to complete the SSQ again. The process of completing the VR scavenger hunt (about 2 min) and completing the SSQ (about 2–3 min) was then repeated for the four experimental conditions in the AMR. All participants completed the Free Walk condition first, as this condition did not include RDW or resets and therefore was less likely to produce CS symptoms. This was done to limit the likelihood participants would experience CS prior to experiencing RDW or resets, which were hypothesized to increase CS symptoms. The last three conditions, RDW-Only, Reset-Only, and RDW-Reset, were presented in a randomized order. Participants spent approximately two minutes in VR for each condition. After completing all the VR scavenger hunts, participants took off the VR system and finished the surveys.

3   Results

The total SSQ score was calculated as per Kennedy et al. [40]. Upon examining the means and standard deviations, we observed a noticeably wide range of SSQ scores within each condition, particularly for the two RDW conditions. For the primary analysis, we conducted a within-subjects ANCOVA using condition as the within-subjects variable and SSQ total scores as the dependent variable. Baseline SSQ scores (i.e., SSQ score measured prior to any VR exposure) were entered into the model as a covariate to account for any pre-VR symptoms. Based on Mauchly's test, the assumption of sphericity was violated ($W = .252, p < .001$); therefore, within-subjects F-ratios are reported using the Greenhouse-Geisser correction. Baseline SSQ was not a significant covariate and did not significantly interact with condition indicating the covariate did not violate the homogeneity of regression slopes assumption. There was a significant main effect for condition, $F(1.72, 39.55) = 3.93, p = .033, \eta_p^2 = .146$. Post-hoc analyses were conducted to further investigate the main effect using Tukey's HSD. As seen in Fig. 2, results from this analysis revealed significant differences between the Free Walk condition and the two RDW conditions, such that participants reported lower SSQ scores in the Free Walk condition than in both RDW conditions, which was supported by large effect sizes. Additionally, participants reported significantly higher SSQ scores in the RDW-Reset condition than in the Reset-Only condition. No significant differences were uncovered between the RDW-Only and Reset-Only conditions. Scores for the Free Walk and Reset-Only conditions were also not significantly different, though total SSQ scores in the Free Walk condition were still lower on average than scores in the Reset-Only condition.

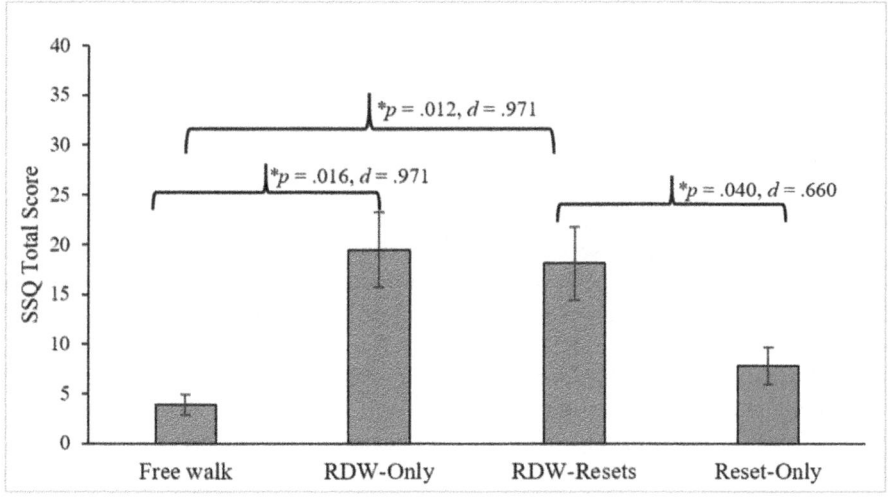

Fig. 2. Bar graph of SSQ total scores by condition. Estimated marginal means reported. Error bars represent standard errors.

Previous research has suggested that CS levels can be affected by whether or not the user notices the RDW manipulations [31]. Therefore, we conducted further exploratory analyses to investigate whether noticeability of RDW affected SSQ scores. We divided scores from the RDW-awareness question into high and low groups using a median split with those scoring 2 or below categorized as "Low," ($n = 13$), and those above 2 categorized as "High." SSQ scores across groups were not normally distributed. Therefore, Welch's t-tests were conducted using RDW-awareness as the grouping variable and SSQ total scores for each condition as dependent variables. Significance was assessed using a Bonferroni-adjusted p-value. Results from the analysis can be found in Table 1. No group differences were uncovered in the non-RDW conditions (i.e., Free Walk and Reset-Only), which is unsurprising given no space compression algorithms were included in these conditions. A significant difference was uncovered for the RDW-Only condition, such that those in the High awareness group reported significantly higher SSQ scores than those in the Low awareness group. However, no significant differences were uncovered in the RDW-Reset condition. Overall, these results indicate that noticing the RDW manipulation may impact whether individuals experience elevated levels of CS.

Table 1. Differences in SSQ Scores by condition and noticeability

	High ($n = 12$)	Low ($n = 13$)			
Condition	M (*SD*)	M (*SD*)	Welch's t (*df*)	p	d
Free Walk	4.68 (*5.99*)	3.16 (*4.79*)	0.692 (*21.1*)	0.496	0.278
RDW-Only	32.10 (*25.29*)	7.77 (*8.70*)	3.165 (*13.4*)	0.007	1.287
RDW-Resets	26.18 (*24.91*)	10.64 (*10.22*)	2.010 (*14.4*)	0.064	0.816
Reset-Only	10.29 (*12.05*)	5.47 (*5.84*)	1.256 (*15.6*)	0.228	0.509

4 Discussion

In this experiment, we compared three conditions that employed different combinations of RDW techniques and 2:1 resets in an applied setting to a control condition that allowed users to walk freely around the environment without scene manipulations. Overall, our hypothesis that the locomotion manipulations would elicit higher CS was supported. CS levels were highest in the two RDW conditions (i.e., RDW-Only and RDW-Reset) as compared to the Free Walk condition. The findings from this experiment are consistent with Schmitz et al. [32] and Hildebrandt et al. [30], who reported elevated SSQ scores after exposure to RDW in VR. This may be because RDW affects optic flow, as it creates a mismatch between movement in the physical space and the virtual space, which has been shown to heighten CS [29, 46, 47]. However, our findings contradict the conclusions of other studies, which report no or minimal effects of RDW on CS [34], or attribute CS symptoms to other factors such as experimental design [25], the VE [31], or predispositions to CS symptoms [45]. Our within-subjects design enabled us to directly compare RDW approaches to a free walking control to better isolate the effects of these locomotion techniques on CS. Interestingly, the SSQ scores from the current experiment were generally lower than those reported in previous experiments, which range from 24.0 [28] to 50.05 [30]. We also had no participants drop out, which is a distinction from other studies where participants had to stop due to experiencing severe CS symptoms [e.g., 31, 32]. This may be a result of the relatively short time participants spent in VR during our experiment (i.e., 2 min per scenario). In contrast, Hodgson et al.

[31] observed that with 6-min VR scenarios, about 25% of participants were unable to complete their study due to CS symptoms. However, we were still able to detect CS in spite of the short VR exposure times.

Our exploratory analysis also revealed that noticeability had a significant effect on SSQ in the RDW-Only condition, such that participants who noticed the manipulation had significantly higher SSQ scores compared to those who did not. Whereas previous studies have asserted that noticeability of RDW is likely to increase CS [31], our implementation of RDW had lower curvature and rotation gains settings than typical noticeable thresholds [40]. Thus, it is surprising that about half of our participants still noticed the redirection. This may be because most previous studies that have examined noticeability thresholds used unconstrained, open VEs [e.g., 27, 28, 36], whereas the current study utilized a very constrained space. Our findings are similar to that of Hodgson et al. [31], who also found that CS and noticeability of RDW was higher when implemented in a constrained space.

4.1 Practical Implications

Based on our findings, there are several practical implications to consider when implementing RDW. First, RDW may work best with VEs that are wide, open spaces, as it is likely that more constrained VEs might aggravate CS symptoms. Additionally, shorter session times might help with lowering CS severity and attrition rates while utilizing RDW. The findings from this experiment also indicate that the negative effects of CS were much lower when only 2:1 resets were implemented. Therefore, 2:1 resets can be a viable alternative to RDW approaches when space is limited, especially if the VE features a confined, high-detail space such as the AMR used in this study. However, it is unclear to what degree 2:1 resets or RDW would interfere specific training requirement, such as spatial knowledge acquisition.

4.2 Limitations and Future Directions

Although our findings are somewhat consistent with others in the literature, the current experiment is not without its limitations. First, the design of the experiment had participants experience the Free Walk condition prior to interacting with the locomotion conditions. The design decision was made to ensure that the Free Walk condition captured a CS assessment without possible interference from residual effects from the other manipulations. However, this design choice may have influenced the results, as CS may have naturally increased as a result of more time in the VE. We attempted to address this limitation by randomizing the order of the remaining conditions for each participant and giving a break from VR after each scavenger hunt, but carry-over effects may still be possible. The short exposure time for all conditions (~2min each) could have also led to the overall low CS levels. The different conditions still revealed results in a pattern similar to previous studies, though the effects might have been stronger if the study was fully between-subjects and utilized longer exposure times. Additionally, the RDW settings used in the study included a steer-to-center curvature algorithm with rotation gains. The default settings for the gains used in this experiment were based on previous RDW detection threshold research [39]. However, based on findings from the current experiment, some participants were able to detect inconsistencies between their physical movements and the rendered VE, which in turn were related to higher levels of CS. It is an open question as to whether reducing the gain values or incorporating a different curvature algorithm (e.g., steer-to-orbit) could mitigate CS levels, though at the expense of saving space. Moreover, the extant literature highlights individual differences that may be related to CS within VR, including sex and previous VR experience. Although these variables were measured during the experiment and examined, the analyses were not significant and possibly underpowered due to the sample size collected. Therefore, these tests were not reported.

Our findings in this study demonstrate various ways that the effects of RDW could be explored through further research. A study that makes direct experimental comparisons between RDW in both open and enclosed VEs could provide evidence as to whether these types of VEs indeed increase noticeability of RDW manipulations, as well as clarify the connection between noticeability and CS. This line of research is especially important given that enclosed VEs are prevalent in many military applications. Because the current experiment only evaluated the user experience, it is unclear whether the levels of CS experienced by participants would have affected learning outcomes in a training situation. If training outcomes are indeed acceptable with RDW, future applications should consider whether elevated levels of CS are a worthy tradeoff. Future research should also examine if RDW and resets, regardless of CS, have their own unique impact on training outcomes.

5   Conclusion

The findings from this experiment contribute to the literature by demonstrating a causal link between elevated levels of CS and RDW approaches in VR. Overall, CS symptoms were higher in the RDW conditions compared to a Free Walk condition that allowed users to walk the VE with a 1:1 mapping of the space. However, the experiment found a relationship between CS symptoms and noticing the RDW manipulation, suggesting that sensitivity to RDW algorithms may affect the user experience. Additionally, the experiment explored the unique contribution of 2:1 resets on CS and found no evidence that this approach increases CS symptoms compared to a similar Free Walk experience.

Acknowledgments. We gratefully acknowledge Mr. Kevin Nguyen and Mr. Eric Peterson for their assistance with testbed development. This work was funded under the Naval Innovative Science and Engineering program established by the National Defense Authorization Act, Section 219. Presentation of this material does not constitute or imply its endorsement, recommendation, or favoring by the U.S. Navy or the Department of Defense (DoD). The opinions of the authors expressed herein do not necessarily state or reflect those of the U.S. Navy of DoD.

References

1. Bailey, S.K., Johnson, C.I., Schroeder, B.L., Marraffino, M.D.: Using virtual reality for training maintenance procedures. In: Interservice/Industry Training, Simulation, and Education Conference (I/ITSEC), vol. 17108, pp. 1–11. Orlando, FL (2017)
2. Kaplan, A.D., Cruit, J., Endsley, M., Beers, S.M., Sawyer, B.D., Hancock, P.A.: The effects of virtual reality, augmented reality, and mixed reality as training enhancement methods: a meta-analysis. Hum. Factors **63**(4), 706–726 (2021)
3. Abich, J., IV., Parker, J., Murphy, J.S., Eudy, M.: A review of the evidence for training effectiveness with virtual reality technology. Virtual Reality **25**(4), 919–933 (2021)
4. Cherep, L.A., et al.: Spatial cognitive implications of teleporting through virtual environments. J. Exp. Psychol. Appl. **26**(3), 480–492 (2020)
5. Ruddle, R.A., Lessels, S.: The benefits of using a walking interface to navigate virtual environments. ACM Trans. Comput.-Hum. Interact. **16**(1), 1–18 (2009)
6. Xie, X., Paris, R.A., McNamara, T.P., Bodenheimer, B.: The effect of locomotion modes on spatial memory and learning in large immersive virtual environments: a comparison of walking with gain to continuous motion control. In: Creem-Regehr, S., Schöning, J., Klippel, A. (eds.) Spatial Cognition XI. Spatial Cognition 2018. LNCS, vol. 11034. Springer, Cham (2018). https://doi.org/10.1007/978-3-319-96385-3_5
7. Caserman, P., Garcia-Agundez, A., Gámez Zerban, A., Göbel, S.: Cybersickness in current-generation virtual reality head-mounted displays: a systematic review and outlook. Virtual Reality **25**(4), 1153–1170 (2021)
8. Boletsis, C.: The new era of virtual reality locomotion: a systematic literature review of techniques and a proposed typology. Multimodal Technol. Interact. **1**(4), 24 (2017)
9. Bozgeyikli, E., Raij, A., Katkoori, S., Dubey, R.: Point & teleport locomotion technique for virtual reality. In: Proceedings of the 2016 Annual Symposium on Computer-Human Interaction in Play, pp. 205–216 (2016)
10. Di Luca, M., Seifi, H., Egan, S., Gonzalez-Franco, M.: Locomotion vault: the extra mile in analyzing VR locomotion techniques. In: Proceedings of the 2021 CHI Conference on Human Factors in Computing Systems, pp. 1–10 (2021)
11. Sargunam, S.P., Ragan, E.D.: Evaluating joystick control for view rotation in virtual reality with continuous turning, discrete turning, and field-of-view reduction. In: Proceedings of the 3rd International Workshop on Interactive and Spatial Computing, pp. 74–79 (2018)
12. Martinez, E.S., Wu, A.S., McMahan, R.P.: Research trends in virtual reality locomotion techniques. In: 2022 IEEE Conference on Virtual Reality and 3D User Interfaces (VR), pp. 270–280 (2022)
13. Bachmann, E.R., Hodgson, E., Hoffbauer, C., Messinger, J.: Multi-user redirected walking and resetting using artificial potential fields. IEEE Trans. Visual Comput. Graph. **25**(5), 2022–2031 (2019)
14. Kuo, C., Allison, R.S.: Motion matters: Comparing naturalness of interaction with two locomotion interfaces using decision-making tasks in virtual reality. In: 2020 IEEE International Conference on Systems, Man, and Cybernetics (SMC), pp. 3283–3290 (2020)
15. Klatzky, R.L., Loomis, J.M., Beall, A.C., Chance, S.S., Golledge, R.G.: Spatial updating of self-position and orientation during real, imagined, and virtual locomotion. Psychol. Sci. **9**(4), 293–298 (1998)
16. Wraga, M., Creem-Regehr, S.H., Proffitt, D.R.: Spatial updating of virtual displays. Mem. Cognit. **32**(3), 399–415 (2004)
17. Sharples, S., Cobb, S., Moody, A., Wilson, J.R.: Virtual reality induced symptoms and effects (VRISE): comparison of head mounted display (HMD), desktop and projection display systems. Displays **29**(2), 58–69 (2008)

18. Fan, L., Li, H., Shi, M.: Redirected walking for exploring immersive virtual spaces with HMD: a comprehensive review and recent advances. IEEE Trans. Visual. Comput. Graph. **29**(10), 4104–4123 (2022)
19. Nilsson, N.C., et al.: 15 years of research on redirected walking in immersive virtual environments. IEEE Comput. Graphics Appl. **38**(2), 44–56 (2018)
20. Razzaque, S., Kohn, Z., and Whitton, M.: Redirected walking. In: Proceedings of Eurographics, pp. 289–294. Manchester, United Kingdom (2001)
21. Kruse, L., Langbehn, E., Steinicke, F.: I can see on my feet while walking: sensitivity to translation gains with visible feet. In: 2018 IEEE Conference on Virtual Reality and 3D User Interfaces (VR), pp. 305–312. IEEE (2018)
22. Paludan, A., et al.: Disguising rotational gain for redirected walking in virtual reality: effect of visual density. In: 2016 IEEE Virtual Reality (VR), pp. 259–260 (2016)
23. Neth, C.T., Souman, J.L., Engel, D., Kloos, U., Bulthoff, H.H., Mohler, B.J.: Velocity-dependent dynamic curvature gain for redirected walking. IEEE Trans. Visual Comput. Graphics **18**(7), 1041–1052 (2012)
24. Williams, B., et al.: Exploring large virtual environments with an HMD when physical space is limited. In: Proceedings of the 4th Symposium on Applied Perception in Graphics and Visualization, pp. 41–48 (2007)
25. Grechkin, T., Thomas, J., Azmandian, M., Bolas, M., Suma, E.: Revisiting detection thresholds for redirected walking: combining translation and curvature gains. In: Proceedings of the ACM Symposium on Applied Perception, pp. 113–120 (2016)
26. Langbehn, E., Lubos, P., Bruder, G., Steinicke, F.: Application of redirected walking in room-scale VR. In: 2017 IEEE Virtual Reality (VR), pp. 449–450 (2017)
27. Steinicke, F., Bruder, G., Jerald, J., Frenz, H., Lappe, M.: Analyses of human sensitivity to redirected walking. In: Proceedings of the 2008 ACM Symposium on Virtual Reality Software and Technology, pp. 149–156 (2008)
28. Steinicke, F., Bruder, G., Jerald, J., Frenz, H., Lappe, M.: Estimation of detection thresholds for redirected walking techniques. IEEE Trans. Visual Comput. Graphics **16**(1), 17–27 (2009)
29. LaViola, J.J., Jr.: A discussion of cybersickness in virtual environments. ACM Sigchi Bull. **32**(1), 47–56 (2000)
30. Hildebrandt, J., Schmitz, P., Calero Valdez, A., Kobbelt, L., Ziefle, M.: Get well soon! Human factors' influence on cybersickness after redirected walking exposure in virtual reality. In: Chen, J., Fragomeni, G. (eds.) Virtual, Augmented and Mixed Reality: Interaction, Navigation, Visualization, Embodiment, and Simulation. VAMR 2018. LNCS, vol. 10909. Springer, Cham (2018). https://doi.org/10.1007/978-3-319-91581-4_7
31. Hodgson, E., Bachmann, E., Thrash, T.: Performance of redirected walking algorithms in a constrained virtual world. IEEE Trans. Visual Comput. Graphics **20**(4), 579–587 (2014)
32. Schmitz, P., Hildebrandt, J., Valdez, A.C., Kobbelt, L., Ziefle, M.: You spin my head right round: threshold of limited immersion for rotation gains in redirected walking. IEEE Trans. Visual Comput. Graphics **24**(4), 1623–1632 (2018)
33. Chang, E., Kim, H.T., Yoo, B.: Virtual reality sickness: a review of causes and measurements. Int. J. Hum.-Comput. Interact. **36**(17), 1658–1682 (2020)
34. Langbehn, E., Lubos, P., Steinicke, F.: Evaluation of locomotion techniques for room-scale VR: joystick, teleportation, and redirected walking. In: Proceedings of the Virtual Reality International Conference - Laval Virtual (VRIC '18), Article 4, pp. 1–9. Association for Computing Machinery, New York, NY, USA (2018)
35. Paris, R.A., Buck, L.E., McNamara, T.P., Bodenheimer, B.: Evaluating the impact of limited physical space on the navigation performance of two locomotion methods in immersive virtual environments. In: 2022 IEEE Conference on Virtual Reality and 3D User Interfaces (VR), pp. 821–831. IEEE (2022)

36. Gao, Y., Li, L., Wang, J., Zheng, L.: Redirected walking for virtual environments: Investigation and evaluation. In: 2022 8th International Conference on Virtual Reality (ICVR), pp. 147–154 (2022)
37. Gibson, J.J.: The perception of the visual world (1950)
38. Faul, F., Erdfelder, E., Lang, A.-G., Buchner, A.: G*Power 3: a flexible statistical power analysis program for the social, behavioral, and biomedical sciences. Behav. Res. Methods **39**, 175–191 (2007)
39. Azmandian, M., Grechkin, T., Bolas, M., Suma, E.: The redirected walking toolkit: a unified development platform for exploring large virtual environments. In: 2016 IEEE 2nd Workshop on Everyday Virtual Reality (WEVR), pp. 9–14. IEEE (2016)
40. Kennedy, R.S., Lane, N.E., Berbaum, K.S., Lilienthal, M.G.: Simulator sickness questionnaire: an enhanced method for quantifying simulator sickness. Int. J. Aviat. Psychol. **3**(3), 203–220 (1993)
41. Stanney, K.M., Kennedy, R.S., Drexler, J.M.: Cybersickness is not simulator sickness. In: Proceedings of the Human Factors and Ergonomics Society Annual Meeting, vol. 41, no. 2, pp. 1138–1142. Los Angeles, Sage, CA (1997)
42. Bruck, S., Watters, P.A.: The factor structure of cybersickness. Displays **32**(4), 153–158 (2011)
43. Bimberg, P., Weissker, T., Kulik, A.: On the usage of the simulator sickness questionnaire for virtual reality research. In: 2020 IEEE Conference on Virtual Reality and 3D User Interfaces Abstracts and Workshops (VRW), pp. 464–467 (2020)
44. Brown, P., Spronck, P., Powell, W.: The simulator sickness questionnaire, and the erroneous zero baseline assumption. Front. Virtual Real. **3**, 1–14 (2022)
45. Steinicke, F., Bruder, G., Jerald, J., Frenz, H., Lappe, M.: Estimation of detection thresholds for redirected walking techniques. IEEE Trans. Visual Comput. Graphics **16**(1), 17–27 (2010)
46. Kim, J., Park, T.: The onset threshold of cybersickness in constant and accelerating optical flow. Appl. Sci. **10**(21), 7808 (2020)
47. Wu, F., Suma Rosenberg, E.: Adaptive field-of-view restriction: lLimiting optical flow to mitigate cybersickness in virtual reality. In: Proceedings of the 28th ACM Symposium on Virtual Reality Software and Technology, pp. 1–11 (2022)

Towards a VR Environment for Desensitization of Ecological Anxiety

Amadeu Quelhas Martins[1,2,3]($\boxtimes$) (iD), Paulo Ferrajão[2,3] (iD), Bianca Revés[2], and Nuno Torres[4] (iD)

[1] UNIDCOM/IADE, Lisboa, Portugal
`amadeu.martins@universidadeeuropeia.pt`
[2] Universidade Europeia, Lisboa, Portugal
[3] CIDESD, UTAD, Vila Real, Portugal
[4] William James Center for Research, ISPA – Instituto Universitário, Lisboa, Portugal

Abstract. The therapeutic use of virtual reality (VR) is well established in the treatment of anxiety disorders. As an early step to develop a VR environment to desensitize people suffering from eco-anxiety, we created an "emotion-to-picture match" task to characterize their behavioral and physiological responses during exposure to neutral and threatening environmental stimuli. Twenty-nine participants who were identified as "high" or "low" scorers in the Hogg Eco-Anxiety Scale (Hogg et al. 2021) were exposed to three blocks of randomized "eco-anxiety" and "neutral" images, while their electrocardiogram and skin conductance level was recorded. In each trial, participants had to choose from six emotions the one that would closely match their feelings towards the image. During "eco-anxiety" images, the "high" scorers addressed significantly more "anger" than the "low" scorers, whereas "seeking" emotions were more frequent among the latter. In addition, "neutral" images also evoked significantly more "panic" among the "high" eco-anxiety participants, whereas "seeking" emotions were more frequently experienced by the "low" eco-anxiety participants. Surprisingly, "high" eco-anxiety participants displayed higher heart rate variability and lower electrodermal activity than "low" eco-anxiety participants throughout the task, a finding that is at odds with the current understanding of physiological symptoms of anxiety. The design of therapeutic VR environments should forecast all sorts of discomfort that patients are willing to tolerate during VR exposure therapy.

Keywords: UX design · VR exposure therapy · ecological anxiety · autonomic control · emotion · heart rate variability · skin conductance level

1 Introduction

1.1 Changing Behavior by UX Design: The Use of VR Exposure Therapies

Substantial design research has focused on the deliberate guiding of people's behavior towards the improvement of social, environmental, and health challenges (e.g., Lee et al. 2023; Mantzari et al. 2022). User experience (UX) design operates on many of our daily environments and can potentially contribute to tackle detrimental social and environmental issues. However, there is some lack of consensus on how to direct design outputs to change behavior (Niedderer et al. 2016). A few reasons might explain this hindsight. On the one hand, design is conventionally associated with the creation of *tangible* "products" such as packaging, furniture, etc. On the other hand, advances in co-design, service design, and in "virtual world" design made such *tangible* outputs lose traction, contributing to some fuzziness of perspectives.

The therapeutic use of VR is a good example of a widespread contribution of UX design to change behavior. Although VR exposure therapies (VRET) were initially targeted for the treatment of anxiety disorders (e.g., phobias), their use has been expanded to different areas of health care, ranging from stroke rehabilitation (Demeco et al. 2023) to chronic pain management (Ahmadpour et al. 2019), to name a few. Typically, the effectiveness of VRET relies on the sense of immersion that the virtual environment provides, which can be attained within a few minutes (Krzystanek et al. 2021). But other factors are at stake. First, both the frequency and the intensity of cues or target stimuli should match the patient's tolerance, otherwise the sense of immersion can be compromised. Moreover, this calibration is particularly challenging for pain management applications or VRET for phobias, since mistakes can jeopardize the patients' compliance (Krzystanek et al. 2021). Second, the habituation to the whole environment should match the rate of habituation to the target stimuli. Often this is accomplished through the design of multiple scenarios, thus counteracting the former. Further, the addition of automated speech recognition or other feedback systems based on the physiological responses of the patient (e.g., electrocardiogram, electrodermal response) can guide system algorithms to set the pace and intensity of stimuli exposure to the patient's habituation rates.

From the above, it is crucial to characterize the impact that both the target stimuli and the whole environment have in users at the initial stage of designing a VRET environment. In our laboratory, we merge psychophysiology methods with UX design to study and induce behavior changes. As part of a larger project aiming to design a VRET environment for eco-anxiety, we sought to study the impact of eco-anxiety evoking stimuli (providing a proxy for target stimuli) and neutral stimuli (providing a proxy for the whole environment stimuli) in terms of emotional appraisal and physiological responses. Indirectly, we also reasoned that the physiological results could inform the type of human-computer interface to be chosen as biofeedback control device.

1.2 Eco-Anxiety, an Emerging Concept of Emergency

Anxiety disorders are among the top ten largest contributors to global disability (GDB 2016), seemingly evolving with societary changes. Recently, "eco-anxiety" was introduced to encompass the anxiety symptoms resulting from global environmental threats (Kurth & Pihkala 2022), be it potential natural disasters or anthropogenic climate changes such as global warming (Clayton 2020; Kurth & Pihkala 2022). For this reason, eco-anxiety has been interpreted as a *"Pre-Traumatic Stress Syndrome"* because sufferers present with nightmares, flashbacks, and fear-induced dissociation, all those experienced *before* any traumatic consequences of climate change take place (Kaplan 2020).

Stable brain circuitry appears to maintain those negative emotions (Clayton 2020), and to trigger the expression of basic innate emotions due to a perceived threat to survival.

According to Panksepp (2016), mammalian brain's older circuits generate those innate emotions. The deep *reptilian brain* underlies basic instinctual actions for seeking, anger, and fear, whereas the *limbic system* encodes the social emotions of caring, sadness, and play (Davis & Panksepp 2011; Panksepp 2016). Although the link between these primary emotions and psychological symptoms has been identified (e.g., Talarowska et al. 2022), it is unknown whether it stands for people who fear extreme climate events and/or report extreme eco-anxiety symptoms in questionnaire measures.

1.3 Anxiety Correlates and Hypotheses Under Study

The autonomic nervous system plays an important role in both anxiety states and emotional appraisals. Accordingly, increases in sympathetic nervous system (SNS) activity during responses to acute stress are considered adaptive because they promote survival in threatening situations (Porges 1995). Conversely, a chronic/prolonged SNS reactivity is strenuous to the individual, increasing the risk for debilitating health outcomes and emotional dysregulation (Brosschot et al. 2017). Among the available measures to assess the autonomic control of the heart, heart rate variability (HRV) is a well-established non-invasive method (Cacioppo et al. 2016). HRV is derived from the timing differences between successive heartbeats, which result from the fast action of parasympathetic vagal enervation of the heart. Further, HRV can be computed in the time-domain (e.g., the root-mean-square of successive differences; RMSSD), in the frequency-domain (e.g., the absolute or relative amount of signal energy within frequency bands), or through non-linear metrics (see Shaffer and Ginsberg 2017 for review). In this study, we applied a discrete Fourier spectral analysis on the interbeat time series extracted from the electrocardiogram to obtain the high frequency (0.15–0.40 Hz; HF) and the low frequency (0.04–0.15 Hz) HRV components.

Most studies examining anxiety disorders such as posttraumatic stress disorder, panic disorder and generalized anxiety disorder, consistently report a *diminished* HRV at rest and during experimental challenges in those participants (Chalmers et al. 2014; Cheng et al. 2022; Pittig et al. 2013). Group differences between patients with anxiety disorders and matched controls are reliably obtained with the most parasympathetic-specific indices of HRV, namely the RMSSD and the HF (Cheng et al. 2022). As such, we expected that "high" eco-anxiety participants would yield a significantly *lower* HF (reflecting parasympathetic withdrawal) during our "emotion-to-picture match" task, in comparison to "low" eco-anxiety participants.

Adding to the HRV findings, increases in the skin conductance level (SCL) are also known to reflect rises in autonomic arousal that are automatically triggered during emotional experiences (Cacioppo et al. 2016). This tonic response is generated by the sweat glands, builds up over time (i.e., tens of seconds to minutes) and is exclusively driven by the sympathetic nervous system (Cacioppo et al. 2016). Therefore, we expected that "high" eco-anxiety participants would yield a significantly *higher* SCL reactivity during the experiment (i.e., stress challenge), than "low" eco-anxiety counterparts.

Finally, the "Affective Neuroscience Personality Theory" (Panksepp 2016) guided our predictions regarding the participants' emotional appraisal during the "Emotion-to-picture match" task. On the one hand, we expected the "high" eco-anxiety group to address significantly more negative emotions (anger, fear, and sadness) to the environmental challenge stimuli than the "low" eco-anxiety group. On the other hand, we had no specific prediction regarding the neutral nature pictures.

2 Method

2.1 Participants

Twenty-nine healthy right-handed participants (9 male) with a mean age of 29 (SD = 13.2) years, gave informed consent and volunteered to participate. They had a mean resting systolic blood pressure of 125.3 (SD = 6.6) mmHg, diastolic blood pressure of 76.9 (SD = 6.0) mmHg, and heart rate of 75.9 (SD = 6.7) bpm. Exclusion criteria comprised any known cardiovascular disease, diabetes, hypertension, hypo or hyperthyroidism, or any medication except birth control. Participants were asked to refrain from caffeine, alcohol, and exercise for 2 h before testing. The local research ethics committee approved the study protocol.

2.2 Apparatus and Instruments

Participants sat 80 cm far from a Full HD 21,5" screen connected to a Dell OptiPlex 3070 (8 GB DDR4 2666 MHz RAM) where the experimental instructions and stimuli were presented. An optical mouse (Dell MS116) was used for response collection. An upper arm blood pressure monitor (OMRON BP7100) was employed for baseline blood pressure and heart rate recordings.

The Hogg Eco-Anxiety Scale (HEAS-13; Hogg et al. 2021). The HEAS is a validated 13-item scale that assesses feelings about climate change over the past two weeks, being regarded as a measure of persistent eco-anxiety. Each item is scored from 0 to 4 hence, total score ranges between 0 and 52. The scale comprises four factors or subscales namely, four items that cover feelings of anxiety, three items that cover ruminative thoughts about negative environmental events, three items that cover behavioral symptoms of eco-anxiety (e.g., sleeping problems, occupational difficulties), and three items that cover anxiety about one's personal impact on the planet. Internal consistency of the affective symptoms (.92), rumination (.90), behavioral symptoms (.86), and anxiety about personal impact (.88) scales were considered excellent. As part of our current project, an online survey collected data from over 600 respondents to the HEAS and other self-report psychometric instruments. Exploratory descriptive statistics ran on the survey participants HEAS total scores allowed us to establish cutoff scores for "low" (< 16) and "high" (> 33) scorers. We then successively invited the participants from this pool to the current experiment.

Electrophysiological Signals. An ambulatory monitoring VU-AMS (Vrije Universiteit-Ambulatory Monitoring System; http://www.vu-ams.nl) amplifier collected the physiological signals during the experiment.

Electrocardiogram (ECG). ECG recording sites were exfoliated (Nuprep, D.O. Weaver & Co) and degreased with isopropyl alcohol until contact impedance was < 10 kΩ. The ECG was recorded with three disposable spot electrodes (Kendall™ Medi-Trace®) in a modified Einthoven triangle configuration. Specifically, the active electrodes were placed on the right clavicle and lower left rib and a ground electrode was placed on the left clavicle. The ECG signal was acquired at a 500 Hz sampling rate. Signal processing was performed offline with the VU- DAMS software package. In detail, QRS detector algorithms ran three separate automated analyses. First, periods with missing data or signal clipping were detected and marked. Second, automated analysis of the QRST waveform detected the occurrence of all R-peaks. Those R-peaks were then converted into the "inter beat interval" (IBI) time series (in milliseconds) and plotted as a continuous signal. A smoothing method ($\lambda = 500$) was applied to detrend inter-beat time series. The third automated analysis checked the plausibility of each IBI latency, considering its surrounding IBIs. Next, all ECG data were visually inspected to correct for omitted (or displaced) R-peaks and to exclude remaining artifacts (e.g. ectopic beats) from further analyses. Finally, a power spectral analysis was performed on the IBI time series to obtain high frequency (HF) and low frequency (LF) HRV. Specifically, the IBI time series within the baseline and each block was interpolated with a cubic spline, resampled at 4 Hz, and split into overlapping periods of 256 s with 1024 data points each. Each period was convoluted with a smoothness prior matrix and submitted to a discrete Fourier analysis using a quadratic window. Power values were then averaged in baseline and block periods (Welch method), and the power in the 0.04–0.15 Hz band (LF) and the 0.15–0.40 Hz band (HF) were extracted. Following the guidelines of the Task Force of the European Society for rigorous HRV data quality (TFES 1996), two "low" and one "high" ecoanxiety participants were excluded from data analysis due to insufficient ECG signal quality. We considered the HF (in squared milliseconds, ms^2) component as a frequency-domain output variable of HRV, computed for the first 240 s into baseline and each of the experimental blocks.

Skin Conductance Level (SCL). Two Ag-AgCl non-polarizable skin conductance transducers (Biopac TP–TSD203) filled with isotonic electrode gel (4OZ–GEL101) were applied on the medial phalanges (volar surface) of the index and middle fingers of the non-dominant hand. Skin conductance was sampled at a rate of 10 Hz within a 0 to 95 microSiemens (μS) signal range. EDA signal was filtered in forward and reverse directions with a low pass cut frequency of 2 Hz. Computation and processing of the EDA signal was performed with the VU- DAMS software package. Data periods where signal clipping levels arose were automatically detected and removed from further analyses. The average skin conductance level (μS) was considered as the output variable computed for the first 240 s into baseline and each of the experimental blocks.

2.3 Procedure

Participants Completed a Single 1-hr Session. Upon arrival, participants provided their informed consent and exclusion criteria were revised. After instrumentation, they rested for 5 min. During this period, blood pressure and heart rate readings were initiated at minutes 1, 3 and 5. Participants were then instructed about the task and electrophysiological recordings were initiated for the baseline period. At the end of the baseline period, participants performed 12 practice trials and then started the task.

"Emotion-to-Picture Match" Task. Participants attended to a series of pictures presented on the screen. Three blocks of 72 trials were presented with 2-min breaks in between.

Stimuli. An initial pool of 200 images depicting environmental crises and calamities (such as wildfires, flooding, high winds; 100 images) and conventional forest and nature environments (100 images) was classified into two categories ("neutral" versus "eco-anxiety" evoking) by two independent research assistants who were blind to the current study. The final pool comprised 29 "eco-anxiety" and 47 neutral pictures achieving an almost perfect agreement (Cohen's Kappa > .95) between the raters. The stimuli employed in this task were drawn from this pool.

18 grey scale pictures of environmental threats ("eco-anxiety" condition) and 18 similar others of nature environments ("neutral" condition) were pseudorandomly presented in each block. Each trial started with a fixation point (latency = 2000 ms) followed by either a "neutral" or an "eco-anxiety" image that stood on the screen. Four seconds later, a series of seven options – six synonyms to each of Davis's and Panksepp's (2011) "primary emotional systems" and a "none of these words" option; see Table 1 – were displayed on the screen around the initial image to prompt a behavioral response. The participant was instructed to choose the option that best matched the emotion that the image has caused in him/her. An ISI randomized from 500 to 1000 ms was employed. Figure 1 presents a typical trial sequence in the "emotion-to-picture match" task.

Table 1. Synonyms employed during the emotional appraisal (Davis & Panksepp 2011).

Anger	Fear	Sadness	Seeking	Care	Play
Resentment	Anxiety	Loss	Novelty	Protection	Liveliness
Disgust	Nervousness	Rejection	Curiosity	Dedication	Amusement
Rage	Worry	Anguish	Interest	Assistance	Laughter
Irritation	Restlessness	Hopelessness	Discovery	Empathy	Happiness
Wrath	Panic	Despair	Creativity	Affection	Cheer

2.4 Data Reduction and Analysis

All analyses were performed with IBM SPSS Statistics for Windows, Version 23.0. Variables were first screened for outliers (3 × interquartile range). Regarding the "emotion-to-picture match" behavioral data, responses with the option "None of these" selected were discarded (220 for the "eco-anxiety" condition, 650 for the "neutral" condition). The remainder responses (2792 in the "eco-anxiety" condition, and 2431 in the "neutral" condition) were inspected through descriptive statistics. All physiological data were normalized and differences from baseline were computed. Most distributions of outcome variables indicated considerable skewness; therefore, non-parametric tests were employed for statistical analysis. Effect sizes for Mann-Whitney U tests were computed as r = |z|/$\sqrt{n}$. An alpha of 0.05 was considered in all analyses.

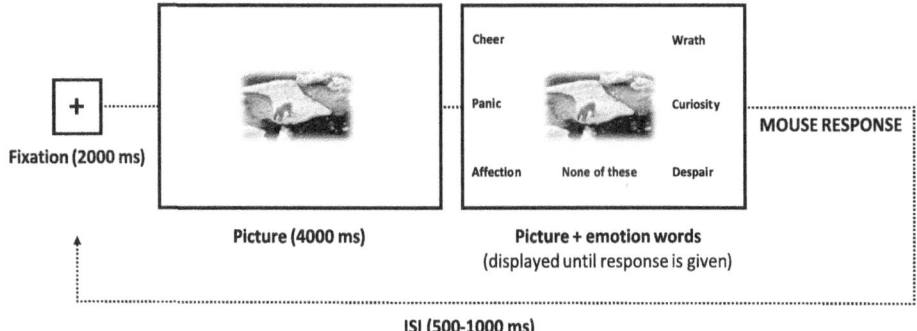

Fig. 1. Typical trial sequence in the "emotion-to-picture match" Task.

3   Results

3.1   Preliminary Analyses

We first examined whether condition allocation could be associated with group differences in demographic and baseline variables. The main characteristics of the participants are presented in Table 2. Mann-Whitney U tests revealed no significant group differences for age (U = 92.00, z = −·044, p = .657), resting heart rate (U = 92.00, z = −0.45, p = .656), resting systolic blood pressure (U = 93.50, z = -0.38, p = .706) and diastolic blood pressure (U = 86.50, z = −0.69, p = .492). However, a Yates corrected chi-square test indicated that the high eco-anxiety group had significantly fewer male participants than the low eco-anxiety group [$\chi^2(1) = 5.12$, p = .024].

3.2   "Emotion-To-Picture Match" Task

Table 3 displays the mean (±SD) frequencies of emotion categories attributed to either neutral or environmental threat pictures. There was considerable variability in mean frequencies per group depending on the type of picture. Considering the "eco-anxiety" images, "anger" emotions were significantly more frequent among the high eco-anxiety group (Md = 21.00) compared to the low eco-anxiety group (Md = 7.00), U = 38.00, z = −2.84, p = .005, with a large effect size r = .53. Conversely, "seeking" emotions were marginally more frequent in low (Md = 2.50) than in high (Md = 0.00) eco-anxiety participants (U = 62.00, z = −1.90, p = .058). Regarding the "neutral" images, "panic" emotions were significantly more frequent in high (Md = 1.00) than in low (Md = 0.00) eco-anxiety participants (U = 61.00, z = −2.08, p = .037), with a large effect size r =

Table 2. Characteristics of the participants allocated to each group condition.

	Low eco-anxiety (N = 12)	High eco-anxiety (N = 17)
Sex (N, %) *		
Males	7 (58.3)	2 (11.8)
Females	5 (41.7)	15 (88.2)
Age (mean, SD) in years	28.7 (12.0)	30.3 (14.5)
Resting HR (mean, SD) bpm	75.4 (6.6)	76.2 (6.9)
Resting systolic BP (mean, SD) mmHg	124.6 (5.6)	125.8 (7.4)
Resting diastolic BP (mean, SD) mmHg	76.3 (5.3)	77.3 (6.5)

Note. BP = blood pressure, HR = heart rate, SD = standard deviation. * $p < .05$.

.39. Again, a statistical trend was found for "seeking" emotions to be more frequent in low (Md = 37.00) than in high (Md = 22.00) eco-anxiety participants (U = 62.50, z = −1.75, p = .08).

Table 3. Mean (±SD) frequencies of emotion categories per image and group condition.

Image condition	Low eco-anxiety (N = 12)	High eco-anxiety (N = 17)
Eco-anxiety		
Anger (mean, SD)*	9.58 (9.53)	23.41 (13.39)
Fear (mean, SD)	38.58 (17.69)	32.00 (10.89)
Panic (mean, SD)	23.42 (15.08)	27.65 (15.86)
Care (mean, SD)	16.42 (9.50)	13.59 (10.09)
Play (mean, SD)	1.25 (2.30)	1.06 (2.02)
Seeking (mean, SD)#	3.50 (3.83)	1.06 (2.63)
Neutral		
Anger (mean, SD)	0.17 (0.58)	0.53 (1.07)
Fear (mean, SD)	2.42 (3.90)	6.65 (11.13)
Panic (mean, SD)*	0.33 (0.89)	2.41 (3.66)
Care (mean, SD)	26.08 (11.78)	29.82 (18.69)
Play (mean, SD)	21.17 (10.49)	15.41 (8.37)
Seeking (mean, SD)#	36.33 (11.49)	27.12 (14.03)

Note. SD = standard deviation. * $p < .05$; # $p < .1$.

3.3 Electrophysiological Responses

Heart Rate Variability. Mean differences in HF-HRV from each block to baseline during the task are depicted in Fig. 2. Reductions in HF-HRV were solely apparent among the low eco-anxiety participants. In other words, an unexpected increase in vagally-mediated HRV occurred throughout the task for the high eco-anxiety group. A Friedman test confirmed this effect across blocks for the high eco-anxiety group [$\chi^2_{(2)} = 6.00$, p < .05]. Despite superior HF-HRV among high eco-anxiety participants, group differences failed to reach statistical significance in all three Mann-Whitney tests.

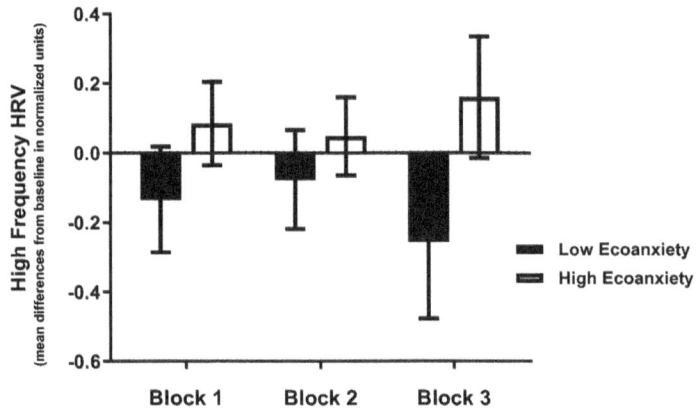

Fig. 2. Mean differences from baseline (expressed in normalized units) in high frequency HRV across the experimental blocks of the "emotion-to-picture match" task.

Skin Conductance Level. Mean differences in SCL from each block to baseline during the task are shown in Fig. 3. Contrary to our prediction, the high eco-anxiety group presented progressive *decreases* in the sympathetic-driven SCL during the task [$\chi^2_{(2)} = 4.63$, p = .09, ns], whereas low eco-anxiety subjects increased the SCL across blocks [$\chi^2_{(2)} = 5.40$, p = .07, ns].

Furthermore, group differences in SCL changes from baseline emerged for the second (U = 37.00, z = −2.27, p = .02) and the third (U = 43.00, z = −1.95, p = .05) blocks, with effect sizes of r = .45 and r = .38, respectively.

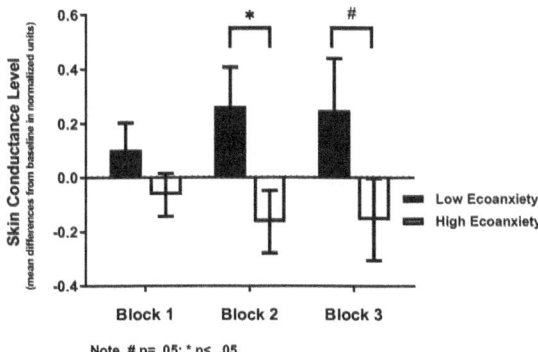

Fig. 3. Mean differences from baseline (expressed in normalized units) in the SCL across the experimental blocks of the "emotion-to-picture match" Task.

4 Discussion

The cost-effectiveness of virtual reality exposure therapies (VRET) has quickly made them popular in recent years, expanding their use in many health applications. VRET have nonetheless important technical demands in the conception and synchronization of both the target (therapeutical) and the whole environment (neutral context scenarios) stimuli, to provide a smooth and an effective immersion in the real experience of the digital environment. Part of these is usually accomplished by coupling brain-computer interfaces or biofeedback devices to the VRET controlling system. Other demands, however, depend on the properties and impact of stimulation. As such, we characterized both the behavioral and the physiological responses of eco-anxious people - who have been previously screened for eco-anxiety – facing either "neutral" or "environmental threat" images. Our main findings are broadly opposite to our hypotheses, thus leading us to dispute the concept of eco-anxiety on several grounds.

First, high eco-anxiety participants seem to address environmental threat stimuli with significantly more anger than low eco-anxious people. Crucially, the groups did not significantly differ in the mean frequencies of 'fear' and 'panic' attributed to those stimuli. However, both 'fear' and 'panic' are core emotions in anxiety disorders and are often engaged with hypervigilance in chronic anxious people (Chalmers et al. 2014; Forte et al. 2021). Such behavioral outcome is therefore incompatible with an anxiety concept. Nonetheless, eco-anxious people did report significantly more 'panic' than non-eco-anxious people when facing neutral stimuli. This could reflect an overall 'catastrophizing' approach to the task.

Second, both the HRV and the SCL results yielded by eco-anxious people are at odds with an anxious condition. Decreases in HF-HRV (reflecting parasympathetic withdrawal) and increases in SCL reactivity (reflecting sympathetic arousal) were strikingly produced by the 'low' but not the 'high' eco-anxiety group. On the one hand, emotions such as 'worry' (Brosschot et al. 2007) and 'panic' (Pittig et al. 2013) have usually been associated with chronic reductions in HRV and form the cognitive core of anxiety disorders. Neither of those were more prevalent among the eco-anxious participants during the environmental threat stimuli. On the other hand, both 'worry' and 'panic' are known to promote steady increases in SCL (Cacioppo et al. 2016). But it's not a rule of thumb that all negative emotions lead to an augmented SCL. Skin conductance responses after a sadness induction can be significantly lower than those after a neutral emotion induction, irrespectively of the stress experienced (Zhan et al. 2017).

Although this study is underpowered to detect subtle task effects in the participants' physiological responses – the large SEM suggested high interindividual variability –, we unveiled a pattern of fast parasympathetic responses among the high eco-anxiety scorers, likely mediated through anger and resentment. Likewise, Wu and colleagues (2019) compared the effects of video induction of 'amusement', 'anger' and 'fear' and found significantly larger HRV in the angry condition than in the fearful condition, as it might be the case in our data.

The generalized unsafety theory of stress (Brosschot et al. 2017; Thayer & Lane 2009) proposes that the stress response is usually active per default, but that it is inhibited whenever safety is perceived. With this in mind, we cannot rule out the possibility that the interspersed neutral stimuli presented throughout the task could have provided a safety cue to those who are generally more concerned with environmental threats, thereby preventing both the increase in the sympathetic response (SCL) and the parasympathetic withdrawal (HF-HRV). Nevertheless, an increased HF-HRV also could contribute to maintain an intense attention to the task cognitive demands, something that has been observed in both healthy (Siennicka et al. 2019) and anxious individuals (Ramírez et al. 2015).

Our analysis did not account for the symptom severity. It is conceivable that a mild or subclinical form of eco-anxiety might not induce overt parasympathetic withdrawal and/or tonic sympathetic activation as typically seen in anxiety disorders. Indeed, one study examining young participants with or without subclinical anxiety has also failed to detect differences in HRV between them (Forte et al. 2021). In addition, although participants were asked to refrain from caffeine, alcohol, and exercise for 2 h before testing, we did not control for other confounders such as substance use, exercise habits and nutritional status, all known to influence the autonomic control of the heart and the sympathetic control of the electrodermal response (Cacioppo et al. 2016).

Taken together, this study emphasizes the need for carefully planning of the graphic elements that make up both the therapeutic and the scenario stimuli when designing virtual reality therapeutic environments. In the specific case of "eco-anxious" people, their dysphoric anticipation of climate catastrophes could be a "hard nut to crack" through VRET given that anger and resentment emotions aroused by the target stimuli may eventually compromise treatment compliance. Future studies should clarify the nature of "eco-anxiety" by employing an event-related analysis to elucidate which physiological responses are evoked on a trial-by-trial basis.

Acknowledgments. This study was supported by UNIDCOM under a grant from the Fundação para a Ciência e Tecnologia (FCT) No. UIDB/00711/2020 attributed to UNIDCOM – Unidade de Investigação em Design e Comunicação, Lisbon, Portugal.

Disclosure of Interests. The authors have no competing interests to declare that are relevant to the content of this article.

References

Ahmadpour, N., Randall, H., Choksi, H., Gao, A., Vaughan, C., Poronnik, P.: Virtual reality interventions for acute and chronic pain management. Int. J. Biochem. Cell Biol. **114**, 105568 (2019). https://doi.org/10.1016/j.biocel.2019.105568

Brosschot, J.F., Verkuil, B., Thayer, J.F.: Exposed to events that never happen: Generalized unsafety, the default stress response, and prolonged autonomic activity. Neurosci. Biobehav. Rev. **74**(Pt B), 287–296 (2017)

Cacioppo, J.T., Tassinary, L.G., Berntson, G.G. (eds.): Handbook of psychophysiology, 4th edn. Cambridge University Press, Cambridge (2016)

Chalmers, J.A., Quintana, D.S., Abbott, M.J., Kemp, A.H.: Anxiety Disorders are Associated with Reduced Heart Rate Variability: A Meta-Analysis. Front. Psych. **5**, 80 (2014)

Cheng, Y.C., Su, M.I., Liu, C.W., Huang, Y.C., Huang, W.L.: Heart rate variability in patients with anxiety disorders: a systematic review and meta-analysis. Psychiatry Clin. Neurosci. **76**(7), 292–302 (2022)

Clayton, S.: Climate anxiety: psychological responses to climate change. J. Anxiety Disord. **74**, 102263 (2020)

Davis, K.L., Panksepp, J.: The brain's emotional foundations of human personality and the Affective Neuroscience Personality Scales. Neurosci. Biobehav. Rev. **35**(9), 1946–1958 (2011)

Demeco, A., et al.: Immersive virtual reality in post-stroke rehabilitation: a systematic review. Sensors **23**(3), 1712 (2023)

Forte, G., Favieri, F., Oliha, E.O., Marotta, A., Casagrande, M.: Anxiety and attentional processes: the role of resting heart rate variability. Brain Sci. **11**(4), 480 (2021)

GDB. Global, regional, and national incidence, prevalence, and years lived with disability for 310 diseases and injuries, 1990-2015: a systematic analysis for the Global Burden of Disease Study 2015. Lancet **388**, 1545–602(2016)

Hogg, T., Stanley, S., O'Brien, L., Wilson, M., Watsford, C.: The Hogg Eco-Anxiety Scale: development and validation of a multidimensional scale. Glob. Environ. Chang. **71**, 102391 (2021)

Kaplan, E.A.: Is climate-related pre-traumatic stress syndrome a real condition? American Imago **77**(1), 81–104 (2020)

Krzystanek, M., et al.: Tips for effective implementation of virtual reality exposure therapy in phobias-a systematic review. Front. Psych. **12**, 737351 (2021)

Kurth, C., Pihkala, P.: Eco-anxiety: what it is and why it matters. Front. Psychol. **13**, 981814 (2022)

Lee, I., et al.: Cigarette pack size and consumption: a randomized cross-over trial. Addiction **118**(3), 489–499 (2023)

Mantzari, E., Ventsel, M., Ferrar, J., Pilling, M.A., Hollands, G.J., Marteau, T.M.: Impact of wine bottle and glass sizes on wine consumption at home: a within- and between- households randomized controlled trial. Addiction **117**(12), 3037–3048 (2022)

Niedderer, K., et al.: Design for behaviour change as a driver for sustainable innovation: implementation in the private and public sectors. Int. J. Des. **10**(2), 67–85 (2016)

Panksepp, J.: The cross-mammalian neurophenomenology of primal emotional affects: from animal feelings to human therapeutics. J. Comp. Neurol. **524**(8), 1624–1635 (2016)

Pittig, A., Arch, J.J., Lam, C.W., Craske, M.G.: Heart rate and heart rate variability in panic, social anxiety, obsessive-compulsive, and generalized anxiety disorders at baseline and in response to relaxation and hyperventilation. Int. J. Psychophysiol. **87**(1), 19–27 (2013)

Porges, S.W.: Orienting in a defensive world: mammalian modifications of our evolutionary heritage. A polyvagal theory. Psychophysiology **32**(4), 301–318 (1995)

Ramírez, E., Ortega, A.R., Reyes Del Paso, G.A.: Anxiety, attention, and decision making: yhe moderating role of heart rate variability. Int. J. Psychophysiol. **98**(3 Pt 1), 490–496 (2015)

Shaffer, F., Ginsberg, J.P.: An overview of heart rate variability metrics and norms. Front. Public Health **5**, 258 (2017)

Siennicka, A., et al.: Resting heart rate variability, attention and attention maintenance in young adults. Int. J. Psychophysiol. **143**, 126–131 (2019)

Talarowska, M., Wysiadecki, G., Chodkiewicz, J.: Affective neuroscience personality scales and early maladaptive schemas in depressive disorders. Int. J. Environ. Res. Public Health **19**(13), 8062 (2022)

Task Force of the European Society, 1996.Task Force of the European Society. Guidelines - heart rate variability. Euro Heart J. **17**, 354–381 (1996)

Thayer, J.F., Lane, R.D.: Claude Bernard and the heart-brain connection: further elaboration of a model of neurovisceral integration. Neurosci. Biobehav. Rev. **33**(2), 81–88 (2009)

Wu, Y., Gu, R., Yang, Q., Luo, Y.J.: How do amusement, anger and fear influence heart rate and heart rate variability? Front. Neurosci. **13**, 1131 (2019)

Zhan, J., et al.: Regulating anger under stress via cognitive reappraisal and sadness. Front. Psychol. **8**, 1372 (2017)

Are We There Yet? Unravelling Usability Challenges and Opportunities in Collaborative Immersive Analytics for Domain Experts

Fahim Arsad Nafis[1]([⊠])(iD), Alexander Rose[1](iD), Simon Su[2](iD), Songqing Chen[1](iD), and Bo Han[1](iD)

[1] George Mason University, Fairfax, VA 22030, USA
{fnafis2,arose23,sqchen,bohan}@gmu.edu
[2] Montgomery College, Rockville, MD 20850, USA
simon.su@montgomerycollege.edu
https://www.gmu.edu/ , https://www.montgomerycollege.edu/

Abstract. In the ever-evolving discipline of high-dimensional scientific data, collaborative immersive analytics (CIA) offers a promising frontier for domain experts in complex data visualization and interpretation. This research presents a comprehensive framework for conducting usability studies on the extended reality (XR) interface of ParaView, an open-source CIA system. By employing established human-computer interaction (HCI) principles, including *Jakob Nielsen's Usability Heuristics, Cognitive Load Theory, NASA Task Load Index, System Usability Scale, Affordance Theory,* and *Gulf of Execution and Evaluation,* this study aims to identify underlying usability issues and provide guidelines for enhancing user experience in scientific domains. Our findings reveal significant usability challenges in the ParaView XR interface that impede effective teamwork and collaboration. For instance, the lack of synchronous collaboration, limited communication methods, and the absence of role-based data access are critical areas that need attention. Additionally, inadequate error handling, insufficient feedback mechanisms, and limited support resources during application use require extensive improvement to fully utilize the system's potential. Our study suggests potential improvements to overcome the existing usability barriers of the collaborative immersive system.

Keywords: Immersive Analytics · Collaboration · Usability Study · Scientific Data Visualization

1 Introduction

Visualizing high-volume scientific data is crucial in a wide range of domains, such as space weather forecasting [10,77], medical imaging [9,64], and high-performance computing (HPC) [40,59], as shown in Fig. 1. Immersive analytics (IA) [46] is a groundbreaking way to drastically improve engagement with

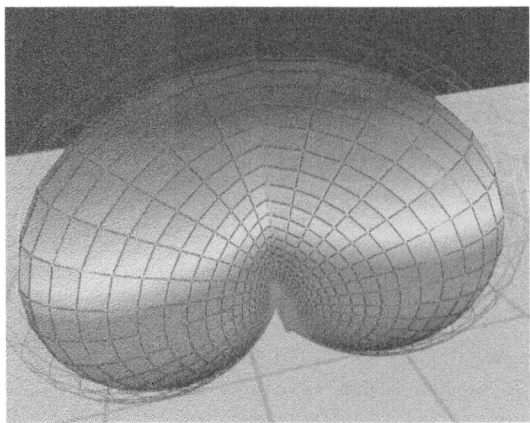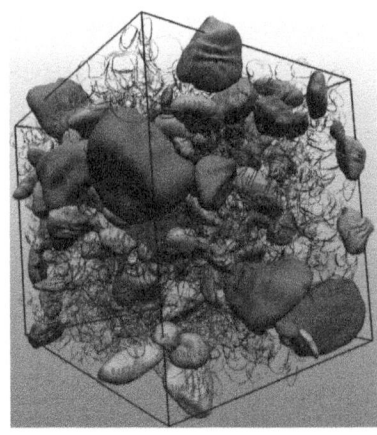

Fig. 1. Visualization of 3D scalar active region magnetic field (left), visualization of the concrete modelling and simulation on a high-performance computer (right).

complex datasets by granting six degrees of freedom (6DoF) movement for the users [43,72]. As the next generation of immersive analytics, collaborative immersive analytics (CIA) [16] has emerged as a transformative approach to data exploration and decision-making. Compared to the traditional IA approach, the CIA empowers domain experts to dive deeper into complex datasets, allowing them to gain richer insights and facilitating interdisciplinary collaboration.

In this paper, we investigate ParaView [7,11], a popular platform to visualize scientific data. Specifically, we examine the ParaView XR interface, as shown in Fig. 2, to explore its challenges and opportunities in usability in the context of CIA. It extends the traditional capabilities of ParaView by incorporating virtual reality (VR) [17] and augmented reality (AR) [12] technology, allowing users to freely navigate and interact with large-scale scientific datasets [67]. Its significance lies in facilitating collaborative exploration and decision-making among multiple domain experts.

The potential of the CIA to revolutionize the scientific workflow is immense, yet several usability challenges hinder its full integration [19,26,58]. Different from traditional interfaces, immersive environments require users to engage with the data through diverse methods. It poses unique challenges in collaborative settings where multiple users must effectively share and manipulate data, yet potentially without physical cues. Although ParaView has significantly advanced the integration of XR features in data visualization, the usability of these tools in collaborative scientific environments remains uncharted [41,42]. Therefore, conducting a usability study in this virtual environment is crucial to identifying and overcoming barriers to effective collaboration and data exploration.

Specifically, our study aims to answer the following four research questions (RQs), designed to meticulously examine multiple aspects of usability and collaborative efficacy of the ParaView XR interface:

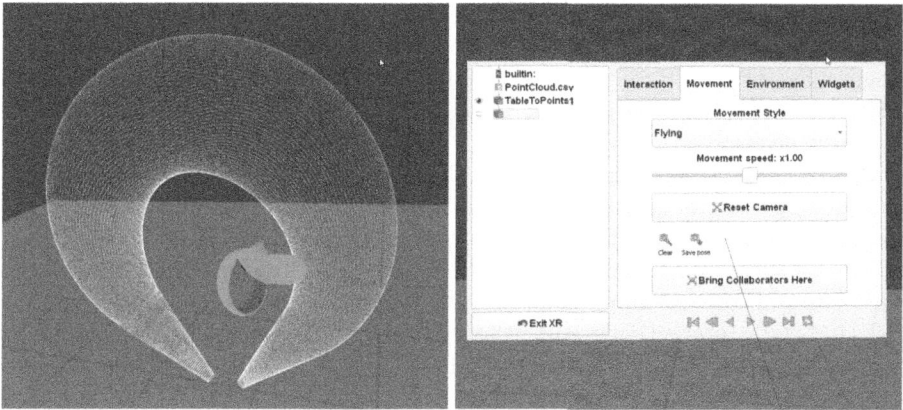

Fig. 2. Interaction with the visualization of 3D vector dipole magnetic field in ParaView XR interface (left), a screenshot of ParaView XR interface user menu (right).

- **RQ1:** How easily can domain scientists individually learn and utilize the immersive visualization capabilities of ParaView?
- **RQ2:** How effective are the collaborative tools within ParaView when used in a multi-user immersive environment by domain scientists?
- **RQ3:** What usability challenges do domain scientists encounter while using the ParaView XR interface in a collaborative setting?
- **RQ4:** What improvements or additional features can be implemented to enhance the collaborative user experience of the ParaView XR interface?

In this research, we present a comprehensive framework for conducting usability studies on CIA systems. Specifically, we make the following contributions:

- Design an experimental framework tailored specifically for usability studies in CIA by utilizing established principles in the HCI area.
- Conduct a pilot study to validate the effectiveness of this framework.
- Investigate the usability issues of the ParaView XR interface and analyze its user experience in individual and collaborative contexts.
- Provide recommendations and enhancements for CIA systems to improve their usability and user experience.

2 Background

2.1 Collaborative Immersive Analytics

Immersive analytics is an emerging field that combines data visualization and analytics with immersive technologies, such as VR and AR [46]. Utilizing human natural spatial skills by presenting data in three-dimensional settings makes exploring and comprehending complex datasets easier. This approach promotes a more intuitive understanding by visually representing information in an engaging immersive environment [14, 29]. Several research directions in IA are actively being pursued to enhance usability. Recent studies systematically review the design space of IA [60], introduce a toolkit to facilitate the development of IA applications [20], and provide a web-based framework to simplify the creation of IA experiences [18].

CIA extends the paradigm of IA by allowing multiple users to simultaneously visualize, and interact with data within shared virtual environments. A recent study shows that the use of shared surfaces and spaces can enhance collaborative data visualization in immersive co-location environments [45]. Another investigation focuses on the design of collaborative frameworks, aiming to improve teamwork and data interaction within the virtual environment [50]. A recent pilot study examines how different modes of collaboration and positional arrangements affect user performance on IA tasks in VR [19].

2.2   Human-Computer Interaction Principles

In this section, we introduce several established principles of HCI that are fundamental to designing and evaluating user interfaces for this study.

Jakob Nielsen's 10 Heuristics [51] are a widely adopted set of principles for assessing and improving user interface design. This principle covers multiple aspects of a system to examine its efficacy. These heuristics cover aspects, such as visibility of system status, the match between the system and the real world, user control and freedom, consistency and standards, error prevention, recognition rather than recall, flexibility and efficiency of use, aesthetic and minimalist design, help for users to recognize and recover from errors, and adequate help and documentation. Jakob Nielsen's heuristic principle has been extensively applied in various studies [23, 73] assessing the usability of virtual environments, making it a suitable choice for evaluating the experiments in this study.

Cognitive Load Theory (CLT) [68] explains how information processing demands can affect a user's ability to perform tasks effectively. According to this theory, human memory can be divided into three main types of cognitive load: intrinsic, extraneous, and germane [55]. The intrinsic load relates to the complexity of the learning material itself. The extraneous load comes from how the information is shown, which can make learning harder if it is not done well. The german load involves mental activities that help to understand and organize new information. This theory can help in understanding how immersive environments impact the cognitive processing of complex datasets. Several studies [36, 65] use this theoretical strategy to minimize unnecessary cognitive load improving learning and data comprehension.

Affordance Theory [32] describes how an object's perceived properties influence its usability. It is relevant in VR and AR environments where user interaction modes are not standardized. When a system includes perceptible affordances, users find its features easy to use. Hidden affordances keep users unaware of certain features resulting in a less effective user experience. Users face false affordances of the system while interacting with elements that misleadingly suggest functionality.

System Usability Scale (SUS) [15] provides a reliable tool to measure the usability of a system. It offers quantitative data that help to assess how users can utilize these advantages in practice. Numerous studies [57,75] have used SUS to assess the usability of VR platforms in formal research.

Gulf of Execution and Evaluation [52] addresses the gap between users' intentions of a system and their actual experiences. The gulf of execution refers to the challenge of determining the necessary steps to achieve desired outcomes. The gulf of evaluation involves understanding the current state of the system and how it aligns with the user's objectives. Recent studies utilize this concept to analyze usability across diverse applications, such as VR video editing [49], and mediating human-robot interactions through mixed reality [69].

NASA Task Load Index (TLX) [35] is a widely used tool that measures workload to assess the user experience. It evaluates factors, such as mental, physical, and temporal demand, satisfaction, effort and frustration caused by performing a certain task [34]. A fixed questionnaire helps to identify potential overloads in a system. Several studies have used this questionnaire to evaluate the usability of VR software in various domains [27,80].

2.3   Usability Study of CIA Systems

As CIA systems gain attention, there is a growing need to understand and address their usability challenges [44]. Several critical factors, such as user interface design, interaction techniques, and collaboration mechanisms, can significantly impact the usability and effectiveness of these systems [26]. Existing works offer crucial insights into IA systems, emphasizing opportunities for improvement in graphical perception, and the broad applicability in mixed reality [38,74].

A recent study has explored the challenges and opportunities within the CIA, particularly through the use of hybrid user interfaces [76]. Another study has addressed the importance of group awareness in collaborative environments that integrate VR and desktop platforms [62].

Despite these studies, there remains a gap in fully understanding how domain experts utilize CIA in real-world scenarios. Most of the existing studies focus on generic tasks or user groups causing a lack of detailed insights into specific domain challenges and workflow integration. This study aims to bridge this gap by exploring the unique usability challenges and opportunities of a CIA system, mostly used by domain experts.

3   Methodology

This section outlines the comprehensive methodology used for the study. Experiment setup, participant demographics, experiment design, and evaluation metrics are briefly discussed to ensure clarity and reproducibility of the study.

Table 1. PC configurations for the experiment settings.

	PC 1	PC 2
CPU	Intel i7-13700K @3.4 GHz	Intel i9-9900X @3.4 GHz
RAM	32GB at 4800 MHz	32 GB at 4800 MHz
GPU	NVIDIA GeForce RTX 4070 Ti	NVIDIA GeForce RTX 3060 Ti

3.1   Experiment Setup

The experiments are conducted using ParaView Version 5.12.0 which is the latest public release during the study. The immersive visualization is facilitated through Meta Quest 2 headsets [47].

The hardware setup includes two high-performance PCs with the specifications mentioned in Table 1. Both Meta Quest 2 headsets are attached to PCs using USB-C cables during the experiments. Remote participants are allowed to use their desktops equipped with Oculus Rift headsets in the experiments.

3.2   Participants

The study involves ten participants, which comprises a diverse group of individuals concerning age, gender, and educational background. The gender distribution includes eight men and two women. The age range is broad, with six participants between 20 and 29 years, one from 30 to 39, one from 40 to 49, and two aged between 50 and 59. Considering the highest education level, participants are also varied, with five holding bachelor's degrees, three with master's degrees, and two with doctoral degrees. It ensures a wide range of educational backgrounds from basic university education to advanced research qualifications. Having four participants with a history of motion sickness provides an opportunity to explore motion sickness-related issues in our experiments.

The group offers a rich blend of expertise in data visualization, including seven researchers, one developer, and two analysts. It helps to get a comprehensive understanding of the usability challenges from different professional viewpoints. Most of the participants are familiar with ParaView (7 out of 10), complemented by their proficiency with other data visualization tools, such as Python Matplotlib [3] and Seaborn [5], Tableau [1], R [4], MATLAB [2], etc.

The participants' experience with VR technologies varies, with five classifying themselves as novices, three as intermediates, and two as experts. Participants specialize in data visualization across various fields such as scientific data, high-performance computing data, solar physics data, etc. However, only three participants have prior experience working on CIA projects.

3.3   Experiment Design

The study is structured into two distinct experiments. Each experiment is designed to evaluate different aspects of interaction within IA environments.

Experiment 1 is conducted individually. Experiment 2 is structured to investigate collaborative dynamics by pairing participants to work together.

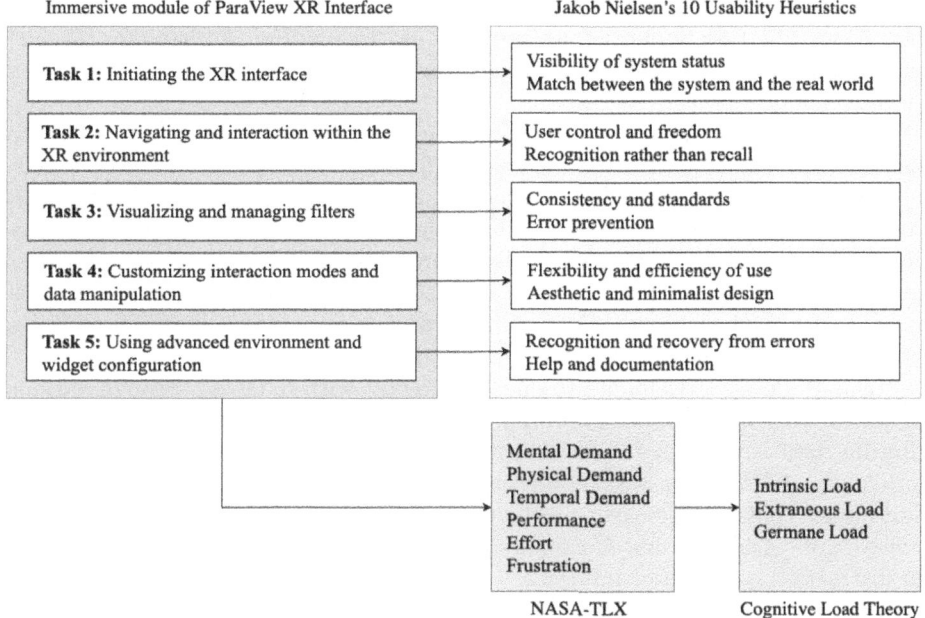

Fig. 3. Experiment design of the individual immersive analytics session.

Design of Experiment 1. The first experiment, as illustrated in Fig. 3, is divided into five major tasks, each consisting of several subtasks that participants are required to demonstrate under the guidance of a research coordinator. Each task is designed to align with two of Jakob Nielsen's usability heuristics. Furthermore, the overall experience of the experiment incorporates CLT, with the application of the NASA TLX questionnaire to evaluate the cognitive demands imposed on participants.

Task 1 focuses on initiating the XR interface, where participants are required to locate and activate the plugin, initiate the immersive experience from the ParaView desktop application, and familiarize themselves with the XR environment. This sequence is designed to ensure participants can transition smoothly from the desktop application to the XR environment. The task leverages the heuristic principle of *"Visibility of System Status"* by ensuring users are aware of the system's status during the transition. Participants are allowed sufficient time to get familiarized with the virtual environment to examine the *"Match between the System and the Real World"* heuristic.

Task 2 involves participants using hand controllers to interact within the XR space. The subtasks include user control, icon identification, and menu navigation through different activities such as moving toward data sets and accessing menus. This task examines the heuristic of *"User Control and Freedom"* allowing participants with the autonomy to navigate within the XR environment at their discretion. The task supports the heuristic of *"Recognition Rather than Recall"* by enabling users to independently perform tasks after their initial exposure in the user menu.

Task 3 asks participants to use existing filters within the XR interface to visualize and interact with data. This task includes adjusting camera positions, interacting with data, enabling and disabling filters, and managing environmental settings, such as floor visibility. The design of this task adheres to the heuristic of *"Consistency and Standards"* by maintaining familiar and consistent user interface conventions, which reduces the learning curve for the users. The task incorporates the heuristic of *"Error Prevention"* to minimize potential user errors by expecting clear warnings before potential mistakes in the user journey.

Task 4 allows participants to engage directly with datasets through various interaction methods such as grabbing, interactive cropping, scaling datasets, and altering data coordinates. This task promotes the heuristic of *"Flexibility and Efficiency of Use"* by assessing adaptability and personalization in the interaction modes that enhance user productivity. In addition, the task adheres to the heuristic of *"Aesthetic and Minimalist Design"* by examining participants' views on distraction on the user interface.

Task 5 involves participants in configuring the XR environment through various widgets, such as measuring the distance with scale and locating a certain data point in the virtual environment with a navigation panel. The design of this task is integrated with the heuristic of *"Recognition and Recovery from Errors"* which provides users with the ability to identify and correct errors easily. Lastly, the task incorporates the heuristic of *"Help and Documentation"* by requiring users to locate and access assistance resources within the system.

These five tasks collectively aim to explore usability within the XR environment through the lens of CLT, using the NASA-TLX questionnaire as an evaluation tool. The questionnaire helps quantify the cognitive load imposed on participants by assessing mental demands, effort, and stress levels in different tasks. The insights gained from this questionnaire are critical to ensure an efficient and satisfying user experience in IA environments.

Design of Experiment 2. The second experiment, as illustrated in Fig. 4 consists of five major tasks, each comprising several subtasks that participants are instructed to demonstrate under the guidance of a research coordinator. This experimental setup utilizes affordance theory and the gulf of execution and evaluation to provide a thorough understanding of the user experience and efficiency of the CIA.

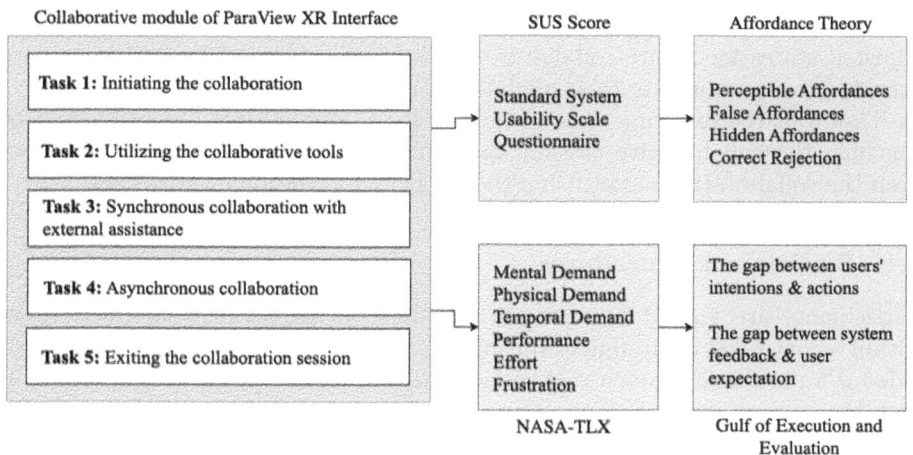

Fig. 4. Experiment design of the collaborative immersive analytics session.

During task 1, participants are provided with a pvsm[1] file to launch their interaction with the collaborative module using ParaView's desktop application. It requires users to activate the plugin, followed by selecting the appropriate XR runtime. Participants are instructed to modify the default identifier to their name for better recognition within the collaborative environment. At the end, they connect to the collaborative server and launch the collaborative setting.

Task 2 requires participants to engage directly with the collaborative features of the system at the beginner level. Users are asked to verbally recognize and call out the name or identifier of another collaborator within the virtual environment. They are instructed to make a gesture (waving) using the hand controller. Participants use the *"Bring Collaborator Here"* button to reposition the collaborator's avatar to a new location. Finally, they are asked to explore the availability of various collaborative tools, such as note-taking, data manipulation, and annotation.

Task 3 asks participants to attempt several synchronous collaborative tasks. Participants are tasked to perform various interactive operations such as grab, pick, and interactive crop on the data and show the modifications to their collaborator. Participants are also instructed to specifically point out areas of interest within the dataset to their collaborator, facilitating focused discussion. They are asked to use any existing widget (for example, ruler, navigation panel, etc.) of their choice to show its implementation to the collaborator. In the end, participants try to be involved in real-time communication between collaborators with and without external assistance.

Task 4 instructs participants to perform non-simultaneous collaborative work within the XR environment. Participants are asked to perform data manip-

---

[1] The pvsm file format stands for "ParaView State Machine", saves the state of a ParaView session, including data sources, filters, views, and other settings.

ulations, such as altering parameters or applying filters, and then save these adjusted states for future collaborators. The annotations and saved states are expected to communicate their analytical process asynchronously.

Task 5 of the experiment is straightforward. Participants are instructed to conclude the collaborative session, quit the XR environment, and disconnect from the collaborative server using the desktop application of ParaView.

3.4   Experiment Procedures

Participants are guided by research coordinators to perform specified tasks within a controlled environment during the experiments. Assistance is only provided if a participant fails a task three times, ensuring independent interaction with the system. After each experiment session, participants are asked verbally about any sensations of motion sickness.

Data Collection. User response is collected immediately following each experiment through a structured survey. The surveys are tailored to the specific requirements of the respective experiment session.

Following the first experiment, the first survey consists of 16 questions. The initial 10 questions target specific usability heuristics defined by Jakob Nielsen. The remaining six questions are based on the NASA-TLX, using a scale from *Low* (1) to *High* (10). This second part of the survey is designed to assess the cognitive load experienced by participants.

Following the second experiment, the second survey consists of 16 questions. The first 10 questions use the established SUS questionnaire. This standard questionnaire allows participants to rate their agreement on a scale ranging from *"Strongly Disagree"* to *"Strongly Agree"*, including options for *"Disagree,"* *"Neutral,"* and *"Agree."*. The following six questions, which are identical to the second part of Experiment 1, are based on the NASA-TLX focusing on evaluating the cognitive load concerning the gulf of execution and evaluation.

4   Results and Discussions

This section presents the results of two experiments aimed at assessing the usability of the ParaView XR interface. These experiments systematically evaluate the tool's performance and user interaction dynamics, with subsequent analysis based on established principles in HCI.

4.1   Results of Experiment 1

In the analysis of experiment 1, user responses are evaluated using Jakob Nielsen's heuristics, as shown in Fig. 5 and 6. The cognitive load during the individual interaction is assessed through the NASA-TLX questionnaire, as shown in Fig. 7.

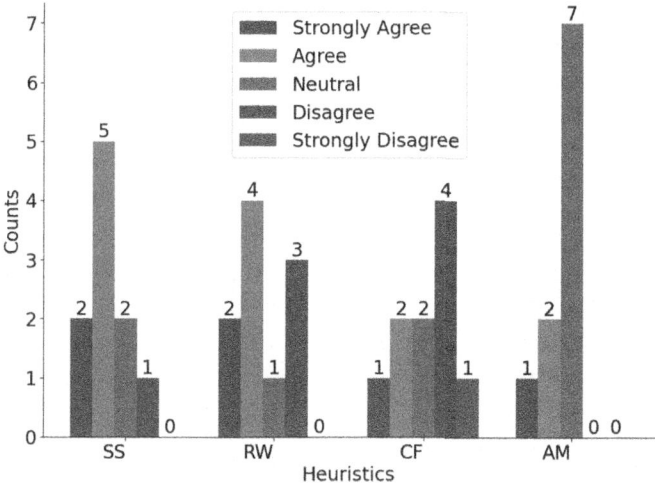

Fig. 5. Results of experiment 1 based on Jakob Nielsen's Heuristics. SS, RW, CF, and AM represent the visibility of system status, the match between the system and the real world, user control and freedom, and aesthetic and minimalist design, respectively.

Visibility of System Status. Most of the participants perceive the system to maintain the visibility of its status effectively, as denoted by **"SS"** in Fig. 5. The system is successful in informing users about its status. Most users receive clear indicators during their interactions, successfully informing them of the transition from the desktop application to the XR interface.

Match Between the System and the Real World. While the system partially meets real-world expectations, there are notable variances that impact user experience, as reflected by **"RW"** in Fig. 5. The fact that 6 out of 10 respondents agree or strongly agree with the statement indicates that the system generally uses terms that are familiar to users. However, the users who disagree highlight a critical area where the system's terminology may not align well with user expectations.

User Control and Freedom. It is essential to improve the undo and redo functionality to offer users more flexibility and control. Participants experience several challenges performing undo actions or reverting to a previous state, as presented by **"CF"** in Fig. 5, drastically impacting user control in the virtual environment. This result indicates a notable deficiency in the system's response to user errors.

Recognition rather than Recall. Identifying the icons and their functionalities within the ParaView XR interface indicates a strong alignment with the heuristic. The majority of participants, 8 out of 10, can identify the icons and their functionalities within the ParaView XR interface, as denoted by **"IR"** in Fig. 6. The interface elements are recognizable without needing to recall information from memory, which supports an intuitive user experience.

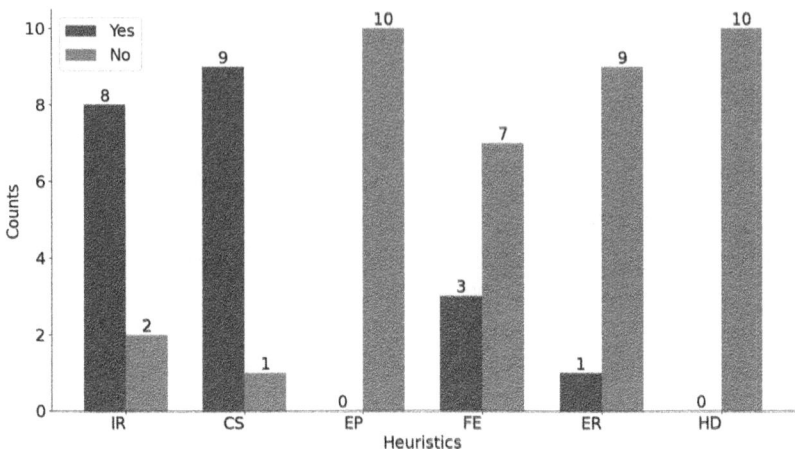

Fig. 6. Results of experiment 1 based on Jakob Nielsen's Heuristics. IR, CS, EP, FE, ER, and HD represent recognition rather than recall, consistency and standards, error prevention, flexibility and efficiency of use, recognition and recovery from error, and help and documentation, respectively.

Consistency and Standards. The majority of participants, with 9 out of 10 responses, find the interface actions and terms to be consistent throughout their use, as shown by **"CS"** in Fig. 6. Consistency is crucial to improve user familiarity and reduce the learning curve. The consistent interface of ParaView XR interface allows users to rely on past experiences rather than relearning new interactions.

Error Prevention. All 10 participants reported the absence of warnings or indicators before making mistakes, as reflected by **"EP"** in Fig. 6. It is crucial to recognize errors by offering users clear warnings or indicators, assisting in the avoidance of potential issues. The lack of such features in the system suggests critical oversight in interface design, which can lead to increased user frustration.

Flexibility and Efficiency of Use. The majority, consisting of 7 users share an opinion of a potential shortfall in the system's design to provide efficient tools that cater to diverse user requirements, as shown by **"FE"** in Fig. 6. The goal of the IA environment is to streamline and enhance user interactions. A lack of an effective workflow acceleration mechanism can lead to increased operational times and reduced overall productivity.

Aesthetic and Minimalist Design. The result highlights a predominantly neutral perspective, with 7 out of 10 users not particularly in favour or against the minimalism of the design, as referred by **"AM"** in Fig. 5. Immersive applications are expected to provide an intuitive experience by focusing on essential elements and minimizing unnecessary information. The outcome supports that the user interface in the existing system adequately delivers information.

Recognition and Recovery from Error. A crucial aspect of maintaining user confidence and minimizing frustration during interaction is helping users recognize and recover from errors efficiently. However, 9 out of 10 participants indicate that the system does not help them in this regard, as denoted by **"ER"** in Fig. 6. The system lacks the necessary feedback mechanisms or instructional guidance to alert users about errors and guide them towards solutions effectively.

Help and Documentation. A system should offer accessible and useful documentation or on-the-spot help to assist users in resolving issues or uncertainties. However, the result shows unanimous user feedback, indicating that no help or documentation is provided when stuck on a task in the system, as reflected by **"HD"** in Fig. 6. The absence of such support in the system can lead to increased frustration, as users are left to troubleshoot issues without guidance.

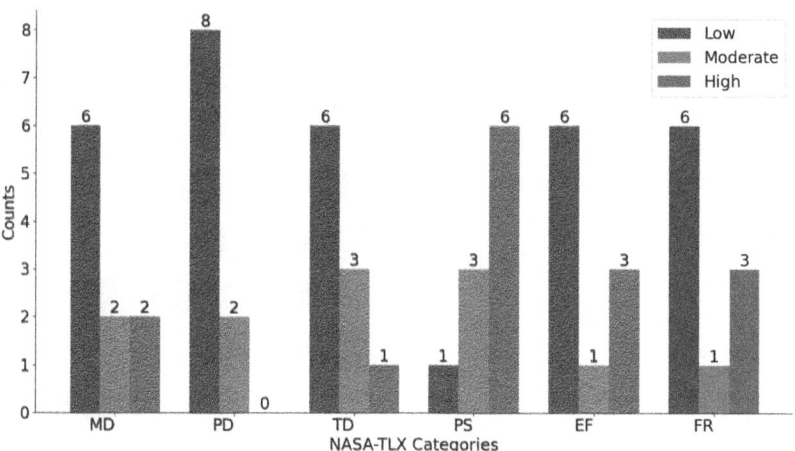

Fig. 7. Results of experiment 1 based on NASA-TLX. MD, PD, TD, PS, EF, and FR represent mental demand, physical demand, temporal demand, performance satisfaction, effort, and frustration, respectively.

Analyzing the Cognitive Load. The responses from the NASA-TLX questionnaire, as shown in Fig. 7, indicate a lower trend of mental, physical, and temporal demands experienced by participants during the individual task. It suggests that the tasks do not require significant cognitive resources and physical effort. A significant majority feel satisfaction with their performance while experiencing the immersive experience individually. Although the task is challenging for some, the majority of participants report for low level of effort and frustration. Overall, participants face fewer challenges and cognitive load while experiencing the ParaView XR interface individually without any requirement of collaboration.

4.2   Results of Experiment 2

In the analysis of results from experiment 2, user responses will be evaluated by combining the SUS and the affordance theory. In addition, the execution and evaluation will be assessed using the NASA-TLX questionnaire, providing information on user expectations in the collaborative environment.

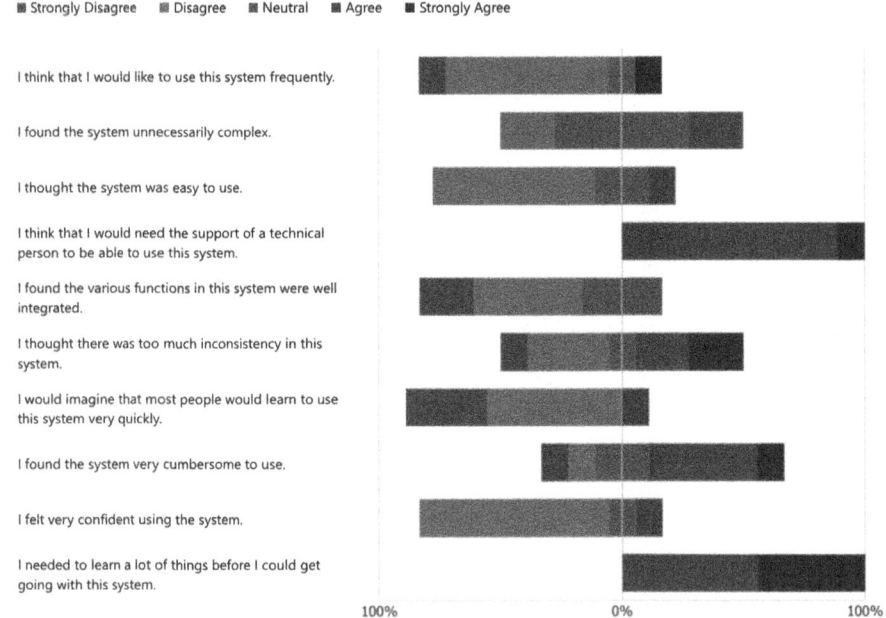

Fig. 8. Results on experiment 2 based on the SUS questionnaire.

System Usability Scale is used to assess the usability of the CIA system used in this experiment, as shown in Fig. 8. The SUS score obtained for the collaborative module of the ParaView XR interface is **32.78**, which significantly indicates the challenges encountered by participants during collaborative sessions. This

SUS score marks below the threshold of 68 which is considered as the benchmark for above-average usability. This low score reflects substantial usability barriers that hinder effective user interaction and collaboration.

Task-Wise Analysis Based on Affordance Theory. The underlying cause of the low score in SUS is evident in the achievement of the tasks in experiment 2.

In task 1, participants effectively engage with the collaborative module by activating the plugin, selecting the appropriate XR runtime and customizing the default identifier, demonstrating an example of perceptible affordance. However, they encounter difficulties in launching the collaborative settings due to an inactive button, indicating a false affordance in the system.

In task 2, participants experience perceptible affordance by successfully recognizing other collaborators and performing gestures using hand controllers. However, while using the *"Bring Collaborators Here"* button to reposition avatars, participants face false affordance in the system causing unexpected overlap of the avatars. The system's inability to accurately locate users in both real-world and virtual environments is observed during the experiment, highlighting an inadequacy in environmental knowledge and contextual understanding. Participants faced a limitation of collaborative tools for data manipulation or annotation, which is a design gap in the system.

In task 3, though participants perform the interactive operation, they are unable to share it with their collaborators because of the asynchronous nature of the system. All participants fail to point out areas of interest within the data set and showcase the implementation of existing widgets to their collaborators due to the same challenge of inability to synchronize. The absence of any communication method in the system, such as voice or text, hinders the ability to synchronize. All of these issues are identified as a design deficiency in the capabilities of the system.

In task 4, participants encounter false affordance in the system while engaging in nonsimultaneous collaborative work in the CIA system. Despite completing the required subtasks, participants fail to save the modified states to be shared with future collaborators due to system constraints. The lack of role-based access control in the system prevents effective management of user roles, such as collaborator, reviewer and observer, causing challenges to ensuring seamless collaboration among participants.

In task 5, participants face challenges when trying to disconnect from the collaborative server within the virtual space. There is no visible button on the XR interface to disconnect directly from the collaborative server, reflecting a hidden affordance in the system.

In general, the system contains numerous false affordances, hidden affordances, and design deficiencies which result in significant usability challenges.

Analyzing Gulf of Execution and Evaluation. The responses from the NASA-TLX questionnaire, as shown in Fig. 9, indicate varying levels of mental,

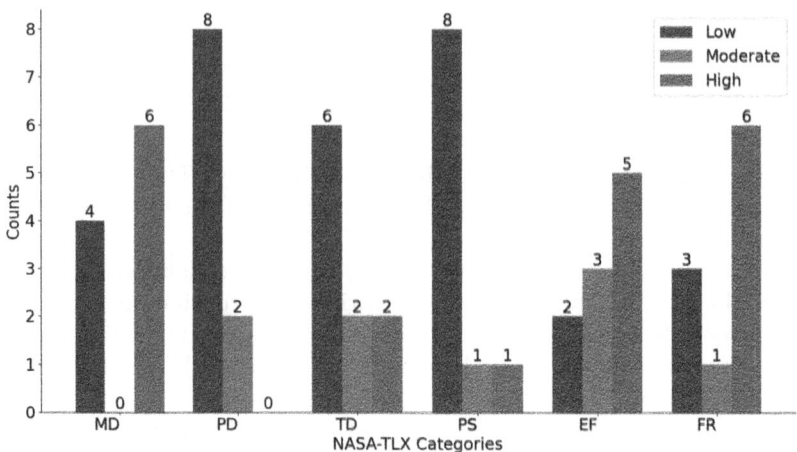

Fig. 9. Results of experiment 2 based on NASA-TLX. MD, PD, TD, PS, EF, and FR represent mental demand, physical demand, temporal demand, performance satisfaction, effort, and frustration, respectively.

physical, and temporal demands experienced by participants. Mental demand appears to be high for the majority of the participants suggesting tasks require a significant level of cognitive processing. Temporal demand varies from user to user due to inconsistent performance and unexpected behaviour of the system. There is a negative trend of performance satisfaction, effort, and frustration among participants in the collaborative experience compared to the individual experience.

The result highlights a significant gulf in execution, where the actions required by the system do not align with the mental models of the participants. This suggests that efficiently translating intentions into actions is a challenge in the CIA system. The recurring system lags and unexpected behaviour worsen the gulf of evaluation, as these issues hinder users' ability to interpret system responses accurately. The observed decline in performance satisfaction highlights disparities between expected and actual system performance. The increased frustration and required efforts, in collaborative settings, compared to individual scenarios, reflect the gulfs of execution and evaluation becoming more noticeable in the CIA system.

4.3   Key Findings in the CIA Module

This section presents the key findings derived from the experimental evaluation of the CIA module of the ParaView XR interface.

- The CIA module lacks support for synchronous collaboration and communication techniques for users.
- The CIA system cannot assign user roles among collaborators, affecting uninterrupted user experience.

– The CIA system is ineffective in resolving conflict resolution in shared spaces between collaborators due to insufficient contextual awareness.

5 Recommendations

This section shares a set of strategic recommendations aimed at enhancing the capabilities of the ParaView XR interface. These recommendations are specifically tailored for domain experts engaged in complex data visualization tasks.

Real-Time Synchronization in Collocated and Distributed Environments. Real-time synchronization is important in CIA. It becomes even more crucial especially when domain experts work in both collocated and distributed settings [24,56]. The goal is to ensure that all participants have a consistent and up-to-date view of the data, irrespective of their physical location, facing the challenge of minimizing latency across varied network conditions [30].

One approach to address this issue is implementing a differential synchronization algorithm [31] which allows the system to transmit the changes made in the shared environment instead of the entire data set. Adding a local caching scheme can significantly enhance real-time synchronization in collocated and distributed environments by reducing the frequency of data transmissions [79].

Adaptive synchronization [33] strategies based on the type of data and the specific collaboration context can further optimize the synchronization process. For example, prioritizing the synchronization of critical data or using delta encoding techniques to minimize the amount of transmitted data can be utilized [70].

Furthermore, modern network protocols such as WebRTC [37] can enhance the communication infrastructure of the CIA, maintaining a secure and reliable channel to transmit data [54]. It can be an ideal choice for handling the complexities of interactive data visualizations involving high-dimensional data sets because it supports real-time media and data channels [48].

Dynamic Role-Based Access Control (RBAC) in CIA. Implementation of RBAC [61] can improve security and ensure appropriate access permissions in CIA environments. Traditionally, RBAC models statically assign permissions based on predefined policies [28]. However, permissions may need to be adjusted in real-time for a dynamic collaborative environment based on various contextual factors, such as user roles, location, current activities, etc. [53].

Another advanced approach can be attribute-based access control [39] which allows access based on attributes associated with users, resources, and environmental conditions. It provides more flexible access control policies which are dynamically evaluated and enforced based on the changing attributes within the collaborative environment [63]. Integrating advanced machine learning algorithms can facilitate the automatic adjustment of access controls based on behaviour patterns [6].

Integrating Environmental Context Awareness into Simultaneous Localization and Mapping (SLAM). To enable the construction of 3D maps and the tracking of user positions and orientations within the environment for CIA applications, SLAM [25] algorithms are essential [21]. Sole dependency on sensor data, such as depth cameras makes traditional SLAM algorithms ineligible for the collaborative environment. This limitation can be addressed by integrating environmental context awareness into the mixed reality-based systems [22].

By leveraging computer vision and machine learning techniques, semantic SLAM [78] algorithms can identify and recognize specific objects, surfaces, or environmental features. It uses this semantic information to improve the accuracy of mapping and localization. Deep learning-based SLAM [66] approaches leverage deep neural networks to improve the reliability of SLAM algorithms. It can perform better in challenging environments or when dealing with dynamic scenes. Utilizing recurrent neural networks (RNNs) or long short-term memory (LSTM) networks ensures accurate tracking and mapping in dynamic scenes [8,13]. Convolutional neural networks (CNNs) can assist in feature extraction and improve the correctness of feature tracking [71].

6   Conclusion

This study conducts an extensive experiment on ParaView's capabilities in facilitating CIA. It uncovers important insights into both the platform's strengths and the areas needing improvements. Our findings from this research demonstrate that the collaboration mode of ParaView currently presents significant usability issues that hinder effective teamwork. Considering the unsatisfactory sentiment among users, the CIA system demands an urgent need for enhancements. As CIA becomes increasingly ubiquitous in professional settings, the simplicity of tool navigation and the clarity of the feedback provided is paramount for user experience.

Usability in the CIA is not a feature anymore. When the usability barriers are high, it can obstruct user engagement, leading to underutilization of potential technology. Therefore, it is essential to fully leverage the collaborative capabilities and innovative potential of immersive analytics tools by optimizing their usability. Developers, practitioners and the research community can significantly enhance the usability and effectiveness of the CIA by considering the recommendations. We wish our research paves the way for more insightful, inclusive, and impactful CIA endeavours.

A   Ethics

This study has been approved by the Institutional Review Board (IRB) and does not raise ethical issues.

References

1. Business Intelligence and Analytics Software — Tableau. https://www.tableau.com/. Accessed 24 May 2024
2. MATLAB. https://www.mathworks.com/products/matlab.html. Accessed 24 May 2024
3. Matplotlib - Visualization with Python. https://matplotlib.org/. Accessed 24 May 2024
4. R: The R Project for Statistical Computing. https://www.r-project.org/. Accessed 24 May 2024
5. Seaborn: Statistical Data Visualization. https://seaborn.pydata.org/. Accessed 24 May 2024
6. Afshar, M., Samet, S., Usefi, H.: Incorporating behavior in attribute based access control model using machine learning. In: Proceedings of IEEE International Systems Conference (SysCon). pp. 1–8 (2021). https://doi.org/10.1109/SysCon48628.2021.9447115
7. Ahrens, J., Geveci, B., Law, C., Hansen, C., Johnson, C.: 36-paraview: an end-user tool for large-data visualization. Visualizat. Handbook **717**, 50038-1 (2005). https://doi.org/10.1016/B978-012387582-2/50038-1
8. Alam, M.S., Mohamed, F.B., Selamat, A., Hossain, A.B.: A review of recurrent neural network based camera localization for indoor environments. IEEE Access **11**, 43985–44009 (2023). https://doi.org/10.1109/ACCESS.2023.3272479
9. Alzubaidi, L., et al.: Novel transfer learning approach for medical imaging with limited labeled data. Cancers **13**(7), 1590 (2021). https://doi.org/10.3390/cancers13071590
10. Angryk, R.A., et al.: Multivariate time series dataset for space weather data analytics. Sci. Data **7**(1), 227 (2020). https://doi.org/10.1038/s41597-020-0548-x
11. Ayachit, U.: The ParaView Guide: A Parallel Visualization Application. Kitware, Inc., Clifton Park (2015). https://dl.acm.org/doi/book/10.5555/2789330
12. Azuma, R.T.: A survey of augmented reality. Pres. Teleoper. Virtual Environ. **6**(4), 355–385 (1997)
13. Azzam, R., Alkendi, Y., Taha, T., Huang, S., Zweiri, Y.: A stacked LSTM-based approach for reducing semantic pose estimation error. IEEE Trans. Inst. Meas. **70**, 1–14 (2021). https://doi.org/10.1109/TIM.2020.3031156
14. Bach, B., Dachselt, R., Carpendale, S., Dwyer, T., Collins, C., Lee, B.: Immersive analytics: exploring future interaction and visualization technologies for data analytics. In: Proceedings of ACM International Conference on Interactive Surfaces and Spaces (2016). https://doi.org/10.1145/2992154.2996365
15. Bangor, A., Kortum, P.T., Miller, J.T.: An empirical evaluation of the system usability scale. Int. J. Hum.-Comput. Interact. **24**(6), 574–594 (2008). https://doi.org/10.1080/10447310802205776
16. Billinghurst, M., Cordeil, M., Bezerianos, A., Margolis, T.: Collaborative immersive analytics. In: Immersive Analytics, pp. 221–257 (2018). https://doi.org/10.1007/978-3-030-01388-2_8
17. Burdea, G.C., Coiffet, P.: Virtual Reality Technology. John Wiley & Sons, Hoboken (2003)
18. Butcher, P.W.S., John, N.W., Ritsos, P.D.: VRIA: a web-based framework for creating immersive analytics experiences. IEEE Trans. Visual Comput. Graph. **27**(7), 3213–3225 (2021). https://doi.org/10.1109/TVCG.2020.2965109

19. Chen, L., Liang, H.N., Lu, F., Wang, J., Chen, W., Yue, Y.: Effect of collaboration mode and position arrangement on immersive analytics tasks in virtual reality: a pilot study. Appl. Sci. **11**(21), 10473 (2021). https://doi.org/10.3390/app112110473

20. Cordeil, M., et al.: IATK: an immersive analytics toolkit. In: Proceedings of IEEE Conference on Virtual Reality and 3D User Interfaces (VR), pp. 200–209 (2019). https://doi.org/10.1109/VR.2019.8797978

21. Covolan, J.P.M., Sementille, A.C., Sanches, S.R.R.: A mapping of visual SLAM algorithms and their applications in augmented reality. In: Proceedings of Symposium on Virtual and Augmented Reality (SVR), pp. 20–29 (2020). https://doi.org/10.1109/SVR51698.2020.00019

22. Dasgupta, A., Manuel, M., Mansur, R.S., Nowak, N., Gračanin, D.: Towards real time object recognition for context awareness in mixed reality: a machine learning approach. In: Proceedings of the 2020 IEEE Conference on Virtual Reality and 3D User Interfaces Abstracts and Workshops (VRW), pp. 262–268 (2020). https://doi.org/10.1109/VRW50115.2020.00054

23. DeYoung, J., Berry, J., Riggs, S., Wesson, J., Wertz, L.C.: Evaluating embodied navigation in virtual reality environments. In: Proceedings of IEEE Games, Entertainment, Media Conference (GEM), pp. 1–9 (2018). https://doi.org/10.1109/GEM.2018.8516499

24. Du, J., Zou, Z., Shi, Y., Zhao, D.: Zero latency: real-time synchronization of BIM data in virtual reality for collaborative decision-making. Autom. Constr. **85**, 51–64 (2018). https://doi.org/10.1016/j.autcon.2017.10.009

25. Durrant-Whyte, H., Bailey, T.: Simultaneous localization and mapping: part I. IEEE Rob. Autom. Maga. **13**(2), 99–110 (2006). https://doi.org/10.1109/MRA.2006.1638022

26. Ens, B., et al.: Grand challenges in immersive analytics. In: Proceedings of CHI Conference on Human Factors in Computing Systems, pp. 1–17 (2021). https://doi.org/10.1145/3411764.3446866

27. Feick, M., Kleer, N., Tang, A., Krüger, A.: The virtual reality questionnaire toolkit. In: Adjunct Proceedings of Annual ACM Symposium on User Interface Software and Technology, p. 68–69 (2020). https://doi.org/10.1145/3379350.3416188

28. Ferraiolo, D.F., Sandhu, R., Gavrila, S., Kuhn, D.R., Chandramouli, R.: Proposed NIST standard for role-based access control. ACM Trans. Inf. Syst. Secur. (TISSEC) **4**(3), 224–274 (2001). https://doi.org/10.1145/501978.501980

29. Fonnet, A., Prié, Y.: Survey of immersive analytics. IEEE Trans. Visual Comput. Graph. **27**(3), 2101–2122 (2021). https://doi.org/10.1109/TVCG.2019.2929033

30. Fraser, M., et al.: Revealing the realities of collaborative virtual reality. In: Proceedings of International Conference on Collaborative Virtual Environments (2000). https://doi.org/10.1145/351006.351010

31. Fraser, N.: Differential synchronization. In: Proceedings of ACM Symposium on Document Engineering, pp. 13–20 (2009). https://doi.org/10.1145/1600193.1600198

32. Gibson, J.J.: The Theory of Affordances. Hilldale, USA **1**(2), 67–82 (1977). https://hal.science/hal-00692033

33. Ginosar, R., Kol, R.: Adaptive synchronization. In: Proceedings International Conference on Computer Design. VLSI in Computers and Processors (Cat. No. 98CB36273), pp. 188–189 (1998). https://doi.org/10.1109/ICCD.1998.727042

34. Hart, S.G.: NASA-task Load Index (NASA-TLX); 20 years later. In: Proceedings of Human Factors and Ergonomics Society Annual Meeting, pp. 904–908 (2006). https://doi.org/10.1177/154193120605000909

35. Hart, S.G., Staveland, L.E.: Development of NASA-TLX (Task Load Index): results of empirical and theoretical research. In: Advances in Psychology, vol. 52, pp. 139–183. Elsevier, North-Holland (1988). https://doi.org/10.1016/S0166-4115(08)62386-9

36. Haryana, M.R.A., Warsono, S., Achjari, D., Nahartyo, E.: Virtual reality learning media with innovative learning materials to enhance individual learning outcomes based on cognitive load theory. Int. J. Manag. Educ. 20(3), 100657 (2022). https://doi.org/10.1016/j.ijme.2022.100657

37. Holmberg, C., Hakansson, S., Eriksson, G.: Web Real-Time Communication Use Cases and Requirements. RFC 7478 (2015). https://rfc-editor.org/rfc/rfc7478.txt

38. Hoppenstedt, B., et al.: Applicability of immersive analytics in mixed reality: usability study. IEEE Access 7, 71921–71932 (2019). https://doi.org/10.1109/ACCESS.2019.2919162

39. Hu, V.C., Kuhn, D.R., Ferraiolo, D.F., Voas, J.: Attribute-based access control. Computer 48(2), 85–88 (2015). https://doi.org/10.1109/MC.2015.33

40. Isaacs, K.E., et al.: State of the art of performance visualization. EuroVis (STARs) 3, 6 (2014). https://doi.org/10.2312/eurovisstar.20141177

41. Isenberg, P., Elmqvist, N., Scholtz, J., Cernea, D., Ma, K.L., Hagen, H.: Collaborative visualization: definition, challenges, and research agenda. Inf. Vis. 10(4), 310–326 (2011). https://doi.org/10.1177/1473871611412817

42. Kerren, A., Schreiber, F.: Toward the role of interaction in visual analytics. In: Proceedings of Winter Simulation Conference (WSC), pp. 1–13 (2012). https://doi.org/10.1109/WSC.2012.6465208

43. Kraus, M., et al.: Immersive analytics with abstract 3D visualizations: a survey. In: Proceedings of Computer Graphics Forum, vol. 41, pp. 201–229 (2022). https://doi.org/10.1111/cgf.14430

44. Kraus, M., Klein, K., Fuchs, J., Keim, D.A., Schreiber, F., Sedlmair, M.: The value of immersive visualization. IEEE Comput. Graph. Appl. 41(4), 125–132 (2021). https://doi.org/10.1109/MCG.2021.3075258

45. Lee, B., Hu, X., Cordeil, M., Prouzeau, A., Jenny, B., Dwyer, T.: Shared surfaces and spaces: collaborative data visualisation in a co-located immersive environment. IEEE Trans. Visual Comput. Graph. 27(2), 1171–1181 (2021). https://doi.org/10.1109/TVCG.2020.3030450

46. Marriott, K., et al.: Immersive Analytics, vol. 11190. Springer, Heidelberg (2018)

47. Meta: Quest 2. https://www.meta.com/quest/products/quest-2/. Accessed 24 May 2024

48. Nakazato, J., Nakagawa, K., Itoh, K., Fontugne, R., Tsukada, M., Esaki, H.: WebRTC over 5 G: a study of remote collaboration QoS in mobile environment. J. Netw. Syst. Manage. 32(1), 1 (2024). https://doi.org/10.1007/s10922-023-09778-5

49. Nguyen, C., DiVerdi, S., Hertzmann, A., Liu, F.: Vremiere: in-headset virtual reality video editing. In: Proceedings of CHI Conference on Human Factors in Computing Systems, pp. 5428–5438 (2017). https://doi.org/10.1145/3025453.3025675

50. Nguyen, H., Marendy, P., Engelke, U.: Collaborative framework design for immersive analytics. In: Proceedings of Big Data Visual Analytics (BDVA), pp. 1–8 (2016). https://doi.org/10.1109/BDVA.2016.7787044

51. Nielsen, J.: Usability inspection methods. In: Proceedings of Conference Companion on Human Factors in Computing Systems, pp. 413–414 (1994). https://dl.acm.org/doi/pdf/10.1145/259963.260531

52. Norman, D.A.: Cognitive engineering. User Cent. Syst. Des. 31(61), 2 (1986). https://doi.org/10.1201/b15703

53. Park, J.S., Sandhu, R., Ahn, G.J.: Role-based access control on the web. ACM Trans. Inf. Syst. Secur. **4**(1), 37–71 (2001). https://doi.org/10.1145/383775.383777

54. Petrangeli, S., Pauwels, D., van der Hooft, J., Wauters, T., De Turck, F., Slowack, J.: Improving quality and scalability of WebRTC video collaboration applications. In: Proceedings of ACM Multimedia Systems Conference, pp. 533–536 (2018). https://doi.org/10.1145/3204949.3208109

55. Plass, J.L., Moreno, R., Brünken, R.: Cognitive Load Theory. Cambridge University Press, Cambridge (2010)

56. Radu, I., Joy, T., Bowman, Y., Bott, I., Schneider, B.: A survey of needs and features for augmented reality collaborations in collocated spaces. In: Proceedings of the ACM on Human-Computer Interaction, vol. 5, no. (CSCW1) (2021). https://doi.org/10.1145/3449243

57. Ramaseri Chandra, A.N., El Jamiy, F., Reza, H.: A review on usability and performance evaluation in virtual reality systems. In: Proceedings of International Conference on Computational Science and Computational Intelligence (CSCI), pp. 1107–1114 (2019). https://doi.org/10.1109/CSCI49370.2019.00210

58. Reski, N., Alissandrakis, A., Kerren, A.: An empirical evaluation of asymmetric synchronous collaboration combining immersive and non-immersive interfaces within the context of immersive analytics. Front. Virtual Real. **2**, 743445 (2022). https://doi.org/10.3389/frvir.2021.743445

59. del Rosario, E., et al.: Gauge: an interactive data-driven visualization tool for HPC application I/O performance analysis. In: Proceedings of IEEE/ACM Fifth International Parallel Data Systems Workshop (PDSW), pp. 15–21 (2020). https://doi.org/10.1109/PDSW51947.2020.00008

60. Saffo, D., et al.: Unraveling the design space of immersive analytics: a systematic review. IEEE Trans. Visual Comput. Graph. **30**(1), 495–506 (2024). https://doi.org/10.1109/TVCG.2023.3327368

61. Sandhu, R.S.: Role-based access control. In: Advances in Computers, vol. 46, pp. 237–286. Elsevier (1998). https://doi.org/10.1016/S0065-2458(08)60206-5

62. Seraji, M.R., Stuerzlinger, W.: XVCollab: an immersive analytics tool for asymmetric collaboration across the virtuality spectrum. In: Proceedings of IEEE International Symposium on Mixed and Augmented Reality Adjunct (ISMAR-Adjunct), pp. 146–154 (2022). https://doi.org/10.1109/ISMAR-Adjunct57072.2022.00035

63. Servos, D., Osborn, S.L.: Current research and open problems in attribute-based access control. ACM Comput. Surv. **49**(4), 1–45 (2017). https://doi.org/10.1145/3007204

64. Shamshad, F., et al.: Transformers in medical imaging: a survey. Med. Image Anal. **88**, 102802 (2023). https://doi.org/10.1016/j.media.2023.102802

65. Souchet, A.D., Philippe, S., Lourdeaux, D., Leroy, L.: Measuring visual fatigue and cognitive load via eye tracking while learning with virtual reality head-mounted displays: a review. Int. J. Hum.-Comput. Interact. **38**(9), 801–824 (2022). https://doi.org/10.1080/10447318.2021.1976509

66. Su, P., Luo, S., Huang, X.: Real-time dynamic SLAM algorithm based on deep learning. IEEE Access **10**, 87754–87766 (2022). https://doi.org/10.1109/ACCESS.2022.3199350

67. Su, S., Lopez-Coto, I., Sherman, W.R., Sayrafian, K., Terrill, J.: Immersive ParaView: an immersive scientific workflow for the advancement of measurement science. In: Proceedings of IEEE International Symposium on Mixed and Augmented Reality Adjunct (ISMAR-Adjunct), pp. 139–145 (2022). https://doi.org/10.1109/ISMAR-Adjunct57072.2022.00034

68. Sweller, J., Van Merrienboer, J.J., Paas, F.G.: Cognitive architecture and instructional design. Educ. Psychol. Rev. **10**, 251–296 (1998). https://doi.org/10.1023/A:1022193728205
69. Szafir, D.: Mediating human-robot interactions with virtual, augmented, and mixed reality. In: Proceedings of the Virtual, Augmented and Mixed Reality, pp. 124–149 (2019). https://doi.org/10.1007/978-3-030-21565-1_9
70. Tan, H., Zhang, Z., Zou, X., Liao, Q., Xia, W.: Exploring the potential of fast delta encoding: marching to a higher compression ratio. In: Proceedings of IEEE International Conference on Cluster Computing (CLUSTER), pp. 198–208 (2020). https://doi.org/10.1109/CLUSTER49012.2020.00030
71. Tateno, K., Tombari, F., Laina, I., Navab, N.: CNN-SLAM: real-time dense monocular SLAM with learned depth prediction. In: Proceedings of the IEEE Conference on Computer Vision and Pattern Recognition, pp. 6243–6252 (2017). https://doi.org/10.48550/arXiv.1704.03489
72. Wagner, J., Stuerzlinger, W., Nedel, L.: The effect of exploration mode and frame of reference in immersive analytics. IEEE Trans. Visualizat. Comput. Graph. **28**(9) (2022). https://doi.org/10.1109/TVCG.2021.3060666
73. Wang, W., Cheng, J., Guo, J.L.: Usability of virtual reality application through the lens of the user community: a case study. In: Proceedings of Extended Abstracts of CHI Conference on Human Factors in Computing Systems, pp. 1–6 (2019). https://doi.org/10.1145/3290607.3312816
74. Whitlock, M., Smart, S., Szafir, D.A.: Graphical perception for immersive analytics. In: Proceedings of IEEE Conference on Virtual Reality and 3D User Interfaces (VR), pp. 616–625 (2020). https://doi.org/10.1109/VR46266.2020.00084
75. Wijaya, A.C., Munandar, M.W.A., Utaminingrum, F.: Usability testing of augmented reality for food advertisement based on mobile phone using system usability scale. In: Proceedings of International Conference on Sustainable Information Engineering and Technology (SIET), pp. 266–269 (2019). https://doi.org/10.1109/SIET48054.2019.8986118
76. Zagermann, J., Hubenschmid, S., Fink, D.I., Wieland, J., Reiterer, H., Feuchtner, T.: Challenges and opportunities for collaborative immersive analytics with hybrid user interfaces. In: Proceedings of IEEE International Symposium on Mixed and Augmented Reality Adjunct (ISMAR-Adjunct), pp. 191–195 (2023). https://doi.org/10.1109/ISMAR-Adjunct60411.2023.00044
77. Zhang, J., et al.: Earth-affecting solar transients: a review of progresses in solar cycle 24. Prog. Earth Planet. Sci. **8**(1), 56:1–56:102 (2021). https://doi.org/10.1186/s40645-021-00426-7
78. Zhang, L., Wei, L., Shen, P., Wei, W., Zhu, G., Song, J.: Semantic SLAM based on object detection and improved octomap. IEEE Access **6**, 75545–75559 (2018). https://doi.org/10.1109/ACCESS.2018.2873617
79. Zhang, W., Han, B., Hui, P.: SEAR: scaling experiences in multi-user augmented reality. IEEE Trans. Visual Comput. Graph. **28**(5), 1982–1992 (2022). https://doi.org/10.1109/TVCG.2022.3150467
80. Zheng, B., Jiang, X., Tien, G., Meneghetti, A., Panton, O.N.M., Atkins, M.S.: Workload assessment of surgeons: correlation between NASA TLX and blinks. Surg. Endosc. **26**, 2746–2750 (2012). https://doi.org/10.1007/s00464-012-2268-6

The Effect of Visual Design Using Biomorphic Designs on Walking Behavior in Virtual World

Mana Nakai[1] ⓘ, Misuzu Hasegawa[1], and Daiji Kobayashi[2]([✉]) ⓘ

[1] Graduate School of Chitose Institute of Science and Technology, Hokkaido, Japan
{m2230250,m2240360}@photon.chitose.ac.jp
[2] Chitose Institute of Science and Technology, Hokkaido, Japan
d-kobaya@photon.chitose.ac.jp

Abstract. In recent years, services enabling users to experience walking within virtual spaces have become increasingly available. As a result, there is a growing popularity in services that enable individuals to navigate virtual environments, using virtual reality technology, without physically visiting the places such as museums or shopping malls. When moving in a virtual space, users operate a user interface, such as a controller, and perceive movement visually. Because the feedback to the movement of users in the virtual space is primarily visual, users lack recognition of spatial information, thus making it difficult for them to remember the space and their location. Mirkia et al. (2022) found that visual attention was heightened in spaces incorporating a 'biomorphic design,' which mimics living organisms and water, representing a curvilinear and fluid nature, and that it improved the ease of memorizing the space. Therefore, the purpose of this study was to investigate the relationship between the number of biomorphic elements in a virtual space and their effect on the experiments of walking through this space performed by participants. The results of the experiment, conducted in a virtual-maze environment and a shopping-mall-like environment indicated that incorporating a biomorphic design decreased the walking time of the participants in the space. These findings suggest that conducting experiments in a more precise environment can further elucidate the effect of biomorphic design in virtual environments.

Keywords: Virtual Reality · Biomorphic Design · Indoor Navigation

1 Introduction

Virtual museum visits and shopping experiences in virtual worlds have gained popularity in recent years. In these virtual environments, users can navigate through galleries, exhibits, and virtual stores by controlling the movement of their avatars. This navigation is typically facilitated by head-mounted displays and motion controllers, allowing the users to interact with the virtual environment. In real-world navigation, a cognitive process known as 'spatial cognition' utilizes various sensory inputs, including visual, auditory, and proprioceptive cues, as well as bodily movements, such as walking, to gather, store, organize, and recognize spatial information [1]. While virtual navigation

© The Author(s), under exclusive license to Springer Nature Switzerland AG 2025
J. Y. C. Chen et al. (Eds.): HCII 2024, LNCS 15377, pp. 182–192, 2025.
https://doi.org/10.1007/978-3-031-76812-5_13

in environments such as metaverses differs from walking in the real world, proposing visual design concepts for virtual spaces can enhance the navigation experiences for users.

Ruddle et al. (2011) reported that a controller-based movement in virtual reality (VR) environments reduced the spatial cognition accuracy of the experimental participants compared to movement involving physical locomotion [2]. To promote spatial cognition in a virtual space, it is imperative to devise methods that can direct attention to the space.

With regards to the human perception of the environment, Stephen (1995) pointed out that connecting with nature has various benefits, including reduced mental fatigue, enhanced concentration, and improved visual attention [3]. Hasti et al. (2022) indicated that spaces incorporating biomorphic designs, which emulate elements such as living organisms and water, featuring curvilinear and fluid natural forms, attracted visual attention and improved spatial memory of the users compared to those lacking such designs [1]. Thus, integrating biomorphic designs holds promise for enhancing spatial cognition. However, their study did not explore visual attention or ease of spatial memory in virtual environments involving walking or controller-based movement. Therefore, this study aimed to investigate the effect of biomorphic designs on walking in the virtual world.

2 Method

2.1 Experiment to Investigate the Effect of Biomorphic Designs in a Virtual Maze

Participants. Twenty healthy students of age between 20 and 24 years (mean = 22.2, SD = 1.5), participated in the study. Before commencement, all participants received a comprehensive explanation of the experiment and provided informed consent.

Experimental Environment. In the experiment, participants navigated through five virtual mazes featuring varying proportions of biomorphic design walls (Environment 1: 0%, Environment 2: 5%, Environment 3: 20%, Environment 4: 30%, Environment 5: 100%). The accompanying figures illustrate the layout of each environment. In Fig. 1, 'S' denotes the starting point, whereas 'G' represents the goal.

All environments had identical dimensions, with the entire maze and the width of the aisles being consistent. Three distinct sizes of walls were employed uniformly across all environments. The goal was positioned diagonally from the starting point, necessitating seven directional changes to reach it, with four of these alterations constituting intersections.

Each of the five virtual maze walls featured a unique proportion of biomorphic design. The design walls were crafted by employing Blender, a 3D modeling tool supplied by the Blender Foundation. Seven variations of biomorphic designs, as shown in Fig. 2, were generated and implemented.

In Environment 3, biomorphic designs were positioned at the second, third, and fourth branching paths. In Environment 4, biomorphic designs adorned all turning points and were strategically placed at the shortest distance between the starting point and the goal. In Environment 5, biomorphic designs embellished all walls uniformly throughout the maze.

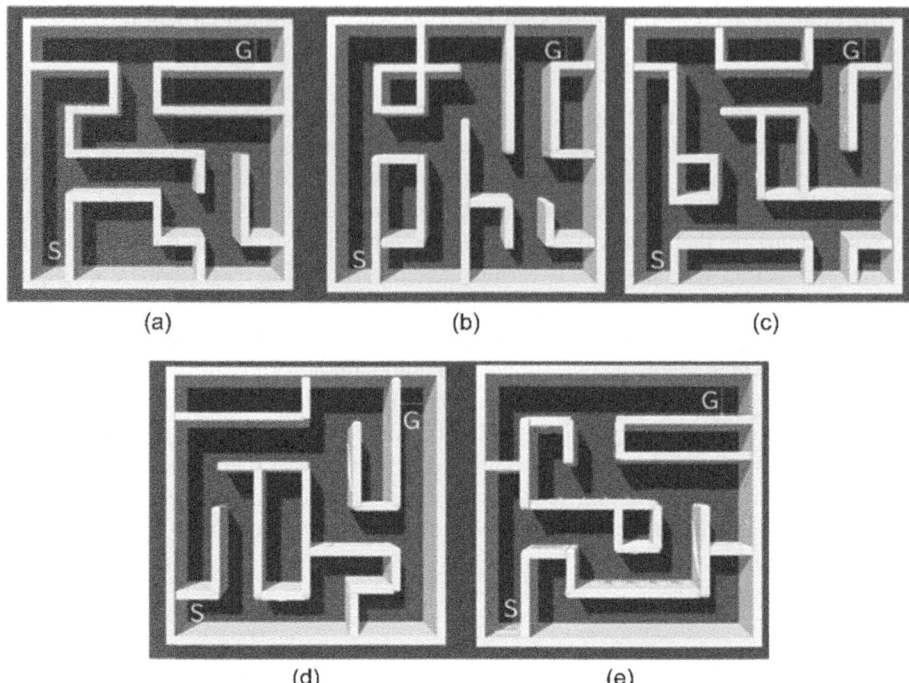

Fig. 1. Schematics of Environment 1 (a), Environment 2 (b), Environment 3 (c), Environment 4 (d), and Environment 5 (e).

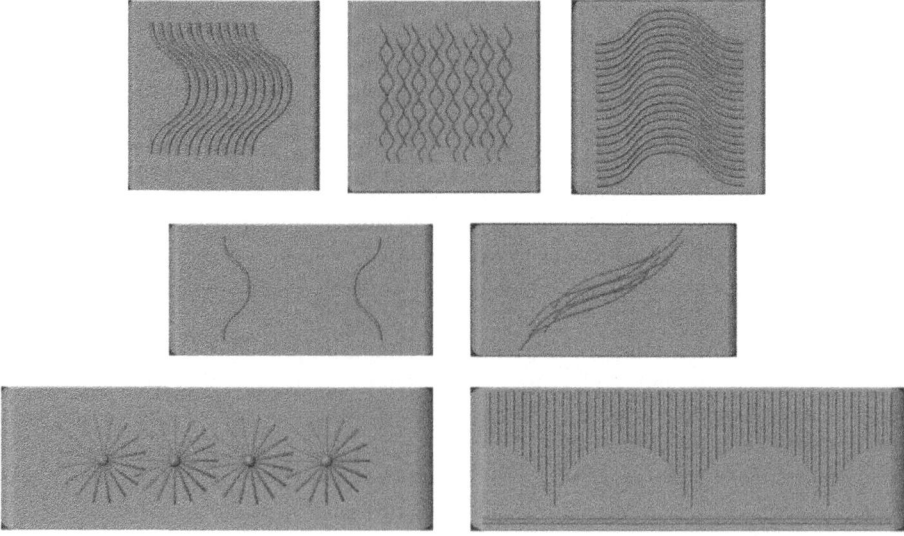

Fig. 2. Seven types of biomorphic designs.

Procedure. The challenge of navigation and orientation in real-world scenarios can fluctuate depending on every individual's sense of direction. Therefore, to explore the relationship between characteristics of the participants and their performance in navigating a virtual maze, we initially assessed the sense of direction of the participants using the simplified version of the Sense of Direction Questionnaire–Short Form (SDQ-S) developed by Takeuchi (1990) [4]. In addition, we surveyed the self-assessment done by the participants of their sense of direction and confidence in navigating the virtual maze.

During the experiment, participants endeavored to navigate through five virtual mazes featuring varying proportions of biomorphic design walls. They completed both outbound tasks, moving from the starting point to the goal within 180 s, and return tasks, returning from the goal to the starting point within the same time limit. After completing the experiment, we performed a questionnaire survey following each task in every virtual maze to collect subjective evaluation of the biomorphic design walls from the participants.

2.2 Experiment to Investigate the Effect of Biomorphic Designs in a Virtual Environment that Simulates a Shopping Mall

Participants. Ten healthy students, of age between 21 and 27 years (mean = 22.6, SD = 1.89), participated in the study. Prior to commencement, all participants received a detailed explanation of the experiment and provided informed consent.

Experimental Environment. In the experiment, participants navigated two virtual environments with differing proportions of biomorphic design walls (Environment 1: with design, Environment 2: without design) as shown in Fig. 3, where 'S' denotes the starting point and 'G' represents the goal.

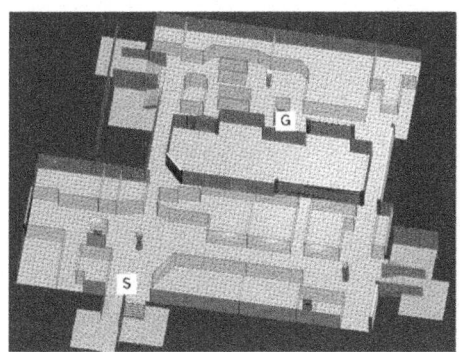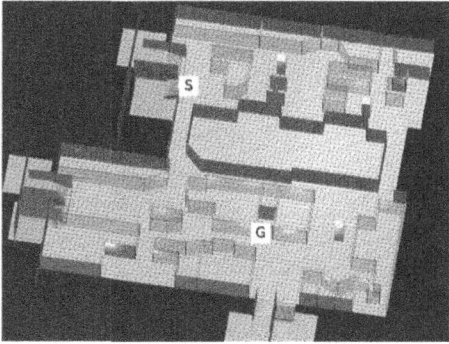

Fig. 3. Schematics of Environment 1 (left) with a biomorphic design and Environment 2 (right) without it.

The walls in Environment 1 featured various proportions of biomorphic design. These design walls were crafted using Blender, a 3D modeling tool provided by the Blender

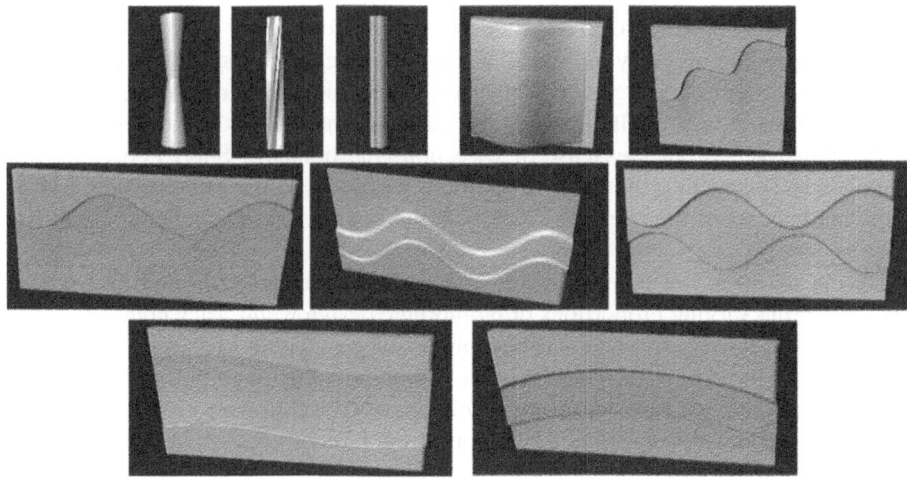

Fig. 4. Ten types of biomorphic designs incorporated in Environment 1.

Foundation, and 10 distinct types of biomorphic designs were generated, as shown in Fig. 4, and implemented in this environment.

Each environment featured designated landmarks serving as reference points. Participants were tasked with locating a specific target. There were two types of targets: one designated and two undesignated targets in each environment, as depicted in Fig. 5.

Fig. 5. Designated (left) and undesignated (right) targets that the users were required to find by navigating both environments.

Procedure. First, the SDQ–S score was given, followed by a self-assessment of their sense of direction and whether or not they had ever gotten lost in a shopping center. Then, to familiarize the participants with moving using a controller in a virtual environment, they practiced moving. Next, we explained the tasks of the experiment to the participants.

There were two types of tasks: an outward task and a return task. The outward task was to find the target object in the virtual environment. The return task was to move from the point where the target was found to the starting point via the shortest path. The onward and return tasks were limited to 240 s each and no instructions were given regarding the objects to be used as landmarks.

In addition, the order of trials of the virtual environment by each participant was counterbalanced to eliminate order effects. During the outward and return tasks, the time required to complete each task and the pupil diameters were measured and recorded. In addition, in order to collect the opinions of the participants about the virtual maze, a questionnaire survey related to the virtual maze they experienced was done after the completion of the task in each virtual maze and after the completion of the task in all virtual mazes, respectively.

Subjective evaluation, psychological stress, and subjective mental workload were also assessed for each environment. Subjective fatigue was assessed using the subjective fatigue factor (SFF). The SFF is a questionnaire developed by the Occupational Fatigue Working Group of the Japan Society for Occupational Health to assess changes in work-related fatigue over time [5], including sleepiness, instability, discomfort, localized pain and fatigue, and eye strain [6].

Psychological stress was assessed using the Brief Job Stress Questionnaire (BJSQ). The BJSQ is a questionnaire provided by the Ministry of Health, Labor, and Welfare that measures work stressors, psychological stress reactions, and physical stress reactions [7]. This study used only 18 items on psychological stress reactions. Participants were asked to rate the 18 items on a 4-point scale. The results of the responses were categorized into five groups: lively, irritable, tired, anxious, and depressed. Depression included six items and was scored on a 24-point scale. The other four groups contained three items each, and thus, scores were calculated on a 12-point scale.

Subjective mental workload was assessed after completion of the return task using the National Aeronautics and Space Administration Task Load Index (NASA-TLX). Participants were asked to rate six items on a visual analog scale from 0 to 100, and mean scores from them were computed. All subjective checklists were presented on a PC screen and participants responded with a mouse click. After the completion of the tasks in all virtual environments, a questionnaire survey related to the virtual environment experienced was done in each case. The raw TLX (RTLX), a simple average of the six items [8], was also calculated in this study.

3   Results

3.1   Experiment to Investigate the Effect of Biomorphic Designs in a Virtual Maze

Participants were categorized into two groups based on their scores on the SDQ–S: those scoring above average (63.55 points) were placed in Group A, whereas those scoring below it were placed in Group B. When comparing the mean achievement times for outbound and return tasks between Groups A and B, significant differences were found in Group A for Environments 1, 2, 3, and 5 at the 1% significance level. In Group B, significant differences were observed in Environments 2 and 5 at the 5% significance level, and in Environment 4 at the 10% significance level.

Gaze times of participants on biomorphic designs within Environments 3, 4, and 5 were analyzed. Each biomorphic design was considered as observed if it was looked at for 300 ms or more. The total gaze times on each biomorphic design during outbound and return tasks were calculated separately for Groups A and B in each environment. A test was conducted to compare the differences in the mean values. In Environment 3, one biomorphic design significantly reduced the average gaze time for Group B during outbound tasks ($p = 0.04$), whereas two biomorphic designs increased the average gaze time for Group B during return tasks ($p = 0.09$, $p = 0.10$). In Environment 4, one biomorphic design significantly reduced the average gaze time for Group B during outbound tasks ($p = 0.09$), but another increased it during return tasks ($p = 0.07$). In Environment 5, one biomorphic design significantly reduced the average gaze time for Group B during outbound tasks ($p = 0.08$).

In Group A and Group B, the average difference in the completion time between the outbound and return tasks was examined in Environment 1 and other environments. Significant differences were observed in Group B for Environment 2 ($p < 0.03$) and Environment 5 ($p < 0.01$).

3.2 Experiment to Check the Effect of Biomorphic Designs in a Virtual Environment that Simulates a Shopping Mall

Participants were divided into two groups based on their SDQ–S scores: those scoring above the average (67.4 points) were allocated to Group C, whereas those scoring below were assigned to Group D.

Two participants whose task completion time exceeded the 240 s limit were excluded from the analysis. On comparing the mean task completion times between Groups C and D, no significant differences were observed in either virtual environment. However, when examining the mean difference between the time taken to complete the outbound task and the time taken to complete the return task for each environment within Groups C and D, a significant difference was found in Group D ($p < .04$), as illustrated in Fig. 6.

Consequently, in Group D, the time disparity between the outbound and return tasks was significantly shorter in the environment including a biomorphic design compared to one lacking it.

The calculation results of SFF are shown in Fig. 7. While no significant differences were observed in all items, Environment 2 exhibited a tendency to have higher values than Environment 1 across all items.

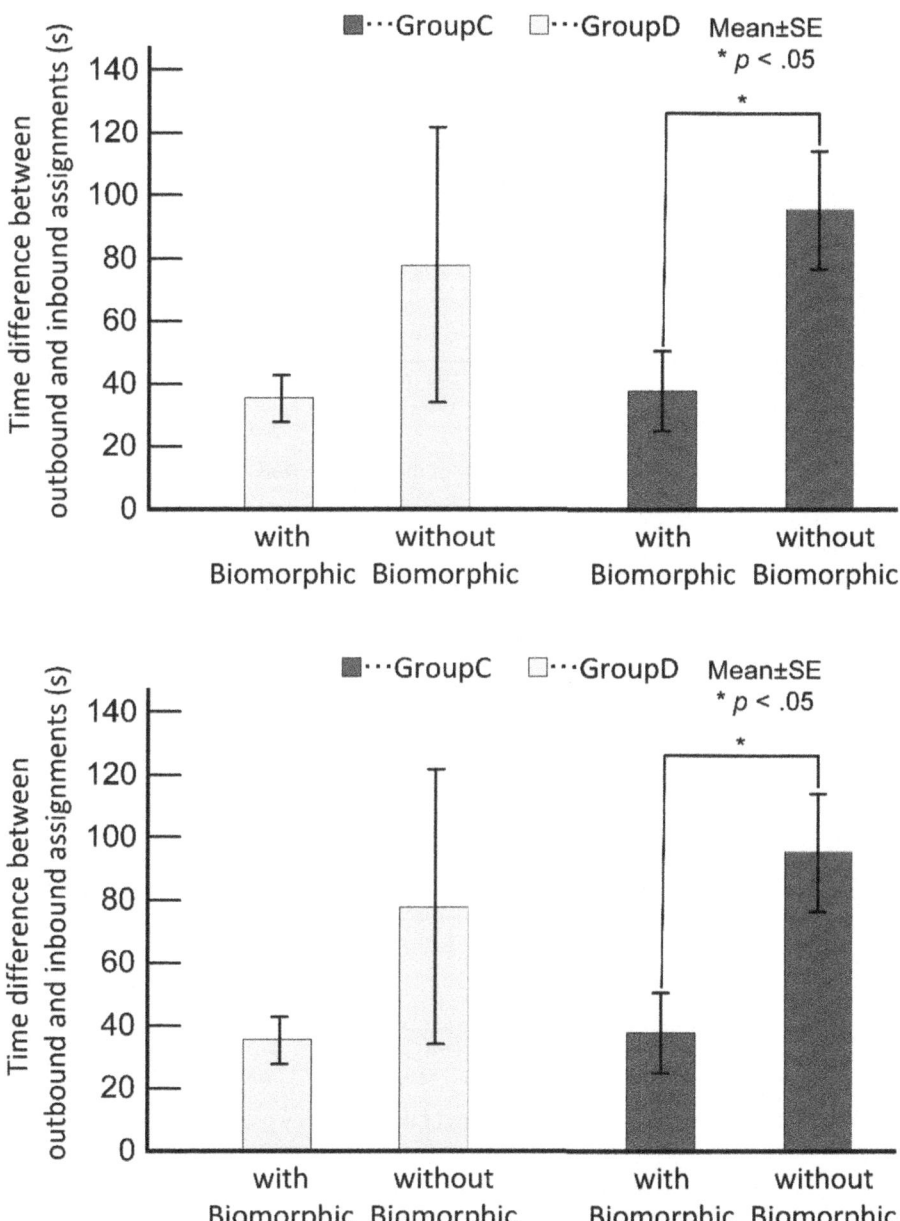

Fig. 6. Time difference between outbound and inbound assignments for Groups C and D in each environment.

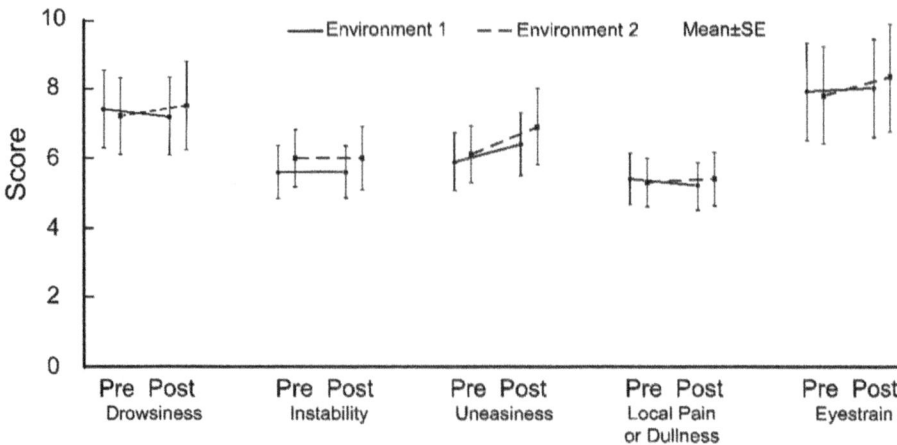

Fig. 7. **SFF** scores of the participants in terms of the different work-fatigue factors (n = 10).

Figure 8 shows the calculation results of BJSQ. No significant differences were observed in all items. Although there was no change in 'irritation', the 'fatigue', 'anxiety', and 'depression' factors tended to be higher in Environment 2 compared to Environment 1.

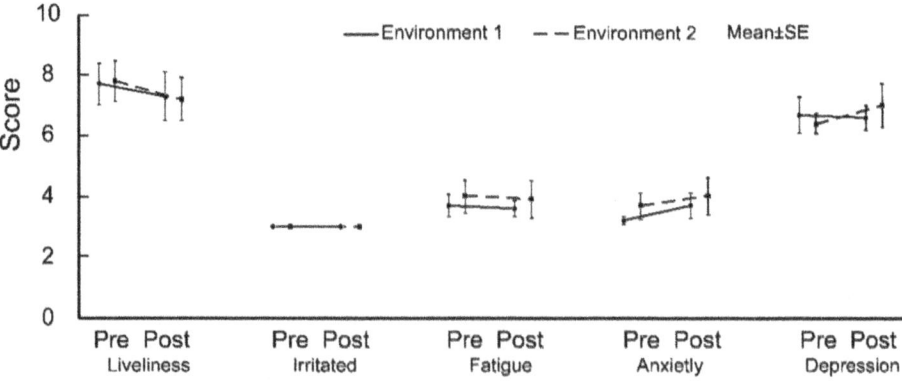

Fig. 8. BJSQ scores of the participants in terms of the different work-fatigue factors (n = 10).

Figure 9 presents calculation results of NASA–TLX. There were no significant differences in all items.

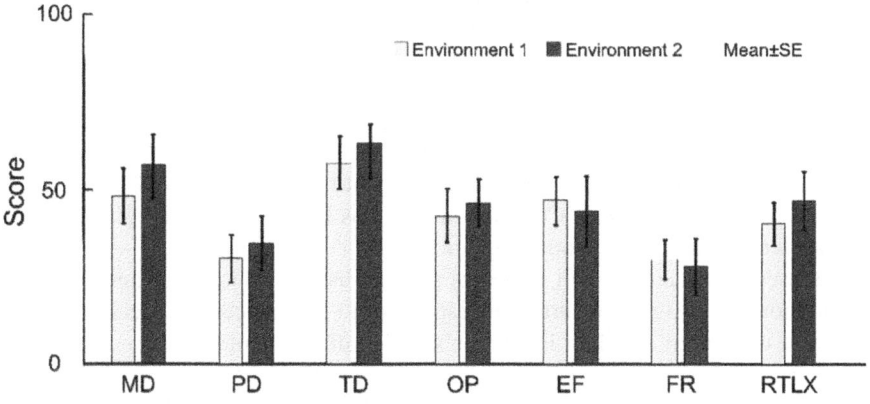

Fig. 9. NASA–TLX scores of the participants (n = 10).

4 Discussion

Integrating biomorphic designs into environments may enhance the spatial cognition of users, potentially facilitating navigation, particularly for individuals with a stronger sense of direction. Future research endeavors will concentrate on refining user standard error and selecting specific biomorphic designs for further investigation, aiming to gain a deeper understanding of their effective utilization and their impact on the sense of direction.

In Group D, the time discrepancy between the outbound and inbound tasks was notably shorter in the environments including a biomorphic design compared to the environment lacking it, indicating that users with low SDQ–S score and a weaker sense of direction can potentially reduce their traversal time.

Despite the SFF and BJSQ results revealing no significant differences, it is plausible that the absence of any biomorphic design in the virtual environment causes psychological stress to users when searching for specific landmarks within the shopping mall. When participants were queried about their preference for a shopping mall environment for daily use, all ten participants selected an environment incorporating biomorphic design. Participants expressed sentiments such as, 'The presence of landmark pillars and patterns made navigation easier,' and 'I feel more adventurous and excited in a space with these patterns.' These findings suggest that environments featuring biomorphic designs are highly valued by users as a customer experience in shopping malls.

5 Conclusion

The two experiments performed in this study demonstrated that while spaces incorporating biomorphic designs enhanced performance ratings of the participants, the impact varied across environments. In a confined space, such as virtual mazes and virtual exhibition, users with higher SDQ–S score and better sense of direction reduced their traversal time. On the other hand, in a space resembling a shopping mall, users with lower SDQ–S score and poorer sense of direction required less time than that taken to complete the outbound task. Therefore, to further elucidate the influence of biomorphic designs, it is imperative to align the environment more closely with the actual VR environment utilized.

A relationship between the SDQ scores and the biomorphic design has been revealed from the results of this study. Furthermore, it was found that for individuals with low SDQ–S scores, who are prone to getting lost easily, it became easier to remember the paths they had previously taken. Consequently, it was found that biomorphic designs have a considerable impact on spatial cognition.

Future research endeavors will prioritize refining user standard error and selecting specific biomorphic designs for further investigation to gain a deeper understanding of their effective utilization and their impact on sense of direction of the user.

Acknowledgments. We thank all participants who gave their time to participate in this study.

References

1. Mirkia, H., Nelson, M.S.C., Abercrombie, H.C., Thorleifsdottir, K., Sangari, A., Assadi, A.: Recognition memory for interior spaces with biomorphic or non-biomorphic interior architectural elements. J. Inter. Des. **47**(3), 47–66 (2022)
2. Ruddle, A.R., Volkova, E., Bülthoff, H.H.: Walking improves your cognitive map in environments that are large-scale and large in extent. ACM Trans. Comput.-Hum. Interact. **18**(2), 1–20 (2011)
3. Kaplan, S.: The restorative benefits of nature: toward an integrative framework. J. Environ. Psychol. **15**(3), 169–182 (1995)
4. Takeuchi, K.: Constructing "Sense of Direction Questionnaire": I. Collecting the items and examining the results of factor analysis. Aichi Univ. Educ. Res. Report Educ. Sci. **39**, 127–140 (1990)
5. "Subjective Fatigue Feelings", Working Group for Occupational Fatigue of Japan Society for Occupational Health. https://square.umin.ac.jp/of/service.html
6. Sasaki, T., Matsumoto, S.: Actual conditions of work, fatigue and sleep in non-employed, home- base female information technology workers with preschool children. Ind. Health **43**(1), 142–150 (2005)
7. "Brief Job Stress Questionnaire," Ministry of Health, Labour and Welfare. https://www.mhlw.go.jp/bunya/roudoukijun/anzeneisei12/dl/stress-check_j.pdf
8. Hart, S.G., Staveland, L.E.: Development of NASA-TLX (Task Load Index): results of empirical and theoretical research. Adv. Psychol. **52**, 139–183 (1988)

Interactive Visual Narrative (IVN) Model: Understanding Discourse Production in IVNs

Krishna Kumar Radhakrishnan$^{(\boxtimes)}$ and Ravi Poovaiah

IDC School of Design, Indian Institute of Technology, Bombay, Mumbai, India
{krishnarkumar,ravi}@iitb.ac.in

Abstract. Our paper focuses on Interactive Visual Narratives (IVNs), a digital storytelling mode where users can interact, manipulate and co-create narratives. We propose a unified IVN Model that facilitates discourse production in IVNs, providing users control while generating narratives. We aim to bring a design perspective to IVN studies by reconsidering narrative discourse production techniques. Our study aims to identify the elements and structure of an IVN and how they integrate to form the structure. We conducted a morphological study to answer questions about narrating and visually presenting a story.

The IVN Model, which explains the structure and production of discourse, comprises Story (What) and Discourse (How). The IVN Construction Method and IVN Discourse Mode visualize the discourse and its manifestation. There is an Order of presentation and an Order of telling. The elements of IVN include the Key Elements, Formation Devices and Presentation Devices.

Our study found a set of consistent elements present across all IVNs. The Key Elements are the foundational elements without which an IVN cannot exist. The Formation Devices help decipher the discourse mode used, while the Presentation Devices facilitate the stylistic presentation of an IVN.

Keywords: Interactive Visual Narrative (IVN) · IVN Model · Discourse in IVN

1 Introduction

An oral or written story can be represented in many ways as Visual Narratives [1]. Our concern in this paper is with Interactive Visual Narratives, henceforth IVNs [2], a mode of visual storytelling through a digital medium where users can experience, interact, manipulate, and co-create narratives.

Scholars have viewed discourse in IVNs from the perspectives of Artificial Intelligence, Cinema, Video Games and Human-Computer Interaction. They, in their respective domains of Artificial Intelligence [3, 4], Computational Linguistics [5], Game Design and Ludology [6–9], Interactive Cinema [10], Neo-Aristotelian Dramatics [11], Victorian Literature [12], Contemporary Narratology [13] have suggested theories that provide diverse vantage points to IVNs. The emphasis of these investigations varied from the arrangement of the incidents or events that form the overall plot structure from a narratological perspective, creating micro-narratives – narrative segments that coalesce to form

© The Author(s), under exclusive license to Springer Nature Switzerland AG 2025
J. Y. C. Chen et al. (Eds.): HCII 2024, LNCS 15377, pp. 193–203, 2025.
https://doi.org/10.1007/978-3-031-76812-5_14

the narrative arc, authoring non-linear narratives with causal integrity, development of synthetic characters or believable agents with a varying spectrum of autonomy ranging from strong to weak; providing agency that varies from strong autonomy to strong story; solving the narrative paradox or provide a dramatic experience outside the boundaries of authored content.

The researchers have conducted these studies in distinct genres with their respective agendas different from ours. The method of investigation for these studies was suited for the genre, and the outcomes are disparate. Furthermore, the scholars have not adequately borrowed methodologies from each other. We propose to observe IVN as a hypernym of these genres, a unified model that brings in heterogeneity. This approach will allow us to understand the discourse mechanism across IVNs and facilitate designers to explore various aspects of discourse production. This viewpoint has helped us conclude that IVN as a universal phenomenon is possible. Despite the shortcomings we have identified from a design perspective, we do not unconditionally disregard the prior research put forward by scholars. We believe that we can gather substantial understanding from these studies. This perspective can lay the foundation for generating novel knowledge through empirical and systematic analysis.

We suggest relooking at the mechanics of discourse production in IVN by situating IVN as a universally existent phenomenon. This viewpoint opens up a large set of IVN samples that researchers can subject to rigorous scrutiny. The enhanced approach to the study is at a structural level, focusing on discourse production in IVNs. The proposal examines discourse in IVNs by reviewing the 'order of presentation' and the 'order of telling'. In discursive forms where the units of meaning are combinable into larger units, Langer [14] suggests that we can understand the function of elements through their structural relationship as they are 'involved in a simultaneous, integral presentation'.

2   The IVN Model

We present a new model of the IVN in this paper. It consists of the structure of IVN in the context of the form and content of a story. We developed the IVN Model to address the need – to describe and analyze the form and function of elements of IVN. It provides a conceptual framework to understand the dynamics of the structure and elements in the IVN and the vocabulary to facilitate further discussion.

The proposed IVN Model is outlined in Fig. 1. The model indicates the following:

1. IVN Model consists of Story (What) and Discourse (How). We drew this model from the work of Seymour Chatman [15].
2. The Discourse, Manifestation and Structure of IVN Transmission have an IVN Construction Method and IVN Discourse Mode. We aligned this to the thoughts of Susan Langer [14] – that there is an Order of Presentation and an Order of Telling.
3. We draw the Elements of IVN from the works of Hanfmann [16], Bal [17], Aarseth [6], Chen [18] and Jenkins [19]. The elements include the Key Elements and Formation Devices.
4. From the works of Arheim [20], we draw the Presentation Devices

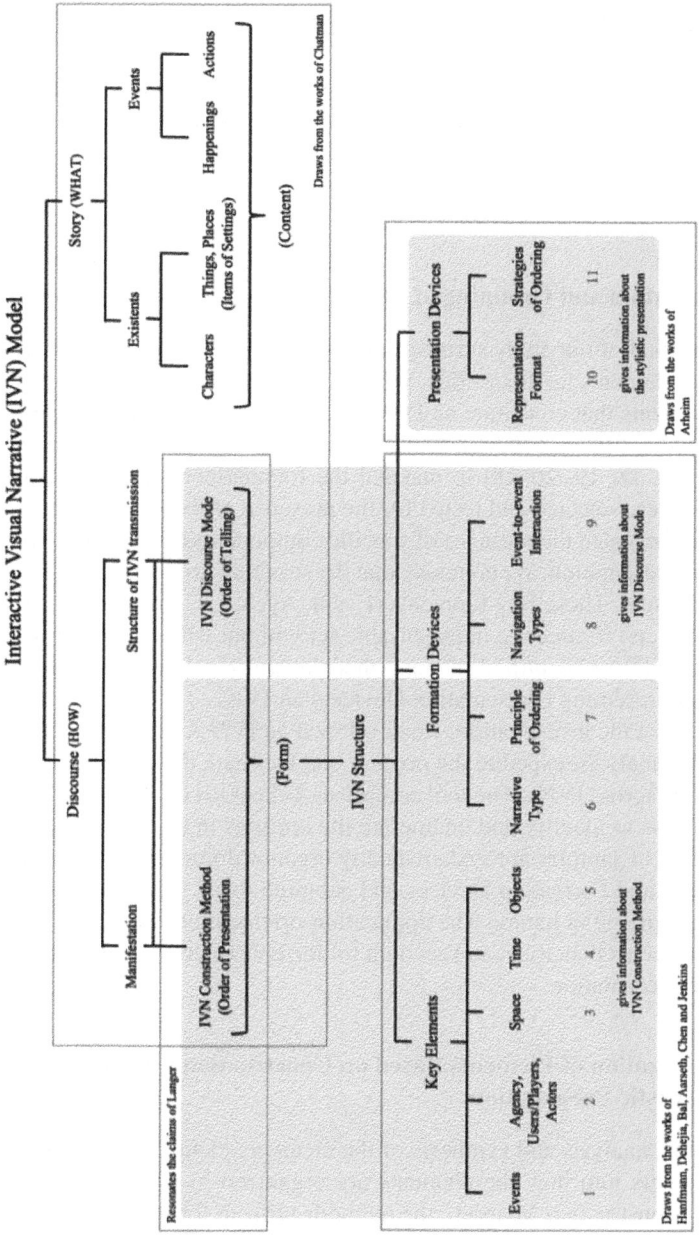

Fig. 1. The proposed IVN Model.

3   Methodology for Looking at the IVN

We employed Structuralist Narratological methods to resolve the structure and working of IVNs in this study. We address the model from a bottom-up approach, starting by finding the elements and then working our way up the model to understand the Key Elements, Formation Devices and Presentation Devices and finally unravelling the structure of the IVNs.

3.1   Identification and Grouping of Elements that Are Present Across IVNs

The starting point of our study surmises that we can represent IVNs in many ways, and a finite set of elements facilitates this. We begin our study by examining and identifying the finite elements that constitute an IVN and provide for its innumerable possibilities. We evaluate the studies conducted in Narratology, Ludology and Interactive Digital Storytelling [6, 18, 19, 26–28] to marshal the foundational set of elements. A set of fifteen IVNs were selected and tested for the presence of the identified elements.

The study revealed the presence of specific components that appeared irrespective of the kind of representation. We conclude that the structure drove the presence of elements and not its content. These Key Elements (Event, Agency, Users/Players, Actors, Space, Time and Objects) formed the indispensable set without which one cannot construct an IVN. Additionally, we identified elements that play a vital role in constructing (Formation Devices) and presenting (Presentation Devices) an IVN.

To systemize the investigation, we developed an IVN Analysis Tool to bring homogeneity to the analysis, expedite the process and facilitate the correlation of similitudes and disparities across IVNs. The tool comprises a checklist of elements. We followed an iterative process to identify and enumerate the sections in the tool. The notes from the Close Reading of samples are systematically organized into the Key Elements, Presentation Devices and Formation Devices and captured using the IVN Analysis Tool. The approach is heuristic in nature. The application-oriented tool expedites the scanning of numerous elements that affect and account for the construction method, discourse mode and stylistic presentation.

3.2   Categorization of Elements Based on Construction Method, Discourse Mode and Stylistic Presentation

Morphological analysis and synthesis of the elements identified using the tool provide valuable insights into how the elements are organized in an IVN to effectively convey a story (Construction Method), the methods utilized for discourse production (Discourse Mode), and the stylistic presentation employed. Insights on how the elements are arranged in a particular manner to communicate a story gave rise to the concept of 'order of presentation'. The elements responsible for forming the IVN gave rise to the 'order of telling' concept.

4 Data Collection

We depend on two sets of sources - primary and secondary for data collected. The IVN sample in which we participated is the primary source. The secondary sources include video walkthroughs, journal papers, websites, and forums.

4.1 Sample Selection

To execute our qualitative study, we selected fifteen samples. We ensured that they represented different genres of IVNs, constructed and presented using diverse technological platforms, and had varying release timelines. We looked for the availability of reference material in an easily accessible medium or with documentation or expert review as a video walkthrough. We took additional references from the journal write-up describing the artefact's purpose, nature, and outcome. We prioritized the IVNs referenced previously by scholars, highlighting the intrinsic interactive narrative qualities. Popularity in vernacular communities, highest-grossing, high accolades for build and qualities of its narrative, and highest in expert reviews were secondary criteria we considered for the selection.

4.2 Close Reading

Our study focuses on components, their variations, functions, and the structure of the IVN and on understanding what is interactive. It does not concern the behavioural and social aspects of the player's interaction with the IVN or the variations in the story due to the influence of events happening in the world. Our quest is to understand better the components and how they work. Therefore, our observations are empirical, and other researchers can reproduce them reliably. This treatment aligns with the formalist method, where we treat IVN as text.

Carr et al. [21] propose that an interactive artefact can be treated as text. Based on the insight that we can analyze IVNs as text, we employ the humanities methodology of Close Reading [22], closely associated with formalism and structuralism for our study. The intent is to unravel the usage of narrative elements and their interrelationship in an IVN that leads to the various levels of interactivity. Close Reading is a methodology adapted to media forms such as cinema from literature. It poses unique challenges while reading interactive media [23, 24]. To reconcile our observations from the Close Reading exercise, we relied on several strategies like undertaking multiple playthroughs of the same sample, meticulously capturing detailed review notes when the playthroughs were complete and adhering to intense documentation techniques through digital notetaking and screenshots. We use walkthroughs, wikis and information from journals to deputize the knowledge we otherwise would have lost due to the unique challenges of accessing interactive media. We use Close Reading for detailed observations and as a pre-study [25], leading to a higher-order formal analysis using our proposed IVN Model.

5   Morphology of an IVN

We identified that IVNs attain their final form through the coalescence of the elements through our preliminary study in chapter four. We grouped the elements into three categories based on their role in IVNs. The categories that form the IVN structure are 1) Key Elements, 2) Formation Devices and 3) Presentation Devices.

The Key Elements are crucial to constructing IVNs and correspond to the IVN Construction Method. The elements within the second category, Formation Devices, assist in deciphering the Discourse Mode employed in an IVN. The elements within the last category, Presentation Devices, draw on the Stylistic Presentation of an IVN.

5.1   Key Elements

Key Elements are the fundamental building blocks of an IVN. It comprises 1) Events, 2) Agency, 3) Users/ Players, 4) Actors, 5) Space, 6) Time, and 7) Objects. We will set out to familiarize ourselves with the Key Elements, their subcategories and variations.

Events. An IVN is essentially a story that its users can experience interactively. When presenting a story, the designer of the narrative or the system decides to represent the story visually. The smaller part of the story, where an action occurs at a point in time, unfolds at a particular place and occupies a specific space [28], is an event. These events depict the pre-scripted actions (presentation) or the enactment, the actions generated while characters interact (representation) of the part of the story. The integration of events at multiple levels forms episodes and, finally, the story. The events anchor the other Key Elements, without which the representations become meaningless. Designers can use two aspects to establish the significance and demeanor of events in IVNs: the type of event [26] and the status and presence of kernels and satellites [6].

Agency. The agency is the feeling experienced when a user can influence the virtual story world, which in turn responds to the action. The agency sets the platform for the participant to interact with the narrative. It could play the role of the author, guiding the users through various plot options for structured narratives or setting the platform for the participants to interact and unravel the narrative in emergent narratives. Five aspects of agency required to understand the phenomenon in IVNs are agency type, level of control [29], interactivity, actions of participants and reactions.

Users/Players. A person receiving a traditional narrative could be termed a viewer, listener or spectator. They are passive receptors of the narrative. We use the term user/player to depict the beneficiaries of the interactive narratives. Although they are not embedded in the system like other Key Elements, they play a vital role as they interact with the narrative and, on certain occasions, even play the role of a co-author of the narrative. We use this specific term to facilitate the differentiation of their intrinsic characteristics and their role in the narrative. Two aspects of the user/player foregrounding this element are the user role and the number of users involved with the IVN [30].

Actors. Actors are the characters in the narrative, analogous to characters in a play. They are the most visible element in the IVN. They are the inhabitants of the story world and communicate directly or indirectly to the users of the IVN. Interactions of the actor with the user or amongst other actors within the narrative lead to the events in the IVN. They are agents who carry out the actions required to further the plot; hence, an IVN cannot be devoid of actors. In an IVN, they can be considered a fundamental element. The five aspects concerning actors in an IVN are characters, narrative voice, narrative distance, focalization and grammatical person [26]. The first one, characters, is to understand the landscape of behaviors in an IVN. In contrast, the succeeding four are primarily regarding the player's character.

Space. In narratives, we reference two key dimensions – the dimension of story events, time, and that of story-existence, space [15]. In IVN, the usage of the term space has many implications. Space can be the geographical or virtual space, the story space, or the location or place where the events in the narrative occur. It is essential to distinguish story space from discourse space and study them separately. Events are not spatial in nature, even though they occur in space. Story space contains the existents, and the entities within it perform the actions or are affected by them. Three aspects that facilitate understanding the concept of space and how it affects discourse production in the context of IVN are geographical and static setting design, conceptual narrative space and location or place.

Time. Stories are temporal in nature [15]. One of the challenges the designers of IVNs face is the representation of the temporally discrete sets of events into a sequential narrative. The two aspects of time crucial to comprehending the usage of temporality in IVNs are conceptual narrative time and temporal movement.

Objects. Numerous storytelling artefacts are available in the narrative space that the actors and characters can interact with, manipulate or create. While some are ornate, others are available for the characters to discover, utilize and move the narrative ahead, making it one of the critical elements facilitating narrative control. The four parameters of objects relevant to IVNs are malleability [6], ordering [27], availability and mechanical significance.

5.2 Formation Devices

The Formation Devices bring the elements together to tell the story. These elements correspond to the discourse mode employed in an IVN. The elements in the Formation Device include 1) Narrative Type, 2) Principles of Ordering, 3) Navigation Type and 4) Event-to-event Interaction,

Narrative Type. Events in stories unfold in space over a given time. The interactive narrative authors and designers must systematically set the environment, providing cues and possibilities for users to unravel the narrative. The spatial design thus becomes an essential aspect of storytelling where the designer or author of the narrative must meticulously design the story world and sculpt spaces. Narrative Type refers to the design of the preconditions and the organization of narrative possibilities and consequences into the narrative space for an immersive narrative experience. The five possibilities for spatial storytelling are evoked, enacted, embedded, emergent [19] and framing narratives [31].

Principles of Ordering. Our examination revealed that the designers of IVN use a rationale to arrange events in the virtual story space. We term this rationale as the

Principle of Ordering. The three possible ways of arranging the events that we identified are Predefined, Conditional and Arbitrary ways of ordering.

Navigation Type. The narrative designer follows some order of placement while sequencing multiple events to form a story in an IVN composition. The Navigation Type depicts the rationale used by the designer of the IVN to lay out the events. The designer could place the events successively one after the other or portray them as happening Simultaneously or Concurrently [28].

Event-to-Event Interaction. We can represent the transition from one event to another in an IVN differently. Event-to-event Interaction deals with how the events are connected and transitioned to the next. The change in the event could be represented as a change in time that transitions across to another place or by remaining in the same place. A change in the state could also facilitate the transition of events. Another device used to represent the change is to show the cause and effect of the events.

5.3 Presentation Devices

Presentation Devices are elements that work together to give a visual form, facilitating the stylistic presentation of an IVN that designers can present to the viewer. These elements are controlled and manipulated by the designer of the IVN to create signifiers that help the viewer visualize the represented event. Presentation Devices comprise Representation Format and Strategies of Ordering. The first element deals with creating an IVN into a visual form, while the second deals with how the narrative segments are connected to form the narrative whole.

Representation Format. The Representational Format is the element responsible for giving a story its visual form [28]. It deals with the Scheme of Presentation or directions on the stylistic presentation that the designers of the IVN choose to employ while representing the IVN.

Strategies of Ordering. The narrative designers employ specific rationale to arrange the visual events in the narrative timeline and compositional space. We refer to these as Strategies of Ordering. The commonly used strategies are Event, Actor, Space, Time and a Space-time-based arrangement.

6   Conclusion

6.1   Research Findings

We arrive at a new model of the IVN. It consists of the structure of IVN in the context of the form and content of a story. The form explains the Discourse (How), and the content explains the Story (What). The Discourse, Manifestation and Structure of IVN Transmission have an IVN Construction Method that explains the order of presentation and an IVN Discourse Mode that explains the order of telling.

We can construct IVNs using a finite set of universally found elements. We found the persistent presence of these eleven elements in all the samples analyzed in the morphological study. The elements we identified are Events, Agency, Users/Players, Actors, Space, Time, Objects, Narrative Type, Principles of Ordering, Navigation Type, Event-to-event Interaction, Representation Format and Strategies of Ordering.

The morphology study revealed the role and function of all the elements in the IVN structure. They are grouped under three categories – Key Elements, Formation Devices and Presentation Devices, and help explain discourse production in IVNs.

The Key Elements are the fundamental building blocks crucial to constructing IVNs and correspond to the IVN Construction Method. The Formation Devices bring the elements together to tell the story, corresponding to the Discourse Mode, and the elements in Presentation Devices work together to give a visual form to IVNs. The Key Elements, Formation Devices and Presentation Devices, together help us understand how discourse production happens in IVNs.

6.2 Reflection on the Research Process

We conducted the research to address the specific objectives within the defined scope. These objectives bring forward certain constraints and are not thorough in all aspects.

The formalist perspective we have followed in this thesis provides a strong foundation for the discovery and comprehension of elements that make the structure and the relationship of the elements, which was one of our prime concerns. However, this approach is not suitable for deciphering certain other aspects, like gauging the emotional impact it has on its participants.

Despite providing detailed parlance, the researcher's understanding of the terms, meaning, and proficiency in using the tool is pivotal in the data logging and analysis phase. Any erroneous deductions of these variables could lead to inaccurate conclusions about the analyzed IVN.

The study maintains a media-agnostic viewpoint and provides a model that aligns with this perspective. It disregards the impact of the medium through which IVNs are designed, presented and instantiated. Conscious scrutiny of the effects of the medium on IVNs could reveal unique constraints and exciting opportunities regarding the construction and delivery through a specific medium.

References

1. Dehejia, V.: On modes of visual narrtion in early buddhist art. Art Bullet. **72**(3), 374–392 (1990)
2. Radhakrishnan, K.K., Poovaiah, R.: On defining interactive visual narratives (IVNs). In: Chakrabarti, A., Singh, V. (eds.) Design in the Era of Industry 4.0, Volume 1. ICORD 2023. Smart Innovation, Systems and Technologies, vol. 343. Springer, Singapore (2023). https://doi.org/10.1007/978-981-99-0293-4_44
3. Bates, J.: The Nature of Character in Interactive Worlds and The Oz Project. (Technical Report CMU-CS-92–200) School of Computer Science, Carnegie Mellon University (1992)

4. Cavazza, M., Charles, F., Mead, S.J.: Characters in search of an author: AI-based virtual storytelling. In: Proceedings of the First International Conference on Virtual Storytelling. ICVS 2001. Lecture Notes in Computer Science, vol. 2197, pp. 145–154 (2001). https://doi.org/10.1007/3-540-45420-9_16

5. Young, R.M.: Notes on the use of plan structure in the creation of interactive plot. In: Mateas, M., Sengers, P. (eds.) Narrative Intelligence: Papers from the AAAI Fall Symposium (Technical Report FS-99-01), pp. 164–167. AAAI Press, Menlo Park (1999)

6. Aarseth, E.J.: A narrative theory of games. In: FDG 2012: Proceedings of the International Conference on the Foundations of Digital Games, pp. 129–133 (2012). https://doi.org/10.1145/2282338.2282365

7. Crawford, C.: Chris Crawford on Interactive Storytelling. New Riders Games (2005)

8. Juul, J.: A Clash between Game and Narrative. [Master's Thesis. University of Copenhagen] Available from Jesperjuul.net (1999)

9. Frasca, G.: Ludology meets Narratology: Similitude and differences between (video) games and narrative. Ludology (1999). https://ludology.typepad.com/weblog/articles/ludology

10. Davenport, G.: Smarter tools for storytelling: are they just around the corner? IEEE Multimedia 3(1), 10–14 (1996). https://doi.org/10.1109/MMUL.1996.486700

11. Laurel, B.: Computers as Theatre. Addison-Wesley Publishing Company, Reading (1993)

12. Murray, J.H.: Hamlet on the Holodeck: The Future of Narrative in Cyberspace. Free Press, New York (1997)

13. Ryan, M.: Narrative as Virtual Reality: Immersion and Interactivity in Literature and Electronic Media. Johns Hopkins University Press (2001)

14. Langer, S.K.: Philosophy in a New Key: A Study in the Symbolism of Reason, Rite and Art (6th Printing). The New American Library (1954)

15. Chatman, S.: Story and Discourse - Narrative Structure in Fiction and Film. Cornell University Press (1978)

16. Hanfmann, G.: Narration in Greek Art. Am. J. Archeol. 61(1), 71–78 JSTOR. IIT Bombay Lib., Mumbai, Maharashtra (1957). <http://www.jstor.org>

17. Bal, M.: Narratology: Introduction to the Theory of Narrative (2nd ed.). University of Toronto Press (1999)

18. Chen, F.: Toward a hermeneutic narratology of interactive digital storytelling. In: Mitchell, A., Fernandez-Vara, C., Thue, D. (eds.) Interactive Storytelling. ICIDS 2014. Lecture Notes in Computer Science, vol. 8832. Springer, Cham (2014). https://doi.org/10.1007/978-3-319-12337-0_12

19. Jenkins, H.: Game design as narrative architecture. In: Wardrip-Fruin, N., Harrigan, P. (eds.) New Media as Story, Performance, and Game, pp. 118–130. First Person (2004)

20. Arheim, R.: Visual Thinking. University of California Press, Berkeley (1969)

21. Carr, D., Buckingham, D., Burn, A., Schott, G.: Computer Games: Text. Polity Press, Narrative and Play (2006)

22. Bizzocchi, J.: Games and narrative: an analytical framework. Loading J. Can. Games Stud. Assoc. 1(1) (2007)

23. Bizzocchi, J., Tanenbaum, T.J.: Well read: applying close reading techniques to gameplay experiences. in well played 3.0: video games. Value Meaning 3, 262–290 (2011)

24. Tanenbaum, J.: Hermeneutic inquiry for digital games research. Comput. Games J. 4(1–2), 59–80 (2015)

25. Mäyrä, F.: An Introduction to Game Studies. Games in Culture. SAGE Publications Ltd (2008). https://doi.org/10.4135/9781446214572

26. Abbott, H.P.: The Cambridge Introduction to Narrative (2nd ed.). Cambridge University Press (2008). https://doi.org/10.1017/CBO9780511816932

27. Krainert, T.: Storytelling artifacts. In: Mitchell, A., Fernández-Vara, C., Thue, D. (eds.). Interactive Storytelling. ICIDS 2014. Lecture Notes in Computer Science, vol. 8832, pp. 113–124. Springer, Cham (2014). https://doi.org/10.1007/978-3-319-12337-0_11
28. Krishna Kumar, S.: Moment and Moments: Discourse in Static Visual Narratives. [Unpublished doctoral dissertation]. Indian Institute of Technology Bombay (2011)
29. Koenitz, H., Haahr, M., Ferri, G., Sezen, T.I., Sezen, D.: Mapping the evolving space of interactive digital narrative - from artifacts to categorizations. In: Koenitz, H., Sezen, T.I., Ferri, G., Haahr, M., Sezen, D., Çatak, G., (eds.). Interactive Storytelling. ICIDS 2013. Lecture Notes in Computer Science, vol. 8230, pp. 55–60. Springer, Cham (2013). https://doi.org/10.1007/978-3-319-02756-2_6
30. Radhakrishnan, K.K., Poovaiah, R.: Audience, participant and agency: need for role definition in interactive visual narratives. In: Chakrabarti, A., Chakrabarti, D. (eds.) Research into Design for Communities, Volume 1. ICoRD 2017. Smart Innovation, Systems and Technologies, vol. 65. Springer, Singapore (2017). https://doi.org/10.1007/978-981-10-3518-0_9
31. Lindley, C.A.: Story and narrative structures in computer games. In: Brunhild, B., (ed.). Developing Interactive Narrative Content. Sagas-sagasnet reader (2005)

Effects of Basic Movement Characteristics and Cognitive Load on Performance Indicators in VR-IADLs

Haruki Ueshima[1], Tania Giovannetti[2], Hayato Ohwada[1],
and Takehiko Yamaguchi[3(✉)]

[1] Tokyo University of Science, Yamazaki, Noda-Shi 2641, Japan
7424504@ed.tus.ac.jp, ohwada@rs.tus.ac.jp
[2] Temple University, 1801 N Broad Street, Philadelphia, PA 19122, USA
tgio@temple.edu
[3] Suwa University of Science, Toyohira, Chino-Shi 5000, Japan
tk-ymgch@rs.sus.ac.jp

Abstract. Dementia is a progressive ailment characterized by irreversible symptoms, but the early detection of mild cognitive impairment (MCI), can halt its progression. Thus, the early detection of MCI is crucial for dementia management. A study developed a tablet-based virtual kitchen challenge system that reproduced the instrumental activities of daily living tasks through virtual reality technology. In addition, indicators, such as task completion time and number of screen touches, were automatically measured by the tablet-based VKC and correlated with the frequency of human errors. Cognitive function tests exhibited significant differences between the young adults and healthy older subjects. Therefore, these indicators might be effective for the early detection of MCI. However, previous studies may implicitly assume that the basic movement characteristics without cognitive load are the same. Given that basic movement characteristics vary considerably among subjects, this study investigated the differences owing to basic movement characteristics using a group difference test. In addition, significant differences observed in the basic movement characteristics were compared with the indices of the breakfast and lunch tasks, and the effects of added cognitive load were investigated. The results showed significant differences in indices related to basic movement characteristics among the subjects, and that subjects with MCI were more affected by the application of cognitive load than healthy older subjects. Prospects include creating a classification model between healthy older subjects and those with MCI, including indicators of basic movement tasks.

Keywords: Mild Cognitive Impairment · Virtual Reality · Tablet Device

1 Introduction

1.1 Increase in the Number of Patients with Alzheimer's Disease

According to a report by the International Alzheimer's Association, the number of people with dementia reached approximately 57 million in 2015 globally and is expected to increase to 115.4 million by 2050 [1]. This trend is also evident in Japan, where the birth

© The Author(s), under exclusive license to Springer Nature Switzerland AG 2025
J. Y. C. Chen et al. (Eds.): HCII 2024, LNCS 15377, pp. 204–223, 2025.
https://doi.org/10.1007/978-3-031-76812-5_15

rate is declining and the population is aging, with a reported 4.62 million people in 2012 and an increase to approximately 7 million by 2025 [2]. Alzheimer's disease is the most common type of dementia, accounting for approximately 67.6% of all cases of dementia [2]. However, no fundamental treatment for dementia has yet been discovered, and when it does occur, the only measures that can be taken are to impede the progression of the disease or to temporarily alleviate symptoms.

1.2 Mild Cognitive Impairment (MCI)

MCI) is a precursor stage of dementia and refers to a condition between healthy individuals and patients with dementia. Winblad et al. proposed the following points [3].

1. The person is neither normal nor demented.
2. Evidence of cognitive deterioration includes objectively measured decline over time or a subjective report of decline by self or informants in conjunction with objective cognitive deficits.
3. Activities of daily living (ADLs) are preserved, and complex instrumental functions are either intact or minimally impaired.

Approximately 1%–2% of normal older people transition to dementia, whereas 10% transition to MCI every year [4]. However, some patients with MCI recovered to a normal cognitive status through appropriate treatment [5]. Therefore, an important issue in coping with cognitive impairment involves understanding of the state of cognitive function of patients, specifically in terms of prevention, and detecting MCI at an early stage. Cognitive function tests, such as the mini mental state examination and revised Hasegawa simplified intelligence scale, are currently used as screening methods for cognitive impairment. However, their accuracy for MCI is low despite their high discrimination accuracy for dementia patients, with sensitivity in the range of 45%–60% and specificity in the range of 65%–90% [6–8]. Therefore, evaluating cognitive and activity functions, such as planning and thinking skills, is essential for MCI screening.

1.3 ADL

Studies have focused on ADL as a screening method for activity function, and ADL are divided into two types: basic activities of daily living (BADL) and instrumental activities of daily living (IADL). Compared with BADL, IADL include the high-level activities of daily living, such as shopping, meal preparation, and property management. IADL are the preferred means of assessing cognitive impairment because they are more complex processes and require more thinking than BADL. Indeed, adults with MCI are more inefficient in IADL tasks than healthy older adults and take more time to complete these tasks [9]. The informant report and naturalistic action test (NAT) are evaluation methods based on IADL.

1.4 Informant Report

Currently, self- and informant reports are commonly used to assess daily functioning in MCI and patients with dementia. The results of these methods are easy to collect and

provide essential information if used with reliable informants. However, these methods were not useful in the absence of informants Even when informants are available,
the results can be biased toward patients and informants. For example, in self-reported
results, patients with MCI tend to underestimate functional difficulties compared with
informants, whereas healthy older adults often overestimate functional difficulties compared with informants [10]. In addition, race, ethnicity, and education may influence
self-report and informant report ratings [10]. Because there are currently no criteria for
determining whether self-reports and informant reports are reliable, an objective method
for assessing IADL competence is required.

1.5   NAT

The NAT, which is a performance-based measurement method using IADL, is an evaluation method that ensures objectivity [11]. Human errors analyzed by the NAT consist
of omission, commission, and micro errors [12, 13].

Omission error occurs when a target task is not performed, commission error occurs
when the task is not performed correctly, and micro errors are subtle action difficulties
not included in omission and commission errors (Tables 1 and 2).

Table 1. Omission and commission errors (modified from [12]).

Error Category		Definitions
	Omission	A step or subtask is not performed
Commission	Substitution	Semantically related or perceptually similar alternate object used in place of target object
	Anticipation-omission	Anticipation of a step that entails a subsequent omission (anticipation-omission); steps or subtasks are performed in reverse order (reversal)
	Perseveration	A step or subtask is performed more than once
	Quality	An action is performed repetitively or for an excessive amount of time
	Gesture Substitution	Task performance is grossly inadequate
	Spatial Misorientation	Correct object is used but with an inappropriate gesture

Previous research on this human error has shown significant differences in the total
scores of omission and commission errors between healthy older and MCI subjects [12].
In subjects with mild cognitive disabilities, micro errors considerably increased with
increasing task difficulty compared with omission and commission errors [13]. Task
difficulty was controlled by the number of actions required to complete a task and the
number of distractor objects (DO), which are objects that are not related to the task but
have a similar shape to the objects required for the task and invite action errors.

However, NAT has various problems because it is performed in a real space (Fig. 1).
For example, the preparation of a task is time consuming and generates waste after the

Table 2. Micro error (modified from [13]).

Error Category	Definitions
Reach, Touch	Unwanted object is reached for and touched
Reach, No Touch	Unwanted object is reached for but not touched
Reach With Object	While holding an object, hand is moved towards a non-target location
Extra Action	Object is lifted and moved or put back down
Sequence	Without purpose and without increasing efficiency

task is completed. Scoring results require expertise, and each patient is diagnosed for several hours to days. Therefore, the NAT is not considered suitable for mass screening.

Fig. 1. The scene of NAT being performed.

1.6 Virtual Kitchen Challenge (VKC)

To address issues related to NAT, virtual reality (VR)-IADL, which uses VR to reproduce IADL, has been developed [14]. It is also referred to as VKC. The VKC was modified into a tablet application, a tablet-based VR-IADL, considering the burden imposed by VR on older people and its use for mass screening. After the VKC was completed, data on a subject's operations were output in the form of a CSV file after the VKC was completed. After the task was completed on the tablet, the equipment and space required for the task were significantly reduced, and the contents of the VKC from the output data were analyzed. Figure 2 shows the VKC execution screen.

1.7 VKC Tasks

The VKC comprises two tasks: a breakfast task, which prepares breakfast, and a lunch task, which prepares lunch. In these two tasks, a main task was defined for each task in

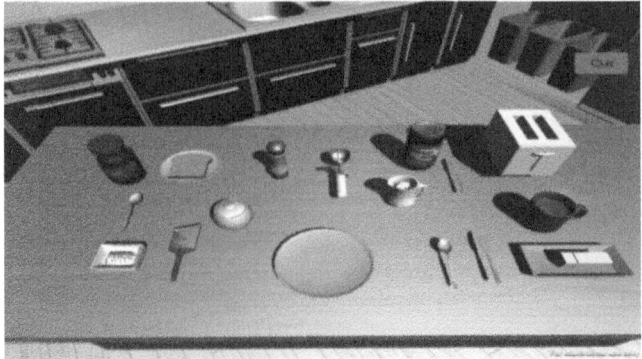

Fig. 2. VKC execution screen.

terms of the number of items created, and each main task consisted of subtasks defined in terms of the number of times the screen was touched.

Examples of the main tasks and subtasks based on the breakfast task are provided below. In the breakfast task, toast and coffee were prepared, representing two main tasks: the toast and coffee tasks. The coffee task has subtasks such as putting a piece of bread in the toaster and pressing the toaster lever. The hierarchical structure of the tasks in the VKC is shown in Fig. 3.

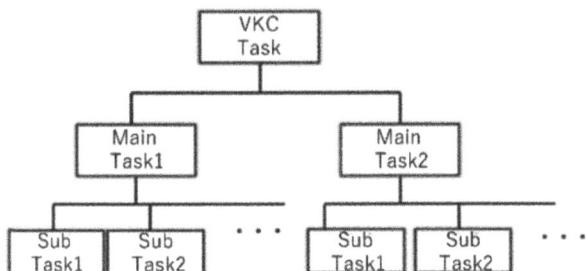

Fig. 3. Hierarchy of VKC tasks.

1.8 VKC Objects

In the VKC, each breakfast or lunch task has a target object (TO), which is an object needed to perform the task, and a DO, which is an object that invites errors in actions that are unrelated to the task. Examples of each object are provided according to the breakfast task (Fig. 4). In the breakfast task, spreading the jam on toast using a knife is essential. Thus, examples of TOs include a piece of bread, a knife, and a jar of jam. However, paintbrush and ice cream scoops are irrelevant for toast and coffee making and are examples of DOs.

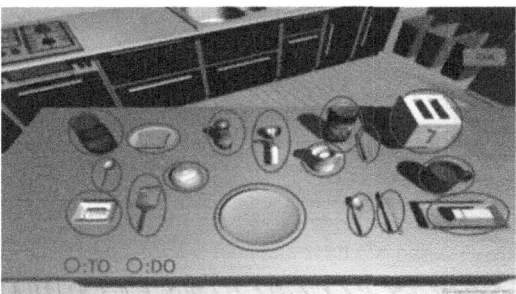

Fig. 4. TO and DO.

1.9 Indicators from the Automatic Measurement of VKC

In the transition from the NAT to the VKC, the diagnostic criteria are diversified. In the NAT, error-based scoring, such as omission, commission, and micro errors is conducted by experts and is based on videos of subjects performing tasks. By contrast, VKC can automatically record a subject's actions from a tablet PC. Therefore, it can measure indicators, such as completion time, number of screen contacts, and screen on or off time. If screening for cognitive dysfunction can be carried out using only these indicators, the diagnosis can be automated.

1.10 Previous Research on VKC

A previous study [14] obtained data from 14 healthy older adults and 21 young adults who performed IADL tasks in real space and on a tablet VKC system. The results in real space were scored by an expert using omission and commission errors. In addition to error-based scoring, the VKC results were measured using indicators automatically obtained by the tablet PC, such as task execution time, number of screen contacts, and percentage of screen on or off time. A comparison of the obtained measurements revealed significant correlations between the total omission and commission error scores obtained from the IADL task in real space and the number of micro errors for all indicators automatically measured by the VKC [14]. In addition, the completion time and number of screen contacts were significantly correlated with the results of tests assessing attention, processing speed, and episodic memory. The usefulness of tablet-type VKC as an objective and efficient method for detecting MCI has been explored.

1.11 VKC Task Behaviors and Human Cognitive and Behavioral Models

A simplified diagram of the behavioral processes that occur in the VKC, which is based on a human cognitive model is shown in Fig. 5.

The model is explained using the act of transferring a piece of bread to a plate as an example, which is one of the subtasks of the VKC.

– Attention

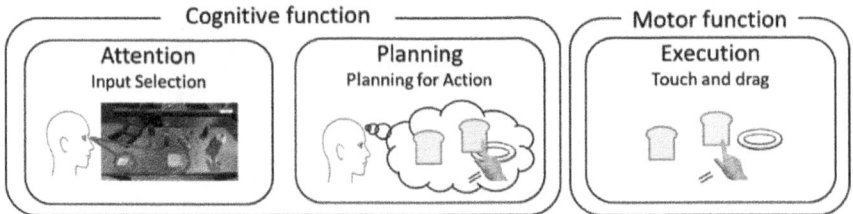

Fig. 5. VKC behaviors and cognitive and behavioral models (modified from [15]).

Discard and select information from a number of TOs and DOs and capture only information on objects (bread and plate) that are relevant to the task.

– Planning

Plan the process of moving the bread to the plate (touch the bread, slide it to the plate, and release the finger to finish).

– Execution

The planned action is executed by basic actions, including touch and drag.

Thus, the performance indicators obtained in the VKC facilitate the evaluation of actions performed through attention and planning by the cognitive function and execution by the motor function. In other words, previous studies have used performance indicators influenced by cognitive and motor functions.

1.12   Assumptions in Previous Studies

However, VKC indices generated by cognitive and motor functions have only been compared with values assessing cognitive functions, such as cognitive function tests and human error [14]. Therefore, simple motor functions, such as dragging and touching, that is, basic movement characteristics, can be implicitly assumed to be the same across subjects. However, the differences in basic movement characteristics remain unclear.

In addition, significant differences were found between young and healthy older adults in the number of motor errors in the NAT and VKC, which are environments that require attention and planning, that is, cognitive load. Examples of motor errors include scooping coffee grounds with a spoon and their spilling. Therefore, differences in basic movement characteristics between healthy elderly (HE) and patients with MCI may be observed when cognitive loads, such as attention and planning, are removed.

1.13   Focus of This Study

Therefore, the differences between subjects in basic movement characteristics when cognitive load is excluded should be investigated. In addition, if significant differences are found between subjects, it is essential to investigate whether a synergistic effect with cognitive load occurs to clarify whether the significant differences shown by the VKC are due to basic movement characteristics alone or whether they include the effects of added cognitive load, such as attention and planning. A synergistic effect suggests that the differences between subjects are further increased by the cognitive load. Conversely, the absence of a synergistic effect suggests that the differences between the subjects are due to basic movement characteristics.

1.14 Basic Movement Task

In this study, a basic movement task was set up to measure the differences in basic movement characteristics in the VKC. In the basic movement task, the movements required in the breakfast and lunch tasks were specified and explained individually, and no objects were required for the task. This approach removes the cognitive load of attention and planning, and only the characteristics of basic movement can be captured. Figure 6 shows the differences between the basic movement task and the breakfast and lunch tasks.

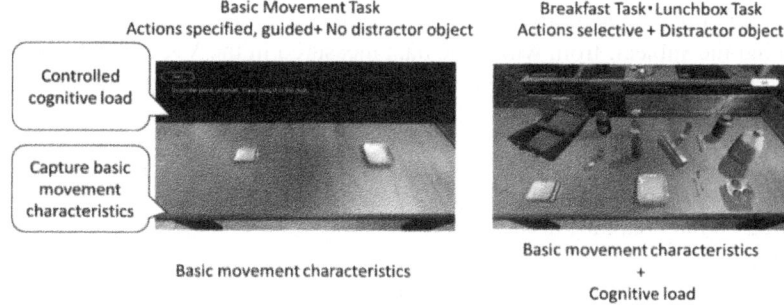

Fig. 6. Differences between basic movement tasks and breakfast and lunch tasks.

1.15 Effects of Basic Movement Characteristics and Cognitive Load

In this study, we used the indicators in the basic movement task to investigate whether the differences between HE and MCI were due to basic movement characteristics. In addition, we compared the indices of the basic movement task, which were influenced by basic movement characteristics, with those of the breakfast and tasks, which were influenced by basic movement characteristics and cognitive load, to investigate whether a synergistic effect occurred between subjects (HE and MCI) and cognitive load (with or without).

2 Objective

In this study, we used the indicators in the basic movement task to investigate whether the differences between HE and MCI are due to basic movement characteristics. In addition, we compared the indicators of the basic movement task, which were influenced by basic movement characteristics, with those of the breakfast and tasks, which were influenced by both basic movement characteristics and cognitive load, to investigate whether a synergistic effect occurred between subjects (HE and MCI) and cognitive load (with or without).

3 Method

3.1 Participant

The present study used a dataset obtained from the measurements of Giovannetti et al. Specifically, we used experimental data from 83 subjects (66 HE: HE and 17 MCI) with a mean age of 73.61 years (SD = 6.85).

3.2 Measurement Environment

The measurement environment in this study is shown in Fig. 7, which consists of a tablet PC with VKC implemented and a camera recording the entire screen of the tablet PC from behind the subject, from which the data measured in the VKC (CSV file) and the subject's video during the experiment were obtained. The subjects performed the VKC tasks in the following order.

1. Training of the basic movement task
2. Test of the basic movement task (with measurement)
3. Training on the breakfast task
4. Training on the lunch task
5. Test of the breakfast task (with measurement)
6. Test of the lunch task (with measurement)

The order of the breakfast and lunch tasks was counterbalanced between subjects.

Fig. 7. Measurement environment

3.3 Details of the VKC

In this study, subjects' data were measured and used for analysis in three tests: breakfast, lunch, and basic movement tasks. The breakfast and lunch tasks in this study consisted of a main task and a subtask. In addition, TO and DO were placed in each task in this study as in previous studies; the number of DO was standardized to four. The VKC execution screen, list of tasks, and list of placed objects used are described in the supplementary material.

3.4 Data Output from the VKC

The VKC used in this study was designed to output a CSV file containing information on each task at the end of the breakfast, lunch, and basic movement training tasks. The following information was included in this CSV file:

1. Time: time from the start to the end of the task
2. Subject's screen interaction: subject's movement on the screen
3. Names of the objects touched
4. Coordinates of each object
5. Rotational coordinates of each object

The data obtained from these CSV files were used to calculate each indicator.

3.5 Calculated Indicators and Calculation Method

In this study, two indicators were calculated for the breakfast or lunch task and the basic movement task: task completion time (completion time) and number of screen touches (total touch number). Each indicator was calculated using MATLAB. A program was set up to calculate each indicator from a CSV file, and each indicator was graphed and compared with the subject's video data to ensure that the calculations were correct. Figure 8 shows the calculation steps conducted using MATLAB.

3.6 Evaluation of Indicators

In this study, an unpaired two-sample test was used to investigate whether significant differences were found between HE and MCI in each of the indices of the basic movement task described in the previous section. An unpaired t-test was used when normality was found in the index data, and a Mann–Whitney U-test was used when normality and equal variance were not found. Effect sizes were calculated using Cohen's d (small $=$ 0.2, medium $=$ 0.5, large $=$ 0.8) for the t-test and Cliff's δ (small $<$ 0.33, medium $<$ 0.47, large $>$ 0.47) for the Mann–Whitney U test.

Moreover, I initially planned to perform an analysis of variance (mixed design) on the indicators that exhibited significant differences between HE and MCI in a two-sample test with no correspondence to investigate how cognitive load affected the differences between the subjects. However, given that no index of normality was found, a non-parametric method, the generalized linear mixed effects model (GLMM), was used instead. The order in which the GLMM was conducted is summarized below.

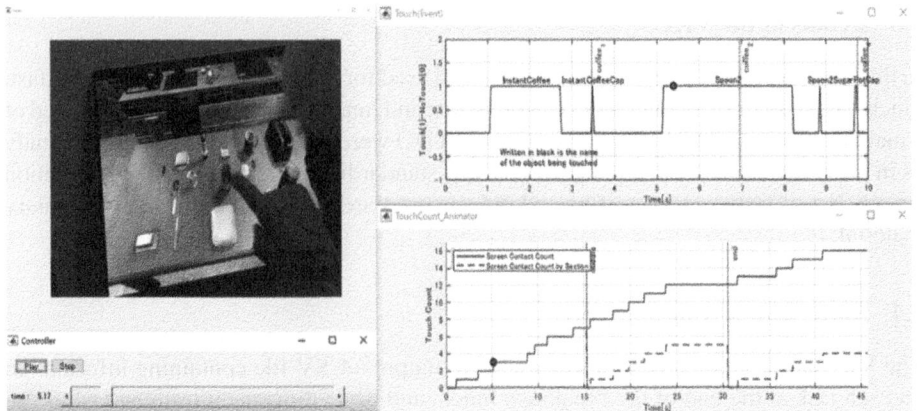

Fig. 8. Environment in which the calculations were carried out.

1. Each indicator was set as the dependent variable, and the between-subjects parameters (HE and MCI) and between-tasks parameter (sum of basic movement, breakfast, and lunch tasks) were used as fixed effects, and the number of subjects as random effects.
2. All streets were generated from each full model to the null model. When the index data were continuous values, the gamma distribution was specified for the family and log for the link function, whereas the Poisson distribution was specified for the family and log for the link function when the index data were discrete values.
3. The model equation with the lowest BIC value among all the models was adopted, and the coefficient of the interaction term was assessed for significance using the Wald test.

4   Result

4.1   Effects of Basic Movement Characteristics on Differences Between Subjects

Whether normality and equal variance were found for completion time and the total touch number in the basic movement task was investigated, and tests of group differences were conducted. The results are shown in Table 3. Given that normality and equal variance were not found for all indicators, Mann–Whitney's U-test was used for the tests.

Table 3.   Result of Mann–Whitney's U-test.

	z	p	Cliff's δ
Completion Time	-3.24	0.00117	-0.51
Total Touch Number	-2.02	0.0376	-0.33

The mean and standard error plots for completion time and screen contact time are shown in Fig. 9.

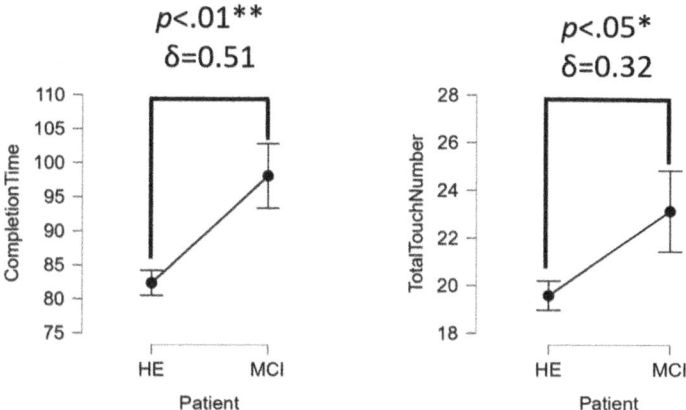

Fig. 9. The mean and standard error plots.

The above results show that MCI has significantly larger values than HE for completion time (z = −3.24, p < .01, δ = 0.51) and total touch number (z = −2.02, p < .05, δ = 0.32). The effect size Cliff's δ was small (0.32) for the number of screen contacts but large (0.51) for the task completion time, suggesting that the VKC can capture differences between HE and MCI according to the basic movement characteristics.

4.2   Effects of Adding Cognitive Load on Between-Subject Differences

The results of a two-factor and two-level GLMM for the two indicators of completion time and total number of touches are shown in Figs. 10 and 11.

```
Fixed effects:
                      Estimate Std. Error t value Pr(>|z|)
(Intercept)            4.39627    0.03582 122.741  <2e-16 ***
PatientMCI             0.16718    0.07911   2.113  0.0346 *
TaskB+L                0.68400    0.02362  28.964  <2e-16 ***
PatientMCI:TaskB+L     0.10772    0.05224   2.062  0.0392 *
---
Signif. codes:  0 '***' 0.001 '**' 0.01 '*' 0.05 '.' 0.1 ' ' 1
```

Fig. 10. GLMM results for completion time.

```
Fixed effects:
                      Estimate Std. Error z value Pr(>|z|)
(Intercept)            2.93255    0.04847  60.507  < 2e-16 ***
PatientMCI             0.08701    0.10518   0.827  0.408
TaskB+L                1.06423    0.03218  33.068  < 2e-16 ***
PatientMCI:TaskB+L     0.28777    0.06501   4.426 9.59e-06 ***
---
Signif. codes:  0 '***' 0.001 '**' 0.01 '*' 0.05 '.' 0.1 ' ' 1
```

Fig. 11. GLMM result for total touch time.

Fixed effects estimates in the above figures exhibited significant interactions for completion time ($t(160) = 2.06$, $p < .05$) and total touch number ($t(160) = 2.67$, $p < .01$). The estimated means and 95% confidence intervals for both indicators are plotted in Figs. 12 and 13.

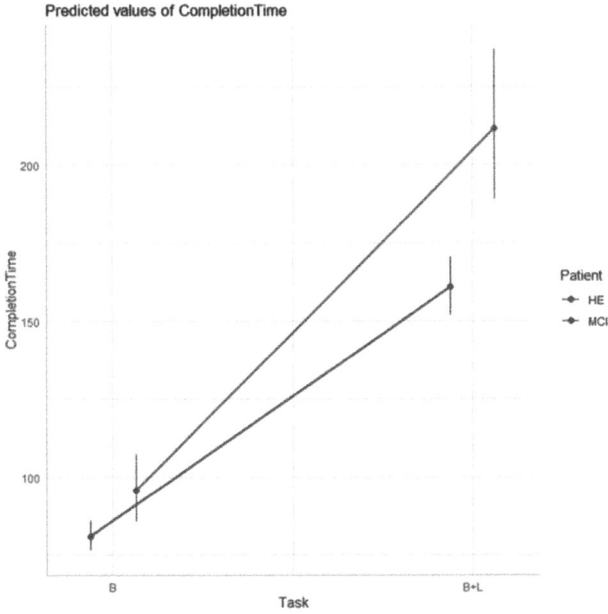

Fig. 12. Estimated mean and 95% confidence intervals for completion time.

The increase in value after the addition of the cognitive load of MCI was greater than the increase in value in HE.

5   Discussion

Substantial differences were observed between the HE and MCI according to the basic movement characteristics of the VKC, and MCI values increased significantly when cognitive load was added, compared with the HE groups.

First, significant differences were observed in the basic movement characteristics; that is, the indices of the basic movement task, which were discussed. We also discussed the significantly greater completion time of MCI compared to that of HE. An example of the on-screen finger velocity waveforms of the HE and MCI is shown in Fig. 14.

The velocity waveforms of the HE and MCI from the above diagram were compared. The velocity waveform of MCI had a tail to the right compared to that of HE. This result suggested that the MCI had a larger adjustment time for pointing movements compared with HE, which might result in increased completion time. During the adjustment time, a visual feedback loop controls the hand to move precisely toward the target

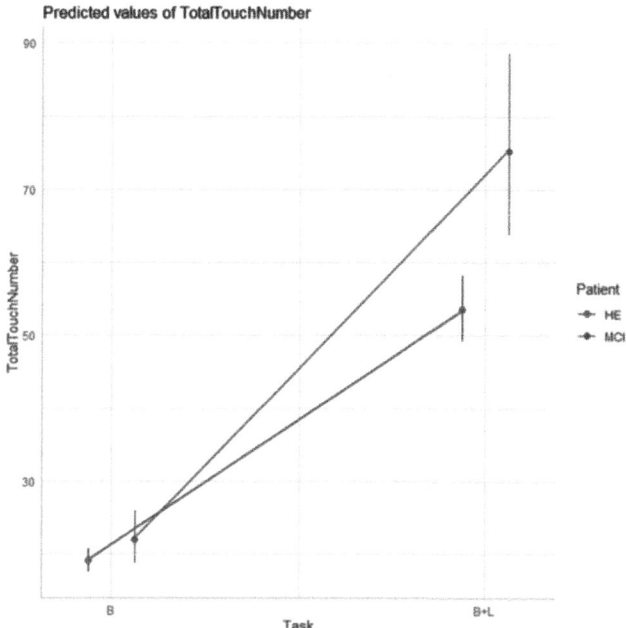

Fig. 13. Estimated mean and 95% confidence intervals for total touch number.

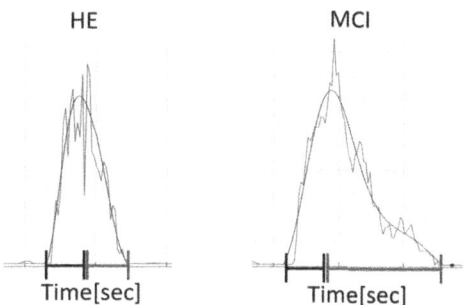

Fig. 14. Velocity waveforms of the HE and MCI.

by adjusting its velocity [16]. Therefore, patients with MCI might exhibit less control over finger movements than those with HE. Similar tendency was observed for off-screen movements; therefore, it is essential to investigate the differences between MCI and HE subjects in terms of finger velocity waveforms. Figure 15 shows the adjustment time for pointing.

Next, a discussion of the significantly higher total touch number in MCI compared with HE was presented: in the movements of MCI, few actions caused a subject to release his fingers during the task due to errors in the strength of the finger force. Therefore, there is a possibility that a decrease in the sense of agency might occur due to

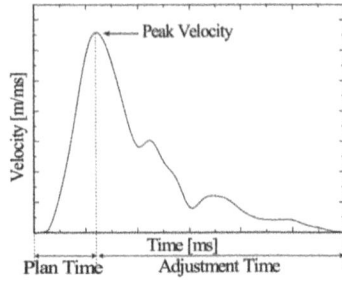

Fig. 15. Velocity waveform during pointing operation [16].

the discrepancy between the predicted movement and the movement performed by the subjects themselves.

Finally, the results of the GLMM suggested that the difference between HE and MCI increased after the addition of cognitive load because MCI was severely affected by an increase in cognitive load compared to HE.

6   Conclusion

The study highlighted that the performance indicators automatically measured by the VKC exhibited significant differences between HE and patients with MCI in terms of basic movement characteristics, and these differences were considerably increased by cognitive load. Prospects include investigating whether speed waveforms can show differences between HE and patients with MCI because MCI may increase the adjustment time. Moreover, because the VKC project ultimately aims to automatically discriminate between HE and MCI, the creation of a classification model for HE and MCI with indicators, including the basic movement task indicators that exhibited significant differences in this study, is necessary.

Acknowledgments. This study was funded by National Institute of Health (NIH) (grant number 1R01AG062503-01A1).

Appendix

This section describes the VKC execution screen, task list and object list used in this study. In this study, subjects' data were measured and used for analysis in three tests: breakfast task, lunch task and basic movement task. Figure 16 below shows the display screens for each task.

Breakfast Task	Lunch Task	Basic Movement Task

Fig. 16. Display screen for each task.

The breakfast and lunch tasks in this study also consist of a main task and subtasks, as in previous studies. The main task and subtasks in the breakfast and lunch tasks are listed below.

Breakfast task (number of main tasks: 4)
Toast task (number of subtasks: 7)

1. Place the bread in the toaster
2. Lower the toaster lever
3. Wait until the toast is cooked
4. Move the toast to the plate
5. Open the grape jam lid.
6. Take a knife and spread the grape jam on the bread.
7. Take the butter with the knife and spread it on the bread
8. Coffee task (Number of subtasks: 6)
9. Open the lid of the instant coffee jar.
10. Take the instant coffee powder with a spoon and put it into the mug
11. Stir the contents of the mug with a spoon
12. Open the lid of the sugar pot
13. Take the sugar with the spoon and put it into the mug
14. Pour the cream into the coffee

Quit button task (number of subtasks: 1)

1. Press the Quit button

Lunch task (number of main tasks: 5)
Sandwich task (number of subtasks: 9)

1. Move one piece of bread to the plate
2. Open the lid of the grape jam
3. Take the grape jam with a knife and spread it on the bread
4. Open the lid of the peanut butter
5. Take the peanut butter with a knife and spread it on the bread.
6. Place the two slices of bread on top of the other
7. Take out the aluminum foil
8. Wrap the sandwich in the aluminum foil
9. Put the sandwich in the box

Juice task (number of subtasks: 5)

1. open the lid of the juice
2. pour the juice into the water bottle
3. close the lid of the water bottle
4. close the cup of the water bottle
5. put the canteen in the box

Snack task (number of subtasks: 3)

1. take out the aluminum foil
2. wrap the cookies in aluminum foil
3. Place the snacks in the box

Box task (Number of subtasks: 1)

1. Close the lunch box

Quit button task (Number of subtasks: 1)

1. Press the Quit button

The basic action task consists of eight actions that are required when performing the breakfast and lunch tasks. When performing each movement, only the objects required for the movement are displayed on the screen. The subject can also perform the movements while reading the explanations displayed at the top of the screen. The eight movements of the basic movement task are described below.

List of actions for basic movement tasks.

1. Move a piece of bread to a plate
2. Stir the contents of the mug with a spoon
3. Open the lid of the juice bottle and pour the juice into the canteen
4. Places the canteen in the lunch box and occupies the lid
5. Open the jam lid, remove the jam with a knife and spread it on the bread
6. Take out the aluminum foil and wrap the cookies in it
7. Place the bread in the toaster and pull down the toaster lever
8. Open the lid of the sugar pot, take out the sugar with a spoon and put it in the mug

Of the above, items 2, 5, 7 and 8 are movements required for the breakfast task and items 1, 3, 4, 5 and 6 for the lunch task. The order of the movements for each task is also counterbalanced.

The objects in the VKC are described next. In this study, as in previous studies, TO and DO were placed in each task; the number of DO was controlled to four. Tables 4 and 5 below show the list of objects for each task.

Table 4. Objects for Breakfast task

#	Object Type	Object
1	Target	Bread Dish
2	Target	Butter Dish
3	Target	Creamer
4	Target	Grape Jelly
5	Target	Grape Jerry Cap
6	Target	Instant Coffee
7	Target	Instant Coffee Cap
8	Target	Knife
9	Target	Mug
10	Target	Spoon
11	Target	Sugar Pot
12	Target	Sugar Pot Cap
13	Target	Toast
14	Target	Toast Dish
15	Target	Toaster
16	Target	Toaster Lever
17	Target	White Dish
18	Distractor	Ashtray
19	Distractor	Ice Cream Scoop
20	Distractor	Paint Brush
21	Distractor	Saltshaker

Table 5. Objects for Lunch task

#	Object Type	Object
1	Target	Aluminum Foil
2	Target	Bread
3	Target	Cap
4	Target	Cookie
5	Target	Cookie Dish
6	Target	Foil
7	Target	Grape Jelly

(*continued*)

Table 5. (*continued*)

#	Object Type	Object
8	Target	Grape Jelly Cap
9	Target	Juice
10	Target	Kitchen Paper
11	Target	Knife
12	Target	Lunchbox
13	Target	Peanut Butter
14	Target	Peanut Butter Cap
15	Target	Salad Bowl
16	Target	Thermos
17	Target	Thermos Cap
18	Target	Thermos Cup
19	Target	Upper Pivot
20	Target	White Dish
21	Target	Wrapped Cookie
22	Target	Wrapped Sandwich
23	Target	Wrapped Snack
24	Distractor	Fork
25	Distractor	Glass
26	Distractor	Razor
27	Distractor	Spray Bottle

References

1. Christina, P.: World Alzheimer Report 2018. World Alzheimer Report 2018: The State of the Art of Dementia Research: New Frontiers (1). 34. (2018)
2. Comprehensive promotion of dementia policies. https://www.mhlw.go.jp/contsent/12300000/000519620.pdf. Accessed 25 March 2023
3. Winblad, B., et al.: Mild cognitive impairment–beyond controversies, towards a consensus: report of the international working group on mild cognitive impairment. J. Intern. Med. **256**(3), 240–246 (2004). https://doi.org/10.1111/j.1365-2796.2004.01380.x
4. Yamamoto, S.: Current topics on mild cognitive impairment (MCI). J. Neuropsych. **133**(6), 584–592 (2018)
5. Malek-Ahmadi, M.: Reversion from mild cognitive impairment to normal cognition: a meta-analysis. Alzheimer Dis. Assoc. Disorders **30**(4), 324–330 (2016). https://doi.org/10.247/NDT.s223958

6. Tariq, S.H., Tumosa, N., Chibnall, J.T., Perry, M.H., Morley. J.E.: Comparison of the saint louis university mental status examination and the mini-mental state examination for detecting dementia and mild neurocognitive disorder–a pilot study. Am. J. Geriatric Psych. Offic. J. Am. Assoc. Geriatric Psych. **14**(11), 900–910 (2006). https://doi.org/10.1097/01.JGP.000022 1510.33817.86

7. Judith, S., Morrow, L., Eschman, A., Archer, G., Luther, J., Zuccolotto. A.: Computer assessment of mild cognitive impairment. Postgrad. Med. **121**(2), 177–185 (2009). https://doi.org/ 10.3810/pgm.2009.03.1990

8. Kaufer, D.I., Williams, C.S, Braaten, A.J., Gill, K., Zimmerman, S., Sloane. P.D.: Cognitive screening for dementia and mild cognitive impairment in assisted living: comparison of 3 tests. J. Am. Med. Direct. Assoc. **9**(8), 586–593 (2008). https://doi.org/10.1016/j.jamda.2008. 05.006

9. Schmitter-Edgecombe, McAlister, C.C., Weakley, A.: Naturalistic assessment of everyday functioning in individuals with mild cognitive impairment: the day-out task. Neuropsychology **26**(5), 631–641 (2012). https://doi.org/10.1037/a0029352

10. Edmonds, E.C., et al.: Susceptibility of the conventional criteria for mild cognitive impairment to false-positive diagnostic errors. Alzheimer's Dementia **11**(4), 415–424 (2015). https://doi. org/10.1016/j.jalz.2014.03.005

11. Giovannetti, T., Bettcher, B.M., Libon, D.J., Brennan, L., Sestito, N., Kessler. R.K.: Environmental adaptations improve everyday action performance in alzheimer's disease: empirical support from performance-based assessment. Neuropsychology **21**(4), 448–457 (2007). https://doi.org/10.1037/0894-4105.21.4.448

12. Giovannetti, T., et al.: Characterization of everyday functioning in mild cognitive impairment: a direct assessment approach. Dementia Geriatric Cogn. Disorders **25**, 359–365 (2008). https://doi.org/10.1159/000121005

13. Seligman, S.C., Giovannetti, T., Sestito, J., Libon. D.J.: A new approach to the characterization of subtle errors in everyday action: implications for mild cognitive impairment. Clin. Neuropsychol. **28**(1), 97–115 (2014). https://doi.org/10.1080/13854046.2013.852624

14. Giovannetti, T., Yamaguchi, T., Roll, E., Harada, T., Rycroft, S.S., Divers. R.: The virtual kitchen challenge: preliminary data from a novel virtual reality test of mild difficulties in everyday functioning. Aging, Neuropsychol. Cogn. **26**(6), 823–841 (2019). https://doi.org/ 10.1080/13825585.2018.1536774

15. Remington, R.W., Loft, S.: Attention and multitasking. In: APA Handbook of Human Systems Integration (1), pp. 261–277 (2015). https://doi.org/10.1037/14528-017

16. Tsukitani, T., Takashima, K., Kitamura, Y., Kishino, F.: Effects of target attributes on trajectory and motion characteristics in mouse pointing. Trans. Hum. Interface Soc. **10**(1), 95–102 (2008). https://doi.org/10.11184/his.10.1_95

Factors Influencing the Purchase Intention of Consumer VR All-In-One Headsets

Ruoyu Yang[2(✉)], Ruiqing Ma[3], and Min Hua[1]

[1] Shanghai Jiao Tong University, Shanghai, China
[2] City University of Hong Kong, Hong Kong, China
ruoyuyang3-c@my.cityu.edu.hk
[3] Arizona State University, Tempe, AZ, USA
alex.ma@asu.edu

Abstract. The recent breakthroughs in Virtual Reality (VR) technology have heightened public interest - as evidenced by initiatives such as the launch of Apple's Vision Pro. However, there is a lack of research exploring consumer acceptance of all-in-one VR headsets. This study aims to address this research gap by investigating the key factors that influence consumers' purchase intentions for VR headsets. In this study, an integrated theoretical framework was employed, combining elements from the Technology Acceptance Model, the Theory of Planned Behavior, and the Value Acceptance Model. This allowed for a comprehensive examination of a variety of influencing factors, including perceived usefulness, content enjoyment, ease of use, price, and physical risk, and their impacts on attitudes towards VR headsets. Furthermore, the study investigated the effect of attitudes and subjective norms on purchase intentions, with a particular focus on the moderating role of prior traditional gaming habits. Data collected through an online survey revealed that perceived usefulness, content enjoyment, and price significantly influenced attitudes, while ease of use and physical risk did not show a significant impact. Both attitudes and subjective norms significantly affected purchase intentions. The proposed model demonstrated robust explanatory power in predicting attitudes and purchase intentions. A multi-group analysis further revealed that prior traditional gaming habits moderate the effects of price on attitude, as well as the impact of attitude on purchase intention. In sum, the study expands existing acceptance models and provides valuable insights into the development, pricing, and marketing strategies for VR content.

Keywords: Consumer VR all-in-one Headset · Virtual Reality · Technology Acceptance Model · Value Acceptance Model · Metaverse

1 Introduction

The development of computer science has led to the emergence of the metaverse, a post-reality multiuser virtual space that merges physical reality with digital virtuality (Mystakidis 2022). The metaverse can develop in two directions: from real to virtual, enhancing individual experiences and efficiencies (consumer metaverse), and from virtual to real, improving industrial efficiency and generating new industries (industrial metaverse) (Deloitte 2022). While research has traditionally focused on the industrial

© The Author(s), under exclusive license to Springer Nature Switzerland AG 2025
J. Y. C. Chen et al. (Eds.): HCII 2024, LNCS 15377, pp. 224–243, 2025.
https://doi.org/10.1007/978-3-031-76812-5_16

metaverse due to its direct profitability, recent years have seen growing interest in the consumer metaverse. Thus, understanding individual consumers' experiences in the metaverse has become increasingly important.

The metaverse is still in its early stages of development, with ongoing advancements in VR technologies that connect physical and virtual spaces (Deloitte, 2022). Virtual Reality (VR) is defined as an immersive technology that being used to simulate interactive virtual spaces in which users can actively participate and feel truly "being there" (Wohlgenannt 2020). Hence, VR technologies play a crucial role in developing the metaverse (Mystakidis 2022). To broaden access to the metaverse, it is essential for consumers to adopt innovative products, especially consumer VR headsets, which serve as accessible portals to the virtual world. From 2022 to 2024, Meta's Oculus Quest series has dominated the consumer VR headset market, and the launch of Apple's mixed reality (XR) headset, Vision Pro, is expected to boost the market despite a recent decline in VR headset shipments (IDC 2024).

As a type of consumer electronics, VR headsets offer both hedonic and utilitarian value (Pal et al. 2022; Han et al. 2001). Currently, gaming is the primary use case for consumer VR headsets, driving the development of the metaverse. However, exploring more mature usage scenarios, such as remote working, virtual socializing, and fitness, is crucial for the long-term development of the metaverse (McKinsey 2022).

VR headsets are categorized into three types: PC-tethered VR, mobile-based VR, and VR all-in-one headsets (Papachristos et al. 2017). PC-tethered VR offers the best visual quality but requires a high-performance computer, making it expensive and technically demanding. Mobile-based VR is the least expensive and technically accessible but suffers from poor quality and limited functionality. VR all-in-one headsets balance price, technical requirements, and visual quality, functioning as standalone products with good visual quality and a rich content ecosystem. Therefore, this study focuses on VR all-in-one headsets.

Studying consumer VR all-in-one headsets is significant for understanding users' purchase intentions and identifying factors influencing them, which can inform product improvements and support the growth of the virtual reality industry and the metaverse.

Thus, this study aims to investigate the factors and mechanisms affecting consumers' purchase intentions for VR all-in-one headsets. Using the technology acceptance model and the value acceptance model, the study examines the impact of perceived benefits and sacrifices on attitude. Additionally, it explores the influence of attitude and subjective norm on purchase intention through the theory of planned behavior. Also, prior traditional game habits is introduced as a moderating variable. The study seeks to build a theoretical framework explaining consumers' purchase intentions toward VR all-in-one headsets, providing both academic and practical implications.

2 Literature Review and Research Hypothesis

2.1 Related Works on VR Technology Acceptance

VR technology acceptance has aroused research interest for years. The related researches could be categorized into two types. First, most research focused on the VR technology could help other domains' development, such as education, clinical medicine, tourism, etc. For instance, Jang et al. (2021) applied extended technology acceptance model to explore teachers' willingness to integrate AR and VR technologies for teaching practice, finding that perceived usefulness and perceived ease of use would affect the attitude toward technology use and attitude would affect the technology use intention. Glegg et al. (2013) applied decomposed theory of planned behavior to examine the factors influencing therapists' adoption of virtual reality for brain injury rehabilitation, revealing that social influence and knowledge would have positive impact on adoption intention, while time would have negative impact on adoption intention. Vishwakarma et al. (2020) investigated the travelers' intention to adopt VR technology through the consumer value perspective, showing that perceived immersion, perceived physical risk, perceived enjoyment and perceived usefulness would have positive impact on perceived value. Perceived complexity would have negative impact on perceived value and perceived value would have positive impact on using intention of VR.

The first type of research has two limitations. Firstly, current research on the acceptance of VR technology predominantly focus on enterprise-level VR technology and how such technology can better drive developments in other fields. In contrast, there is a lack of academic research on the consumer VR technology. Second, these studies lack attention to the acceptance of actual VR technology experiencers, especially the active consumers. Therefore, this research gap needs to be addressed.

The second type of research focuses on how users accept VR technologies. Sagnier et al. (2020) examined the intention to use VR technology within the context of organizational communication by applying an extended technology acceptance model. Manis and Choi (2019) investigated the mechanism behind VR hardware acceptance intention through the technology acceptance model. These studies, however, have limitations as they do not specifically consider consumer VR all-in-one headsets, which are important due to their promising future. Additionally, most studies related to VR technology acceptance are based on the technology acceptance model, incorporating various extended variables according to their research objectives. It is imperative to review the classical technology acceptance models.

2.2 Classical Technology Acceptance Models

Since the 1970s, scholars have worked on understanding why users accept innovative technologies (IT), resulting in the development of various IT acceptance theories at both organizational and individual levels. The Technology Acceptance Model (TAM) stands out as a foundational theory predicting user acceptance of innovative technology (Davis 1989). Perceived usefulness and perceived ease of use are fundamental determinants in TAM, influencing users' acceptance of innovative technologies. In Davis' research, perceived usefulness and perceived ease of use have significant impact on attitude, while attitude affects the acceptance intention siginifically. Empirical researches extensively support TAM's ability to explain various technology acceptance intentions.

The theory of planned behavior (TPB), introduced by Ajzen (1991), explores individuals' behavioral intentions from a social psychological perspective. Attitude, subjective norm and perceived behavioral control shape behavioral intentions. TPB has successfully explained and predicted behavior across domains, including technology adoption and consumer behavior (Ajzen 2020). Moreover, subjective norm is an important variable that scholars use to enrich the TAM (Taylor & Todd 1995).

Another theory that greatly enriching the TAM is value acceptance model (VAM) proposed by Kim et al. (2007). They found that users in the Internet era, unlike the organizational environment in which the TAM originated, can voluntarily choose to adopt innovative technology from an individual perspective, with the gains and losses evaluated by the individual. Therefore, the perceived value theory was introduced based on the TAM. Zeithaml (1988) believed that the antecedents influencing perceived value are perceived benefits and perceived sacrifices. Babin et al. (1994) divided perceived value into perceived utilitarian value and perceived hedonic value. Sweeney and Soutar (2001) proposed the "PERVAL" model, dividing perceived value into perceived emotional value, perceived social value, perceived quality, and perceived price. Wang et al. (2004) based on "PERVAL," divided perceived value into perceived functional value, perceived emotional value, perceived social value, and perceived losses, with perceived losses compensating for the shortcomings of perceived price by covering losses other than monetary ones. In empirical researches, specific sub-dimensions of perceived value are adjusted according to the research purpose.

2.3 Hypotheses

The theoretical model is shown in (Fig. 1). This model presents the factors and relationships that affecting the purchase intention towards consumer VR all-in-one headsets.

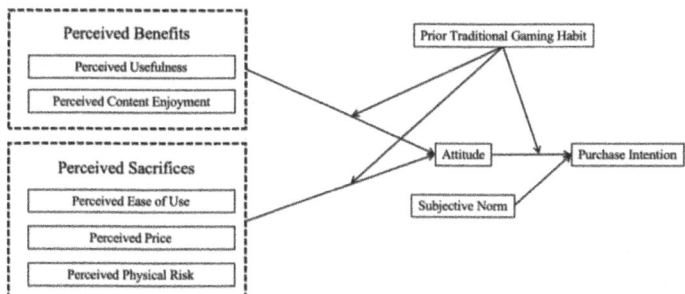

Fig. 1. Theoretical model of influencing factors of purchase intention of consumer VR all-in-one headsets

Purchase Intention, Attitude and Subjective Norm. Combining the definition that Davis provided in the TAM, the purchase intention in this study is defined as the degree that a consumer wants to purchase consumer VR all-in-one headsets (Davis 1989). According to the TPB, an important determinant of behavior intention is attitude (Ajzen 1991). Attitude is defined as the degree to which a consumer has a favorable or unfavorable evaluation of purchasing consumer VR all-in-one headsets in this study. When considering the innovative technologies use intention, such as free trials of technology-based services, attitude is examined as a predictor of trial intention (Zhu & Chang 2014).

Attitude also has impact on the purchase intention towards electronic vehicles (Tunçel 2022). Therefore, this study assumes that attitude would have effect on purchase intention towards consumer VR all-in-one headsets.

According to the TPB, subjective norm is also an important determinant of behavior intention (Ajzen 1991). In this study, subjective norm is defined as the degree to which a consumer perceives social pressure to purchase consumer VR all-in-one headsets. Different from perceived social value, subjective norm emphasizes on the social pressure from important others, while perceived social value emphasized on the association with one or more specific social groups. In the context of this study, subjective norm is believed to be more explanatory towards purchase intention. Subjective norm is proved to be a significant determinant of luxury products among Gen Y consumers (Jain 2020). Thus, this study supposes that subjective norm will have effect on purchase intention towards consumer VR all-in-one headsets. The H1 and H2 are presented below.

H1: Attitude will influence the purchase intention towards consumer VR all-in-one headsets.

H2: Subjective norm will influence the purchase intention towards consumer VR all-in-one headsets.

Perceived Benefits. According to the perceived value, the assessment of a product is determined by comparing the perceived benefits and perceived sacrifices. Various empirical studies have demonstrated that perceived benefits impact attitudes toward specific behaviors. For example, research conducted by Al-Debei et al. (2015) indicated that perceived benefits positively affect consumer attitudes towards online shopping. In the VAM, perceived benefits include two sub-dimensions: perceived usefulness and perceived enjoyment, corresponding to perceived utilitarian value and hedonic value (Kim et al. 2007; Babin et al. 1994). Given that the development of these products is trending towards multifunctional and utilitarian uses, it is important to evaluate whether perceived usefulness is a determinant of attitudes towards consumer VR all-in-one headsets. Thus, this study posits that perceived usefulness, defined as the degree to which a consumer believes the consumer VR all-in-one headsets will increase their work performance, will influence attitude towards purchasing consumer VR all-in-one headsets.

Similarly, perceived enjoyment is considered important to consumers, as the main function of consumer VR all-in-one headsets is still gaming. Since the primary enjoyment comes from the applications rather than the hardware, this study considers perceived content enjoyment, defined as the degree to which a consumer believes the content of consumer VR all-in-one headsets will be enjoyable, as a factor influencing attitude. The H3 and H4 are presented below.

H3: Perceived usefulness will influence the attitude towards purchasing consumer VR all-in-one headsets.

H4: Perceived content enjoyment will influence the attitude towards purchasing consumer VR all-in-one headsets.

Perceived Sacrifices. In VAM, Kim et al. (2007) deemed perceived technicality as one of the sub-dimensions of perceived sacrifices. According to Kim et al. (2007), perceived ease of use has been widely used as an element of technicality, which refers to the degree to which a user believes the operation of a product or system would be free of effort. Perceived ease of use has been considered as an important determinant of attitude towards electric vehicles (Jaiswal et al. 2021). This study assumes the perceived ease of use will influence the attitude towards purchasing consumer VR all-in-one headsets.

Perceived fee, or perceived price, is another sub-dimension of perceived sacrifices. Chiang and Jang (2007) defined perceived price as consumers' relative evaluation of price. Yu et al. (2017) thought repair fee should be considered into perceived price when it comes to consumer electronics. Therefore, this study defines perceive price as consumers' relative evaluation of the sum of the price and repair fee of consumer VR all-on-one. Perceived price is reported as an important predictor of attitude in many empirical studies. Ashfaq et al. (2021) indicated that perceived price significantly affects the consumer attitude towards smart speakers. Hence, this study proposes the perceived price will influence the attitude towards purchasing consumer VR all-in-one headsets.

Perceived risk is an important sub-dimension of perceived sacrifices. According to comments feedback on social media platform, some VR all-in-one headsets users feel sick and dizzy because the 3D vision. Some of them even get hurt because they can't see the real-world obstacle. Therefore, this study assumes perceived physical risk as an indicator towards attitude, which is defined as the degree to which a consumer believes consumer VR all-in-one headsets may be dangerous to health or safety (Derbaix, 1983). The H5, H6 and H7 are listed below.

H5: Perceived ease of use will influence the attitude towards purchasing consumer VR all-in-one headsets.

H6: Perceived price will influence the attitude towards purchasing consumer VR all-in-one headsets.

H7: Perceived physical risk will influence the attitude towards purchasing consumer VR all-in-one headsets.

Prior Traditional Gaming Habits. Prior habit is defined as the combination of experience and automatic behavior. Habit is identified as a significant moderating variable influencing behavioral intention (Venkatesh et al. 2012). Yu et al. (2017) validated that consumer with prior smartphone usage habit perceive greater usefulness of media tablets compared to those without such habit; similarly, Kosa and Uysal (2021) found that the impact of perceived relatedness on the willingness to play Pokémon GO is significantly higher among players with previous gaming habits than those without. Since the main function of consumer VR all-in-one headsets is still perceived as playing game, this study supposes that consumers' prior traditional gaming habits may moderate the effect that perceived value on the attitude and the attitude on the purchase intention. Consequently, this study posits the following hypotheses.

H8a: Prior traditional gaming habits will moderate the effect of perceived usefulness on attitude.

H8b: Prior traditional gaming habits will moderate the effect of perceived content enjoyment on attitude.

H8c: Prior traditional gaming habits will moderate the effect of perceived ease of use on attitude.

H8d: Prior traditional gaming habits will moderate the effect of perceived price on attitude.

H8e: Prior traditional gaming habits will moderate the effect of perceived physical risk on attitude.

H8f: Prior traditional gaming habits will moderate the effect of attitude on purchase intention.

3 Methods

3.1 Data Collection

An online questionnaire survey was conducted to collect data and explore the factors that influencing the purchase intention of consumer VR all-in-one headsets. Questionnaire was distributed from November 2023 to February 2024 through social media platforms in China. To ensure the quality of data, consumer VR all-in-one headset was introduced at the beginning of the questionnaire and the respondents were asked to answer if they ever heard of this type of VR product. Then the purpose of this study was explained. After deleting the respondents who (1) failed the attention-check questions, (2) filled the questionnaire within 60 s, and (3) never heard of the consumer VR all-in-one headset, 371 valid respondents were left for data analysis. Table 1 shows the demographic profile of the respondents.

Table 1. Descriptive statistics of respondents' demographic information

Variable	Category	Frequency (%)
Gender	Male	51.2%
	Female	48.8%
Age	24 or below	20.2%
	25–34	56.6%
	35–44	18.1%
	45 or above	5.1%
Education	Primary school	1.9%
	Junior or senior school	11.6%
	Junior college	28.0%
	Bachelor's degree	33.2%
	Master's degree or above	25.3%
Income per month (RMB)	5000 or below	30.2%
	5000–9999	40.2%
	10000–14999	24.3%
	15000 or above	5.4%

3.2   Measurement Development

To ensure the validity of variable measurement, the measurement items of all variables in this study are developed from the previous studies that exhibited high reliability and validity. All items are adapted according to the research purpose of this study. The measurement included 27 items describing 8 latent variables. This study applies the 7-Likert point scale, as 1 stands for "strongly disagree" and 7 stands for "strongly agree". Table 2 shows the measurement items.

Table 2.   Measurement Items

Variable	Items	Sources
Perceived Usefulness	PU1: Using consumer VR all-in-one headsets would help my daily life and work	Davis 1989; Moon & Kim 2001; Kim & Kyung 2023
	PU2: Using consumer VR all-in-one headsets would improve my working quality	
	PU3: Using consumer VR all-in-one headsets would improve my working efficiency	
	PU4: Using consumer VR all-in-one headsets is useful to work	
Perceived Content Enjoyment	PCE1: The content of consumer VR all-in-one headsets would give enjoyment to me	Kim et al. 2007; Moon and Kim 2001; Yu et al. 2017
	PCE2: The content of consumer VR all-in-one headsets would keep me happy	
	PCE3: The content of consumer VR all-in-one headsets would leads to my exploration	
	PCE4: The content of consumer VR all-in-one headsets would arouse my imagination	
Perceived Ease of Use	PEOU1: It's difficult to learn how to use consumer VR all-in-one headsets	Davis 1989; Kim & Kyung 2023; Moon and Kim 2001
	PEOU2: It takes too long a time to learn to use consumer VR all-in-one headsets	

(*continued*)

Table 2. (*continued*)

Variable	Items	Sources
	PEOU3: It is difficult to remember how to use consumer VR all-in-one headsets	
Perceived Price	PP1: The cost for purchasing consumer VR all-in-one headsets is burdensome to me	Yu et al. 2017
	PP2: Additional A/S costs will be incurred when consumer VR all-in-one headset is out of order	
	PP3: The cost for purchasing the content and applications of consumer VR all-in-one headsets is burdensome to me	
Perceived Physical Risk	PPR1: Using consumer VR all-in-one headsets would make me feel uncomfortable	Developed by researchers
	PPR2: Using consumer VR all-in-one headsets would make me feel dizzy or sick	
	PPR3: Using consumer VR all-in-one headsets would make me feel heavy	
	PPR4: Using consumer VR all-in-one headsets would make me get injured	
Attitude	ATT1: Using consumer VR all-in-one headsets would be beneficial	Ajzen 2002; Taylor & Todd 1995
	ATT2: The advantages of the consumer VR all-in-one headsets outweigh its disadvantages	
	ATT3: Using consumer VR all-in-one headsets would be helpful	

(*continued*)

Table 2. (*continued*)

Variable	Items	Sources
Subjective Norm	SN1: I will be influenced by friends and classmates to purchase consumer VR all-in-one headsets	Ajzen 1991; Taylor&Todd 1995
	SN2: I will be influenced by family members to purchase consumer VR all-in-one headsets	
	SN3: I will be influenced by media content to purchase consumer VR all-in-one headsets	
Purchase Intention	PI1: I will use consumer VR all-in-one headsets in the future	Moon & Kim 2001; Yu et al. 2017
	PI2: I will purchase consumer VR all-in-one headsets in the future	
	PI3: I will recommend others to purchase consumer VR all-in-one headsets	

4 Results

4.1 Measurement Model

This study employed SPSS 28.0 and AMOS 29.0 to conduct structural equation model analysis. To examine the reliability and validity, confirmatory factor analysis (CFA) is conducted. In this study, Cronbach's α coefficient was used to detect the internal consistency of the scale. There is some debate about the exact acceptable size of Cronbach's α coefficient. In the social sciences study, because it is often necessary to measure more abstract variables, many scholars believe that a Cronbach's α coefficient greater than 0.65 is acceptable (Vaske et al. 2017). Besides, the composite reliability (CR) and the average variance extracted (AVE) should exceed 0.7 and 0.5 respectively to denote a good convergent reliability (Hair et al. 2009; Fornell & Larcker 1981). Table 3 shows the results of reliability test, showing that all the metrics are meet.

Table 4 shows the discriminative validity test results of each construct. The square root of the AVE of each construct is higher than the correlation coefficient with other constructs, indicating the discriminant validity is acceptable (Fornell & Larcker 1981).

Table 3. Results of reliability test

Construct	Item	Factor Loading	Cronbach's α	CR	AVE
Perceived Usefulness	PU1	0.681	0.820	0.820	0.532
	PU2	0.718			
	PU3	0.762			
	PU4	0.755			
Perceived Content Enjoyment	PCE1	0.740	0.790	0.810	0.518
	PCE2	0.731			
	PCE3	0.729			
	PCE4	0.676			
Perceived Ease of Use	PEOU1	0.745	0.793	0.795	0.564
	PEOU2	0.729			
	PEOU3	0.778			
Perceived Price	PP1	0.684	0.681	0.755	0.508
	PP2	0.745			
	PP3	0.707			
Perceived Physical Risk	PPR1	0.668	0.793	0.803	0.506
	PPR2	0.735			
	PPR3	0.682			
	PPR4	0.757			
Attitude	ATT1	0.696	0.793	0.759	0.513
	ATT2	0.744			
	ATT3	0.707			
Subjective Norm	SN1	0.734	0.742	0.768	0.524
	SN2	0.717			
	SN3	0.721			
Purchase Intention	PI1	0.664	0.713	0.752	0.505
	PI2	0.709			
	PI3	0.755			

4.2 Structural Model Fit

This study evaluates the fit of the structural model, with specific fit indices presented in Table 5. According to Table 5, the indices are the ratio of χ^2 and degrees of freedom ratio (χ^2/df), Root Mean Square Error of Approximation (RMSEA), Comparative Fit Index (CFI), Goodness-of-fit Index (GFI), Incremental Fit Index (IFI), Parsimony Goodness of Fit Index (PGFI). Based on the evaluation of these model fit indices, it can be concluded that the theoretical model in this study has a good fit and can be used to explain consumers' purchase intention.

Table 4. Discriminant validity test

	PU	PCE	PEOU	PP	PPR	ATT	SN	PI
PU	**0.729**							
PCE	0.461	**0.720**						
PEOU	0.394	0.226	**0.751**					
PP	0.092	0.159	0.303	**0.713**				
PPR	0.013	0.069	0.336	0.537	**0.711**			
ATT	0.603	0.56	0.29	0.05	0.013	**0.716**		
SN	0.592	0.544	0.336	0.047	0.02	0.652	**0.724**	
PI	0.456	0.42	0.263	0.009	0.002	0.551	0.689	**0.711**

Table 5. Structural model fit

Fit Indices	χ^2/df	RMSEA	CFI	IFI	PGFI
Recommended guidelines	<3	<0.06	>0.9	>0.9	>0.5
Structural model	2.14	0.056	0.912	0.913	0.706

4.3 Hypotheses Testing

The structural equation modeling results are shown in Table 6 and the hypotheses testing results are presented in Table 7. With the exception of three hypotheses that are not significant, all other hypotheses are significant. The perceived usefulness (H1), perceived content enjoyment (H2), and perceived price (H4) of consumer VR all-in-one headsets significantly influence consumer attitude. According to Table 6, perceived usefulness ($\beta = .50, p < .01$) and perceived content enjoyment ($\beta = .52, p < .01$) have a significant positive impact on consumer attitudes. Conversely, perceived price ($\beta = -.23, p < .05$) has a significant negative impact on attitude, while perceived ease of use and perceived physical risk do not significantly affect attitude.

Additionally, consumer attitudes (H6) and subjective norm (H7) significantly influence purchase intention. According to the results in Table 6, consumer attitudes ($\beta = .44, p < .01$) and subjective norms ($\beta = .64, p < .01$) have a significant positive impact on purchase intention. Consequently, the hypotheses of this study can be preliminarily validated, and the structural model path coefficient of this study are shown in Fig. 2.

Table 6. Hypotheses testing results

Hypothesis	Path	β	p	Result
H1	PU → ATT	0.50	***	Supported
H2	PCE → ATT	0.52	***	Supported
H3	PEOU → ATT	0.08	0.532	Not Supported
H4	PP → ATT	−0.23	0.038*	Supported
H5	PPR → ATT	0.08	0.229	Not Supported
H6	ATT → PI	0.44	***	Supported
H7	SN → PI	0.64	***	Supported

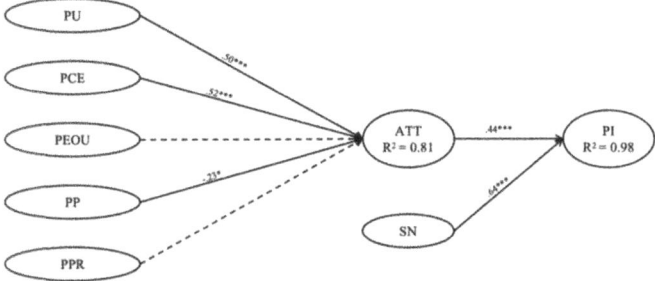

Fig. 2. Structural model path coefficient (Only significant paths are shown; *$p < .05$; **$p < .01$; **$p < .001$)

4.4 Moderating Effect

Since the moderating variable in this study is a categorical variable (having traditional gaming habits or not having traditional gaming habits), multi-group analysis will be used to test the moderating effect. Multi-group analysis in structural equation modeling is frequently employed to analyze moderating effects of categorical variables, specifically to determine whether the path coefficients of one group can be applied to other groups.

This study follows the steps recommended by Awang (2012) to conduct multi-group analysis. First, the unconstrained model fit indices, RMSEA, should be lower than the threshold 0.06. Second, the chi-square differences of measurement weights, structural weights, structural covariances and structural residuals models should be significant. Then, the moderation effect of each individual path is investigated. The criteria for moderation for individual paths are: (1) if the beta value for consumer with prior traditional gaming habit is significant, the beta value for consumer without prior traditional gaming habit must be non-significant; and (2) if the beta values for both types of consumers are significant, one value must be positive while the other must be negative (Hair et al. 2012). The results are presented in Table 7, Table 8 and Table 9. The results indicate that the prior gaming habit possesses a moderating effect on the relationship between PP and ATT, as well as ATT and PI.

Table 7. Moderation with Chi-square significance

Model	RMSEA	DF	CMIN	Δdf	Δx^2	p
Unconstrained	.047	604	1087.252			
Measurement weights	.047	623	1125.443	19	38.191	.006
Structural weights	.047	630	1148.173	26	60.921	.000
Structural covariances	.047	651	1185.064	47	97.812	.000
Structural residuals	.047	653	1185.977	49	98.725	.000

Table 8. Results of Chi-square difference test for multi-group analysis

Hypotheses	Path	DF	CMIN	p
H8a	PU → ATT	1	0.113	0.737
H8b	PCE → ATT	1	7.748	0.005**
H8c	PEOU → ATT	1	0.33	0.566
H8d	PP → ATT	1	8.376	0.004**
H8e	PPR → ATT	1	1.789	0.181
H8f	ATT → PI	1	9.405	0.002**

Table 9. Beta value for multi-group analysis

	With Prior Gaming Habit		Without Prior Gaming Habit	
Path	β	p	β	p
PCE → ATT	0.619	***	0.383	***
PP → ATT	−0.594	0.012*	−0.009	0.932
ATT → PI	0.258	0.076	.625	***

5   Discussions and Implications

5.1   Findings

Perceived Benefits and Their Impact on Attitude. Firstly, consumers' perceived usefulness of VR all-in-one headsets significantly positively influence their attitude, echoing the results of previous researches. This aligns with consumers' functional demand for VR all-in-one headset. It is believed that consumer VR all-in-one headsets could enhance efficiency and work motivation in certain professions and activities. For instance, for consumers with design needs, consumer VR all-in-one headsets could improve the quality of drawing and design. Also, for people who work remotely, the virtual office and social environments presented by VR all-in-one headsets would be potentially promising. Currently, major brands of VR all-in-one headsets have introduced numerous applications to enhance perceived usefulness, such as the floor-cleaning assistant and 3D scanning apps on Vision Pro, and virtual fitness apps on Pico4. These applications leverage virtual reality technology to make certain aspects of consumers' lives more convenient and efficient.

Simultaneously, another sub-dimension of perceived benefits, perceived content enjoyment of VR all-in-one headsets significantly positively influences their attitude. This result aligns with the definition of consumer electronics, which aims to satisfy consumers' entertainment needs. It also corresponds with most consumers' expectations of the usage experience of VR all-in-one headsets for now. Most consumers believe these games and applications offer a unique entertainment experience through virtual reality technology.

Therefore, it can be concluded that VR all-in-one headsets likely create perceived benefits by renewing many conventional applications and content through virtual reality technology, which in turn positively influences consumers' attitude toward these devices.

Perceived Sacrifices and Their Impact on Attitude. Perceived sacrifices consist of three sub-dimensions: perceived ease of use, perceived price, and perceived physical risk. From the model's overall effects, only perceived price had a significant negative impact on attitude, while perceived ease of use and perceived physical risk did not have significant negative effects on attitude. When introducing prior traditional gaming habits as a moderating variable, perceived ease of use and perceived physical risk still have no significant impact on attitude. For consumers with prior traditional gaming habits, perceived price continued to significantly affect attitude. For consumers without prior traditional gaming habits, perceived price did not have a significant impact on attitude.

First, despite the majority of previous research suggesting that perceived ease of use has a significant positive impact on attitude or acceptance intention, this study found that perceived ease of use does not significantly affect consumer attitude. Some prior studies have reached similar conclusions. The qualitative research conducted by Pikkarainen et al. (2004) demonstrated that internet technology greatly improved the ease of use of mobile banking, leading to the finding that perceived ease of use did not significantly influence Finns' willingness to use mobile banking. Similarly, Nathania et al. (2021) found no significant impact of perceived ease of use on Indonesian seniors' attitude and usage intention towards smartphones. Luo et al. (2022) confirmed that perceived ease of use did not significantly affect attitude towards agricultural e-commerce platforms in western China, suggesting that the technicality of internet platforms is no longer a major barrier. These studies indicate that the explanatory power perceived ease of use has diminished for internet-era users who frequently use mobile technologies.

Three reasons could explain this result. First, today's internet users frequently encounter new hardware and software technologies, such as changing phones, computers, or using new apps, and may no longer focusing on the perceived ease of use. Second, most products offer clear and detailed usage guides for new users, which can help consumers to deal with technical issues. Finally, the sample structure of this study shows that over 70% of the sample is under 34 years old. Previous researches have shown that perceived ease of use does not significantly lead to negative attitudes among younger groups (Chien et al. 2019). Therefore, it can be concluded that the internet users for consumer VR all-in-one headsets is not sensitive to the operation.

Second, the results of this study indicate that for consumer VR all-in-one headsets, perceived price remains an important variable with theoretical significance. Additionally, the results of the multi-group anaylsis reflect that consumer with traditional gaming habits have a higher price sensitivity towards consumer VR all-in-one headsets and form their attitudes towards consumer VR all-in-one headsets based on more dimensions (perceived usefulness, perceived content enjoyment, perceived price).

Third, perceived physical risk has no significant impact on attitude, which echos with Molina-Castillo et al. (2012)' research. This may be because the innovation level of consumer VR all-in-one headsets is relatively low since this product is not radical innovations. Previous researches indicated that consumers' perceived risk would be less sensitive if the innovation level of a product is low (Sarin et al. 2003).

In summary, it can be concluded that the influence of perceived sacrifices on attitude is relatively weak. The primary factors influencing attitude are still the perceived benefits directly linked to the content.

Attitude, Subjective Norm and Their Impact on Purchase Intention. The result demonstrated that attitude is a significant direct influencing factor for purchase intention. However, multi-group analysis results show that the attitude of consumers with traditional gaming habits does not significantly affect purchase intention, whereas the attitude of consumers without traditional gaming habits does significantly affect purchase intention. This may be because consumers may tend to compare relative advantage when evaluating consumer VR headsets (Veryzer 1998; Sarin et al. 2003). Consumers with traditional game habits may compare consumer VR all-in-one headsets with gaming consoles, perceiving that the new products do not add significant value to their gaming experience beyond these existing products. Conversely, consumers without traditional gaming habits may not have similar products to compare about. They are more inclined to focus on diverse content instead of focusing on game, leading their attitude toward the product to have a significant positive impact on their purchase intention.

The results of this study show that subjective norm significantly positively influences the purchase intention towards consumer VR all-in-one headsets. When considering buying a VR all-in-one headset, consumers would be influenced by important others. Meanwhile, the introduction section of this study has already discussed consumers' expectations for virtual social interactions, and the result of this study may echo this envision.

In conclusion, attitude and subjective norm are direct influencing factors of purchase intention. Based on the above conclusions, it can be stated that the proposed model for the mechanism influencing the purchase intention of consumer VR all-in-one headsets is well-supported, generally consistent with previous research findings and practical realities, and extends previous research with certain practical implications.

5.2 Practical Implications

Content-Driven Hardware: Quality Enhancement and Innovation. Based on data analysis results, both perceived usefulness and perceived content enjoyment are directly related to content. Thus, the first practical recommendation of this study is that current consumer VR all-in-one headsets should focus heavily on content development and utilize content to attract potential consumers.

There are numerous examples were content drives sales of consumer electronics. For instance, Nintendo's release of "The Legend of Zelda" converted many potential users into paying consumers who purchased switches. Similarly, Apple's iPad and Apple Pencil were complemented by applications like Procreate, Notability, and GoodNotes, which greatly enhanced work efficiency and provided enjoyment to non-professional users, prompting them to purchase the hardware. If high-quality and diverse content were developed, not only VR games, consumer VR all-in-one headsets would gain broader acceptance.

Tiered Pricing: Technology-Driven Price Rationalization. Currently, the price range of consumer VR all-in-one headsets varies widely. The research results indicate that perceived price significantly negatively impacts attitude, making pricing a critical factor. Prices for these products range from 2,00 to 3,000 dollars, with a significant gap between the low and high ends. For example, Pico series products are priced around 200 dollars, Oculus Quest series around 250 dollars, and Vision Pro at about 3,000 dollars, with few options in between. This wide price disparity narrows the choice for consumers, possibly deterring them from purchasing. This study suggests that manufacturers and operators of consumer VR all-in-one headsets should develop more mature technologies to enable tiered pricing, offering a wider range of price options, thereby increasing purchase intentions.

Targeted Marketing: Different Strategies for Different Groups. The study's examination of moderating effects shows that prior traditional gaming habits significantly influence the path from attitude to purchase intention, providing important insights for marketing strategies. To improve marketing conversion rates, more precise marketing is needed, including more detailed audience targeting, marketing channels, and specific marketing content.

This study recommends that the marketing departments of consumer VR all-in-one headset companies conduct further research on users with and without traditional gaming habits, refine user profiles, and allocate different promotional channels for each group to increase conversion rates. In terms of specific marketing content, for users with traditional gaming habits, who are more sensitive to perceived price and likely to compare relative products, marketing should emphasize the cost-effectiveness of the product, highlighting the alignment of the experience content with the product price. For users without traditional gaming habits, who are less sensitive to perceived price but whose positive attitude significantly influence purchase intention, marketing should use positive language to leave a favorable impression.

6 Conclusions, Limitations and Future Research

This study, based on classical technology acceptance models, proposes a theoretical framework for understanding consumer attitudes and purchase intentions towards consumer VR all-in-one headsets. The model demonstrates good reliability and validity, while also highlighting the diminishing influence of classical variables and the emergence of new variable relationships in the context of the metaverse era.

However, this study has limitations that future research could address. First, the data was collected before the launch of the Vision Pro. As noted in the introduction, the VR headset market experienced a decline last year. The launch of the Vision Pro has improved shipments and sparked extensive social media discussions. More social media influencers are now posting content about their experiences with the Vision Pro, which may alter consumer perceptions and purchase intentions. Future studies could examine user attitudes and purchase intentions post-launch of the Vision Pro. Second, the constructs in the theoretical framework are limited. Future research could introduce more variables, such as individual characteristics and external product cues, to enhance the explanatory power of the theoretical framework. Third, this study focuses solely on purchase intentions without considering purchase scenarios. Future research could control for different purchase scenarios, such as online versus physical store shopping, to compare the differing influence mechanisms. By addressing these limitations, future research can provide a more comprehensive understanding of consumer behavior in the evolving VR market.

Acknowledgments. The authors thank the respondents for filling the questionnaire.

Disclosure of Interests. The authors have no competing interests to declare that are relevant to the content of this article.

References

Mystakidis, S.: Metaverse. Encyclopedia **2**(1), 486–497 (2022)

Deloitte. Metaverse Report—Future is here Global XR Industry insight. Deloitte China. (2022)

IDC. AR & VR Headsets Market Share. https://www.idc.com/promo/arvr. Accessed 16 May 2024

Wohlgenannt, I., Simons, A., & Stieglitz, S.: Virtual reality. Bus. Inf. Syst. Eng. **62**, 455-461 (2020)

Han, S.H., Yun, M.H., Kwahk, J., Hong, S.W.: Usability of consumer electronic products. Int. J. Ind. Ergon. **28**(3–4), 143–151 (2001)

Pal, D., Roy, P., Arpnikanondt, C., Thapliyal, H.: The effect of trust and its antecedents towards determining users' behavioral intention with voice-based consumer electronic devices. Heliyon **8**(4) (2022)

Papachristos, N.M., Vrellis, I., Mikropoulos, T.A.: A comparison between oculus rift and a low-cost smartphone VR headset: immersive user experience and learning. In: 2017 IEEE 17th International Conference on Advanced Learning Technologies (ICALT), pp. 477–481. IEEE (2017)

Value creation in the metaverse: the real business of the virtual world. In: McKinsey & Company (2022)

Jang, J., Ko, Y., Shin, W.S., Han, I.: Augmented reality and virtual reality for learning: an examination using an extended technology acceptance model. IEEE Access **9**, 6798–6809 (2021)

Glegg, S.M., Holsti, L., Velikonja, D., Ansley, B., Brum, C., Sartor, D.: Factors influencing therapists' adoption of virtual reality for brain injury rehabilitation. Cyberpsychol. Behav. Soc. Netw. **16**(5), 385–401 (2013)

Vishwakarma, P., Mukherjee, S., Datta, B.: Travelers' intention to adopt virtual reality: a consumer value perspective. J. Destin. Mark. Manag. **17**, 100456 (2020)

Sagnier, C., Loup-Escande, E., Lourdeaux, D., Thouvenin, I., Valléry, G.: User acceptance of virtual reality: an extended technology acceptance model. Int. J. Hum.-Comput. Interact. **36**(11), 993–1007 (2020)

Manis, K.T., Choi, D.: The virtual reality hardware acceptance model (VR-HAM): extending and individuating the technology acceptance model (TAM) for virtual reality hardware. J. Bus. Res. **100**, 503–513 (2019)

Davis, F.D.: Perceived usefulness, perceived ease of use, and user acceptance of information technology. MIS Q. 319–340 (1989)

Ajzen, I.: The theory of planned behavior. Organ. Behav. Hum. Decis. Process. **50**(2), 179–211 (1991)

Ajzen, I.: The theory of planned behavior: frequently asked questions. Hum. Behav. Emerg. Technol. **2**(4), 314–324 (2020)

Kim, H.W., Chan, H.C., Gupta, S.: Value-based adoption of mobile internet: an empirical investigation. Decis. Support. Syst. **43**(1), 111–126 (2007)

Zeithaml, V.A.: Consumer perceptions of price, quality, and value: a means-end model and synthesis of evidence. J. Mark. **52**(3), 2–22 (1988)

Babin, B.J., Darden, W.R., Griffin, M.: Work and/or fun: measuring hedonic and utilitarian shopping value. J. Consum. Res. **20**(4), 644–656 (1994)

Sweeney, J.C., Soutar, G.N.: Consumer perceived value: the development of a multiple item scale. J. Retail. **77**(2), 203–220 (2001)

Wang, Y., Po Lo, H., Chi, R., Yang, Y.: An integrated framework for customer value and customer-relationship-management performance: a customer-based perspective from China. Managing Serv. Qual. Int. J. **14**(2/3), 169–182 (2004)

Venkatesh, V., Thong, J.Y., Xu, X.: Consumer acceptance and use of information technology: extending the unified theory of acceptance and use of technology. MIS Q. 157–178 (2012)

Kosa, M., Uysal, A.: The role of need satisfaction in explaining intentions to purchase and play in Pokémon Go and the moderating role of prior experience. Psychol. Popular Media **10**(2), 187 (2021)

Moon, J.W., Kim, Y.G.: Extending the TAM for a world-wide-web context. Inf. Manag. **38**(4), 217–230 (2001)

Kim, E., Kyung, Y.: Factors affecting the adoption intention of new electronic authentication services: a convergent model approach of VAM, PMT, and TPB. IEEE Access **11**, 13859–13876 (2023)

Yu, J., Lee, H., Ha, I., Zo, H.: User acceptance of media tablets: an empirical examination of perceived value. Telematics Inform. **34**(4), 206–223 (2017)

Zhu, D.H., Chang, Y.P.: Investigating consumer attitude and intention toward free trials of technology-based services. Comput. Hum. Behav. **30**, 328–334 (2014)

Tunçel, N.: Intention to purchase electric vehicles: evidence from an emerging market. Res. Transp. Bus. Manag. **43**, 100764 (2022)

Jain, S.: Assessing the moderating effect of subjective norm on luxury purchase intention: a study of Gen Y consumers in India. Int. J. Retail Distrib. Manag. **48**(5), 517–536 (2020)

Al-Debei, M.M., Akroush, M.N., Ashouri, M.I.: Consumer attitudes towards online shopping: the effects of trust, perceived benefits, and perceived web quality. Internet Res. **25**(5), 707–733 (2015)

Jaiswal, D., Kaushal, V., Kant, R., Singh, P.K.: Consumer adoption intention for electric vehicles: Insights and evidence from Indian sustainable transportation. Technol. Forecast. Soc. Chang. **173**, 121089 (2021)

Ashfaq, M., Yun, J., Yu, S.: My smart speaker is cool! perceived coolness, perceived values, and users' attitude toward smart speakers. Int. J. Hum.-Comput. Interact. **37**(6), 560–573 (2021)

Chiang, C.F., Jang, S.S.: The effects of perceived price and brand image on value and purchase intention: leisure travelers' attitudes toward online hotel booking. J. Hosp. Leis. Mark. **15**(3), 49–69 (2007)

Derbaix, C.: Perceived risk and risk relievers: an empirical investigation. J. Econ. Psychol. **3**(1), 19–38 (1983)

Ajzen, I.: Constructing a TPB questionnaire: Conceptual and methodological considerations (2002)

Taylor, S., Todd, P.A.: Understanding information technology usage: a test of competing models. Inf. Syst. Res. **6**(2), 144–176 (1995)

Vaske, J.J., Beaman, J., Sponarski, C.C.: Rethinking internal consistency in Cronbach's alpha. Leis. Sci. **39**(2), 163–173 (2017)

Hair, J.F., Black, W.C., Babin, B.J., Anderson, R.E.: Multivariate data analysis (7th ed.). Prentice-Hall (2009)

Fornell, C., Larcker, D.F.: Evaluating structural equation models with unobservable variables and measurement error. J. Mark. Res. **18**, 39–50 (1981)

Awang, Z.: Strutural equation modeling using AMOS graphic. Penerbit Universiti Teknologi MAR. (2012)

Hair, J.F., Sarstedt, M., Ringle, C.M., Mena, J.A.: An assessment of the use of partial least squares structural equation modeling in marketing research. J. Acad. Mark. Sci. **40**, 414–433 (2012)

Pikkarainen, T., Pikkarainen, K., Karjaluoto, H., Pahnila, S.: Consumer acceptance of online banking: an extension of the technology acceptance model. Internet Res. **14**(3), 224–235 (2004)

Nathania, L., Anandya, D: The effects of external factors on perceived ease of use, perceived usefulness, attitude towards use, and behavioral intention of older adults in Indonesia. In: 18th International Symposium on Management (INSYMA 2021), pp. 152–156. Atlantis Press (2021)

Luo, S., Wang, S., Xu, L.: Research on the use intention of agricultural products e-commerce platform in Western China from the perspective of agricultural production organizations. Sci.Decis. Making **07**, 105–120 (2022)

Veryzer, R.W., Jr.: Key factors affecting customer evaluation of discontinuous new products. J. Prod. Innov. Manag. **15**(2), 136–150 (1998)

Sarin, S., Sego, T., Chanvarasuth, N.: Strategic use of bundling for reducing consumers' perceived risk associated with the purchase of new high-tech products. J. Mark. Theory Pract. **11**(3), 71–83 (2003)

Molina-Castillo, F.J., Lopez-Nicolas, C., Soto-Acosta, P.: Interaction effects of media and message on perceived complexity, risk and trust of innovative products. Eur. Manag. J. **30**(6), 577–587 (2012)

Chien, S.E., Chu, L., Lee, H.H., et al.: Age difference in perceived ease of use, curiosity, and implicit negative attitude toward robots. In: Jenkins, O.C., Sabanovic, S. (eds.) ACM Transactions on Human-Robot Interaction (THRI) 2019, vol. 8, no. 2, pp. 1–19 (2019)

HoloCook: A Real-Time Remote Mixed Reality Cooking Tutoring System

Liuchuan Yu$^{(\boxtimes)}$ (iD), Bo Han (iD), Songqing Chen (iD), and Lap-Fai Yu (iD)

George Mason University, Fairfax, VA 22030, USA
{lyu20,bohan,sqchen,craigyu}@gmu.edu

Abstract. Advancements in extended reality (XR) technology have spurred research into XR-based training and collaboration. On the other hand, mixed reality (MR) fuses the real and the virtual world in real time and provides interaction, which brings the possibility of completing real-world tasks collaboratively through MR headsets. We present HoloCook, a novel real-time remote cooking tutoring system utilizing HoloLens 2. HoloCook is a lightweight system that doesn't require any additional devices. HoloCook can not only synchronize the coach's action with the trainee in real time but also provide the trainee with animations and 3D annotations to aid in tutoring process. HoloCook supports tutoring two recipes: pancakes and cocktails. Our user evaluation with one coach and four trainees establishes HoloCook as a feasible and usable remote cooking tutoring system in mixed-reality environments.

Keywords: Mixed reality · Cooking tutoring · Real-time remote system

1 Introduction

Virtual reality (VR) and augmented reality (AR) have been demonstrated effectiveness comparable to conventional training methods [14]. Creating real-world training setups can be costly and time-intensive [15], while VR training significantly reduces costs and enhances performance [16]. Additionally, AR holds promising potential for future training applications [18]. Beyond training, VR and AR find applications in education [17], assistive technology [3], manufacturing [34], and collaboration [36]. However, VR environments are entirely virtual, posing challenges for authoring, while AR primarily overlays virtual objects onto real ones, limiting interactivity.

Mixed reality (MR) combines aspects of both VR and AR, integrating digital and physical objects to interact and coexist in the same space [26]. With the progression of MR headsets like Microsoft HoloLens, Meta Quest Series (Quest Pro/Quest 3), and the newly launched Apple Vision Pro, MR is gaining considerable research interest, often surpassing VR and AR in various aspects. Because of its seamless blending of the digital and physical realms, MR provides a more immersive and interactive experience.

J. Y. C. Chen et al. (Eds.): HCII 2024, LNCS 15377, pp. 244–264, 2025.
https://doi.org/10.1007/978-3-031-76812-5_17

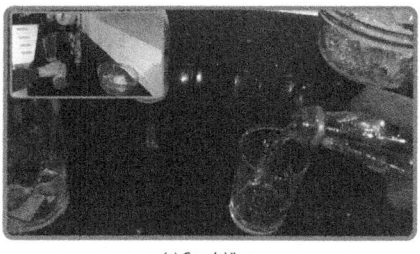

(a) Coach View   (b) Trainee View

Fig. 1. An illustration of HoloCook. Two individuals, one as a coach and the other as a trainee, each equipped with HoloLens 2, are situated in separate kitchens. As the system starts, the coach's actions are live-streamed to the trainee's end. The trainee observes and replicates the actions to complete tasks. (a) and (b) depict the coach's and the trainee's perspectives, with side camera views indicated by the top-left orange boxes. In this cocktail-making instance, the coach pours lime juice (0.75 oz) into a measuring cup. Simultaneously, the trainee sees an overlay of the lime juice, the measuring cup, and 3D texts indicating the amount. The trainee follows suit accordingly.

The initial release of the Microsoft HoloLens occurred in 2016, followed by its successor, HoloLens 2, in 2019. Researchers have extensively employed HoloLens for investigations across various domains [30]. HoloLens 2 serves as an apt platform for mixed-reality research due to its Windows-like operating system and provision of multimodal interactions, including hand-tracking, gaze input, and voice recognition. While some research works utilize HoloLens 2, certain projects necessitate additional devices or sensors [28,42], are limited to single-user scenarios [29,45], or entail complex setup procedures [31,41].

To explore multiplayer mixed-reality systems with simplified setup, we introduce HoloCook, a real-time remote mixed-reality cooking tutoring system utilizing HoloLens 2. HoloCook is a lightweight peer-to-peer tutoring system comprising two clients: one running on a standard PC and the other on HoloLens 2, without the need for additional devices or sensors. Additionally, HoloCook features a symmetric design, where both coach and trainee utilize identical clients, ensuring ease of extension and maintenance. To enhance the tutoring experience, we incorporate animations and 3D annotations. Key contributions of HoloCook include:

1. Proposing a novel lightweight real-time remote cooking tutoring system, symmetrically designed and devoid of additional devices or sensors;
2. Implementing two recipes, pancake and cocktail, based on our system; and
3. Conducting user evaluation experiments involving one coach and four trainees for pancake-making and cocktail-making tutoring.

HoloCook code is available at https://github.com/luffy-yu/HoloCook.

2   Related Work

2.1   XR Training

VR and AR serve as effective training mechanisms comparable to conventional methods [14]. Establishing real-world training environments can be costly and time-intensive [15], whereas VR training significantly reduces costs and enhances performance [16]. VR finds applications across various fields, including first responder training [11], medical training [12], military training [39], sports [22], recycling behaviors [6], construction safety [20], mining [24,25], and evacuation [19,21]. Additionally, AR demonstrates positive potential for future [18], such as medical training [38], industry training [37], corporate training [23], and vocational training [4].

Unlike prior XR training approaches, HoloCook focuses on real-time tutoring, enabling learners to complete real-world tasks in authentic environments, diverging from training solely within synthetic environments.

2.2   XR Education and Tutoring

XR demonstrates positive impacts in education, accommodating various learning styles and aiding in teaching methods [35]. Several studies highlight XR's utility in secondary education: Ray et al. [33] developed a VR application for teaching micro-controllers and Arduino boards using Google Cardboard headsets, showcasing VR's affordability in education. Dieker et al. [5] described TLE TeachLivE, a VR application from the University of Central Florida. Villanueva et al. [43] introduced Meta-AR-App, a collaborative AR platform leveraging cloud computing. Villanueva et al. [44] presented ColabAR, enhancing AR laboratories with physical proxies.

While previous works relied on additional infrastructure [43], sensors [44], or complex setups [5,33], HoloCook stands out as a lightweight system requiring only a PC and HoloLens 2 headset on one side. No extra devices or sensors are necessary, and both coach and trainee can share the same PC, provided it's networked and accessible to both HoloLens 2 headsets.

2.3   XR Collaboration

With network connectivity, XR finds applications in collaborative human scenarios. Various frameworks have been proposed to facilitate collaboration in virtual environments. For instance, Elvezio et al. [7] introduced a method supporting remote collaboration in AR and VR through virtual replicas, enabling remote users to manipulate virtual replicas of physical objects locally. Teo et al. [40] implemented a similar framework for MR remote collaboration, combining 360-degree video and 3D reconstruction. Nebeling et al. [27] presented XRDirector, a collaborative immersive authoring system allowing designers to express interactions through AR and VR devices, effectively manipulating virtual objects within physical space. Piumsomboon et al. [32] introduced CoVAR, a remote collaborative system blending VR and AR seamlessly, employing natural communication cues to foster novel collaboration. Liu et al. [21] proposed a networked training drill system supporting remote collaboration in virtual environments and locomotion in large shared virtual environments using treadmills.

Previous works often exhibit asymmetric designs [7], require additional devices [21,40], or involve different hardware and software on both ends [27,32]. In contrast, HoloCook is symmetrically designed, with both coach and trainee utilizing the same hardware and software. Each end can assume either role, selected before tutoring begins. This symmetry enhances HoloCook's extendability and maintainability.

2.4 MR Applications on HoloLens

Microsoft HoloLens debuted in 2016, followed by the release of HoloLens 2 in 2019, serving as a pivotal tool for research across diverse domains. Orts-Escolano et al. [28] developed Holoportation, showcasing real-time 3D reconstructions of spaces using new depth cameras. Piumsomboon et al. [31] introduced Mini-Me, an adaptive avatar enhancing mixed-reality collaboration between local AR users and remote VR users. Loki [41] facilitated remote instruction for physical tasks through bi-directional mixed-reality telepresence, with one side in AR and the other in VR. ARTEMIS [9] enabled immersive surgical telementoring, employing AR for novices and VR for experts. Zhao et al. [46] developed a visual and audio wayfinding guidance app on HoloLens for individuals with low vision. Yu et al. [45] introduced HoloAAC, an augmentative and alternative communication app on HoloLens 2 that aids individuals with expressive language difficulties in grocery shopping. Farouk et al. [8] presented an app on HoloLens 2 enhancing collaboration on visualized data through Kinect-captured remote user movements. Ihara et al. [13] introduced HoloBots, a mixed-reality collaboration platform improving holographic telepresence via synchronized mobile robots, integrating Kinect and tabletop robots.

These applications often involve disparate hardware and technologies [9,31, 41] or necessitate additional devices and sensors [8,13,28]. Some lack multiplayer support [45,46]. In contrast, HoloCook is a networked real-time tutoring system with identical hardware and software on both ends, supporting peer-to-peer coaching in real time. Furthermore, HoloCook's design facilitates easy extension for one-to-many coaching applications.

3 Overview

The overall workflow of HoloCook is depicted in Fig. 2. HoloCook comprises two clients at each end, one running on HoloLens 2 and the other on PC. It's noteworthy that the PC clients can operate on the same PC, provided both HoloLens clients can access it. Initially, both the coach and the trainee wear HoloLens 2. Subsequently, the PC client can initiate, followed by the coach and

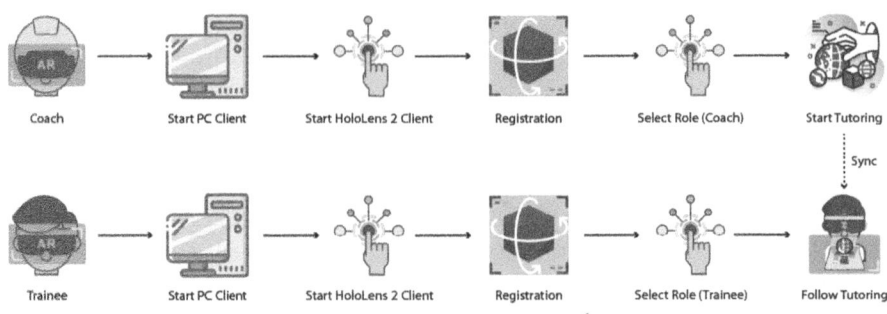

Fig. 2. Overall system workflow. Please refer to the main text for explanation.

the trainee starting their respective HoloLens clients. Registration is necessary on both ends before tutoring commences. The coach can initiate tutoring after selecting the coach role, while the trainee can view and follow tutoring upon selecting the trainee role. An example of this tutoring process is illustrated in Fig. 1.

4   Technical Approach

4.1   Network Data Flow

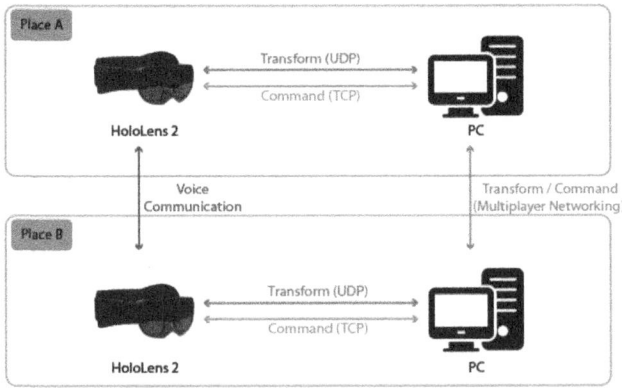

Fig. 3. Network data flow. Please refer to the main text for explanation.

In order to facilitate communication between two HoloLens 2 headsets situated in separate physical locations (kitchens in our scenario), we employ the PC as an intermediary. Figure 3 illustrates the network data flow and communication mechanisms employed. In our setup, both place A and place B are equipped with identical hardware, comprising a HoloLens 2 and a PC. Each endpoint, comprising the HoloLens and the PC, can engage in bidirectional communication. We employ two distinct network protocols for data transmission: TCP (Transmission Control Protocol) and UDP (User Datagram Protocol). TCP is utilized for sending command data due to its reliability. Here, "command" refers to actions such as controlling the HoloLens and the PC, enabling/disabling virtual objects, altering transform synchronization, displaying animations, etc. UDP, on the other hand, is used for synchronizing transform data of objects at a specific frequency. Given that the volume of data is relatively larger compared to command data and the loss of some packets is tolerable, UDP proves to be more suitable than TCP.

Regarding synchronization between the local and remote ends, we employ an off-the-shelf multiplayer networking framework. This framework automatically synchronizes objects' transforms (position and rotation). For command information, we utilize RPC (Remote Procedure Call) between two PCs. To enhance the tutoring experience, we enable verbal communication between the coach and the trainee.

One potential advantage of using PCs as bridges is the visualization of transform synchronization through the PC. Additionally, various post-processing tasks such as video/image processing and trajectory mapping can be applied.

Consider the scenario where the coach is situated in place A, and the trainee is in place B. During tutoring sessions, the data flow unfolds as follows: transforms are sent from the HoloLens 2 in place A to the PC in place A; these transforms are synchronized from the PC in place A to the PC in place B; finally, the transforms are sent from the PC in place B to the HoloLens 2 in place B. Command information follows a similar schema.

4.2 Clients

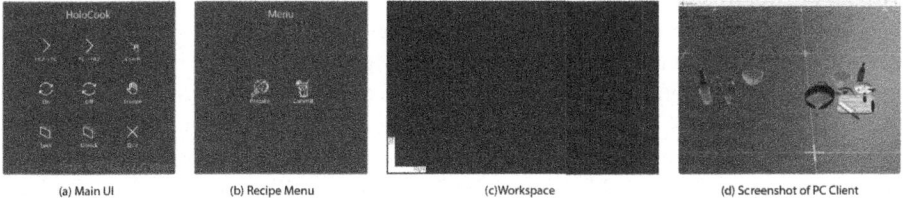

(a) Main UI   (b) Recipe Menu   (c)Workspace   (d) Screenshot of PC Client

Fig. 4. Screenshots of HoloCook. (a), (b), and (c) refer to the HoloLens 2 client. (d) shows the PC client. Please refer to the main text for their explanation.

As aforementioned, at each end, HoloCook comprises two clients, of which one runs on HoloLens 2 (HoloLens 2 client) and the other runs on Windows (PC client). Figure 4 shows some screenshots. Figure 4(a), Fig. 4(b), and Fig. 4(c) belong to the HoloLens 2 client. Figure 4(d) shows the screenshot of the PC client.

HoloLens 2 Client. Figure 4(a) illustrates the screenshot of the main menu, which is comprised of three primary components arranged from top to bottom:

(a) **Title:** The title dynamically changes throughout interactions. Initially, it displays as "HoloCook." The format of the title follows the pattern *HoloCook-role-direction*, where *role* denotes either "Coach" or "Trainee," and *direction* indicates the synchronization direction: $HL2->PC$ (default, from HoloLens 2 to PC) or $PC->HL2$ (from PC to HoloLens 2).

(b) **Buttons:** This panel hosts nine buttons:
  (1) $HL2->PC$: Adjusts synchronization direction to from HoloLens 2 to PC.
  (2) $PC->HL2$: Adjusts synchronization direction inversely.
  (3) *Coach*: Sets this side as the coach and initiates the tutoring process.
  (4) *On*: Enables transformation synchronization.
  (5) *Off*: Disables transformation synchronization.
  (6) *Trainee*: Sets this side as the trainee and joins the tutoring process.
  (7) *Lock*: Locks the workspace (Fig. 4(c)), preventing user manipulation.
  (8) *Unlock*: Unlocks the workspace, allowing user manipulation.
  (9) *Quit*: Exits the application.

(c) **Status Bar:** A line of text displays the IP address and port of the PC client.

Figure 4(b) illustrates the recipe menu. Currently, HoloCook supports tutoring in making pancakes and cocktails. However, it is designed to be flexible and can be easily extended to accommodate other recipes.

Figure 4(c) showcases the workspace, which essentially constitutes a plane with its origin positioned at the bottom left corner. We devised this workspace for two primary purposes: 1) It facilitates the conversion of coordinate systems between the coach and trainee ends. 2) It aids in detecting the drop-off action. Upon launching the HoloLens client, a coordinate system is initialized based on its own spatial context. Consequently, there are intrinsic variations in coordinate systems between the coach and trainee ends. Hence, it is imperative to incorporate such a conversion to ensure that tutoring appears correctly. Furthermore, although hand-tracking is well-supported on HoloLens 2, detecting the drop-off action poses a challenge. The workspace functions as a collider, enabling the detection of drop-offs. When objects, including hands, intersect with the plane, it triggers the drop-off action, releasing the object. In the bottom-left corner, we have incorporated an "L" symbol with the words **Top** and **Right**, denoting the origin. This signifies that the user should orient the plane correctly, with **Right** indicating the right direction and **Top** indicating the upward direction. The workspace allows for translation, rotation, and scaling. Additionally, it can be rendered invisible during tutoring sessions.

PC Client. The PC client interface is depicted in Fig. 4(d). During the tutoring process, there is no direct interaction with the PC client; instead, it functions solely as a conduit for transferring transform and command data between the local and remote ends. At the top left corner, four lines of text are displayed: 1) The first line exhibits the application title, HoloCook. 2) The second line displays the Role, with three possible values: Unknown, Coach, and Trainee.

In the current screenshot, it indicates Unknown because the HoloLens 2 device hasn't connected to it yet. 3) The third line reveals the IP address and port of the PC, facilitating connectivity for HoloLens 2. 4)The fourth line presents the IP address and port of the HoloLens 2 device. It's noteworthy that even though the HoloLens 2 hasn't established a connection with the PC at this moment, it is essential to have prior knowledge of both the PC and HoloLens 2 addresses.

4.3   3D Models

Fig. 5. Screenshot of the real objects (kitchen wares, tools, and ingredients) and their virtual counterparts. The first row and the second row show the real and virtual objects, respectively. From left to right and from top to bottom: pan, whisk, turner, knife, spoon, oil, banana, egg, egg, cutting board, plate, bowl, ice, measuring cup (small cup), large cup, lime juice, beer, and rum.

In order to enhance the tutoring experience, particularly for the trainee, it is imperative to utilize realistic 3D models (Fig. 5). While some models can be readily acquired from online sources, certain objects may not be readily available (e.g., oil, lime juice, beer, and rum). To address this issue, we employ an iPad application called *Reality Composer*[1] to first scan these objects and then refine the scanned models using Blender. For the models obtained online, we manually adjust their scales to ensure they match real-world objects.

---

[1] https://apps.apple.com/au/app/reality-composer/id1462358802.

4.4   Pose Estimation

Pose estimation poses a significant challenge in tutoring scenarios, as poor estimation can severely degrade the user experience. Achieving real-time tutoring necessitates a pose estimation algorithm that operates swiftly and can effectively handle various lighting conditions and occlusions. Despite conducting initial research, we found no off-the-shelf solution that met our expectations. Consequently, we pursued an alternative approach: hand tracking.

4.5   Hand Tracking

Microsoft HoloLens 2 leverages hand tracking to facilitate various interactions, including object manipulation (translating, rotating, and scaling), button clicks, and air-tap gestures. However, determining the pose of objects held by the hand poses a challenge, given that the hand pose is generally known. To address this challenge, we propose the following approach:

Upon object registration, the object intended for manipulation attaches to the hand when the hand collides with it. Consequently, the object tracks hand movements, including translation and rotation. To prevent unintentional pick-ups resulting from collisions, we employ two strategies: 1) Defining handedness. Certain objects are designated as right-handed, meaning they can only be picked up by the right hand. For instance, a banana may be defined as right-handed, allowing only the right hand to grab it. 2) Determining effective collisions. Due to the limited workspace and close proximity of objects, full-hand collisions may lead to inadvertent pickups. Therefore, we consider a hand-object collision effective for grabbing only if the *ThumbTip* joint collides with the object. Here, we refer to the *ThumbTip* joint as defined in the default hand joint representation (Fig. 6).

As mentioned earlier, we utilize the workspace (depicted in Fig. 4(c)) to aid in detecting the drop-off action. When a virtual object is already attached to the hand, it becomes detached once the object collides with the workspace. Initially, we perform manual registration to ensure that the virtual object models align accurately with their real-world counterparts.

5   Experiments and Results

5.1   Development Environment

We developed HoloCook using a Windows 11 PC equipped with a Nvidia GTX 3070 GPU, running Unity 2020.3.20, Microsoft Visual Studio 2019, and JetBrains Rider 2023.2.

5.2   Implementation

Networking. For communication between HoloLens 2 and PC, we utilize an off-the-shelf Unity Asset called Netly[2]. To facilitate communication between PCs, we employ Photon Fusion. Additionally, we integrate Photon Voice, an off-the-shelf implementation, for voice communication purposes.

---

[2] https://assetstore.unity.com/packages/tools/network/netly-tcp-udp-225473.

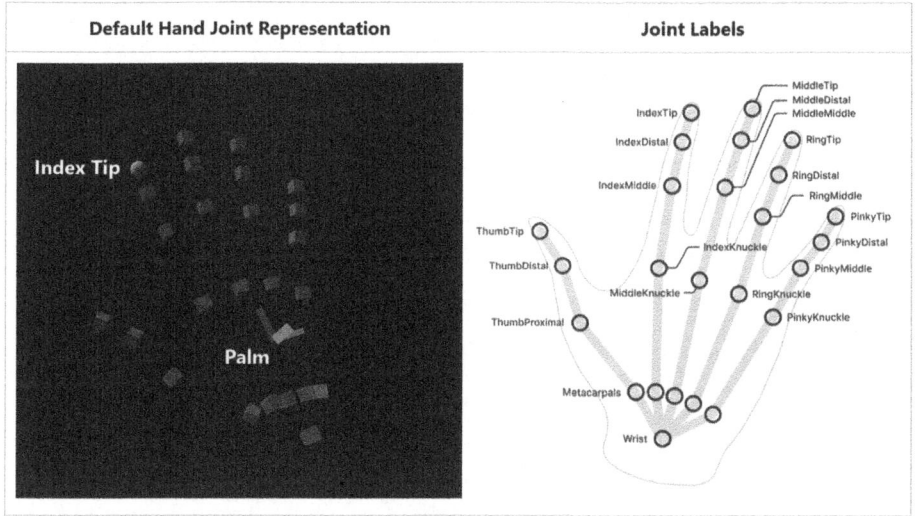

Fig. 6. Default hand joint representation (source: MRTK 2 official website).

Fig. 7. Banana slices-falling animation. This dynamic animation is triggered as the coach maneuvers banana slices atop the bowl using the knife (Fig. 12(c)).

Animation. Transformation synchronization via the network effectively handles many aspects of the tutoring process. However, certain behaviors, such as cracking eggs and dropping off ice, pose challenges for synchronization. To enhance the tutoring experience, particularly for the trainee, we have developed several animations including dropping banana slices (Fig. 7), cracking eggs (Fig. 8), pouring cooked pancakes (Fig. 9), and dropping ices (Fig. 10).

To ensure that these animations function as intended, we have implemented trigger areas positioned strategically above their expected destinations. For instance, for the banana and eggs animations, the trigger area is located above the bowl; for the pancake animation, it is positioned above the plate; and for the ice animation, it is situated above the large cup. These trigger areas facilitate the seamless execution of animations in response to specific actions or events during the tutoring process.

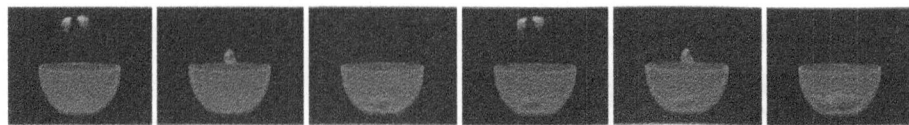

Fig. 8. Eggs-cracking animation. This animated sequence is activated as the coach cracks the two eggs. The first three frames depict the cracking of the left egg above the bowl (Fig. 12(d)). Subsequently, the following three frames illustrate the cracking of the right egg above the bowl (Fig. 12(e)).

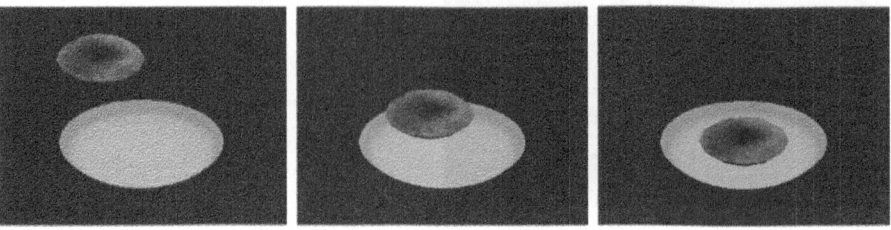

Fig. 9. Pancake-pouring animation. This animation will be activated as the coach holds the pan and prepares to pour the pancake onto the plate (to Fig. 12(g)).

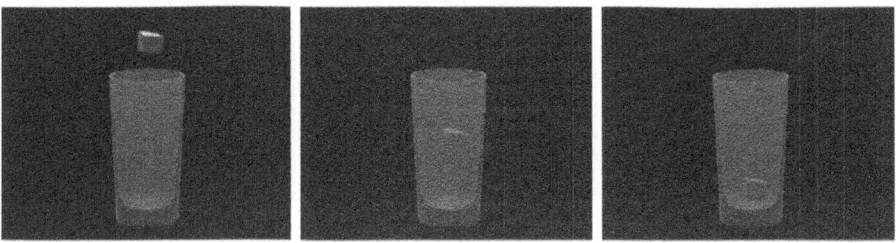

Fig. 10. Ice-dropping animation. This animation plays as the coach prepares to release the ice from his hand above the large cup (Fig. 13(c)).

Fig. 11. Annotations. (a) occurs when the torn banana is placed on the board. (b) occurs when the lime juice is grabbed. (c) occurs when the rum is grabbed.

Annotations. In addition to animations, we have incorporated several annotations to enrich the tutoring experience. Tearing a banana is challenging to simulate and visualize, so we have introduced a virtual representation of a torn banana to illustrate the action when the coach tears the banana and places it on the board. This visualization is demonstrated in Fig. 11(a).

Furthermore, to alleviate the memorization burden for the trainee during tutoring sessions, we have integrated 3D texts onto the measuring cup. These texts are displayed when the coach retrieves the lime juice and the rum, respectively. Figure 11(b) and Fig. 11(c) showcase these annotations. They serve to provide helpful guidance and instruction, enhancing the trainee's learning experience.

5.3 Cooking Recipes

HoloCook currently supports tutoring two recipes: pancakes and cocktails.

Table 1. The procedure for making a pancake[4]

Step	Action
1	Grabbing the banana and tearing it (Fig. 12(a))
2	Placing the torn banana on the board
3	Using a knife to cut the torn banana into pieces (Fig. 12(b))
4	Transferring banana slices into the bowl by placing them on the side of the knife (Fig. 12(c))
5	Mashing the banana slices with a spoon
6	Grabbing the left egg and cracking it above the bowl (Fig. 12(d))
7	Grabbing the right egg and cracking it above the bowl (Fig. 12(e))
8	Whisking with a whisk (Fig. 12(f))
9	Grabbing the oil bottle and pouring it into the pan
10	Grabbing the bowl and pouring its contents into the pan
11	Cooking with a turner
12	Pouring the cooked pancake onto the plate (Fig. 12(g))

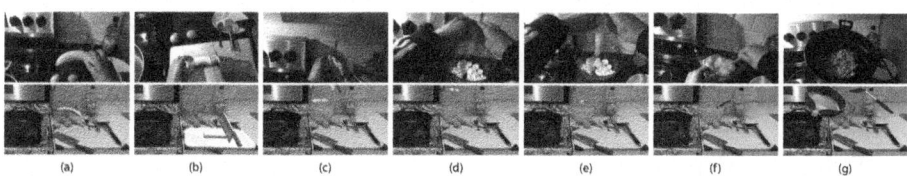

(a)   (b)   (c)   (d)   (e)   (f)   (g)

Fig. 12. An illustration of pancake-making tutoring. The first row depicts the coach's view. The second row represents the trainee's view. (a) shows the coach grabbing the banana; (b) illustrates the coach cutting the banana using a knife; (c) displays the movement of banana slices into the bowl; (d) shows the cracking of the left egg; (e) captures the cracking of the right egg; (f) demonstrates the coach whisking; and (g) depicts the coach pouring the pancake onto the plate.

---

[4] Adapted from: https://www.instagram.com/p/Bv4AWJ6nedf.

Pancake. Following the preparation depicted in Fig. 14, the step-by-step process of making pancakes is outlined in Table 1. Certain steps illustrating the perspectives of both the coach and the trainee are depicted in Fig. 12.

Cocktail. Table 2 shows the procedures to make the cocktail. Some steps are visualized in Fig. 13.

Table 2. The procedure for making a cocktail[6]

Step	Action
1	Pouring 0.75oz lime juice into the measuring cup (Fig. 13(a))
2	Pouring lime juice from the measuring cup into the large cup (Fig. 13(b))
3	Grabbing some ice from the bowl and placing it into the large cup (Fig. 13(c))
4	Pouring some beer (Fig. 13(d))
5	Pouring 2oz rum into the measuring cup (Fig. 13(e))
6	Pouring rum from the measuring cup into the large cup

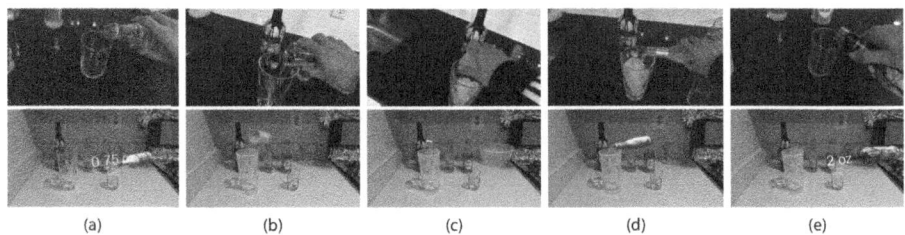

(a)   (b)   (c)   (d)   (e)

Fig. 13. An illustration of cocktail-making tutoring. The first row represents the coach's view. The second row depicts what the trainee will observe. (a) depicts the coach measuring 0.75oz lime juice; (b) shows the coach pouring lime juice into the large cup; (c) illustrates the coach grabbing ice; (d) displays the coach pouring beer; and (e) captures the coach measuring 2oz rum.

6   User Evaluation

We conducted case studies to validate the usability of HoloCook and gather feedback. We used two kitchens as depicted in Fig. 14 for our experiments. The coach's kitchen was situated in an apartment, while the trainee's kitchen was located in a townhouse. During tutoring sessions, both the coach and the trainee wore the HoloLens 2. Additionally, each side was equipped with a common PC capable of running the PC client.

---

[6] Source: https://www.youtube.com/watch?v=c6GV_vRlIIA&t=462.

Table 3. Participants' demographics. Note that P5 served as the coach and the others served as the trainees in our user evaluation.

Participant	Years of Cooking Experience	Years of Making Pancake	Years of Making Cocktail	VR/AR Experience	Way of Learning Cooking
P1	5	0	0	2	Youtube Video
P2	15	10	5	3	Apps
P3	10	0	0	0	Youtube Video
P4	1	0.5	0	0	Friends
P5	5	2	0	1	Youtube Video

Fig. 14. Kitchen layouts for the user evaluation. The first row and the second row show the coach side and the trainee side, respectively. The first column refers to making a pancake, and the second column refers to making a cocktail.

6.1 Participants

We recruited five participants, each with specific roles: one participant (P5) served as the coach, while the remaining four participants (P1, P2, P3, P4) acted as trainees. The participants' ages ranged from 23 to 32, with a mean age of 28 and a standard deviation of 3.03. Their demographic details are presented in Table 3.

6.2 Experiment Objects

The majority of the ingredients were purchased from local stores or markets, including bananas, eggs, oil, lime juice, beer, and rum. Additionally, we utilized various kitchen tools that were readily available in the kitchen such as pans, cutting boards, and knives.

6.3 Questionnaire

Each participant was asked to fill out a questionnaire. The questionnaire was composed of four sections: demographics, NASA Task Load Index (TLX) [10], System Usability Scale (SUS) [2], and general feedback.

6.4 Procedure

At the outset of each case study, all items were arranged neatly as depicted in Fig. 14. Subsequently, we provided instructions to the coach on registration and coaching procedures. For the trainees, we advised them to register objects first and then observed and followed the coach's actions. Both the coach and trainee were encouraged to communicate during the tasks. The first task involved making pancakes, followed by preparing cocktails. At the conclusion of each case study, we organized all items in preparation for the next session.

Trainees were instructed to finish a questionnaire after both tasks, while the coach was asked to finish the same questionnaire after coaching all four trainees.

6.5 Result Analysis

We collected all questionnaire responses and analyzed them from three aspects: NASA TLX, SUS, and general feedback.

NASA TLX. The original ratings are depicted in Fig. 15. Observation reveals that a majority of ratings fall at or below 5. The top three highest ratings pertain to *Performance Dissatisfaction*, provided by P1, P3, and P4. This is largely due to their minimal experience in making pancakes and cocktails, except for P4 who possesses 0.5 years of pancake-making experience, as shown in Table 3.

Mental Demand. Trainees (P1, P3, and P4) rated mental demand at 2, while P2 rated it 5. The average rating across all trainees stands at 2.8, indicating a better than neutral (4) perception. The coach's rating is 5, implying a need for increased attention to ensure effective tutoring.

Physical Demand. Ratings for physical demand include two 1 s (from P2 and P4), one 2 (from P1), and one 3 (from P3), yielding an average rating of 1.8. This suggests a level of physical demand nearing very low (1). The coach's rating of 5 indicates a higher demand perceived by them compared to the trainees.

Temporal Demand. All ratings for temporal demand are at or below 4 (Neutral). The average rating across all trainees is 2.0, implying that participants do not feel rushed during the experience.

Performance Dissatisfaction. Ratings for performance dissatisfaction are uniformly at or above 4 (Neutral). Trainees' average rating is 5.5, the highest among all aspects. The coach also rated it 5. Notably, P2, with significant prior experience, provided the lowest rating. This suggests that participants with prior experience tend to be more satisfied.

Effort. All ratings for effort are at or below 4 (Neutral). The average rating across all trainees is 3.0, indicating a perception better than Neutral (4).

Frustration. Trainees' ratings for frustration are uniformly at or below 2, with the coach rating it 5. The trainees' average rating is 1.3, significantly better than Neutral (4).

Overall, trainees consistently provided lower ratings compared to the coach. Trainees rated five out of six aspects better than neutral: mental demand (2.8), physical demand (1.8), temporal demand (2.0), effort (3.0), and frustration (1.3). They rated performance dissatisfaction higher (5.5) likely due to their lack of experience in pancake and cocktail making.

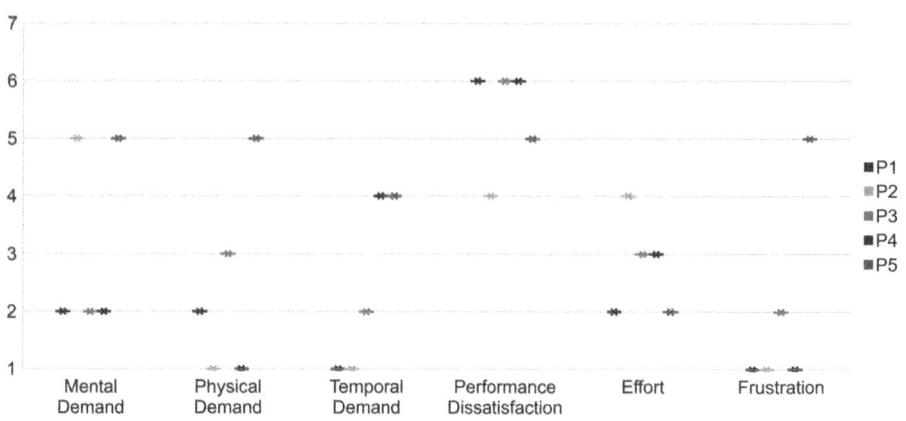

Fig. 15. NASA TLX ratings given by the five participants. 1 means very low, 4 means neutral, and 7 means very high. Refer to the main text for an explanation.

Table 4. Participants' answers to the ten SUS questions.

Participant	Q1	Q2	Q3	Q4	Q5	Q6	Q7	Q8	Q9	Q10
P1	4	2	4	2	4	2	3	3	4	2
P2	3	1	5	2	2	3	5	3	5	1
P3	3	3	2	2	4	1	5	1	5	1
P4	4	1	4	3	4	2	3	1	4	3
P5	4	3	3	5	4	2	3	2	4	5

The coach assigned four 5-ratings for mental demand, physical demand, performance dissatisfaction, and frustration, a 1-rating for temporal demand, and a

2-rating for effort. This indicates the coach's need to ensure synchronization with the trainees' actions, emphasizing the importance of object registration offset in coaching experiences.

SUS. Table 4 presents participants' responses to the ten SUS questions. Following the original methodology by Brooke et al. [2], the SUS scores for the five participants are 70 ("OK"), 75 ("Good"), 77.5 ("Good"), 72.5 ("Good"), and 52.5 ("OK") with corresponding approximate adjectives as per Bangor et al. [1]. According to conventional standards, a score exceeding 68 indicates above-average usability, while a score below 68 indicates below-average usability. As the results show, all trainees rated HoloCook's usability above-average, whereas the coach's rating is below-average. This pattern mirrors NASA TLX ratings. Given that the coach typically requires more attention than the trainees during tutoring sessions, it is reasonable to infer that the trainees would have a more positive experience than the coach. Overall, all participants perceived HoloCook to be **OK** or better, with three of them rating it as **Good**.

General Feedback. P1 appreciated the overall organization but expressed dissatisfaction with the limited field of view. P2 admired the real-time tutoring approach and recommended providing textual instructions alongside. Both P3 and P4 enjoyed the visual guidance provided. P3 eagerly expressed, **"I can't wait to use it to learn some new cuisines."** Meanwhile, P4 exclaimed, **"This experience is fantastic and new to me."** P5 appreciated the straightforward communication of complex actions but found hand tracking to be unreliable sometimes. P5 proposed enhancing user experience by incorporating textual or visual prompts for feature activation or instructions and optimizing the user interface to let the coach conveniently reset tutoring and register objects.

7   Limitations and Future Work

Accurate object registration forms the foundation of HoloCook's functionality. Presently, manual registration suffices; however, enhancing precision through computer vision techniques, such as semi-automatic or automatic approaches, represents a potential solution. For instance, initial rough registration by the user followed by refinement using computer vision techniques can significantly improve accuracy, leveraging the locatable feature of HoloLens 2 camera.

HoloCook operates on identical relative layouts for objects on both the coach and trainee sides, enabling real-time operation streaming but limiting deployability. Extending HoloCook to comprehend the semantic significance of coach operations and intentions presents an opportunity for enhancement. Additionally, implementing recording and relaying features can further augment the system's utility. For example, coaches can record operations for some recipes, which trainees can then replay and learn from independently.

To address complex actions involving deformable objects, HoloCook incorporates animations to convey meaning, albeit not as realistically as synchronized transformations. Future research avenues may explore segmenting objects of interest from camera streams and transferring relevant clips to the trainee side, leveraging HoloCook's PC client for efficient video/image processing.

8   Conclusion

We introduced HoloCook, a novel lightweight real-time remote cooking tutoring system harnessing HoloLens 2. HoloCook exhibits several distinctive features. First, it adopts a symmetric design, eliminating the need for additional devices or sensors. Both the coach and the trainee use the same client interface, simplifying setup and operation. Second, HoloCook offers comprehensive instruction for two complete recipes: pancake and cocktail. These recipes are meticulously crafted to be taught seamlessly via the HoloCook system. Third, we incorporated animations and annotations into HoloCook to enhance tutoring, providing visual aids for clearer understanding and guidance. We conducted a user evaluation session to assess HoloCook's usability and gather valuable user feedback, which helps refine HoloCook and inspires future research.

Acknowledgments. We are grateful to the participants for their feedback on Holo-Cook. We thank Huizhen Zhou for his generously providing the kitchen. This project was supported by NSF grants (award numbers: 2235049 and 2128867) and the GMU IDIA P3 Faculty Fellowship.

Disclosure of Interests. The authors have no competing interests to declare that are relevant to the content of this article.

References

1. Bangor, A., Kortum, P., Miller, J.: Determining what individual sus scores mean: adding an adjective rating scale. J. Usability Stud. **4**(3), 114–123 (2009)
2. Brooke, J., et al.: Sus-a quick and dirty usability scale. Usability Evaluation Ind. **189**(194), 4–7 (1996)
3. Bryant, L., Brunner, M., Hemsley, B.: A review of virtual reality technologies in the field of communication disability: Implications for practice and research. Disabil. Rehabil. Assist. Technol. **15**(4), 365–372 (2020)
4. Chiang, F.K., Shang, X., Qiao, L.: Augmented reality in vocational training: a systematic review of research and applications. Comput. Hum. Behav. **129**, 107125 (2022)
5. Dieker, L.A., Hynes, M.C., Hughes, C.E., Hardin, S., Becht, K.: Tle teachlive^{TM}: using technology to provide quality professional development in rural schools. Rural Special Educ. Quart. **34**(3), 11–16 (2015)
6. Do, T.D., Dylan, S.Y., Katz, A., McMahan, R.P.: Virtual reality training for proper recycling behaviors. In: ICAT-EGVE (Posters and Demos), pp. 31–32 (2020)

7. Elvezio, C., Sukan, M., Oda, O., Feiner, S., Tversky, B.: Remote collaboration in ar and vr using virtual replicas. In: ACM SIGGRAPH 2017 VR Village, pp. 1–2 (2017)
8. Farouk, P., Faransawy, N., Sharaf, N.: Using hololens for remote collaboration in extended data visualization. In: 2022 26th International Conference Information Visualisation (IV), pp. 209–214. IEEE (2022)
9. Gasques, D., et al.: Artemis: a collaborative mixed-reality system for immersive surgical telementoring. In: Proceedings of the 2021 CHI Conference on Human Factors in Computing Systems, pp. 1–14 (2021)
10. Hart, S.G.: Nasa task load index (tlx) (1986)
11. Heirman, J., et al.: Exploring the possibilities of extended reality in the world of firefighting. In: 2020 IEEE international conference on artificial intelligence and virtual reality (AIVR), pp. 266–273. IEEE (2020)
12. Hurd, O., Kurniawan, S., Teodorescu, M.: Virtual reality video game paired with physical monocular blurring as accessible therapy for amblyopia. In: 2019 IEEE Conference on Virtual Reality and 3D User Interfaces (VR). IEEE (2019)
13. Ihara, K., Faridan, M., Ichikawa, A., Kawaguchi, I., Suzuki, R.: Holobots: Augmenting holographic telepresence with mobile robots for tangible remote collaboration in mixed reality. In: Proceedings of the 36th Annual ACM Symposium on User Interface Software and Technology, pp. 1–12 (2023)
14. Kaplan, A.D., Cruit, J., Endsley, M., Beers, S.M., Sawyer, B.D., Hancock, P.: The effects of virtual reality, augmented reality, and mixed reality as training enhancement methods: a meta-analysis. Hum. Factors 63(4), 706–726 (2021)
15. Karabiyik, U., Mousas, C., Sirota, D., Iwai, T., Akdere, M.: A virtual reality framework for training incident first responders and digital forensic investigators. In: International Symposium on Visual Computing, pp. 469–480. Springer (2019)
16. Koutitas, G., Smith, S., Lawrence, G.: Performance evaluation of ar/vr training technologies for ems first responders. Virtual Reality, pp. 1–12 (2020)
17. Law, E.L.C., Heintz, M.: Augmented reality applications for k-12 education: a systematic review from the usability and user experience perspective. Int. J. Child-Comput. Inter. 30, 100321 (2021)
18. Lee, K.: Augmented reality in education and training. TechTrends 56(2), 13–21 (2012)
19. Li, C., Liang, W., Quigley, C., Zhao, Y., Yu, L.F.: Earthquake safety training through virtual drills. IEEE Trans. Visual Comput. Graphics 23(4), 1275–1284 (2017)
20. Li, W., Huang, H., Solomon, T., Esmaeili, B., Yu, L.F.: Synthesizing personalized construction safety training scenarios for vr training. IEEE Trans. Visual Comput. Graphics 28(5), 1993–2002 (2022)
21. Liu, H., Choi, M., Yu, L., Koilias, A., Yu, L.F., Mousas, C.: Synthesizing shared space virtual reality fire evacuation training drills. In: 2022 IEEE International Symposium on Mixed and Augmented Reality Adjunct (ISMAR-Adjunct), pp. 459–464. IEEE (2022)
22. Liu, H., Wang, Z., Mousas, C., Kao, D.: Virtual reality racket sports: virtual drills for exercise and training. In: 2020 IEEE International Symposium on Mixed and Augmented Reality (ISMAR), pp. 566–576. IEEE (2020)
23. Martins, B.R., Jorge, J.A., Zorzal, E.R.: Towards augmented reality for corporate training. Interactive Learning Environments, pp. 1–19 (2021)
24. McMahan, R., Bowman, D., Schafrik, S., Karmis, M.: Virtual environment training for preshift inspections of haul trucks to improve mining safety. In: International Future Mining Conference & Exhibition, pp. 520–528 (2008)

25. McMahan, R.P., Schafrik, S., Bowman, D.A., Karmis, M., Brune, J.: Virtual environments for surface mining powered haulage training. In: Proceedings of SME Symposium Celebrating, vol. 100, pp. 520–528 (2010)
26. Milgram, P., Kishino, F.: A taxonomy of mixed reality visual displays. IEICE Trans. Inf. Syst. **77**(12), 1321–1329 (1994)
27. Nebeling, M., et al.: Xrdirector: a role-based collaborative immersive authoring system. In: Proceedings of the 2020 CHI Conference on Human Factors in Computing Systems, pp. 1–12 (2020)
28. Orts-Escolano, S., et al.: Holoportation: virtual 3d teleportation in real-time. In: Proceedings of the 29th Annual Symposium on User Interface Software and Technology, pp. 741–754 (2016)
29. Park, B.J., Hunt, S.J., Nadolski, G.J., Gade, T.P.: Augmented reality improves procedural efficiency and reduces radiation dose for ct-guided lesion targeting: a phantom study using hololens 2. Sci. Rep. **10**(1), 18620 (2020)
30. Park, S., Bokijonov, S., Choi, Y.: Review of microsoft hololens applications over the past five years. Appl. Sci. **11**(16), 7259 (2021)
31. Piumsomboon, T., et al.: Mini-me: an adaptive avatar for mixed reality remote collaboration. In: Proceedings of the 2018 CHI Conference on Human Factors in Computing Systems, pp. 1–13 (2018)
32. Piumsomboon, T., Lee, Y., Lee, G., Billinghurst, M.: Covar: a collaborative virtual and augmented reality system for remote collaboration. In: SIGGRAPH Asia 2017 Emerging Technologies, pp. 1–2 (2017)
33. Ray, A.B., Deb, S.: Smartphone based virtual reality systems in classroom teaching-a study on the effects of learning outcome. In: 2016 IEEE Eighth International Conference on Technology for Education (T4E), pp. 68–71. IEEE (2016)
34. Sahu, C.K., Young, C., Rai, R.: Artificial intelligence (ai) in augmented reality (ar)-assisted manufacturing applications: a review. Int. J. Prod. Res. **59**(16), 4903–4959 (2021)
35. Sala, N.: Virtual reality, augmented reality, and mixed reality in education: a brief overview. Current and prospective applications of virtual reality in higher education, pp. 48–73 (2021)
36. Schäfer, A., Reis, G., Stricker, D.: A survey on synchronous augmented, virtual and mixed reality remote collaboration systems. ACM Comput. Surv. (CSUR) (2021)
37. Sorko, S.R., Brunnhofer, M.: Potentials of augmented reality in training. Procedia Manufacturing **31**, 85–90 (2019)
38. Tang, K.S., Cheng, D.L., Mi, E., Greenberg, P.B.: Augmented reality in medical education: a systematic review. Canadian Med. Educ. J. **11**(1), e81 (2020)
39. Taupiac, J.D., Rodriguez, N., Strauss, O., Rabier, M.: Ad-hoc study on soldiers calibration procedure in virtual reality. In: 2019 IEEE Conference on Virtual Reality and 3d User Interfaces (VR), pp. 190–199. IEEE (2019)
40. Teo, T., Lawrence, L., Lee, G.A., Billinghurst, M., Adcock, M.: Mixed reality remote collaboration combining 360 video and 3d reconstruction. In: Proceedings of the 2019 CHI Conference on Human Factors in Computing Systems, pp. 1–14 (2019)
41. Thoravi Kumaravel, B., Anderson, F., Fitzmaurice, G., Hartmann, B., Grossman, T.: Loki: Facilitating remote instruction of physical tasks using bi-directional mixed-reality telepresence. In: Proceedings of the 32nd Annual ACM Symposium on User Interface Software and Technology, pp. 161–174 (2019)
42. Vidal-Balea, A., et al.: Analysis, design and practical validation of an augmented reality teaching system based on microsoft hololens 2 and edge computing. Eng. Proc. **2**(1), 52 (2020)

43. Villanueva, A., Zhu, Z., Liu, Z., Peppler, K., Redick, T., Ramani, K.: Meta-ar-app: an authoring platform for collaborative augmented reality in stem classrooms. In: Proceedings of the 2020 CHI Conference on Human Factors in Computing Systems, pp. 1–14 (2020)
44. Villanueva, A., Zhu, Z., Liu, Z., Wang, F., Chidambaram, S., Ramani, K.: Colabar: a toolkit for remote collaboration in tangible augmented reality laboratories. Proc. ACM Hum.-Comput. Interact. **6**(CSCW1), April 2022
45. Yu, L., et al.: Holoaac: a mixed reality aac application for people with expressive language difficulties. In: International Conference on Human-Computer Interaction. Springer (2024)
46. Zhao, Y., Kupferstein, E., Rojnirun, H., Findlater, L., Azenkot, S.: The effectiveness of visual and audio wayfinding guidance on smartglasses for people with low vision. In: Proceedings of the 2020 CHI Conference on Human Factors in Computing Systems, pp. 1–14 (2020)

Conceptual Design Ease of Use MR-PACS

Zeyu Zhou[1(✉)], Lingjing Liu[2], and Yidan Cong[2]

[1] Georgia Institute of Technology, Atlanta, GA 30332, USA
gcwpf@outlook.com
[2] Northeastern University, Boston, MA 02115, USA
{liu.lingj,cong.yi}@northeastern.edu

Abstract. Medical professionals are frequently burdened by the extensive, routine tasks associated with patient care, one of which includes navigating and interpreting patient information through medical PACS (Picture Archiving and Communication System) systems. Complex visual elements detract from the system's usability by overcrowding the interface and perplexing the end-users. Since 2022, the remarkable development and breakthroughs in Large Language Models (LLMs) have transformed the way we analyze and access both structured and unstructured data. Furthermore, the enhanced hardware capabilities of Virtual Reality (VR) devices have ushered in the era of Spatial Computing, a paradigm that transcends the limitations of physical space, allowing for unprecedented interaction and creativity. In response to the convergence of these technological advancements, we have conceptualized and developed a Virtual Reality (VR)/Mixed Reality (MR) application designed to enhance the operational efficiency of medical workflows. We designed engineering aesthetic visual elements to minimize discomfort for the user. Additionally, it incorporates a virtual medical assistant powered by a sophisticated Large Language Model (GPT-4), facilitating the analysis of patient information through intuitive voice commands. This integration not only liberates medical professionals from the constraints of physical space and hardware but also empowers them to efficiently process a greater volume of patient data. Through this exploration, we aim to streamline medical workflows, and utilize those techniques for digital transformation of traditional medical practices.

Keywords: Mixed Reality · Large Language Model · Spatial computing · Medical PACs · information retrieval · medical images · Unity · Virtual Assistant

1 Introduction

Medical Picture Archiving and Communication Systems (PACS) have long been a standard approach in healthcare, extensively used by medical professionals to manage and view medical images and patient information effectively [16]. These systems are integral to the day-to-day operations of healthcare facilities, ensuring efficient storage, retrieval, presentation, and dissemination of patient imaging

J. Y. C. Chen et al. (Eds.): HCII 2024, LNCS 15377, pp. 265–282, 2025.
https://doi.org/10.1007/978-3-031-76812-5_18

data. Despite their widespread utility and importance in providing a centralized image viewer, PACS come with inherent limitations. These include limited capabilities for data mining, challenges in integrating with external knowledge bases, and constraints in workspace efficiency. Additionally, the financial cost associated with implementing and maintaining PACS is significant, necessitating substantial investment in both the systems themselves and the high-quality monitors needed for optimal image display.

Virtual reality (VR) technology has rapidly evolved, becoming increasingly accessible, cost-effective, and powerful. Once a niche and expensive tool limited to specific industries, VR devices are now widely available to the general public, offering a diverse array of applications from entertainment to education, and notably, healthcare. This widespread availability is attributed to significant advancements in computing power, miniaturization of components, and competitive market dynamics, which have collectively driven down costs while enhancing the capabilities of these devices. As VR technology continues to mature, it promises to unlock unprecedented opportunities for immersive experiences across various sectors, transforming how we interact with digital content.

To address these challenges and limitations associated with traditional PACS, our team has explored integrating Mixed Reality (MR) technology into our imaging workflows. By utilizing MR, we aim to significantly reduce reliance on expensive, specialized monitors, opting instead for more versatile and widely available devices. This approach not only cuts down on the substantial costs linked to high-end hardware but also enhances display performance by providing a more immersive and interactive viewing experience. Furthermore, MR technology improves data transfer speeds and operational efficiency, effectively addressing both spatial and financial constraints commonly faced in traditional PACS setups.

The foremost advantage of this application is its ability to significantly enhance the capabilities of existing PACS systems. It provides medical professionals with an advanced visual display and an intuitive user interface for efficient management of patient data. Utilizing Mixed Reality (MR) technology, the system facilitates dynamic interactions with medical images and associated text, which deepens the understanding of patient conditions. By integrating cutting-edge visualization and interaction techniques, our solution streamlines the diagnostic process and substantially improves the efficiency of medical imaging workflows.

To further enhance the utility of MR technology in medical imaging, we have introduced a virtual assistant powered by advanced large language models, complemented by ChatTTS technology for voice-to-text conversion. This integration significantly streamlines various operational processes, including data retrieval, data mining, and medical report generation [22]. The virtual assistant not only assists in routine tasks but also brings external medical knowledge into the MR environment, facilitating more informed and accurate medical diagnoses. This addition effectively removes operational barriers, enabling more efficient and comprehensive assistance during medical operations. Additionally, the ChatTTS feature reduces the need for manual text inputs, thereby increasing the efficiency and effectiveness of operations. This comprehensive approach not only removes operational barriers but also enhances the overall user experience in medical settings.

2   Related Work

The research landscape in medical Picture Archiving and Communication Systems (PACS) design is notably diverse and innovative, focusing on several key areas aimed at enhancing functionality, efficiency, and user experience. Prominent areas of interest include the development of advanced PACS architectures, the integration of Virtual Reality (VR) and Mixed Reality (MR) technologies, and the implementation of Large Language Models (LLMs).

Medical PACS Architecture. The adoption of PACS systems has led to substantial cost reductions and streamlined workflows within healthcare settings. By transitioning away from physical films, associated storage expenses are minimized, and the reduction in manual administrative tasks enhances the efficiency of imaging processes. Medical PACS system closely integrated with Hospital Information Systems (HIS) has been shown to streamline the radiology workflow significantly by enabling more efficient access to both images and electronic health records (EHR) [19]. This integration allows healthcare providers to access patient images and comprehensive medical history in one place, reducing the need for toggling between systems and minimizing errors related to dual data entry. This setup enhances the coordination of patient care and ensures that healthcare professionals can make informed decisions quickly [6]. This enables healthcare providers to focus more on delivering high-quality patient care instead of being bogged down by paperwork, optimizing resource allocation and improving overall healthcare delivery [4]. Thin client architectures for PACS systems are increasingly being utilized to streamline the management and viewing of medical images across healthcare organizations. This approach centralizes image processing tasks on a high-performance server, while client devices utilize lightweight, often web-based applications for image display and interaction [12]. Such a configuration facilitates real-time image rendering and user interactions like zooming and annotating, processed on the server side, enhancing system efficiency and security by minimizing data storage on local devices [5,24].

VR/MR Display Application. Virtual reality (VR) technology is transforming medical imaging and healthcare by creating immersive and interactive environments that surpass traditional boundaries. In the realm of medical imaging, VR enhances how radiologists view diagnostic images by introducing high-quality 3D imaging, allowing for flexibility and remote operation without needing a traditional workstation. Devices like the Meta Quest 3 are increasingly incorporated into medical PACS systems, offering applications crucial for surgical planning, medical education, and collaborative medical teamwork. These applications convert complex medical images into three-dimensional, interactive models that significantly improve surgical planning and patient care understanding [7,8]. This advanced visualization allows medical professionals to view and manipulate detailed 3D images directly in the virtual environment, eliminating the need for high-end monitors. The technology maintains the grayscale and intricate details of the images, ensuring that critical information is preserved and accessible. Additionally, this approach reduces the need for extensive device setup and allows medical professionals to access and interact with these images from various locations, enhancing flexibility and efficiency in medical analysis and decision-making.

Advanced AI/Large Language Model Integration. Artificial intelligence (AI), particularly Large Language Models (LLMs), is increasingly instrumental in enhancing the efficiency and effectiveness of medical PACS systems [13,15,18]. These advanced AI technologies automate labor-intensive tasks within radiology workflows, such as image sorting, preliminary analysis, and sophisticated report generation. Such automation frees up significant time for radiologists and improves the accuracy and speed of diagnostics [9]. LLMs, specifically, are highly effective in refining PACS functionalities like worklist optimization and report structuring. Some researchers employ deep learning algorithms to prioritize urgent cases, which not only expedites the diagnostic process but also ensures critical conditions receive timely attention, thereby enhancing patient care outcomes. The integration of LLMs into PACS extends to broader clinical decision support roles [10]. These models leverage their vast training data to provide enhanced diagnostic insights and manage complex clinical data across various sources seamlessly [14]. This capability helps in generating enriched, structured reports that are crucial for clinicians, making the information more comprehensive and easier to navigate, ultimately improving the decision-making process in clinical settings.

Voice Control. Speech recognition systems have significantly enhanced the efficiency and accuracy of radiology reporting. These systems enable radiologists to dictate their findings directly into the PACS, which are transcribed in real-time, facilitating faster and more precise documentation. Early speech recognition systems for report generation were described, but broad adoption did not occur until the mid-2000s. This delay was due to the need for context-sensitive integration with PACS and RIS and improvements in voice recognition technology [20,21]. Recent progress in technologies like ChatTTS has further revolutionized real-time voice control systems [23]. These advancements have made it feasible to implement highly accurate, real-time speech recognition in medical settings, providing seamless voice control for radiologists. Despite these advancements, existing research indicates that integration with Electronic Medical Records (EMR) systems remains minimal and suboptimal, highlighting the need for further development in this area.

3   Proposed Approach

The primary objective of this project is to demonstrate the potential of Mixed Reality (MR) technology in the context of medical PACS (Picture Archiving and Communication Systems). This paper explores the integration of MR technology and Large Language Models (LLMs) within traditional healthcare frameworks, leveraging the capabilities of the Meta Quest 3. The research focuses on the user-friendly interface design and the integration of emerging technologies into the medical PACS imaging pipeline. Through this work, We aim to create a strong link between modern MR and LLM technologies and traditional medical imaging systems, showcasing their combined potential to enhance user interaction, data retrieval, and overall system efficiency in healthcare settings.

3.1   Hardware/Software Platform

To begin, we evaluated popular VR devices in the North American market, focusing on Apple Vision Pro and Meta Quest 3 [11]. After careful comparison, we chose the Meta Quest 3. Although the Apple Vision Pro excels in performance and display quality, the Quest 3 is better suited for prototyping and testing conceptual implementations. Additionally, the Quest 3 is more cost-effective, offering significant value for our budget (Table 1).

Table 1. Apple Vision Pro vs Meta Quest 3: Specifications

Specification	Apple Vision Pro	Meta Quest 3
Release date	US: Febr. 02 2024	Oct. 10 2023
Starting price	$3,499	$499
Refresh rate	90 Hz/96 Hz/100 Hz	72 Hz/80 Hz/90 Hz/120 Hz
Display resolution	$3,660 \times 3,142$ px per eye	$2,064 \times 2,208$ px per eye
Display technology	micro-OLED	LCD
Field of view	around $110°$	$110°$ (horizontal), $96°$ (vertical)
Weight	600–650 g	515 g
Storage sizes	215 GB/512 GB/1 TB	128 GB/512 GB
Processor	M2 processor and an R1 chip	Snapdragon XR2 Gen 2 processor
Battery life	2 h (general use), 2.5 h (watching video)	Up to 2 h
Audio	Two speakers, spatial audio-enabled	Near-field

The Quest 3's ability to seamlessly merge real-world objects with virtual representations provides a compelling sense of immediacy. We also chose the Meta Quest 3 platform for its advanced mixed reality capabilities, including full-color pass-through, suggested boundary, assisted Space Setup, and Direct Touch [3]. These features significantly enhance user immersion and presence, making the Quest 3 ideal for our MR applications.

To develop for the Quest 3, we selected Unity 3D as our development platform. Unity provides a comprehensive toolkit for creating interactive content, including scene visualization and dynamic 3D modeling. Its use of C# as the primary scripting language ensures a user-friendly and secure environment suitable for developers at all skill levels. This ease of use boosts productivity and simplifies problem-solving in development projects. The platform's support for advanced functionalities, such as collision detection and ergonomic analysis, is essential for developing intuitive and interactive virtual user interfaces. These interfaces are crucial for translating user interactions into digital signals, thereby optimizing the operator's interaction with the digital environment.

3.2   Workflow Design

Figure 1 illustrates the workflow of a medical imaging system integrating various components through standardized protocols. It begins with a medical imaging device, such as a CT scanner, capturing images and transmitting them to a Gateway using the DICOM protocol. Simultaneously, the Hospital Information System (HIS) or Radiology Information System (RIS) exchanges patient information and order details with the Gateway using HL7 standards [17]. For long-term storage, the PACS Server archives the images in the PACS Image Archive using the DICOM protocol. When these images need to be retrieved, the PACS Server fetches them from the archive, making them available for review and diagnosis. This workflow ensures efficient and standardized handling of medical images and patient data within the healthcare system.

Compared to the traditional workflow, our design incorporates a VR/MR module that offers functionality similar to the workstation show in Fig. 1. This module includes several key components: the VR/MR device, which interacts with a medical report generating engine, a medical image viewer, and a voice control system. Additionally, a large language model facilitates access to external knowledge databases, enhancing the overall capability and efficiency of the system.

Communication Module. The communication module functions as a crucial link between the Meta Quest 3 and the Medical PACS Server, as shown in Fig. 1. This system uses a client/server (C/S) architecture to facilitate real-time transmission of user commands. The Meta Quest 3, acting as the client, handles various tasks including retrieving patient data, loading models, executing model operations, performing spatial computing, and managing human-computer interactions. These functions significantly enhance the mixed reality experience by leveraging data from the medical PACS server.

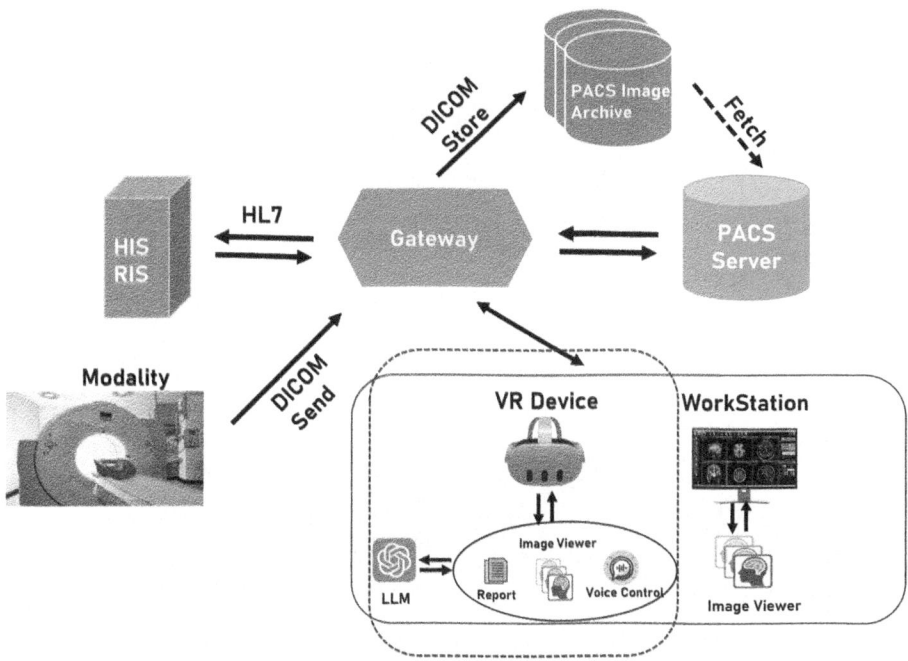

Fig. 1. Workflow Design of MR-PACs system

AI/Large Language Model Module. Introduced in late 2022, the ChatGPT large language model has been pivotal in numerous visual-text application trials. It excels in converting unstructured natural language data into structured formats, interpreting meanings, and providing the most appropriate responses. This module allows users to interact directly via voice, bypassing manual controls, and leverages a well-configured LLM API to potentially automate the PACS system either partially or fully. Such automation not only saves time for medical professionals but also enhances capabilities in generating medical reports, diagnosing diseases, and identifying potential patient risks through pattern recognition. Voice Recognition Module acts as a submodule within the larger LLM framework, enhanced by ChatTTS technology. It captures natural human voice inputs, converting them into textual data for further processing by the NLP engine. This integration ensures seamless voice-to-text conversion, facilitating intuitive user interactions without the need for manual input (Fig. 2).

Mixed Reality User Interface. In this system, the user interface enables interactive operations with digital content, facilitating database queries through hand gestures, voice commands, and text inputs. This design allows users to seamlessly interact with the system, enhancing the efficiency and intuitiveness of data retrieval and manipulation within medical applications (Fig. 4).

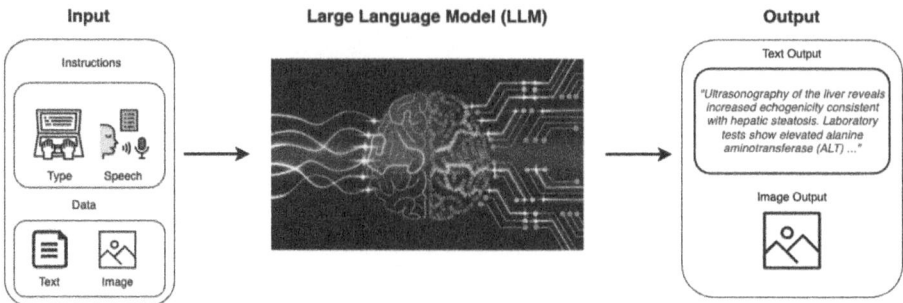

Fig. 2. LLM workflow

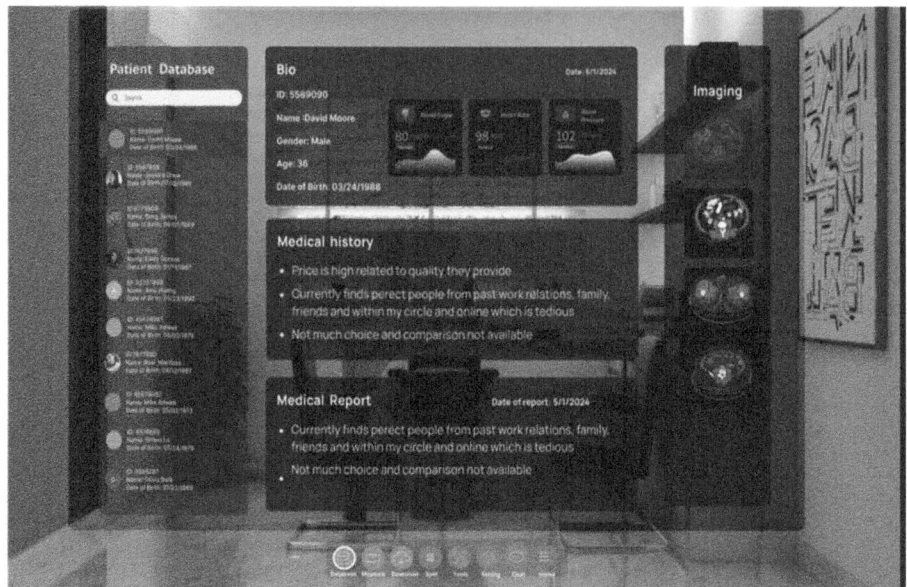

Fig. 3. Main Interface in Plain View

In this workflow design, we would like to achieve design goals: To ensure users are fully absorbed in the environment, advanced VR/MR technologies are employed to create natural and engaging interactions. Interactive elements and intuitive interfaces are incorporated to encourage continuous engagement and maintain user interest. The interfaces are designed to be simple to navigate, featuring clear instructions and minimal learning curves. Additionally, features like voice control and customizable settings are included to accommodate diverse user needs.

From Fig. 3, 5, 6, 7, 8, we implement the designed key features by incorporating 3D UI elements that can be manipulated in the virtual space, providing a more intuitive and engaging user experience. The system supports voice

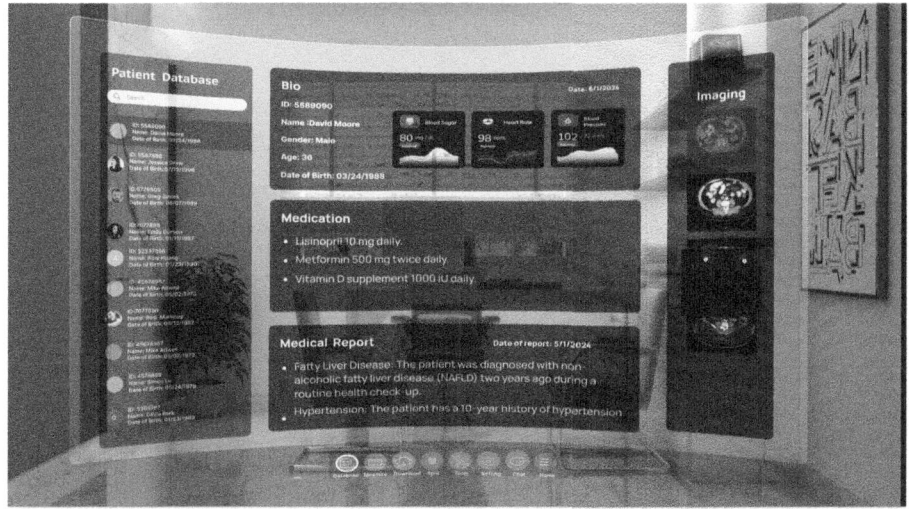

Fig. 4. Main Interface in Expand View

commands, hand tracking, and eye-gaze controls to ensure natural interactions. Sensors and AI are utilized to understand the user's environment and actions, offering relevant information and controls based on context. High-contrast visuals, clear labels, and straightforward navigation paths are employed to prevent confusion and enhance usability.

Figure 3 illustrates the four-region layout design. The left side features the patient database, where users can search and select patient records. The middle region displays detailed patient information, including bio, medication, and medical reports. The right region serves as the patient images bar, showcasing relevant medical images for detailed examination. The bottom bar functions as a toolbar, providing quick access to various tools and settings. Additionally, raising a hand activates the handtool bar, offering further interactive capabilities for manipulating the interface and data.

Figure 5 shows a hand gesture being used to interact with a floating menu. The menu includes various icons such as Home, Settings, Download, Database, Tool, Chat, Measure, Split, and an additional tool. The menu items are designed with clear, recognizable icons and distinct colors, ensuring that users can quickly identify and select the necessary tools. Users can perform tasks without the need to switch devices, maintaining their focus and reducing workflow interruptions. This integration of gesture recognition minimizes the need for physical interactions with hardware. The interface is highly customizable, allowing users to personalize the layout and functionality of the menu based on their preferences. This flexibility ensures that each user can optimize the UI for their specific workflow needs.

In the MR-PACS design, Fig. 6, multiple datasets can be shown in different windows side-by-side, significantly extending the limitations of traditional PACS,

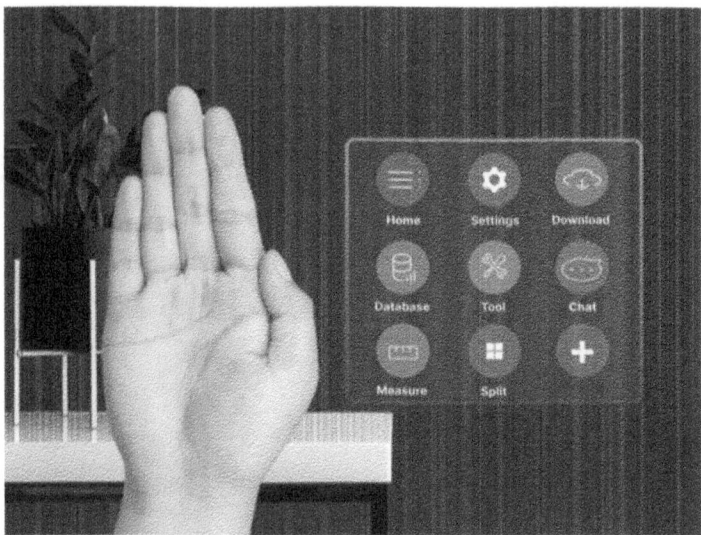

Fig. 5. Hand tools

Fig. 6. Image Viewer in Immersive Environment

which typically allow only one dataset to be reviewed at a time. This new feature leverages advanced multitasking capabilities, improving efficiency by enabling healthcare professionals to compare and analyze multiple patient records or imaging studies simultaneously. This enhanced functionality attributes to a more efficient and effective workflow in medical imaging.

The user interface features an intuitive layout with hand gesture controls for seamless interaction. Users can manipulate 3D medical images using hand

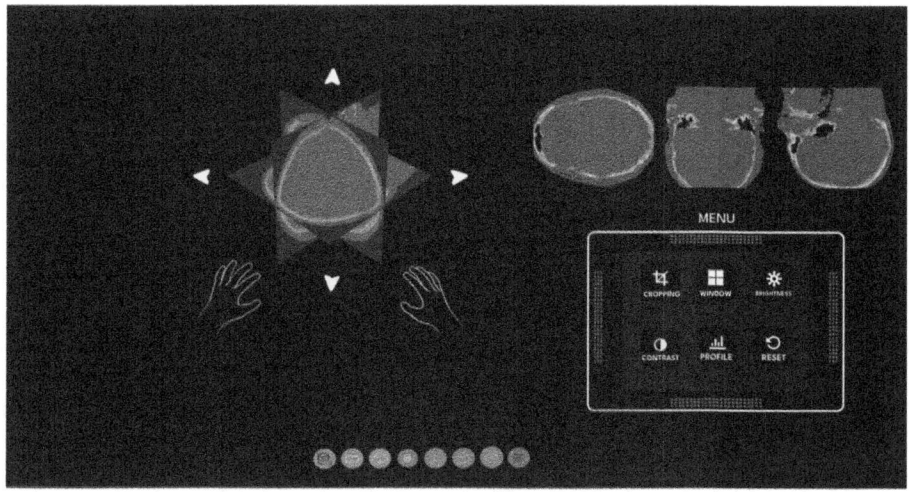

Fig. 7. High Contrast Environment

Fig. 8. PACS Assistance Bot

movements, providing a more immersive and interactive experience Fig. 7. The central area displays a 3D model of the scanned organ, which can be rotated and adjusted from various angles using simple hand gestures. On the right side, multiple 2D slices of the scan are displayed, enabling detailed examination of different cross-sections. The menu located in the lower-right corner includes essential tools such as cropping, window adjustment, brightness control, contrast settings, profile adjustments, and a reset function. Additional customizable buttons offer advanced image processing operations like zooming, panning, edge detection, noise reduction, segmentation, sharpening, smoothing, measurement tools, and annotation capabilities are also available for selections. These tools are easily accessible and designed to enhance the user's ability to customize and analyze medical images efficiently.

Voice commands are seamlessly integrated into the MR system, providing corresponding visual responses to enhance multi-modal interaction. When a voice command is recognized, related UI elements react visually-such as lighting up or animating-to confirm that the command has been processed. This immediate feedback not only validates the user's input but also enhances the overall interactivity and engagement of the system. Furthermore, text buttons are made interactive through a sophisticated speech recognition module from the Quest 3, transforming spoken words into operational commands. This capability allows users to send commands directly to the AI system, enabling it to process these instructions for various tasks such as data processing, data retrieval, and assisted diagnosis. The system's interactive capabilities are highly customizable, adapting to the specific needs of different scenes or applications. This flexibility ensures that the user experience is both tailored and efficient, catering to various user requirements and scenarios.

With the capabilities of a large language model, the system can also provide preliminary diagnoses for abnormal regions in medical images and identify unusual points in medical texts. It autonomously pinpoints areas of concern within medical images by scrutinizing patterns and deviations from standard anatomical structures, flagging potential abnormalities such as tumors, lesions, and other pathologies. Additionally, the LLM vision capability extends to analyzing medical texts, identifying anomalous points, including atypical symptoms or inconsistencies in clinical reports. The integration of abnormal region detection with VR/MR display technology further facilitates the visualization of highlighted regions in a 3D context, aiding in enhanced understanding and accurate diagnosis.

Report generation module automatically drafts initial medical reports based on the analysis of medical images and patient data, significantly reducing the time clinicians spend on documentation. Users can select from predefined templates below tailored to various imaging studies, ensuring consistent and complete documentation. The module integrates seamlessly with imaging data, allowing clinicians to include annotated images and key findings in reports, thus providing visual context to the written analysis. Voice dictation and natural language processing further expedite report creation, while real-time collaboration enables multiple healthcare professionals to contribute simultaneously, which is especially useful for complex cases. AI-driven contextual recommendations ensure that reports align with the latest medical literature and best practices. The review and approval workflow ensures accuracy and compliance with institutional guidelines, while secure storage and controlled access protect patient privacy and data security. Integration with the hospital's EHR system ensures that reports are automatically added to the patient's medical record, facilitating a comprehensive view of the patient's health history. By incorporating these features, the report generation module significantly enhances the efficiency, accuracy, and comprehensiveness of medical reporting, ultimately improving patient care and clinical outcomes.

Medical Report Template

Patient Information:
Name: [Patient Name]
ID: [Patient ID]
Date of Birth: [MM/DD/YYYY]
Gender: [Male/Female/Other]
Date of Report: [MM/DD/YYYY]

Referring Physician:
Name: [Physician Name]
Department: [Department Name]
Contact Information: [Phone/Email]

Examination Details:
Type of Examination: [CT/MRI/X-ray/Ultrasound/etc.]
Date of Examination: [MM/DD/YYYY].
Study Description: [Description of the study].
Indications for Study: [Reason for the examination, symptoms, or condition being investigated].

Clinical History:
Brief History: [Relevant medical history, previous conditions, surgeries, medications].

Findings:
1. [Description of finding 1].
2. [Description of finding 2].
3. [Description of finding 3].

Impressions/Diagnosis:
1. [Summary of the main findings and interpretation].
2. [Diagnosis if applicable].
3. [Recommendations for further tests or follow-up].

Conclusion:
A brief summary of the key findings and their implications for the patient's health.

Recommendations:
1. [Follow-up procedures or consultations].
2. [Suggested treatments or interventions].
3. [Lifestyle changes or patient instructions].

Attached Images/Annotations:.
1. [Include any relevant annotated images from the study].

Radiologist/Technician Information:
Name: [Radiologist/Technician Name]
Signature: [Signature if applicable]
Contact Information: [Phone/Email].

3.3   Usability Survey

To better understand the usability of our design, we also conducted a post-usage survey for users. To begin the experiment, each participant was required to sign a consent form detailing the procedures and data usage policies for the collected data. A concise tutorial on how to operate the medical PACS application using the VR/MR headset is given, participants began by interacting with a series of panels containing medical images and text data. They were instructed to read each section and answer a question at the end of the experiments. This questions were designed to assess their ability to navigate and understand the information presented within the VR/MR environment, ensuring a comprehensive evaluation of the application's usability. Below is the survey used Table 2:

Table 2. Usability Survey Questions

Section 1: User Experience	
How easy was it to navigate the VR environment?	1 2 3 4 5
Were the controls intuitive?	Yes No
Please describe any difficulties you encountered.	[Open-ended]
Section 2: Comfort	
Did you experience any discomfort while using the VR application?	Yes No
How comfortable was the VR headset?	1 2 3 4 5
How long were you able to use the application before needing a break?	[<30 min, 30 min - 1 h, 1–2 h, >2 h]
Section 3: Functionality	
How would you rate the VR application?	1 2 3 4 5
Did you experience any technical issues?	Yes No
Are there any features you found particularly useful or lacking?	[Open-ended]
Section 4: Visual and Audio Quality	
How would you rate the quality of the graphics?	1 2 3 4 5
How would you rate the audio quality?	1 2 3 4 5
Section 5: Overall Satisfaction	
How satisfied are you with your overall experience?	1 2 3 4 5
Would you recommend this VR application to others?	Yes No
Any additional suggestions for improvement:	[Open-ended]

4   Results

The usability survey, completed by 15 participants, provides valuable insights into the MR-PACS system. The results are summarized below in Table 3. In terms of user experience, most participants found the VR environment easy to navigate, with 46.7% rating it a 4 and 20% rating it a 5. The controls were considered intuitive by 80% of users, though some encountered difficulties selecting small text items. Regarding comfort, 73.3% of participants did not experience any discomfort while using the VR application. The VR headset was generally comfortable, with most users rating it between 3 and 4. Participants could use the application for 1–2 hours before needing a break, with 40% indicating this usage duration. Functionality received generally positive feedback, with 53.3% of users rating the application a 4. However, 33.3% experienced technical issues. Users appreciated the clarity of the graphics but suggested the need for more interactive tutorials. Visual and audio quality were rated positively, with 53.3% giving the graphics a 4 and 46.7% giving the audio quality a 4.

Overall satisfaction was above average, with 53.3% rating their experience a 4, and 80% would recommend the VR/MR application to others. Suggestions

Table 3. Usability Survey Questions and Responses

Section 1: User Experience	
How easy was it to navigate the VR environment?	1: 0%, 2: 13.3%, 3: 20%, 4: 46.7%, 5: 20%
Were the controls intuitive?	Yes: 80%, No: 20%
Please describe any difficulties you encountered.	Several participants mentioned difficulty in selecting small text items.
Section 2: Comfort	
Did you experience any discomfort while using the VR application?	Yes: 26.7%, No: 73.3%
How comfortable was the VR headset?	1: 6.7%, 2: 13.3%, 3: 33.3%, 4: 33.3%, 5: 13.3%
How long were you able to use the application before needing a break?	<30 min: 20%, 30 min - 1 h: 33.3%, 1–2 h: 40%, >2 h: 6.7%
Section 3: Functionality	
How would you rate the VR application?	1: 0%, 2: 6.7%, 3: 26.7%, 4: 53.3%, 5: 13.3%
Did you experience any technical issues?	Yes: 33.3%, No: 66.7%
Are there any features you found particularly useful or lacking?	Participants appreciated the clarity of the graphics but suggested more interactive tutorials.
Section 4: Visual and Audio Quality	
How would you rate the quality of the graphics?	1: 0%, 2: 6.7%, 3: 13.3%, 4: 53.3%, 5: 26.7%
How would you rate the audio quality?	1: 0%, 2: 13.3%, 3: 20%, 4: 46.7%, 5: 20%
Section 5: Overall Satisfaction	
How satisfied are you with your overall experience?	1: 0%, 2: 6.7%, 3: 20%, 4: 53.3%, 5: 20%
Would you recommend this VR application to others?	Yes: 80%, No: 20%
Any additional suggestions for improvement:	Many participants suggested adding more customizable settings and improving the response time of controls.

for improvement included adding more customizable settings and improving the response time of controls.

5   Conclusions

In conclusion, while traditional medical PACS systems have proven effective, they often require significant financial and logistical investments. Our development of an innovative MR-based medical PACS application, enhanced by the integration of a large language model, represents a substantial advancement in medical imaging technology. This new system significantly improves the integration of external medical knowledge, enhances information retrieval, and provides stronger diagnostic support, thereby pushing the boundaries of conventional medical imaging capabilities.

Our preliminary evaluation, which involved 15 participants utilizing a usability survey, indicated that the application is user-friendly, achieving an average score of 2.07 out of 5 points. This positive feedback highlights the ease of use, although there are opportunities to further improve the user interface to enhance overall usability. However, some participants reported difficulties with certain features, such as small text selection and navigation complexity, indicating areas where the system did not perform as well as expected.

Additionally, the system's performance in real-world settings remains to be fully tested. The lack of extensive real-world medical data integration has limited the practical applicability and realism of the application so far. Addressing this gap is crucial for enhancing its utility in clinical environments.

Moving forward, we aim to increase the realism and practical applicability of the application by integrating real-world medical data, thereby enhancing its utility in clinical environments. We also plan to refine the user interface based on the feedback received to resolve the reported issues and improve overall user experience. Furthermore, we plan to conduct a more extensive user study involving a diverse range of healthcare professionals to gather deeper insights and more comprehensive feedback. This will guide targeted enhancements to our MR-PACS system. Our ultimate goal is to ensure that the system meets the evolving needs of the medical community, addresses its current shortcomings, and continues to improve patient care.

Acknowledgments. The author(s) would like to thank everyone who contributed to the development and completion of this research project.

Disclosure of Interests. The authors declare no potential conflict of interest with respect to the research, authorship, and/or publication of this article.

References

1. Andriole, K.P.: SPIE medical imaging 50th anniversary: history of the picture archiving and communication systems conference. J. Med. Imaging **9**(Suppl 1), 12210 (2022). https://doi.org/10.1117/1.JMI.9.S1.S12210
2. Andriole, K.P.: Picture archiving and communication systems: past, present, and future. J. Med. Imaging. **10**(6), 061405 (2023). https://doi.org/10.1117/1.JMI.10.6.061405
3. Meta Quest 3 Homepage. https://www.meta.com/help/quest/articles/getting-started/getting-started-with-quest-3/mixed-reality-quest-3/. Accessed 10 Dec 2023
4. Role of Pacs in medical imaging. https://techperia.com/the-role-of-pacs-systems-in-medical-imaging/. Accessed 12 Nov 2023
5. What is a thin client solution in PACS? https://www.openrad.com/news/thin-client/. Accessed 28 July 2023
6. Integration of PACS and EHR: Streamlining PACS for Radiology Workflow. https://www.postdicom.com/en/blog/integration-of-pacs-and-ehr. Accessed 25 Oct 2023
7. Virtual and Augmented Reality in Medical Imaging. https://www.medical-professionals.com/en/virtual-augmented-reality-medical-imaging. Accessed 01 Jan 2024
8. AI, Automatic Segmentation, Smart Medical Data. In Augmented and Virtual Reality. https://www.medicalholodeck.com/en/. Accessed 01 Jan 2024
9. PACS RIS and AI: a fully integrated radiology workflow. https://www.aidoc.com/learn/blog/pacs-ris-ai-workflow/. Accessed 01 Jan 2024
10. AI applications to PACS systems - challenges and understanding the impact on workflows. https://www.healthcareitnews.com/news/asia/ai-applications-pacs-systems-challenges-and-understanding-impact-workflows. Accessed 03 Oct 2019
11. Meta Quest 3 vs. Apple Vision Pro: How accurate was Zuckerberg's review? https://www.zdnet.com/article/meta-quest-3-vs-apple-vision-pro/. Accessed 14 Feb 2024
12. Nieh, J., Yang, S.J., Novik, N.: A comparison of thin-client computing architectures (2000). https://doi.org/10.7916/D8Z329VF
13. Yang, Y., et al.: Design and implementation of a new generation of PACS based on artificial intelligent visualization. In: Medical Imaging 2020: Imaging Informatics for Healthcare, Research, and Applications, vol. 11318, pp. 214–222(2020). https://doi.org/10.1117/12.2548921
14. D'Asseler, Y., et al.: PACS and multimodality in medical imaging. Technol. Health Care **8**(1), 35–52 (2000). https://doi.org/10.3233/THC-2000-8104
15. Taira, R.K., Breant, C.M., McNitt-Gray, M.F., Sinha, S., Huang, H.K.: Adding intelligence to PACS. In: Medical Imaging VI: PACS Design and Evaluation, vol. 1654, pp. 476–484 (1992). https://doi.org/10.1117/12.60302
16. Meyer-Ebrecht, D. Picture archiving and communication systems (PACS) for medical application. Int. J. Bio-medical Comput. **35**, 91–124 (1994). https://doi.org/10.1109/SCAMC.1983.764774
17. Ratib, O., Swiernik, M., McCoy, J. M. From PACS to integrated EMR. Comput. Med. Imaging Graph. **27**, 207–215 (2003). https://doi.org/10.1016/s0895-6111(02)00075-7
18. Faggioni, L., Neri, E., Castellana, C., Caramella, D., Bartolozzi, C. The future of PACS in healthcare enterprises. Eur. J. Radiol. **78**(2), 253–258 (2011). https://doi.org/10.1016/s0895-6111(02)00075-7

19. Cohen, S., Gilboa, F., Shani, U.: PACS and electronic health records. In: Medical Imaging 2002: PACS and Integrated Medical Information Systems: Design and Evaluation. SPIE, vol. 4685, pp. 288–298 (2002). https://doi.org/10.1117/12.467019
20. Rokhsaritalemi, S., Sadeghi-Niaraki, A., Choi, S.M.: A review on mixed reality: current trends, challenges and prospects. Appl. Sci. **10**(2), 636 (2020). https://doi.org/10.3390/app10020636
21. Ruksakulpiwat, S., Kumar, A., Ajibade, A.: Using ChatGPT in medical research: current status and future directions. J. Multidisc. Healthc., 1513–1520 (2023). https://doi.org/10.2147/JMDH.S413470
22. Zhou, Z.: Evaluation of ChatGPT's capabilities in medical report generation. Cureus **15**(4), 37589 (2023). https://doi.org/10.7759/cureus.37589
23. Guo, H., Zhang, S., Soong, F.K., He, L., Xie, L.: Conversational end-to-end tts for voice agents. In: 2021 IEEE Spoken Language Technology Workshop (SLT), pp. 403–409 (2021). https://doi.org/10.1109/SLT48900.2021.9383460
24. Huang, H.K.: Pacs-Based Multimedia Imaging Informatics: Basic Principles and Applications. John Wiley & Sons, Hoboken (2019). https://doi.org/10.1002/9781118795552

Playing Experiences

Alien Mystery Scavenger Hunt: Enhancing Intergenerational Interaction with Physical Web Technologies Through Location-Based Games

Fatima Badmos[1]([⊠]) [iD], Emma Murphy[2] [iD], Michael Ward[1], Mayanka Parmar[1], Paula Kelly[1], and Damon Berry[1] [iD]

[1] School Electric Electrical Engineering, Technological University Dublin, Dublin, Ireland
fatima.badmos@tudublin.ie
[2] School of Computer Science, Technological University Dublin, Dublin, Ireland

Abstract. The Physical Web is a powerful, easy-to-implement and inexpensive way to bridge the gap between the digital and physical realms compared to other technologies used for web location-aware interaction. In this study, we propose a Physical Web for an intergenerational game through the Alien Mystery scavenger hunt. Through the design and implementation of a Physical Web for outdoor intergenerational games, we show the potential of Physical Web technologies in presenting different interactions between the web and the user's physical environment. The game utilises the ubiquity of QR codes and NFC in modern mobile devices, enabling users to seamlessly interact with physical objects and locations while accessing location-specific digital content. The user observation and anonymous feedback revealed that participants enjoyed the intergenerational aspect of the game and the two-way interaction between their mobile devices and the physical artefacts without the need to download an application on their devices before engaging in the game.

Keywords: Physical Web · Location-based game · Intergenerational

1 Introduction

Intergenerational outdoor games provide an inclusive environment that fosters social connections across generations. Understanding the dynamics of these games, facilitated by physical artefacts and digital clues, is crucial to designing physical-digital experiences that stimulate interactions and promote intergenerational relationships. Contemporary mobile devices incorporate technologies like Bluetooth, NFC (Near Field Communication), accelerometers, and cameras. This development has facilitated the emergence of interconnected and dynamic digital ecosystems that shape how people interact with the physical environment. Merging digital with physical worlds has been explored to varying extents in location-based games and, in general, Physical Web technologies using QR Codes, NFC and IoT (Internet of Things) [20]. However, an area that has remained underexplored is the creation of digital clues to facilitate interactions with physical objects

J. Y. C. Chen et al. (Eds.): HCII 2024, LNCS 15377, pp. 285–295, 2025.
https://doi.org/10.1007/978-3-031-76812-5_19

in outdoor gaming without companion mobile applications. This paper presents "Alien Mystery Scavenger Hunt", a multigenerational outdoor game developed with Physical Web technologies and designed to foster intergenerational interaction. Our study aims to explore how tangible interactions with physical objects, guided by digital clues accessed via QR codes and NFC technology, can improve the user experience in intergenerational contexts without the need to download companion apps.

1.1 Background and Related Literature

The convergence of the digital and physical worlds has ushered in a new era of human interaction, transforming how we engage with our environment. This paradigm shift, driven by the growing ubiquity of internet-connected devices and the rapid increase in smart technologies, has given rise to innovative approaches to bridging the gap between the physical and virtual worlds. Many modern versions of outdoor games have employed IoT technologies using NFCs and QR codes [4, 16], Augmented Reality [5], and Proximity-Based AI games [7]. However, many games require dedicated mobile phone applications that users must install to participate. For example, Kanjo et al. and Gama et al. focused on a specific niche in their designs, which require users to download purpose-built companion apps [10, 12]. Similarly, other games like "Stroll Around Yesterday", an intergenerational location-based Games [18, 19] Ingress, Geo- catching [20] followed the same trend.

Compared to other technologies, such as RFID, Bluetooth, Beacon or augmented reality, which have been used to develop outdoor games. The choice of QR codes and NFC technology demonstrates benefits in terms of deployment, simplicity, cost-effectiveness, and cross-device compatibility [14, 24]. The minimal infrastructure requirements and low entry barriers contribute to the scalability and accessibility of QR codes and NFC technologies, ensuring a broader reach among diverse participants. Although Google used Google Eddystone for their original support for Physical Web [21], it discontinued the project in 2019 due to challenges in deployment and adoption [22], while Apple continues to support the iBeacon protocol. Research has shown that the concept of the Physical Web interaction on demand with smart devices - remains a powerful idea that still significantly impacts how we interact with the physical environment [14]. In addition, in many cases, technologies like QR codes, NFC, and Bluetooth cited in the above research are only sometimes labelled as Physical Web technologies in literature. The key innovation behind the Physical Web is to enable quick and seamless interactions with physical objects and locations without users downloading an app [21]. It provides a unique design opportunity to create an interface that works for older and younger people because not all older people or children are digitally proficient [25]. Additionally, some older people or children might find it difficult to install apps because some application installation processes are not always intuitive.

The gamification of tangible interface technologies has the potential to bring out a hybrid of physical and web components, which has mutual advantages for different generations [13]. An intergenerational outdoor game changes the medium of communication and the traditional roles of young and older people, providing new ways and opportunities for connecting the two age groups [2].

Intergenerational outdoor games enable adults and children to engage in productive and meaningful activities and provide opportunities for different generations to learn from each other and build healthy, mutually beneficial relationships [1]. Unlike traditional outdoor games that may be age-specific, intergenerational outdoor games aim to create an inclusive environment that fosters social connections across generations. Intergenerational collaborative games combine fun and interaction, allowing younger and older people to make creative, playful and social use of their leisure time [8]. Understanding the dynamics of intergenerational outdoor activities, facilitated by physical artefacts and digital games, is beneficial to designing outdoor physical-digital games to stimulate intergenerational interactions and promote meaningful intergenerational relationships and learning. Research has shown that intergenerational plays are valuable for promoting social interaction and well-being across age groups [6]. The positive impact extends beyond the physical benefits, encompassing cognitive stimulation, emotional well-being, and a strengthened sense of community [2, 9]. As communities seek to create environments that support holistic well-being for individuals of all ages, incorporating Physical Web technologies for intergenerational outdoor digital games emerges as a promising and enriching approach.

2   Alien Mystery Scavenger Hunt

The Alien Mystery was inspired by the study of related work and literature supported by the location-based pervasive game design using physical web technologies like QR codes and NFC for outdoor family activities like scavenger hunts [4]. The game was deployed on a university campus as part of a campus event to engage the local community, with a storyline intended to garner the whole family's attention irrespective of age. The story concept was designed to engage the players in an immersive and interactive experience of the physical artefact without downloading an app first. The aim was to stimulate cooperation and teamwork between the (grand) parents and their children as they played the game.

2.1   Game Design

Technology: The technological elements of the game encompassed the media or devices that allowed the participants to play the game and the digital skills required. The Physical Web approach employed in the game development of Alien Mystery Hunt was purposefully tailored with the intention of ensuring seamless interactions and minimal experience of technology. Therefore, the focus was to use Physical Web-compatible technologies such as QR codes and NFC to launch each user interaction, which are familiar technologies, since millions of people use their mobile devices daily to interact with their physical environment using these technologies, for instance, scanning QR codes to access menus at the restaurants and using NFC to make payments. Using QR codes and NFC facilitated tap/scan and play with minimal other required digital skills, enables accessibility and improves user engagement with the game.

Story Plots: The success of every outdoor intergenerational game depends on a good storyline with an engaging plot twist [17]. If the scenarios in the game are too simplistic and tailored primarily for children, they may not be sufficiently compelling and exciting enough to attract the interest of adults. Similarly, if the scenarios in the game are too challenging, the younger participants may not be interested in participating. The plot of Alien Mystery was created to appeal to young and older participants. We developed a story about aliens invading a university campus and capturing a professor. As part of the gameplay, participants were tasked with finding the aliens and rescuing the professor. The participants solved puzzles at each location to find clues to lead them to the subsequent location.

Game Mechanics: Dynamic game mechanics were integrated into the Alien Mystery Hunt game to foster an intergenerational experience. Videos, audio, interactive web animation, and physical cues were designed to engage participants and promoted communication. The mechanics were designed to prompt participants of various ages to work together to solve puzzles and chase imagery and alien clues across the campus.

Aesthetics: The overarching aim of the alien hunt was to design a game experience that stimulated the participants visually and ensured that all participants could actively participate and enjoy the game. We started the game aesthetics with a visually engaging theme that resonated with the intrigue of an extra-terrestrial invasion adventure on a university campus. Alien-inspired costumes, colour, alien fonts, alien animations on the webpages, videos, and laser cuts QR codes were woven into the game visually, setting the stage for an engaging and visual "physical world" experience.

3   Different Physical Web Interactions at Each Location

Location 1: In this location, participants were encouraged to test their devices to see if they could scan the QR codes and tap the NFC. A quick introduction to QR code and NFC was given to participants who had no idea what these technologies were or how they worked (Fig. 1).

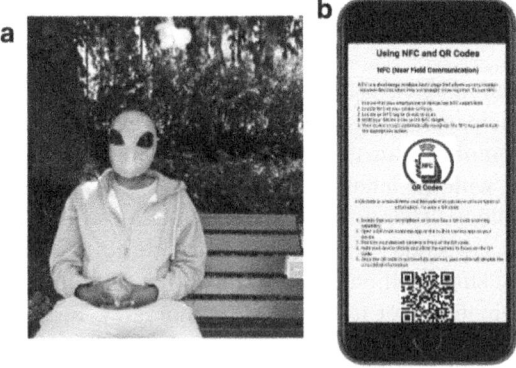

Fig. 1.   (a) Location 1 visual alien reference artefact near QR Code/NFC (b) Introduction webpage

Location 2: The participants scanned the QR code and interacted with the associated webpage. There, a video of a university professor asking for participants' help gave background as to why he needed help and a clue to the next location (Fig. 2).

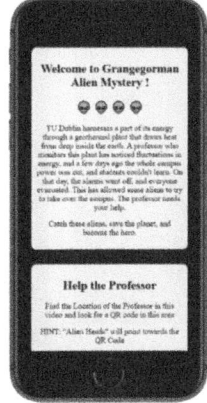

Fig. 2. The webpage screen of the game introduction.

Location 3: The participants scanned the QR code they found at the next location, which opened a webpage asking them to translate 'alien code' messages into English on their device. The user found the keys to translate the message using a substitute cypher in the location (Fig. 3).

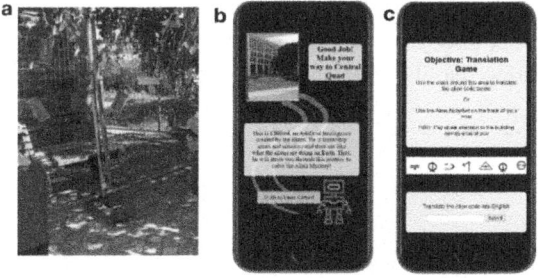

Fig. 3. Location three (a) alien clues (b) given user confirmation on successfully completed the game on location (c) webpage screen to translate alien code into English.

Location 4: This game is centred around a tree; the participants found a QR code around this tree, which opened instructions on the webpage about the ID game. Participants were presented with several ID cards and had to find the correct ID among several fakes. The fake and correct IDs were embedded with QR codes and NFCs, that led to many web pages. The user had to find the correct one to complete this challenge and progress to the next one. There were error messages for the fake scans, and participants were given clues to the next location when they scanned the right card (Fig. 4).

Location 5: The QR code at the location led the participant to a webpage that plays a sequence of notes. At this location, a custom-built' alien' music box' was stationed that produced musical sounds upon pressing labelled buttons on the box. The partici-pants were asked to reproduce the sequence of notes they heard on the web page on the

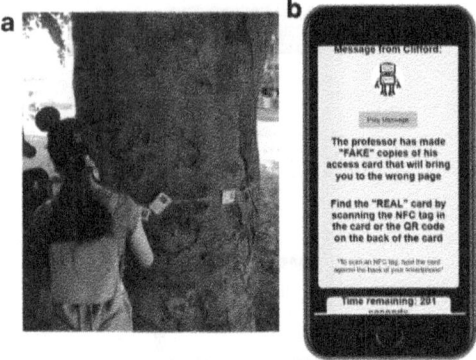

Fig. 4. (a) ID game with several ID for the users to pick from (b) webpage screen showing professor instruction on finding the real ID.

music box in the physical environment. Once the participants identified the sequence of the notes on the music box, they were required to enter the sequence of the button labels from the music box that corresponded with the music notes on the webpage. Designing this involved connecting a keypad to an Arduino and programming the system to produce different tones when specific keys are pressed. The wiring includes connecting the keypad to digital pins for input and a speaker to an output pin for generating tones. The authors developed an Arduino program to detect keypad presses and generate corresponding tones. This gave the participants the opportunity to not only interact with the web on their phone but also interact with electronics in the physical environment (Fig. 5).

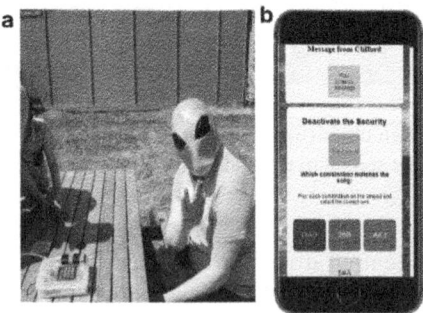

Fig. 5. Location 5 (a) alien artefact and music game box (b) webpage screen for the music combination.

Location 6: There was a QR code at this location, which opened a webpage where participants were prompted with an English question and were asked to input the correct answer using alien code. To answer the question, the webpage presented a selection keyboard containing alien code symbol as the keys input; there was a prompt to get a hint, if they got the answer wrong and the correct answer gave the participants clues to the next location (Fig. 6).

Fig. 6. Location 6 (a) QR Code interface (b) Webpage screen showing alien codes to solve the mystery

Location 7: In this location, participants played a button pushing game using both digital and physical buttons. Its location was hidden and could only be found when the participants completed the previous game. A QR code was placed on a table near the physical button device to direct the participant to the game web interface. The button device is Arduino-based, and its physical buttons are connected to specific digital pins on the Arduino board. The Arduino board monitors the state of these buttons. The participants were presented with multiple button sequences on the webpage to play on the physical button device. Participants had to test the various input sequences by pressing the physical buttons. Once they input the correct sequence, a green status light would turn on otherwise a red status light would turn on and reset the game (Fig. 7).

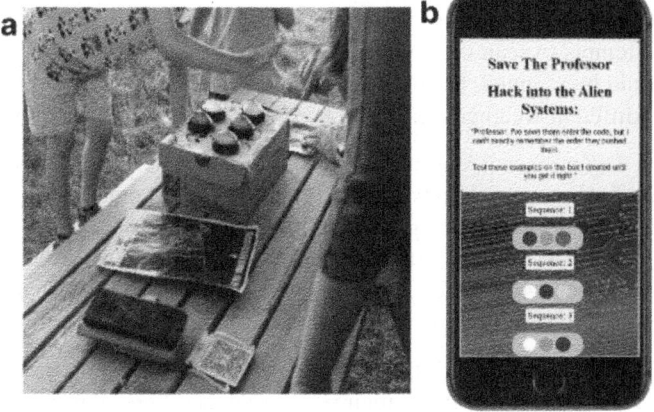

Fig. 7. Location 7 pushing button game, (a) pushing button game device (b) webpage playing interface

3.1 Method

Thirty families, including children, parents, and grandparents aged between 6 and 65, participated in the Alien Mystery Hunt events at the Technological University Dublin campus Grangegorman. These events created an avenue for families as they moved around looking for clues to uncover the complex 250 years of history of Grangorgeman's campus. Participants registered through the Eventbrite set-up for the event. Promotional materials were shared on social media platforms to create awareness. A university grounds survey was first conducted to identify accessible and functional locations around which to base the story and the technologies. Seven different Alien Hunt game scenarios were created to evaluate participants' engagement when playing at each location. We employed a mixed methods approach to evaluate the game, combining qualitative insights from detailed observation of the participant's interactions and engagement with the Physical Web technologies. Twenty-five participants answered the quantitative anonymous feedback, including closed-ended and open-ended questions at the end of the game.

4 Observations and Preliminary User Feedback

Participants were invited to provide feedback on their experiences. Our research reveals several significant findings contributing to intergenerational outdoor games and the merging of the physical and digital worlds in HCI literature. 68% of participants found the game entertaining and engaging, and 32% found it relatively entertaining and engaging. However, 92% of the participants found the game very satisfying, and 8% reasonably satisfying. Nevertheless, many participants reported that the tangible aspect of the game, like solving puzzles on the web to unlock physical objects, added layers of excitement and immersion that purely digital or physical standalone games could not replicate.

Weather: During the event, it became apparent that environmental factors like sunlight posed a challenge when using the QR code scanning process. The sun's glare disrupted participants' attempts to scan the codes. We had shaded these QR codes in some cases before they could be scanned, highlighting the need for adaptive technologies that can accommodate different weather conditions.

Device-specific Differences: Another interesting finding was the device-specific differences discovered when participants scanned the QR code. Some participants encountered challenges and needed to bring their devices closer to the QR codes for successful scanning. This indicates the importance of researching device-specific differences in QR code scanning behaviour when developing a Physical Web outdoors application to ensure optimal functionality across diverse smartphone device platforms.

User Experience: We discovered during our observation that not all participants could locate the QR code scanner feature on their mobile devices. Several participants reported difficulty locating the scanner feature, hinting at a potential usability issue, highlighting the importance of user-friendly design considerations and instructional prompts for the participant, as we did in location 1, to enhance the overall accessibility of the QR code and NFC for the whole family.

Interactive Game: Including interactive games within the Physical Web application gathered positive feedback from the participants. Participants expressed enthusiasm for the game that involved all members of their families and promoted a sense of inclusivity, fostering shared experiences and collaboration. Additionally, the scan-and-play function of the Physical Web resonated well with the participants, as it eliminated the need to download a separate app before they could play the game. This finding aligns with the desire for seamless and hassle-free interactions, indicating that families value simplicity and accessibility in intergenerational technology-enabled activities. The strategic puzzles embedded in the game heighten excitement and ensure a thrilling experience for all ages. Adopting the Physical Web through QR codes, NFC, and location-based physical-digital challenges added a modern twist to the game. This immersive gameplay improves cognitive engagement and encourages physical activity and meaningful interactions among all participants.

5 Discussion

Observation of the Alien Mystery event and participants' feedback provided valuable insight into the user experience of families engaging with a Physical Web application featuring QR codes and NFC for outdoor games. Families that participated in the game engaged in interactive, collaborative problem-solving activities to solve the puzzles in the game. This interaction fosters connections between the younger members of the family and the older members. Teamwork became evident as different generations engaged in collaborative problem-solving activities and combined their skills to decipher extraterrestrial clues scattered across the campus. The challenges identified in the study, such as sunlight interferences with scanning and device-specific scanning, highlight the importance of considering the environmental factors and device variance in intergenerational outdoor technology. The observed participants' problem in locating the QR code and NFC features on their phones suggests a digital skills gap in relation to this technology and a potential design improvement opportunity. Intuitive design features and clear instructions can reduce usability issues and ensure a more user-friendly experience for all generations engaging with the technology in outdoor settings. The positive feedback on the interactive game aligns with the broader theme of promoting intergenerational outdoor activities. Designing outdoor technology supports shared family experiences, promotes well-being, and improves familial bonds through collaborative outdoor activities. The challenges identified with scanning QR codes on some phones raised a crucial consideration for device compatibility. They highlight the importance of rigorous testing of applications across various device models to identify and address potential problems and ensure a user experience devoid of usability issues. These findings contribute valuable perspectives to the ongoing discourse on creating inclusive and enjoyable intergenerational outdoor technology solutions.

6   Conclusion and Future Work

The Alien Mystery intergenerational game represents a significant contribution to the field of HCI by showcasing the potential of visually appealing design and interactive Physical Web technologies in fostering inclusive and engaging physical-digital inter-generational experiences outdoors. As technology advances, the intersection of Human-Computer Interaction and digital-physical interactions in outdoor gaming provides a rich landscape for exploration, offering new possibilities for meaningful intergenera-tional interactions and impactful interventions in health and well-being. A Physical Web based approach has great potential to enhance the design of inclusive tangible interactive technologies outdoors and bring about a hybrid of digital and physical components that mutually benefit different generations. In our future work, we aim to find ways to harness the power of AI embedded with the Physical Web for different age groups and conduct a detailed user evaluation of the application with different user groups.

Acknowledgments. This work was conducted with the financial support of the Science Founda-tion Ireland Centre for Research Training in Digitally Enhanced Reality (d-real) under Grant No. 18/CRT/6224. For the purpose of Open Access, the author has applied a CC BY public copyright licence to any Author Accepted Manuscript version arising from this submission.

Disclosure of Interests.   The authors have no competing interests to declare that are relevant to the content of this article.

References

1. Couto, R., Leal, J., Costa, P.M., Galvão, T.: 2015. Exploring ticketing approaches using mobile technologies: QR codes, NFC and BLE. In: IEEE Conference on Intelligent Transportation Systems, Proceedings, ITSC 2015-October (10 2015), pp. 7–12 (2015). https://doi.org/10.1109/ITSC.2015.9
2. De la Hera, T., Loos, E., Simons, M., Blom, J.: Benefits and factors influencing the design of intergenerational digital games: a systematic literature review. Societies **7**(3), 18 (2017). https://doi.org/10.3390/SOC7030018
3. Fränti, P., Fazal, N.: Design principles for content creation in location-based games. ACM Trans. Multimedia Comput. Commun. Appl. **19**(5), 1–30 (2023). https://doi.org/10.1145/3583689
4. Gama, K., Wanderley, R., Maranhão, D., Garcia, V.C.: A web-based platform for scavenger hunt games using the Internet of Things. In: 2015. 12th Annual IEEE Consumer Commu-nications and Networking Conference, CCNC 2015, pp. 835–840 (2015). https://doi.org/10.1109/CCNC.2015.7158085
5. Gleue, T., Dähne, P.: Design and implementation of a mobile device for outdoor aug-mented reality in the ARCHEOGUIDE project. In: Proceedings VAST 2001 Virtual Real-ity, Archeology, and Cultural Heritage, pp. 161–168 (2001). https://doi.org/10.1145/584993.585018
6. Gualano, M.R., Voglino, G., Bert, F., Thomas, R., Camussi, E., Siliquini, R.: The impact of intergenerational programs on children and older adults: a review. Int. Psychogeriatr. **30**(4) , 451–468 (2018). https://doi.org/10.1017/S104161021700182X

7. Kanjo, E., Woodward, K.: Tag in the park: paving the way for proximity-based AI pervasive games. IEEE Commun. Mag. **61**(8), 161–167 (2023). https://doi.org/10.1109/MCOM.003. 230004
8. Drs Kaufman, D., Sauvé, L.: Playful Aging: Digital Games for Older Adults (2020)
9. Khalili-Mahani, N., et al.: For whom the games toll: a qualitative and intergenerational evaluation of what is serious in games for older adults. Comput. Games J. **9**(2), 221–244. (2020). https://doi.org/10.1007/S40869-020-00103-7
10. Kanjo, E., Woodward, K.: Tag in the park: paving the way for proximity-based AI pervasive games. IEEE Commun. Mag. (2023)
11. Schell, J.:. The Art of Game Design: A Book of Lenses (1 2008), pp. 1–489 (2008). https://doi.org/10.1201/9780080919171 ART-GAME-DESIGN-JESSE-SCHELL-JESSE-SCHELL
12. Gama, K., Wanderley, R., Maranhão, D., Garcia, V.C.: A web-based platform for scavenger hunt games using the Internet of Things. In: 2015 12th Annual IEEE (CCNC), pp. 835–840 (2015)
13. Tran, K.D., Blackler, A., Ploderer, B., Vickery, N.E.: Intergenerational active play: a scoping review. In: ACM International Conference Proceeding Series, pp. 88–96 (2022). https://doi.org/10.1145/3572921.3576217
14. Vazquez-Briseno, M., et al.: Using RFID/NFC and QR-Code in mobile phones to link the physical and the digital world. Interactive Multimedia (2012). https://doi.org/10.5772/37447
15. Vermesan, O., Friess, P.: Internet of Things: converging technologies for smart environments and integrated ecosystems. Internet of Things, 3–27 (2013). https://riverpublishers.com/book_details.php?book_id=176
16. Vieira, L., Coutinho, C., Graça, J.: The implementation of mobile location based-games and QR codes: the case of Mobigeo. In: International Technology, Education and Development Conference (2014)
17. Zhang, F.: Intergenerational play between young people and old family members: Patterns, benefits, and challenges. In: Lecture Notes in Computer Science (including subseries Lecture Notes in Artificial Intelligence and Lecture Notes in Bioinformatics) 10926 LNCS (2018), pp. 581–593 (2018). https://doi.org/10.1007/978-3-319-92034-4_44/TABLES/7
18. Kopeć, W., et al.: A location-based game for two generations: teaching mobile technology to the elderly with the support of young volunteers. In: Giokas, K., Bokor, L., Hopfgartner, F. (eds.) eHealth 360°. Lecture Notes of the Institute for Computer Sciences, Social Informatics and Telecommunications Engineering, vol. 181, pp. 84–91. Springer, Cham (2017). https://doi.org/10.1007/978-3-319-49655-9_12
19. Ulysses, S., et al.: The hybrid space of collaborative location-based mobile games and the city: a case study of ingress. Urban Planning **5**(4), 358–370 (2020). https://doi.org/10.17645/up.v5i4.3487
20. Fornasini, S., et al.: Using geocaching to promote active aging: qualitative study. J. Med. Internet Res. **22**(6), e15339 (2020)
21. Bhattacharya, D., Canul, M., Knight, S.: Case study: impact of the physical web and BLE beacons (2017)
22. Discontinuing support for Android nearby notifications (no date) Android Developers Blog. https://android-developers.googleblog.com/2018/10/discontinuing-support-for-android.html. Accessed 24 May 2024
23. Walk up and use anything (no date) The Physical Web. https://google.github.io/physical-web/. Accessed 24 May 2024
24. Sneps-Sneppe, M., Namiot, D.: On physical web models. In: 2016 International Siberian Conference on Control and Communications (SIBCON), Moscow, Russia, pp. 1–6 (2016). https://doi.org/10.1109/SIBCON.2016.7491675
25. Pirhonen, J., et al.: These devices have not been made for older people's needs–Older adults' perceptions of digital technologies in Finland and Ireland. Technol. Soc. **62**, 101287 (2020)

Augmented Motion Representation Learning Based on Virtual Reality Sports Game Review Data

Jing Cao[1], Gang Zhao[2], Siming Li[1], Jingting Sun[3], and Zhiqiang Wu[1](✉)

[1] College of Design and Innovation, Tongji University, Shanghai, China
wus@tongji.edu.cn
[2] Shanghai Research Institute for Intelligent Autonomous Systems, Tongji University, Shanghai, China
[3] Future Architecture and Urban Research Institute, Tongji Architectural Design (Group) Co., Ltd. Urban Planning, Tongji University, Shanghai, China

Abstract. Introduction: Virtual reality (VR) sports games have gained prominence as both a novel form of entertainment and an effective tool for rehabilitation and fitness. VR technology has revolutionized sports by offering immersive environments that enhance training, performance analysis, and user engagement. Despite numerous studies confirming the effectiveness of VR in improving physical abilities, understanding user experience (UX) remains crucial for optimizing these systems for usability, satisfaction, and effectiveness. This study aims to explore an augmented motion representation learning framework based on VR sports game review data to empower UX research in VR sports applications.

Methods: To analyze user experiences in VR sports games, we collected a comprehensive dataset of user reviews from the Steam platform, focusing on VR sports games. The dataset included 1,803,946 reviews from 1,512,851 unique users, filtered to 306,001 reviews for 354 VR sports games, dating from 2010/10/19 to 2024/05/14. We employed the DeepCoNN model, a deep cooperative neural network, to generate vector representations for users and games. This model consists of two parallel neural networks: one learns user behaviors from reviews, while the other learns item features from related reviews. By integrating these networks, the model overcomes the sparsity problem and incorporates review information to provide better recommendations. Additionally, we constructed a motion glossary based on the KIT Whole-Body Human Motion Database to enhance the extraction quality of user body-motion features.

Results: The DeepCoNN model was trained for 300 epochs, achieving a final mean squared error (MSE) of 1.975 on a test set comprising 10% of the dataset for training. The analysis revealed significant user behaviors and preferences clusters, demonstrating the model's effectiveness in capturing complex interactions. For instance, in the game "Crazy Kung Fu," the model successfully extracted body-motion features, identifying personalized patterns of user interactions. Augmented semantic networks provided a detailed understanding of user behaviors and preferences, enabling the identification of motion clusters such as inspect-nod-pick-shake and diagonal-hold-rotate-swim.

Conclusion: Our findings validate the applicability of the DeepCoNN model for VR game review data, offering a robust framework for understanding and

J. Y. C. Chen et al. (Eds.): HCII 2024, LNCS 15377, pp. 296–310, 2025.
https://doi.org/10.1007/978-3-031-76812-5_20

improving UX in VR sports applications. By leveraging big data from user reviews, we can comprehensively understand user experiences, complementing traditional laboratory-based methods. The augmented motion representation learning approach facilitates personalized recommendations and motion feature extraction, proving particularly valuable when review data is limited. Future research will focus on training conversational embodied agents using deep learning models and body-motion description datasets to enhance personalized virtual sports coaching services, thereby improving users' VR gaming experiences.

Keywords: Virtual reality · Augmented learning · Embodied Interaction · Game Review · Motion Representation

1 Introduction

The COVID-19 pandemic has brought changes to lifestyles globally, including a significant increase in demand for indoor activities [1]. Virtual reality (VR) sports games have emerged as popular forms of entertainment [2] and effective tools for rehabilitation and fitness [1]. VR has revolutionized sports and physical activities by providing immersive environments that enhance training, performance analysis, and user engagement. Numerous empirical studies have validated the effectiveness of VR games in improving users' physical abilities. Consequently, understanding user experience (UX) in VR sports applications is crucial for optimizing these systems for usability, satisfaction, and effectiveness. Various research methods have been employed to evaluate user-embodied experiences.

1.1 Questionnaires and Interviews

Dong et al. (2022) analyzed head movement data and SSQ scores to understand VR sickness, emphasizing the need to monitor physical responses [2]. Du et al. (2023) identified novelty and vividness as key factors in viewer responses to AR sports videos [3]. Alvarez et al. (2024) point out that user feedback through questionnaires and interviews remains a crucial method for assessing the usability and acceptance of VR systems [4].

1.2 Integration of Physiological Sensors and AI

Integrating physiological sensors and AI technologies enhances the effectiveness and personalization of VR sports applications. Wang et al. (2024) used machine learning algorithms like support vector machines (SVM) and particle swarm optimization (PSO) to create an interactive VR environment for physical education, significantly improving student performance and engagement [5]. Téllez et al. (2023) developed a VR videogame for stress management in athletes, demonstrating significant stress reduction through optical heart rate sensor monitoring in a week-long study with ten football players [6]. Van Biemen et al. (2023) studied football referees' visual behavior using motion capture and eye tracking in on-field, VR, and video conditions, showing that VR effectively replicates on-field visual-motor behavior [7]. Goutsu and Inamura (2023) applied a Gaussian process dynamical model (GPDM) to predict user success rates in a VR Kendama game, allowing for instant difficulty adjustment based on user skill levels [8]. Lo et al. (2023) examined technical factors in AR sports spectating, finding that latency and registration accuracy had the highest disruptive impacts on user experience [9]. Krupitzer et al. (2022) developed an immersive VR system to train executive functions of soccer players, using machine learning to monitor performance and adapt training sessions [10]. Mun et al. (2022) enhanced VR sports' realism by combining multimodal vibration and impact data [11], and Dong et al. (2022) also highlighted the importance of physical well-being in VR UX research by studying head movement and VR sickness [2]. Tsai et al. (2022) designed ungrounded directional force feedback for virtual racket sports, showing that perceptual designs significantly improve realism and user preference [12]. Zhang et al. (2022) developed a virtual golf putting simulator, analyzing the relationship between motion performance and user experience, and optimizing system design for improved rendering efficiency [13].

1.3   Challenges and the Dawn of the Big Data Era

The majority of investigations primarily rely on interviews, and laboratories rely on behavioral experiments, and most of them remain limited in data volume. Besides, Jean Lave's work "Cognition in Practice" explains that conducting user research in a laboratory is no more instructive than ordinary people describing their daily lives [14]. People usually flexibly use available resources or structures to cope with a problem or complete a task in a given situation, which emphasizes the difference between cognition in the wild and classical cognitive theories, in which people do not always rely on pre-planned or involved approaches to solving problems [14]. Lucy Suchman emphasized that developers should not develop human-computer interaction interfaces using so-called scientific behavioral models but should draw experiences from people's daily behaviors and reactions [15].

In contrast to the aforementioned studies, Deng et al. (2023) and Dong et al. (2024) show the advantages of involving big data of user reviews to advance research on the user experience with avatars in VR. Deng et al. used Structural Topic Model (STM) based text mining of VRChat's Steam reviews to explore factors impacting user experience, categorizing topics into clusters such as avatars, complaints, hardware, and recommendations [16]. Dong et al. conducted a comprehensive analysis of 6,206 avatar-related user reviews from social VR applications on the Steam platform. By studying examined avatar customization, diversity, and theft, Dong et al. suggest that developers should support extensive avatar customization and implement mechanisms to prevent avatar theft [17].

While big data analysis offers valuable insights, it also presents challenges. The extensive information embedded in user reviews is not fully leveraged initially. For example, the selection process of typical cases, such as research on VRChat, relied on the number of reviews and utilized Collaborative Filtering (CF) techniques. These techniques operate on the fundamental premise that individuals with similar past preferences will likely make similar choices in the future [18].

1.4   Game Reviews as a Form of Embodied Interactive Evidence

Each user review is a kind of self-report on embodiment in the virtual wild that reflects the authors' understanding of actual embodied perceptions and reactions, which are shaped by a multifaceted embodied cognition process. Glenberg & Kaschak's work, 'Perception of Motion Affects Language Processing,' elucidates the significance of motor cognition in the process of constructing action-sentence descriptions [19]. This process involves an intricate integration of motor activity [20], perceptual information [21], and emotional systems [22]. Consequently, descriptions related to motion offer a more holistic understanding of the development and interplay between motor and cognitive systems within embodied interaction. By detecting a broad range of body-motion descriptions gleaned from user reviews, we may discern patterns and trends and identify areas where Action Compatibility Effects [19] are more pronounced.

Through this analysis, we aim to provide researchers and developers with methods for detecting and augmenting virtual embodied motion-representation, thereby creating more user-friendly embodied interactions in virtual sports environments.

Our research contributes in the following three ways:

1. validated a deep learning and recommender system combined approach for both user and game representation learning based on VR game review data;
2. proposed a motion glossary to construct body-motion descriptions of users and games based on semantic network analysis of review data;
3. established an augmented motion-representation learning framework for users and games with limited review data based on (1) and (2).

2   Data

2.1   Reviews Data

Data on user reviews were collected from the Steam platform, filtering out 779 games that matched both "sports" and "VR" keywords, totaling 1,803,946 reviews from 1,512,851 unique users and 779 apps, dating from 2010/10/19 to 2024/05/14. After verifying VR modes with "VR Support" or "VR Only," 354 VR sports games were identified, yielding 306,001 reviews. Each review included details such as the user's SteamID, language, review text, playtime when the review was written, recommendation status, helpfulness score, and the app's ID. For our research, only English reviews with a helpfulness score of 0.65 or higher were selected, resulting in a final dataset of 12,345 reviews from 482 users across 253 apps. Additionally, a rating score was added to each review: 5 for recommended and 1 for not recommended.

2.2   Motion Data

Embodied cognition and embodied interaction refer to the concept of using the human body as a medium for interaction, where information is transmitted and communicated through actions, postures, expressions, and other physical movements [23]. In a narrow sense, embodied interaction specifically focuses on this bodily engagement as the primary means of interaction. This type of interaction is commonly utilized in virtual reality, augmented reality, games, interactive devices, and other fields to enhance user immersion and engagement. However, a review might cover various aspects of a VR game, such as gameplay, tasks, cost, visuals, sounds, avatars, devices, etc. [17]. Thus, embodied movement related vocabulary may be submerged in a large number of body-irrelevant vocabulary.

To ensure a higher extraction quality of the user body-motion feature, a specific motion glossary was constructed based on the KIT Whole-Body Human Motion Database [24]. The keywords of motion information, including locomotion, manipulation, grasps, gesticulation, sport, direction, body parts, and poses, a total of 146 words were selected as the nodes of co-occurring word network to discover the user perception structure and represent the structure of body movement descriptions in Steam user reviews in this paper [25].

3   Method

3.1   Deep Cooperative Neural Networks

The core idea of the Deep Cooperative Neural Network, first proposed by Zheng et al. (2017), is to train two parallel neural networks that are concatenated through one layer to improve the quality of recommendations [26]. This is in line with our research goal of this paper, which is to study the relationship between users and Apps by vectorizing them through review data. While one network focuses on learning user behaviors by reading specific user-written reviews, another one learns item features by reading reviews that are related. Latent factors are learned for user and item interactions in a way similar to factorization machine approaches, which are made possible by a shared layer connecting these two networks at the top. Experimental findings show that on a range of datasets, DeepCoNN performs noticeably better than baseline recommender systems. Compared to traditional Collaborative Filtering (CF) techniques [18], DeepCoNN can overcome the sparsity problem, as well as bring in review information to achieve better recommendations [26].

Figure 1 shows how the user or App-related reviews are merged into one single document and transferred into a word vector matrix through a word embedding dictionary. After passing through CNN layers, vector representations are achieved and connected, and then the Factorization Machine is adopted as the estimator of the corresponding rating to train the whole network. The final optimization function can be written as:

$$J = \widehat{w}_0 + \widehat{w}^T \hat{z} + \hat{z}^T V \hat{z} \tag{1}$$

where $\widehat{w}_0$ is bias term, $\widehat{w}^T$ is the weight vector, $\hat{z}$ is the concatenated input vector, V is a matrix that captures the interactions between the components of $\hat{z}$.

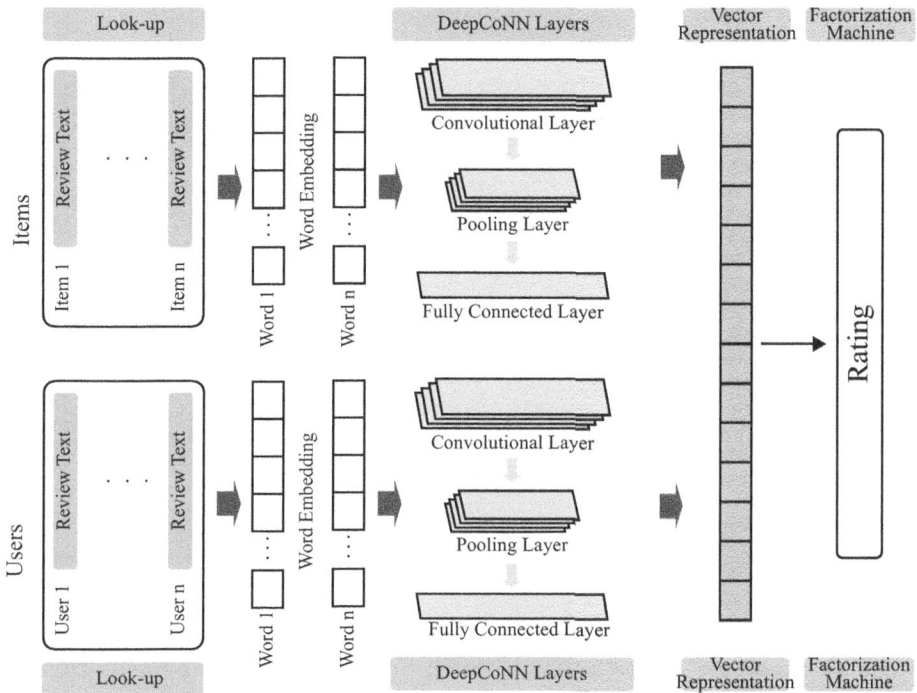

Fig. 1. Augmented process of semantic networking based on collective review data of 1 user

3.2 Semantic Network

Given a user review, the recommender system built by DeepCoNN would be able to identify all the relative user samples from the review dataset, and then a co-occurring word network can be constructed from the augmented review data of the user as Fig. 2, which is denoted as $G = (V, E)$ where V is the node of motion data, E is the edge between nodes if two words appear simultaneous in one review. The same logic is also applicable to Apps as Fig. 3, as the DeepCoNN can also recommend users when given App reviews. With this graph representation of users or Apps, a number of downstream tasks are available, such as user feature extraction, App feature extraction, or causal learning of user and App interactions, based on graph-level learning techniques.

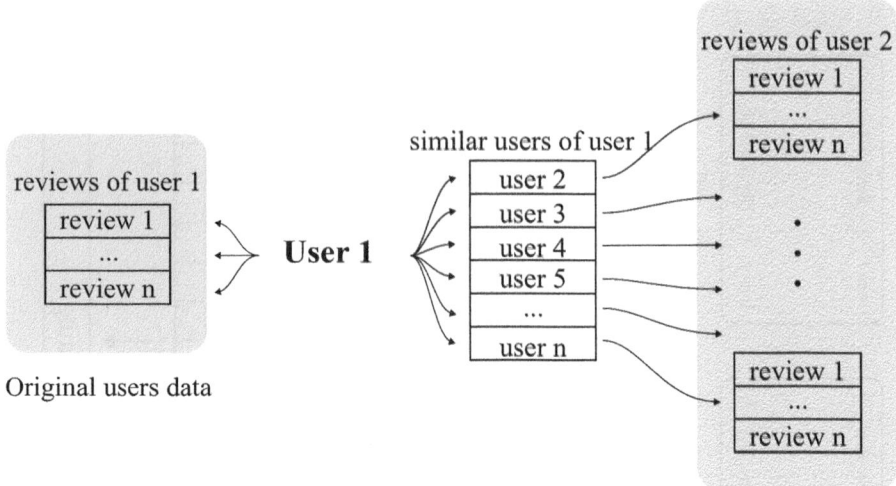

Fig. 2. Augmented representation of semantic network based on collective review data of 1 user

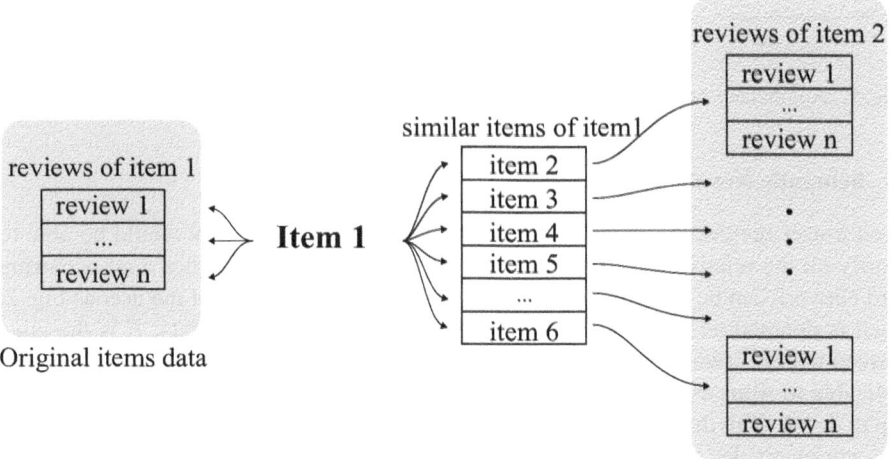

Fig. 3. Augmented representation of semantic network based on collective review data of 1 item

4   Result

4.1   Establishing an Augmented Motion-Representation Learning Framework for Users or Games with Limited Review Data

The DeepCoNN model was trained for 300 epochs, and the final MSE is 1.975 tested on 10% randomly sampled reviews of training data. The average review number of a typical user is 1.20. Thus, the semantic network achieved is limited, and a sample user with dozens of reviews can get a network like in Fig. 4. After feeding the user reviews into the DeepCoNN model, a list of recommended Apps is identified, and based on all the related reviews, an augmented version network appears, like Fig. 5. Comparing these two networks, the augmented network provides more information about motion nodes, as well as the clusters detected. Through community detection on the augmented network, motion clusters, like inspect-nod-pick-shake cluster, diagonal-hold-rotate-swim cluster, balance-grasp-wave cluster, etc., are identified, which greatly helps to understand the motion perception structure of specific users and Apps that lack review data. Ed Hutchins advocates for cognitive research that considers the distributive qualities of cognitive phenomena across individuals, tools, and internal and external representations [23]. The augmented semantic network approach offers a more collective comprehension and co-creation view of how embodied cognition develops and operates.

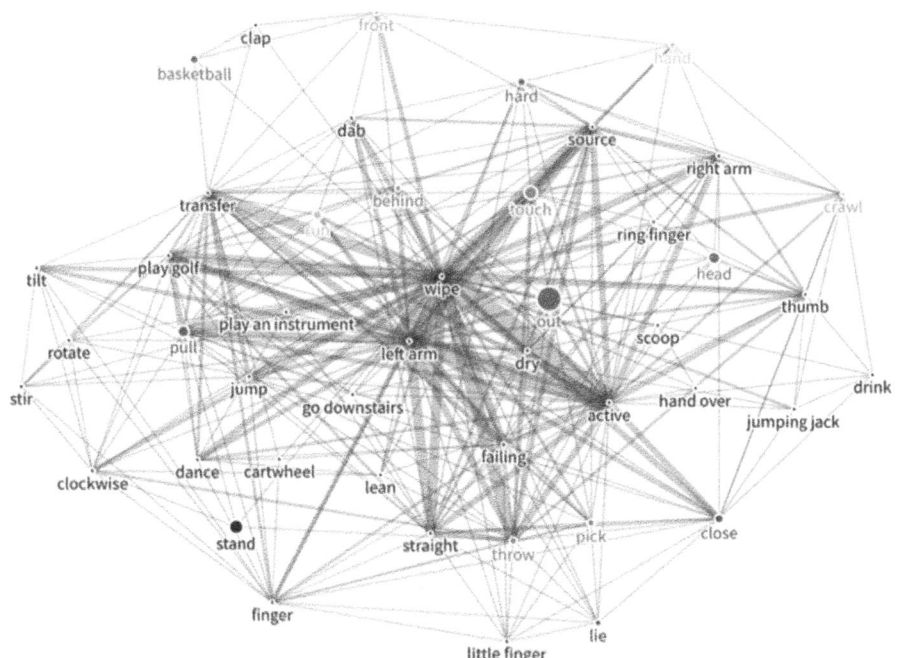

Fig. 4. User sample semantic network

4.2 Validating a Deep Learning and Recommender System Combined Approach for User and Game Representation Learning Based on VR Game Review Data

Based on the vector representations of users and games, we can calculate similarity matrices of users and games and then implement a spectral clustering method to find clusters of users and games, as well as the centers of these clusters based on the mean

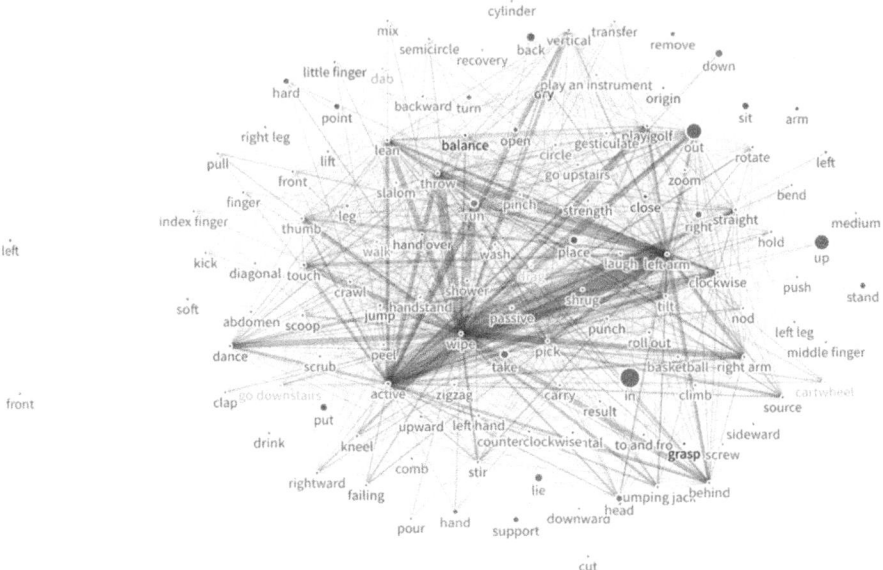

Fig. 5. User sample augmented semantic network

values of users or games vectors in these clusters. There are mainly two user clusters, with 362 and 101 users separately; games are also divided into two clusters, with 158 and 71 games separately.

By simulating a selection process of typical cases, we can see in Table 1, the homogeneity of the ranking lists based on a single index and the diversity of the list by cluster centers of games. Worthy of note top 10 games recommended by artificial intelligence algorithms are all fully immersive virtual reality games that require wearing a head-mounted display. While 9 of 10 games recommended by most reviews, are VR-supported games. That means users might not play these games in an immersive mode. There may be a large number of game reviews that only reflect the 2D interactive behavior of players in front of a desktop computer, while their interactive perception and operational postures will be completely different from those of fully immersive 3D interactive players. In total, there are 354 games, of which 286 are fully immersive games with VR mode, and 68 games can be played in either semi-immersive or fully immersive mode. However, the total number of reviews for the latter game accounts for 72% of the total reviews for the 354 games. To ensure the validity of review data in line with research goals on embodied interactivity, researchers must further identify the context in which users are playing.

4.3 Proposing a Motion Glossary to Construct Body-Motion Descriptions of Users or Games Based on Semantic Network Analysis of Review Data

The DeepCoNN model consists of two parallel neural networks: one focuses on learning user behaviors from user-written reviews, while the other learns game features from

Table 1. Simulating a selection process of typical cases

Ranked by Number of Reviews		Ranked by Center Similarity Matrices 1 Cluster	
App Name	Sport Type	App Name	Sport Type
Assetto Corsa	*Driving*	Crazy Kung Fu	*Kung Fu*
CarX Drift Racing Online	*Driving*	Let's Bowl VR - Bowling Game	*Bowling*
Beat Saber	*Dancing*	Little Witch Academia: VR Broom Racing	*Hurtling*
Rec Room	*Social Sporting*	VRSailing by BeTomorrow	*Sailing*
DiRT Rally 2.0	*Driving*	Mutant Boxing League VR	*Boxing*
Assetto Corsa Competizione	*Driving*	Stunt Kite Masters VR	*Glidering*
Golf It!	*Golfing*	Golf Pool VR	*Golfing*
RaceRoom Racing Experience	*Driving*	Legendary Hunter VR	*Hunting*
F1 23	*Driving*	Tahko Alpine Ski	*Skiing*
Automobilista 2	Driving	Down Fast VR	Driving

related reviews. Body-Motion description tags enable structured queries, allowing us to efficiently search for specific body-motion types, ensuring that specific motion data can be accessed quickly and intuitively Table 2. Shows Top 10 key words in 72 reviews of App ID:1340300, named Crazy Kung Fu.

The ID of the App nearest to the center of the first cluster is 1340300, named Crazy Kung Fu, which has 72 reviews and an average playtime of 191 min before giving a review. Figure 7. Shows 2 clusters of the body-motion feature clearly extracted. The model successfully extracted body-motion features, Figs. 6 and 7 illustrate the differences between initial semantic networks and those augmented with motion-representation features.

The ID of the user nearest to the center of the first cluster is 76561198049000736, who has only 2 reviews and an average playtime of 494 min before giving a review. Figure 8. Shows 3 clusters of personal interest. Figure 9. Shows a very personalized pattern of the body-motion feature with turning direction. Even with very limited two review of user, but the augmented networks in Fig. 9. Provide a more detailed understanding of body-motion behaviors and preferences from the perspective of collective users in the same cluster, which could highly enrich our imagination of their body-motion diversity. The DeepCoNN model networks are connected through a shared layer that captures interactions between users and items. This setup allows the model to overcome the sparsity problem commonly faced by traditional collaborative filtering techniques and to incorporate review information for better recommendations.

Table 2. Top 10 key words in 72 reviews of App ID:1340300, named Crazy Kung Fu

Word	Word Frequency	Reviews Mentioned	Example
game	82	44	Overall, this is a good game, but it requires a lot of movement
training	29	17	I use it for a daily work out and reflex training
fun	27	21	We need more healthy, useful & fun learning games like this one!
vr	23	18	Probably the most physically engaging VR game I've played since Beat Saber
block	17	14	Why would I block Punches that I already dodged?
feel	17	12	I wanna swing these meat hands and feel the impact
workout	16	15	It's a nice workout, bit of cardio and reflexes
dummy	16	10	Please add a wing chun dummy mode that doesn't move or have blades
level	16	14	As someone that is looking to achieve the level of kung fu master in the next few years, this game is fun
martial	14	10	I feel like a martial arts master

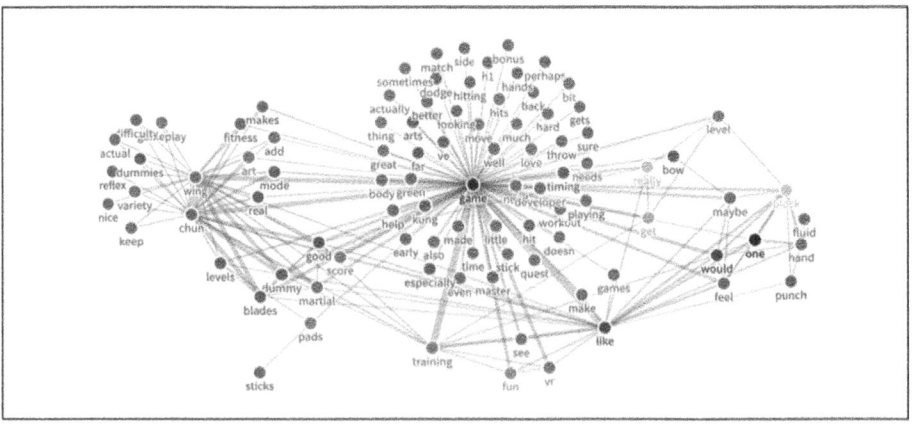

Fig. 6. Kungfu App Initial semantic network without extracting body-motion feature

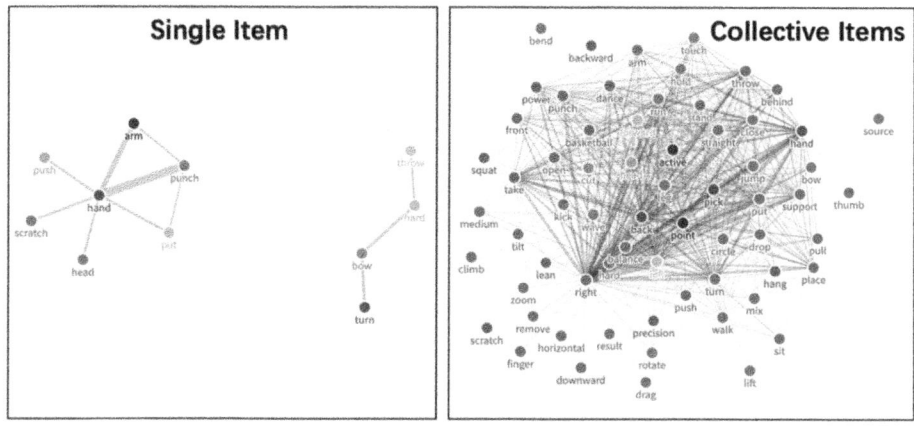

Fig. 7. Augmented motion-representation semantic network of Kungfu

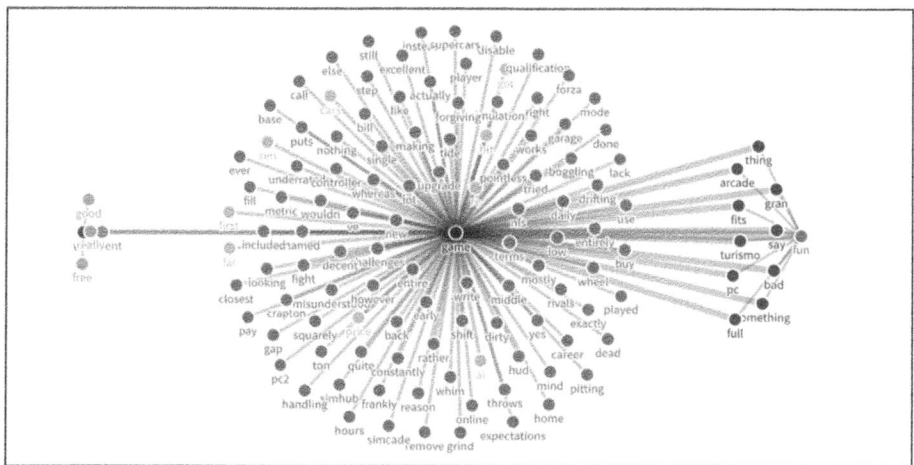

Fig. 8. Initial semantic network of 76561198049000736 without extracting body-motion feature

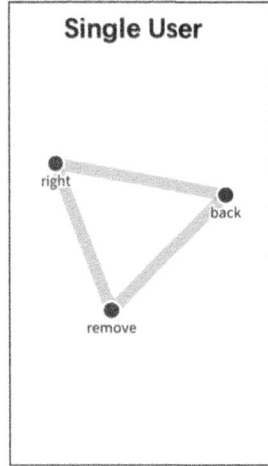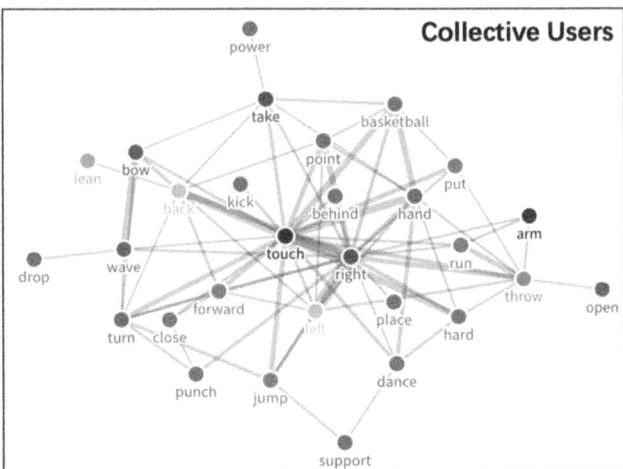

Fig. 9. Augmented motion-representation semantic network of 76561198049000736 (User ID)

5 Conclusion

The emerging trend of leveraging big data from user comments offers a larger-scale, more comprehensive understanding of user experiences, complementing traditional laboratory-based methods.

Our results verified the applicability of the DeepCoNN model with VR game review data from the Steam Platform. The unique deep cooperative learning framework combined with the recommender system and deep learning succeeded in generating vector representations for users and games. This approach enables the extraction of meaningful patterns from user interactions and experiences, facilitating various downstream tasks such as personalized recommendations and motion feature extraction. Based on the similarities between users or games, the augmented sample dataset for a particular user or game would be available, and then the body-motion description semantic network using the collected glossary can also be established. This augmented user and game feature learning approach would be extremely helpful when the review data is limited for a user or game. These networks are connected through a shared layer that captures interactions between users and items. This setup allows the model to overcome the sparsity problem commonly faced by traditional collaborative filtering techniques and to incorporate review information for better recommendations.

In the ongoing study, we plan to train conversational embodied agents using deep learning models and body-motion review datasets to generate personalized virtual sports coaching services, thereby enhancing users' virtual sports gaming experiences.

Acknowledgments. The study was financially supported by the China Ministry of Science and Technology (STI 2030-Major Projects-2022ZD0213100), Shanghai Brain Health Foundation Grant (SHBHF 2016001) and Tongji University Teaching Reform Project "Design and Usability Evaluation Based on Virtual Simulation".

References

1. Yang, H., Li, J., Liu, J., Bian, Y., Liu, J.: Development of an indoor exergame based on moving-target hitting task for COVID-19 epidemic: a comparison between AR and VR mode. IEEE Trans. Games **14**(3), 511–521 (2022)
2. Dong, J., Ota, K., Dong, M.: Why VR games sickness? an empirical study of capturing and analyzing VR games head movement dataset. IEEE Multimedia **29**(2), 74–82 (2022)
3. Du, Z., Wang, T., Wang, F., Wang, S.: Augmented reality experience: an examination of viewer responses to sports videos. J. Consum. Behav. **23**(3), 1307–1328 (2024)
4. Álvarez, I.M., Manero, B., Romero-Hernández, A., Cárdenas, M., Masó, I.: Virtual reality platform for teacher training on classroom climate management: evaluating user acceptance. Virtual Reality **28**(2), 78 (2024)
5. Wang, J., Yang, Y., Liu, H., Jiang, L.: Enhancing the college and university physical education teaching and learning experience using virtual reality and particle swarm optimization. Soft. Comput. **28**(2), 1277–1294 (2024)
6. Téllez, A.M., Castro, L.A., Tentori, M.: Developing and evaluating a virtual reality videogame using biofeedback for stress management in sports. Interact. Comput. **35**(2), 407–420 (2023)
7. Van Biemen, T., Müller, D., Mann, D.L.: Virtual reality as a representative training environment for football referees. Hum. Mov. Sci. **89**, 103091 (2023)
8. Goutsu, Y., Inamura, T.: Instant difficulty adjustment: predicting success rate of VR kendama when changing the difficulty level. In: Augmented Humans Conference, Glasgow, pp. 346–348. ACM, United Kingdom (2023)
9. Lo, W.H., Regenbrecht, H., Zollmann, S.: Sports visualization in the wild: the impact of technical factors on user experience in augmented reality sports spectating. IEEE Comput. Graph. Appl. **43**(6), 64–74 (2023)
10. Krupitzer, C., et al.: CortexVR: Immersive analysis and training of cognitive executive functions of soccer players using virtual reality and machine learning. Front. Psychol. **13** (2022)
11. Mun, M., Oh, S., Park, C., Seungmoon, C.: Multimodal haptic rendering for interactive VR sports applications. J. KIISE **49**(2), 97–105 (2022)
12. Tsai, C.-Y., et al.: AirRacket: perceptual design of ungrounded, directional force feedback to improve virtual racket sports experiences. In: CHI Conference on Human Factors in Computing Systems, pp. 1–15. ACM, New Orleans LA USA (2022)
13. Zhang, Q., Li, Z., Liu, M.: Research on the relationship between motion performance and user experience of golf virtual simulation putting simulator. Math. Probl. Eng. **2022**, 1–10 (2022)
14. Lave, J.: Cognition in Practice: Mind, Mathematics and Culture in Everyday Life. Cambridge University Press (1988)
15. Clark, A., Chalmers, D.: The extended mind. Analysis **58**(1), 7–19 (1998)
16. Deng, D., Bujic, M., Hamari, J.: Understanding multi-platform social VR consumer opinions: a case study in VRChat using topics modeling of reviews. In: Tu, Y., Chi, M. (eds.) E-Business. Digital Empowerment for an Intelligent Future. WHICEB 2023. Lecture Notes in Business Information Processing, vol. 481, pp. 35–46. Springer, Cham (2023). https://doi.org/10.1007/978-3-031-32302-7_4
17. Dong, J., Ota, K., Dong, M.: Exploring avatar experiences in social VR: a comprehensive analysis of user reviews. IEEE Consumer Electron. Mag. **13**(3), 53–60 (2024)
18. Koren, Y., Bell, R., Volinsky, C.: Matrix factorization techniques for recommender systems. Computer **42**(8), 30–37 (2009)
19. Glenberg, A.M., Kaschak, M.P.: Grounding language in action. Psychon. Bull. Rev. **9**, 558–565 (2002)

20. Bub, D.N., Masson, M.E.J.: On the nature of hand-action representations evoked during written sentence comprehension. Cognition **116**(3), 394–408 (2010)
21. Kaschak, M.P., et al.: Perception of motion affects language processing. Cognition **94**(3), B79–B89 (2005)
22. Havas, D.A., Glenberg, A.M., Gutowski, K.A., Lucarelli, M.J., Davidson, R.J.: Cosmetic use of botulinum toxin-a affects processing of emotional language. Psychol. Sci. **21**(7), 895–900 (2010)
23. Clark, A.: An embodied cognitive science? Trends Cogn. Sci. **3**(9), 345–351 (1999)
24. The KIT whole-body human motion database Homepage. https://motion-database.humano ids.kit.edu/list/motions/. Accessed 31 May 2024
25. Mandery, C., Terlemez, O., Do, M., Vahrenkamp, N., Asfour, T.: The KIT whole-body human motion database. In: 2015 International Conference on Advanced Robotics (ICAR), pp. 329–336. IEEE, Istanbul, Turkey (2015)
26. Zheng, L., Noroozi, V., Yu, P.S.: Joint deep modeling of users and items using reviews for recommendation. In: Proceedings of the Tenth ACM International Conference on Web Search and Data Mining, pp. 425–434. ACM, Cambridge United Kingdom (2017)

Exploring Virtual Chess Personalities: Analyzing Class-C Players vs. Nimzowitsch and Fine Virtual Grandmasters

Khaldoon Dhou[(✉)]

College of Business Administration, Texas A&M University-Central Texas,
Killeen, TX, USA
kdhou@tamuct.edu

Abstract. This study investigates the impact of chess personalities on game outcomes. To this end, the author utilizes two virtual chess grandmasters, Nimzowitsch and Fine, and three class-C players who vary in their chess personalities. Chess personality is defined as the style of a chess player during their games against other players in the community. The present study analyzed the Chessmaster agreement percentages on moves made by class-C players while competing against Nimzowitsch and Fine. Specifically, Cole and Ginger demonstrated superior performance compared to Kanna, which highlights the influence of player personality and grandmaster color on game outcomes. Additionally, consistent with previous research in this area, players performed better when competing against Fine than Nimzowitsch. The results were analyzed through the lens of cognitive load theory and social cognitive theory. These findings underscore the importance of understanding individual player characteristics and contextual factors in shaping dynamics and strategic decision-making in chess. Such insights can be valuable in the development of tailored training programs and in helping businesses formulate effective strategies.

Keywords: chess · virtual chess players · chess personality · Fine · Nimzowitsch · cognitive load theory · social cognitive theory

1 Introduction

Chess plays a pivotal role in exploring numerous facets of computer science, business, and psychology. Through the lens of chess, researchers have delved into complex decision-making problems and cognitive heuristics. Existing literature highlights notable advancements in computerized chess, notably the momentous achievement of a computer defeating Gary Kasparov, the reigning World Chess Champion, in 1997 [12]. Furthermore, the field of artificial intelligence has witnessed significant strides, particularly in the development of virtual humans

J. Y. C. Chen et al. (Eds.): HCII 2024, LNCS 15377, pp. 311–321, 2025.
https://doi.org/10.1007/978-3-031-76812-5_21

capable of emulating various chess players' personalities, including elite figures such as Judit Polgar, among others.

A chess player is distinguished by two fundamental attributes: rating and chess personality. Rating is a numerical value assigned to a player based on their performance against others within the research community. Numerous organizations, such as the World Chess Federation (FIDE) and the United States Chess Federation, administer ratings. These ratings categorize players into various tiers, including grandmaster, international master, class-A, and class-B, providing a standardized measure of skill. While rating serves as the predominant metric for assessing a player's proficiency, recent research suggests that chess personality significantly influences outcomes, even when ratings are identical [3,6–8,10,11]. Chess personality refers to a player's demeanor and approach when competing against others in the community [6]. For example, some players exhibit an aggressive style, while others adopt a more defensive strategy. Understanding the nuances of chess personality can offer valuable insights into player behavior and strategic decision-making on the board.

Although existing literature reveals numerous studies that explore chess players of various skills (e.g., [14,19]), utilizing virtual chess players in research yields numerous advantages. Firstly, they enable the examination of a diverse array of chess players, including historical figures, facilitating comprehensive comparative analyses across varying playing styles and historical periods. Secondly, virtual chess players offer a practical means to gather gameplay data from top-tier grandmasters under specific settings, a task often logistically challenging or unattainable with real-life counterparts. Thirdly, they facilitate studies comparing grandmasters from different epochs, elucidating the evolution of strategic approaches and playing techniques over time. Furthermore, virtual chess players afford researchers the flexibility to manipulate parameters, facilitating hypothesis testing in controlled experimental settings. Additionally, they serve as invaluable educational tools for chess learners, providing opportunities to compete against players of varying skill levels and playing styles, thereby enhancing proficiency in the game.

In the present study, the author explores the chess personalities exhibited by three class-C players as they engage in matches against two distinguished grandmasters: Nimzowitsch and Fine. Nimzowitsch is renowned for his adeptness at center control through varied means, favoring closed and cramped positions, while Fine adopts an aggressive, open style. The three class-C players manifest distinct chess personalities: one who exposes their king to potential attacks, another who strategically lays traps, and a third who adopts a balanced approach, prioritizing domination of the board's center. In this study, the author employs the Chessmaster's agreement percentage to analyze the performance of class-C players against the two grandmasters and to discern variations in their respective performances.

2   Related Work

The extensive search reveals that the exploration of chess personalities has been a subject of investigation since the early work of Karpman in 1937 [13], where he identified distinct traits of chess players. Industrial developments in the field of artificial intelligence (AI) have reignited interest in exploring chess personalities. This renewed interest has paved the way for more innovative studies, especially those that involve virtual chess players, to explore chess personalities and how they influence game outcomes. In other words, notable chess figures such as Kasparov and Waitzkin have been subjects of exploration [7,10,11] via the involvement of virtual chess players that simulate real styles of these players.

Early work in the field of chess psychology was conducted by de Groot, who focused his research on chess masters and beginners [5]. In his experiments, he presented players with meaningful chess positions for some time, and they asked them to reconstruct them from memory. He found that chess experts outperformed beginners in this task. Later, a similar experiment was conducted by Chase and Simon [4], who instructed players to look at meaningless chess positions and to reconstruct them and found that the performance of chess beginners and experts dropped. These early works laid the foundation for understanding the cognitive processes that underlined chess expertise and became the basis of more research in chess psychology.

The initial comprehensive exploration of virtual chess players delved into the personalities of two contrasting grandmasters: Anderssen and Leko [6]. Anderssen was characterized by his aggressive playing style, while Leko was known for his solid defensive approach. These grandmasters were pitted against class-B players with diverse strengths in opening and endgame strategies. The findings revealed that Anderssen exhibited fewer errors compared to Leko, and his opponents also demonstrated lower error rates. Additionally, games involving Anderssen tended to be longer, indicating greater resistance from his opponents. Later, Dhou [9] explored the personalities of the same virtual grandmasters in the games against three class-A players that vary in their involvements of knight and bishop chess pieces. The outcomes were generally consistent with the first study in [6], where class-A players did better while competing against Anderssen.

To further explore chess personalities, Dhou [7] investigated the personality of Kasparov via the involvement of a simulation that replicates the strategies of Gary Kasparov at a grandmaster's level. Kasparov's virtual player competed against three class-A players. Consistent with previous research, Kasparov's performance varied depending on the personalities of his opponents. Additionally, attack strategies were also investigated via the involvement of virtual chess players. In one study, Dhou [10] conducted an experiment that features the virtual grandmaster Josh Waitzkin and three additional class-A players. While Waitzkin epitomized a fearless attacker, other class-A players have distinct chess personalities. These personalities included prioritizing managing the center, an inclination towards capturing more pieces, and the tendency to offer opening traps. The results showed that among the three class-A players, the one that controlled the center exhibited the highest performance. Likewise, Waitzkin demonstrated excellent performance when pitted against this particular player compared to others.

Interestingly, chess outcomes can be explained through the lens of many theories that have deep roots in psychology. In this research, the author employs two theories: the social cognitive theory [2], and the cognitive load theory [15]. According to the social cognitive theory, human functioning can be explained via a model of triadic reciprocal causation, where behavior, cognitive and personal factors, and environmental events interact as mutual determinants. For more information on the social cognitive theory, the author refers readers to [1]. On the other hand, the cognitive load theory is an instructional theory that relies on human cognition. According to the theory, cognitive load pertains to the overall mental effort that is needed by the working memory at any given time. A major contributor to cognitive load is the quantity of elements that demand attention simultaneously. However, working memory is highly restricted, and under certain conditions, these limitations can hinder the learning process.

Although existing studies have provided valuable insights into the employment of virtual humans to explore the personalities of chess players, there is still a large gap in the literature regarding the exploration of chess personalities. The current study further contributes to the field, and it advances our understanding of new chess personalities.

3   Method

3.1   Participants

In this experiment, the author employed five virtual chess players from the Chessmaster (Grandmaster Edition), which is a highly reputable software in the chess community. The five chess players consist of two grandmasters and three class-B players, as follows:

- Nimzowitsch: a top-rank grandmaster whose style is focused on the strategic control of the center without necessarily filling it with pawns. Additionally, he performs well when his opponent's center is vulnerable.
- Fine: a top-rank grandmaster who favors an aggressive, open style that aims at controlling the game since its beginning. Fine has an extensive knowledge of opening strategies, but he remains dangerous at the end of the game.
- Cole: a class-C player who believes that it is essential to free up tight positions and unleash the power of his pieces. However, this often causes his king to be exposed to attacks.
- Ginger: a class-C player who enjoys setting up subtle traps when the game starts. If her opponent recognizes and takes advantage of these opportunities, they have a good chance of winning the game against her. On the other hand, if her opponent cannot recognize traps, Ginger adopts a determined approach and refuses to accept a draw.
- Kanna: a class-C player who likes to dominate the center of the board and prioritizes the mobility of her pieces

All these descriptions of the virtual players were offered by the Chessmaster (Grandmaster Edition) [18]. All of them represent real-life players.

3.2   Materials

In the current experimental design, we employ two independent variables:

- Chess personality of grandmasters: This variable is manipulated by selecting two distinct personalities, Nimzowitsch and Fine, which are to be associated with different sets of games. Half of the games feature Nimzowitsch's personality, while the rest are associated with Fine's personality.
- Chess personality of class-C players: This variable varied between the three personalities of Cole, Ginger, and Kanna. The participant's subsection provides the descriptions of the three personalities.

The current design has one dependent variable: the Chessmaster agreement percentage on the moves made by class-C players. The color of the grandmaster was used as a between-subjects factor. This experimental design results in a two-way repeated measures ANOVA that considers the interaction between grandmaster personality (Nimzowitsch vs. Fine) and class-C player personality (Cole, Ginger, and Kanna). It is essential to mention that while the virtual grandmasters in the experiment have identical USCF ratings, the ratings of the class-C players are very close to each other. Additionally, players within the same category (i.e., grandmasters and class-C players) exhibit different personalities. Each grandmaster participated in 39 games against each class-C player within the experiment.

4   Results

- All the effects were considered significant at $p < 0.05$. The main effect of the chess personality of grandmasters was significant, $F(1, 76) = 27.394$, $p < 0.001$. Post-hoc tests revealed that Chessmaster agreement percentage was significantly higher for class-C players when games were associated with Fine's personality ($M = 80.628$) compared to Nimzowitsch's personality ($M = 77.632$).
- The main effect of the chess personality of class-C players was also significant, $F(2, 152) = 6.66$, $p = 0.002$. Post-hoc comparisons indicated that the Chessmaster agreement percentage varied significantly across the personalities of Cole ($M = 80.013$), Ginger ($M = 79.929$), and Kanna ($M = 77.449$). Paired samples t-tests revealed that there is a significant difference between the mean Chessmaster agreement percentages for the moves made by Cole ($M = 80.01$, $SD = 8.099$) and Kanna ($M = 77.45$, $SD = 6.915$), $t(155) = 2.939$, $p = 0.004$. Additionally, there was a significant difference between the mean Chessmaster agreement percentages for the moves made by Ginger ($M = 79.39$, $SD = 6.915$) and Kanna, $t(155) = 3.268$, $p = 0.001$.

- There was a significant interaction effect between player personality and the color of the grandmaster, $F(2, 152) = 3.502$, $p = 0.033$. For the white color, paired samples t-tests between each pair of players revealed no significant differences. However, for the black color, paired samples t-tests showed significant differences. The mean Chessmaster agreement percentage for the moves made by Cole ($M = 81.73$, $SD = 7.284$) was significantly higher than that for the moves made by Kanna ($M = 77.08$, $SD = 6.736$), $t(77) = 3.783$, $p < 0.001$. Additionally, the mean Chessmaster agreement percentage for the moves made by Ginger ($M = 80.78$, $SD = 6.559$) was significantly higher than that for the moves made by Kanna ($M = 77.08$, $SD = 6.736$), $t(77) = 3.604$, $p = 0.001$.
- There was a significant interaction between the grandmaster and class-C player, $F(2, 152) = 5.068$, $p = 0.007$. This interaction suggests that the performance of the class-C players varied depending on which grandmaster they were competing against, and this variation was different for each player. In other words, the performances of the class-C players were not consistent, and each player's performance changed depending on the grandmaster's personality. Figure 1 shows the average Chessmaster agreement percentages for the moves made by the class-C players when competing against the two grandmasters, Nimzowitsch and Fine. To further explore this interaction, paired samples t-tests were conducted to compare the performances of each pair of class-C players for each grandmaster. To investigate this interaction further, paired samples t-tests were conducted to compare the performances of each pair of class-C players for each grandmaster. Interestingly, for the games against Nimzowitsch, there were no significant differences between any of the pairs. On the other hand, for the games against Fine, the mean Chessmaster agreement percentage for Cole's games ($M = 82.94$, $SD = 7.558$) was significantly higher than for Kanna's games ($M = 77.92$, $SD = 7.516$), $t(77) = 3.987$, $p < 0.001$. Similarly, the mean Chessmaster agreement percentage for Ginger's games ($M = 81.03$, $SD = 6.746$) was significantly higher than that for Kanna's games ($M = 77.92$, $SD = 7.516$), $t(77) = 2.746$, $p = 0.007$.

There was a significant interaction between the grandmaster, class-C player, and the color of the grandmaster, $F(2, 152) = 5.682$, $p = 0.004$ (See Fig. 2). To break down the interaction, paired samples t-tests were conducted to analyze the effect of the color of the grandmaster for each combination of grandmaster and class-C player.

For the white color:

- The Chessmaster agreement percentage was significantly higher for Ginger ($M = 79.03$, $SD = 5.504$) than Cole ($M = 73.9$, $SD = 7.993$) while competing against Nimzowitsch, $t(38) = 3.279$, $p = 0.002$.
- The Chessmaster agreement percentage was significantly higher for Cole ($M = 82.69$, $SD = 6.662$) than Kanna ($M = 78.95$, $SD = 7.067$) while competing against Fine, $t(38) = 2.086$, $p = 0.044$.

- The Chessmaster agreement percentage was significantly higher for Cole ($M = 82.69$, $SD = 6.662$) than Kanna ($M = 79.05$, $SD = 8.159$) when competing against Fine, $t(38) = 2.185$, $p = 0.035$.

For the black color:

- The Chessmaster agreement percentage for Cole ($M = 83.18$, $SD = 8.441$) was significantly higher than that for Kanna ($M = 76.79$, $SD = 6.728$) while competing against Fine, $t(38) = 3.398$, $p = 0.002$.
- The Chessmaster agreement percentage for Ginger ($M = 83.10$, $SD = 5.780$) was significantly higher than that for Kanna ($M = 76.79$, $SD = 6.728$) while competing against Fine, $t(38) = 4.498$, $p < 0.001$.

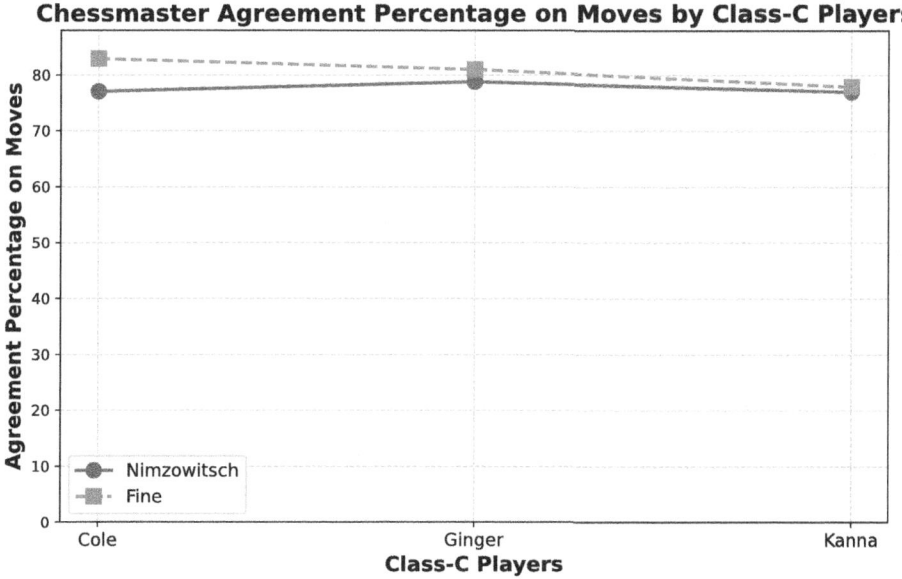

Fig. 1. The Chessmaster agreement percentage on moves by class-C players against Nimzowitsch and Fine

5 Discussion

The present study was designed to explore the chess personalities of three class-C players while competing against two top chess grandmasters: Nimzowitsch and Fine. All the players were virtual, and they simulated real players. The current investigation found that chess players can perform differently according to their chess personalities and the personality of the grandmaster they compete against.

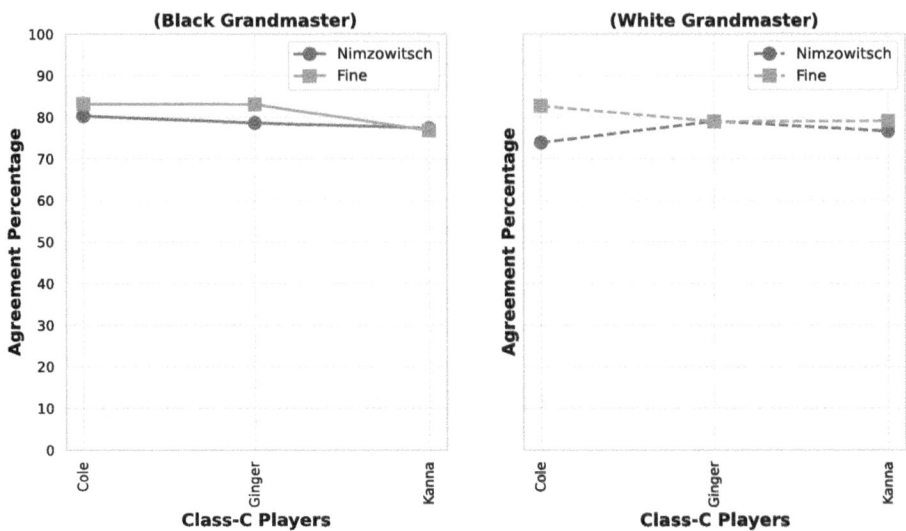

Fig. 2. The Chessmaster agreement percentages by player with grandmasters playing white and black

Interestingly, players did better while competing against Fine as opposed to Nimzowitsch (Fig. 1). One possible explanation is that Fine's aggressive personality might lead to more predictable patterns that are recognized by class-C players. On the other hand, the Nimzowitsch style might introduce more complexity, which would cause the class-C player to perform at a lower level. Interestingly, these findings are consistent with the previous findings in [6], where players did better with Anderssen, who adopts an aggressive style, as opposed to Leko, who is a defensive grandmaster. This finding is in alignment with Bandura's social cognitive theory [2], which suggests that people may struggle to model behaviors that they perceive as more complex or less predictable, leading to less performance in these situations. This can probably be applied to Nimzowitsch's chess personality, which follows a strategic approach to controlling the center, emphasizes long-term planning and spatial relationships on the board. This cognitive style can be particularly challenging for class-C players, who generally have less developed pattern recognition skills and may struggle to counter these sophisticated strategies compared to elite players. Conversely, Fine's aggressive style might have provided players with a clear expectation and more recognizable patterns to respond to.

Interestingly, the outcomes revealed that Cole and Ginger did significantly better than Kanna. This findings can probably be explained by the cognitive load theory that addresses the allocation of mental resources during learning and problem solving activities [15]. These activities impose a substantial 'extraneous cognitive load,' which hinders the main objectives of the task. This extraneous load arises from the organization and presentation of the task instead of the activities that are needed to complete the relevant goals. Some instructional approaches can impose a significant cognitive load before learning. This happens because the way information is presented might demand extensive initial reorganization and processing of various elements [17]. On the other hand, part of the working memory load comes from the inherent complexity of the material itself, which is referred to as the 'intrinsic cognitive load' [16]. Additionally, the 'germane cognitive load' pertains solely to the attributes of the learner and denotes the mental capacity allocated by the learner to manage the intrinsic cognitive load linked with the information. The germane cognitive load operates autonomously from the presented information. In the context of this paper, Cole's approach of opening the board will probably reduce extraneous load, which makes it easier for him to focus on the main strategic aspects. Similarly, Ginger's personality focuses on setting traps at an early stage of the game, which might reduce the extraneous cognitive load by narrowing the focus of her cognitive efforts to certain key actions. However, Kanna's personality requires meticulous control and frequent adjustments, which could add more cognitive load that can affect her overall performance.

The study unveiled a significant interaction between the class-C players' personalities and the color of their opponents. It implies that the performance of class-C players depended on both their own personalities and the color of the grandmaster they were facing. Notably, when confronted with a black grandmaster, Cole and Ginger exhibited notably superior performance compared to Kanna. This indicates that Cole and Ginger's chess personalities were more adept at facing black-colored grandmaster opponents. An additional explanation can be found through the lens of cognitive load theory, which suggests that playing against a black grandmaster may impose additional cognitive demands compared to competing against a white grandmaster. Cole and Ginger may possess chess personalities that are better equipped to handle these additional cognitive demands when facing a black grandmaster.

The outcomes also show that the players' performances were not consistent and varied according to the personality of the grandmaster they were playing against. Further analysis was conducted by comparing the performances of each pair of class-C players for each grandmaster using paired samples t-tests. When playing against Nimzowitsch, there were no significant differences between any of the pairs, which suggests a consistent performance regardless of the opponent's personality. On the other hand, when facing Fine, significant differences emerged. When facing Fine, Cole and Ginger did significantly better than Kanna, which highlights the importance of understanding the interplay between the chess personalities of class-C players and grandmasters in determining chess performance.

6   Conclusion

The findings of the current study shed light on the intricate dynamics between the chess personalities of class-C players and grandmasters in determining how class-C players perform. This study examines the chess personalities of two grandmasters while competing against three class-C players. Overall, these findings underscore the complex interplay between player personality and grandmaster characteristics in shaping chess gameplay outcomes, offering valuable insights into the factors influencing competitive performance in the game. These outcomes also showed the complexity of chess as a strategic domain to be explored by psychologists, computer scientists, and business researchers.

One implication could be the employment of similar strategies in competitive arenas where the personalities of individuals and opponents play an important role in performance outcomes. For instance, in strategic decision-making, understanding one's own cognitive style and decision-making patterns could provide more effective negotiation strategies and better decision-making processes. Leveraging insights from cognitive psychology and behavioral economics, businesses might be able to customize their strategies to meet certain needs and preferences. For instance, understanding the requirements and communication preferences of each client allows businesses to deliver personalized services and better address issues, and therefore, they can build long-lasting relationships.

References

1. Bandura, A.: Social foundations of thought and action. Englewood Cliffs, NJ **1986**(23–28), 2 (1986)
2. Bandura, A.: Social cognitive theory of self-regulation. Organ. Behav. Hum. Decis. Process. **50**(2), 248–287 (1991)
3. Caci, B., Dhou, K.: The interplay between artificial intelligence and users' personalities: a new scenario for human-computer interaction in gaming. In: Stephanidis, C., et al. (eds.) HCI International 2020 - Late Breaking Papers: Cognition, Learning and Games, pp. 619–630. Springer, Cham (2020). https://doi.org/10.1007/978-3-030-60128-7_45
4. Chase, W.G., Simon, H.A.: The mind's eye in chess. In: Visual Information Processing, pp. 215–281. Elsevier (1973)
5. De Groot, A.D.: Thought and choice in chess, vol. 4. Walter de Gruyter GmbH & Co KG (1978)
6. Dhou, K.: Towards a better understanding of chess players' personalities: a study using virtual chess players. In: Kurosu, M. (ed.) HCI 2018. LNCS, vol. 10903, pp. 435–446. Springer, Cham (2018). https://doi.org/10.1007/978-3-319-91250-9_34
7. Dhou, K.: An innovative employment of virtual humans to explore the chess personalities of Garry Kasparov and other class-a players. In: Stephanidis, C. (ed.) HCI International 2019 - Late Breaking Papers, pp. 306–319. Springer, Cham (2019). https://doi.org/10.1007/978-3-030-30033-3_24
8. Dhou, K.: A novel investigation of attack strategies via the involvement of virtual humans: a user study of Josh Waitzkin, a virtual chess grandmaster. In: Stephanidis, C., et al. (eds.) HCI International 2020 - Late Breaking Papers: Cognition, Learning and Games, pp. 658–668. Springer, Cham (2020). https://doi.org/10.1007/978-3-030-60128-7_48
9. Dhou, K.: An exploration of chess personalities in grandmasters and class-a players using virtual humans. Int. J. Entertain. Technol. Manag. **1**(2), 126–145 (2021)

10. Dhou, K.: An exploration of the fear of attack strategy in chess and its influence on class-a players of different chess personalities: an exploration using virtual humans. In: Fang, X. (ed.) HCI in Games: Experience Design and Game Mechanics, pp. 185–195. Springer, Cham (2021). https://doi.org/10.1007/978-3-030-77277-2_15

11. Dhou, K.: An exploration of feared versus fearless attack attitudes using the chess personalities of virtual chess players. In: Fang, X. (ed.) HCI in Games, pp. 176–185. Springer, Cham (2023). https://doi.org/10.1007/978-3-031-35979-8_14

12. Goodman, D., Keene, R.: Man versus machine: Kasparov versus deep blue. ICGA J. **20**(3), 186–187 (1997)

13. Karpman, B.: The psychology of chess: (richard reti). Psychoanalytic Rev. (1913–1957) **24**, 54 (1937)

14. Küchelmann, T., Velentzas, K., Essig, K., Koester, D., Schack, T.: Expertise-dependent perceptual performance in chess tasks with varying complexity. Front. Psychol. **13**, 986787 (2022)

15. Sweller, J.: Cognitive load during problem solving: effects on learning. Cogn. Sci. **12**(2), 257–285 (1988)

16. Sweller, J.: Element interactivity and intrinsic, extraneous, and germane cognitive load. Educ. Psychol. Rev. **22**, 123–138 (2010)

17. Sweller, J., Chandler, P., Tierney, P., Cooper, M.: Cognitive load as a factor in the structuring of technical material. J. Exp. Psychol. Gen. **119**(2), 176 (1990)

18. Ubisoft: Chessmaster grandmaster edition. http://chessmaster.uk.ubi.com/xi/index.php

19. Vollstädt-Klein, S., Grimm, O., Kirsch, P., Bilalić, M.: Personality of elite male and female chess players and its relation to chess skill. Learn. Individ. Differ. **20**(5), 517–521 (2010). http://www.sciencedirect.com/science/article/pii/S1041608010000403

Storytelling, Worlds and Game Design: Viewer Experience and Interaction in "Sky, Children of the Light"

Carlos M. Figueiredo(✉) ⓘ and Sofia M. Santos ⓘ

CIAUD, Lisbon School of Architecture, Universidade de Lisboa, Lisbon, Portugal
cfigpt@gmail.com, smachado@ga-s2.com

Abstract. The game "Sky: Children of the Light" is a foremost example of how storytelling, world-building, game design, game interaction, and community building can create an engaging and emotional player experience. Its dreamlike realms, storytelling techniques, game design, non-orthodox interaction design, communication design, and community building, unique and original features (such as its cutscenes, 3d filming messages), and a lavish deep immersive tale, can make us learn new ways in Game Design, Storytelling, Player Agency and Game community interaction.

Keywords: Emotion motivation and persuasion design · Metaphor mental-model navigation design · Player Immersion · World and Spatial Design · Interaction · Storytelling · Player Gaze · Player's Sense of Presence and Agency

1 Introduction

1.1 A Subsection Sample

"Sky; Children of the Light" is a game created by Jenova Chen for "ThatGameCompany" in 2019. This paced adventure combines elements of poetry, music, nature themes, and motion controls to offer a sensory-rich social experience. Originally available on iOS the game later expanded to Android Nintendo Switch, PlayStation 4, and PlayStation 5. It follows in the footsteps of the company's titles like Journey (2012) and Flower (2009) which focus on interactions over traditional win-lose dynamics since its inception in 2008, under Kellee Santiago's guidance.

2 Development Philosophy and Emotional Storytelling

2.1 Emotion in Games

"ThatGameCompany", the developer of Sky, began life to establish human bonds using ecological, positive, emotional 'gameplay' experiences. The system operates on emotions, rather than on the usual theories of technical, mathematical gameplay. Images, storylines, and soundtracks all correlate to an experience of emotions beyond the usual excitement or drama of most action games, adding mystery, harmony, and peace.

© The Author(s), under exclusive license to Springer Nature Switzerland AG 2025
J. Y. C. Chen et al. (Eds.): HCII 2024, LNCS 15377, pp. 322–340, 2025.
https://doi.org/10.1007/978-3-031-76812-5_22

The universality of the story and the fact that the experience the player has is immersive and invites projection from each player, help give players of different cultures the ability to metaphorically empathize with the game on a deeper level: "We wanted to create a game where players feel a genuine sense of connection and empathy towards others, using the game's mechanics to build relationships and share experiences" [1].

This inclusive playful storytelling approach allows players of all stripes to develop powerful bonds with more than the game itself. As Kellee Santiago says: "The goal was really to create a game that promotes real connections and empathy, so we designed the mechanics to help grow relationships between the players and exchange experiences" [2].

2.2 Core Principles and Founding Mission

"Thatgamecompany" studio focuses on creating games that offer experiences for players of all ages. Their main aim is to revolutionize game design pushing the limits of the gaming industry to build relationships and foster a community feeling among players.

The path of "Sky: Children of the Light" is more about a feeling in your heart than anything else. In this game, you play as a Child of Light who navigates through the fallen world and through different realms to get lost winged lights to return the stars to their constellations, like the ones twinkling at night. Sky feels like there are too many areas, quests, and foes to ever be completed by the players acting as children of light. However, its biggest story is presented in the visual gameplay aspect, so, for this reason, walking on themed landscapes makes it appear like all kingdoms should be filled with love until they are illuminated.

Studio designers worry about how to make games that transcend the flat space of the monitor to draw remote players into a community. 'ThatGamecompany' makes emotionally fulfilling games for players of all ages.

As the players were interviewed, they talked about how their gameplay had changed them. As Jenova Chen later put it: What the players are experiencing has a deeper impact on their lives individually: "Our games are designed to inspire wonder and self-reflection encouraging players to contemplate their experiences and relationships". [3].

The foundation of that in turn is just wanting to make games that hopefully people are going to love and replay for years to come. People still remember games. Games remind us of life when we were kids; of sentiment; of ideas. Video games have the power to pull us in, to unite us, as Jenova Chen says. You are simply pulling strings from that emotional structure to elicit an emotion from people to keep you tapping into that emotion to send people on their way happy and wanting to play your game. But we do that by getting people organized together.

Our objective is to create timeless games that evoke emotions and spark reflections that cater to an audience while nurturing meaningful connections, according to Jenova Chen [3]. He designs its games to inspire awe and self-reflection, encouraging players to contemplate their experiences and connections. The goal is to create enduring games that evoke emotions, provoke a deep appeal to a range of players, and foster meaningful connections.

3 Concept and Narrative

3.1 Premise and Plot

The entirety of the core challenges revolves around radiating light in a world full of darkness. The complex emotional story, the core mechanics of the game, and its foolproof romance options push 'Sky' players to seek relationships in the game that can also span to real life. A gaming space that prescribes positivity, and spreads light as you glide through the stars and skies, is, in many ways, a unified, new, and powerful experiment.

We designed "Sky: Children of the Light" with a clear vision to create an emotional and social gaming experience. The concept emphasizes exploration, cooperation, and the sharing of light as central themes. In the game, players take on the role of a child of light to bring hope to a kingdom that is suffering from darkness. Players are "children of light," with an explicit mission given to bring hope to the desolate kingdom and restore light in their realms. The main goal is to guide fallen stars to their places in the sky, in heaven. This means the return of the heaven lights and stars to the shadowed lands. This journey encapsulates themes of illumination and mysticism, at the core of the game's storytelling.

The spirits need to be found by the player as well as deliver illumination into captivity among inhabitants who have been stuck within different realms so that they may be freed by children's candlelight, so their spirits can ascend spiritually.

This game requires every player to reach the highest part of the sky where fallen stars gather at night in Eden. Such "winged stars" are dispersed throughout all realms; one child of light can save many falling stars. In Sky's most difficult level, players must fight with enormous hazards ascending through Eden until it tops out, endure fire and rock storms, give away fallen winged light, and then certainly die. After that run into paradise beyond its gates and resurrect. Next rise over heaven! Pass beyond its gates and reborn upon the earth again.

The player has also to find and give light to the imprisoned spirits of the inhabitants, trapped through all realms, so they can be freed, to be able to ascend. The collecting of the scattered stars of light, the "winged lights", from all the realms, also allows the player to gain wings so he can fly through the kingdom, higher and farther. The player must also seek out and illuminate the trapped spirits of the residents spread across all realms, making them free, and allowing them to ascend.

In this game, the "Children of Light" embark on quests with companions to bring light back to darkened realms. Along their adventure, they will discover knowledge and hidden truths of the Sky Kingdom. Jennie Kong says this tale of brightness and hope plays a role in shaping the game's storyline [4].

The game's story aims to create an experience that resonates beyond linguistic boundaries. Players strive to convey a sense of purpose fostering a journey that extends beyond themselves; "The narrative is carefully designed to be inclusive and relatable to players, from diverse backgrounds and cultures promoting a shared adventure of wonder and discovery" [1].

3.2 Realms and Eye of Eden

The role of image discourse syntaxes is of primary importance to convey the game's narrative atmosphere: The structures and subsequences of the game's visual telling syntaxes are created with attention to the paralinguistic, ludic, and emotional immersion of the player. 'In the fictional characteristics of the script, the visual telling syntaxes are staged in combination, time and time again, to create image projects of the cinematic and visual spaces, providing emphasis for the pretended interactions [5].

Triumph Valley acts as a domain for competitions and challenges that symbolize power and achievements for adults. There players feel an exhilarating surge of adrenaline as they forge alliances to overcome obstacles. Within the Golden Wasteland perilous creatures roam, amidst ruins denoting time's passage and decline. To conquer threats and unearth buried legends players must collaborate effectively. The Knowledge Vault resembles a library beckoning players to explore its wealth of knowledge representing enlightenment. As players navigate its corridors they will delve into a repository of information.

The Eye of Eden acts as the final challenge in the player's adventure. Obstructed and filled with precipitous death traps, it assesses all the skills that have been acquired so far, structuring a narrative linked to issues of mortality and regeneration. Players face various trials that result in significant transformative changes. Jennie Kong says players rely on each other to overcome obstacles, working towards a primal sense of accomplishment and closure that promotes the kind of selflessness, teamwork, and strategic thinking [4]. Each Eden completion lets you get Ascended Candles that unlock more powerful permanent upgrades and better spirit interactions. This breeds helpfulness, team spirit, and a strategic mindset.

Having obstacles that cannot be overcome singularly, but rather exclusively by players leaning on each other, The journey through Eden often elicits deep emotional responses. Eden is the ultimate test: anarchy, rebirth. They go through storms, they make sacrifices—it is about redemption. The Eye of Eden is the endpoint, death, and rebirth. It is where you must face your final trials, leading to an emotional transformation. According to Indie Ranger, this is the peak of the game for us in terms of narrative - where everything comes together in a deeply affecting finale [4].

3.3 Narrative Syntactic Approach

The game employs nonverbal storytelling strategies that involve body language, gestures, and atmosphere factors. This method allows individuals across numerous cultures to communicate beyond linguistic limitations. The handling of non-verbal communication guarantees that the narrative is accessible to all, creating mutual comprehension and psychological connection across players from diversified cultures.

Spirits in the game relate their memories using visual recalls told in silent cutscenes. This approach, if paired with the emotional journey through multiple dimensions, produces a very immersive insight [4].

4   Visual and Artistic Design

4.1   Art Style and Environmental Storytelling

The artwork in Sky is just beautiful, each location has such an impressive style and mood. The soft color palettes and particle effects in each realm are intentionally created so you can 'feel' something and see how 'dynamic lighting and shadows work to give a sense of motion across the game platform. Zhao's illustrations [6] portray the otherworldly and peaceful environment of "Sky: Children of the Light" with the highlights being broad landscapes in soft light and references to the exploration and spiritual journey themes of the game.

Every scene captures the highs and lows of the kingdom, from the peaceable islands of wind to the harsh trials within the Cave of Prophecy, enjoying the symbolism of sunshine and darkness alongside, to offer us glimpses of a compelling story and the broader "sky" global myths. His scenes portray the contrasts of the Realm's lands, playing on and around the symbolism of sunshine and darkness [6].

These visual elements are carefully crafted to enhance the player's immersion and emotional engagement: "The multiple visual syntaxes used, optimized for their media supports, must create a cinematic telling flow portraying the tale of fictional worlds that induce the viewer's percepts of immersion, presence, and feedback" [7].

The art book certainly nails the delicate, calming atmosphere of "Sky: Children of the Light". Details are given with spotted lighting and airy panoramas, making these worlds seem other, turning them into a vision of discovering what you want to do. The big contrast of light and dark and hope and despair are reflected in the central narrative of the game, that light is in a dark place: "Zhao's visual development of the lush prairies, misty forests, and desolate wastelands through which the player will adventure; his complex and emotional early designs of the Children of Light" [6].

His drawings of those sunny skies, full of the ellipses in which people find themselves. It helps to tell the story better while talking about sacrifice, the most important thing for the one you love, a new beginning, and eternal life. The aesthetic of "Sky" appeals: to beautiful landscapes, mystical and genuine, never fails to be captivating. Zhao's visual design adopts an environmental storytelling approach allowing him to create a powerful, living game space. There, players are directed through visual landmarks and hints at strange stories: "Many games put narrative information into designed space. The more visuals can become part of the story, the less space there is for the audience" [7].

Every kingdom's realm and thematic areas seek to generate the desired emotional response using particle systems, soft color schemes, and dynamic lighting. Zhao's drawings make it feel like other worlds exist within these places; peacefulness is heightened during massive journeys toward spiritual awareness while basking in different lights: "The emotions of the characters in each (..) scene must be expressed simply by the storyboard artist and the mood must be established through each scene" [5].

Storytelling and visuality form the principal foundation of Sky's functional design. The primary means used to animate the game world is via these kinds of narrating visual cues that guide players while also enriching narratives. They leave less interpretive space to the audience than do games designed with design as opposed to story: "The more visuals doing storytelling, the less space the audience can put themselves in" [7].

4.2 Sound and Music

The "Sky: Children of Light" soundtrack is composed by Vincent Diamante. It combines orchestral and ambient music to heighten the emotional impact of the game. Sound design includes ambient noises that surround players, as well as musical cues leading them through key events. The depth of this game increases dramatically with directional and guiding sound effects which draw players into an environment abundant in such cues. Acoustic hints act out parts of the script's fictional stories by guiding players through situations and events. These also serve to enhance narrative development while eliciting emotions in the players. So intimate are these sounds; one might easily think of them part-and-packing within any given level or scene, with all storytelling devices working together towards a common goal: making worlds more real than ever before experienced is possible for those who play "Sky".

The first three CDs (later, four) soundtrack releases with the game have a marvelous quality, fitting and adapted to the space where events and action take place in each realm, spatial and dynamic, related to the space, to the materiality of the realms: every track signal and complements the surrounding space, the ambiance and player feeling, its characters or inhabitants, and the actions or tasks that need to be accomplished. Jennie Kong stands: "The music in 'Sky' is not just background sound; it is integral to the emotional experience, guiding players through the narrative and enhancing the overall sense of immersion" [4].

Emotional and philosophical themes play a significant role in the plot of "Sky. "The game explores concepts of connection, memory, and hope, inviting players to reflect on their own experiences and relationships. Through interactions with the spirits of past inhabitants, players uncover touching stories of loss, redemption, and love. This emotional depth adds a layer of meaning to the gameplay, creating a profound and immersive experience that resonates on a personal level. For Cody Crumley, "Playing music together in 'Sky' is a magical experience that raises a sense of community" [8].

The "Sky" game invests in the concept of connection, memory, and hope, encouraging players to think about what they have been through and their relations with others. By communicating with the spirits of previous residents, one learns touching tales about losing everything, making up for it, or falling in love again. This level of depth in feeling adds another dimension to sound and music, moreover when the visual and sound are perfectly tuned. Then, a very deep involvement place, one that touches players' selves at a personal level. According to Cody Crumley, "Playing music together in 'Sky' is a magical experience that raises a sense of community" [8].

5 Gameplay Mechanics

5.1 Exploration and Flying

Flight is key to the gameplay loop and central to the core of this game. It's all about freedom, self-direction, and finding new things. In terms of mechanics, players can regain their energy by either sticking close to one another—thus fostering social connections—or seeking out light sources scattered throughout the world like clouds, radiant manta rays, or phosphorescent plants sprouting from trees and underwater cliffsides.

The first-person challenges in "Sky" significantly improve the player's sense of presence and immersion: "Eventually games gave the player realistic first-person challenges. The user's sense of presence and immersion increases as interactivity does" [7].

Santiago [9] states that in "Sky" the freedom of flight is a metaphor for exploration, discovery, and findings, allowing players to have an immersed experience of the world of 'Sky', felt as a uniquely personal path. Exploration involves discovering hidden paths, secret areas, scattered memories of lost spirits, touching spaces, or appealing landscapes. This mechanic gives the player a sense of adventure and wonder.

5.2 Exploration and Flying

Players team up to solve quests that require a group to solve and access new areas, requiring cooperation to progress. The game seamlessly integrates social mechanics, enhancing the sense of community and shared goals. Cooperation is not just encouraged but regularly necessary, as well as help from other players to learn how to handle a quest, action, or explore a space. "The cooperative gameplay in 'Sky' is designed to foster genuine connections and teamwork, making each interaction meaningful and rewarding [1].

This produces a feeling of companionship and reciprocal assistance among players, which eventually leads to friendships. This encourages a sense of companionship and mutual support among players, that evolves into friendship in time.

To solve complex tasks and get into new places that are unavailable for an individual player, players must act in groups. The social mechanics of the game promote community building and shared purpose. Collaboration is not only advice but also sometimes mandatory when assistance from other gamers is needed to understand how to cope with a quest or action or just when exploring some areas: "Sky has cooperative gameplay that encourages genuine connections between people who work together towards common goals" [9, 10]. According to Jenova Chen [11], such attitudes create an atmosphere of brotherhood where players help each other, promoting friendships along the way.

5.3 Candles and Light

The idea of light is central to both the mechanics of gameplay and the theme of spreading joy throughout the world of Sky: Children of the Light. You gather light to charge your cape and fly with it. Candles, on the other hand, are the main form of currency in the game and are formed when you collect light along all realms. This collected light is then used to craft candles, that can be used to unlock emotes (to express yourself), cosmetics (to create a personalized avatar), and or obtain items. Light as a medium for crafting candles endorses the theme of light and positivity: "Sky" encourages acts of kindness, developing a positive community atmosphere.

Again, light plays an important role in unlocking certain objects of the environmental setting, as well as creating a sequence of game events – adding an unexpected centrality for light in Sky – says Chen - and a light-driven storyline to the player: "By allowing players to use light to unlock new areas and solve quests, you add a new layer of depth to a game's exploration mechanics" [11].

Winged Light fragments help with the flight energy the player can have, so the more you have, the higher and the longer you can fly, which leads to exploration and facilitates the flow of the game by rewarding persistence. This gives a meaning layer of the mechanics used with light and candles in the themes of sociability of the game itself: light is obtained by collecting and sharing, letting players level up in the game, progress further in it, and come closer to each other. This serves to underline the game's central belief: the sharing of light and, most importantly, of joys: "Sky's innovative combination of light and candles reinforces the game's focus on positive social interactions and cooperative gameplay.

There are three kinds of candles:

- Normal Candles: candles forged from light collected along the realms, in candles (or cakes of candles) become normal candles. Normal candles serve all purposes of daily activities. Awake spirits buy cosmetics, social interactions… everything to progress in the game, and you need to play it, without great levels of progress.
- Season Candles – when in a season I collect light from that season candles in the realms, when I forge a candle, it becomes a Season Candle.
- Ascended candles – those are a level of candles higher than regular candles, which can be earned in-game based on significant achievements: defeating ruthless falling shards or as a reward for defying the Eden forces and evil creatures, lighting fallen stars with collected winged lights and accomplishing their release, to allow them to ascend to their sky constellations: "Ascended Candles provide a meaningful reward for players who achieve significant milestones in the game" [8].

Besides candles, there's a whole bunch of collectibles that enhance your experience – for instance, pieces of Winged Light for your flight energy (wing): the more you find, the more you can fly, and the longer. You earn wings to fly farther distances to earn more wings, which in turn encourages exploration and facilitates the flow of the gameplay. Socialization awards you hearts that you can use to buy special items, which therefore also makes the game more social, and you want to be more social to further missions within the gameplay as well.

Cosmetics form an essential part of the wild and expressive avatar-customization possibilities: capes, masks, outfits, face-wear, hairstyles, and tools. Each option allows for a richer way to explore and develop the boundaries of their individuality, and then continue their journey deeper into the worlds of 'Sky'. Cosmetic items, available both seasonally and event-related, offer special rewards and customization unlocks merely by playing the seasonal events. 'Sky' contains a vast number of cosmetic options to create attractive but distinct avatars.

This gives a meaning layer of the mechanics used with light and candles in the themes of sociability of the game itself, therefore in the most exploration side of the game and under the core mechanics in the game: light is obtained by collecting and sharing, letting players level up in the game, to progress further in the game and to come closer to each other. Jennie Kong says this serves to underline the game's central motif: the sharing of light and most importantly of joys: "Sky's innovative combination of light and candles reinforces the game's focus on positive social interactions and cooperative gameplay [4].

6 Collectibles and Accessories

6.1 Types of Collectibles

Light plays a key role in Sky: Children of the Light's mechanics and theme of bringing happiness to others. You collect light to charge your cape and then fly with it. In essence, it lets players travel through beautifully crafted worlds and find hidden optional content. Candles act as the main currency in the game, which are created by collecting light during gameplay.

Aside from candles, the game boasts countless collectibles that improve the player's journey. The term Collectibles in the game" Sky, Children of Light" means all that a player can collect in the realms of the game. It was referred already three of them: Winged Lights, Regular Candles, which are forged with the light collected through the realms of Sky, and Hearts, which are earned exclusively through social interactions, from other players who are our friends, or from Spirits as a gift of friendship. It is a currency earned by interaction and friendship, relating to other players or the dormant inhabitants of "Sky", and it is always from benevolent action of giving light to friends and players we met in the friend's constellation.

There are items a player pays for items with regular or seasonal candles, others only with hearts. A player can buy more regular or seasonal candles by spending real money, but he cannot buy hearts, because they symbolize companionship and friendship, and that is not for sale! Socialization grants hearts to a player, which can be used to purchase items in that currency, most of them owned in the spirit's tree. This makes the game more social and invites players to engage with others and form relationships within the gameplay.

So, a player can collect Winged Lights, light to forge Candles, and Hearts he uses to get exclusive items. All these currencies allow to unlock Emotes (gestures or mimic expressions for an avatar, to improve the mute player's self-expression) and cosmetics, which are of an enormous variety, and be grouped into items for avatar visual look, tools for the player to use or Musical Instrument to Play.

In "Sky: Children of the Light", light is central to both the mechanics of the game and its central theme of bringing happiness into the world. You gather light so that you can charge your cape and fly using it; basically, players can explore beautifully designed realms and look for optional secrets and content hidden in far-off places. On the other hand, candles are the main currency in the game—they represent collected light.

However, these collected lights are still used in crafting candles which can also be used to unlock emotes (to communicate better), cosmetics (for a more personalized avatar), and other interactive features. Another use for light is enabling certain environmental pieces as well as game progressions. There are quests or challenges where players must activate sources of light for them to move forward, therefore further fueling curiosity ignited by the game already. This gives a narrative driven by light which adds more depth to their experience as explorers: "Using light to unlock new areas and solve quests adds depth to the game's exploration mechanics" [11].

6.2 Cosmetics

Cosmetics are a big part of what lets players go wild with their avatar customization: capes, masks, outfits, face accessories, hairstyles, and tools. This provides players with a deeper way to experience and customize their individuality and then venture deeper into the realms of "Sky". Seasonal cosmetics, set to be available during their events, allow players to earn exclusive customization options by simply engaging with those events. "Sky" has a wide range of cosmetics in which players can create their own unique and individual avatars, express themselves, and communicate and interact creatively with others [6].

Describing better the kinds of cosmetics there are:

– Capes: the most visible piece of clothing, essential for flight and appearance, with all kinds of colors and designs various colors and designs
– Hairstyles: allow players to customize their avatar's hair, there are a wide variety of styles
– Masks: change the facial appearance of the player's avatar, adding personality and mystery. They can range from unusual to intimidating (Animal Masks, Themed Masks, Seasonal Masks)
– Outfits: they include pants and leggings that are visible under the cape. They provide the base layer for the player's (avatar) appearance
– Face Accessories: headphones, horns, earrings, and sunglasses, necklaces
– Hair Accessories: to use over selected hairstyles and include items like hats, headpieces, crowns, hairpins and small ornaments
– Musical Instruments: they are playable and there are also music scores we can get. Some of them are Piano, Harp, Flute, Drum, Guitar, Saxophone, Violin
– Tools: these items are usable, and the player employs them during his journeys. You can take with you just one of these tools or musical instruments. Just at the Home entry spaces of each realm, it is possible to exchange one tool for another, and in the Theatre and Coliseum, created in the Season of Performance and of Aurora). Tools can be torches, lanterns, tables, chairs, tea tables, boats, tents, umbrellas, fireplaces, fireworks, photographic machines, and so many more. They are interactive with the environment and other players.

Tools and Instruments: these are objecting the player can utilize as he makes his way through the game. One tool or musical instrument can be taken with you at any given time. Tools or musical instruments can be swapped for one another at Home (there is one Home in each realm), and in Theatre/Coliseum (created in Season of Performance/Aurora). Torches and lamps, tables and chairs, tea tables, boats, tents, umbrellas, fire, and fireplaces are examples of tools; and there are many more (fireworks, photographic machines, etc.) that interact with their surroundings and with other players.

Musical instruments have another use in the game besides creativity and community: they facilitate shared music experiences among players and help overcome the social realities of the person behind the music: 'Play music together in the Sky, it creates a magical atmosphere that encourages a lot of camaraderie between those participating together' [8].

7 Seasons and Events

Typical seasonal-themed events provide you with fresh tales, scripts, and a plot of land, characters, as well as quests, usually a fresh area of one of the Circles, that is often associated with real seasons of the year. Seasonal Redeemable Events, Spirits, and sometimes a season-guiding bot character incentive engagement with each signed-in season.

This also means fresh blood for the game as far as player experience; each season offers players new and ever-changing sub-plots to keep them motivated and excited. Seasons along with seasonal events bring new stories, characters, and additions that come to enrich the already existing long-term core plot of the game. Each new season features a theme and associated quests to complete, keeping the game fresh. A cleverly crafted incentives system, centered around the theme and objectives of the season is included to add depth to the game and keep people engaged so that seasonal events and tasks offer must-have rewards and items.

These seasonal events return regularly, and they deliver new tales, characters, and challenges. Seasonal cosmetics are unique to the season, and all refer to season rewards, so players have a reason to keep playing and then participate all over again in the next season. That's a breath of fresh air to the game, new content that makes the game "alive" and that the players can play with enthusiasm.

The new lands, tasks, challenges, and some cosmetics of the Seasons remain available in the game after the season ends, and this adds content permanently to the game, increasing the library indefinitely. Traveling Spirits are seasonal spirits that return from previous seasons (along with their unique trees of cosmetics), regularly and for a few days at a time.

Some of the past seasons and their themes were:

- Season of Gratitude: Focuses on thankfulness, introducing quests emphasizing giving thanks.
- Season of Lightseekers: Explores curiosity, adding new areas and characters.
- Season of Enchantment: Features magical elements and whimsical rewards.
- Season of Sanctuary: Introduces tranquil, summer-themed areas.
- Season of Dreams: Encourages artistic expression and creativity.
- Season of Assembly: Focuses on community and teamwork.
- Season of Prophecy: adds mystical trials and ancient-themed rewards.
- Season of Belonging: Highlights family and connections with heartwarming stories.

Many others brought important expansions to the game, where the Seasons of Shards, of the Little Prince, of Performance, and the Season of Aurora. >

A third series of parallel plots (added to the game with the 5th Birthday celebration) is the yearly environmental and other themed quests. Much of what you will have to do requires creativity and/or social collaboration with other players to complete these annual thematic events. The threats are there to encourage mutual play among players and allow cooperative gameplay as a behavior to emerge. Players must play together, which in many tasks of the game, means that the tasks will need two or more players passing the various obstacles and completing the quests that they come across.

Event Currency: these temporary annual thematic quests or events have their associated currency so that you can buy encounter-related currency-only goods. That does at least lend some fresh and real challenge to the gameplay.

So, in addition to core challenges and seasonal challenges, you can also hunt down new spirits in a few limited annual thematic events, so Sky has created some different parallel gameplay plots to keep players busy and always returning to "Sky."

8   Core Challenges and Plot

In "Sky: Children of the Light", a story is told in an environment that has been created with extreme detail; in this game, the players are explorers who have to fix fallen stars and return them into constellations. One of the main challenges of "Sky" is finding your way around its sprawling, atmospheric realms. What sets these apart from other encounters is that there are environments as you move through a realm. Those environments present quests or obstacles that need to be overcome before progressing: "Agency can be purely practical, or it can involve elements of creativity, roleplaying, and identification. Empathy is the potential for players to form emotional bonds with the character, identify with their goals and hence the game's objectives" [12].

The serene landscapes of the Isle of Dawn give way to hidden caves filled with mystery in the Valley of Triumph where different skill-based puzzles await players' intelligence. To proceed further in the game world, one must solve environmental quests mostly centered around using light as a means of activation for various mechanisms leading to unlocking more areas, thereby fueling the exploration mood even deeper.

The exploration of the realms, the loneliness of the environment, and the encounters with stories, Sky features multiple seasons of events that tie back to the lore of the world and provide an ongoing story for the players. Every season has updated stories, characters, and unique rewards to expand the lore in the game, each of the seasons features a quest line for the player to follow and complete.

Season of Enchantment and the Season of Prophecy are seasonal events that add extra elements and quests to the game ensuring that the gameplay always remains as challenging as it is, and deeply emotional and related to nature, ancient inhabitants of "Sky" and their past, or interaction, bonds, and friendship with other players. Which will also help push players to come back to the game and be involved in the community movements.

The central quests are where players will become a Child of Light and try to realize the story of the kingdom. And they'll be playing to counteract the destruction, the darkness all around. That's a central quest because the narrative essence, the thematic substance of the flowering and spread of light and life forms – that's threaded through the entire work here.

This affective, philosophical aspect of Sky is likewise central to its story. The narrative game is an empathetic, evocative, and connective, one that, at intervals, asks its players to look at their own lives and connections around them. The story does descend into the previous lives of the spirits they met, in other worlds, in other skies, in tales of loss and reparation and love. This element of emotional investment is vital to the story in the game, and to the resultant translation of emotional consequence into the gameplay elements, the plot of the game's events in the tasks and quests where a real resonance is placed, a sensitivity and feeling driving the loop.

This emotional and philosophical aspect of Sky is also pivotal to its plot. The narrative game is one about connection, memory, and hope, and encourages its players to look at their own experiences and connections as well. The story sometimes slopes into the past lives of the spirits who met in the different realms with beautiful stories of loss, redemption, and love. It is imperative to the narrative in the game that this emotional resonance exists and the translation to the gameplay mechanics, placing in the tasks and quests an actual deeper sensibility and emotion.

9   Player Interaction and Community Feedback

9.1 Social Gameplay

In a cooperative game, over-assigning workload creates stronger relationship-biasing encouragement of cooperation and goals, which in turn leads to larger social networks and thus more advanced social coordination and development. That is the key step for each collaboration to become a process. The ability of the team to cooperate instead of competing was stressed again during recent playtesting. This is how gaming changed to foster such play [1].

Satisfying their player base can be achieved by being open-minded about what people want to play with while checking in with the community occasionally for feedback. Feedback comes from TGC-playing developers; these suggestions keep it going. Game development means getting input from gamers themselves regularly so that the game can be shaped toward its audience more. When future updates are implemented based on conversations between "devs" (developers) and players, communities' opinion gets heard [13].

There are also issues in Sky such as social interaction and collaboration. This title aims at coaxing people to cooperate to get by the matters and progress in the story as a unit. Most quests and goals are meant to be solved together, asserting the value of working as a team and bonding over the experience. It doubles down on this social element with the use of emotes and candles, which players can always use to convey their emotions and find new friends. The developers designed the game to have a gift economy, which is unusual for a game of this type: players are free to help with collectibles like light and resources or fight fatal "Krills" together, but there's little exchange of items between players.

Inspired to foster a community rather than toxic antisocial habits, "Sky" incentivizes gamers to perform a suite of emotes including hugging, interacting, and even holding hands. All these minute interactions are plain, yet organic, resulting in a feeling of companionship between the players, quotes Indie Ranger.

9.2 Community Features

"Sky" emphasizes communal storytelling and shared memories through group activities and events. In social play (or cooperative play, halfway), the game needs places that call and gather players to meet and communicate. "Sky" had thought about them, since the beginning: there were "cozy places", areas of peace, comfort, and protection in the middle of harsh terrain or foes! These locations always had a fireplace in the center because its light recharges the player's capes. But also, because anthropologically fireplaces endorse protection, being with others, and mutual protection. Also, these cozy places were somehow hidden, totally, or in a way one couldn't find them.

Besides, there were in these "cozy places" or in places without danger to relax and communicate, the" homes": of "Sky" and one in each Realm, benches that allow two players to chat, if they light the candle in the middle. So, they were places to recover from hard and dangerous journeys and fights, as were places to play, get to know others, play or listen to music, to foster friendships and groups of friends.

Then the game began to have shared places, in "homes" or isolated ones. Shared places are parallel places that each player can customize with his own tools and cosmetics, chairs, tents, web beds, coffee, tents, and lighting, and give that version of the place a "shared place". Any player could use those shared places, real customized cozy places, come together, and socialize.

But "Thatgamecompany", TGC as all players know it, invented the concept of mobile shared places, which means that any player, in any place, could create a "shared place" a shelter all players could use. But these "user-shared places" last for a few days, then vanishes.

So, there are, in the loneliness of big and dangerous extensions of the realms, warm peaceful places that contrast, where "sky kids" stay for hours! "Sky" promotes cooperative gameplay, fostering a sense of community and shared goals, and players bond with others and groups of others, creating a sense of community, of helping someone we don't know but who needs help!

Moreover, two friends (they are, after spending two candles to give hands and fly together) have a tree of progressive features to be able to go deeper into that Friendship. Just two steps of it:

1 – They can reach the capacity in that tree, to chat between themselves, everywhere, and always they are in the same area of a Realm. The chat translates to English any known language, all can speak!

2 – A friend can teleport to where the other is, in any area of ant Realm. Very useful to dangerous combat, of fights together, to assist each other.

Also, anyone can leave a message to another gamer that later passes by. If he likes, he can give hearts to the message writer. Now messages can be placed anywhere, and they are filming the sender does, not just written messages.

Living life events are based on communal storytelling and anything that bonds us together as a group. Players can group up, take part in events, and make memories together, or so says Jenny Kong: "The closed loop of community feedback is at the heart of the way the game is developed, where the players make their voices heard and direct their experiences and opinions into shaping the updates to come" [4].

10   Unique Features and Philosophical Appeal

More broadly, ethical monetization of markets helps to create the right atmosphere for harmonious negotiation and cooperation amongst all players, and no one is privileged over the others due to their balance on their bank statements. Ethical Monetization: indeed, while the game is free, to play the only items available for purchase are cosmetics and gifts. This approach aims to highlight a system to fellow players. By ensuring everyone is on the footing we avoid turning into a 'pay to win' scenario where spending money becomes essential to compete with wealthier players. Additionally, it fosters generosity and community spirit by allowing players to purchase items for others.

Altruism in this sense is seen as enhancing gameplay. It is important to note that while in-game goods have value only when translated into actions, the main goal of Sky is to brighten up its game world and, by extension, the lives of its players, Sky children connecting with their fellow players leading to greater unity, empathy and closer connections between them in the real world. The gifts emphasize the aspect of giving is Sky's core values, each action feeds into the above principles of philanthropy and empathy.

Overall, the ethical monetization of markets is essential in setting a tone for peaceful exchanges and interactions between all players, with no one having any distinct advantages based on their bank balance.

11   Development and Technical Innovations

Festival Tech: Amplifies social relations, massive player congregations, and decade-lasting memories. But what we aim for are genuine human bonds; so, we look for individuals capable of fostering such emotional links where players feel acknowledged and understood. Rocket Construction: Festival Tech development—medium.com 1.6 million people were seeking connections to be among the first 400 visitors to the Aurora concert that was held in virtual space. Refined through Player Feedback.

Iterative Development and Player Feedback [13]: We continuously monitor the feedback from players through the ongoing beta test with thousands of players. By focusing on the emotional and multiplayer core, we can identify what's more fun, and what can be further improved iteration by iteration. We develop this game hand in hand with the many hundreds of players who are now participating in the beta phase – the player feedback is what drives our development and allows the game to grow according to the needs and interests of the community.

12   Accessibility and Gameplay

Inclusive Design: The game Sky: Children of the Light is pampered for her heterodox design philosophy by new game players. This game was originally a mobile game, but then she expanded to all platforms. Her choice of play made it more inclusive, giving players of all skill levels content, from lighter to harder. This inclusive design made her appeal to multi-generational players, like me; And the inclusion aspect of multiplatform made her get to the masses; which gave her a massively multi-player accessibility game.

Free-to-Play Model: that's the free-to-play model where the game costs nothing to play on a basic level, but contains a staggering number of cosmetics, as well as cosmetic seasonal stuff, which is purchasable in real currency. They're considered to be the 'ethical' ways to monetize in-game good things, and nobody will ever be able to squash the emotional bonds these players have for each other. It is gifting, not buying for yourself.

Performance and Controls: control can be problematic on ported versions (anything but mobile), and this can spoil the experience. Above are all points you should remember before any decisions play into protecting the integrity of the play experience between devices. On the other hand, performance-wise, the game can be a bit choppy and lagging, on a few platforms. We work daily to enhance performance, and at launch, we are 100% confident all our players will have a smooth experience [8].

13 Future Directions

13.1 Building Meaningful Connections

"Sky: Children of the Light" is centered around creating a community atmosphere and shared moments. The game's design is focused on cooperative play and meaningful social interactions. Developers depend on community feedback to make improvements, often involving players in discussions about what they think should be done for future updates. Ultimately aiming at developing a fantastic festival experience for players; it involves plans such as expanding interactive events' scale/scope by taking cues from real-world festivals or large gatherings [13] For player satisfaction to stay high while also making sure that the game continues to evolve with each passing season; this means adding seasonal events as well as working on performance/control enhancements which can keep them engaged longer and improve their overall experience too.

13.2 Emotional Impact and Player Feedback

Games can provide emotional experiences, and "Sky" is one of them. Such types of games are good at making people feel strongly and remember for a long time. The ongoing development of the game is closely tied to the feedback from players because these opinions help determine what the next step should be in creating this world together as community participants. It enables developers to keep changing it so that more people like playing this game. Developers ask players what they think about their product so far before releasing new versions; Cody Crumley [8] states that developers should ask for thoughts or comments from gamers on current features and then take those back into account during future iterations.

13.3 Innovative Game Design

Through a minimalist style of art, the visual design of "Sky" represents hope and connection. This decision about how to design not only makes the game look better but also supports its narrative and emotional objectives. The combination of beautiful graphics, immersive soundscapes, and innovative gameplay mechanics in "Sky" makes it a significant achievement for game design. Therefore, showing that games can be both artful and profitable. It is successful in terms of setting new records for emotional depth and social interaction among games. Consequently, it has motivated developers to explore similar ideas thereby impacting positively on the growth of the gaming industry. The creators made non-verbal storytelling methods that are universal and emotionally powerful when crafting the story structure for Sky which transcends culture or language barriers used so anyone can feel included this approach creates deep engagement with players at every level possible without always using words. Non-verbal communication coupled with cooperative playing sets this game apart from others because it emphasizes innovation as well as creating unique player experiences.

14 Conclusion

The beautiful landscapes of "Sky", the immersive soundtracks, and the innovative gameplay elements make Sky a benchmark in game design. Sky focuses heavily on the emotional journey of the players that are required to get through the encounter, which should hopefully make the following games even better. The game has been praised for the narrative and emotionally engaging elements that the players can play through and experience that would stick with the player for a long time.

The stark graphic simplicity and the overall lightness in the presentation work perfectly when it comes to delivering its message of hope and hearts beating as one, especially considering the beauty of the sky. The result is that it achieves its narrative and emotional goals while also looking and feeling like a better game.

The main strong and inspiring tale of the kingdom of "Sky," its fate, and the hope that players have (and are endorsed) to reestablish fallen stars and lighten all Realms, attach to the game (to that world) players that become children of light, ready to fight to.

The game's emphasis on positive social interactions and community building challenges the often competitive and solitary nature of traditional games, offering a refreshing alternative that appeals to a broad audience. Peace is the goal in "Sky: Children of the Light".

Unlike other transformative hands-on experiences, Sky deliberately leverages visual gestures and expressions to demonstrate how it's feasible to interact with players in a simple way that is original and playful. With Emotes, "Sky" designed their story system as questionless to be understood by all peoples, in any language, no matter cultural background.

"Sky" shows a more attractive possibility truly universal of games that are rewarding based on social interactions and that are engaging beyond performance but removing the competitive and loneliness characteristics of traditional win-or-die games.

But some ideas could maybe make "Sky" even greater:

"Sky: Children of the Light" combines ethereal aesthetics, emotive storytelling, and social mechanics to create an immersive, heartwarming adventure. Its focus on altruism, cooperation, and non-verbal communication offers a unique and rewarding experience, inspiring players to connect meaningfully with each other. The game's evolving content and ethical monetization further enhance its appeal, making it a beloved title in the gaming community.

The huge amount of time that takes to collect the light from the Realms, (the famous Candlerun), to forge some regular candles, daily, is very repetitive and boring. To do it hundreds of times (of days) just kills the game to pro players being kids of light for years or months. Players give up playing because the option would be to buy each day's candles with real money, extremely expensive.

There is no information about events, seasons, or about sky itself easily accessible, the answer cannot be some friends that can or cannot know the answers. All of Sky's current information, about events, seasons, and active quests, which are presently active in Sky, should be easily accessible, in-game or on a website linked to the game. Best if the player remains inside the game while reading about it.

The price of cosmetics is extremely high, in candles, seasonal candles, hearts, or real money. In the end, all players must pay lots of true money for in-game currency to get some of the season or core cosmetics that can be useful tools to fight in quests or to be able to socialize, not just fancy clothes. Some important tools can be lost forever. This drives old players away.

The high, sometimes crazy prices of all kinds of cosmetics, are erasing the fundamental principle of "Sky": the ethics of monetizing are falling apart. We are not already in a pay-to-win, but we are already in a pay-to-socialize, and that is against the fundamental principles of "sky"! The price of cosmetics to wear can be high, but those cosmetics to use in shared spaces, and in the fight against the dark skies, should be not to buy but to earn by merit.

What about players that arrive now, how do they get all cosmetics and other items from past events and seasons, sometimes essential items to progress in the game? Never? They are too good to be inaccessible forever, all in years. That is a big loss of invested talent from a game!

Some spirit-owned items, and not only cosmetics, cannot be paid in time to the traveling spirit before he goes away. "Candle Run" for a few days is not enough. Make spirits stay longer or lower the item's prices! Traveling spirits items are treasures that we can never see again! Why not have a Sky shop, with all the items of seasons and events there, more expensive but possible to afford, anyway? Imagine the splendor of that shop! Could be made like the instruments shop, where players can try or buy musical instruments and music sheets. The boredom of long days can make players leave.

– The core tale of Sky and its resolution is what makes "sky" so special and unique, above all. But after a few months, the player made all progress in that plot, and there is no more progress a player can make in it, for the resolution to the darkness of "Sky". That story and plot should have given progress chances, not to make the loop of all Reals and find them all destroyed again, the darkness freezing temples or mantas, again. And so many talents and resources were made in so beautiful seasons, that tell stories related to the core, but that make no progress in it. Core tale and seasons tales are related, but not linked! This drives players away, tired of little stories, not able to progress in the mission given in Dawn caves …

– Even with Seasons, a player takes fifteen minutes to get the season candles of the day, more than thirty if there is a season quest to solve, which happens once in 7 to

10 days or so. Then we have the "candle run", boring, or repeat already solved quests, boring again. To socialize with friends makes sense in it is a time of rest before the action. Much time a day doing the same boring things, in terms of progress and facing quests, little fighting o progress in the resolution of plots, none for the main plot. To change that would be the most wonderful thing for "Sky".

– In annual events or thematic events, with their currency, when the event ends its currency vanishes and should be converted, like it is when seasons end.
– The new home is beautiful, but the central skating space with sea waves all around gave more space for activities with other sand to play or socialize. The center of the old home is free, and the center of the new one is occupied. It should not, it should have a huge "cozy space" in the center, surrounded by the same shop houses that already are there.
– To bring real-life friends to "Sky" should be easier, and the compartments in small groups where the millions of players are sliced up should be flexible. So, any player could face many more "Sky" players than now he does. Why not a rotation cycle, chained by friendship relationships relations? Why not be able to jump to parallel "sky" games, each in their own set of friends, a multiverse approach?

References

1. Designing Social Play for Sky: Children of the Light (2020)
2. GDC 10: ThatGameCompany interview (2010)
3. Game UX Summit '19|Keynote|Jenova Chen|From Journey to Sky-Lessons learned (2019)
4. Evolving Emotional Storytelling in thatgamecompany's Sky (2021)
5. Byrne, M.T.: Animation: the art of layout and storyboarding: complete step-by-step techniques in drawing layout and storyboards for classical, TV, and computer game animation. Mark T. Byrne Production, Leixlip, Co Kildare (1999)
6. Sky - Children of the Light. https://www.tomzhao.com/sky1. Accessed 10 June 2024
7. Bucher, J.K.: Storytelling for Virtual Reality: Methods and Principles for Crafting Immersive Narratives. Routledge, Taylor & Francis Group, New York; London (2018)
8. Crumley, C.: [Review] Sky: Children of Light. https://indieranger.com/review-sky-children-of-light/. Accessed 10 June 2024
9. Sky: Children of the Light - Explained (no spoilers) (2021)
10. 1Art of Sky Children of the Light (2020)
11. Sky: Children of the Light - Breaking a World Record|Gamescom 2023 (2023)
12. Miller, C.H.: Digital Storytelling: a Creator's Guide to Interactive Entertainment. Focal Press, Amsterdam; Boston (2004)
13. Developer Update: Festival Tech|Sky: Children of the Light (2023)

A Review of Cultural Impact on Children's Play Perception and Digital Games

Nandhini Giri$^{(\boxtimes)}$

Purdue University, West Lafayette, IN 47907, USA
girin@purdue.edu

Abstract. This paper reviews existing research articles to understand how cultural factors play a role in children's perception of play, especially within the digital gaming and interactive applications domain. The review investigates interrelated themes on cultural influences in play perception, cultural representation in games and the role of culture in digital character and narrative design. Children interact with digital characters and engaging narrative structures through games and interactive entertainment applications for learning, play and social activities. The pervasive nature of games in children's technology mediated environment makes the medium a powerful tool that shapes children's lived experiences. Designing games with diverse characters, narratives with cultural context and interaction mechanics that align with cultural practices and traditional play artifacts, improve children's engagement with games. This paper presents the findings of this literature review through a framework and discusses cultural factors that influence qualities of play among children from diverse cultural backgrounds.

Keywords: children's perception of play · cross-cultural design in games · cultural representation

1 Introduction

Games and interactive entertainment applications are increasingly being used by children both in and outside classrooms for various purposes that include learning and play activities (C.S. & Rao, 2008). Children live in a technology pervasive environment, and they are constantly interacting with digital applications in the form of games, mobile or browser play apps and other social platforms. Digitally animated characters play a major role in communicating with children through these graphical interfaces. These characters take up social roles by being part of the narrative in interactive games, animation, virtual tutoring, and mobile applications. Narratives are also embedded in these playful interactions to add meaning to children's life experiences.

As the use of games and related entertainment platforms steadily increase, game designers have also started focusing on topics of diversity and cultural representation, to design more inclusive games and interactive media content. Themes which are not often explored and narratives from underrepresented groups are showcased more. There is also a need for diversity and authentic representation of digital characters for gamers to

© The Author(s), under exclusive license to Springer Nature Switzerland AG 2025
J. Y. C. Chen et al. (Eds.): HCII 2024, LNCS 15377, pp. 341–351, 2025.
https://doi.org/10.1007/978-3-031-76812-5_23

identify better with the game characters and feel more engaged in player communities. It helps them learn more about their own cultural identity and voice out their unique perspectives to the corresponding gaming communities.

Play is influenced by cultural practices which in turn affects the way children perceive play tasks. Socio-cultural interactions shape children's experience of playful activities and collaborative task performances. It also raises the question of the extent to which games represent cultural artifacts and provide opportunities for global collaborations. An area of ongoing research work is to answer the question of how these research articles and findings inform game designers in designing culturally inclusive games for children. This review paper approaches the body of research done in the child-computer interaction community through the lens of culture and children's contextual understanding of life experiences. Elements of game play that include digital character interaction, narrative structures and playful interactions are the topics that will be analyzed in the review process. A summary of the research articles and opportunities for future research work in this area will be discussed in subsequent sections.

2   Background

The research work reviewed in this section explore generic design frameworks for children as audiences and collaborative designers. The literature review on the topic of children's lived experiences and digital game design and collaborating with children as co-creators lead to interesting research questions that will be reviewed in this paper.

Carter et al. (2016) studied the influence of stylistic elements of animated characters on targeted child audiences of various age groups. The study highlighted professional practices of animators who varied head size, eye size and eye roundedness when designing characters for various age groups of child audiences. The researchers concluded that the current artistic trends do not accurately reflect the character design preferences of children. Moreover, when children were asked to create their own characters, they preferred regular sized heads and wide-set eyes. This was quite contrary to the general assumptions and popular design trends for child audiences.

Gray et al. (2017) published a paper that describes their decade long experimentation at Sesame Workshop, building media characters that create strong bonds with children. They explain methodologies like "Breaking the fourth wall" as a design technique that helps children interact with and build empathy towards media characters. An example is when media characters pause and look at the camera to ask a direct question and engage a child audience. Media characters that portray rich facial expressions in life situations that are contextually familiar to children promote greater character affinity. The designers also discuss design frameworks beyond television characters. Interactive characters as in games can be more engaging with children and afford social play if they are designed to integrate with classic playthings. The paper also discusses procedurally generated dynamic content that allows interactive digital characters to respond to children's actions in real-time that leads to meaningful interactions.

Walsh et al. (2016) used a distributed participatory research approach with game worlds as co-design spaces for involvement of a globally distributed child audience. A virtual sandbox game environment was used as a co design tool to leverage children's experiences and enrich the design process through global collaboration. Participatory design projects (Grundy et al., 2012) have also explored activities that involve children creating personas as fictitious characters (Itenge-Wheeler et al., 2018) that capture other children's life stories. This activity helps children empathize with other children's diverse perspectives and can be used as a tool to bring out their own inner needs. Designing characters is a fun activity and characters as mediators of emotions can help investigate children's feelings towards sensitive issues. Benton et al. (2014) explain that young children can comprehend narrative structures and that by including them in the narrative design process, they can help game designers to build products that are contextually, temporally, and culturally relevant to children's life experiences.

3   Research Methodology and Analysis

A systematic literature review was conducted to review papers published in the ACM digital library with a focus on journal articles and conference proceedings. The review process also includes relevant research findings from other mediums like storybooks, online collaborative software, technological interfaces, and others that have relevant design implications for game design. The literature review was driven by the following overarching research goals:

- What are the key research studies undertaken in the scholarly areas of culture, gaming technology design practices and children's play perceptions?
- What are the key cultural factors that influence children's play perceptions within the gaming and digital gaming technology platforms?
- How do researchers and practitioners apply these findings in co-designing/co-creating play experiences for and with children in digital gaming technology platforms?

The following inclusion search criteria were used to make a list of research papers that focus on the area of play, culture, and children. Search keywords were applied to the abstract instead of the full text to narrow down the review to research papers that focus specifically in the research work on play, culture, and children.

- Query Syntax: Abstract:(play) AND Abstract:(culture)
- Query Syntax: Abstract:(games) AND Abstract:(culture)
- Query Syntax: Fulltext:(character OR avatar) AND Fulltext:(culture)
- Query Syntax: Abstract:(narrative OR story) AND Abstract:(culture)

A total of 47 research articles were listed by the search queries. A second round of review with 'relevance to the research objective' as the exclusion criteria resulted in the removal of 9 articles leading to a total of 38 research articles. The articles were ordered based on the research objectives. A qualitative approach was employed to textually analyze the insights and research findings on the list of articles obtained through the search queries. A summary of the research findings that are most relevant to the research questions explored in this review paper are presented here:

3.1 Play and Culture

In one of the studies the researchers focused on the role of cultural differences in mediating the effects of interactivity on learning gains (Apostolellis & Bowman, 2015).

Culture-specific cognitive styles affect the way information is perceived by children leading to various levels of cognitive engagement with the game play tasks. Based on sociocultural mediations in orchestrated learning, their hypothesis was that culturally driven prior exposure to and interest in the subject would improve game play experience leading to efficient learning. They observed that in collectivist cultures, children playing games were more concerned about in-group relationships and equal collaboration opportunities. They undervalued the fact that this was detrimental to the game experience and learning. Sociocultural theories have been studied further to derive principles and design decisions that allow children separated by physical and cultural distances to collaborate by building narratives for games together (Campos et al., 2017; Gelderblom, 2004; Chu et al., 2015; Charoenying, 2008).

Research work also draws inspiration from cultural practices to design more engaging and playful interfaces. Researchers have explored the socio-cultural forces that motivate students to play games while building knowledge structures through playing. Children's natural inclination to play is leveraged to derive elements of game design that facilitate efficient learning. A similar approach is taken to study food related culture and traditional practices for designing playful interactions with technology (Chisik, 2020). Oriental calligraphy techniques (Kim, 2010) have been used to derive design elements that encourage well-being through technology interactions. Studies also draw connections between materiality, body, and practice to understand the relationship between human interaction with technology. It suggests that the approach to testing interactive technologies should not be about usability but as a broader cultural practice (Karoff & Johansen, 2009).

3.2   Games and Culture

The papers that were reviewed under this search query used games as a medium for cultural education (Muravevskaia et al., 2016). Culture box (Griffith et al., 2018) is a tablet-based learning game that allows children to navigate through different time periods and experience various cultural locations. The researchers who developed this game found that children are not often exposed to cultures outside their own surroundings and that the Culture box will be an opportunity to experience other cultures through an interactive process of discovery. With the help of augmented reality technology, a narrator leads children through a map letting them collect travel posters of the time and have a unique cultural experience. Mini games, sound, visuals, fun facts, and character accessories entertain and simultaneously teach children about various cultures around the world. Ilha Musical (Gomes et al., 2012) is yet another interactive panoramic experience that features traditional Madeiran cultural practices for children to learn and enjoy. A rhythm game is used in the design to engage children with the traditional folk music, architectural visuals, dance, and cultural motifs from the island of Madeira in this interactive game environment.

The other research papers in this review criteria focus on globally inclusive online collaborations for school children and ways to overcome socio-technical challenges for cross cultural collaborative applications. CityCompass (Sharma et al., 2019; Sharma et al., 2018) an online virtual navigational application for conversational language learning was presented to school children from India and Finland. User studies with Indian children showed several communication and collaborations barriers due to limited access to gaming technology and socio-cultural issues like power distances and face saving. On the other hand, students from Finland showed reduced motivation due to previous computer and gaming experience. The study concluded that online collaboration is affected by differences in computer skills, video gaming experiences and social norms. The researchers also propose a methodology called Bollywood method that is characterized by emotional narratives from popular Indian cinema style. Introducing the Bollywood method with dramatized scenarios facilitated meaningful collaborations for Indian school children. It helped them overcome the socio-technical challenges and limitations of reduced gaming experience. This study shows that more efficient cross-cultural online collaborations across children from different cultures and varying computer skills is quite possible.

3.3 Digital Characters and Culture

Research articles that fall under this theme address various aspects of character design, cultural differences, and design impact on children's interaction with gaming technologies. Maker culture and participatory design are design methodologies that researchers have explored in this area – in terms of character design with children. Researchers have used participatory design initiatives in Namibia for a school library renovation project. Children were asked to create personas that will make them empathize with other children and create diverse perspectives. Designing personas as fictitious characters is a fun activity (Itenge-Wheeler et al., 2018) that can help bring out the feelings and emotional needs of children. It also helps children as creators to understand the perspectives of other children in the process. Research papers explore how mixed ability maker culture supports self-expression in children through virtual avatars in Minecraft's (a popular game) online community (Ring-land, 2017). Research shows that the maker movement can encourage more underrepresented groups to be engaged with science in non-traditional ways by employing cultural historical activity theory (Xu & Nicholson, 2003; McBeath et al., 2017; Benton & Johnson, 2015; Chu et al., 2015). Maker Theatre, which is a storytelling toolkit encourages children to draw story characters on character cards to instill a maker mindset in them.

Studies on interaction show that the physicality of cultural artifacts and affordances of cul-tural objects support children's imagination (Kosmyna, 2020; Isbell & Raines, 2012; Chu & Quek, 2013) to extend broader (Anastasious, 2016). Digible pets project (DuMont & Lee, 2012) combines novel computational technologies with traditional aspects of children's toys and cultural artifacts. The hypothesis is that computationally enhanced tangible toys will motivate children to feel more empowered and capable when interacting with technology. Studies also bring out the impact of cultural differences in gestures for collaborative problem-solving tasks for children interacting with tangible user interfaces. Blended space is another project for children to design heritage stories, by combining physical spaces with digital tourism of a living historic village (O'Keefe & Benyon, 2015). Studies conclude that technology design is integral to culture. Research also shows that serious games designed for classroom engagement through avatar creation and interaction, have varying levels of engagement that questions prior assumptions (Deater-Deckard et al., 2014; Bers, 2017).

3.4 Narratives and Culture

Research work studies the question of how computer games can be developed to engage children in critical discussions of cultural awareness inside and outside classroom (Muravevskaia et al., 2016). Researchers answer the question of "how to expose children to different cultures and help them develop cultural awareness and empathy?". This led to a game prototype based on a Russian traditional fairy tale. The design framework for this game on cultural awareness was developed based on early child development theories, fairy tale literature and game design practices. The paper also highlights the importance of children's agency to make key game design decisions on their own. Supporting children through the reflective process makes them understand what and why something is important.

Stories are powerful tools to share life and cultural experiences. Research papers discuss the use of digital storytelling for knowledge creation in cross-cultural settings (Multisilta et al., 2017; Silver, 2009). A global sharing pedagogy approach involves students sharing their digital stories globally and learning through collaboration on videos. Video inquiry learning approach promotes learning through investigation of questions, scenarios and problems using videos created and shared by students. A third approach features aspects of the first two approaches along with assistive and participatory teaching through a network of media making clubs.

One study also revealed that British born Chinese children require age-appropriate stories that use a lot more simplified language to interpret stories compared to Chinese born children. Children's comprehension of stories also does not vary between physical and digital storybook reading, although parent-child engagement with storybooks may differ as a function of the platform (Lauricella et al., 2014; Eisenberg, 2009; Horn et al., 2013; Horn, 2013). One argument is that it is advantageous to present strong recognizable cultural forms in novel technological interactions to help children structure their interactions around familiar artifacts. This helps in the activation of cognitive, physical, and emotional resources of parents and children with new tasks. This informal learning activity also supports emerging computational literacy skills in a fun and engaging way for children. The affordances of digital storytelling have also been experimented with a group of high school Alaska native youth to promote indigenous voices and encourage reflection (Coenraad, 2019).

4 Discussion

This review summarizes key research insights focusing on the cultural factors that influence children's perception of play and how these findings are employed in co-creating better play experiences for and with children in the digital gaming platforms.

Culture specific cognitive styles have a major role to play when designing games for children from different cultures. Play activities vary through children's early cognitive development stages which determines how they engage with various game tasks and consider them to be significant or not. Decisions made by children in cooperative game tasks is also influenced by cultures. Collective cultures nurture equal opportunities while undermining the game's learning objectives. This is a key insight that designers need to consider when designing inclusive games and winning strategies across multiple cultural demographics. Again, research work also explores food practices and traditional methods like calligraphy to draw inspiration for novel interaction with technology interfaces. The idea that usability testing of novel interfaces should be expanded to blend with cultural practices is a key step towards designing more inclusive applications. Some of the research articles focused more on technology and computational applications in a broad sense. However, they are also applicable to games and online collaborative gamer communities. Another take away from the first list of review articles is to leverage children's natural inclination to play for better design of engaging education games.

The next set of review articles on games as a medium for cultural representation brings up a variety of discussions on the relationship between games and culture exploration. Researchers have explored participatory environments and augmented reality technologies to create opportunities for children to explore cultures beyond their own immediate surroundings. Often children are confined to their physical surroundings and are unaware of global cultures beyond their own geographic limits. Interactive games provide mechanics to reward cultural explorations beyond the constraints of time and space. Games also provide children with an opportunity to collaborate online with children from other cultures. Computer skills and level of gaming experience play a role in the engagement level of children with games. This engagement varies between children from different cultures. However, adapting methodologies to regional cultural settings can provide the necessary support for children from technology deprived regions to develop these skills over a short period of time.

Maker culture and participatory design (Walsh et al., 2016; Kafai, 2010) are key approaches that researchers have explored in digital character design and cultural representation. Children empathizing with other children's perspectives through persona building activities is a great way to understand each other's emotional needs, likings, and dislikes. The research articles in this review list also emphasize the blend of digital and tangible artifacts and cultural forms for better engagement with children. Digital pets in virtual spaces with tangible extensions are a great way to experiment children's engagement with toys and digital characters. Translation of playful interaction with tangible toys into transmedia storytelling and digital character interaction is one direction that the community can conduct further research work. This will help researchers understand the significance of embodied learning experiences with physical artifacts in cultural contexts that extend into digital spaces.

Finally, narratives are envisioned by researchers as powerful tools in empowering children to share life experiences. There is a lot of opportunities for children to be culturally aware and develop empathy through reflection in the game design process. Children, when given the agency to make decisions about narratives and related elements in the game design process, helps them appreciate the significance of cultural practices. Digital storytelling is also a learning tool in cross-cultural settings where children learn by sharing videos of stories and create bonds by investigating problems together through collaborative story building. Studies show that cultural representation in digital mediums foster seamless engagement between traditional storytelling methods and digital counterparts. Further work in this area can investigate the affordances of digital storytelling and the inclusion of cultural forms for better narrative engagement.

5 Conclusion and Future Work

This review article highlights the major research findings and design implications on the major cultural factors that influence children's play perceptions and how these findings can help co-create digital game technology platforms for and with children. The review also shows that further work can be done in this specialized area as there are huge opportunities for researchers and practitioners to partner with children and co-create gaming content that is meaningful to them and represents their everyday lived experiences. It also provides a connection for children from different parts of the world to share experiences, empathize with other children and understand diverse perspectives.

The research community can also benefit by probing deeper into the effectiveness of incorporating cultural artifacts in game narratives and digital character representations. Moving beyond physical attributes, it will be interesting to understand the concept of cultural authenticity in gameplay interactions from a child's perspective. Evaluating culturally critical designs in games can help bridge the divide between gaming content created for children in different demographics. Games have a huge impact on children's learning and cultural understanding of self and other children. Building authentic design frameworks that support children as cultural ambassadors and developing design guidelines that are culturally sensitive can help practitioners create more child-centric culturally authentic games. This will lead to more engaging experiences for children interacting with games for both educational and entertainment purposes.

References

Lauricella, A.R., Barr, R., Calvert, S.L.: Parent-child interactions during traditional and computer storybook reading for children's comprehension. Int. J. Child-Comp. Interact. 2(1), 17–25 (2014). https://doi.org/10.1016/j.ijcci.2014.07.001

Gomes, A., Oh, H., Chisik, Y., Chen, M.: Ilha Musical: a CAVE for nurturing cultural appreciation. In: Proceedings of the 11th International Conference on Interaction Design and Children (IDC 2012), pp. 232–235. Association for Computing Machinery, New York (2012). https://doi.org/10.1145/2307096.2307133

Griffith, A., Vigne, F., McCormick, J., Kovach, S.: Culture box: education app on the world through history and time. In: Proceedings of the 17th ACM Conference on Interaction Design and Children (IDC 2018), pp. 757–760. Association for Computing Machinery, New York (2018). https://doi.org/10.1145/3202185.3214122

Benton, L., Vasalou, A., Gooch, D., Khaled, R.: Understanding and fostering children's storytelling during game narrative design. In: Proceedings of the 2014 Conference on Interaction Design and Children, pp. 301–304 (2014)

O'Keefe, B., Benyon, D.: Using the blended spaces framework to design heritage stories with schoolchildren. Int. J. Child-Comp. Interact. 6(C), 7–16 (2015). https://doi.org/10.1016/j.ijcci.2016.02.001

Ang, C.S., Rao, G.R.K.: Computer game theories for designing motivating educational software: a survey study. Int. J. E-Learn. 7(2), 181–199 (2008)

Anastasiou, D., Maquil, V., Ras, E., Fal, M.: Design implications for a user study on a tangible tabletop. In: Proceedings of the 15th International Conference on Interaction Design and Children (IDC 2016), pp. 499–505. Association for Computing Machinery, New York (2016). https://doi-org.proxyiub.uits.iu.edu/10.1145/2930674.2935982

Xu, D., Nicholson, I.: Multimedia software to motivate ethnic minority children to learn about their culture and language of origin. In: Proceedings of the 2003 Conference on Interaction Design and Children (IDC 2003), p. 159. Association for Computing Machinery, New York (2003). https://doi-org.proxyiub.uits.iu.edu/10.1145/953536.953569

Muravevskaia, E., Tavassoli, F., Gardner-McCune, C.: Developing children's cultural awareness and empathy through games and fairy tales. In: Proceedings of the 15th International Conference on Interaction Design and Children (IDC 2016), pp. 701–706. Association for Computing Machinery, New York (2016). https://doi.org/10.1145/2930674.2935998

Carter, E.J., Mahler, M., Landlord, M., McIntosh, K., Hodgins, J.K.: Designing animated characters for children of different ages. In: Proceedings of the 15th International Conference on Interaction Design and Children, pp. 421–427 (2016)

Campos, F., Blikstein, P., Azhar, A.: The conference of the birds: a collaborative storytelling environment for literacy development. In: Proceedings of the 2017 Conference on Interaction Design and Children (IDC 2017), pp. 729–732. Association for Computing Machinery, New York (2017). https://doi-org.proxyiub.uits.iu.edu/10.1145/3078072.3091991

Grundy, C., Pemberton, L., Morris, R.: Characters as agents for the co-design process. In: Proceedings of the 11th International Conference on Interaction Design and Children, pp. 180–183 (2012)

Gelderblom, H.: Designing software for young children: theoretically grounded guidelines. In: Proceedings of the 2004 Conference on Interaction Design and Children: Building a Community. IDC 2004, pp. 121–122. Association for Computing Machinery, New York (2004). https://doi-org.proxyiub.uits.iu.edu/10.1145/1017833.1017851

Karoff, H., Johansen, S.L.: Materiality, practice, body. In: Proceedings of the 8th International Conference on Interaction Design and Children (IDC 2009), pp. 238–241. Association for Computing Machinery, New York (2009). https://doi-org.proxyiub.uits.iu.edu/10.1145/1551788.1551840

Itenge-Wheeler, H., Winschiers-Theophilus, H., Soro, A., Brereton, M.: Child designers creating personas to diversify design perspectives and concepts for their own technology enhanced library. In: Proceedings of the 17th ACM Conference on Interaction Design and Children (IDC 2018), pp. 381–388. Association for Computing Machinery, New York (2018). https://doi-org.proxyiub.uits.iu.edu/10.1145/3202185.3202760

Itenge-Wheeler, H., Winschiers-Theophilus, H., Soro, A., Brereton, M.: Child designers creating personas to diversify design perspectives and concepts for their own technology enhanced library. In: Proceedings of the 17th ACM Conference on Interaction Design and Children, pp. 381–388 (2018)

Gray, J.H., Reardon, E., Kotler, J.A.: Designing for parasocial relationships and learning: linear video, interactive media, and artificial intelligence. In: Proceedings of the 2017 Conference on Interaction Design and Children, pp. 227–237 (2017l)

Multisilta, J., Niemi, H., Hamilton, E.: Children designing videos: tools, pedagogical models, and best practices for digital storytelling and media-making in the classroom. In: Proceedings of the 2017 Conference on Interaction Design and Children (IDC 2017), pp. 693–696. Association for Computing Machinery, New York (2017). https://doi-org.proxyiub.uits.iu.edu/10.1145/3078072.3091982

McBeath, J.K., Durán, R.P., Harlow, D.B.: Not my gumdrop buttons! youth tool use in designing an electronic Shrek-themed bean bag toss. In: Proceedings of the 2017 Conference on Interaction Design and Children (IDC 2017), pp. 61–72. Association for Computing Machinery, New York (2017). https://doi-org.proxyiub.uits.iu.edu/10.1145/3078072.3079721

Silver, J.: Awakening to make methodology: the metamorphosis of a curious caterpillar. In: Proceedings of the 8th International Conference on Interaction Design and Children (IDC 2009), pp. 242–245. Association for Computing Machinery, New York (2009). https://doi-org.proxyiub.uits.iu.edu/10.1145/1551788.1551841

Ringland, K.E., Boyd, L., Faucett, H., Cullen, A.L.L., Hayes, G.R.: Making in minecraft: a means of self-expression for youth with Autism. In: Proceedings of the 2017 Conference on Interaction Design and Children (IDC 2017), pp. 340–345. Association for Computing Machinery, New York (2017). https://doi-org.proxyiub.uits.iu.edu/10.1145/3078072.3079749

Deater-Deckard, K., El Mallah, S., Chang, M., Evans, M.A., Norton, A.: Student behavioral engagement during mathematics educational video game instruction with 11–14-year-olds. Int. J. Child-Comp. Interact. **2**(3), 101–108 (2014). https://doi.org/10.1016/j.ijcci.2014.08.001

Benton, L., Johnson, H.: Widening participation in technology design. Int. J. Child-Comp. Interact. **3**(C), 23–40 (2015)

DuMont, M., Lee, V.R.: Material pets, virtual spaces, isolated designers: how collaboration may be unintentionally constrained in the design of tangible computational crafts. In: Proceedings of the 11th International Conference on Interaction Design and Children (IDC 2012), pp. 244–247. Association for Computing Machinery, New York (2012). https://doi-org.proxyiub.uits.iu.edu/10.1145/2307096.2307136

Bers, M.U.: The Seymour test. Int. J. Child-Comp. Interact. **14**(C), 10–14 (2017). https://doi.org/10.1016/j.ijcci.2017.06.004

Coenraad, M.: Youth design of digital stories to promote indigenous voices. In: Proceedings of the 18th ACM International Conference on Interaction Design and Children (IDC 2019), pp. 728–731. Association for Computing Machinery, New York (2019). https://doi-org.proxyiub.uits.iu.edu/10.1145/3311927.3325353

Eisenberg, M., Elumeze, N., MacFerrin, M., Buechley, L.: Children's programming, reconsidered: settings, stuff, and surfaces. In Proceedings of the 8th International Conference on Interaction Design and Children (IDC 2009), pp. Association for Computing Machinery, New York, NY, USA, 1–8. https://doi-org.proxyiub.uits.iu.edu/10.1145/1551788.1551790

Horn, M.S., Al Sulaiman, S., Koh, J.: Translating Roberto to Omar: computational literacy, sticker-books, and cultural forms. In Proceedings of the 12th International Conference on Interaction Design and Children (IDC 2013), pp. 120–127. Association for Computing Machinery, New York (2013). https://doi-org.proxyiub.uits.iu.edu/10.1145/2485760.2485773

Horn, M.S.: Interaction design, books, and cultural forms. In: Proceedings of the 12th International Conference on Interaction Design and Children (IDC 2013), pp. 628–631. Association for Computing Machinery, New York (2013). https://doi-org.proxyiub.uits.iu.edu/10.1145/2485760.2485892

Kosmyna, N., Gross, A., Maes, P.: "The thinking cap 2.0": preliminary study on fostering growth mindset of children by means of electroencephalography and perceived magic using artifacts from fictional sci-fi universes. In Proceedings of the Interaction Design and Children Conference (IDC 2020), pp. 458–469. Association for Computing Machinery, New York (2020). https://doi-org.proxyiub.uits.iu.edu/10.1145/3392063.3394424

Apostolellis, P., Bowman, D.A.: Small group learning with games in museums: effects of interactivity as mediated by cultural differences. In: Proceedings of the 14th International Conference on Interaction Design and Children (IDC 2015), pp. 160–169. Association for Computing Machinery, New York (2015). https://doi-org.proxyiub.uits.iu.edu/10.1145/2771839.2771856

Isbell, R., Raines, S.: Creativity and the arts with young children. Cengage Learning (2012)

Chu, S.L., Quek, F.: Things to imagine with: designing for the child's creativity. In: Proceedings of the 12th International Conference on Interaction Design and Children (IDC 2013), pp. 261–264. Association for Computing Machinery, New York (2013). https://doi-org.proxyiub.uits.iu.edu/10.1145/2485760.2485793

Chu, S.L., Quek, F., Bhangaonkar, S., Ging, A.B., Sridharamurthy, K.: Making the maker. Int. J. Child-Comp. Interact. **5**(C), 11–19 (2015). https://doi.org/10.1016/j.ijcci.2015.08.002

Sharma, S., Kallioniemi, P., Hakulinen, J., Keskinen, T., Turunen, M.: Exploring globally inclusive online collaboration for Indian and Finnish schoolchildren. In: Proceedings of the 18th

ACM International Conference on Interaction Design and Children (IDC 2019), pp. 153–160. Association for Computing Machinery, New York (2019). https://doi.org/10.1145/3311927. 3323119

Sharma, S., Kallioniemi, P., Heimonen, T., Hakulinen, J., Turunen, M., Keskinen, T.: Overcoming socio-technical challenges for cross-cultural collaborative applications. In: Proceedings of the 17th ACM Conference on Interaction Design and Children (IDC 2018), pp. 325–336. Association for Computing Machinery, New York (2018). https://doi.org/10.1145/3202185. 3202730

Charoenying, T.: Accountable game designs for classroom learning. In: Proceedings of the 7th International Conference on Interaction Design and Children (IDC 2008), pp. 1–5. Association for Computing Machinery, New York (2008). https://doi-org.proxyiub.uits.iu.edu/10.1145/146 3689.1463703

Walsh, G., Donahue, C., Pease, Z.: Inclusive co-design within a three-dimensional game environment. In: Proceedings of the 15th International Conference on Interaction Design and Children, pp. 1–10 (2016)

Kafai, Y.B., Peppler, K.A., Burke, Q., Moore, M., Glosson, D.: Fröbel's forgotten gift: textile construction kits as pathways into play, design and computation. In: Proceedings of the 9th International Conference on Interaction Design and Children (IDC 2010), pp. 214–217. Association for Computing Machinery, New York (2010). https://doi-org.proxyiub.uits.iu.edu/10. 1145/1810543.1810574

Chisik, Y., Bertran, F.A., Schaper, M.-M., Segura, E.M., Vidal, L.T., Wilde, D.: Chasing play potentials in food culture: embracing children's perspectives. In: Proceedings of the 2020 ACM Interaction Design and Children Conference: Extended Abstracts (IDC 2020), pp. 46–53. Association for Computing Machinery, New York (2020). https://doi-org.proxyiub.uits.iu. edu/10.1145/3397617.3398062

Kim, Y.: Oriental well-being design. In: Proceedings of the 9th International Conference on Interaction Design and Children (IDC 2010), pp. 286–289. Association for Computing Machinery, New York (2010). https://doi-org.proxyiub.uits.iu.edu/10.1145/1810543.1810593

Head and Shoulder (e)Sports Event Organization Tools: A User-Based Study

George Margetis[1]([⊠]) [iD], Eirini Sykianaki[1], Ioannis Chatzakis[1],
Emmanouil Adamakis[1] [iD], Stavroula Ntoa[1] [iD], Konstantinos C. Apostolakis[1] [iD],
Ioannis Markopoulos[3], and Constantine Stephanidis[1,2] [iD]

[1] Institute of Computer Science, Foundation for Research and Technology—Hellas (FORTH),
70013 Heraklion, Crete, Greece
{gmarget,eirinisi,johnhatz,madamakis,stant,kapostol,
cs}@ics.forth.gr
[2] University of Crete, Heraklion, Crete, Greece
[3] NOVA, Athens, Greece
ioannis.markopoulos@novaict.gr

Abstract. Driving engagement among the numerous (e)sports broadcasts requires professionals to discover innovative methods to maintain audience interest. Creating a compelling narrative for (e)sports events is a highly effective strategy for achieving desired outcomes. In this paper, a suite of tools for (e)sports professionals is presented, aimed at facilitating transmedia storytelling before, during, and after the event based on cross-channel narratives. Through these tools, professionals can collaboratively create graphics and posts, generate transmedia storytelling narratives, display graphic overlays in live streams, and access enriching information to elevate their commentary. The tools have been evaluated and improved to meet professionals' needs through two phases and have also been validated in realistic eSports game scenarios.

Keywords: Transmedia storytelling · Data-driven production · (e)Sports broadcasting

1 Introduction

In the last few years, sports broadcasting has experienced rapid growth and currently generates more revenue than ticket sales at stadiums [1]. Consequently, sports have become one of the most valuable forms of broadcast entertainment. Alongside, esports viewership and professionals' salaries have reached the same level as those in traditional professional sports [2]. With eSports' growth, traditional sports are increasingly integrating new technologies, such as computerized broadcasting, including internet streaming [3]. Initially, the live stream experience used to be similar to a television broadcast, but later advancements led to a new type of non-linear broadcasting, featuring user-generated content with high interaction between creators and viewers [4].

J. Y. C. Chen et al. (Eds.): HCII 2024, LNCS 15377, pp. 352–372, 2025.
https://doi.org/10.1007/978-3-031-76812-5_24

However, with so much content being provided through numerous TV channels and internet streaming platforms, it is difficult to attract a large viewership for a single broadcast [5]. Transmedia storytelling addresses this issue by creating cohesive narratives across different platforms and unifying audiences around a shared narrative experience. For example, in the field of sports and eSports, collectively referred to as (e)sports, instead of just streaming the games, a complete narrative can be created by providing information about players and teams through commentary and social media posts. This would engage viewers more with the event and provide greater entertainment [6, 7].

Therefore, the production teams must create a captivating narrative supporting audience engagement before, during, and after the event following a head-and-shoulder programming approach [8], which ensures that the audience's interest remains undiminished before-during-after the event. Commentary and visual techniques, such as graphic overlays, can contribute to achieving this objective [9]. Commentators not only enhance the entertainment value of an event but also significantly shape viewers' perceptions of it [10]. Hence, they need timely access to information that can assist them in composing a compelling narrative. Furthermore, it has been proven that even simple data-driven graphical overlays can significantly improve both the commentary and the quality of coverage [11]. Thus, streamlining graphics production and seamlessly integrating them into live streams can yield significant value.

In this paper, we present a suite of tools specifically designed for (e)sports broadcasting teams, aimed at assisting professionals in optimizing their performance. The suite comprises three tools designed to support different aspects of (e)sports production. Starting with the transmedia storytelling platform, which aids professionals in scheduling posts and conveying multimedia messages to fans and interested audiences, across various media channels, an engaging event storytelling experience is commenced. The storytelling platform comprises three different management environments (i.e., for graphic generation, social media post creation, and event production). Additionally, it enables professional teams to collaboratively create dynamic graphics with data-driven content, ready-to-use or customizable post templates, and the event timeline, with other professionals (e.g., artists, graphics designers, social media content creators) or just fans. The second tool is the data-driven graphics director dashboard, which allows the production crew to display graphic overlays with data-driven information overlayed on the live stream. The last tool discussed is the data-driven graphics commentator dashboard, which provides professionals with insights about an ongoing game, useful for enhancing the commentary, filling pauses, and ensuring no important moments go uncommented.

The rest of the paper is stranded as follows: Sect. 2 provides an overview of related works, Sect. 3 presents the suite of tools for (e)sports professionals, Sect. 4 elaborates on the way the tools were implemented, Sect. 5 discusses the procedures and outcomes of the evaluation and validation processes, and Sect. 6 concludes the study.

2   Related Work

In recent years, research has focused more and more on fostering (e)sports user experience [12, 13]. Especially during the COVID-19 pandemic, the production of (e)sports media proved compelling in terms of maintaining viewership [14]. Conversely, despite the increased demand for enticing (e)sports online events, a mere sparsity of works aiming to utilize technology for developing tools that assist broadcasting professionals emerged, and an even more limited number of works focused on comprehensive technology-driven solutions appeared aiming at integrating various aspects of production.

An example of technology creating visuals for esports events is presented by Block et al. [11], initially introduced as Echo. It is a data-driven tool that utilises historical data to identify highlights in live esports games and automatically converts them into graphics that are eventually displayed to the audience. Block was evolved to Echo Show and included in the Echo Suite software along with its extension, Echo NE, employing an AI-driven engine that generates personalized viewer experiences [15].

Arguably, more research tools have been developed for supporting the live casting of (e)sports events. For example, MELISA [16] is a platform for program directors to display interactive, real-time data within game scenes for advertising and live gaming betting purposes. Similarly, Weavr Companion [17] is a mobile application that turns real-time game data into interactive stories and visualizations for esports viewers. Another solution to help viewers better understand games and support esports commentators was introduced by Wang and Yoshinaga [18], towards using game data to generate textual commentary. Moreover, Zhi et al. [19] presented two prototypes for esports, one targeting sportswriters to help them rapidly extract essential game information for reports or recaps and the other aiming at fans to enhance their game-viewing experience and facilitate data-driven commentary.

The topics of engaging narrative and transmedia storytelling for (e)sports are still under-researched. However, some works are worth mentioning, such as PISTE [20], which enables users to import templates created manually or online using the PISTE Template Editor, which is then parsed by the Dynamic Scene Generator integrating virtual object models and animation data from video streams, and utilizes operator parameters to produce virtual scene representations. Moreover, Jeffery-Poulter [21] discusses the creation of flexible templates that can be posted across multiple platforms. Finally, Gürel et al. [22] examine how transmedia storytelling can shape media content and narratives.

Although some research efforts for supporting (e)sports events production, in terms of programming and engaging audience participation, already exist [23–25], to the best of our knowledge, none presents a comprehensive approach that fosters a head-and-shoulder production life-cycle as a continuous transmedia storytelling approach. In this respect, we present an (e)sports toolkit that brings together (e)Sports professionals, other professionals, and (e)sports communities for the creation of non-linear (e)sports content. The presented work is the evolution of the color casting and direction tools introduced in [26], offering a solution for streamlining established workflows and managing multiple scenes and graphics from a single point of access for (e)sports events.

3   System Overview

A human-centered design approach [27, 28] was followed to create the suite of tools for (e)sports professionals. In particular, the target users and the context of use were identified. Then, the user requirements were specified in collaboration with (e)sports professionals during online workshops. Based on these requirements and the information collected, the first mockups were designed. Following this, the mockups were evaluated against the requirements, and changes were made. This process was repeated until the mockups met the requirements, at which point implementation began.

The implemented (e)sports toolkit that emerged from this process includes: (i) the transmedia storytelling platform, (ii) the data-driven graphics director dashboard, and (iii) the data-driven graphics commentator dashboard. In the next sections, the description of each tool is provided.

3.1 Transmedia Storytelling Platform

The transmedia storytelling platform enables professionals to streamline the process of scheduling (e)sports events to facilitate a smooth flow before, during, and after the live event. It is a collaborative platform that allows broadcast teams to work together on scheduling and managing (e)sports events. Moreover, it supports the creation of transmedia storytelling narratives for (e)sports events across multiple media channels, while a diversity of stakeholders, professionals, and fans, can design dynamic graphics that are used as overlayed information in the live stream media channels or as content for the transmedia storytelling narratives. The aforementioned functionalities which are provided to the users through a dashboard are presented below.

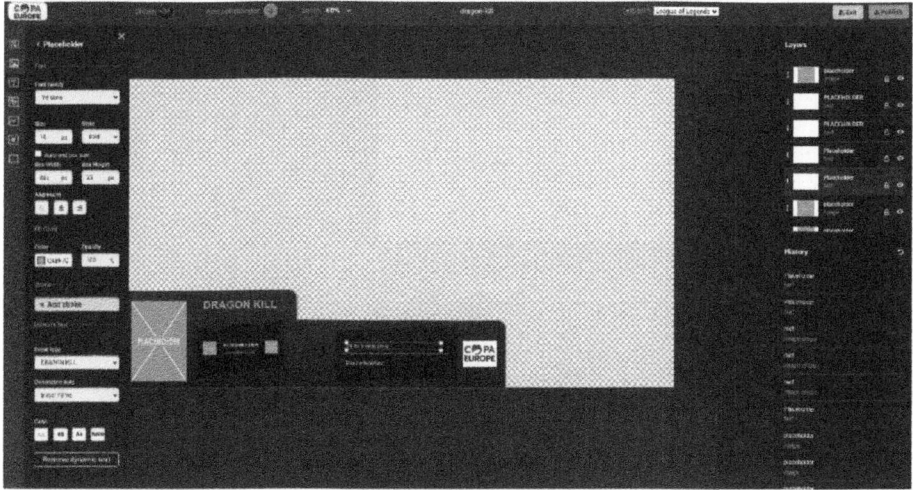

Fig. 1. The graphics editor while editing dynamic text.

Graphics Editor. The graphics editor allows users to build graphics with dynamic data-driven content that is being updated automatically in real-time (e.g., a scoreboard graphic that displays the game score live). Professionals can use the editor to create simple graphics from scratch or they can edit premade graphics, since they likely already work with their advanced editing tools, to incorporate dynamic data-driven content, which is the innovative feature of the editor.

To create or edit graphics using the platform, users have at their disposal fundamental editing features, such as canvas editing, as well as the ability to add images, text, shapes, charts, stickers, and frames. Users can also modify various style properties of the added components (e.g., text color, add stoke, image dimensions), and make the text, images, and charts dynamic so that they update their content in real-time during the event. To make a component dynamic, users need to add a placeholder at their desired location on the canvas and style it as they wish (see Fig. 1). Then they have to select the type of data-driven event (e.g., first blood) and the corresponding data they wish to showcase instead of the placeholder (e.g., the name of the player who achieved the first blood). Another important aspect of the platform is that it promotes collaboration. Two or more users can work simultaneously to create a graphic.

The created content can be published on the platform and be available for use for a fee. To this end, (e)sports producers can purchase them and use them as-is or customize them according to their preferences. For each content created and made available on the platform, creators can view information and statistics about revenue, ratings, buyers, and projects (i.e., events and posts) in which it has been included. On the other hand, buyers can rate the content and report it in case of any violations of the community rules.

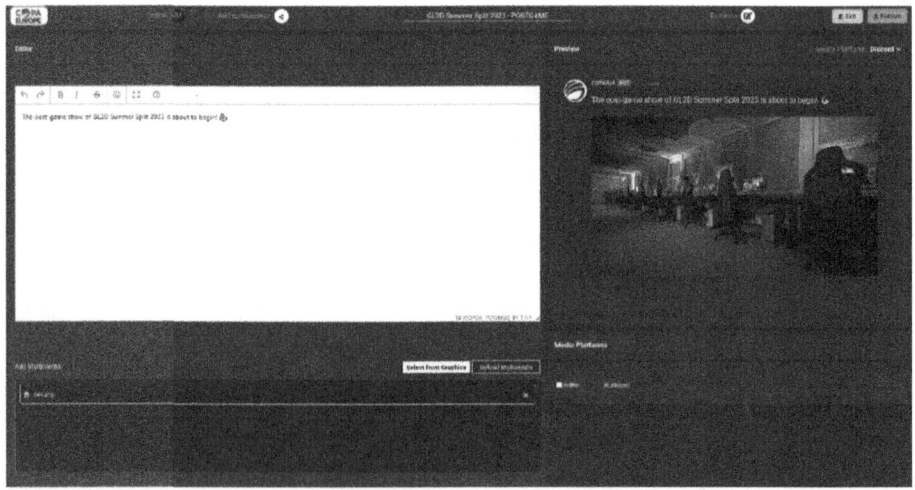

Fig. 2. The post editor.

Post Editor. The post editor can assist professionals in creating and scheduling posts to be published on different social media channels. The tool can be used for creating fully-fledged posts or just templates that are quick and easy to edit during the live event. Through the tool, users can schedule when and to which media channels the post will be published and preview how it will look on each one as they make changes.

The available editing features depend on the capabilities of the selected publishing channels, but in general, the post editor resembles a text editor (see Fig. 2). It allows users to write and edit text by selecting paragraph style, font family, background color, text decoration (i.e., bold, italic, underline, and strikethrough), and adding bullets, numbering, decreased or increased indent, hyperlinks, emoticons, and polls. Moreover, users can add multimedia to their posts by uploading files from their devices or browsing through the platform to select graphics they have already created.

Similar to the graphics editor, the post editor is a collaborative tool. Users can simultaneously collaborate to create a post as a team. Also, professionals can sell their posts to the community for other members to use as-is or customized for their events. Statistics are once again available regarding the published posts, and buyers can rate or, if necessary, report any post.

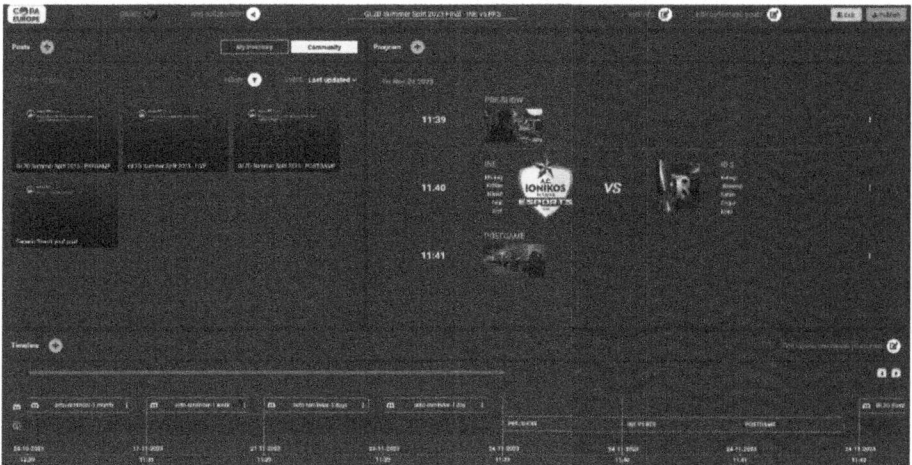

Fig. 3. The event editor.

Event Editor. The event editor enables professionals to create stories that contribute to a transmedia storytelling narrative around an event and post them on different social media channels. Through the platform, users can specify automated posts and timelines indicating when and where to post stories about the event. It determines the entire scheduling and event flow, offering numerous automations.

Through the provided timeline users can schedule posts for specific days, times, and social media channels (see Fig. 3), before, during, or after the event happens. These posts can be selected from their inventory, which consists of posts created in the post editor, or can be purchased from the community. Users can also promptly create or edit posts directly within the event editor, otherwise, they can use the post editor to access more advanced options. Furthermore, they can add automatic posts with event reminders, highlights, and statistics. For each post, they have to select the media platforms on which it is going to be published, the content format (e.g., image, text, video), and whether they prefer automatic publication or if they want to approve it before it goes live. In the case of reminders, they also need to specify the time (e.g., one day before the event), while for highlights and statistics, the content type (e.g., best moments, funny moments, achievements, past performance, global high scores). As a result, the system will automatically generate posts based on users' preferences and it will directly add them to the timeline or ask for approval through a popup.

In addition to the timeline, the event schedule can be also customized through the event editor. More specifically, users can add scheduled entries, such as interviews, podcasts, or games, to the program. Each entry consists of a title and an image, or in the case of a game, team names, players, and logos.

Professionals can collaboratively use the platform to schedule the event flow before-hand, but they can also edit and monitor the timeline during the event. While the event is ongoing, live feedback is displayed on the editor, including statistics and information about user engagement (e.g., number of viewers, ratings, mentions). On the event's game page, even more information is available, such as revenue charts and viewer demographics.

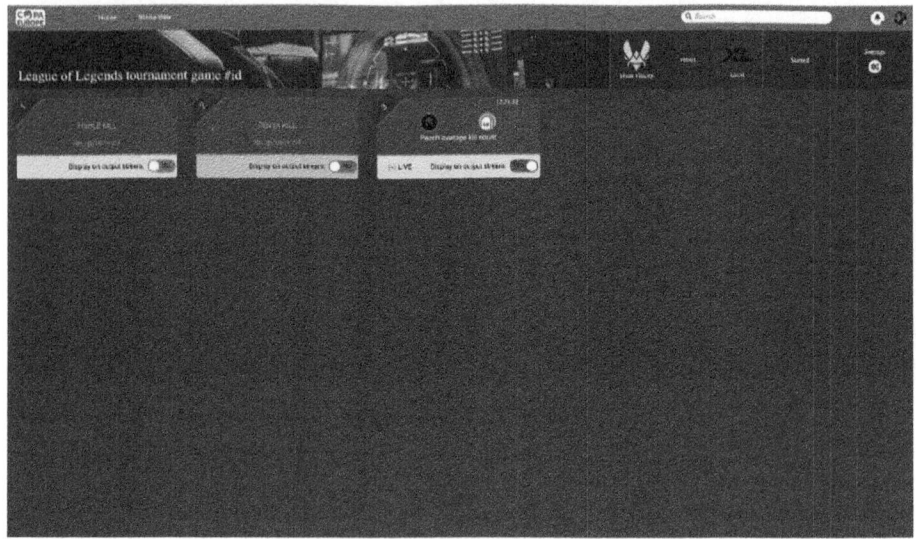

Fig. 4. The data-driven graphics director dashboard.

3.2 Data-Driven Graphics Director Dashboard

The data-driven graphics director dashboard is a web-based application that aims to support directorial teams of (e)sports events. Directors using the dashboard can manage the data-driven graphics and select the scenes they will be displayed on (see Fig. 4).

The dashboard is customizable to the directors' preferences, who can determine the scenes they want to monitor during the event and as a result, what should be displayed on the dashboard. Each scene is defined by the type of action occurring in the game (e.g., a triple kill) and the corresponding graphic that can be used to visualize it. Users can also prioritize the scenes based on their importance using color coding (i.e., green for high, purple for medium, and yellow for low) and enable or disable automatic display on the screen when the defined action takes place.

Each time an action included in a scene occurs, its card is highlighted to enhance visibility. The director can activate at any time the scene of which the graphic will be displayed as an overlay in the livestream. Moreover, users can adjust how long a newly activated scene remains highlighted and an activated graphic is displayed.

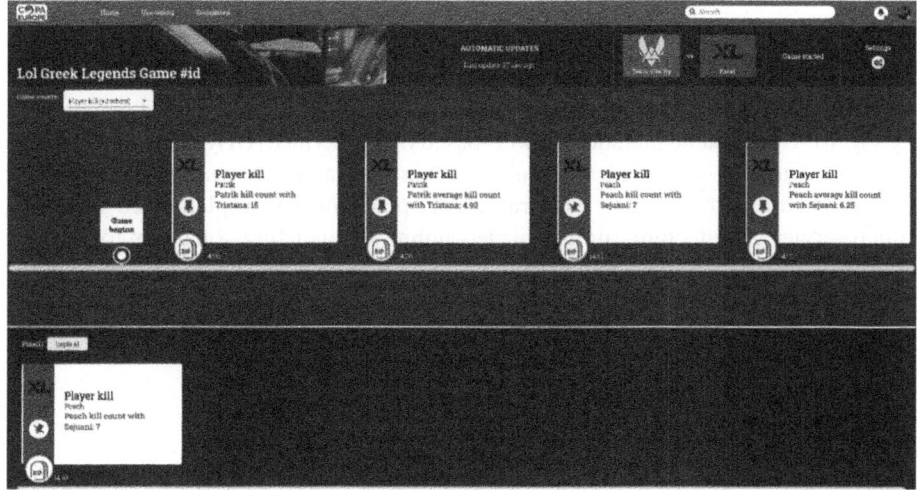

Fig. 5. The data-driven graphics commentator dashboard.

3.3 Data-Driven Graphics Commentator Dashboard

The data-driven graphics commentator dashboard is a web-based application that assists the commentator team during live streams of (e)sports events. The dashboard provides real-time data about ongoing events to professionals who may be commentators, spotters (individuals who identify the player or players involved in a particular action), or statsmen (the crew responsible for keeping the game statistics). The provided data is enriched with additional information that enhances the commentary on the event. For example, when a player scores a goal, the history of the goal ratio for the player can be displayed.

Through the dashboard, users can filter the displayed data based on the game events (e.g., show only records related to a particular event type, such as penalties for football or pentakills for League of Legends tournaments) and pin records they intend to comment on later for quick access (see Fig. 5). Furthermore, they can select whether they want the dashboard to be updated manually by pressing the corresponding button or automatically when new information becomes available.

Initially, the system presents system-generated information on the dashboard, but users can further customize it and specify what they would like to be informed about. To showcase tailored information, they should select the type of game events they are interested in, and for each one, the related statistics to be displayed. Finally, they can choose which of them will be automatically pinned.

4   Implementation

The following sections provide detailed information about the implementation of the (e)sports toolkit.

4.1 Transmedia Storytelling Platform

The transmedia storytelling platform comprises the frontend and backend components (see Fig. 6). The frontend includes the web-based User Interface (UI) of the tool, while the backend includes the technical components that provide all the necessary functionalities to the frontend of the system. The transmedia platform was implemented following a microservice architecture, aiming at decoupling distinct functionalities to separate services, while at the same time providing the set of advanced functionalities required from the frontend of the platform.

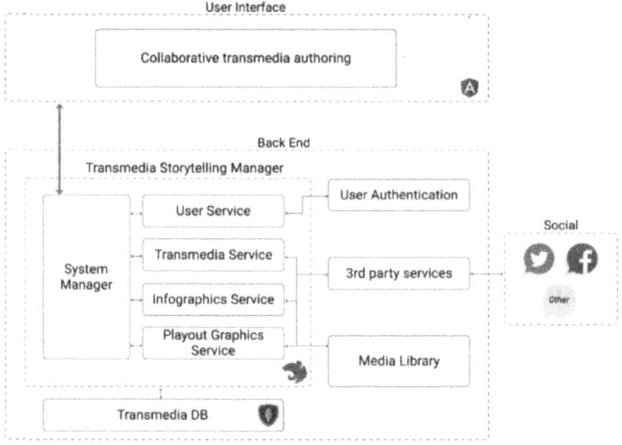

Fig. 6. Transmedia storytelling platform system architecture.

The UI of the transmedia platform was implemented as a Single Page Application (SPA), offering a desktop-application-like experience while at the same enabling its easy deployment and operation on most end-user computers that support a web browser.

Regarding the backend of the transmedia platform, it comprises the Transmedia Storytelling Manager as well as the Transmedia Database (DB), and the Media Library. The Transmedia Manager, through its System Manager component, coordinates all the provided services and acts as a mediator between the backend services and the frontend clients through a REST API gateway, offering a single point of entry. The backend services are responsible for processing the information related to the functionalities of the platform, the communication with the Transmedia DB and Media Library, as well as the communication with the User Authorization and other third-party services, including social media.

Online collaboration between users provided by the platform is achieved with the use of the User Service of the Transmedia Manager, which coordinates and synchronizes the input/output of different web clients operated by various users who edit the same content so that they can view the result of the other users' actions in real-time. The communication between the platform and the users' web browsers is achieved through Web Sockets. Any action performed by a user is first processed by the User Service, which is responsible for communication with other services that apply the changes to the content. Afterward, the results are propagated to the other browsers as a changed state event to update the rendered content. This way, all the online collaborators can view the latest version of the content, without losing any of their local changes, ensuring consistent content parallel editing. Furthermore, a common history of actions is also provided, with users being able to revert changes made either by them or by other users.

4.2 Data-Driven Graphics System

The data-driven graphics system comprises three components (Fig. 7): the data-driven graphics director dashboard, the data-driven graphics commentator dashboard, and the decision-making back-end server. The functionality of the first two components, which constitute the front end of this tool has already been described in the previous sections.

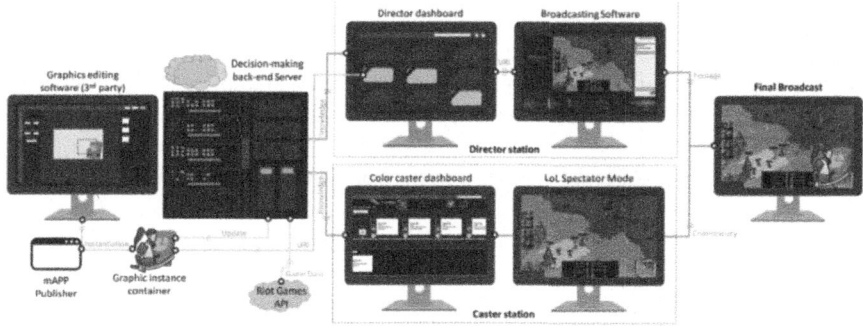

Fig. 7. Data-driven graphics architecture.

These two dashboards have been developed in a way similar to the transmedia storytelling platform UI implementation as a SPA. Essentially, both dashboards connect to the same decision-making back-end server, via web socket connections, which enable near-immediate updates for the contents displayed on both dashboards. Each dashboard upon connecting to the back-end server, transmits the game ID it expects to receive data for. When an event occurs in the game with the ID specified during the initial "handshake", the back-end server transmits over the web sockets an update object, containing the new data that needs to appear to the user, as well as the game ID based on which the dashboards will discern messages that are meant to be rendered and ones that can be discarded. The back-end server has been developed using Node.js[1] and a rudimentary MongoDB database. The server is responsible for connecting to the RIOT Games Tournament Realm API[2] and polling for game event updates every half a second. The connection is enabled via REST API and with each request the game ID, a pagination token, and the authentication token are supplied. Upon a dashboard connecting to the server, an asynchronous thread is generated, which is responsible for querying data from the API for the requested game ID every half a second. In case the game ID already exists in a running thread, no additional thread is created since the data retrieved will be broadcasted to all clients connected to the specific socket and each additional client requesting the data will receive the data and update the UI accordingly.

Additionally, for each game ID that a thread is running for, a unique entry is created in a hash map (with the game ID as a key) which contains an array of all data shared between the backend server and the dashboard instance(s) that have requested the specific game ID. In this manner, each new client (dashboard instance) that connects can receive the entire history of data that has been shared for this game thus far.

Furthermore, in case a user decides to "pin" a statistic on the dashboard, a new entry is created in the database which links the user ID, who pinned the statistic, with a unique identifier of the statistic. Consequently, when a user reloads their commentator dashboard page two actions are taking place automatically upon connection of the dashboard to the back-end. Firstly, the entire history of the game event-based statistics will be reloaded in the order they occurred, and secondly, pinned statistics are retrieved from the database and shared with any dashboard that has just connected and requested such information.

Finally, concurrently with the statistic retrieval for a specific game event, the data of the event are forwarded to the Graphics Instance Container. The Graphics Instance Container is responsible for updating the graphics that are attached to each scene card of the director dashboard. After the pertinent graphic related to the game event has been updated, a signal is transmitted to the director dashboard, to highlight the appropriate scene cards.

While both the frontend tools connect to the backend server, the director dashboard and the commentator dashboard intercommunications are quite different. The director dashboard is waiting for a signal that will trigger a reaction that will cause the pertinent scene cards to light up. Additionally, it is responsible for connecting to broadcasting software, through which the toggling of the graphics (scenes) can seamlessly occur. The commentator dashboard, on the other hand, is configured to automatically receive statistics and render statistics cards for the user to refer to when commentating. Additionally, it is responsible for requesting or updating pinned statistics via REST API endpoints configured on the back-end server. The retrieval of pinned statistics happens once, during the first connection with the backend server.

The combination of the two dashboard applications enables a straightforward user experience, while the system handles most of the decision-making and statistic generation, allowing the casters to remain focused on the in-game action.

---

[1] Node.js—About Node.js® (nodejs.org).

[2] Riot Developer Portal (riotgames.com).

5 Evaluation and Validation

The tools were evaluated at two different stages of development to ensure they meet the needs of professionals. More specifically, considering the results from the first evaluation, they were improved and then re-evaluated and also validated.

5.1 Methodology

The procedure followed to evaluate the suite of tools for (e)sports professionals was the same for both evaluation trials. However, in the second trial, there was also a validation phase. The aim was to assess the data-driven graphics dashboards' performance within the context of an actual live (e)sports game. A user-based evaluation [29] was conducted to collect feedback from user interactions with the system. The methodology adopted involved direct user observation, task execution using the think-aloud protocol, performance measurement, questionnaires, and interviews, thus using a comprehensive approach to data collection [30].

Before the evaluation process, participants were asked to complete a questionnaire with information about their age, gender, and interest in (e)sports. Then, during the evaluation sessions, they were assigned various tasks to perform. While attempting to complete a task, they were instructed to think aloud [31, 32] to provide information about their thought processes to the evaluation facilitators. Moreover, the completion success rate (i.e., success, partial success, failure) was used to determine how effective each participant was in completing each task [33]. After evaluating each tool, participants filled out the System Usability Scale (SUS) [34] and the shorter version of the Usability Metric for User Experience (UMUX-LITE) [35] questionnaires to rate each application's usability and user experience (UX). Afterward, a semi-structured interview approach [36] was followed to gather additional insights from them. Finally, after testing all applications, the User Experience Questionnaire (UEQ) [37] and the Net Promoter Score (NPS) [38] questionnaires were utilized.

The validation phase was integrated as an additional step during the second round of trials. It involved the assessment of data-driven graphics director and commentator dashboards in a real-time scenario during a live esports game. In this phase, participants used the dashboards in pairs to collaboratively broadcast the live game to their hypothetical audience. Simultaneously, the actual broadcasting was conducted by two of their colleagues who operated as usual, without the dashboards. Both broadcasts were recorded for later analysis and the same questionnaires used in the evaluation process were provided to participants to collect their feedback.

5.2 Participant Demographics

A total of 21 experts with work experience in the eSports industry participated in the assessment of the suite of tools for (e)sports professionals. All participants were male except one in the second evaluation phase. Although the participants' sample was not well-balanced, this was a realistic deviation, as the esports industry is heavily male-dominated [39, 40]. Participants' ages ranged from 18 to 54. Five of them participated in the first evaluation, twelve in the second evaluation, and four in the validation phase.

They held distinct job titles, which included: live broadcast producer, broadcast director, commentator, league operator, commercial director, creative project manager, graphic designer, art director, film post-production specialist, and technical director. Moreover, three participants had over ten years of experience in the field of eSports, eleven had between five to ten years, and seven had less than five years of experience (see Table 1).

Table 1. Participant demographics.

	First evaluation	Second evaluation	Validation
Gender			
Male	*5*	*11*	*4*
Female	*0*	*1*	*0*
Age			
18–24	*2*	*1*	*0*
25–34	*1*	*10*	*4*
35–44	*1*	*1*	*0*
45–54	*1*	*0*	*0*
Experience			
Less than 5 years	*1*	*5*	*1*
5–10 years	*3*	*5*	*3*
Over 10 years	*1*	*2*	*0*

5.3   Results

The feedback received from participants who took part in the evaluation and validation processes of the suite of tools for (e)sports professionals was extremely positive. Most participants successfully completed the assigned tasks and provided favorable responses through questionnaires. They also offered suggestions for improvements.

Transmedia Storytelling Platform. During the first evaluation, the transmedia story-telling platform had a 100% success rate for nine out of thirteen tasks, an 80% success rate for three tasks, and a 60% success rate for one task (see Table 2). The UMUX-LITE questionnaire received an average score of 58.33%, while the SUS questionnaire had an average score of 68%. It is notable that although they were highly effective in the tasks they were asked to perform, they were not very satisfied with their interaction with the system. Participants' feedback was constructive and their comments led to changes in the platform, such as the addition of editing properties in the graphics editor, the improvement of the process of adding entries and social media platforms to the event editor, and the inclusion of brief explanatory descriptions in the publishing screens.

In the second evaluation, success rates were 100% for eight out of eleven tasks, 91.67% for two tasks, and 83.33% for one task (see Table 3). The UMUX-LITE and

Table 2. Success rates in the first transmedia storytelling platform evaluation.

Task	Success	Partial success	Failure
1. Log in to the platform	100%	0%	0%
2. Create a graphic			
2.1 Set general graphic information	100%	0%	0%
2.2. Adjust the canvas size and opacity	100%	0%	0%
2.3 Add an image from the computer	80%	20%	0%
2.4 Add regular text	100%	0%	0%
2.5 Add dynamic text	100%	0%	0%
2.6 Publish the graphic	100%	0%	0%
3. Create a story			
3.1 Set general event information	100%	0%	0%
3.2 Connect the Discord media platform	80%	0%	20%
3.3 Create and add a post to the timeline	80%	0%	20%
3.4 Add an entry to the schedule	60%	20%	20%
3.5 Publish the story	100%	0%	0%
3.6 Check Discord for the generated post	100%	0%	0%

SUS questionnaires had average scores of 77.08% and 78.10%, respectively, marking a considerable increase, which testifies that the results were significantly better after the implemented changes. The platform was better received by participants, who highlighted more opportunities for potential improvements, including the implementation of confirmation popups during purchases, easier access to the user's balance, and adding labels when hovering over card buttons.

Data-Driven Graphics Director Dashboard. The director dashboard was evaluated in the first evaluation through one task that had a 100% success rate (see Table 4). The UMUX-LITE and SUS questionnaires garnered average scores of 71.67% and 81.50%, respectively. Participants provided positive comments on the director dashboard during the interviews and some areas for improvement were identified. These enhancements included the development of a preference page, enabling users to customize the director dashboard, and the implementation of color coding based on importance.

In the second evaluation, two tasks achieved a 100% success rate (see Table 5). The average scores for the UMUX-LITE and SUS questionnaires were 81.25% and 83.50%, respectively. Once more, we observe an important improvement. Participants also expressed more positive feedback about their experience using the dashboard and new modifications proposed, such as improving the organization of the dashboard, an option to set how long an activated layout is displayed, and a quick action to delete from the dashboard.

Table 3. Success rates in the second transmedia storytelling platform evaluation.

Task	Success	Partial success	Failure
1. Log in to the platform	*100%*	*0%*	*0%*
2 Purchase a graphic	*100%*	*0%*	*0%*
3. Edit a collaborator's graphic	*91.67%*	*8.33%*	*0%*
4. Create a post			
4.1 Set general post information	*100%*	*0%*	*0%*
4.2 Add content	*100%*	*0%*	*0%*
4.3 Publish the post	*100%*	*0%*	*0%*
5. Create a story			
5.1 Set general event information	*100%*	*0%*	*0%*
5.2 Connect the Twitter media platform	*100%*	*0%*	*0%*
5.3 Add automated reminder	*91.67%*	*8.33%*	*0%*
5.4 Add a post to the story timeline	*83.33%*	*16.67%*	*0%*
5.5 Publish the story	*100%*	*0%*	*0%*

Table 4. Success rates in the first data-driven graphics director dashboard evaluation.

Task	Success	Partial success	Failure
1. Display graphics on the livestream	*100%*	*0%*	*0%*

Table 5. Success rates in the second data-driven graphics director dashboard evaluation.

Task	Success	Partial success	Failure
1. Set preferred game events	*100%*	*0%*	*0%*
2. Display graphics on the livestream	*100%*	*0%*	*0%*

In the validation phase, a single task was performed from participants with a 100% success rate (see Table 6) and the UMUX-LITE and SUS questionnaires had average scores of 75% and 80%, respectively. Participants provided encouraging comments regarding their experience and proposed organizing the dashboard based on the scenes' importance. Moreover, it is evident that the director dashboard significantly enhanced the stream by introducing more graphic overlays during the simulations, 18 in total, while in actual streams, no overlays were presented during the game.

Data-Driven Graphics Commentator Dashboard. One task was performed in the first evaluation to assess the commentator dashboard and achieved a 100% success rate (see Table 7). The UMUX-LITE and SUS questionnaires received average scores of

Table 6. Success rates in the data-driven graphics director dashboard validation.

Task	Success	Partial success	Failure
1. Display graphics on the livestream	*100%*	*0%*	*0%*

71.67% and 64%, respectively. During the debriefing interview, participants provided favorable feedback, and some of their suggestions were to implement a preference page to enable customization and add filtering.

Table 7. Success rates in the first data-driven graphics commentator dashboard evaluation.

Task	Success	Partial success	Failure
1. Pin game events and cast the game	*100%*	*0%*	*0%*

On the other hand, two tasks were used in the second evaluation, both achieving a 100% success rate (see Table 8). The average scores obtained were 80.56% for the UMUX-LITE questionnaire and 83.80% for the SUS, which have significantly improved. In addition, the following adjustments were recommended by participants, who generally liked the dashboard: group similar game events into one card and add dragged and dropped functionality for pinning records.

Table 8. Success rates in the second data-driven graphics commentator dashboard evaluation.

Task	Success	Partial success	Failure
1. Pin game events and cast the game	*100%*	*0%*	*0%*
2. Display graphics on the livestream	*100%*	*0%*	*0%*

In the validation phase, one task was conducted and achieved a 100% success rate (see Table 9), while the UMUX-LITE and SUS questionnaires received average scores of 70.83% and 71.90%, respectively. Participants in the debriefing interview provided positive feedback and suggested grouping similar game events into one card and implementing color coding based on importance.

Table 9. Success rates in the data-driven graphics commentator dashboard validation.

Task	Success	Partial success	Failure
1. Pin game events and cast the game	*100%*	*0%*	*0%*

Additionally, the validation results from comparing the simulation using the dashboard with those from the actual stream were remarkably close, as can be seen in Table 10, so further testing is required to form conclusions. Specifically, in the first game, the professional streamers covered 43 events with a total of 6 s of pauses and the simulation streamers using the dashboard covered 38 events with a total of 5 s of pauses. In the second game, the professional streamers covered 20 events with 2-s pauses, and the simulation streamers covered 27 with 19-s pauses. Commentary times in total were 80 s for the professional stream and 77 s for the simulation stream in the first game, while they were 60 and 65 s, respectively, in the second game. However, it is important to note that the results are quite encouraging, demonstrating that users may experience improved outcomes upon becoming familiar with the dashboard. In addition, it is worth mentioning that professionals involved in the dashboard simulation study, although experts in their field, were not thoroughly acquainted with the particular stream they were assigned to describe. In particular, a caster devotes substantial prep time before each event, studying the teams, reviewing recent matches, analyzing the current meta, and sometimes even conducting research on individual players. In the case of the simulation event, participants spent less prep time before the game, considering the voluntary and simulation nature of the event. In addition, during the validation phase, they were often eager to provide comments and suggestions on the system, which although valuable may affect the performance metrics recorded. For example, the increased pause durations during the simulations sometimes occurred when participants were providing comments or seeking clarification about the dashboards.

Table 10. Comparison of professional streams versus commentator dashboard simulations.

	esports game 1		esports game 2	
	Professional stream	Dashboard simulation	Professional stream	Dashboard simulation
Number of game events commented	*43*	*38*	*20*	*27*
Longest pause time between commenting	*2 s*	*2 s*	*1 s*	*2 s*
Total time of pauses between commenting	*6 s*	*5 s*	*2 s*	*19 s*
Average game event commenting time	*1.84 s*	*2.02 s*	*3 s*	*2.40 s*
Total game events commenting time	*80 s*	*77 s*	*60 s*	*65 s*

Overall User Experience and Satisfaction. To evaluate overall user experience and satisfaction, users completed the UEQ questionnaire. Their answers were transformed on a scale from –3 to 3 (see Table 11) to indicate positive or negative values. Additionally, users completed the NPS questionnaire to assess the likelihood of promoting the tools. The results for both questionnaires are presented below.

In the first evaluation, the results from the UEQ questionnaire indicated that the stimulation and novelty of the tools were excellent, whereas attractiveness received good feedback, and perspicuity, efficiency, and dependability achieved an above-average rating. Furthermore, the result analysis yielded an NPS score of 60, which is considered excellent because it surpasses the benchmark of 50 [41], and shows that participants are very likely to recommend the tools to their friends or colleagues.

In the second evaluation, the results from the UEQ questionnaire indicated that attractiveness, efficiency, dependability, stimulation, and novelty received good feedback, and perspicuity achieved an above-average rating. Moreover, the NPS score was 8.33, which is considered good as it surpasses the benchmark of 0 [41].

In the validation phase, the aspect of novelty was rated as excellent from the UEQ questionnaire results, whereas attractiveness, perspicuity, and stimulation received good feedback, and efficiency and dependability achieved an above-average rating. Also, the analysis of the results produced an NPS score of 25, which is considered good. Overall, the results suggest a positive user experience and strong potential for adoption within the user community.

Table 11. UEQ scale values.

Scale	Mean		
	First evaluation	Second evaluation	Validation phase
Attractiveness	1.80 (SD: 1.07)	1.71 (SD: 0.40)	1.63 (SD: 0.48)
Perspicuity	1.35 (SD: 1.28)	1.60 (SD: 0.73)	1.94 (SD: 0.66)
Efficiency	1.35 (SD: 0.89)	1.81 (SD: 0.43)	1.31 (SD: 0.87)
Dependability	1.40 (SD: 0.74)	1.63 (SD: 0.48)	1.44 (SD: 0.77)
Stimulation	1.95 (SD: 0.82)	1.63 (SD: 0.45)	1.44 (SD: 0.66)
Novelty	1.95 (SD: 0.60)	1.44 (SD: 0.93)	1.81 (SD: 0.47)

6 Conclusion

In this paper, a toolkit for (e)sports professionals has been presented. It features a trans-media storytelling platform for collaboratively creating graphics, posts, and event narratives, a data-driven graphics director dashboard for seamlessly displaying graphic overlays during live streams, and a data-driven graphics commentator dashboard for enhancing broadcast commentary. The tools aim at enhancing professionals' performance by creating more engaging narratives for (e)sports events and attracting a larger audience to broadcasts.

To study its usability and effectiveness, the suite of tools has been tested by eSports professionals, who constitute the main target user group. More specifically, two user-based evaluation trials were conducted at two different stages of development to collect user feedback, along with a validation process to test the data-driven dashboard under realistic circumstances. The results of the user-based evaluation trials were not only very encouraging, with high scores and positive user feedback, but also improved in the second stage, attributed to the implementation of changes informed by the first evaluation. Moreover, the validation results revealed that the data-driven graphics director dashboard enhanced the stream by incorporating additional graphic overlays in comparison to a traditionally directed stream. On the other hand, more testing is needed for the data-driven graphics commentator dashboard, as the outcomes from the simulation and the actual stream were similar. However, participants might have performed better using the commentator dashboard if they had been more familiar with it. Overall, the suite of tools has demonstrated its effectiveness in assisting (e)sports professionals, and it is a promising solution.

Acknowledgments. The authors would like to thank the evaluation participants for their valuable feedback that has contributed to platform improvements, and the **pixel-perfect gaming & esports company**[3] for their collaboration throughout the requirements elicitation, evaluation, and validation phases.

References

1. Gratton, C., Solberg, H.A.: The economics of sports broadcasting. Routledge (2007)
2. Steinkuehler, C.: Esports research: critical, empirical, and historical studies of competitive videogame play. Games Cult. **15**, 3–8 (2020). https://doi.org/10.1177/1555412019836855
3. Hamari, J., Sjöblom, M.: What is eSports and why do people watch it? Internet Res. **27**, 211–232 (2017). https://doi.org/10.1108/IntR-04-2016-0085
4. Jang, W.W., Byon, K.K., Baker, T.A., III., Tsuji, Y.: Mediating effect of esports content live streaming in the relationship between esports recreational gameplay and esports event broadcast. Sport Bus. Manag. Int. J. **11**, 89–108 (2020). https://doi.org/10.1108/SBM-10-2019-0087
5. AC/E: AC/E Digital Culture Annual Report 2014: Focus 2014: The Use of New Technologies in the Performing Arts. Dosdoce (2014)
6. Lewis, N., Weaver, A.J.: More than a game: sports media framing effects on attitudes, intentions, and enjoyment. Commun. Sport **3**, 219–242 (2015). https://doi.org/10.1177/216747951 3508273
7. Abbasi, A.Z., Alqahtani, N., Tsiotsou, R.H., Rehman, U., Ting, D.H.: Esports as playful consumption experiences: examining the antecedents and consequences of game engagement. Telemat. Inform. **77**, 101937 (2023)
8. Deninger, D.: Sports on Television. Routledge (2012)
9. Lee, M., Kim, D., Williams, A.S., Pedersen, P.M.: Investigating the role of sports commentary: an analysis of media-consumption behavior and programmatic quality and satisfaction. J. Sports Media **11**, 145–167 (2016). https://doi.org/10.1353/jsm.2016.0001

---

[3] https://pixel-perfect.gr/.

10. Comisky, P., Bryant, J., Zillmann, D.: Commentary as a substitute for action. J. Commun. **27**, 150–153 (1977). https://doi.org/10.1111/j.1460-2466.1977.tb02141.x

11. Block, F., Hodge, V., Hobson, S., Sephton, N., Devlin, S., Ursu, M.F., Drachen, A., Cowling, P.I.: Narrative bytes: data-driven content production in esports. In: Proceedings of the 2018 ACM International Conference on Interactive Experiences for TV and Online Video, pp. 29–41. ACM, SEOUL Republic of Korea (2018)

12. Hagelgans, M.: The Impact of Digitalization on Sports Broadcasting: An Analysis of how Streaming Changed the German Sports Broadcasting Market. Springer Fachmedien Wiesbaden, Wiesbaden (2022)

13. Sell, J.C.: E-sports broadcasting (2015). https://dspace.mit.edu/handle/1721.1/97996

14. Goldman, M.M., Hedlund, D.P.: Rebooting content: broadcasting sport and esports to homes during COVID-19. Int. J. Sport Commun. **13**, 370–380 (2020)

15. Block, F.O., et al.: Echo Suite of Software (Showcase Brochure) (2020)

16. Papaioannou, E., et al.: Melisa - a distributed multimedia system for multiplatform interactive sports content broadcasting. In: Proceedings of the 30th Euromicro Conference, 2004, pp. 222–229. IEEE, Rennes (2004)

17. DAX: Data-driven audience experiences in esports. In: Proceedings of the 2020 ACM International Conference on Interactive Media Experiences. https://dl.acm.org/doi/https://doi.org/10.1145/3391614.3393659

18. Wang, Z., Yoshinaga, N.: From eSports Data to Game Commentary: Datasets, Models, and Evaluation Metrics (2021)

19. Zhi, Q., Lin, S., Talkad Sukumar, P., Metoyer, R.: GameViews: understanding and supporting data-driven sports storytelling. In: Proceedings of the 2019 CHI Conference on Human Factors in Computing Systems, pp. 1–13. ACM, Glasgow (2019)

20. Demiris, A.M., et al.: Enhanced sports broadcasting by means of augmented reality in MPEG-4. In: International Conference on Augmented, Virtual Environments and Three-Dimensional Imaging, Mykonos, Greece. Citeseer (2001)

21. Jeffery-Poulter, S.: Creating and producing digital content across multiple platforms. J. Media Pract. **3**, 155–164 (2003). https://doi.org/10.1386/jmpr.3.3.155

22. Gürel, E., Tığlı, Ö.: New world created by social media: transmedia storytelling. J. Media Crit. **1**, 35–65 (2014)

23. Ntoa, S., et al.: User generated content for enhanced professional productions: a mobile application for content contributors and a study on the factors influencing their satisfaction and loyalty. Multimed. Tools Appl. **80**, 33679–33699 (2021). https://doi.org/10.1007/s11042-021-11381-2

24. Carter, M., Egliston, B.: The work of watching Twitch: Audience labour in livestreaming and esports. J. Gaming Virtual Worlds **13**, 3–20 (2021). https://doi.org/10.1386/jgvw_00025_1

25. Pedrassoli Chitayat, A., et al.: From passive viewer to active fan: towards the design and large-scale evaluation of interactive audience experiences in Esports and beyond. In: Proceedings of the 2024 ACM International Conference on Interactive Media Experiences, pp. 94–107. Association for Computing Machinery, New York (2024)

26. Margetis, G., et al.: Visual summarisations for computer-assisted live color casting and direction in league of legends. In: Fang, X. (eds.) HCI in Games. HCII 2023. Lecture Notes in Computer Science, vol. 14046, pp. 133–153. Springer, Cham (2023). https://doi.org/10.1007/978-3-031-35930-9_10

27. Norman, D.A., Draper, S.W.: User centered system design; new perspectives on human-computer interaction. L. Erlbaum Associates Inc. (1986)

28. ISO: 9241–210: 2019 Ergonomics of human-system interaction—Part 210: human-centred design for interactive systems (2019)

29. Dumas, J.S.: User-based evaluations. In: The Human-Computer Interaction Handbook: Fundamentals, Evolving Technologies and Emerging Applications, pp. 1093–1117. L. Erlbaum Associates Inc., USA (2002)
30. Ntoa, S.: Usability and user experience evaluation in intelligent environments: a review and reappraisal. Int. J. Hum.-Comput. Interact., 1–30 (2024). https://doi.org/10.1080/10447318.2024.2394724
31. Wright, P.C., Monk, A.F.: The use of think-aloud evaluation methods in design. ACM SIGCHI Bull. **23**, 55–57 (1991). https://doi.org/10.1145/122672.122685
32. Eccles, D.W., Arsal, G.: The think aloud method: what is it and how do I use it? Qual. Res. Sport Exerc. Health. **9**, 514–531 (2017). https://doi.org/10.1080/2159676X.2017.1331501
33. Albert, B., Tullis, T.: Measuring the User Experience: Collecting, Analyzing, and Presenting Usability Metrics. Newnes (2013)
34. Brooke, J.: SUS: A "Quick and Dirty" usability scale. In: Usability Evaluation in Industry. CRC Press (1996)
35. Lewis, J.R., Utesch, B.S., Maher, D.E.: UMUX-LITE: when there's no time for the SUS. In: Proceedings of the SIGCHI Conference on Human Factors in Computing Systems, pp. 2099–2102. Association for Computing Machinery, New York (2013)
36. Wilson, C.: Interview Techniques for UX Practitioners: A User-Centered Design Method. Newnes (2013)
37. Schrepp, M., Thomaschewski, J., Hinderks, A.: Construction of a benchmark for the user experience questionnaire (UEQ) (2017). https://doi.org/10.9781/ijimai.2017.445
38. Krol, M.W., de Boer, D., Delnoij, D.M., Rademakers, J.J.D.J.M.: The Net Promoter Score – an asset to patient experience surveys? Health Expect. **18**, 3099–3109 (2015). https://doi.org/10.1111/hex.12297
39. Rogstad, E.T.: Gender in eSports research: a literature review. Eur. J. Sport Soc. **19**, 195–213 (2022). https://doi.org/10.1080/16138171.2021.1930941
40. Stamou, S., Apostolakis, K.C., Margetis, G., Ntoa, S., Stephanidis, C.: The current situation and debate on gender segregation in Esports tournaments. In: Proceedings of the 2024 IEEE Gaming, Entertainment, and Media Conference (GEM), pp. 1–6. IEEE, Turin (2024)
41. Lee, S.: Net promoter score: using NPS to measure IT customer support satisfaction. In: Proceedings of the 2018 ACM SIGUCCS Annual Conference, pp. 63–64. Association for Computing Machinery, New York (2018)

SDG Quest: Leveraging Mobile Game-Based Learning to Foster Environmental, Social, and Economic Sustainable Development Goals

Andriani Piki[1]([✉]), Iraklis Tchanturia[1], Nicos Kasenides[1], Nearchos Paspallis[1], and Susana Leal[2]

[1] University of Central Lancashire Cyprus (UCLan Cyprus), Larnaca, Cyprus
{APiki,ITchanturia,NKasenides,NPaspallis}@uclan.ac.uk
[2] Santarém Polytechnic University, Life Quality Research Centre (CIEQV), Santarém, Portugal
Susana.Leal@esg.ipsantarem.pt

Abstract. Amid the quest for sustainable development, education can serve as a catalyst for incentivising people of all ages and backgrounds to realise the vision towards a healthier planet, a fairer society, and a more peaceful and prosperous future for all. This study presents the design and evaluation of 'SDG Quest' - a novel mobile educational game crafted for raising awareness about environmental, social, and economic Sustainable Development Goals. Embracing gamification features and game mechanics such as rewards, points, milestones, challenges, badges, and mentor personalisation, SDG Quest aims to advance players' understanding of all dimensions and goals of sustainable development, captivate their interest through an engaging, gamified learning experience, and ultimately, nurture the right mindset required for realising the goals. This paper discusses the design and empirical evaluation of SDG Quest. The evaluation involving both users (n = 73) and experts (n = 12) reflects a positive user experience and highlights the game's usability, appealing design, and learning effectiveness. Creative ideas and suggestions for further enhancing the game's features and impact are also captured. The findings illuminate the beneficial contribution of mobile game-based learning in the sphere of education for sustainable development.

Keywords: Sustainable Development Goals · Mobile Game-Based Learning · Education for Sustainable Development · Usability Evaluation

1 Introduction

The United Nations' 2030 Agenda for Sustainable Development (SD) provides a global plan leveraging strategic partnerships, to eradicate poverty and reduce

J. Y. C. Chen et al. (Eds.): HCII 2024, LNCS 15377, pp. 373–392, 2025.
https://doi.org/10.1007/978-3-031-76812-5_25

inequality, expand social protection and decent jobs, address the crises in education and climate change, and strengthen universal peace [34]. At the heart of this agenda lie the UN's 17 Sustainable Development Goals (SDGs) which, along with 169 associated targets and 232 indicators, propagate an urgent call for action by all countries and stakeholders for the betterment of our world [33]. To realise the complexity of the SDGs and better assess progress towards achieving them, they have been organised into five principles (5 Ps): People, Prosperity, Planet, Peace, and Partnership which extend the three core pillars of sustainable development: Economic, Social and Environmental [32,34].

We are currently traversing the second half of the strategic plan towards the 2030 Agenda. Yet, despite worldwide initiatives, the most recent progress report on the SDGs presents a negative picture, with more than 50% of the SDG targets demonstrating weak progress, while for another 30% progress has stalled or declined [35]. The outbreak of Covid-19 pandemic [17] and the ongoing three-fold crisis of climate change, biodiversity loss, and environmental pollution are having a devastating and lasting impact deteriorating progress towards the SDGs [35]. These negative impacts have been further amplified by recent conflicts driving increases in the prices of food and energy and constraining access to economic resources, spurring a global cost-of-living crisis affecting billions of people globally [35]. The current situation calls for an urgent and critical need to (re)act. Addressing this need, however, presupposes 'sustainability literacy'. Towards this end, Education for Sustainable Development (ESD) and mobile Game-Based Learning (mGBL) constitute key drivers for behavioural change, knowledge acquisition, and awareness raising among all stakeholders [29,37].

Having established the problem context, Sect. 2 presents a review of related literature nto the interplay between ESD and mGBL. Section 3 describes the design, navigation, game mechanics and gamification features of SDG Quest. Section 4 discusses key findings from user and expert evaluation and ideas for future research and development. Finally, Sect. 5 synthesises the key findings.

2   Background and Related Work

The positive outcomes associated with the use of games in teaching and learning are unquestionable. Still, before embarking on the development of a new mobile educational game for raising awareness on the SDGs, it is essential to critically review related research and explore existing serious games developed in the realm of ESD. This investigation has a two-fold aim: to discover the most prevailing features and benefits of educational games, and to reveal the inherent barriers and gaps associated with mGBL in sustainability education with the view to inform the design and implementation of a new mobile educational game.

2.1   Key Features and Educational Benefits of GBL for ESD

Quality education and educational technology are inextricably interwoven. Quality education strives to ensure inclusive and equitable education and promote lifelong learning opportunities for all [36]. Obtaining these goals underpins a range of fundamental development drivers, one of which is technology. Educational technology, including educational games [15,26], can contribute to widening access to all levels of education and vocational training, including people with disabilities and children in vulnerable situations [36], and have a synergistic role enhancing other drivers towards promoting the knowledge, attitudes, and behaviours associated with the SDGs [15,29].

The benefits of games, gamification, and GBL, such as increased engagement, motivation, learner satisfaction, and autonomy, are central for promoting impactful educational experiences, especially in complex, multidisciplinary fields like sustainability [21,26]. GBL is also associated with enhanced comprehension, critical thinking, curiosity, and problem-solving skills development. Such competencies are essential when aiming to face multilayered real-world issues such as the ones encompassed by sustainability development [21]. The utilisation of GBL (including mobile games, video games, virtual reality and augmented reality (VR/AR) games [19], gamified educational robotics, virtual tutors driven by Artificial Intelligence (AI), and web-based games) has heightened in recent years with applications extending across all dimensions of SD and levels of education. Implementing GBL into ESD can lead to effective teaching and learning processes, enhance learners' awareness on the SDGs, and enable them to become active agents driving sustainable solutions [26].

Various studies have demonstrated the positive learning outcomes associated with the use of educational games and mGBL towards raising awareness on SD and the SDGs [2–5,7,10,12,19,22,27]. These studies highlight the role of games in fostering environmental awareness, promoting sustainable behaviours, and cultivating a sense of responsibility towards addressing pressing sustainability challenges. Games present opportunities for edutainment, combining education and entertainment to positively impact the learning outcomes [15].

Conclusively, employing GBL endeavours in ESD can equip learners with a deep understanding of complex, inter-disciplinary knowledge areas [7,10,13,16, 27,28] and enhance their attention and interest leading to an enjoyable learning experience about the SDGs [19]. The integration of mobile, experiential, and game-based educational approaches can form the basis for action-oriented, transformative pedagogies which are deemed essential for the development of key competencies, knowledge, behaviours, and attitudes for SD [7,10,27].

2.2 Inherent Barriers and Gaps Associated with mGBL for ESD

While there are many benefits and positive learning outcomes associated with using GBL strategies, there are also significant challenges and hurdles [23]. Understanding how games can exert a lasting and constructive influence on citizens [7], as well as identifying ways to mitigate the weaknesses of mobile games [25] and mobile learning [30], are imperative steps to undertake in the context of ESD.

First and foremost, it is important to consider whether the technology or game is being used merely for the sake of playing or whether it is purposefully embedded in the learning process to improve learning [23]. This brings forward important considerations regarding assessment and learner engagement [14]. A myriad of mobile applications and games, whose content or objectives address SD are readily available falling under different genres and categories. However, not all SDG-themed mobile apps declare an educational purpose or provide gamified content. Similarly, not all SDG-related games are mobile-based, thus aspects of educational inclusion and technological accessibility are also raised. Although a thorough discussion of all available SDG games and mobile apps is beyond the scope of this study, existing games and mobile apps were explored with the view to identify additional limitations and gaps that can inform the design and development of new mobile educational games.

The first gap has to do with game design and appeal. Despite the rich affordances of many educational games and the benefits they present for ESD, SDG-related serious games are (still) a long way from attaining the diffusion levels or commercial, entertainment games [7]. Even for experienced game designers creating a good educational game - one that effectively teaches and engages players - is challenging [23]. The second gap concerns the learning theme/scope. There is an evident tendency in ESD initiatives to focus more on environmental sustainability [2,9,12,40] or accentuate a particular goal or target, rather than holistically embracing serious games to establish a systemic understanding of all pillars of SD [19,31]. Furthermore, although most SDG-related mobile apps capture all 17 SDGs, they do not explicitly connect the content to the three core pillars of environmental, social, and economic sustainability.

There are also evident gaps related to accessibility and game mechanics. Many mobile apps are only available to download from Google Play store, restricting access to Android devices alone. At the same time, very few SDG-related mobile apps feature gamified content or game mechanics such as rewards, points, milestones, leaderboards, challenges, badges/achievements, experience-based in-game progression, and avatar/mentor personalisation. These features are essential for engaging users with the learning content and triggering their interest. Instead, many SDG-related mobile apps are informational, encourage users to donate a monetary amount to help implement the SDGs, or allow them to view progress on selected goals and targets. Although these tools have merit and can contribute towards attaining the SDGs, they often presume that users are aware about SD and have the necessary prior understanding on how to act. Additionally, students' proficiency with mobile learning should be addressed, so that the technology itself does not become a barrier to learning [23].

Novel ESD initiatives should aim to adopt a holistic, interdisciplinary approach integrating mGBL and modern gamification techniques to empower learners to reflect on their actions, develop sustainability competencies, behave in a responsible way, and embrace positive changes towards a sustainable future. These observations have led to the proposed game which leverages mGBL and aims to offer an enriched learning experience towards fostering the SDGs.

3   The 'SDG Quest' Mobile Educational Game

To address the identified gaps and contribute to existing ESD efforts, a novel mobile educational game was designed, developed, and evaluated aiming to raise awareness on environmental, social, and economic SDGs. A user-centred, iterative, and incremental mobile application development approach was employed.

A hybrid system development lifecycle methodology was adopted combining features from traditional, waterfall methodology (structured user requirements gathering and analysis) and agile development (prototyping, requirements prioritisation, timeboxing). On one hand, conducting a comprehensive stakeholder needs analysis and in-depth exploration of existing solutions' strengths and weaknesses offer a strong foundation during initial stages of the development lifecycle (ideation, planning, analysis). On the other hand, the iterative and incremental process in agile approaches helps deliver a quality product within a given time frame by actively involving key stakeholders throughout the development lifecycle, embracing change, and incrementally improving the final application [6,11]. The following paragraphs describe the user requirements, gamified features and game mechanics, key learning objectives and thematic content of SDG Quest.

3.1   User Requirements Gathering and Analysis

The extracted list of user requirements was informed by four primary sources: (a) relevant literature on ESD and mGBL, including educational theories and underlying pedagogical constructs (experiential learning, playful learning, and learner engagement); (b) existing mobile apps and educational games; (c) User Interface (UI) design principles and usability goals; and (d) primary data gathered through an online survey from a convenience sample of potential users (n = 35) (including both male and female participants, from different academic backgrounds (computing, engineering, web design, business administration, sports science, law, etc.), representing different age groups (18–54 years old)).

Although the sample size was limited, it was useful for verifying what was suggested in the literature in terms of (lack of) awareness about the SDGs and environmental, social, and economic sustainability. Specifically, none of the participants responded they strongly agree with for the statement *"I am familiar with the term Sustainable Development Goals"* and only 9 agreed (25.7%). For the statement *"I am familiar with the term Sustainable development"* only 2 participants (5.7%) strongly agreed and 11 agreed (31.4%). Regarding the three pillars of SD, 71.4% are mostly familiar with environmental sustainability, with only 14,3% and 8,6% reporting they are mostly familiar with social and economic sustainability, respectively, while another 5,7% are not familiar with any of the three. This also reinforces what was suggested by the studied literature. The respondents' lack of awareness of the 17 SDGs was also portrayed in their answers to the question *"Are you satisfied with the current progress of the implementation of the 17 SDGs"*, whereby only 2 participants (5.7%) responded positively, 9 responded negatively (25.7%), and the remaining 24 participants

(58.6%) responded *"I don't know"*. These findings strengthen the initial motivation behind the need for more initiatives to raise awareness across all dimensions of SD and the 17 SDGs. The data analysis also helped gain deeper insights on both functional and non-functional requirements.

3.2 Functional and Non-functional Requirements

To elicit the app's functional requirements, participants were asked to express their preferences in terms of potential game features, their opinion about aspects that can facilitate learning about the SDGs, and their perceptions regarding features that can improve the overall educational effectiveness of the proposed app. Based on the gathered responses (n = 35), the most popular game features include: a rewards system (69%), daily trivia/challenges (60%), interactive learning modules (57%), instructions on how to play (51%), and quizzes (46%). These were consequently prioritised during system design and development. Furthermore, participants were asked to rank various features based on their contribution toward a successful SDG-related educational mobile app. The most highly rated features involve content quality, usability and design, and learning outcomes, followed by performance, accessibility, personalisation, and competitive activities. The insights informed the implementation of SDG Quest.

Non-functional requirements, such as preferred technological platform, and degree of competence and familiarity with similar GBL applications, were also captured. These informed the decision to opt for cross-platform development over a native development approach, since both Android and iOS usage was substantially represented in the responses. Although native applications outperform cross platform ones and have access to a larger feature set [1,39], cross platform paradigm is more suitable when users utilise diverse devices and platforms. Furthermore, significant advancements have been observed recently regarding the performance of cross-platform software. Frameworks such as Flutter [8] help bridge the performance gap significantly, offering similar performance with that of native applications while dramatically reducing development time, effort, and maintenance costs [1]. Since the goal of this project is to raise awareness of the UN's 17 SDGs, creating an application that can run on multiple platforms can help reach a wider user base satisfying inclusiveness and accessibility principles.

3.3 User Interface Design, Usability, and Game Mechanics

Engagement by Design. A well-designed and appealing UI is essential for a successful mobile application as it greatly affects the users' interest and their long-term engagement. This is crucial since the success of educational applications presupposes learner engagement [24]. Mobile games exhibit inherent constraints such as limited screen size, hence the various widgets that will comprise the UI need to dynamically adjust to varying screen sizes, while offering clear and consistent information with as little visual noise as possible, to prevent confusion. To create the application in a systematic way, and enable 'engagement by design' [14], we embraced UI design principles based on Nielsen's 10 usability heuristics [18] which were adapted to the context of mobile applications [20] and mGBL for sustainability education.

UI Design and Navigation System. When launching SDG Quest, only the *Standard* game mode is unlocked by default, while locked content appears with faded colours and is clearly signposted (Fig. 1a). Progressively releasing locked content, along with achieving milestones and earning rewards constitute key gamification principles for engaging learners. The app features a background with a smoothly-changing colour gradient which makes the brighter-coloured, floating widgets stand out (Fig. 1b). When unlocked, the *Individual* game mode lists the 17 SDGs leading to the respective themed quizzes. The app maintains the official colours of each SDG logo to strengthen recognition, learnability, and memorability, aiming to enhance the learning experience and the game's educational effectiveness (Fig. 1c).

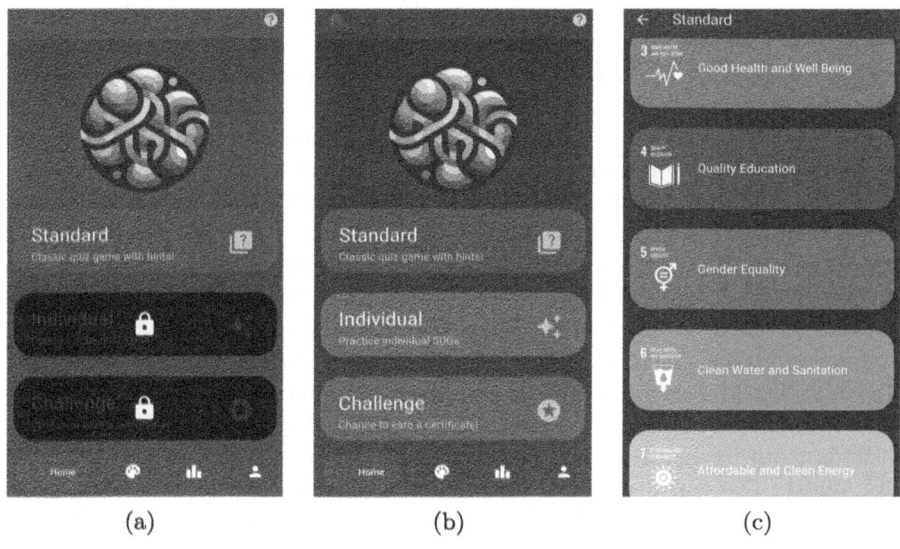

Fig. 1. (a) Main Menu, (b) Game Modes, (c) SDG Quizzes

In addition to choosing an appropriate colour palette, designing an intuitive and responsive navigation system is vital for ensuring an efficient and enjoyable player experience. The top and bottom bars are maintained between the various views providing a smooth and high-performance navigation experience. The top bar provides contextual feedback to the user (e.g., the respective screen's icon, progress bar and hints, pop up feedback messages for points earned, streak mode activation, successfully saving avatar changes, etc.). A dedicated 'Help' page is also accessible from the top navigation bar providing informative content about the (i) purpose of SDG Quest, (ii) game mechanics (gaining points/experience, unlocking levels, enabling streak mode, revealing the answer, entering challenge mode to get a personalised certificate); (iii) rules of the game (progression through *Standard*, *Individual*, and *Challenge* game modes); as well as (iv) tips and instructions for enhancing the learning process and reinforcing key knowledge areas, attitudes, and skills.

Game Mechanics and Game Play. There are 3 game modes (Fig. 1b):

– *Standard* - Classic quizzes categorised into the three dimensions of SD (Fig. 2a). Each category is associated with the respective *Milestone*.
– *Individual* - Themed quizzes focusing on each SDG. Answering correctly unlocks the respective *Badge*.
– *Challenge* - A chance to answer questions across all 17 SDGs and the 3 dimensions of SD and earn a *Certificate*.

Unlocking the *Individual* and *Challenge* modes requires gaining points by correctly answering the quiz questions to 'level up'. Experience and points are used interchangeably to refer to the *Rewards System* of the SDG Quest game. For every 100 points the player accumulates, a new level is earned. This aims to incentivise users to continue learning through play.

The 'Quiz' view (Fig. 2b) comprises multiple-choice questions. It defines the main gameplay loop through which users gain points/experience. Embedded features include a 'Hint' option directing the player to UN's official dedicated pages and learning content on the SDGs [33], a progress indicator, the 'Reveal Answer' option and the 'Streak' mode functionality. Visual feedback is provided, e.g., when an answer is selected this is highlighted and the button changes guiding the user to continue and submit the answer (Fig. 2c).

Game mechanics include *Badges* for each of the 17 SDGs (Fig. 3a), *Milestones* for each of the three sustainability pillars (Environmental, Social, and Economic) (Fig. 3b), and a *Leaderboard*. These are accessible through the respective icons on the bottom navigation bar. The leaderboard adds a competitive element to SDG Quest. The top 3 winners are highlighted to stand out, while the entire list adjusts dynamically based on database updates. The locked/unlocked status for the badges and milestones depends on the points/experience earned while completing the various game modes.

The 'Mentor Palette' (Fig. 3c) constitutes a gamified personalisation feature in SDG Quest, which is unlocked after earning the first 100 points. This aims to make the app more engaging and aesthetically appealing, which is significant since the mentor's avatar appears along with all questions in the Quiz view. Additionally, to simulate the effect of the mentor narrating the question, a type-writer animation is used to gradually present the question text (clicking on the actual text box will skip the animation and present the question in its entirety), while the mentor's backdrop animation adds a fine detail to enhance the overall appearance.

The 'Streak' feature serves as an incentive for learners to read and learn more about the SDGs and the current progress on the related targets by studying the

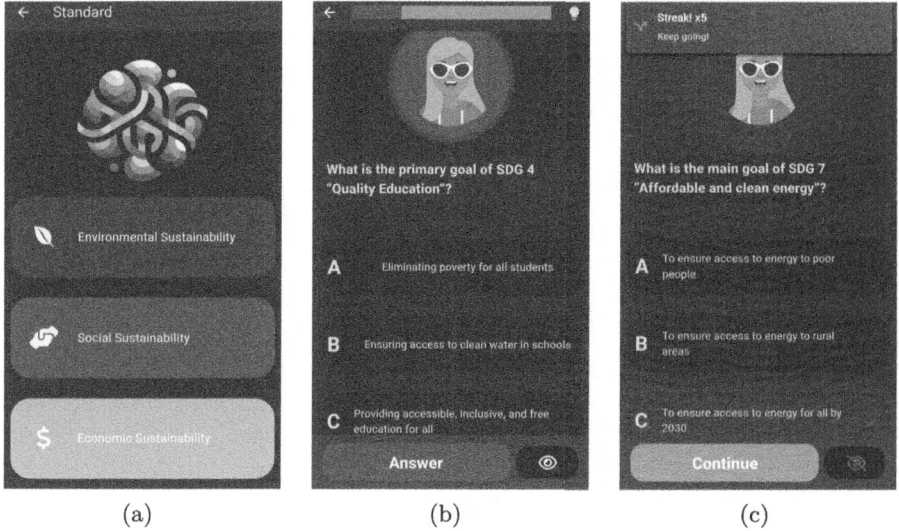

(a)   (b)   (c)

Fig. 2. (a) Themed Quizzes, (b) Quiz Mode, (c) Streak Feature

available learning content (accessed through the 'Hint'), before answering a question. Since the questions are inspired by the latest information presented on the SDGs site, reading this material helps players answer correctly and, by extension, learn about the SDGs. Guiding players to the official UN resources [33] ensures that the content remains relevant and futureproof, rather than embedding static learning content in the app. Every correct answer increments the streakCounter variable while incorrect answers set the counter back to zero. After three consecutive correct answers (i.e., when the counter reaches 3) the question widget enters 'Streak' mode. When this mode is activated UI animations become more noticeable and the backdrop colour changes to shades of green Fig. 2b). The points for any subsequent correct answers are multiplied by the streakCounter, greatly incentivising learning since maintaining a streak (through studying before answering) is the most efficient way to gain experience/points.

The 'Reveal answer' option is another gamified feature. When selected it highlights the correct answer. However, the number of reveals depends on the Quiz mode (3 reveals for *Standard* game mode and 1 reveal for *Individual* game mode). The *Challenge* mode has no reveals as this is the ultimate test leading to a personalised Certificate (generated when 80% of the *Challenge* mode gets unlocked). When choosing to reveal an answer the user maintains their streak, but no points are awarded. Finally, the leaderboard is based on the number of levels each player reaches.

Design features were implemented with Nielsen's heuristics in mind by providing adequate feedback for actions (e.g., for correct/wrong answers), clearly displaying the status of the app, preventing mistakes by utilising two distinct actions for submitting an answer, and displaying dialogue boxes for confirmation

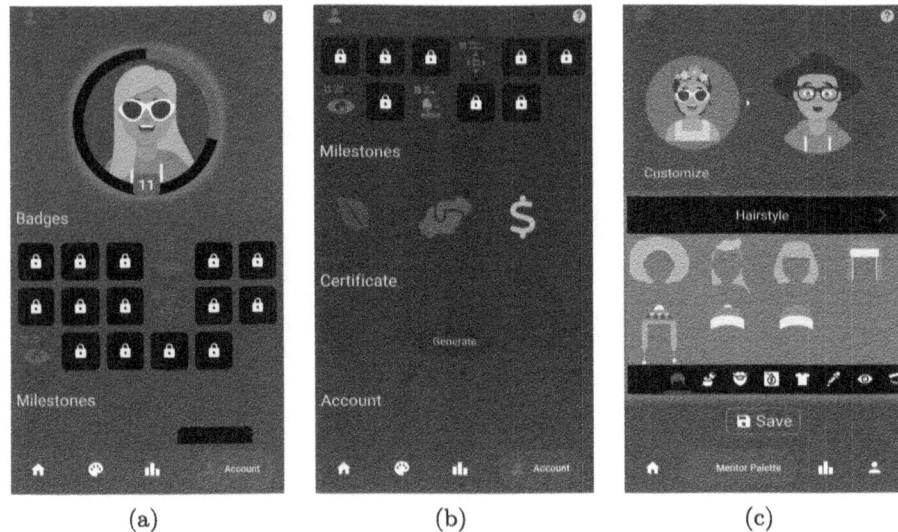

(a)   (b)   (c)

Fig. 3. (a) Badges for the 17 SDGs, (b) Milestones and Certificate, (c) Mentor Palette

before an action is committed (e.g., before redirecting to the external SDGs website, when the exit button is pressed, or to confirm the player wants to leave the quiz page to avoid losing progress). This way accidental errors can be eliminated and contextualised feedback is provided.

Educational Gamification. Gamification principles have greatly influenced the design of SDG Quest. Most of the options, quizzes, and functionalities in the game are initially locked (Figs. 1a, 3a.) and users must engage in learning through play to unlock them. Effectively, the player level increases in tandem with the level of knowledge and understanding of the SDGs. Furthermore, game mechanics, including mentor personalisation, badges, milestones, and certificate generation, serve as incentives to keep players engaged and strive for long-term educational goals, while also addressing the identified gaps.

4   Usability Evaluation and Discussion of the Findings

The purpose of the evaluation was to invite users and experts to playtest SDG Quest, provide insights about their user experience and overall satisfaction with SDG Quest, and give suggestions and feedback to improve its design, overall quality, and educational efficacy. Participation was voluntary and all information gathered was anonymous. Participants were provided with an information sheet describing the evaluation protocol. Specifically, information for accessing the app, playtesting/evaluation guidelines, and the link to the evaluation questionnaire was provided. For consistency, the evaluators were provided with a list of activities to follow during playtesting. They were guided to create an account and log in, access help documentation, and navigate on the various screens to familiarise with the layout before switching to play mode. Indicative tasks were listed on the information sheet (e.g., play the *Standard* quizzes until the 'Mentor Personalisation' feature is unlocked; customise the Mentor's avatar; play to top the Leaderboard or until the *Challenge* mode is unlocked or a Certificate is earned). The minimum playtime was approximately one hour after which participants were requested to fill in the evaluation questionnaire. A total 85 completed questionnaires were received from users (n = 73) and experts (n = 12), providing rich insights which are discussed next.

4.1   User Evaluation Results

User Experience. SDG Quest was evaluated by diverse users, both male (59%) and female (41%), representing different age groups (between 18 and 52 years old, with 30 being the average age), and areas of expertise (including Computer Science, Business Administration, Health and Welfare, Natural Sciences and Mathematics, Engineering and Social Sciences). The overall experience was positively evaluated (with an average rating of 4.11 out of 5). Specifically, users agree or strongly agree that SDG Quest is visually appealing (81%), easy to use (82%), well-designed (81%), enjoyable (74%), has a good performance (80%) and is a satisfying learning game (71%), provides useful help and instructions (70%), and is appropriately challenging (64%). The lower rating on the last three aspects was also addressed in the open-ended questions where users identified the need for customising the level of difficulty, length of quizzes, and other attributes to make the game more appealing and appropriately challenging.

Learning Effectiveness. Users were enquired to evaluate the game's learning effectiveness across various dimensions: enjoyment with learning through playing, sense of accomplishment, knowledge acquisition about SD, learning something new about the SDGs, clarity of content and relevance to the 17 SDGs, preference of mGBL with SDG Quest rather than traditional learning, and usefulness of the 'Hints' feature in guiding users to relevant information just in time. Overall, users highly rated all aspects (Fig. 4) indicating the apps' merits towards engaging players and raising awareness about the SDGs.

Usability Design. Users also assessed SDG Quest based on usability goals. Users agree or strongly agree that SDG Quest is effective (92%), efficient (93%), has good utility and includes useful and meaningful gamified content (86%), does not require personal or confidential information impacting security or privacy (86%), easy to learn how to navigate and intuitive (88%), memorable and easy to remember how to use (90%).

In terms of usability heuristics (Fig. 5), the app was positively evaluated overall. Three aspects received slightly lower ranking which are worth noting: 'User control and freedom': SDG Quest allows me to undo a mistake and go

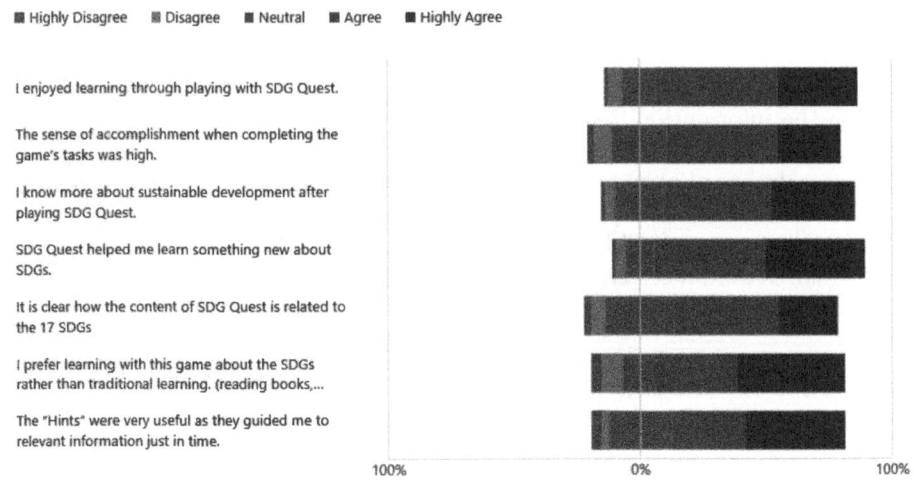

Fig. 4. Learning Effectiveness of SDG Quest

back to a previous state (Highly disagree: 1.4%, Disagree: 8.2%, Neutral 31.5%, Agree: 30.1%, and Highly Agree: 28.8%); 'Recognition rather than recall': SDG Quest has memorable and recognisable actions and elements (Highly disagree: 4.1%, Disagree: 4.1%, Neutral 16.4%, Agree: 38.4 and Highly Agree: 37.0%); and 'Help and documentation': SDG Quest provides documentation that assists in completing the game's tasks (Highly disagree: 2.7%, Disagree: 6.8%, Neutral 19.2%, Agree: 42.5%, and Highly Agree: 28.8%). Therefore, more work is needed for improving the app along these lines.

Strengths, Weaknesses, and Suggestions for Improvement. The users' evaluation questionnaire also included three open-ended questions asking the respondents to provide feedback on the most and least enjoyed aspects of the app as well as inviting general feedback and suggestions for improving its design, content, and learning effectiveness. The provided answers were coded and grouped under thematic areas. The number in brackets indicates the frequency analysis i.e., how many times each aspect was mentioned.

The most enjoyed aspects were grouped under 5 thematic areas representing the main strengths of the app: (a) Visual aesthetics, design, graphics, simplicity, responsiveness, and animations (n = 23); (b) SDG-related knowledge acquisition, learning curve, learning objectives, and certificate (n = 17); (c) Quality of the questions, informative content, quizzes, and hints (n = 17); (d) Game mechanics, gamification, challenges, competitive/leaderboard (n = 12); and (e) Mentor personalisation (n = 8).

The respondents also listed the app's weaknesses and the aspects they enjoyed the least. These were grouped under 7 thematic areas: (a) Style of questions (i.e., repetitive or long questions, questions focusing on numerical data or statistics, challenging and lengthy quizzes) (n = 13); (b) Animations and colour (i.e., distracting animations, avatar animation, blinking options, colour scheme) (n = 7); (c) Performance (i.e., responsiveness, delay in displaying unlocked content) (n = 6); (d) Submitting the answer (i.e., the fact that two steps were required to select and then confirm the answer is counter intuitive) (n = 3); (e) Welcome screen (i.e., lack of orientation and intro to make the user aware of the need to create an account in order to be able to save progress) (n = 3); (f) Leaderboard (i.e., poorly designed leaderboard in relation to the rest of UI design (n = 2). Finally, the last category, (g) Other, was used to group together the remaining weaknesses which were listed only once (e.g., lack of in-app, offline learning content, language barrier, font size, not possible to go back to the previous question, lack of customisation options regarding the difficulty level, quiz length, timer on/off, and lack of sound). Although the negative aspects were less represented in the gathered evaluation data, they still provide a good ground for further improving the app.

While frequency analysis provided useful insights in the cases above, it was not applicable for analysing the textual responses capturing the participants' general feedback and suggestions for improvement, the reason being that the answers were largely unique and demonstrated a great discrepancy in terms of length and breadth of information. Instead, for this question, the responses were tagged/coded based on three thematic areas which were deductively extracted based on the three areas mentioned in the respective open-ended question: (a) Design, (b) Content, and (c) Learning Effectiveness. Representative verbatim quotes showing the interplay between these three aspects are presented below.

Suggestions and Areas of Improvement Related to Design and Content

- *"The game is nice, and I love the UI. However the questions appear repetitive, and it could be exploited to climb up the leader board. I'd recommend randomly picking from a pool of questions. Overall amazing experience"*.
- *"It would be better to see the 3 possible answers ABC at once (instead of having to scroll up and down). Also, instead of the typewriter effect, I prefer the question appearing at once. The question animation is a but distracting"*.
- *"Decrease the size of the avatar's icon so the quiz questions are more visible"*.
- *"The inclusion of sounds (e.g. music track, or sound effect when a button is clicked), would enhance the user experience"*.

Areas of Improvement Related to Content and Learning Effectiveness

- *"There was no immediate feedback on what the correct answer is after giving a wrong answer; being an educational game it should show the correct answer"*.
- *"A recommendation I have in relation to the learning outcomes is the inclusion of explanations. When a user gives an answer, it should explain why the answer is right or wrong. This is especially true for numerical questions since merely indicating the correct answer does not suffice for encoding that fact into memory. An explanation is needed to ensure that the user understands or connects this number with a particular phenomenon"*.

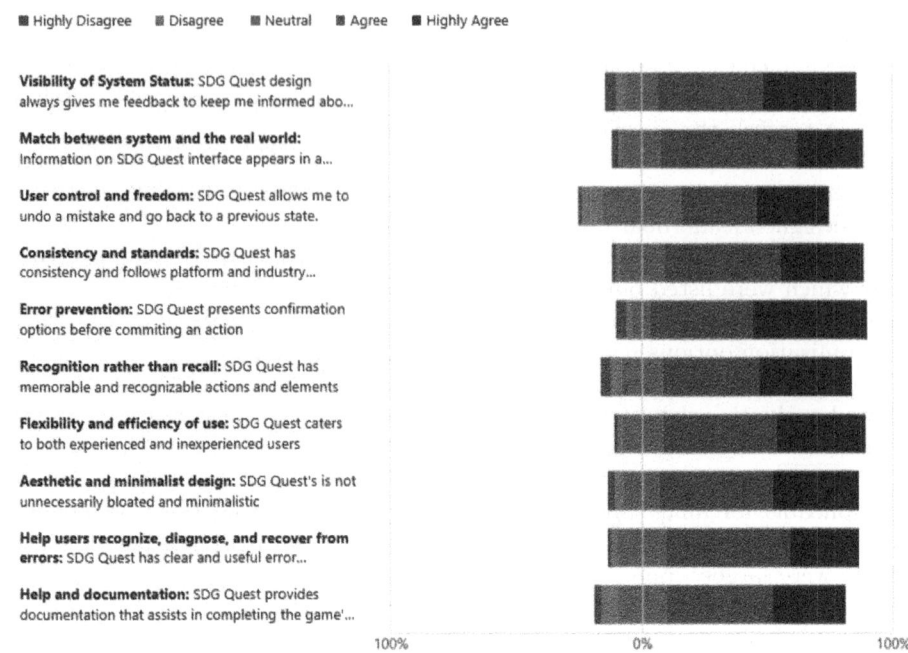

Fig. 5. Usability Evaluation - Users

- *"To really comprehend the role of SDGs there should be an option to customise the content and level of difficulty of the questions, and length of the quizzes, according to prior knowledge, educational level, or other attributes".*
- *"My main feedback concerns the intended learning outcomes. While the questions are meant to provide some practical knowledge in relation to the SDGs, the multiple-choice and True/False format does not support deep learning".*

4.2   Expert Evaluation Results

User Experience. In addition to gathering feedback from users about the app's usability and their user experience, expert evaluation was also conducted. Experts (n = 12) from related specialisation areas (including mobile development, games development, software engineering, computing, and web design and development), and between 3 and 25 years of experience (average: 11 years), were invited to playtest and evaluate SDG Quest.

The experts positively rated their overall experience with SDG Quest (4.17 out of 5). Specifically, experts agree or strongly agree that the app is visually appealing (83%), easy to use (83%), well-designed (67%), enjoyable (67%), has a good performance (92%) and is a satisfying learning game (92%), provides useful help and instructions (50%), and is appropriately challenging (67%). Evidently, experts' evaluation has more discrepancy among different aspects. Performance, user satisfaction, visual appeal, and usability were highly rated, whereas level of challenge, enjoyment, and provision of help and instructions received a lower rating. This observation indicates there is room for improvement, in terms of content customisation and the usefulness and accessibility of the provided help and instructions, for reaching the app's full potential.

Usability Design. Expert evaluation was performed using Nielsen's heuristics. Although the overall evaluation was positive, it is noteworthy that the principle of 'User control and freedom' has the most responses under 'Strongly disagree' (17%) compared to all other principles (Fig. 6). It is also intriguing that this is the same aspect which users rated comparatively lower. In the case of quizzes, the option to undo or go back is naturally restricted. Still, user flexibility can be improved by ensuring the user can easily navigate to a previous state or easily locate the necessary access controls. Experts were also asked to evaluate various design-oriented aspects. They highly rated visual design (11 out of 12 or 92% Good/Excellent, and 1 out of 12 or 8% poor); font size (100% Good/Excellent); font colour and colour palette (11 out of 12 or 92% Good/Excellent, and 1 out of 12 or 8% neutral).

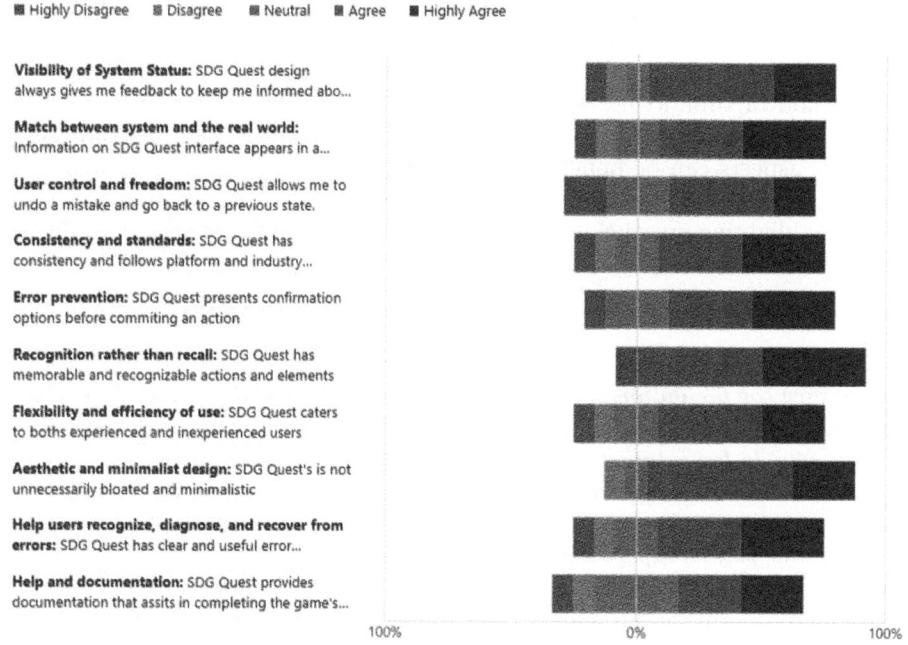

Fig. 6. Usability Evaluation - Experts

Strengths, Weaknesses, and Suggestions for Improvement. The experts were also queried about what they consider as the most and least enjoyed aspects of SDG Quest, and were invited to identify areas of improvement regarding the app's design, content, and learning effectiveness.

Experts' responses about that the aspects they enjoyed the most include: gamification; UI Design and customisation options; step-wise approach to familiarising with the SDGs; learning about SD; hints and links to external sources for further learning; the questions were short and clear; overall design is appealing; game mechanics and rationale on the rewards and achievements is well designed and executed; challenge; the quiz nature of the app, which introduces an aspect of competitiveness into learning; the app also features animated items which make it fun to look at and an enjoyable experience; the personalisation feature, which allows the user to select from a very diverse set of characters, and the streak notifications which makes players feel good for achieving it. The most popular feature, which was explicitly mentioned by half of the experts.however, was the 'Mentor Palette' or character customisation/personalisation.

In addition to identifying strengths, highlighting weaknesses and limitations is imperative. Experts highlighted several recommendations: adding more guidance when first launching the app (on the 'Home' screen); explaining the learning objectives of the educational game in the outset; providing animated instructions on how to unlock the levels; adding more flexibility (e.g., when re-entering the app to resume rather than restart, constraining animations, removing the two-click method of submitting an answer); providing access to the 'Help' screen; and redirecting to key screens to easily locate information. They emphasised that these aspects can be beneficial especially for new users who are unfamiliar with the app and SDG goals. A selection of representative verbatim quotes from experts highlighting creative ideas and areas of improvement is presented below.

Design-Related Suggestions and Areas of Improvement

- *"The animated gradient color at the background and text animations are not necessary (or the option to disable them should exist) as they may make users feel dizzy after playing for a long period of time"*.
- *"Add sounds for interaction feedback as well as ambiance sounds to provide a more immersive experience. Both of these should come with the option to enable or disable them"*.
- *"The total points/experience accumulated should be shown during gameplay without having to leave the quiz or navigate to the Account screen"*.
- *"The bottom navigation should have a different background color, as it may confuse the user if there is more scrolling or not"*.

Functionality and Content-Related Suggestions for Improvement

- *"The first time a user launches SDG Quest, an option should be available to get a short visual tour explaining all functions and game mechanics"*.

- *"Reduce the number of clicks to a single click for answering a question. The option to skip a question should also be available".*
- *"Provide more customisation features and flexibility in terms of level of difficulty/challenge, language, switching sound and animations on/off, etc.".*
- *"Incorporate the option to share the ongoing game progress and achievements on social media, (e.g., how may SDGs are unlocked)".*
- *"Add an option allowing the user to share the application with other learners or have a competitive mode embedded in the app allowing a group of users to join a live competitive quiz for example".*
- *"Provide users with timely and contextual information about their current status, i.e., how many questions out of the total number were answered correctly and what the current score is".*

Learning-Oriented Suggestions and Areas of Improvement

- *"To make the game more interesting update the questions or make them progressively more difficult. This way players are encouraged to actually learn instead of just memorising".*
- *"Adding a chat bot would make the educational side of the game more interesting and help navigate the learning content on SDGs more effectively".*

The verbatim quotes present a more nuanced and contextualised picture of both experts' and users' experiences and perceptions. Future research, development, and pedagogical initiatives in the sphere of ESD can greatly benefit from the empirical evaluation of SDG Quest and the synthesis of insights gathered from diverse participants (n = 85). The findings reflect a positive user experience and highlight the game's usability, appealing design, and learning effectiveness. Creative ideas and suggestions are also captured in the participants' open ended responses highlighting key areas for further enhancing the game's features and the overall impact on fostering sustainability skills, knowledge, and behaviours.

5   Conclusion

Recent ESD initiatives embrace a range of educational technologies, including serious games [7,9,31,40], mobile educational games [27], and VR games [19] to raise awareness and educate learners around the globe on the importance of the SDGs [38]. In this study we focus on mGBL aiming to contribute to existing efforts in the realm of ESD. We present the process of user requirements gathering and analysis, user-centred design, and evaluation of SDG Quest taking a holistic view on SD capturing the knowledge, skills, and attitudes required across Environmental, Social, and Economic SDGs. The results of usability evaluation indicate that the game's appealing design and rich set of features can help promote education on Environmental, Social, and Economic Sustainability, hence addressing the identified gaps. Embracing appealing gamification features and game mechanics such as rewards, points, milestones, challenges, badges, and mentor personalisation, SDG Quest can contribute to advancing players' understanding of SD, captivate their interest through an engaging, gamified learning experience, and ultimately, nurture the right mindset required for realising the SDGs and enabling learners become active agents driving sustainable solutions [26]. The findings also illuminate a rich set of creative ideas and constructive suggestions for leveraging mGBL towards fostering the knowledge and skills required for promoting the SDGs.

Acknowledgments. This work is co-funded under the Erasmus+ Program for the project 'TIME2ACT@SD: Time to Act through Sustainable Experiences for Higher Education Students', Grant Agreement: 2022-1-PT01-KA220-HED-000087984.

References

1. Barros, L., Medeiros, F., Moraes, E., Júnior, A.F.: Analyzing the performance of apps developed by using cross-platform and native technologies. In: International Conference on Software Engineering and Knowledge Engineering (SEKE 2020), pp. 186–191 (2020)
2. Bilancini, E., Bconcinelli, L., Di Paolo, R.: Game-based education promotes sustainable water use. Research Square (2021). https://doi.org/10.21203/rs.3.rs-490913/v1
3. Ceccarini, C., Prandi, C.: EscapeCampus: exploiting a game-based learning tool to increase the sustainability knowledge of students. In: Proceedings of the 2022 ACM Conference on Information Technology for Social Good, pp. 390–396 (2022)
4. Chappin, E.J., Bijvoet, X., Oei, A.: Teaching sustainability to a broad audience through an entertainment game the effect of Catan: oil springs. J. Clean. Prod. **156**, 556–568 (2017). https://doi.org/10.1016/j.jclepro.2017.04.069
5. Chen, F.H., Ho, S.J.: Designing a board game about the united nations sustainable development goals. Sustainability **14**(18), 11197 (2022). https://doi.org/10.3390/su141811197
6. Fagarasan, C., Popa, O., Pisla, A., Cristea, C.: Agile, waterfall and iterative approach in information technology projects. IOP Conf. Ser. Mater. Sci. Eng. **1169**(1), 012025 (2021). https://doi.org/10.1088/1757-899X/1169/1/012025
7. Floricel, S.: Understanding the nature and effects of digital games in promoting sustainability. Glob. Econ. Observer **8**(2), 125–134 (2020)
8. Flutter: flutter documentation: FAQ (2024). https://docs.flutter.dev/resources/faq
9. Hallinger, P., Wang, R., Chatpinyakoop, C., Nguyen, V.T., Nguyen, U.P.: A bibliometric review of research on simulations and serious games used in educating for sustainability. J. Clean. Prod. **256**, 120358 (2020)
10. Ho, S.J., Hsu, Y.S., Lai, C.H., Chen, F.H., Yang, M.H.: Applying game-based experiential learning to comprehensive sustainable development-based education. Sustainability **14**(3), 1172 (2022)
11. Kisielnicki, J., Misiak, A.M.: Effectiveness of agile compared to waterfall implementation methods in it projects: analysis based on business intelligence projects. Found. Manage. **9**(1), 273–286 (2017). https://doi.org/10.1515/fman-2017-0021
12. Janakiraman, S., Watson, S.L., Watson, W.R.: Using game-based learning to facilitate attitude change for environmental sustainability. J. Educ. Sustain. Dev. **12**(2), 176–185 (2018). https://doi.org/10.1177/097340821878328

13. Jouan, J., De Graeuwe, M., Carof, M., Baccar, R., Bareille, N., Bastian, S., et al.: Learning interdisciplinarity and systems approaches in agroecology: experience with the serious game SEGAE. Sustainability. **12**(11), 4351 (2020). https://doi.org/10.3390/su12114351

14. Kasenides, N., Piki, A., Paspallis, N.: Exploring the user experience and effectiveness of mobile game-based learning in higher education. In: Coman, A., Vasilache, S. (eds.) 15th International Conference on Social Computing and Social Media (SCSM 2023) help at 25th International Conference on Human-Computer Interaction (HCII 2023), vol. 14026, pp. 72–91. Springer Nature Switzerland, Cham (2023). https://doi.org/10.1007/978-3-031-35927-9_6

15. Katsaliaki, K., Mustafee, N.: Edutainment for sustainable development. Simul. Gaming **46**(6), 647–672 (2014). https://doi.org/10.1177/1046878114552166

16. Langendahl, P.A., Cook, M., Mark-Herbert, C.: Exploring gamification in management education for sustainable development. Creat. Educ. **8**(14), 2243–2257 (2017). https://doi.org/10.4236/ce.2017.814154

17. Lekagul, A., Chattong, A., Rueangsom, P., Waleewong, O., Tangcharoensathien, V.: Multi-dimensional impacts of coronavirus disease 2019 pandemic on sustainable development goal achievement. Glob. Health **18**(65), 1–10 (2022). https://doi.org/10.1186/s12992-022-00861-1

18. Nielsen, J.: 10 usability heuristics for user interface design, Nielsen Norman Group (2014-2024). https://www.nngroup.com/articles/ten-usability-heuristics/

19. Nistiotis, N., Piki, A., Theodorou, P., Leal, S., Barradas, L.C., Nascimento, J.A.: Evaluation of a serious VR game designed to promote the sustainable development goals. In: IEEE CTSoc Gaming, Entertainment and Media conference (IEEE GEM 2024). IEEE (2024)

20. NNG: User experience for mobile applications and websites, Nielsen Norman Group. https://www.nngroup.com/reports/mobile-website-and-application-usability/

21. Oliveira, R.P., de Souza, C.G., da Cunha Reis, A., de Souza, W.M.: Gamification in e-learning and sustainability: a theoretical framework. Sustainability **13**(21), 11945 (2021). https://doi.org/10.3390/su132111945

22. Ouariachi, T., Olvera-Lobo, M.D., Gutiérrez-Pérez, J.: Serious games and sustainability. In: Leal Filho, W. (eds.) Encyclopedia of Sustain. Higher Education, pp. 1450–1458 (2019). https://doi.org/10.1007/978-3-030-11352-0_326

23. Pho, A., Dinscore, A.: Game-based learning (2015). https://acrl.ala.org/IS/wp-content/uploads/2014/05/spring2015.pdf

24. Piki, A.: Learner engagement in computer-supported collaborative learning environments: a mixed-methods study in postgraduate education. Ph.D. thesis, Royal Holloway University of London, UK (2012)

25. Piki, A., Ştefan, I.A., Stefan, A., Gheorghe, A.F.: Mitigating the challenges of mobile games-based learning through gamified lesson paths. In: World Conference on Mobile and Contextual Learning, pp. 73–80 (2020)

26. Pineda-Martínez, M., Llanos-Ruiz, D., Puente-Torre, P., García-Delgado, M.: Impact of video games, gamification, and game-based learning on sustainability education in higher education. Sustainability **15**(17), 13032 (2023). https://doi.org/10.3390/su151713032

27. Pombo, L.: Exploring the role of mobile game-based apps towards a smart learning city environment-the innovation of EduCITY. Education + Training **65**(2), 253–264 (2023). https://doi.org/10.1108/ET-06-2022-0238

28. Schulze, J., Martin, R., Finger, A., Henzen, C., Lindner, M., Pietzsch, K., et al.: Design, implementation and test of a serious online game for exploring complex relationships of sustainable land management and human well-being. Environ. Modell. Softw. **65**, 58–66 (2015). https://doi.org/10.1016/j.envsoft.2014.11.029

29. SDSN: Accelerating education for the SDGs in universities: a guide for universities, colleges, and tertiary and higher education institutions. Sustainable Development Solutions Network (2020). https://irp-cdn.multiscreensite.com/be6d1d56/files/uploaded/accelerating-education-for-the-sdgs-in-unis-web_zZuYLaoZRHK1L77zAd4n.pdf

30. Sophonhiranrak, S.: Features, barriers, and influencing factors of mobile learning in higher education: a systematic review. Heliyon **7**(4), e06696 (2021)

31. Stanitsas, M., Kirytopoulos, K., Vareilles, E.: Facilitating sustainability transition through serious games: a systematic literature review. J. Clean. Prod. **208**, 924–936 (2019). https://doi.org/10.1016/j.jclepro.2018.10.157

32. Tremblay, D., Fortier, F., Boucher, J.F., Riffon, O., Villeneuve, C.: Sustainable development goal interactions: an analysis based on the five pillars of the 2030 agenda. Sustain. Dev. **28**(6), 1584–1596 (2020). https://doi.org/10.1002/sd.2107

33. UN: The 17 goals — Sustainable Development. United Nations. https://sdgs.un.org/goals

34. UN: transforming our world: the 2030 agenda for sustainable development. United Nations (2015). https://sdgs.un.org/sites/default/files/publications/21252030%20Agenda%20for%20Sustainable%20Development%20web.pdf

35. UN: The Sustainable Development Goals Report 2023. United Nations (2023). https://unstats.un.org/sdgs/report/2023/The-Sustainable-Development-Goals-Report-2023.pdf

36. UN: Quality Education: Ensure inclusive and equitable quality education and promote lifelong learning opportunities for all. United Nations (2024). https://sdgs.un.org/goals/goal4#targets_and_indicators

37. UNESCO: Sustainable development goals - resources for educators (2021). https://en.unesco.org/themes/education/sdgs/material

38. UNESCO: Education for sustainable development (2023). https://www.unesco.org/en/education-sustainable-development

39. Xanthopoulos, S., Xinogalos, S.: A comparative analysis of cross-platform development approaches for mobile applications. In: Proceedings of the 6th Balkan Conference in Informatics, pp. 213–220 (2013)

40. Tan, C., Nurul-Asna, H.: Serious games for environmental education. Integr. Conserv. **2**(1), 19–42 (2023)

Automated Facial Mark Creating Systems Replace Classical Geometric Morphometrics: An Example of How New Technology Can and Should Drive Avatar Creation in a Game Development Pipeline

Hermann Prossinger[1,2] , Daniel Říha[3(✉)] , Violetta Prossinger-Beck[4],
Silvia Boschetti[2] , and Jakub Binter[2,5]

[1] Department of Evolutionary Biology, University of Vienna, Vienna, Austria
`hermann.prossinger@univie.ac.at`
[2] Faculty of Social and Economic Studies, University of Jan Evangelista Purkyně,
Ustinad Labem, Czech Republic
[3] Faculty of Humanities, Charles University, Prague, Czech Republic
`daniel.riha@fhs.cuni.cz`
[4] Technical University, Dresden, Germany
[5] Faculty of Science, Charles University, Prague, Czech Republic

Abstract. In recent years, the field of artificial intelligence (AI) has witnessed significant advancements, particularly with the development of transformer architectures and pre-learned feature extraction techniques. Before this, thousands of high-quality scientific papers using biological landmarks (manually placed by a researcher) on faces have identified relations between facial morphology and various human ratings of them. Geometric Morphometrics provides a framework for quantifying and analyzing shape variations in biological organisms, allowing for the extraction of morphological features that rely on landmark identification. In avatar creation, matters are more complex. Game designers, when attempting to mimic anticipated ratings, oftentimes cannot rely strictly on landmarks. As we document here, we can relax the rigor of constructed, geometrically identifiable landmarks and replace them with characteristic points identified by artificial neural networks (aNNs), obviating the need for tiresome, meticulous landmark identification by human operators. By integrating these features into the avatar generation process, we can ensure that the resulting avatars exhibit desired characteristics, while still adhering to biological constraints. We relate these characteristic points on female face images whose physical attractiveness has been rated by 50 males and 50 females (on a 7-point scale). We construct Dirichlet distributions of the ratings of each face and use these to investigate whether there are trends or biases in face ratings by male raters versus female raters. We use the coordinates of characteristic points on the faces to identify clusters of attractiveness and relate these clusters to heat maps of the ratings. We explore localized pseudo-symmetries, and how they relate to these ratings. Our proposed system aims to leverage the strengths of transformer architectures and pre-trained neural networks, notably their ability to capture contextual information, to enhance the realism and biological accuracy of the avatars.

© The Author(s), under exclusive license to Springer Nature Switzerland AG 2025
J. Y. C. Chen et al. (Eds.): HCII 2024, LNCS 15377, pp. 393–403, 2025.
https://doi.org/10.1007/978-3-031-76812-5_26

Keywords: Avatar · Game Design · Facial Features · Dirichlet Distribution · Geometric Morphometrics · Clustering · DBSCAN · Transformer Architecture · Pseudo-Symmetry · Facial Attractiveness

1   Introduction

With the introduction of transformer architecture, the world of computation has changed. The technology has arrived at a point where we can create not only 'machines' that learn but also those that create. Whether it is a text or an image being created, the speed and accuracy of the outcome is (nowadays) astonishing.

This also means that applied computer graphics, namely avatar generation, is affected and so (asymptotically, perhaps) approaching the world in which an image can emerge by methods that are not necessarily "off the shelf". Thus, the realism is then dependent on the factual knowledge that the algorithms can supply. In this regard, biology, perceptual and cognitive psychology, as well as neuroscience are most dependent on these specialized tools for human-like avatar creation. One of the key elements is the study of symmetry—or lack thereof—which we present in this paper.

Symmetry is a generalized mathematical concept related to conservation laws (Noether's First and Second Theorems; Noether, 1918). In conventional parlance, symmetry is more often than not identified with bilateral symmetry (left/right symmetry)—it is this symmetry which we focus on in this paper. Despite humans' visual system being able to identify bilateral symmetry, it doesn't exist—at least not for faces. Numerous external and internal violations of bilateral asymmetries can be identified, along with functional ones (such as handedness). Blatant examples of the violation of internal bilateral symmetry is the fact that the human heart is on the left, the liver on the right—and there are numerous others.

It may be inferred that human perception of (bilateral) asymmetry has an evolutionary history, because these asymmetries signal (biological) fitness, but is only advantageous if the resultant asymmetry is not too pronounced. Because the asymmetry we perceive visually is subtle, it is conventional to refer to it as pseudo-asymmetry. One signal of biological fitness is, of course, attractiveness. In this paper, we restrict ourselves to the rating of the attractiveness of 15 female faces, as rated by 50 male raters and by 50 female raters. The sample is sufficient for this demonstration as attractiveness is one of the well-studied topics and the ratings are very stable.

Attractiveness is, therefore, an issue for those designing avatars in gaming environments, virtual worlds and metaverses. Game designers, when wishing to infer attractiveness (or at least realism and comfort) of an avatar present in some gaming plot or virtual interaction, need to be aware of (and implement) some degree of pseudo-symmetry in their designs. We specify, in this paper, how subtly and how localized such asymmetries should be implemented.

The (bilateral) symmetry can be studied using Geometric Morphometrics. While Geometric Morphometrics typically relies on experienced researchers to place landmarks, automation offers a promising alternative. However, achieving fully automated landmark placement, particularly for tasks like facial symmetry analysis that involve a large number of landmarks (68 in this paper) per image, remains challenging. Automating this process requires overcoming the issues accuracy and consistency, which are crucial to avoid introducing errors into the analysis. Only then is the "right amount of life-like look of the avatar" meaningful and enhancing the experience. This is further complicated by the preparation of the learning set. Relying on stimuli that are not conventionally standardized—as we do in this article—is more meaningful.

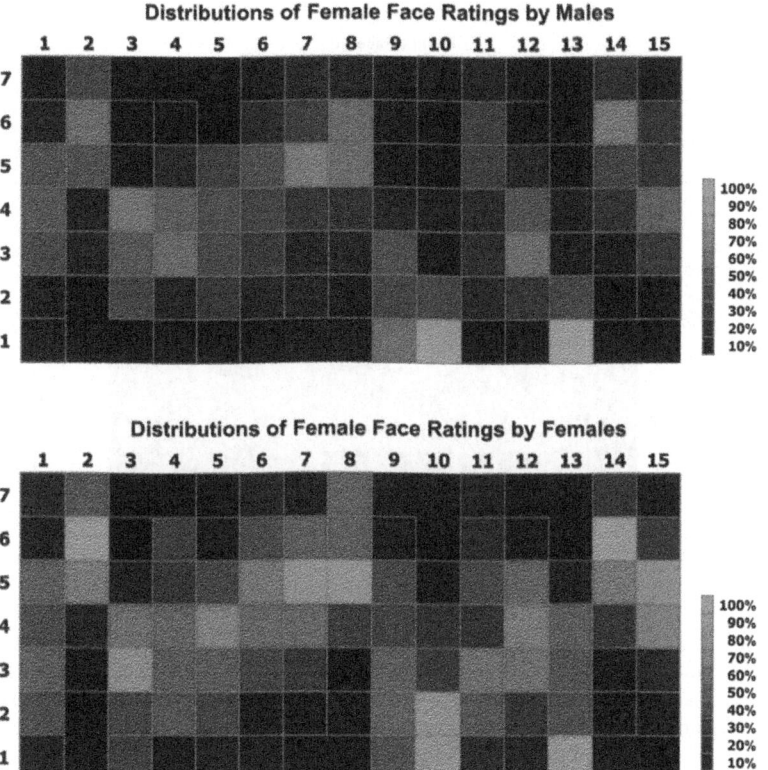

Fig. 1. The heat maps of the rating distributions of the 15 female faces by (above) 50 males and (below) 50 females. Vertical axis: rating score (from A□1 to G□7); horizontal axis: female face number. The brightness of green is determined by the fractions for each rating, scaled by the overall maximum frequency (29 in this manuscript). Squares without a gray boundary are occurrences of no ratings whatsoever. (For example, no male raters and no female raters rated female Face 14 with rating A□1, and no male raters rated female Face 2 with G□7.) Visual assessment apparently shows that some female faces are rated with very low attractiveness by male raters (for example Face 10 and Face 13) yet not so by the female raters. We use the construction of confusion matrices derived from the Dirichlet distributions (see text) to assess any possibly significantly different distributions.

2   Materials

15 color images of female faces of varying characteristics were presented to 50 male raters and 50 female raters; all were students within the age range 18–40 years. These raters were requested to rate the attractiveness of each face on a scale A–G, with A as the most attractive.

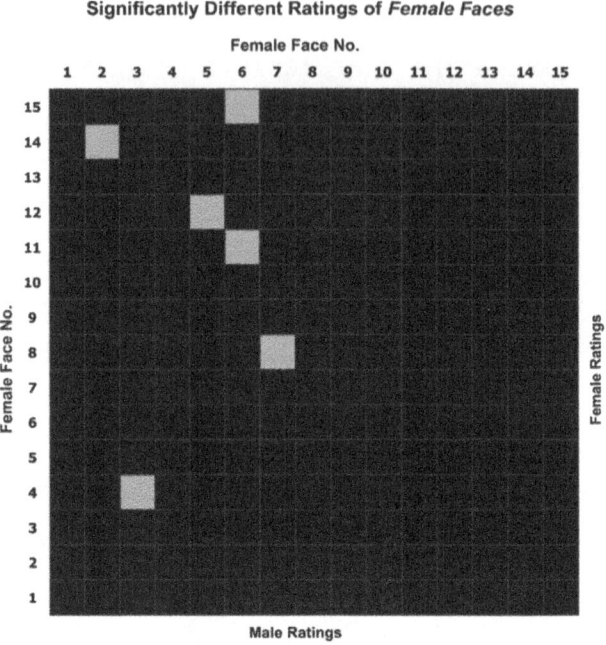

Fig. 2. The heat map of the significance of differences between the male and female ratings of the female faces. If the differences in distributions is not significant, then the entry in the heat map is a yellow square. The heat map shows that, of the 98 comparisons, only 6 are not significantly different. The (Bayesian) probability of finding this many non-significant differences due to chance is 1.9×10^{-21}; in other words, the males and females rate the faces significantly differently with very high significance.

3   Methods

3.1   Detection of Lateral Pseudo-symmetries

A face is not symmetric, so finding an axis of symmetry is impossible. Mardia et al. (2000) had devised a way of finding an axis of pseudo-symmetry for 2D images, which we implement here. The pseudo-symmetry axis is found by Procrustes superimposition of the label-symmetric characteristic points and their reflected-relabeled ones, leaving the label-non-symmetric ones (such as the tip of the nose) untouched. To do so, in this paper, we first find characteristic points (so named because they are not the landmarks in the traditional, established world of Geometric Morphometrics; Bookstein, 1991). These characteristic points are identified with a trained neural network available from Wolfram Technology. The neural network has been trained to identify characteristic points along the eyebrows, the outlines of the eyes, the ridge and lower end of the nose, the outer outlines of the lips, inner points of the mouth, and the outline of the lower edge of the face—largely the chin outline. In Fig. 3, the locations of these 68 points on one face used in the analyses are illustrated.

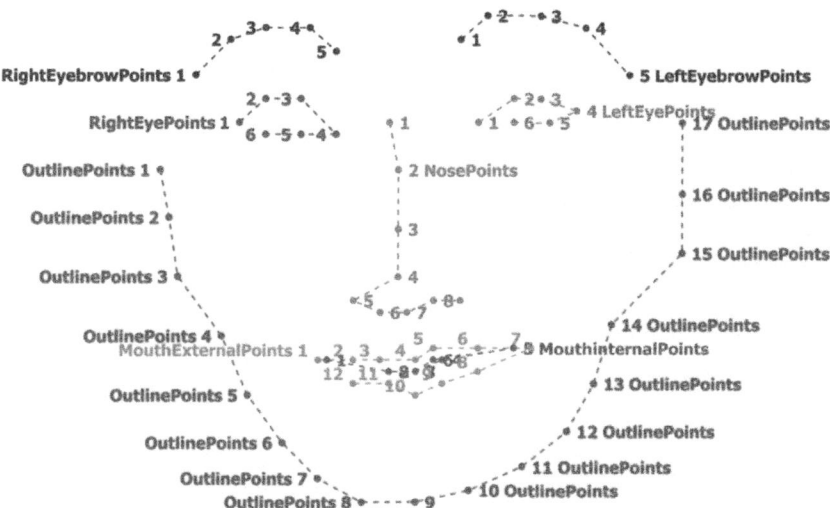

Fig. 3. The characteristic points (so called in the neural network available in Wolfram Technology's MATHEMATICA software package) of a facial image. This neural network has been trained to identify points in images of faces, as labeled. The number of identified points is fixed; it cannot be controlled/altered by the user. There are 17 points in the outline (most of it a contour line along the chin); eyebrow points and eye points are self-explanatory. There are eight nose points, four of them along the ridge. The mouth external points are essentially those along the outer outlines of the lips, while the internal mouth points are along the lips (whenever they are pressed together) or on teeth features in the case of a slightly open mouth (such as a smile with partially revealed teeth). In the data set investigated here, the issue of an open, yet toothless mouth is moot. The (geometric) location of the points is affected by the slight tilt of the head and slight smile.

Not all points are used for the determination of pseudo symmetry. We use: the eyebrows ($k = 1 \cdots 5$), the outlines of the eyes ($k = 1 \cdots 6$) and the lower (chin) outline ($k = 1 \cdots 8$). Let P_{eyek} $k = 1 \cdots 6$ be the coordinates of the outline of the right eye; likewise Q_{eyek} for the left eye. The process of reflecting laterally symmetric points (not mathematically, but biologically or image-wise) is to relabel the points P as Q' and Q as P'; this relabeling is performed for all outline points (listed above) that we used for our pseudo-symmetry investigations. We now have two sets of points and we Procrustes superimpose these, while including all other points in the image, but not reflecting/relabeling the latter prior to the Procrustes superimposition (Slice, 2004). We then obtain distances $||P_{fitk} - Q'_{fitk}||$ for all pseudo-symmetric points. A measure of the asymmetry is the sum of the squares of these distances: $asymm = \sum_k ||P_{fitk} - Q'_{fitk}||^2$. Depending on our choice of k, we obtain various measures of asymmetry: (i) for the lower outline (chin) only, (ii) for the eye outlines only, and (iii) for the eyebrows only. We thus have, for every face, three measures of asymmetry.

We can (and do) investigate whether these asymmetries cluster. In the investigations we present here, we use DBSCAN clustering (Ester et al., 1996).

3.2 Rating Distribution Comparisons

We compare the distributions of ratings by the male raters versus the female raters for each of the clusters for each of the asymmetries. We note that ratings are categorical variables; their (Bayesian) analysis necessitates the use of Dirichlet distributions.

We tally the ratings by the males and females of each female face in a cluster separately. These (tallied) ratings are Dirichlet distributed. Specifically, if $\{n_A, n_B, n_C, n_D, n_E, n_F, n_G\}$ are the tallies of the ratings of the physical attractiveness of a female face in a cluster by the male raters, then the *pdf* of the Dirichlet distribution is $pdf(\Delta Dir((n_A + 1, n_B + 1, n_C + 1, n_D + 1, n_E + 1, n_F + 1, n_G + 1),$ $s_1, s_2, s_3, s_4, s_5, s_6, s_7))$; likewise for the female raters of the same face. In order to determine whether a significant difference between the two distributions exists, we use a Monte Carlo method. We generate $ran_n = 25000$ random 7D vectors twice, one batch for the distribution ΔDir_{male} and a second batch for the distribution ΔDir_{female}. For the male batch, there will be n_{TRUE} occurrences for which $pdf(\Delta Dir_{male}, s_k) > pdf(\Delta Dir_{female}, s_k)$ (where $k = 1 \cdots 7$); $n_{FALSE} = ran_n - n_{TRUE}$. We repeat the same test for the females. We obtain a confusion matrix for the two Dirichlet distributions, namely

$$\frac{1}{ran_n} \begin{pmatrix} n_{TRUE} & n_{FALSE} \\ n_{FALSE} & n_{TRUE} \end{pmatrix}$$

in which the top row is for male raters and the bottom row is for female raters. If the off-diagonal elements are both less than 0.1, then the confusion matrix informs us that the two Dirichlet distributions are significantly different (Caelen, 2017).

We also need to find out whether the occurrences of non-significant differences are due to chance. For $n+m = 98$ comparisons, let n be the number of significant differences, and m the number of non-significant differences. Then the (Bayesian) probability that m is significant is when the significance $sig = const \int_0^{1/2} s^n (1 - s)^m ds < sig.level$, for some chosen $sig.level$.

4 Findings

The distribution of the male and female ratings of the 15 female faces are shown in Fig. 1. We find that the females and the males rate the 15 female faces significantly differently with significance $sig. = 1.9 \times 10^{-21}$ ($m = 92$ and $n = 6$; Fig. 2). We conclude that it is highly unlikely that males and females rate a female face as equally attractive.

Distributions of Female Face Ratings by Males for Procrustes Clusters

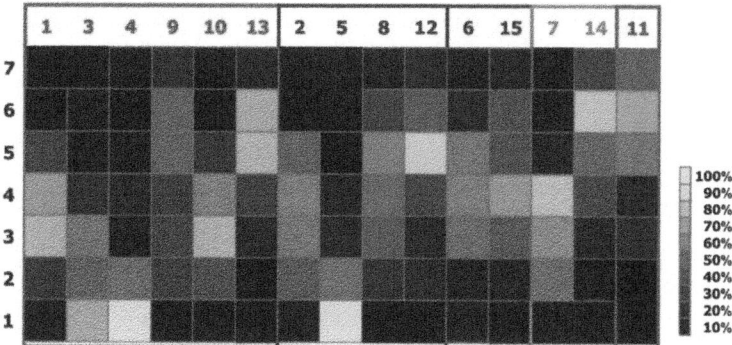

Distributions of Female Face Ratings by Females for Procrustes Clusters

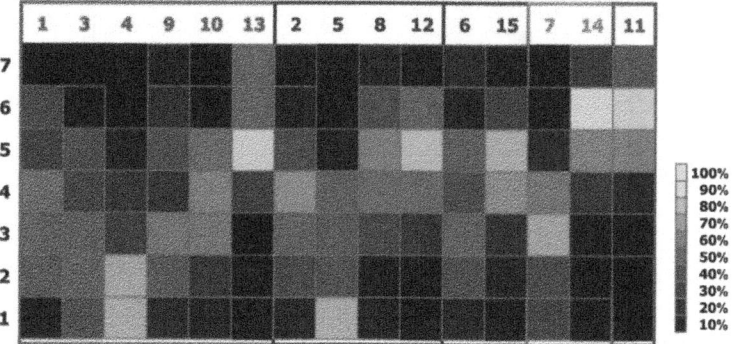

Fig. 4. The clustering of ratings of female faces by (above) males and (below) females. These heat maps show to what extent the distributions of ratings agree among the male and female raters within each of the five clusters. The clusters are identifiable by their colored peripheries.

We find that the both the male ratings and the female ratings of the female faces cluster: there are 5 clusters (Fig. 4), with a different number of faces in each cluster (Fig. 4). Remarkably, the clusters are the same for the male raters and the female raters, although the distribution of ratings is significantly different (Fig. 2).

We find that the localized asymmetries (i.e., the asymmetry of the chin outlines, the asymmetries of the eye outlines, and the asymmetry of the eyebrows) also cluster into five clusters. In Fig. 5, we graph each triple of asymmetries as a point and color-code the clusters. The memberships of faces in these clusters are not the same as in the clusters Fig. 3 (Table 2).

5   Discussion

The novel approach we present in this manuscript is to use a neural network trained to identify the characteristic points on a facial image, rather than using the landmarks identified by some researcher. Careful retrospective inspection (by us) of the output of the neural network produced by Wolfram Technologies confirms a widespread reputation of the company's algorithm's robustness, combined with exquisite quality (and computational speed): we curated the locations of all $15 \times 68 = 1088$ by visual inspection and found the neural network output superior to our characteristic landmark placement suggestions.

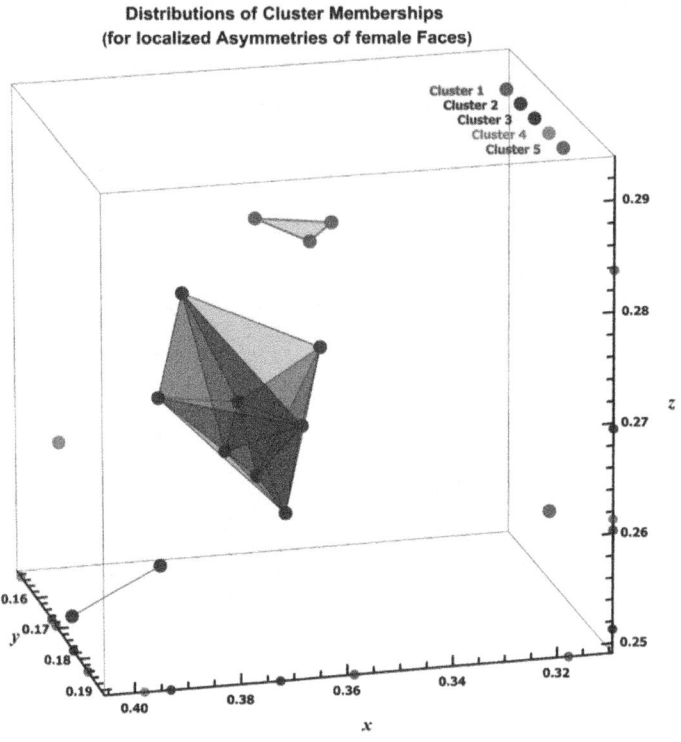

Fig. 5. The distribution of clusters of localized asymmetries of the faces. The asymmetries of the chin outlines (x-axis), eye outlines (y-axis), and the eyebrows (z-axis) were determined by the standard reflection/relabeling procedure of OPA (details in the text). The clusters were determined using the DBSCAN algorithm. Although we (again) detect five clusters with the DBSCAN algorithm, these clusters are not related to those shown in Fig. 3 (Table 2). The colored points on the axes are the mean asymmetries for each cluster (Table 1).

For each face, we superimposed only two sets of characteristic points: the points themselves as one set and the relabeled, reflected ones that are label-symmetric in the other set, while leaving some characteristic points (such as those on the nose and the mouth outlines) in their original position. This superimposition is OPA (ordinary Procrustes analysis; Goodall, 1991), in contrast to GPA (general Procrustes analysis). We did not use GPA in the analysis presented here, because we statistically investigated local asymmetries, face-by-face, and their relation with the ratings by the raters (as exhibited in the heat maps, in Table 2 and in Fig. 5); the analysis was done with a suite of techniques described in the Methods section.

Table 1. The (arithmetic) means of the asymmetries of chin outlines, eye outlines and eyebrows (Fig. 3), cluster-by-cluster. We observe, for example, that the average eye outline asymmetry in Cluster 1 and Cluster 3 are almost equal; also, for example, the mean eyebrow asymmetry for Cluster 4 and Cluster 5. The locations of these average asymmetries are shown on the graph axes in Fig. 5.

Cluster	Chin Outline	Eye Outline	Eyebrow
1	0.359	0.169	0.284
2	0.373	0.177	0.270
3	0.393	0.167	0.251
4	0.398	0.153	0.261
5	0.318	0.184	0.260

Table 2. The membership of the female faces to the five clusters for face ratings and the five clusters for local asymmetries (a triple for each face; Fig. 5). The numerical sequence of cluster membership is determined by the clustering algorithm (the smallest Face ID is the first in each cluster list). The membership of a face in face ratings clusters does not infer the same membership in the clusters of local asymmetries triple, although the DBSCAN algorithm detects five clusters in each data set. The largest cluster for face ratings contains six faces, while the largest cluster for local asymmetries triples contains eight faces (Fig. 5) There are few overlaps and there is no overall pattern. Faces 6 and 15 belong to the same cluster for face ratings and for local asymmetries triples; same cluster membership is also true for the singleton Face 11.

Cluster	Face Ratings	Local Asymmetries
1	{1, 3, 4, 9, 10, 13}	{1, 2, 14}
2	{2, 5, 8, 12}	{3, 4, 5, 7, 8, 9, 12, 13}
3	{6, 15}	{6, 15}
4	{7, 14}	{10}
5	{11}	{11}

In biology, near symmetry is often argued to be a sign of developmental stability and good fitness—indeed, a considerable body of research has demonstrated that "almost symmetric" is the decisive signal of highest attractiveness (Gangestad et al., 1994; Brown et al., 2008). Arguably, the fascination with bilateral symmetry by (classical) anthropologists, image creators, and artists can be traced to this misconception of "perfect symmetry" as an ideal and a (technically) easily achievable product.

As the example of the *Sutura palatina* demonstrates (Manschiebel, 2013), the cause of asymmetry is not always visually accessible, yet its implications are important in the context of attractiveness and, ultimately, in reproductive fitness. For example, the asymmetry of the *Sutura palatina* causes an asymmetry of the dental arches: their asymmetries are detectable in the appearance of the chin outline. Partially rectifying any dental arch asymmetry is the grist of the orthodontics industry.

If the perceived symmetry is too high, images are perceived as unnatural and animation-like in the negative sense—a discomfort caused by artificiality (Geller, 2008). This is most pronounced when perception of faces is involved, and it has been confirmed that AI-generated faces are of lower morphological diversity (Boudníková & Kleisner, 2024). A direct consequence for avatar creators: introduces a mild asymmetry! Specifically, in the face, generate local asymmetries, like the ones we list in Table 1 and graph in Fig. 5. The perception of a generated avatar (and inferentially, its rating) is under the control of its creator and adds quality to the visual impact (and the progression within the temporal evolution of the plot).

Our focusing on local asymmetries avoids both the issue of distinguishing between directed asymmetry (a population phenomenon) and fluctuating asymmetry (the remaining, non-directed component of asymmetry of each individual). The raters did not have knowledge of the population and therefore could not incorporate fluctuating asymmetry in their ratings. Rather, as we found—and present in this paper —, they seem to rate the attractiveness differently, depending on which of the three localized asymmetries (chin outlines, eye outlines, and eyebrows) they were basing their ratings on (Table 1).

These aspects of an avatar generation system further extend the capabilities by the novel incorporation of identifiable rating mechanisms. By defining features desirable in avatars *a priori* (as well as others beyond facial symmetry, namely: body proportions and other visually appealing traits—we note that these can also be modeled), the system can evaluate and assign ratings to the avatars based on their adherence to the features that we have found. This rating system, driven by the perception raters (adjusted to place, culture and historic era), enables the generation of avatars with varying degrees of quality and desirability, thereby enhancing the overall user experience in gaming environments.

In future applications, testing the applicability of latent diffusion algorithms in combination with the above suggested mechanisms of detecting localized asymmetries is strongly recommended; it ensures the perception stability and consistency of the generated avatars. Diffusion techniques, which have shown promise in various image generation tasks, can be utilized to refine the avatars and eliminate artifacts or inconsistencies that may arise during the generation process. Inclusion of ratings ensures that the avatars exhibit high visual credibility and coherence.

Our findings point to the new possibilities for enhancing the visual quality and attendant immersion of game environments. Our statistical analyses contribute to pushing the boundaries of AI-driven avatar generation into new realms that overcome the "Valley of Uncanniness."

Lastly, it should not go unmentioned that, when combined with skin textures, background colors, fashion choice decisions, and grimaces, our recommended approach allows for the generation of stimuli which can concurrently be evaluated by human raters and machine learning algorithms.

Acknowledgments. This work was supported by the *Cooperatio Program* (research area: ARTS).

Conflict of Interest. The Authors Declare no Conflict of Interest.

References

Bookstein, F.L.: Morphometric Tools for Landmark Data: Geometry and Biology. Cambridge University Press, Cambridge (1991)

Boudníková, O., Kleisner, K.: AI-generated faces show lower morphological diversity then real faces do. Anthropol. Rev. **87**(1), 81–91 (2024)

Brown, W.M., Price, M.E., Kang, J., Pound, N., Zhao, Y., Yu, H.: Fluctuating asymmetry and preferences for sex-typical bodily characteristics. PNAS **105**, 12938–12943 (2008)

Caelen, O.: A Bayesian interpretation of the confusion matrix. Ann. Math. Artif. Intell. **8**(13), 429–450 (2017). https://doi.org/10.1007/s10472-017-9564-8

Ester, M., Kriegel, H.-P., Sander, J., Xu, X.: A density-based algorithm for discovering clusters in large spatial databases with noise. In: Simoudis, E., Han, J., Fayyad, U.M. (eds.) Proceedings of the Second International Conference on Knowledge Discovery and Data Mining (KDD-96), pp. 226–231. AAAI Press (1996)

Gangestad, S.W., Thornhill, R., Yeo, R.A.: Facial attractiveness, developmental stability, and fluctuating asymmetry. Ethol. Sociobiol. **15**, 73–85 (1994)

Geller, T.: Overcoming the uncanny valley. IEEE Comput. Graphics Appl. **28**(4), 11–17 (2008)

Goodall, C.R.: Procrustes methods in the statistical analysis of shape. J. Roy Statistical Society, Series B. **53**, 285–339 (1991)

Manschiebel, S.: Die Lage der *Sutura palatina* in Bezug auf die Pseudosymmetrieebenen der Zahnbögen. Master Thesis (in German). Medical University of Vienna, Vienna, Austria (2013)

Mardia, K.V., Bookstein, F.L., Moreton, I.J.: Statistical assessment of bilateral asymmetry of shapes. Biometrika **87**, 285–300 (2000)

Noether, E.: Invariante Variationsprobleme. Nachrichten von der Gesellschaft der Wissenschaften zu Göttingen. Mathematisch-Physikalische Klasse. (in German) **1918**, 235–257 (1918)

Slice, D.E.: Modern morphometrics. In: Tuttle, R.E. (ed.) Developments in Primatology: Progress and Prospects, vol. VI. Kluwer Academic/Plenum Publishers, New York (2004)

UBI Journey: A Tool Against University Student Social Isolation

João Braga Santos[2,3] , Eulerson Rodrigues[2(✉)] , Ernesto Filgueiras[1,2,3(✉)] ,
and Flávio Almeida[2,3(✉)]

[1] Research Centre for Architecture, Urbanism and Design, Lisbon School of Architecture,
CIAUD, Universidade de Lisboa, UBI Polo, Portugal
[2] University of Beira Interior, Convento de Sto. António, 6201-001 Covilhã, Portugal
`joao.braga.santos@ubi.pt`
[3] Labcom-Communication and Arts, University of Beira Interior, Covilhã, Portugal

Abstract. This article explores the development and potential impact of UBI-Journey, a mobile game designed to enhance student socialization and exploration within the University of Beira Interior (UBI) campus environment. Drawing upon principles of gamification and leveraging techniques from successful digital games, UBI Journey aims to address common challenges faced by university students, such as integration into the academic community and navigating unfamiliar campus spaces. The game's development process involved prototyping and initial testing to assess feasibility and user engagement. Results from laboratory tests showed promising levels of user engagement, paving the way for future large-scale testing with students across multiple campus locations. Through the application of gamification mechanics and techniques, UBI Journey represents a step towards promoting socialization, exploration, and community building within the university setting. The article discusses how UBI Journey aligns with Sustainable Development Goals (SDGs) 3, 4, and 11 by fostering student well-being, enhancing educational experiences, and promoting sustainable communities within the university environment. The project contributes to the development of a model for future evaluation of software impact on users, highlighting its potential as a tool for improving student integration and academic success in higher education institutions.

Keywords: Students Social Isolation · Social Games · Geofencing Mobile Game · Augmented Reality

1 Introduction

1.1 Background

The university experience is a significant phase in students' journey, fraught with challenges and potential for personal and academic growth. Social interaction and integration into the educational institution play crucial roles in shaping an enriching experience. Studies demonstrate that successful integration can positively influence students' academic performance and emotional well-being (Tinto, 1993). However, 2 it's important

© The Author(s), under exclusive license to Springer Nature Switzerland AG 2025
J. Y. C. Chen et al. (Eds.): HCII 2024, LNCS 15377, pp. 404–415, 2025.
https://doi.org/10.1007/978-3-031-76812-5_27

to note that many students face obstacles in adapting to new university environments. According to research by the American College Health Association (ACHA), the majority of university students encounter adaptation challenges, with 63.1% reporting feeling very lonely at some point during their first year of college (ACHA, 2020). Therefore, exploring ways to facilitate this transition and promote more effective integration is of utmost relevance for the success and well-being of university students.

In today's age, games and social media have experienced considerable diffusion among young people, substantially reshaping how they relate to and connect with the world around them. Research indicates that these technologies have been effective tools in promoting socialization and exploration among users, providing more informal and dynamic interactions, while also stimulating the exploration of various locations and content.

A survey conducted by the Pew Research Center (2018) revealed that approximately 88% of young adults aged 18 to 29 in the United States regularly use social media, and 97% of them have access to smartphones. Additionally, studies like those by Hamari et al. (2014) explore how gaming elements and gamification can be incorporated into social media platforms and applications to encourage user interaction and engagement. Therefore, the intersection of gaming, social media, and interactivity has been the subject of academic and practical research in seeking more effective ways to promote socialization and exploration. The challenge posed is how we can apply the lessons learned from the success of these popular games to address the integration and socialization difficulties common among university students. The idea is to create a specific social game concept for the academic environment, leveraging the fundamental principles of these games to provide an enriching experience for students, assisting them in university integration and building solid relationships. This study aims to explore this perspective and develop absolution that can be applied in different university contexts. In response to this challenge, the UBI Rectorate initiated the development of the Academic Success Monitoring Platform, which, in partnership with the Faculty of Computer Science and the Game Design and Development Laboratory (G3Dlab), seeks solutions for these and other issues using innovative technologies.

1.2 Motivation

This work was motivated by a central challenge that many university students face: the difficulty of integration and socialization in a new and often unfamiliar academic environment. When entering university, students are confronted with the need to quickly adapt to a complex academic environment, filled with new people, procedures, and expectations.

The lack of successful integration can lead to a series of negative consequences, including social isolation, academic difficulties, and even emotional issues. Many students, especially those who are introverted or face socialization challenges, may feel lost or excluded.

At the same time, we observe that popular commercial games have a remarkable ability to promote social interactions and integration among players. These games provide an environment where people can connect, collaborate, and compete in a relaxed and engaging manner. They also encourage the exploration of virtual worlds, problem-solving, and relationship-building within the game. This research is motivated by the following question: How can we leverage the lessons learned from the success of these popular games to address common integration and socialization difficulties among university students? The proposal was to create a specific social game concept for the academic environment, incorporating the fundamental principles that make these games captivating. This has the potential to significantly enrich the student experience, aiding them in university integration, building strong relationships, and exploring the academic environment in a more engaging and interactive way.

The challenges of integration and socialization faced by university students, particularly in new and unfamiliar academic environments, have been extensively documented in the literature (Bolliger & Halupa, 2012; Elmer et al., 2020; Tinto, 1993). These challenges can result in negative consequences such as social isolation, academic difficulties, and emotional issues, particularly for introverted students or those facing socialization challenges (Freeman et al., 2014). However, research has also highlighted the remarkable ability of popular commercial games to promote social interactions and integration among players (Hamari et al., 2014). Studies suggest that games provide an environment where individuals can connect, collaborate, and compete in a relaxed and engaging manner, ultimately encouraging exploration, problem-solving, and relationship-building (Price & Kirkwood, 2014). Therefore, leveraging the lessons learned from the success of these popular games to address common integration and socialization difficulties among university students holds significant promise (Kahu, 2013). By creating a specific social game concept for the academic environment and incorporating fundamental principles that make games captivating, it is possible to enrich the student experience and facilitate university integration, relationship-building, and exploration of the academic environment (Bueno et al., 2020; Hamari et al., 2014). This work aims to contribute to this area by exploring the potential of gamification to address these challenges, drawing on insights from both existing literature and practical applications.

A notable example of how games can catalyze integration and socialization is evidenced in the work of Halbrook et al. (2019). They highlight how well-planned gamification can be a powerful tool for promoting user interaction, encouraging collaboration, and forming cohesive virtual communities. By applying these principles to the university context, we can create an experience that not only facilitates student integration but also strengthens bonds within the academic community. Thus, the development of a social game tailored to the university environment aligns with research demonstrating the tangible benefits of gamification in promoting interaction and relationship-building. Therefore, this work aimed to explore this unique perspective and develop a practical solution that can be applied in different university contexts, addressing a real and relevant problem for students' lives.

2   Literature Review

In recent years, the use of gamification in various domains, including education, has gained significant attention from researchers and practitioners alike. Gamification refers to the application of game design elements and principles in non-game contexts to engage users and enhance their experiences. Within the realm of education, gamification has emerged as a promising approach to motivate students, facilitate learning, and improve academic outcomes.

Several studies have explored the effectiveness of gamification in educational settings. For example, Hamari et al. (2014) conducted a systematic literature review on gamification research and found that gamification elements such as points, badges, leaderboards, and feedback mechanisms can effectively enhance user engagement and motivation. Similarly, Deterding et al. (2011) identified various game design elements, such as challenges, progression, and social interaction, that contribute to the effectiveness of gamified systems in promoting user engagement and behavior change. Research in the field of gamification has demonstrated its potential to enhance user interaction and collaboration within various contexts. For instance, a study conducted by Deterding et al. (2011) delved into the concept of "gamification" and its impact on user engagement. They highlighted how well-designed gamified systems have the capacity to foster collaboration among users by incorporating game design elements that promote interaction and teamwork. Similarly, Landers et al. (2015) investigated the effects of gamification on student engagement and social interaction in online learning environments and found that gamified activities increased student interaction and collaboration.

Furthermore, gamification has been increasingly used to promote exploration and discovery in educational contexts. Games such as Pokémon GO, which utilize location-based augmented reality technology, have demonstrated the potential to encourage users to explore their physical surroundings and engage with their environment in new ways. Similarly, gamified educational apps and platforms often incorporate features that encourage students to explore new concepts, solve problems, and discover new content through interactive and immersive experiences.

Recent research by Bueno et al. (2020) investigated the uses and gratifications of augmented reality games, focusing on Pokémon GO. The study examined how players engage with augmented reality games and the gratifications they derive from these experiences. The findings shed light on the motivations behind player engagement and the potential benefits of augmented reality games for promoting physical activity, social interaction, and exploration.

Additionally, the utilization of gamification in educational settings aligns with the objectives outlined in the United Nations Sustainable Development Goals (SDGs), particularly Goals 3, 4, and 11. Goal 3 aims to ensure healthy lives and promote wellbeing for all at all ages, which can be supported through gamified interventions that promote physical activity and social interaction. Goal 4 focuses on ensuring inclusive and equitable quality education and promoting lifelong learning opportunities, which can be facilitated by gamified educational platforms that enhance student engagement 5 and motivation. Finally, Goal 11 aims to make cities and human settlements inclusive, safe, resilient, and sustainable, which can be addressed through gamified applications that encourage exploration and interaction within urban environments (United Nations, 2015).

2.1 Social Games

Social games have been recognized for their potential to foster feelings of belonging and camaraderie among participants and create an environment conducive to initiating conversations and establishing social connections (Snodgrass et al., 2017). Group missions, by promoting cooperation and collaboration, contribute to the development of important skills and strengthen bonds among users (Cole & Griffiths, 2007). Through avatar customization and cosmetic stores, games offer players the freedom of individual expression, increasing their sense of autonomy and self-esteem (Fox et al., 2013).

Free Fire, developed by Garena, is one of the most popular social games for mobile devices currently. With its assertive approach, the game has attracted millions of players worldwide and has become a cultural phenomenon. It offers a Battle Royale experience, where players compete against each other in a virtual environment, aiming to survive and become the last player or team standing. Avatar customization in Free Fire plays a crucial role in attracting players and building their virtual identity. Players can customize their avatars with a variety of clothing, accessories, and skins, allowing them to express their individuality and style within the game. This customization possibility contributes to a deeper emotional connection between the player and their avatar, increasing engagement and interest in continuing to play.

Additionally, Free Fire encourages online interactions among players through features such as voice chat and text messages. This real-time communication enables the coordination of strategies, sharing gaming experiences, and teaming up with friends or players from around the world. These social interactions contribute to the creation of a cohesive community around the game, where players can share common interests and connect with people from different cultural backgrounds.

Among Us, developed by InnerSloth, is a notable example of how social games for mobile devices can promote social interactions and build bonds among players. In this immersive digital scenario, players are transported inside a spaceship, where they take on roles as crew members. The core dynamics of the game are twofold: on one hand, players work together to complete vital tasks for the ship's operation, such as system maintenance and specific activities; on the other hand, they also face an additional intriguing challenge. One or more players are designated as sabotaging impostors, whose mission is to destabilize the ship and eliminate crew members without being discovered. This mechanic initiates a cat-and-mouse game, where intrigue, deduction, and strategy become crucial components.

Academic studies have explored the importance of these social interactions in online games, highlighting how games like Among Us can lead to a sense of belonging, cooperation, and even the formation of lasting social bonds (Yee, 2006). Through strategic discussions, careful deductions, and teamwork, this game exemplifies how social games can create a socially enriching experience. In this example, players need to communicate their suspicions, share information, and coordinate efforts to identify impostors, while impostors use deception and deceit to achieve their goals. Among the results of studies on games like Among Us, it has been found that they can contribute to the development of social skills, such as communication enhancement, teamwork ability, and deepening empathy. Additionally, such games provide opportunities for the creation of shared narratives, reinforcing the sense of belonging to the player community. In an academic context, these findings have inspired the creation of an institutional game, aiming to apply similar principles of social interaction and cooperation to enhance students' university experience.

2.2 Location-Based Games

With the advent of geolocation technology and the growing popularity of digital exploration games, new possibilities for integration between the virtual and physical worlds have emerged. In this context, we will analyze relevant academic references that address the impact of games like Pokémon Go, which utilize geocaching in real-world exploration.

Pokémon GO, developed by Niantic, is widely recognized as a pioneer in the use of augmented reality and geolocation in mobile games (Althoff et al., 2016). By combining elements of the Pokémon universe with real-world exploration, the game has attracted millions of players worldwide, demonstrating how technology can be harnessed to engage players in virtual adventures within the context of their physical environments. The game puts players in the role of Pokémon trainers, encouraging them to explore the real world to capture, train, and battle with these virtual creatures.

The gameplay of Pokémon GO is based on the use of geolocation and real maps, allowing players to find Pokémon at physical locations in the real world. By physically moving in their surrounding environment, players can encounter wild Pokémon in various places such as parks, squares, tourist spots, and even their own neighborhoods. This transforms the gaming experience into an adventure, encouraging exploration and social interaction as players seek out different species of Pokémon.

In addition to capturing Pokémon, the game offers the opportunity to participate in battles at Gyms and Raids. Gyms, located at key points in the city, serve as venues for competition and conquest, where players can compete against each other by defending the Gym or attacking other trainers' Pokémon to claim control. Raids, on the other hand, are high-level cooperative battles where players join forces to face powerful d legendary Pokémon, with the chance to capture them after victory.

The article "Influence of Pokémon Go on Physical Activity: Study and Implications" by Althoff (2016) analyzes the impact of the Pokémon GO game on players' physical activity. The study reveals that the game motivated many players to engage in physical activities such as walking, which may have positive implications for public health. The game's geolocation and augmented reality were identified as factors that encouraged exploration and physical movement.

Another article, "Tourism-based regional development: boosting and inhibiting factors" by Alves et al. (2021), presents factors that drive regional development based on tourism. Considering the potential of games in promoting the exploration of physical spaces, these software applications can be seen as an opportunity to boost local tourism. Games like Pokémon GO have demonstrated their potential to boost tourism in various parts of the world. A notable example is the effect the game had on cities like Yokohama, Japan, where themed game events attracted thousands of players and visitors to the region. Additionally, historical sites, monuments, and specific tourist areas were highlighted as points of interest in the game, leading to a significant increase in the number of tourists visiting these locations to explore and capture virtual creatures. This phenomenon illustrates how the interaction between the virtual world of games and the real world can create a powerful synergy that benefits the tourism sector and promotes interest in discovering new places and cultures.

Developed by Niantic, the same company behind Pokémon GO, Ingress combines elements of augmented reality, geofencing, and geocaching with real-world exploration. In Ingress, players take on the role of agents who are part of two conflicting.

factions: Enlightened and Resistance. The main objective is to capture virtual portals, which are located in real-world places such as tourist spots, historical landmarks, and works of art.

Geofencing is used to define virtual areas on the game map, corresponding to specific locations in the real world. When a player approaches these areas, they can interact with the portals and perform actions in the game. Geocaching is incorporated through game items called resonators, which players must collect when visiting the portals. The study conducted by Kosa and Uysal (2022) offers an enlightening perspective on the effects of geocaching activity on players' experience in augmented reality games like Ingress. By analyzing how these games provide an increase in players' well-being, we can better understand how the encouragement of outdoor exploration provided by such games can positively influence players' immersion and satisfaction.

The combination of real-world elements with virtual elements in AR games creates an interaction that encourages players to explore their physical environment while participating in virtual challenges. In this context, the study highlights how the immersion provided by presence and the physical activity involved can enrich players' experience, highlighting the potential of these games to promote not only fun but also discovery and interaction with the real world.

3 Methodology

The development process of UBI Journey began with the conceptualization of the game's design and features, aimed at addressing the challenges of integration and socialization faced by university students. The initial phase involved brainstorming sessions and consultations with stakeholders, including students, faculty members, 8 and educational experts, to identify the key elements and mechanics that would facilitate social interaction and exploration within the academic environment. Once the conceptual framework was established, the development team proceeded to create a prototype of the game using game development tools and software. The prototype was designed to provide a basic representation of the gameplay mechanics, user interface, and interactive features envisioned for the final product. This early prototype served as a proof of concept to test the feasibility of implementing gamification elements to promote student engagement and interaction. Following the development of the prototype, initial tests were conducted to assess the functionality and usability of the game. A small group of participants, including students and faculty members, were invited to playtest the prototype and provide feedback on their experience. The playtest sessions were structured to gather qualitative feedback on various aspects of the game, such as gameplay mechanics, user interface design, and overall enjoyment. It's important to note that these initial tests were conducted as a preliminary exploration of the concept, aiming to evaluate the potential of gamification in addressing the targeted challenges. The focus was on identifying technical issues, user experience preferences, and areas for improvement in the game design. The results of these tests informed further iterations of the game development process and provided valuable insights for refining the gameplay experience.

Moving forward, future studies will involve more extensive testing and evaluation of the UBI Journey game among a larger group of university students. These studies will focus on measuring the potential impact of the game on student integration, socialization, and overall academic experience. Quantitative metrics, such as student engagement levels, social interaction patterns, and academic performance indicators, will be collected and analyzed to assess the effectiveness of the game in achieving its intended objectives. Additionally, qualitative feedback from participants will be gathered to gain deeper insights into their perceptions and experiences with the game.

4 UBI Journey

UBI Journey is a mobile application designed to enhance the university experience by promoting socialization and exploration among students at the University of Beira Interior (UBI). The game incorporates gamification elements to engage users and incentivize participation in various activities within the academic environment.

4.1 Key Features

Below, we present the key features of the game, UBI Journey. Each of these features have been designed to enhance user engagement, promote socialization, and provide an immersive and enjoyable gaming experience. Avatar Customization: Players can create and customize their avatars to represent themselves within the game. This feature allows users to personalize their gaming experience and express their individuality.

Exploration Challenges: UBI Journey offers a series of exploration challenges that encourage players to visit different locations on campus. These challenges are designed to familiarize students with various campus facilities and landmarks while promoting physical activity and social interaction.

Social Interaction: The game facilitates social interaction through features such as in-game messaging, group activities, and collaborative challenges. Players can connect with classmates, form study groups, and participate in multiplayer activities to earn rewards and achievements.

Reward System: UBI Journey implements a reward system based on gamification principles to motivate and incentivize players. Users earn points, badges, and virtual rewards for completing challenges, achieving milestones, and engaging with the game.

Leaderboards: The game features leaderboards that display the rankings of players based on their performance and achievements. This competitive element encourages friendly competition among students and fosters a sense of community within the game.

GPS-Based Navigation: UBI Journey utilizes GPS technology for navigation on the in-game map. This feature enables players to navigate the virtual campus and locate specific points of interest or challenges based on their real-world location.

4.2 Gamification Mechanics

In this section, we will focus on presenting and explaining each gamification element incorporated into the game. This section will provide a details of various gamification components designed to enhance player engagement.

Points and Rewards: Points are awarded to players for completing tasks, participating in activities, and achieving goals within the game. These points can be redeemed for virtual rewards, such as customizations for their avatars or access to exclusive in game content. Badges and Achievements: UBI Journey includes a badge system that rewards players with virtual badges for accomplishing specific milestones or demonstrating particular skills. These badges serve as visual representations of players' accomplishments and can be showcased on their profiles.

Progression System: The game features a progression system where players advance through levels by earning experience points (XP). As players level up, they unlock new features, challenges, and rewards, providing a sense of accomplishment and progression.

Social Challenges: UBI Journey incorporates social challenges that require players to collaborate with their peers to complete tasks or achieve objectives. These challenges promote teamwork and social interaction, fostering a sense of community among players.

5   Results and Discussion

This section provides an analysis of the outcomes observed during the study, including observation on user engagement levels, feedback received from participants, alignment with Sustainable Development Goals, and potential implications for future research and development in the field.

5.1   User Engagement and Feedback

During the iterative process of creating UBI Journey, several prototypes were developed and tested to refine the game mechanics and user experience. These prototypes underwent rigorous testing in laboratory settings, allowing for detailed analysis of user interactions and feedback. Through these iterative design cycles, the team behind UBI Journey sought to strike a balance between engaging gameplay mechanics and intuitive, user-friendly design. Feedback gathered from these tests played a crucial role in shaping the final design of the game, ensuring that it not only captured the interest of users but also provided a seamless and enjoyable experience.

The gamification mechanics and techniques implemented in UBI Journey proved to be highly effective in captivating users during the testing phase. Participants in the laboratory tests expressed a high level of engagement and enthusiasm for the game's features, indicating that the chosen mechanics resonated well with the target audience. This positive feedback validated the design decisions made throughout the development process and underscored the effectiveness of gamification in enhancing user engagement.

Furthermore, the user feedback collected during the testing phase provided valuable insights into areas for improvement and refinement. Suggestions and observations from participants were carefully considered and incorporated into the game's design, resulting in iterative enhancements aimed at optimizing user experience. By leveraging user feedback, UBI Journey was able to evolve into a more polished and compelling product, better suited to meet the needs and preferences of its intended audience.

The refined design of UBI Journey, informed by user feedback and iterative testing, is now ready for the next phase of evaluation: large-scale testing with students across the university's various campuses. This pivotal step will provide an opportunity to assess the game's impact on a broader demographic and gather additional insights into its effectiveness in promoting student engagement and socialization. Ultimately, this project represents a significant milestone in the ongoing development of a model that can be further evaluated and refined to maximize its positive impact on users.

5.2 Sustainable Development Goals (SDGs)

The objectives of UBI Journey align closely with several Sustainable Development Goals (SDGs) outlined by the United Nations, particularly Goals 3, 4, and 11. Goal 3, "Good Health and Well-being," is addressed through the promotion of physical activity and social interaction among students, which contributes to overall well-being and mental health. By encouraging students to explore campus facilities and engage in physical activities, UBI Journey supports a healthier lifestyle and enhances student well-being. Goal 4, "Quality Education," is advanced by UBI Journey's focus on enriching the university experience through gamified learning and socialization opportunities. The game provides a unique platform for students to acquire practical knowledge about campus resources, engage in collaborative learning experiences, and develop essential skills such as teamwork and problem-solving. By enhancing the quality and effectiveness of the educational experience, UBI Journey contributes to the goal of ensuring inclusive and equitable quality education for all. Goal 11, "Sustainable Cities and Communities," is addressed through UBI Journey's emphasis on promoting exploration and engagement within the university campus. By encouraging students to discover and utilize campus facilities and resources more efficiently, the game contributes to the development of sustainable and inclusive communities within the university environment. Additionally, by fostering a sense of community and belonging among students, UBI Journey supports the creation of vibrant and resilient university communities that are essential for sustainable urban development.

5.3 Future Directions and Implications

The findings from this study suggest that gamified interventions such as UBI Journey have the potential to positively impact student socialization, engagement, and wellbeing within the university context. However, further research is needed to assess the long-term effects of such interventions and their broader implications for student success and academic outcomes. Future studies could explore the relationship between student engagement with UBI Journey and indicators of academic performance, retention rates, and overall satisfaction with the university experience.

Moreover, the integration of sustainable development principles into gamified interventions like UBI Journey presents an exciting opportunity to promote social, environmental, and economic sustainability within educational institutions. By aligning gamification strategies with the objectives of the SDGs, universities can leverage technology and innovation to create more inclusive, engaging, and sustainable learning environments that empower students to become active agents of positive change in their communities.

In conclusion, UBI Journey represents a promising approach to enhancing student socialization, exploration, and engagement within the university environment. By incorporating gamification elements and aligning with the objectives of the SDGs, UBI Journey offers a novel platform for promoting student well-being, fostering inclusive learning experiences, and contributing to the development of sustainable university communities. Further research and collaboration are essential to maximize the potential impact of gamified interventions like UBI Journey and advance the goals of quality education, well-being, and sustainable development in higher education settings.

Acknowledgments. This study was also partially supported by national funds through FCT - Fundação para a Ciência e a Tecnologia, I.P., under the Strategic Project with the references UIDB/04008/2020 and UIDP/04008/2020.

Disclosure of Interests. The authors have no competing interests to declare that are relevant to the content of this article.

References

Althoff, T., White, R.W., Horvitz, E.: Influence of Pokémon go on physical activity: study and implications. J. Med. Internet Res. **18**(12), e315 (2016). https://doi.org/10.2196/jmir.6759. PMID:27923778;PMCID:PMC5174727

Alves, H.M.B., Manso, J.R.P., Teixeira, Z.M.S.S., Estevão, C.M.S., Nave, A.C.P.: Tourism-based regional development: boosting and inhibiting factors. Anatolia (2021). https://doi.org/10.1080/13032917.2021.1924211

American College Health Association: American College Health Association National College Health Assessment II: Undergraduate Student Reference Group Executive Summary Spring 2020. American College Health Association (2020)

Bollinger, D.U., Halupa, C.: Student perceptions of satisfaction and anxiety in an online doctoral program. Distance Educ. **33**, 81–98 (2012). https://doi.org/10.1080/01587919.2012.667961

Bueno, S., Gallego, M.D., Noyes, J.: Uses and gratifications on augmented reality games: an examination of Pokémon go. Appl. Sci. **10**(5), 1644 (2020). https://doi.org/10.3390/app10051644

Cole, H., Griffiths, M.D.: Social interaction in massively multiplayer online role-playing gamers. CyberPsychology Behav. **10**(4), 575–583 (2007). https://doi.org/10.1089/cpb.2007.9988

Deterding, S., Dixon, D., Khaled, R., Nacke, L.: From game design elements to gamefulness: defining gamification. In: Proceedings of the 15th International Academic MindTrek Conference: Envisioning Future Media Environments, pp. 9–15. ACM (2011). https://doi.org/10.1145/2181037.2181040

Elmer, T., Mepham, K., Stadtfeld, C.: Students under lockdown: comparisons of students' social networks and mental health before and during the COVID-19 crisis in Switzerland. PLoS ONE **15**(7), e0236337 (2020)

Fox, J., Bailenson, J., Tricase, L.: The embodiment of sexualized virtual selves: the Proteus effect and experiences of self-objectification via avatars. Comput. Hum. Behav. **29**, 930–938 (2013). https://doi.org/10.1016/j.chb.2012.12.027

Freeman, S., et al.: Active learning increases student performance in science, engineering, and mathematics. Proc. Natl. Acad. Sci. **111**(23), 8410–8415 (2014)

Hamari, J., Koivisto, J., Sarsa, H.: Does gamification work? --a literature review of empirical studies on gamification. In: 2014 47th Hawaii International Conference on System Sciences, pp. 3025–3034. IEEE (2014)

Halbrook, Y., O'Donnell, A., Msetfi, R.: When and how video games can be good: a review of the positive effects of video games on well-being. Perspect. Psychol. Sci. **14**, 1096–1104 (2019). https://doi.org/10.1177/1745691619863807

Kahu, E.R.: Framing student engagement in higher education. Stud. High. Educ. **38**(5), 758–773 (2013). https://doi.org/10.1080/03075079.2011.598505

Landers, R., Bauer, K., Callan, R., Armstrong, M.: Psychological theory and the gamification of learning (2015). https://doi.org/10.1007/978-3-319-10208-5_9

Price, L., Kirkwood, A.: Using technology for teaching and learning in higher education: a critical review of the role of evidence in informing practice. High. Educ. Res. Dev. **33**(3), 549–564 (2014)

Snodgrass, J., Dengah II, H., Lacy, M., Bagwell, A., Van Oostenburg, M., Lende, D.: Online gaming involvement and its positive and negative consequences: a cognitive anthropological "cultural consensus" approach to psychiatric measurement and assessment. Comput. Hum. Behav. 66 (2017). https://doi.org/10.1016/j.chb.2016.09.025

Tinto, V.: Leaving College: Rethinking the Causes and Cures of Student Attrition, (2nd ed.) University of Chicago Press (1993)

Yee, N.: Motivations for play in online games. Cyberpsychol. Behav. **9**(6), 772–775, December 2006. https://doi.org/10.1089/cpb.2006.9.772. PMID: 17201605. Accessed 21 Nov 2016

Rhythmic Galaxy: A New Metaverse Concert Empowering Players Through Co-design

Limeng Wang⬤, Yian Wang⬤, Zhongyuan Fan⬤, Yutong Guo⬤, Jingya Li⬤, and Yuan Yao$^{(\boxtimes)}$⬤

School of Architecture and Design, Beijing Jiaotong University, Beijing 100044, China
yuanyao@bjtu.edu.cn

Abstract. How can we redesign the virtual concert experience in Metaverse? Rhythmic Galaxy is an innovative VR music game designed to transcend the boundaries of traditional musical performances, offering a unique and inclusive music experience. Through co-design, we recognize the demand for virtual concerts and explore the innovative experiences that can arise from shifts in player identity. The significance of this design lies in empowering players, transforming the traditional roles of performer and audience into Spatial Artisans, Visual Contributors, Audio Maestros, and Behavior Shapers. By collaborating across these roles, players can engage in the creation of virtual stages, customization of music modules, and audiovisual expression. We discovered that this redistribution of control through musical performance can form a new type of Metaverse concert, expanding the significance of musical works within virtual spaces (Fig. 1).

Keywords: Virtual Reality · Virtual Concert · Game Design · Spatial Interaction

1 Introduction

In recent years, the rise of VR has driven efforts to create an open, inclusive Metaverse, with Metaverse concerts emerging as a social hotspot for music fans globally. These virtual events remove location barriers, allowing global participation and increasing inclusivity. The integration of VR with HCI aims to deliver multimodal, accessible, and immersive interactions [22,24,27,28].

Metaverse concerts typically mimic traditional stage setups with limited roles for actors and audience. VR has been used mainly to enhance visual and auditory effects and provide limited audience interaction, missing the opportunity to deepen musical understanding and connect users psychologically in the Metaverse. There's a gap in addressing the needs of those who wish to express emotions through music communally.

Our design addresses this by exploring future Metaverse concert possibilities. We designed "Rhythmic Galaxy," a multiplayer virtual stage game, with seven

J. Y. C. Chen et al. (Eds.): HCII 2024, LNCS 15377, pp. 416–428, 2025.
https://doi.org/10.1007/978-3-031-76812-5_28

music-affiliated participants. It's a cyberpunk, Chinese-themed concert, offering a game, performance, and co-created social experience. Using the Hexad player model, we redefined roles and interactions, giving players more creative control and "embodied visibility" [11] to perform, direct, or disrupt, allowing for unique collaborative performances and emotional sharing. In the boundless virtual world, audiences will have the opportunity to become integral parts of music and performance creation, evolving from the roles of spectators to those of "spect-actors" [13].

Fig. 1. Rhythmic Galaxy, an innovative VR concert.

2 Background and Related Work

2.1 Virtual Concert and Video Game

As early as 2006, music performances in "Second Life" marked the inception of virtual concerts [2]. That same year, Phil Collins's performance of "In The Air Tonight" in "Grand Theft Auto: Vice City Stories" integrated virtual concerts into gaming experiences [1]. In the past 20 years, there has been a surge in high-quality commercial and gamified virtual concerts. Examples from 2019 include "Fortnite Party Royale [4]", "Only Wanna Be With You (Pokmon 25 Version) [3]" and "Intermundium [5]", among others. Especially since the pandemic in 2020, the emotional suppression of the public has accelerated the development of virtual concerts. The characteristics of these virtual concerts are that they enrich the performance scenarios, support performers and audience members in choosing avatars, and interact within certain areas around the performance zone.

2.2 Virtual Art Performance and HCI

In recent years, research on enhancing VR art experiences within the field of HCI has gradually increased. These studies often employ gamification design principles and multimodal technologies to enhance user engagement with music or artistic performances. At the level of artistic works, artists and HCI designers strive to provide novel forms of artistic engagement for both audiences and performers through diverse and conceptually rich creations. Some relevant works include "The Calling [12]", "Cyberdream VR [29]", "Becoming [31]", "Gumball Dreams [17]", "Anonymous [8]", among others.

In the field of virtual art performance control, several interactive interface designs have emerged to support user participation. For example, users can interact with music and lighting in virtual spaces through the application of embodied cognition technologies. [6,7]. Tools supporting user-generated music and stage designs have been developed [25,26,30], along with VR demonstration systems enhancing user rehearsal effectiveness [15].

As the integration of art performances with VR advances, issues of user participation and social interaction within VR are receiving increasing attention. Typical research areas include: real-time participation methods for multiple musicians and audiences to join virtual concerts from different locations [16,21,22], social interaction methods among multiple individuals within and beyond the virtual world [18], The contribution of music to player experience in VR games [23], positive attitudes of users in VR towards shared experiences, performance, self-expression, and identity [20], User identity transformation and self-reflection in artistic performances [8,13].

Relevant industry and academic works provide experiential support that our designed virtual concert game serves as a form rather than an end goal. The significance of this design is to empower residents of the digital age with a passion for music to participate in virtual concerts, enabling them to find resonance and emotional value within these musical interactions, and to help users have a more proactive and immersive experience in the game's musical exchanges (Fig. 2).

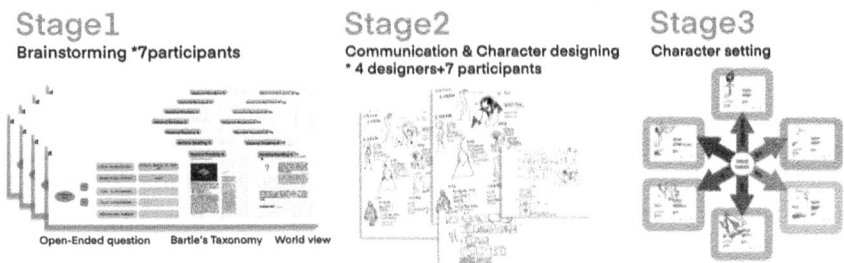

Fig. 2. The process of creative design.

3   Co-design

3.1   Recruitment and Participants

We sought collaboration with music industry professionals to better understand and meet the needs of virtual concert participants, aiming to foster innovation in our design process. A recruitment notice was posted in a Chinese music fan group, from which we selected seven individuals (5 females, 2 males, average age 25.42, SD 6.9) eager for innovative virtual concert participation, with diverse stage-related experience. Our group consisted of a drummer, lead singer, bassist, arranger, stage designer, photographer, and a student experienced in stage lighting. To thank them, we will share our prototype's latest developments to spark their creative input.

We launched our project by emphasizing the aim to empower player engagement in Metaverse concerts, highlighting how participants' concert expertise could enhance our co-design effort. Framing them as "game designers," we encouraged them to extend beyond their usual roles [10] to influence concert game dynamics. Through a Figma interface, they explored identities within both real and virtual concerts and envisioned their ideal Metaverse concert experience. To guide these visions into tangible designs, we presented a game narrative where digital residents call upon humans to use VR for dance and concert creation, an act pivotal to preserving their musical Metaverse. The Hexad model was also provided as a tool to deepen the understanding and design of player identities. This led participants to develop a range of game roles, narratives, and visuals, aligning with diverse player motivations. By this point, participants were fully briefed on their recruitment, the objectives of testing, and had a clear direction for their design contributions.

3.2 Game World View

In the digital realm of infinite possibilities, human forerunners discovered a group of mysterious digital residents, led by the Skydancer, each possessing exceptional musical prowess. After development and experimentation, humans aided these residents in building a lively nexus for music. In this place, the digital denizens dance fervently to the rhythms, enriching their world and thus forging a musical utopia. Yet when the digital matrix detected the tumult, it sought to retract the residents' rights to create these musical congregations. In gratitude to humanity, the residents now wish to urgently transfer this right to us via VR technology. Will you accept the invitation to partake in the grand feast of the stage offered by the digital residents?

3.3 Character and Interaction Strategy Design

Participants aimed to create game roles aligned with their visions. Seven participants, aided by four authors, engaged in deeper discussions with the team on player empowerment in Metaverse concerts and refined their game role designs. Incorporating feedback and using textual and visual formats, they developed the game roles. Seven game role design sets emerged, with each set containing four to seven roles.

We learned that participants wish for virtual concert players to move beyond traditional limits on self-presentation, actively influencing the performance and particularly in expressing "identity" and "emotion" (p2, p3, p4, p5, p7).

We integrated participant feedback into our design by adapting seven proposed game roles with distinct abilities. For instance, participants wanting to "showcase themselves" (p2, p4) inspired roles with social, independent, and competitive traits, allowing players to be conspicuous and change their appearance freely. These were condensed into a "Visual Contributor" role, encapsulating designed skills for interactive design purposes.

Based on participants' design materials, we summarized and defined four player identities: Spatial Builders, Auditory Controllers, Visual Contributors, and Behavioral Shapers, and outlined their in-game interactions. Utilizing a Chinese cyber aesthetic, we created six detailed game roles, elaborated in the following chapter.

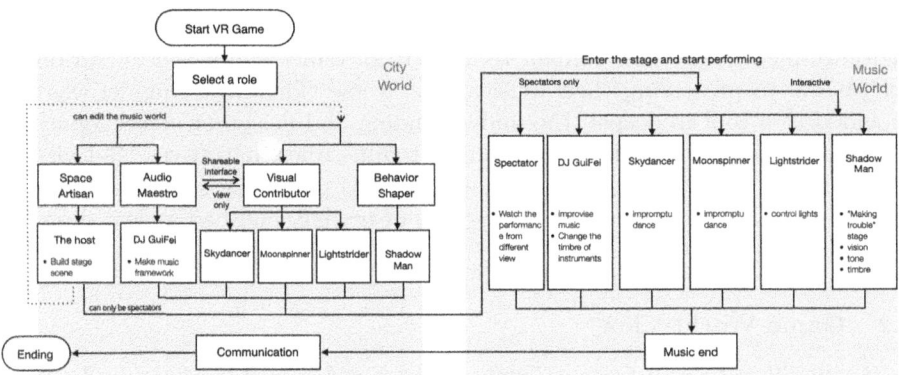

Fig. 3. Game flow chart.

3.4 Game Flow Design

Participants highlighted the psychological transition between real and virtual concerts and issues with stage operations (p2, p4, p5). This shaped a pre-performance module in the game flow (Fig. 3) , allowing players to start the concert game more effectively once they are prepared.

The game features two virtual environments: the "City World" (Fig. 5a) for role selection and social interaction, and the "Music World" (Fig. 5c) for concert creation and performance. Players start in "City World," pick roles, and communicate. "Spatial Artisans" and "Audio Maestros" then build the stage and music in "Music World." During the concert, performers collaborate in "Music World" for an expressive show (Fig. 5f). Post-concert, players reconvene in the "City World" to share experiences, enhancing the game's depth and their collective enjoyment.

Game character settings   Technical support

Fig. 4. Game character settings and technical support.

4 Game Concept Development

4.1 Main Character Design

Space Artisan: The Host. The Spatial Artisan, focused on social engagement and achievements, is tasked with stage construction and coordination. They must build the stage foundation by leveraging player interactions and plan initial placements within the scene. The Host starts by discussing stage designs with players, considers the basic musical structure from DJ GuiFei, and selects scene models to form the stage's core look. After building the stage, The Host may switch roles or watch the show as a spectator. Post-performance, The Host leads a discussion to reflect on the setup and exchange feedback.

The Host acts as the master of the room and the god of the stage, gathering the ideas of other player characters from the beginning to conceive the performance. Much like arranging furniture in a room, The Host designs the stage setting for the players to move and interact within. After completing the preliminary work, The Host has the authority to decide whether to join the guests in the room for an engaging performance or to remain an observer, appreciating any event that unfolds within the space.

Visual Contributors: Skydancer, Moonspinner, Lightstrider. "Visual Contributors" like Skydancer, Moonspinner, and Lightstrider are akin to Socialisers, Free Spirits, and Killers, enabling collaborative creation of emotionally expressive performances. Certain VR players thrive on audience attention [20], finding excitement and a performance drive, and are buoyed by praise for their dance-a fit for expressing themselves as Visual Contributors. Tactile feedback from visual challenges in collaboration becomes a conduit for emotional and informational exchange. We've enhanced visual feedback for subtle emotional expression through body and limb movements [14]. The humanoid Skydancer (Fig. 4a) utilizes gestures to convey feelings. Multiple Visual Contributors can exist on stage; the dancer Moonspinner (Fig. 4b) features dynamic visual mapping for magical effects, with player movements reflecting in its pliable structure's contortions. The Lightstrider (Fig. 4c), a lighting controller, is operated by player hand gestures, where finger spread simulates light emission and gestures dictate light intensity and beams.

The participants envision the Skydancer as an energetic humanoid dancer with a body resembling that of a human, but with various planets replacing the head. The planets radiate immense energy and shine in their uniqueness due to their different types. The Moonspinner is positioned close to the Skydancer on the stage, as they are akin to the lead dancer and the backup dancers, complementing each other. However, the Skydancer is more like a street dancer with a distinctive personality, whose performances feel more direct and robust; whereas the Moonspinner is like a collaborative dancer painting a picture, adept at expressing delicate and expansive emotions. The Lightstrider, designed to resemble lighting, weaves between the Moonspinner and Skydancer, crafting an atmospheric ambiance. These Visual Contributors bestow drama upon the visual center of the stage and infuse the entire space with light and vitality.

Audio Maestro: DJ Guifei. The Audio Maestro is an explorer in sound innovation, with authority over performance assignments. We highlight the importance of body awareness linked to sound elements in the game [19]. They use virtual instruments instead of physical contact, creating sounds with bodily motions and gestures.

We have designed DJ GuiFei (Fig. 4d) , who constructs the basic music framework and segments before the performance and incorporates impromptu Chinese instrumental creativity during the show. Using a moon-shaped spherical controller that resembles a hand, DJ GuiFei manipulates the music through gestures of tapping, striking, and sliding. Integrating classic scenes from traditional Chinese Peking opera, we designed the theme-based interaction of "GuiFei Intoxicated, Gazing at the Moon." The climax of DJ GuiFei's musical performance is marked by the lifting of the controller, signifying the moon's ascent.

DJ GuiFei's appearance is akin to a robot from the future, logical and unquestionable, differing from the "GuiFei" of Chinese Peking opera. This suggests to players that they are about to embody a new "GuiFei," one that originates from traditional culture but transcends past and present concepts. DJ GuiFei advances the performance with her skill in creating music, no longer confined to fixed bodily movements at set times with a single story outcome, as in the opera. Instead, she holds the power of movement in her hands, open to the possibilities of multiple storylines.

Behavior Shaper: The Shadow Man. The Behavior Shaper, "The Shadow Man," blends competition with exploration, disrupting the mundane with strategic actions that influence the game. Rhythmic Galaxy introduces this role to break the monotony of past virtual concerts and spark more discussions. This character has unique abilities that can affect the stage's sensory elements and gameplay complexity. It enriches player interactions by varying the degree to which their actions affect other virtual objects [9]. The Shadow Man can manipulate music and visuals locally, changing pitch and tone, impacting all players' visual experiences. He's an agent of chaos and creativity.

The Shadow Man's presence in Rhythmic Galaxy is a subject worth examining for its impact on user experience. He does not make a substantial visual or auditory "contribution" to the stage, but as a game character, he represents a variant with limitless expansion possibilities. Strong recommendations from our participants (p1, p2, p6) have led us to assertively define the player type known as the Behavior Shaper and to create The Shadow Man based on the concept of visual and auditory "filters." This character is conceived as an innovative attempt within the Metaverse concert setting, suggesting a subtle yet significant influence on the overall ambiance and player interaction.

Role Relationships. The Audio Maestro and Space Artisan team up for initial audiovisual setup, while Visual Contributors join the Audio Maestro to finalize the performance's sights and sounds. Behavior Shapers, unique in their impact, can alter other roles positively or negatively, drawing their behavioral influence from players of other roles.

Game composition includes 3–15 players: 1–2 Space Artisans, 1 Audio Maestro, at least 1 Visual Contributor, and any number of Behavior Shapers.

Fig. 5. Game scene settings.

4.2 Game Scene Design

The "City World" (Fig. 5a) acts as a transitional bridge from reality to the "Music World" (Fig. 5c), gathering players in a virtual city. As the show starts, a music airship carries them to the "Music World" (Fig. 5b), where they perform on a vast, irregular stage (Fig. 5e,f). The concert stage setting is closely related to the musical experience, requiring a synesthetic connection from auditory to visual senses. The visual form of the stage originates from The Host's spatial creation, where the model materials crafted by The Host are pre-converted from the music's signal data and sound characteristics provided by us. During the pre-fabrication of the model library, we first analyze some music segments that can be used in the game, using Matlab to read and analyze the audio signal features. Then, we amplify these signal features in Touchdesigner to achieve audio visualization from audio to graphics, forming a basic musical graphic perception. Afterwards, we use Blender and ZBrush to further sculpt the basic shapes and ultimately export them as model library materials.

A model acts like a phase or component of the music; the entire stage composed of multiple models can be seen as a visualization of the performance's music. One of our team members takes on the role of DJ GuiFei, combining pre-show music production with improvisational music production during the performance to create a 2-minute electronic music show. Figure c is a top-down view of the Rhythmic Galaxy stage, which was constructed by another team member playing the role of The Host, based on the music using the model library. Its shape is bizarre and abstract, complementing the style of electronic music. Moreover, the stage also needs to consider the space for players' activities. In this scene, The Host plans to place the main golden stage in the center of the entire larger stage, for Skydancers and Moonspinners to move on; the elongated arc-shaped wall structures on both sides delineate the larger stage space, providing Lightstriders with a movement plan following their contours; a large dynamic mesh-like spherical structure envelops the outside of the stage, serving as decorative lighting for the stage backdrop. Opposite the main golden stage, there is a focal point of the entire stage space-DJ GuiFei's performance area. DJ GuiFei communicates face-to-face with Skydancers, Moonspinners, and Lightstriders in this scene, as if engaging in a dialogue through musical performance from a distance. The other parts of the stage provide a habitat for The Shadow Man, allowing him greater scope for creativity.

5   Participant Feedback

All test subjects were co-design phase participants. We investigated the technical support required for game production (Fig. 4e, f, g, h) and communicated the possible features to them. We created a visual prototype of the game process and, through the testers' explanations, guided the subjects to comprehend interaction within the Metaverse. *"(p1) The idea of different players collaboratively performing a concert with their bodies makes me eager to try it out."* Some subjects were intrigued by the interaction with the concert. *"(p6)Being able to thoroughly observe the stage is fantastic". "(p7)Wearing VR devices being able to emit stage lights with my hands feels novel to me". "(p3) The way DJ GuiFei is operated reminds me of a magic sphere, akin to the methods employed by real-world DJs, yet it introduces innovative elements. I look forward to experiencing this type of narrative-rich interaction with virtual instruments."*

6   Reflection and Future Work

For the new generation of users who are more attuned to virtual and digital experiences, virtual concerts offer a musical experience that aligns with their digitally native lifestyle. This game design represents a modest foray into design exploration. Although the video prototype is virtual, participants were still able to project themselves into the experience, recognizing the potential value that redistributing control through musical performance brings to Metaverse concerts, responding to their aspirations for what a concert could be. However, we lack feedback from actual device usage. At the same time, some test subjects expressed concerns about this new way of engaging with concerts: *"(p5) I feel uncertain about participating in the stage experience in this manner. "* We must also consider measuring user experience across more dimensions.

7   Conclusion

Rhythmic Galaxy aims to revolutionize traditional VR concerts by co-designing with music professionals and learners, resulting in a Metaverse concert prototype that empowers player participation. Utilizing the Hexad player model as a framework, we guided participants to design seven game role concepts. From these designs, we distilled four categories of virtual concert player identities and developed six game roles for prototype usage. Building on this, we crafted deeper role concepts from the perspective of player identities, granting players greater agency to experience different aspects of musical performance.

During the prototype feedback phase, we produced and presented a video prototype. Participants indicated that this type of virtual concert facilitates self-expression and emotional resonance through musical performance. This suggests that redistributing control through musical performance can transform virtual concerts into an even more exciting form of entertainment and social interaction, exploring the potential of future VR concerts.

References

1. "in the air tonight" - Phil Collins concert (2006). https://www.youtube.com/watch?v=gZrcUDRUBjw
2. Second life rocks (2006). http://news.bbc.co.uk/2/hi/technology/5253782.stm
3. Only wanna be with you (pokémon 25 version) (2019). https://www.pokemon.com/us/pokemon-news/a-post-malone-concert-and-pikachu-distribution-for-the-pokemon-25th-anniversary-celebration
4. Fortnite party royale (2020). https://www.fortnite.com/@epic/party-royale
5. intermundium (2023). https://sensoriumgalaxy.com/intermundium
6. Altosaar, R., Tindale, A., Doyle, J.: Physically colliding with music: full-body interactions with an audio-only virtual reality interface. In: Proceedings of the Thirteenth International Conference on Tangible, Embedded, and Embodied Interaction, p. 553–557. TEI 2019, Association for Computing Machinery, New York, NY, USA (2019). https://doi.org/10.1145/3294109.3301256
7. Arterbury, T., Poor, G.M.: 3D positional movement interaction with user-defined, virtual interface for music software: MoveMIDI. In: Extended Abstracts of the 2019 CHI Conference on Human Factors in Computing Systems, pp. 1–6. CHI EA 2019, Association for Computing Machinery, New York, NY, USA (2019). https://doi.org/10.1145/3290607.3312954

8. Bahng, S., Kelly, R.M., McCormack, J.: Reflexive VR storytelling design beyond immersion: facilitating self-reflection on death and loneliness. In: Proceedings of the 2020 CHI Conference on Human Factors in Computing Systems, pp. 1–13. CHI 2020, Association for Computing Machinery, New York, NY, USA (2020). https://doi.org/10.1145/3313831.3376582

9. Chen, C.C., Li, T.Y.: Interactive smart character in a shooting game. In: Proceedings of the 2007 ACM Symposium on Virtual Reality Software and Technology, pp. 231–232. VRST 2007, Association for Computing Machinery, New York, NY, USA (2007). https://doi.org/10.1145/1315184.1315235

10. Dindler, C., Iversen, O.S.: Relational expertise in participatory design. In: Proceedings of the 13th Participatory Design Conference: Research Papers-Volume 1, pp. 41–50 (2014)

11. Freeman, G., Acena, D.: "acting out" queer identity: the embodied visibility in social virtual reality. Proc. ACM Hum. Comput. Interact. 6(CSCW2), 1–32 (2022)

12. Ilongwe, A., Sepulveda, C., Kashani, T.: The calling VR: a musical virtual reality experience. In: ACM SIGGRAPH 2023 Immersive Pavilion. SIGGRAPH 2023, Association for Computing Machinery, New York, NY, USA (2023). https://doi.org/10.1145/3588027.3595598

13. Jdid, F., Richir, S., Lioret, A.: Virtual stage sets in live performing arts (from the spectator to the spect-actor). In: Proceedings of the Virtual Reality International Conference: Laval Virtual. VRIC 2013, Association for Computing Machinery, New York, NY, USA (2013). https://doi.org/10.1145/2466816.2466840

14. Kleinsmith, A., Semsar, A.: Perception of emotion in body expressions from gaze behavior. In: Extended Abstracts of the 2019 CHI Conference on Human Factors in Computing Systems, pp. 1–6. CHI EA 2019, Association for Computing Machinery, New York, NY, USA (2019). https://doi.org/10.1145/3290607.3313062

15. Lalioti, V., et al.: VR rehearse & perform - a platform for rehearsing in virtual reality. In: Proceedings of the 27th ACM Symposium on Virtual Reality Software and Technology. VRST 2021, Association for Computing Machinery, New York, NY, USA (2021). https://doi.org/10.1145/3489849.3489896

16. Lyons, D., Butchko, S.G., Moore, J., Bradley, B., Soto, T.L.: Live performance in VR: live performance in virtual reality by creators from different metaverses discuss the challenges and advantages of performance in this new storytelling platform. In: ACM SIGGRAPH 2021 Panels. SIGGRAPH 2021, Association for Computing Machinery, New York, NY, USA (2021). https://doi.org/10.1145/3450617.3464495

17. Lyons, D.V., Davis, C.L., Butchko, S., Frank, W., Tull, B., Roy, B.: Gumball dreams: live theatre in VR. In: ACM SIGGRAPH 2023 Immersive Pavilion. SIGGRAPH 2023, Association for Computing Machinery, New York, NY, USA (2023). https://doi.org/10.1145/3588027.3595593

18. O'Hagan, J., Williamson, J.R., Khamis, M., McGill, M.: Exploring manipulating in-VR audio to facilitate verbal interactions between VR users and bystanders. In: Proceedings of the 2022 International Conference on Advanced Visual Interfaces. AVI 2022, Association for Computing Machinery, New York, NY, USA (2022). https://doi.org/10.1145/3531073.3531079

19. Palacio, P., Bisig, D.: Piano&dancer: Interaction between a dancer and an acoustic instrument. In: Proceedings of the 4th International Conference on Movement Computing. MOCO 2017, Association for Computing Machinery, New York, NY, USA (2017). https://doi.org/10.1145/3077981.3078052

20. Piitulainen, R., Hämäläinen, P., Mekler, E.D.: Vibing together: dance experiences in social virtual reality. In: Proceedings of the 2022 CHI Conference on Human Factors in Computing Systems. CHI 2022, Association for Computing Machinery, New York, NY, USA (2022). https://doi.org/10.1145/3491102.3501828
21. Ppali, S.: Music from anywhere & everywhere: exploring the design space of remote music performance. In: Companion Publication of the 2023 ACM Designing Interactive Systems Conference, pp. 45–49. DIS 2023 Companion, Association for Computing Machinery, New York, NY, USA (2023). https://doi.org/10.1145/3563703.3593067
22. Ppali, S., et al.: Keep the VRhythm going: a musician-centred study investigating how virtual reality can support creative musical practice. In: Proceedings of the 2022 CHI Conference on Human Factors in Computing Systems. CHI 2022, Association for Computing Machinery, New York, NY, USA (2022). https://doi.org/10.1145/3491102.3501922
23. Rogers, K., Milo, M., Weber, M., Nacke, L.E.: The potential disconnect between time perception and immersion: effects of music on VR player experience. In: Proceedings of the Annual Symposium on Computer-Human Interaction in Play, pp. 414–426. CHI PLAY 2020, Association for Computing Machinery, New York, NY, USA (2020). https://doi.org/10.1145/3410404.3414246
24. Schlagowski, R., et al.: Wish you were here: mental and physiological effects of remote music collaboration in mixed reality. In: Proceedings of the 2023 CHI Conference on Human Factors in Computing Systems. CHI 2023, Association for Computing Machinery, New York, NY, USA (2023). https://doi.org/10.1145/3544548.3581162
25. Schlagowski, R., Wildgrube, F., Mertes, S., George, C., André, E.: Flow with the beat! human-centered design of virtual environments for musical creativity support in VR. In: Proceedings of the 14th Conference on Creativity and Cognition, pp. 428–442. C & C 2022, Association for Computing Machinery, New York, NY, USA (2022). https://doi.org/10.1145/3527927.3532799
26. Soga, A., Matsushita, T.: Movement creation by choreographers with a partially self-controllable human body in VR. In: Proceedings of the 29th ACM Symposium on Virtual Reality Software and Technology. VRST 2023, Association for Computing Machinery, New York, NY, USA (2023). https://doi.org/10.1145/3611659.3617198
27. Tanenbaum, T.J., Hartoonian, N., Bryan, J.: "how do i make this thing smile?": an inventory of expressive nonverbal communication in commercial social virtual reality platforms. In: Proceedings of the 2020 CHI Conference on Human Factors in Computing Systems, pp. 1–13. CHI 2020, Association for Computing Machinery, New York, NY, USA (2020). https://doi.org/10.1145/3313831.3376606
28. Teng, S.Y., Wu, K.D., Chen, J., Lopes, P.: Prolonging VR haptic experiences by harvesting kinetic energy from the user. In: Proceedings of the 35th Annual ACM Symposium on User Interface Software and Technology. UIST 2022, Association for Computing Machinery, New York, NY, USA (2022).https://doi.org/10.1145/3526113.3545635
29. Weinel, J.: CyberDream VR: visualizing rave music and vaporwave in virtual reality. In: Proceedings of the 14th International Audio Mostly Conference: A Journey in Sound, pp. 277–281. AM 2019, Association for Computing Machinery, New York, NY, USA (2019). https://doi.org/10.1145/3356590.3356637

30. Whitley, A., Kirchhof, S., Strutt, D.: Digital dance studio VR (DDS-VR): An innovative user-focused immersive software application for digital choreographic composition, planning, teaching, learning, and rehearsal. In: ACM SIGGRAPH 2023 Immersive Pavilion. SIGGRAPH 2023, Association for Computing Machinery, New York, NY, USA (2023). https://doi.org/10.1145/3588027.3595602
31. Yadegari, S., et al.: Becoming: an interactive musical journey in VR. In: ACM SIG-GRAPH 2022 Immersive Pavilion. SIGGRAPH 2022, Association for Computing Machinery, New York, NY, USA (2022). https://doi.org/10.1145/3532834.3536209

AI-Enhanced Tools for Cross-Cultural Game Design: Supporting Online Character Conceptualization and Collaborative Sketching

Yuanyuan Xu[1(✉)], Xinyang Shan[1], Yin-Shan Lin[2], and Jinyin Wang[3]

[1] Tongji University, Shanghai 200092, China
ecusttethys@foxmail.com
[2] Northeastern University, Boston 02115, USA
[3] Amazon Inc, New York 10001, USA

Abstract. In the context of globalization, game development teams are increasingly demonstrating cross-cultural diversity. However, existing tools often fail to adequately address the unique challenges of cross-cultural design, such as overcoming communication barriers and creative expression difficulties caused by cultural differences. This study explores a tool based on Artificial Intelligence and Computer Graphics (AICG), specifically designed to assist game concept artists from diverse cultural backgrounds in role conceptualization and collaborative sketching, thus addressing the inadequacies in supporting cross-cultural collaboration. We conducted in-depth individual interviews with six designers from different cultural backgrounds in Vancouver to determine their needs. After the first two interviews, we presented a preliminary design prototype with potential practical features to support collaborative ideation. The final four interviews involved a heuristic evaluation of the design. This research revealed several challenges faced by cross-cultural game character designers during the co-creation process, including differences in cultural understanding, language barriers, and limitations in creative expression. We outlined the functionalities required for an online product design collaboration tool: an AICG-enhanced real-time collaborative sketchboard, features for cross-cultural visual analytics, and a hybrid (online and offline) cross-cultural visual repository. This study provides new insights into developing tools that support cross-cultural game concept creation.

Keywords: Cross-cultural · Collaborative sketching · Online character conceptualization · Game concept artists

1 Introduction

In the globalized environment of game development, the integration of teams from diverse cultural backgrounds has not only become common but is also

J. Y. C. Chen et al. (Eds.): HCII 2024, LNCS 15377, pp. 429–446, 2025.
https://doi.org/10.1007/978-3-031-76812-5_29

crucial for tapping into broader markets [1,2]. These cross-cultural teams face unique challenges that can affect both their collaborative efficiency and the innovativeness and relevance of their outputs [3–5].

This study aims to exploring the development and application of tools based on Artificial Intelligence and Computer Graphics (AICG) to support cross-cultural collaboration among game concept artists [6–8]. These artists play a pivotal role in the early stages of game development, but they often encounter significant barriers due to differences in language, cultural expressions, and conceptualization methods [9–11].

As emphasized by some author, overcoming barriers in cross-cultural communication is crucial for enhancing collaboration and ensuring the success of multicultural teams [12–15]. This study delves into these issues through a series of interviews with game designers from diverse cultural backgrounds, based in Vancouver, a city known for its vibrant and diverse gaming industry. The findings of this study aim to contribute to the existing body of knowledge on cross-cultural collaboration tools and are intended to enhance the efficiency and creativity of cross-cultural game design teams.

2   Literature Review

2.1   Creative Conceptualization and Collaborative Sketching Processes in Game Design

Game concept designers play a pivotal role in the creative process, transforming abstract ideas into concrete visual expressions through sketches and digital tools. During the early stages of game development, concept generation is crucial, typically involving brainstorming among team members and exploration of various creative ideas and themes [16,17]. The goal of this phase is to establish the foundational framework of the game, including the narrative background, character settings, and core gameplay mechanics [18]. This leads into the sketching phase, where artists and designers, based on discussions from the concept generation stage, begin to create concept art and preliminary sketches [19]. These sketches often encompass elements such as characters, environments, and props, with the primary function of translating abstract ideas into tangible visual representations, thereby providing team members with a clearer and more concrete understanding and consensus on the game's visual style and design elements [20]. Further, these initial sketches and design concepts are presented to other team members, such as programmers, other game designers, and sound designers, to gather their feedback [21]. Based on this feedback, artists and designers make necessary adjustments and optimizations to the sketches and designs. Through this iterative design and evaluation process, the team can effectively integrate professional opinions from various fields, progressively refining the game design.

This process not only requires a high degree of creativity but also close collaboration with other team members [22]. Collaboration in cross-cultural teams can be particularly complex due to cultural differences and varying communication habits, which may create potential barriers [23]. In the character conceptualization process, designers must consider the adaptability of cultural elements to ensure that the character designs can communicate and resonate across cultures [24]. This requires designers to be well-versed not only in their own cultural backgrounds but also to have an understanding and respect for the cultures of their collaborators [25].

2.2   Collaborative Game Design in Cross-Cultural Contexts

In cross-cultural game design collaboration, differences in cultural understanding, language barriers, and limitations in creative expression are significant challenges that require careful management and technological strategies for resolution.

For example, due to variations in cultural backgrounds, team members might have different perceptions of time management and priorities, potentially leading to discrepancies in project timelines and expectations, which can impact the efficiency of game development and team morale. However, adopting flexible management practices that are sensitive to cultural nuances, and clearly defining the stages of work, can help reduce misunderstandings and conflicts caused by cultural differences.

Language barriers present another critical challenge, thus the choice of communication tools is essential for bridging these differences [26, 27]. Technological support can help team members better understand each other's intentions and feedback. However, it is also necessary to pay attention to the selection and configuration of these tools to ensure they support multiple languages and are adapted to subtle cultural differences [28]. Communication tools need the capacity to handle cultural and linguistic variances to prevent communication breakdowns, ensuring that all team members can accurately understand and execute the details of the game design [29].

Regarding the limitations in creative expression, team members from different cultural backgrounds may have distinct styles of creative expression and understandings of innovation, which can complicate the integration and implementation of creative ideas [30]. Shared platforms, such as collaborative digital whiteboards and shared design platforms, can not only facilitate the generation of ideas but also assist teams in organizing these ideas from a cross-cultural perspective [31]. However, the design and application of these tools must consider the diverse creative outputs and feedback styles across cultures to fully leverage the team's diversity and promote genuine innovation [32].

2.3   Challenges of Collaborative Game Design in Cross-Cultural Contexts

In cross-cultural game design collaboration, differences in cultural understanding, language barriers, and limitations in creative expression are significant challenges that require careful management and technological strategies for resolution.

In cross-cultural teams, the segmentation and management of work phases are essential to ensure timely project completion. Due to varying cultural perceptions of time and priorities, team members often encounter communication barriers and collaborative difficulties, impacting overall efficiency and potentially leading to frustration among the group [10,11]. The research recently indicates that by clearly delineating work phases and adopting culturally sensitive management strategies, teams can significantly enhance their operational effectiveness [33].

Moreover, the appropriate selection of communication tools is critical for enhancing interactions and understanding among team members [7,21]. Although technology can reduce communication gaps, selecting tools that support multiple languages and adapt to cultural differences is crucial for improving the efficiency of cross-cultural team collaboration [24,26]. This perspective is further supported by numerous scholars who stress the importance of choosing communication tools capable of accommodating subtle cultural nuances, ensuring the accuracy and effectiveness of information transmission.

In the process of innovation, the effective evaluation and organization of creative ideas are vital for stimulating the creativity of cross-cultural teams. The literature supports the notion that having shared platforms that embrace multicultural perspectives is essential [13,23]. These platforms not only facilitate the generation of ideas but also assist team members in organizing and assessing these ideas in a culturally comprehensible manner, thereby optimizing creative outcomes.

Regarding software tools, ensuring the intuitiveness of user interfaces and their cultural adaptability is extremely important. Following Nielsen's principles of interface design, software used in cross-cultural settings should undergo iterative testing to accommodate the needs of users from diverse cultural backgrounds [34]. Additionally, collecting and integrating feedback from multicultural users post-testing is crucial for the continuous improvement of design tool functionalities and enhancing user experience.

2.4   AICG-Enhanced Creativity Support Tools

In the field of AICG, the development of creativity support tools is enhancing and simulating the human creative process in unprecedented ways. These tools integrate advanced machine learning algorithms, natural language processing techniques, and in-depth user behavior analytics to foster the generation and realization of creative ideas. For instance, tools such as Adobe Sensei and Autodesk's Dreamcatcher utilize artificial intelligence to analyze users' design habits and preferences, thereby offering personalized design suggestions and automated solutions [35,36]. The application of such technology not only significantly increases the efficiency of design and creation but also enables creators to break free from traditional thinking patterns and explore new creative avenues [37].

Addressing the need for enhanced communication and collaboration across different cultural backgrounds, integrating artificial intelligence and computer graphics into collaborative tools represents a significant advancement [38]. Artificial intelligence aids in generating new ideas, automating repetitive tasks, and providing real-time feedback, thereby enhancing creativity and productivity [39]. These capabilities are particularly valuable in cross-cultural settings, where varying backgrounds and expectations can lead to communication breakdowns. Furthermore, computer graphics play a crucial role in the visualization of complex concepts, allowing team members to more easily share and understand visual ideas across cultures [40]. Recent research indicates that AI-enhanced collaborative tools can improve communication and creativity generation within creative teams, addressing many of the challenges found in cross-cultural game design collaboration.

3   Methods

3.1   Participants

We conducted semi-structured interviews with six game concept artists from diverse cultural backgrounds working in the Vancouver area. The selected artists possess extensive experience in the field of game design, particularly in character conceptualization and collaborative sketching within digital environments. The initial interviews aimed to understand their individual creative processes and their experiences working in cross-cultural teams.

After the first two interviews, we introduced a preliminary design prototype of a tool based on Artificial Intelligence and Computer Graphics (AICG). This was intended to assess the practicality and adaptability of our design in meeting the needs identified during these preliminary discussions. In interviews with the subsequent four participants, we also conducted heuristic evaluations and discussions about their specific needs. Table 1 provides detailed information about the

Table 1. Summary of the participants .

Participants	Age	Gender	Occupation	Team Size	Team was formed	Location
P1	28	M	Game character concept artist at a game development studio	8	3–5 years	CO
P2	30	F	Freelance game character concept artist	5	0–3 years	DT
P3	26	M	Game character concept artist at an indie game studio	6	¿5 years	CO
P4	29	F	Game character concept artist at a large game company	9	¿5 years	DT
P5	25	F	Game character concept artist at a startup game studio	4	0–3 years	DT
P6	27	M	Game character concept artist at a mobile game com-pany	6	3–5 years	CO

Gender: F = Female, M = Male; Location: CO = Co-located, DT = Distributed, but most members were co-located participants, including their age, gender, professional role, team size, duration of team collaboration, and work location.

3.2 Data Collection

The data collection phase consisted of semi-structured interviews with six game concept artists. These interviews were meticulously designed to delve deeply into the participants' needs at various stages of the creative team process, with a particular focus on problem identification, ideation, evaluation, and documentation. We developed a series of six questions to explore different aspects of their experiences in conceptualizing and sketching game characters:

1. Online Collaboration Process: How do you organize and manage the different stages of work during the online character conceptualization process? What is the working process?
2. Digital Communication Tools: Which specific communication tools do you use in your online collaboration process? What difficulties were encountered?
3. Online Evaluation and Management of Creativity: How do you assess and organize creativity within the team in an online environment? Have you utilized any specific tools to support this process?
4. Adaptability of Professional Software: To what extent does the software used for character conceptualization and drawing meet your needs? Are there any specific features that need improvement?
5. Usability Challenges: In line with Nielsen's usability principles, what potential issues do you perceive with the tool? How do these issues impact your creative process?
6. User Interface and Feature Feedback: How would you evaluate the features such as an AICG-enhanced real-time collaborative sketchboard, features for cross-cultural visual analytics, and a hybrid (online and offline) cross-cultural visual repository and more? Do you have any suggestions?

Each interview lasted approximately one hour and was conducted in a manner that encouraged open discussion and detailed feedback. All interviews were recorded and subsequently transcribed to ensure accurate capture of the participants' responses. This comprehensive approach allowed us to gain deep insights into how the tools impact the artists' workflows and to identify areas where our software might need enhancements.

3.3 Data Analysis

After the data collection phase was completed, we utilized affinity diagramming to perform three rounds of structured coding on the interview transcripts, facilitating a comprehensive thematic analysis of the data. Initially, four researchers independently conducted open coding, identifying preliminary themes and patterns from the transcript records. This process generated a total of 232 initial codes, with a high convergence rate of 67% among them. The research team collaboratively discussed these codes and used them to create a preliminary coding manual.

In subsequent rounds, this code set was refined to further clarify and consolidate emerging insights. In the second round, the similarity among the 227 refined codes reached 96%, forming a more comprehensive set of codes. In the final round of coding, a lead researcher applied this refined code set to all the transcripts, focusing on distilling insights into key themes that describe the challenges faced by game concept artists in cross-cultural collaboration and the potential solutions offered by our AICG tools. This structured collaborative approach involving four researchers ensured the robustness of the analysis.

4   Results

4.1   Challenges and Innovative Needs in Cross-Cultural Online Character Design

In our research, we analyzed the characteristics of online character conception and drawing. While the experiences of artists generally aligned with existing literature, significant deviations in specific workflow processes were observed. These deviations highlight unique challenges faced by cross-cultural game design teams during the creative process, particularly in terms of creative expression and innovation, impact on team dynamics, and the supportive needs related to the usability and functionality of digital tools. Additionally, our findings underscore the importance of developing advanced tools that are culturally sensitive, which not only facilitate the ideation of creativity but also effectively manage and integrate diverse inputs.

Understanding Cultural Differences in the Creative Phases. Participants noted that brainstorming methods often fail to fully reflect diverse cultural perspectives, resulting in characters that may not resonate globally (N = 4). The integration of cultural elements in game design tends to be superficial, with important cultural nuances frequently overlooked during the conceptualization phase (N = 6).

Due to similar methodologies adopted by teams from different cultural backgrounds, there is a tendency for creativity to become homogenized, losing its unique cultural depth (N = 4). For instance, P2 shared their experience,

"In the early stages of design, we often struggle to figure out what kind of artistic message we want to get across with our designs. Our research tends to lead us to similar themes, and we end up discussing these themes over and over. Even though our team is diverse culturally, the stuff we create usually shows a pretty narrow view, kind of like we're seeing everything through the same cultural lens."

Moreover, there is a significant gap in delving into cultural backgrounds, which is crucial for shaping characters that are not only visually appealing but also culturally meaningful and authentic (N = 5).

Communication and Collaboration Efficiency. Language differences and cultural misunderstandings frequently impede effective communication within cross-cultural teams, affecting the clarity and efficiency of brainstorming sessions

(N = 4). These barriers complicate the exchange of ideas and often lead to reduced comprehension among team members, thereby hampering the overall collaborative process.

Cultural norms and practices significantly influence how team members interact, occasionally leading to inconsistent collaboration practices (N = 6). For example, P3 noted,

"Our team collaborates in really different ways. Some of us are straight to the point, while others take a more careful way of communicating. This often leads to mix-ups and slows us down during brainstorming, because we're not always on the same page about how to interact. "

Non-verbal cues, which are crucial in some cultures, are often lost in virtual settings, potentially leading to misunderstandings or overlooked contributions (N = 3).

Creativity Expression and Innovation. Participants frequently felt constrained by existing tools that do not always facilitate creativity across different cultural backgrounds (N = 4).

When team members misunderstand subtle cultural nuances, creativity can be adversely affected, leading to designs perceived as inauthentic or insensitive (N = 5). P5 expressed his concerns,

"We want to innovate and add new angles to our game designs. But sometimes, what we think is innovative might accidentally offend, simply because we don't fully get the deeper cultural nuances. "

Additionally, many participants also noted that technical limitations of design tools often stifle the creative potential of artists, preventing them from fully realizing their creative visions (N = 3). These technical restrictions can hinder the implementation of innovative ideas, significantly affecting the quality and depth of the final product.

Usability and Accessibility. If tools are not universally usable by all team members, especially those from diverse cultural backgrounds, it often leads to uneven contributions in the design process (N = 5). Many collaborative tools have interfaces that are not intuitive, particularly for team members who are not tech-savvy (N = 3). P1 shared their frustration,

"As an artist who mainly uses traditional drawing, I find complex design software really challenging. The tough learning curve slows me down and makes it harder to share my ideas effectively."

Additionally, teams often rely on a variety of non-standardized tools, which vary greatly in terms of usability and ease of use, making the collaboration process more complicated (N = 4).

Impact on Team Dynamics. Cultural differences sometimes lead to discord in team interactions, affecting the effectiveness of collaboration (N = 4). Not all team members feel that their voices are heard equally, which can lead to feelings of marginalization, especially among members from less represented cultures (N = 5). This disparity can disrupt team cohesion and reduce the overall productivity and creativity of the group. Concerned by P6,

"Sometimes, cultural differences create a bit of tension in our group. It feels like not everyone's opinions are taken seriously, which can be really disheartening. It tends to be those of us from that aren't as well represented who feel this the most."

Strategic Significance in Game Development. Failing to fully understand and integrate diverse cultural insights can limit a game's appeal in the global market (N = 4).

There is a substantial risk involved in inadvertently including culturally sensitive content, which could damage the game's popularity and the brand's reputation (N = 6). As game development teams grow and become more culturally diverse, adapting development processes to accommodate this diversity becomes increasingly challenging. P3 highlighted the strategic importance of this adaptation,

"When we develop games for a global audience, we need to be very careful about cultural nuances. Misunderstandings can lead to backlash, which not only affects our sales but can also harm our reputation."

As half of participants feel, a lack of genuine multicultural insights can hinder innovation, leading to games that fail to resonate fully with or engage diverse audiences (N = 3).

4.2 Character Concept Design and Sketching Tools

During the character concept design and sketching processes, participants typically utilize communication methods such as messaging apps on smart devices, offline meetings, emails, and video conferencing. For the initial stages of concept generation, software like PureRef, Adobe Bridge, Moodboard, MindMeister, and Autodesk Sketchbook are employed to foster creativity. In later stages, communication and discussion with the team often involve tools like Zoom, Microsoft Teams, and Jira. Most participants find these methods practical because:

1. Efficiency and Organization: The use of these software tools can enhance the efficiency and organization of character creativity generation (N = 6).
2. Visualization of Diverse Visual Themes: Methods that allow for the visualization of multiple visual themes can promote creative thinking and visual exploration in character design (N = 5). For instance, P2 noted, *"Using tools like Moodboard and MindMeister really helps me play around with different looks and feels when I'm designing game characters. I can mix and match colors and ideas visually, which helps me see how everything works together and affects the character's vibe and story. "*
3. Real-Time Sharing and Collaboration: Tools that support real-time sharing and collaboration ensure coherence in design direction and safeguard the final quality of the project (N = 5).

Despite the convenience provided by existing tools during the initial concept stages of game character design, there are still key areas where further improvements could enhance the effectiveness and efficiency of the overall design process:

1. Redundancy and Inefficiency Due to Lack of Smarter Features: There is a need for more intelligent functionality to reduce redundancy and inefficiency (N = 3).
2. Limited Support for Diverse Cultural Artistic Styles: The resources offered by software, such as brushes, often lack adequate support for various cultural artistic styles (N = 4).

4.3   Preliminary Design Assessment

During the preliminary design assessment phase of the project, all game character concept designers participated and provided valuable feedback on their experience using the tool for online character conceptualization and collaborative sketching. The feedback was overwhelmingly positive, with participants noting the tool's effectiveness in streamlining the ideation process.

Some participants (N = 2) requested enhancements to the sketching tools, specifically seeking brushes with more features and faster response times to quickly mimic various artistic styles suitable for rapid ideation phases. Others (N = 3) called for more dynamic integration of existing assets within the tool, allowing designers to manipulate and modify existing character elements in real-time, thus enhancing creativity without compromising performance.

Over half of the participants (N = 4) expressed the need for a more comprehensive asset library. P6 suggested,

"It would be very beneficial if we could have a large library of character components that could be modified and tweaked at any time. For example, if I've designed a fantasy character before, then they should be able to take elements from that design and create a new character with minimal tweaking."

Some participants (N = 2) expressed a desire to use more off-screen indicators during brainstorming sessions to maintain focus and creativity without the distraction of constant online presence. Several designers (N = 3) emphasized the need to strengthen both synchronous and asynchronous communication tools, highlighting that efficient communication is crucial for the collaborative creative process.

Half of the participants (N = 3) recommended meticulous documentation of the entire design process to facilitate post-meeting reviews. P5 noted,

"Ideally, there would be a feature that displays and analyzes the outcomes of our sketching sessions. Contributions from each participant should be clearly marked and archived for future reference."

These feedback comments reveal the potential of the tool and underscore specific improvements that could make it a more valuable asset for game character concept designers during the creative process.

5   Online Character Conceptualization and Collaborative Sketching Product Ideation

In cross-cultural game design, leveraging Artificial Intelligence and Cognitive Graphics (AICG) tools for character conceptualization and collaborative sketching offers significant opportunities to enhance team collaboration and creativity. Based on comprehensive research and feedback from various design teams, we identified several key areas or pain points. These pain points are categorized into innovation objectives, support objectives, and strategic objectives, aimed at maximizing the potential of AICG technology. The objectives are outlined as follows:

5.1 Innovation Objectives

Creativity Expression and Innovation. The core innovation objective is to amplify the creative potential of each team member through the use of AICG tools. These tools employ advanced artificial intelligence algorithms to conduct in-depth analysis of game narratives and scripts, extracting visual cultural insights. These insights are presented alongside culturally relevant reference materials, providing visual feedback suggestions for the cultural contexts of game characters (see Fig. 1). This approach not only reflects the integration of cultural aesthetics and narratives but also enhances the game's appeal and resonance in a multicultural context.

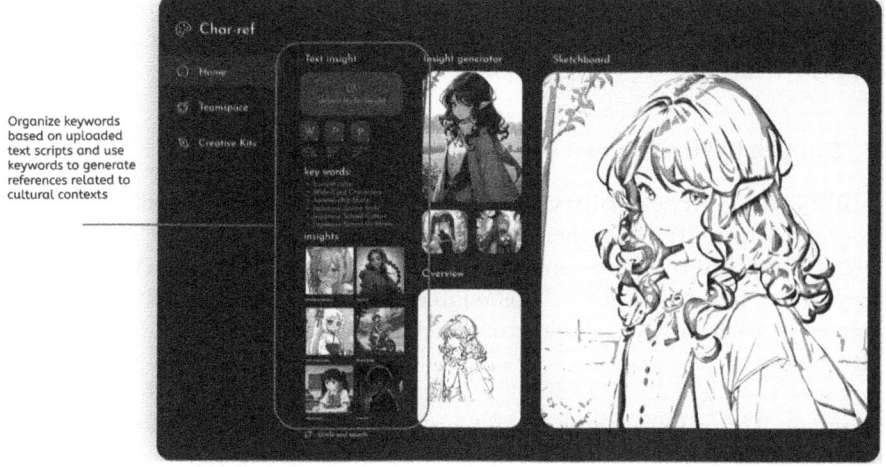

Fig. 1. Home interface, where users can get insights on key words and images through various types of documents

Understanding Cultural Nuances. The image understanding capabilities of AICG technology focus on effectively recognizing and respecting cultural differences. When team members are uncertain about the visual representation of provided reference materials or cultural elements, AICG's image search functionality can assist them in exploring these cultural visual elements more deeply (see

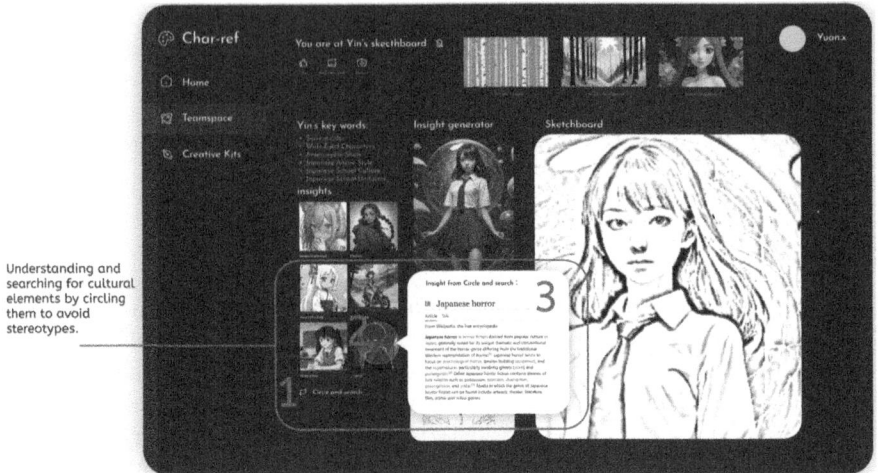

Understanding and searching for cultural elements by circling them to avoid stereotypes.

Fig. 2. Circle and Search feature, users can use this function to explore cultural elements on the insight panel.

Fig. 2). This feature not only supports artists in better understanding cross-cultural content but also enhances information sharing and visual consistency within the team. .

5.2 Support Objectives

Usability and Accessibility. The creative asset packs generated by AICG are designed to unify team members' understanding of cultural elements while allowing designers to create and maintain a personal style library through an integrated system (see Fig. 3). This enables designers to effectively utilize their resources in each project, thereby enhancing the personalization and efficiency of the design.

Impact on Team Dynamics. By integrating AICG tools that feature real-time communication and whiteboarding capabilities, this study aims to foster a more democratic mode of team engagement, positively influencing team dynamics. The system allows all team members to view each other's contributions in real-time and respond promptly, effectively eliminating cultural barriers that might arise in traditional textual communication and meetings (see Fig. 4). This mode of real-time visual communication not only enhances interaction among team members but also ensures that every voice in a culturally diverse team is expressed and understood, thereby enhancing the overall collaborative efficiency and diversity of creative outputs.

Fig. 3. Integrated with OpenAI's toolkit features, as well as functionalities that allow users to create their own offline style libraries .

Fig. 4. Teamspace interface, team users can access open boards and interact with members .

5.3 Efficiency Objectives

integrated sketching capabilities of AICG. By translating verbal descriptions into visual elements and effects, enhance designers' ability to select and iterate on these prompt results (see Fig. 5). This approach significantly improves

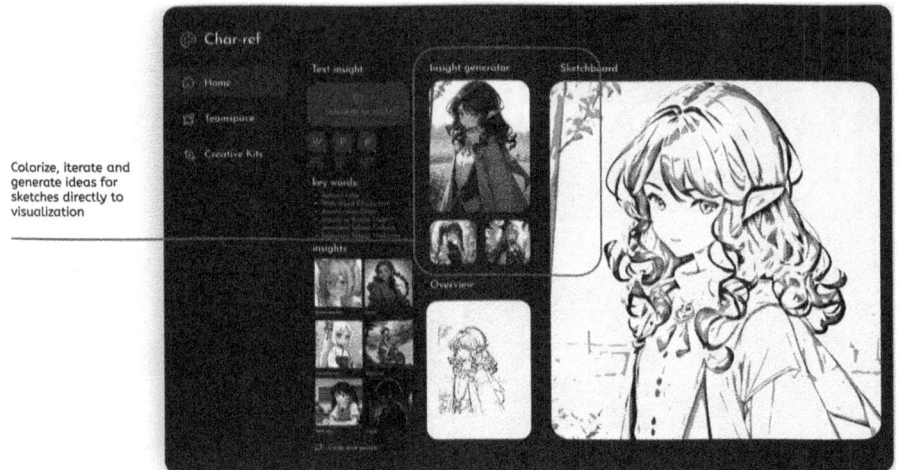

Colorize, iterate and generate ideas for sketches directly to visualization

Fig. 5. Integrated with AICG efficiency tools, empowering the creative process with AI for smoother workflow.

the clarity of design outcomes in communication and exchanges, more effectively reducing misunderstandings and speeding up the design iteration process compared to relying solely on textual communication. The integration of real-time updates, feedback mechanisms, and seamless incorporation of collaborative inputs ensures smoother interactions among team members, thereby increasing overall design efficiency.

6   Discussion and Design Conclusions

6.1   Discussion

The findings of this study underscore the pivotal role of professional tools in optimizing collaboration within cross-cultural game design teams. The AI-enhanced Character Generation (AICG) tool we proposed specifically addresses the multifaceted challenges faced by these teams, including bridging cultural gaps and fostering mutual understanding among artists from diverse backgrounds. By seamlessly integrating various creative inputs, the AICG tool enhances both the creativity and efficiency of the game development process, aligning with the hypothesis that advanced technology can significantly improve creative synergy within diverse teams.

The AICG tool features the capability to directly translate and integrate subtle cultural nuances into the character conceptualization workflow, facilitating this enhancement [41]. This functionality ensures that all team members can make effective contributions and feel valued within the project. Additionally, by simplifying communication and automating parts of the creative process, the tool also helps to reduce common collaborative barriers, such as misunderstandings and repetitive modifications, thus achieving a more cohesive and agile development cycle.

Despite the promising results, it is necessary to acknowledge the limitations encountered, such as the relatively small sample size and the restriction to participants from a specific region like North America. These limitations suggest that the findings should not be generalized without further validation across broader scenarios. Future research could expand demographic diversity and explore more cultural settings to provide a more comprehensive validation of AICG tools.

Nevertheless, our findings add a nuanced layer to the existing body of knowledge by demonstrating the practical application of AICG in real-world settings, particularly in the creative phases of game development. The tool's effectiveness is evident not only theoretically but also in tangible outputs, clearly illustrating the path from conceptualization to final design stages.

6.2   Conclusion

The significance of our findings lies in the clear demonstration of the demand for advanced tools within cross-cultural contexts, a demand that is becoming increasingly prevalent in the globalized game development landscape. This study provides foundational insights into the specific needs of cross-cultural game concept artists and outlines how AI-enhanced tools can revolutionize online character conceptualization and collaborative sketching. The AICG tools designed with these needs in mind are poised to become instrumental in creating game characters that are not only culturally rich and engaging but also resonate with a global audience. Our research confirms the applicative value of AICG technology in cross-cultural game design, particularly in fostering innovation and enhancing collaboration.

For the academic community, this research offers a framework for analyzing and enhancing tools for cross-cultural collaboration. For the industry, particularly in fields like game development and digital content creation, the study provides strong evidence supporting the integration of AICG tools to boost productivity and creativity.

Based on these insights, it is recommended that tool developers focus on improving the intuitiveness of user interfaces and expand the cultural adaptability of their products. Additionally, it is advised to continue exploring the application of these tools in other creative settings, further validating their adaptability and efficacy across different cultural contexts.

Looking ahead, future research should focus on refining AICG tool functionalities based on feedback from practical applications within the game development environment. The effectiveness of the tool in real projects must be assessed, examining its impact on team dynamics, creative output, and project timelines. Further studies could explore the integration of more advanced AI functionalities, such as predictive design analytics, which could anticipate design trends and suggest adjustments based on real-time global cultural shifts[43]. Moreover, expanding the tool's capabilities to support other aspects of game design, such as environment creation and narrative development, could provide comprehensive support to cross-cultural game development teams.

References

1. Author, F.: Article title. Journal **2**(5), 99–110 (2016)
2. Bakhmat, N., Smorgun, M.: On the role of digitalization and globalization for the development of mobile video games in the education of the future: trends, models, cases. Futurity Educ. **2**(4), 77–90 (2022)
3. Witt, M.A., Li, P.P., Välikangas, L., et al.: De-globalization and decoupling: game changing consequences? Manag. Organ. Rev. **17**(1), 6–15 (2021)
4. Gjicali, K., Finn, B.M., Hebert, D.: Effects of belief generation on social exploration, culturally-appropriate actions, and cross-cultural concept learning in a game-based social simulation. Comput. Educ. **156**, 103959 (2020)
5. Iskhakova, M., Ott, D.L.: Working in culturally diverse teams: team-level cultural intelligence (CQ) development and team performance. J. Int. Educ. Bus. **13**(1), 37–54 (2020)
6. Sato Y.: Cross-cultural game studies. In: Lee, N. (eds.) Encyclopedia of Computer Graphics and Games. Springer International Publishing, Cham, pp. 485–490 (2024). https://doi.org/10.1007/978-3-319-08234-9_400-1
7. Cruz, C.A., Uresti, J.A.R.: Player-centered game AI from a flow perspective: towards a better understanding of past trends and future directions. Entertain. Comput. **20**, 11–24 (2017)
8. Robertson, G., Watson, I.: A review of real-time strategy game AI. AI Mag. **35**(4), 75–104 (2014)
9. Perez-Liebana, D., Liu, J., Khalifa, A., et al.: General video game AI: a multitrack framework for evaluating agents, games, and content generation algorithms. IEEE Trans. Games **11**(3), 195–214 (2019)
10. Westera, W., Prada, R., Mascarenhas, S., et al.: Artificial intelligence moving serious gaming: presenting reusable game AI components. Educ. Inf. Technol. **25**, 351–380 (2020)
11. Schöbel, S., Saqr, M., Janson, A.: Two decades of game concepts in digital learning environments-a bibliometric study and research agenda. Comput. Educ. **173**, 104296 (2021)
12. Alam, A.: A digital game based learning approach for effective curriculum transaction for teaching-learning of artificial intelligence and machine learning. In: 2022 International Conference on Sustainable Computing and Data Communication Systems (ICSCDS). IEEE, pp. 69–74 (2022)
13. Fitria, T.N.: Artificial intelligence (AI) in education: using AI tools for teaching and learning process. In: Prosiding Seminar Nasional & Call for Paper STIE AAS, pp. 134–147 (2021)
14. Lee, I., Perret, B.: Preparing high school teachers to integrate AI methods into STEM classrooms. In: Proceedings of the AAAI Conference on Artificial Intelligence, vol. 36, no. 11, pp. 12783–12791 (2022)
15. Aririguzoh, S.: Communication competencies, culture and SDGs: effective processes to cross-cultural communication. Humani. Soc. Sci. Commun. **9**(1), 1–11 (2022)
16. Sousa, M.: Fast Brainstorm techniques with modern board games adaptations for daily uses in business and project managing. In: Proceedings of the International Conference of Applied Business and Management (ICABM2020), pp. 508–524 (2020)
17. Nazarov, Z.S.E.: Using brainstorming and case-study method in practical classes of microbiology. New Day Med. **1**, 79–85 (2021)

18. Naul, E., Liu, M.: Why story matters: a review of narrative in serious games. J. Educ. Comput. Res. **58**(3), 687–707 (2020)
19. Newman, J.I., Xue, H., Watanabe, N.M., et al.: Gaming gone viral: an analysis of the emerging esports narrative economy. Commun. Sport **10**(2), 241–270 (2022)
20. Block, B.: The Visual Story: Creating the Visual Structure of Film, TV, and Digital Media. Routledge (2020)
21. Lai, K.W.K., Chen, H.J.H.: A comparative study on the effects of a VR and PC visual novel game on vocabulary learning. Comput. Assist. Lang. Learn. **36**(3), 312–345 (2023)
22. Peters, D., Loke, L., Ahmadpour, N.: Toolkits, cards and games-a review of analogue tools for collaborative ideation. CoDesign **17**(4), 410–434 (2021)
23. Ratasuk, A., Charoensukmongkol, P.: Does cultural intelligence promote cross-cultural teams' knowledge sharing and innovation in the restaurant business? Asia-Pacific J. Bus. Admin. **12**(2), 183–203 (2020)
24. Haque, A., Yamoah, F.A.: The role of ethical leadership in managing occupational stress to promote innovative work behaviour: a cross-cultural management perspective. Sustainability **13**(17), 9608 (2021)
25. O'Hagan, M.: Towards a cross-cultural game design: an explorative study in understanding the player experience of a localised Japanese video game. J. Specialised Translat. **11**, 211–233 (2009)
26. Tietze, S., Piekkari, R.: Languages and cross-cultural management. In: The SAGE Handbook of Contemporary Cross-Cultural Management, pp. 181–195 (2020)
27. Piekkari, R., Welch, C., Zølner, M.: The uneasy relationship between the case study and cross-cultural management. In: The Sage Handbook of Contemporary Cross-Cultural Management, pp. 156–170 (2020)
28. Tam, K.P., Milfont, T.L.: Towards cross-cultural environmental psychology: a state-of-the-art review and recommendations. J. Environ. Psychol. **71**, 101474 (2020)
29. von Humboldt, S., Mendoza-Ruvalcaba, N.M., Arias-Merino, E.D., et al.: Smart technology and the meaning in life of older adults during the Covid-19 public health emergency period: a cross-cultural qualitative study. Int. Rev. Psychiatry **32**(7–8), 713–722 (2020)
30. Broesch, T., Crittenden, A.N., Beheim, B.A., et al.: Navigating cross-cultural research: methodological and ethical considerations. Proc. R. Soc. B **287**(1935), 20201245 (2020)
31. Rutishauser, L., Sender, A.: Effect of team-member exchange on turnover intention: a cross-cultural perspective on a selected aspect of employee engagement. In: International Perspectives on Employee Engagement. Routledge, pp. 52–71 (2021)
32. Stephan, U.: Cross-cultural innovation and entrepreneurship. Annu. Rev. Organ. Psych. Organ. Behav. **9**, 277–308 (2022)
33. Lansford, J.E.: Annual research review: cross-cultural similarities and differences in parenting. J. Child Psychol. Psychiatry **63**(4), 466–479 (2022)
34. Nielsen, J.: Usability Engineering. Academic Press, Cambridge (1993)
35. Liang, Z., Tao, F.: Research on the application of artificial intelligence in e-commerce design. In: 2020 International Conference on Innovation Design and Digital Technology (ICIDDT). IEEE, pp. 455–458 (2020)
36. Buonamici, F., Carfagni, M., Furferi, R., et al.: Generative design: an explorative study. Comput. Aided Des. Appl. **18**(1), 144–155 (2020)
37. Agostini, M., van Zomeren, M.: Toward a comprehensive and potentially cross-cultural model of why people engage in collective action: a quantitative research

synthesis of four motivations and structural constraints. Psychol. Bull. **147**(7), 667 (2021)

38. Seeber, I., Bittner, E., Briggs, R.O., et al.: Machines as teammates: a research agenda on AI in team collaboration. Inf. Manag. **57**(2), 103174 (2020)

39. Porter, B., Grippa, F.: A platform for AI-enabled real-time feedback to promote digital collaboration. Sustainability **12**(24), 10243 (2020)

40. Cetinic, E., She, J.: Understanding and creating art with AI: review and outlook. ACM Trans. Multimedia Comput. Commun. Appl. (TOMM) **18**(2), 1–22 (2022)

41. Costa-jussà, M.R., Cross, J., Çelebi, O., et al.: No language left behind: scaling human-centered machine translation. arXiv preprint arXiv:2207.04672 (2022)

Author Index

J. Y. C. Chen et al. (Eds.): HCII 2024, LNCS 15377, pp. 447–448, 2025.
https://doi.org/10.1007/978-3-031-76812-5

GPSR Compliance

The European Union's (EU) General Product Safety Regulation (GPSR) is a set of rules that requires consumer products to be safe and our obligations to ensure this.

If you have any concerns about our products, you can contact us on ProductSafety@springernature.com

In case Publisher is established outside the EU, the EU authorized representative is:

Springer Nature Customer Service Center GmbH
Europaplatz 3
69115 Heidelberg, Germany

The manufacturer's authorised representative in the EU is Springer
Nature Customer Service Centre GmbH, Europaplatz 3, 69115 Heidelberg,
Germany. If you have any concerns regarding our products, please
contact ProductSafety@springernature.com

Printed and bound by CPI Group (UK) Ltd, Croydon, CR0 4YY
24/04/2026
02096365-0013